T0374980

PAOLO GIOVIO

◆ ◆ ◆

NOTABLE MEN AND
WOMEN OF OUR TIME

EDITED AND TRANSLATED BY

KENNETH GOUWENS

THE I TATTI RENAISSANCE LIBRARY
HARVARD UNIVERSITY PRESS
CAMBRIDGE, MASSACHUSETTS
LONDON, ENGLAND
2013

Series design by Dean Bornstein

Library of Congress Cataloging-in-Publication Data

Giovio, Paolo, 1483–1552.
Notable men and women of our time / Paolo Giovio ; edited and translated by
Kenneth Gouwens.
pages cm. — (I Tatti Renaissance Library ; 56)
English and Latin parallel text on facing pages.
Includes bibliographical references and index.
ISBN 978-0-674-05505-6 (alk. paper)
1. Authors — Italy — Biography — Early works to 1800.   2. Scholars — Italy —
Biography — Early works to 1800.   3. Nobility — Italy — Biography — Early
works to 1800.   4. Italy — Biography — Early works to 1800.   5. Rome (Italy) —
History — Siege, 1527 — Early works to 1800.   I. Gouwens, Kenneth, editor,
translator.   II. Giovio, Paolo, 1483–1552. Elogia doctorum virorum.
III. Giovio, Paolo, 1483–1552. Elogia doctorum virorum. English.   IV. Title.
CT93.G513   2013
945.63092K2 — dc23   2012037853

Contents

ॐ§?§

Introduction

❧❧❧

Paolo Giovio[1] wrote *Notable Men and Women* in the aftermath of the catastrophic Sack of Rome in May of 1527 by troops of Emperor Charles V.[2] Virtually neglected in modern scholarship, this dialogue provides an informed perspective on the event's causes and consequences: for Giovio was both an intimate of the pope, who was the prime target of the imperial army, and a prominent intellectual who had already embarked upon writing the history of his times. In short, the dialogue constitutes an authoritative contemporary account of a pivotal moment in the history of the Renaissance.

Notable Men and Women is of surpassing importance for two other reasons as well. First, Giovio offers penetrating analyses of the literary style and in some cases the character of famous authors whom he knew personally, including Ludovico Ariosto, Baldassare Castiglione, Niccolò Machiavelli, Jacopo Sannazaro, and Vittoria Colonna. His interlocutors discuss some of the foremost concerns of Renaissance intellectuals: the question of whether the vernacular could rival or surpass Latin as a vehicle for literary expression, the impact of classical learning on the training of elites, and the extent to which education in the liberal arts is integral to the formation of a fully realized human being.

The dialogue's chief significance from a twenty-first century standpoint, however, is neither its political nor its literary content, but its extensive survey of the Italian noblewomen who were Giovio's contemporaries. In recent decades, scholars have given unprecedented attention to the achievements of women both as patrons of artists and scholars and as authors themselves. Giovio sheds new light on the careers and character of many of these outstanding women, in the process showing how integral they

were to the social, cultural, and political interconnections among courts throughout the peninsula, while at the same time highlighting what he saw as distinctive about the women of particular cities and regions.

To be sure, the celebration of illustrious women was an established genre in the Renaissance long before Giovio. The most prominent and influential exempla were Boccaccio's *Famous Women* (1361–62) and Christine de Pizan's *Book of the City of Ladies* (1405), both of which highlighted notable women across the course of centuries.[3] Within Giovio's lifetime, attention in such catalogs had turned to contemporary women, as for example in Giovanni Sabadino degli Arienti's *Gynevera* (ca. 1489–90; 1492) and Mario Equicola's *On Women* (ca. 1501).[4] The sixteenth century saw a proliferation of literary celebrations of noblewomen, ranging from the catalog in Mario di Leo's poem *L'amore prigioniero* (1538) to Giuseppe Betussi's dialogue *Le imagini del tempio della signora donna Giovanna Aragona* (1556).[5] But Giovio's *Notable Men and Women* stands out from the rest not only for the range of women treated but for its admixture of praise and blame. With candor and specificity, he details the respective strengths and weaknesses of women ranging from nobles of distinguished lineage to a courtesan and even a lowly (albeit successful and therefore wealthy) midwife. Admittedly, some of the praises are boilerplate. Yet particularly when acknowledging his subjects' shortcomings, Giovio describes peculiarities that help us to recognize them as distinct from one another. Even in the dialogue's encomium of its patron, Vittoria Colonna, we may discern a critical subtext that adds both depth and humanity to its characterization.

Although wide-reaching in its scope, this dialogue was born of a particular historical moment. The extent to which the Sack of Rome was indeed a watershed remains the subject of scholarly

THE I TATTI
RENAISSANCE LIBRARY

James Hankins, General Editor

GIOVIO

NOTABLE MEN AND
WOMEN OF OUR TIME

ITRL 56

debate.[6] Few specialists today would agree with historian Ludwig von Pastor's influential assertion, around a century ago, that it "marked, in fact, the end of the Renaissance."[7] Inarguably, however, the disaster spurred Italian intellectuals to speculate about its causes, gauge its impact, and assess Italy's prospects for political and cultural recovery in its aftermath.

Among those intellectuals was Giovio, whose own experience of the Sack did not lack drama. As the imperial troops made their way into Rome on May 6, 1527, a desperate Pope Clement VII[8] had fled along a raised passageway from the Vatican Palace to the papal fortress, the Castel Sant' Angelo. Immediately behind him came Giovio, who in addition to being an aspiring humanist historian was also Clement's personal physician. When they reached the exposed bridge that connected the corridor to the fortress, Giovio covered Clement's white vestments with his own scarlet cloak so as to make the pontiff a less obvious target. Once within, they were safe from immediate danger; but by evening the emperor's troops had conquered the city outside. That victory was just the beginning of Rome's ills: the imperial army would not quit Rome for good until the following February.

Clement initially held out hope that relief would come from his allies, but on June 5, 1527, he at last capitulated and agreed to raise the exorbitant ransom demanded for his release. Pending its payment, he was to be held under guard in the Castel Sant' Angelo. Initially Giovio remained with his patron, but when plague struck within the fortress, in order to slow its progress, the pope's captors ordered that he dismiss more men from his retinue. Thus Giovio was forced to leave. On July 17 Clement issued him a safe-conduct which ultimately enabled him to travel to the island of Ischia, off the coast of Naples. There, Giovio would enjoy the hospitality of Vittoria Colonna, scion of one of the most powerful Roman families and widow of the great military commander Ferdinando Fran-

cesco d'Avalos, marquis of Pescara (d. 1525). A poet and a patron of writers and artists, Vittoria was already developing a reputation as the host of literary discussions.[9] At her urging, he says, he composed the present dialogue, which he claims faithfully records actual conversations on Ischia in the autumn of 1527.

In its initial version, the dialogue was dedicated to Gian Matteo Giberti, the papal datary, who was a friend of both the author and Vittoria Colonna. Its purpose, Giovio wrote, was to offer consolation to the datary, who was among those taken hostage by the imperial soldiers in late September to serve as added incentive to the pope to pay the ransom demanded of him. On the night of November 29–30, through the agency of Pompeo Colonna, a cardinal who was Vittoria's kinsman, Giberti, and the other hostages managed to escape their captors.[10] The dialogue, said to have taken place on three consecutive days, is thus set at some point between late September and early December, by which time news of Giberti's escape would surely have reached Ischia.[11] Of course, the dialogue need not have been composed when Giovio claims to have written it. Nonetheless, a passage excised from subsequent redactions, describing Giberti as in captivity, suggests that Giovio did in fact begin the initial draft within weeks of its setting.

The terminus ad quem of composition, however, cannot be established with any certainty. Perhaps because of Giberti's release, Giovio did not complete the dialogue during his year-long sojourn on Ischia. He tried to revise it for publication at least twice, in 1530 and in 1535, but its moment had passed: no amount of rewriting and expansion could sufficiently adjust its contents to fit the drastically changed political circumstances following the reconciliation of Clement VII and Charles V in 1529. A major concern of the dialogue was the *libertà d'Italia*, the freedom of the peninsula from foreign domination—a cause that had exercised numerous other literati, notably Machiavelli. But by the time of the imperial

coronation (February 24, 1530), all hope for that freedom had disappeared: the dialogue's recounting and analysis of the now-failed struggle for Italian liberty and of the wars between pope and emperor were no longer of immediate relevance and were perhaps even painful for those who had endured misfortunes.[12] No part of the *Dialogues* would be published until the eighteenth century, when Girolamo Tiraboschi included a transcription of "day two" in his monumental *History of Italian Literature*.[13] Only in 1984 did the other two "days" join it in print, in the text prepared by Ernesto Travi and Mariagrazia Penco for the National Edition of Giovio's works.[14] The first appearance of the work in a modern language was the 2011 publication of an excellent critical edition and Italian translation.[15] The present volume renders the work into English for the first time.

Giovio's Life and Works

Paolo Giovio was born in Como in 1486.[16] His father died when he was a child, and he was raised by his older brother, Benedetto, whose interests in history, philology, and archaeology inspired him to become a man of letters. After studying in Milan under Demetrius Chalcondyles and Giano Parrasio, by late 1506 he was in Padua taking courses in medicine and philosophy (the latter, taught by Pietro Pomponazzi). Next he went to Pavia, where he studied with the anatomist Marcantonio della Torre and completed his degrees in medicine and philosophy in 1511. Soon thereafter he went to Rome. Initially he joined the household of Cardinal Bendinello Sauli,[17] and by 1514 he was lecturing in moral philosophy at the university ("La Sapienza"). Beyond practicing medicine and teaching philosophy, Giovio took part in the informal gatherings of Roman humanists sponsored by Angelo Colocci and Johannes Goritz which fostered scholarly exchange and liter-

ary composition.[18] In addition, he began to write the history of his own times, a massive project on which he would labor over the course of the rest of his life.

When Sauli was implicated in the "conspiracy of cardinals" against Pope Leo X in 1517, Giovio somehow contrived to move to the protection of Leo's cousin, Cardinal Giulio de' Medici. Upon Giulio's elevation as Pope Clement VII in 1523, Giovio hoped for special consideration, but in fact he received favor less from Clement than from Giberti. Giovio opposed the League of Cognac of 1526, in which Clement joined forces with France, Venice, and other powers against Charles V. Nonetheless, during the Sack of Rome, he remained at the pope's side so long as he was allowed to do so. In gratitude for his fidelity, Clement bestowed on him the bishopric of Nocera dei Pagani.[19] Upon being cast out of the papal fortress, Giovio stayed initially in the house of his banker, Francesco Formento, but soon thereafter accepted Vittoria Colonna's invitation to Ischia. He remained there for over a year, departing only on October 28, 1528.[20]

By November 8 he was again in Rome, and he continued to serve Clement VII thereafter. In the early 1530s, evidently with Clement's blessing, he moved to the court of the pope's *nipote*, Cardinal Ippolito de' Medici. Following the deaths of Clement in 1534 and Ippolito in 1535, Giovio became attached to Cardinal Alessandro Farnese, grandson of the new pope, Paul III (1534–49). In time, Giovio's pro-imperial politics led to his fall from favor with the Farnese: he never attained the cardinalate as he had hoped, nor even the bishopric of Como, which fell vacant in 1548. Evidently his attachment to Ferrante Gonzaga, in particular, militated against his advancement. In 1550, finally, Giovio settled in Florence at the court of Cosimo I de' Medici. On the night of December 11–12, 1552, he died there, the completed *Histories* having been published only that September.

Until recently, Giovio's *Histories* have received little scholarly attention in the English-speaking world. Far more influential has been his *Elogia virorum illustrium*, a collection of encomia (and mock encomia) that he wrote to accompany portraits that he collected in his villa on Lake Como. Of these, only the *elogia* of literati, and not those of outstanding men of arms, have been rendered in English.[21] The *Histories* await translation. And only now does the *Dialogus* appear for the first time in an English edition.

The Interlocutors and Subjects of the Dialogues

The three interlocutors of the dialogues are named for the imperial military officer Alfonso d'Avalos,[22] the Neapolitan jurist Giovanni Antonio Muscettola, and Giovio himself, all of whom were in fact on Ischia in late 1527. D'Avalos, the marquis del Vasto, spent his military career in the service of Spain. Born on Ischia, he was the son of Iñigo (II) d'Avalos, marquis del Vasto, and Laura Sanseverino. Upon being orphaned at an early age, he was raised by his aunt, Costanza d'Avalos.[23] He served in the imperial army initially under the command of his cousin Ferdinando Francesco d'Avalos, the marquis of Pescara, who was Vittoria Colonna's husband.[24] Del Vasto (1502–46) fought with distinction in the Battle of Pavia (February 24, 1525), in which imperial forces defeated the French and took King Francis I prisoner. Thanks to del Vasto's effectiveness and to the recommendation of his cousin, on November 25, 1525, Charles V made him commander in chief of his infantry in Italy. When Pescara died the following month, del Vasto inherited his cousin's rights and titles.[25] He would go on to greater distinction: in 1535 he led the imperial troops that took Tunis from the Moors, and in 1538 the emperor named him governor of Milan. His career would end on a sour note: in 1544 he suffered a crushing defeat by the French at the Battle of Ceresole, and in his

final year he was charged with maladministration of Milan.[26] But at the time of the "Ischian" dialogue, he was a promising young commander ideally suited to speak both to the condition of the soldiery in Italy and to the special prowess of Pescara, upon whom the interlocutor d'Avalos showers praises at the end of Book 1.

Giovanni Antonio Muscettola (1487–1534) was from a respected family in Ravello, a town high above the Amalfi coast in the Kingdom of Naples.[27] While less well known today than Del Vasto, he gained distinction as an orator, lawyer, and statesman. In 1518 he had served as *Guardianatus* (i.e., officer in charge) of the port of Manfredonia, a key locus of grain and wool exports in the kingdom. In 1521 he was president of the *Regia Camera della Sommaria*, the Neapolitan Exchequer or Financial Council. In 1527, at the time the dialogue is set, he was serving on the council of the imperial viceroy of Naples, Hugo de Moncada (1476–1528), and in the early 1530s he would represent the emperor in Rome.[28] Meanwhile, Clement VII held Muscettola in such esteem that in May of 1532 he would make plans (which, however, would go unrealized) to create him cardinal.[29] According to Giovio, the occasion for the present conversation is that Moncada and the Neapolitan government have just sent Muscettola to Ischia on a mission to persuade d'Avalos to resume his military responsibilities on the mainland.[30]

The interlocutors spend the three days of the dialogue discussing outstanding men-of-arms, literati, and noblewomen, respectively. Their congenial if at times heated conversations range widely. The first "day," which focuses on military commanders, does not just provide a descriptive catalog or define an ideal type, it includes as well philosophical debates about fate, the value (or lack thereof) of astrology, and the place of morality in keeping order; assessments of the impact that foreign invasions have had upon the scope for developing and demonstrating prowess; and sophisticated technical discussions of military strategy and the tactics of numerous battles. Why is it, they ask, that Italian troops

have been so unsuccessful in recent campaigns? Does the problem lie primarily with rank-and-file soldiers, or with their leaders? And, if there is a crisis of leadership, what has caused it? Can the root of the problem be found in systems of training, whether in military science or in character? Are inattentive, foolish, or corrupt princes choosing and promoting commanders for reasons other than ability and accomplishment? Or are top talents themselves eschewing military posts, either because they see the cause as already lost, or because they cannot stomach working for the protagonists on either side?

The second day's discussion surveys over a hundred men of letters, ranging from the internationally famous to the third-rate talents of whose works few scraps have survived. The newfound prestige of the vernacular in learned presentations and in written compositions appears to have led to a drop in opportunities for specialists in Latin. The interlocutors consider a variety of possible reasons for this change. Is the *volgare* more pleasing to women and the masses, whose tastes are carrying the day? Is the Tuscan dialect, championed by Bembo, a suitable alternative to Latin, and if so, for what genres and occasions? Many who essayed Latin in earlier years have now switched to writing almost exclusively in the vernacular. Have they done so because of the wider audience it provides and the range of expression it offers, or more because they are either too lazy to master Latin or simply incapable of doing so? Finally, while Italy is in crisis, are humanist Latinists elsewhere in Europe coming to surpass the Italians in talent, productivity, and prestige?

On the third "day," on illustrious women, the interlocutors survey the cities of Italy and single out individuals for praise and blame. The central question, as in the first two discussions, is whether outstanding figures of the present can rival those of earlier generations. Does the perception of a dearth of outstanding noblewomen result from the dim vision of aging men, who cannot

fairly compare women they see now with those they had seen with younger eyes? Is an evident decline in fertility sufficiently offset by other qualities now valued more in women than they used to be, such as political leadership, patronage, taste, and learnedness? Or has the scope for female virtue been narrowed by the occupation of foreign armies, who threaten not only women's livelihood but their chastity?

This "Ischian" dialogue records, or at least imagines, a revealing exchange of ideas at a critical moment in Renaissance history. Although the interlocutor *d'Avalos* speaks with particular authority to the military issues in Dialogue One, throughout the discussions all three offer their opinions and analyses on a range of topics. As a whole, the dialogue raises far more issues than it resolves. This quality of open-ended questioning is in keeping with a long tradition of Renaissance dialogues, and indeed was characteristic of Humanism more generally.[31] Yet the lack of resolution and the many loose ends in *Notable Men and Women* may also reflect its incompleteness, the unresolved internal contradictions giving eloquent voice to the sweeping political and cultural changes in early sixteenth-century Italy that had defied predictions and that resisted satisfactory comprehension by even the best minds of a generation.

Grants from the American Philosophical Society, the Renaissance Society of America, and the University of Connecticut Research Foundation enabled me to consult manuscripts in Como, where I benefited from the generosity of Sergio Lazzarini and Magda Noseda. For help on matters particular to their expertise, I am most indebted to Bill Caferro, Victor Coelho, Tom Cohen, Paul Dover, Anne Dunlop, Paola Farenga, John Gagné, Julia Gaisser, Meredith Gill, Julia Hairston, Colin Imber, Tim Kircher, John Monfasani, Laurie Nussdorfer, Sarah Ross, Barbara Sparti, and Price Zimmermann. Brian Roots, Greg Guderian, and Diana

Robin vetted extensive portions of an early draft of the translation, and John Grant gave a meticulous reading to the penultimate versions of both text and translation. James Hankins, with deft editorial hand, guided me in making the apparatus more systematic, queried potential slips in transcription, and made the English rendition far more felicitous. All remaining errors are, of course, my own.

NOTES

1. The fundamental biography of Giovio is that of Zimmermann (for full bibliographical references, see the list of Abbreviations under Notes to the Translation, pp. 615–624). See also Zimmermann's more recent entry on Giovio in *DBI* 56:430–40.

2. Charles V had inherited his Spanish possessions from his maternal grandfather, King Ferdinand of Aragon (d. 1516). In 1519 he was elected Holy Roman Emperor, in which position he succeeded his paternal grandfather, Maximilian. In the mid-1520s, Pope Clement VII (Giulio de' Medici; pope, 1523–34) tried to keep a balance of power between Spanish and French forces on the Italian peninsula. Initially he was aligned with Charles V, whose support had facilitated his election. But in 1524, in order to counterbalance Spain's growing hegemony, Clement allied the papacy with France. That decision proved disastrous: on February 24, 1525 (the emperor's birthday, as it happened), an imperial army soundly defeated the French at Pavia, taking King Francis I prisoner. As a result, Clement was forced to make peace with the emperor; but the release of the French king the following winter renewed hopes for checking Spain's sway in Italy. And so, on May 22, 1526, urged on by advisors including Francesco Guicciardini, Clement joined the papacy and Florence with Milan, Venice, and France in the League of Cognac. Although the League presented itself as a defensive alliance against the Turks, no one was fooled, least of all Charles V, who intensified his efforts to secure his foothold in Italy. By early 1527, an imperial army led by Charles, duke of Bourbon — the former constable of France who had gone over to the emperor's side — was marching south toward Rome.

3. Giovanni Boccaccio, *Famous Women*, published in this I Tatti Library (2001, vol. 1), ed. and trans. Virginia Brown; Christine de Pizan, *The Book of the City of Ladies*, ed. and trans. Rosalind Brown-Grant (Harmondsworth: Penguin, 1999). Important recent monographs on learned women in the Renaissance include Cox; Robin; and Sarah Gwyneth Ross, *The Birth of Feminism: Woman as Intellect in Renaissance Italy and England* (Cambridge, MA: Harvard University Press, 2009).

4. Stephen Kolsky, *The Ghost of Boccaccio: Writings on Famous Women in Renaissance Italy* (Turnhout, Belgium: Brepols, 2005).

5. Di Leo's poem appears in full in Marc'Antonio Epicuro, *I drammi e le poesie italiane e latine, aggiuntovi l'Amore prigioniero di Mario di Leo*, ed. Alfredo Parente (Bari: Laterza, 1942); Giuseppe Betussi, *Le imagini del tempio della signora donna Giovanna Aragona, Dialogo di M. Giuseppe Betussi, alla illustrissima signora donna Vittoria Colonna di Tolledo*, 2nd ed. (Venice: Giovanni de' Rossi, 1557; 1st ed., Florence: Lorenzo Torrentino, 1556). The dramatis personae of both overlap significantly with that of Book 3 of Giovio's dialogue. On Betussi and on numerous other sixteenth-century Italian books by and about women, see Robin.

6. Noteworthy contributions include André Chastel, *The Sack of Rome, 1527*, trans. Beth Archer (Princeton: Princeton University Press, 1983); *Il Sacco di Roma del 1527 e l'immaginario collettivo*, ed. Alberto Asor Rosa et al. (Rome: Istituto Nazionale di Studi Romani, 1986); Vincenzo De Caprio, *La tradizione e il trauma. Idee del Rinascimento romano* (Manziana: Vecchiarelli, 1991); Gouwens; *Les discours sur le sac de Rome de 1527: pouvoir et littérature*, ed. Augustin Redondo (Paris: Presses de la Sorbonne nouvelle, 1999); and *Pontificate of Clement*.

7. Pastor, 10:443.

8. Clement VII, like his cousin Leo X (1513–21), was a scion of Florence's most powerful family.

9. On Vittoria Colonna's literary sodality and patronage, see Thérault; Robin.

10. On attempts to establish the moment in which the dialogue was set, see Zimmermann, 316–17 n. 21. See also Ernesto Travi and Mariagrazia

Penco's comments in their introduction to the edition of the *Dialogus* in *IO* 9:149–50, 157–58; compare also Vecce (1990b), 73; Minonzio, 1:LV–CIX.

11. A further clue is that in Dialogue Three, the pope is described as still a captive. On December 6, with the assistance of Pompeo Colonna, Clement escaped from Castel Sant' Angelo, and news would surely have reached Ischia soon thereafter.

12. Around the time of the coronation, Giovio requested and obtained from Isabella d'Este seventy reams of top-quality paper, and he got as far as preparing the dialogue for the typesetter, but stopped short of publication. As Zimmermann observes (111), "After an initial rush of enthusiasm, he probably realized how little he stood to gain by opening old wounds now that pope and emperor had composed their quarrels and a new day was dawning."

13. Tiraboschi, *Storia della letteratura italiana*, vol. 7, pt. 2 (Milan: Società Tipografica de' Classici Italiani, 1824), 2444–99.

14. *IO* 9:147–321. In the mid-twentieth century, Carlo Volpati drew upon the third part of the dialogue, without however citing the manuscript, in several articles: "Paolo Giovio e Vittoria Colonna," *Roma* 11 (1933): 501–6; "Paolo Giovio e Venezia," *Archivio veneto* 15 (1934): 132–56; "Paolo Giovio e Napoli," *Nuova rivista storica* 20 (1936): 347–62; "Paolo Giovio e Genova," *Giornale storico e letterario della Liguria* 14 (1938): 92–99, 182–89.

15. Minonzio. For details on that edition and comparisons with the present one, see the Note on the Text and Translation in this volume.

16. Although his birth has traditionally been assigned to 1483, Giovio's own statements indicate that he was born in 1486. The details that follow in this section are drawn substantially from Zimmermann's entry on Giovio in *DBI* 56:430–40.

17. On Bendinello Sauli, see especially Hyde.

18. On the sodalities of Colocci and Goritz, see *DLI*, throughout; Zimmermann, 20–27; Gouwens, 1–30, 103–42; D'Amico, 89–112; Ubaldini; Ingrid D. Rowland, *The Culture of the High Renaissance: Ancients and Moderns in Sixteenth-Century Rome* (New York: Cambridge University Press, 1998), passim.

19. Nocera is near Salerno in the Kingdom of Naples.

20. For these details, see Zimmermann, 86–87, 105, 315 n. 5.

21. In collaboration with Franco Minonzio, I am now preparing a critical edition and translation of the complete *Elogia* for this I Tatti Library.

22. On Alfonso d'Avalos, see *DBI* 4:612–16, from which the following details are drawn.

23. Costanza d'Avalos the Elder (ca. 1460–1541) was the daughter of Iñigo (I) d'Avalos. In 1501, she became duchess of Francavilla and followed her brother Iñigo II to Ischia. After he died in 1503, she personally directed the defense of the island against a French siege. See *DBI* 4:621–22. She was one of Giovio's hosts on Ischia in 1527–28.

24. On Pescara's life and career, see Dialogue One, n. 37.

25. Pescara died the night of December 2–3, 1525, evidently from complications arising from wounds he suffered at the Battle of Pavia.

26. On the Battle of Ceresole (April 11, 1544), see Bert S. Hall, *Weapons and Warfare in Renaissance Europe: Gunpowder, Technology, and Tactics* (Baltimore: The Johns Hopkins University Press, 1997), 185–90.

27. On Muscettola, see Zimmermann, 88–105, 116, and 316 n. 16; Maria Antonietta Visceglia, "La vicenda dei Muscettola tra XV e XIX secolo," in eadem, *Il bisogno di eternità: I comportamenti aristocratici a Napoli in età moderna* (Naples: Guida editori, 1988), 178–262, at 136, 181–84. His upward mobility is evident in his children having married beyond the Ravellese elite, into titled aristocratic families: his daughter, Camilla, to Francesco Antonio Cantelmo, count of Popoli, in 1531; and his son, Giovanni Francesco, to Camilla Carafa, sister of the count of Montecalvo (1544). See Visceglia, 182.

28. Charles V in fact rewarded Muscettola for his services by making him *signore* of Roccadivandro, Camina, and Prata in Terra di Lavoro. See Visceglia, 182.

29. On the reasons for Clement not following through on his intention, see Pastor, 10:209–10. The unfortunate Muscettola had even gone so far as to order his Cardinal's insignia.

30. Muscettola also served the Neapolitan government in 1533 as one of three regents (*reggenti*), special high counselors who also served on the *Camera della Collaterale*, which made political decisions. See Visceglia, 182.

31. On humanist dialogues, see David Marsh, *The Quattrocento Dialogue: Classical Tradition and Humanist Innovation* (Cambridge, MA: Harvard University Press, 1980); Jon R. Snyder, *Writing the Scene of Speaking: Theories of Dialogue in the Late Italian Renaissance* (Stanford: Stanford University Press, 1989); Thomas F. Mayer, "The Dialogue in Classical and 'Medieval' Tradition," chap. 5 in his *Thomas Starkey and the Commonweal: Humanist Politics and Religion in the Reign of Henry VIII* (Cambridge: Cambridge University Press, 1989), 139–68; and Virginia Cox, *The Renaissance Dialogue: Literary Dialogue in its Social and Political Contexts, Castiglione to Galileo* (Cambridge: Cambridge University Press, 1992). On the place of dialogue in a broader humanistic culture of *disputatio*, see Christopher S. Celenza, *The Lost Italian Renaissance: Humanists, Historians, and Latin's Legacy* (Baltimore: The Johns Hopkins University Press, 2004), 86–88, 91, 99.

PAULI IOVII
DE VIRIS ET FEMINIS AETATE
NOSTRA FLORENTIBUS
AD IOANNEM MATTEUM GIBERTUM

PAOLO GIOVIO
NOTABLE MEN AND WOMEN OF
OUR TIME
TO GIAN MATTEO GIBERTI[1]

DIALOGUS PRIMUS

1   Cum[1] in ipso incredibili et longe luctuosissimo totius paene religionis et Romanae civitatis interitu gravis pestilentia super tot ac-
cumulatas clades Hadriani molem invasisset, in qua Clemens iam
deditus et senatus barbarorum custodia servabantur, totque circum me iactis fulminibus totam veteris atque perpetui officii mei
cum pontifice consuetudinem abrupisset, arce eiectus in Aenariam
veni ad Victoriam Columnam, feminam cum forma et pudicitia
illustrem tum omni virili laude longe dignissimam. Sciebam enim
illam tanta esse animi magnitudine atque virtute ut nihil praestantius duceret quam naufragio et saevis adversae tempestatis eiectos
fluctibus excipere, nec eos ulla fortunae iniuria mergi pati, ac demum conservatos benigne et liberaliter recreare, et eos quidem
ante alios qui aliquam ab optimis litterarum studiis commendationem ac laudem meruissent. Neque vero id sum veritus quominus
ab ea insignis humanitas cum summa liberalitate foret exspectanda, ut offenso animo acerbissimarum cladium memoriam retineret, quarum magnitudine Columnius ager Latino bello a nostris
exercitibus atrociter fuerit evastatus; hunc enim domestici doloris
sensum virtutis amor penitus abstersit, ad eam unam siquidem
inflammata plenis passibus fertur, eximiaque pietate reiectis humanae vitae illecebris viam sibi ad gloriam in caelum munire contendit.

2   Itaque ea caritate eoque liberali animo sum receptus ut me non
amicum modo vel necessarium clientem, sed exoptatum aliquem

DIALOGUE ONE

In the very midst of the incredible and most lamentable destruction of practically the whole of religion and of the city of Rome,
on top of so many accumulated disasters, a severe pestilence attacked Castel Sant' Angelo, where Clement, who had already surrendered, and the cardinals were being held in custody by the
barbarians. Amid so many thunderbolts that had fallen round
about me, the pestilence broke off my entire association with the
pope—a longstanding and uninterrupted attendance. Cast out of
the citadel, I came to Ischia—and to Vittoria Colonna.² She is a
woman both outstanding in beauty and purity and worthiest by
far of the kind of praise normally reserved for men. I was aware
that she is endowed with such magnanimity and virtue that she
considers nothing finer than to rescue those cast out by shipwreck
and by the savage waves of a hostile storm and not to allow them
to be drowned by any wrong of Fortune and, once they have been
saved, kindly and generously to restore them to health, especially
those who have derived some commendation and praise from the
excellent study of literature. Nor in fact did I entertain any fears
that her outstanding kindness, combined with exceeding generosity, might not await me or that she would rancorously harbor the
memory of the terrible, large-scale disasters by which, during the
war in Latium, the Colonna estate was shockingly devastated by
our armies.³ Her love of virtue thoroughly cleansed her sense of
domestic grievance, since to virtue alone she is carried with passion and at full stride. With her extraordinary piety she has cast
aside the allurements of human life and hastens to pave for herself
a path to heavenly glory.

And so I was welcomed with such love and generosity that the
others in the household supposed that I had arrived, not just as a

propinquum advenisse ceteri familiares existimarent. Certatum enim est exquisita atque perpetua benignitate cum ab ipso Alfonso Davalo duce ⟨civili⟩ et bellica virtute ⟨clariss⟩imo, tum etiam ab huius amita Constantia Davala, cuius ingenio nihil nobilius aut sanctius reperitur.

3   Venerat tum forte ex Umbris ab exercitu Davalus, ut has illustres feminas sanguine atque amore sibi coniunctissimas inviseret; nam cum, oppressa caesaris classe et Genua subinde capta, Andreas Auria Gallicae praefectus classis a Tyrrheno mari et Venetae triremes a Siculo freto Campaniae oram maxime terruissent, plerique cariores res suas in hanc munitissimam arcem perbeatae insulae conferre coeperant. Ipsique ante alios Ascanius Columna et Alfonsus Amalfius Regulus Ioannam Aragoniam et Constantiam Davalam uxores suas, quibus pulchriores sol non videt, cum infantibus liberis ad Victoriam sororem et Constantiam Davalam Seniorem amitam deduxerant. Itemque Davalus etiam ex ora Picentinorum Mariam uxorem acciverat, quae sicut Aragoniae soror est, ita eius formam atque elegantiam statim aequatura videtur, cum adamati coniugis emollita atque excitata blanditiis puellarem verecundiam exuerit.

4   Has omnes Davalus incredibili studio ita colebat ut nullam omnino praetermitteret occasionem exercitationum varii generis ac ludorum qua muliebris animus iucundissima voluptate posset oblectari. Namque aliquot ingentes cervos sic agitavit et cepit in proximis montibus ut totus venationis apparatus, ferarum fuga, et varius canum et iuvenum discursus e summae arcis fenestris

friend or an invaluable dependent, but as some longed-for close relation. Indeed the commander Alfonso d'Avalos[4] and his aunt Costanza d'Avalos[5] contended with each other in their exquisite and continual kindness toward me. He himself is highly distinguished in statesmanship and martial prowess, and she has the noblest, gentlest, holiest character that one could possibly find.

At that time, as it happened, d'Avalos had come from the army 3 in Umbria to visit these illustrious women, bound to him by ties of blood and affection. Recently, after the emperor's[6] fleet had been defeated and Genoa captured, Andrea Doria,[7] the admiral of the French fleet, had terrorized the coast of Campania from the Tyrrhenian Sea, and Venetian ships had done so from the Straits of Messina. And so, many people had begun to convey their treasures into the exceedingly well-fortified citadel of the blessed isle of Ischia. Above all others, Ascanio Colonna[8] and Alfonso Piccolomini,[9] the duke of Amalfi, had brought to this place their respective wives, Giovanna d'Aragona[10] and Costanza d'Avalos the Younger.[11] No one under the sun is more beautiful than they. Along with their infant children, these women came to stay with Ascanio's sister Vittoria and his wife's aunt, Costanza d'Avalos the Elder. In like manner, Alfonso d'Avalos too had sent for his wife, Maria,[12] from the coast of the Marche. The sister of Giovanna d'Aragona, she appears poised to equal her beauty and elegance as soon as, softened and stimulated by the blandishments of her dearly loved husband, she will have cast off girlish bashfulness.

D'Avalos was looking after all these women with such extraor- 4 dinary zeal that he let slip no opportunity for exercises and games of every sort in order that their womanly minds could be delighted by the most agreeable amusements. In the nearby hills he pursued and captured several large deer in such a way that, from the windows of the highest part of the fortress, the women could look out upon all the preparations for the hunt, the wild beasts in flight,

spectarentur. Ab ea quoque parte qua insula praealtis aspera cotibus sed his summo in vertice peramoeno nemore virentibus ab
oriente in meridiem recurvatur, perdices nobilissimo aucupii genere consectatus est, cum mansuefacti hierofalcones per aera sinuoso praecipitique volatu exturbatas sedibus ac in mare provolantes invaderent.

5   Altera dies, cunctis diis atque deabus maris ad exoptatam tranquillitatem mire faventibus, celeberrima piscatione fuit insignis.
Exquisito enim apparatu ad piscosissimam stationem, quae ambustis adiacet petris, omni prope piscium generi feliciter insidiati
sumus. Horrida est supra litus et confragosa loci facies antiquis
Aenariae incendiis deformata; multis enim ante saeculis quam
Vesevus arserit, Aenariam summo cacumine evomuisse flammas
atque hunc tractum percoctis ac eliquatis cotibus penitus evastasse
constat, natamque exinde fabulam poetarum carminibus de Typhoei gigantis supplicio quem, superbe caelitibus bellum minantem ac saevos ore et naribus spirantem ignes, tota simul insula,
supino reluctantique imposita, Iuppiter iratus et ultor oppresserit.
Sed quantum atrae et squallidae sterilitatis ea incendia proximis
insulae partibus intulerunt, tantum natura, humanis usibus semper benigna, apud subiectum litus certa[2] ac fertili piscatione compensavit.

6   Ultima porro dies iucunditate novitateque spectaculi haud dubie superiores antecessit; cum fulicis enim incredibili cum[3] voluptate uberrimoque victoriae proventu pugnavimus. Lacus est paullo
supra ambustas petras in circuitu decem fere stadiorum naturali et
pulcherrimo inclusus amphitheatro quod undique frondosi colles,
velut circino in orbem circumducti, ad singularem spectantium

and the dogs and young men running about. Next he hunted partridges in that part where the island's high and forbidding cliffs (although these are verdant on top with a very pleasant grove) curve round from the east to the south. This he did with the noblest kind of fowling: trained falcons, wheeling and diving in the air, hunted down partridges which had been disturbed in their nests and were flying out across the sea.

The second day was extraordinary for its successful fishing, 5 since all the gods and goddesses of the sea were wonderfully propitious in providing the longed-for tranquility. With carefully chosen gear, we successfully lay in ambush for nearly every kind of fish at the anchorage near the scorched rocks, which absolutely teems with them. Above the shore, the appearance of the place is rough and rugged, disfigured by the ancient fires of Ischia. For it is known that many centuries before Vesuvius erupted, Ischia spewed forth flames from the highest peak and totally devastated this region with the molten lava it poured out. From this was born the tale in the verses of poets concerning the punishment of the giant Typhoeus:[13] when he arrogantly threatened the gods with war and breathed out savage fires from his mouth and nostrils, angry and avenging Jupiter crushed him, covering him with the whole island as he lay on his back struggling. But to the extent that those fires scorched the nearby regions of the island and made them sterile, nature, always obliging to human needs, has compensated for the damage with reliable and abundant fishing near the shore below.

The final day, in its turn, surely surpassed the earlier ones in 6 pleasantness and novelty of spectacle, for we battled the waterfowl both with immense pleasure and with an abundant yield of victory. A little above the scorched rocks is a lake, enclosed within a circumference of almost ten stadia by a very beautiful natural amphitheater, which the leafy hills on all sides, as if drawn in a circle by a compass, display to the singular delight of observers. Broken

voluptatem repraesentant; verum a septentrionibus effracti ad exitum aquarum depressas fauces praebent, atque inde, velut ab ingenti porta, late maria prospectantur. Ad laevam virentia succedunt prata, quae ab amoenis lacus ripis ad ipsos molliter assurgentes
colles, curvatis spatiis extenduntur. Totae margines partim iuncis
et lentisco, partim frequentibus myrtetis, convestitae[4] consaeptaeque sunt. Ab austro incipiunt altissimi et in summo culmine exesi
montes in quorum radicibus iuxta lacum salubri scaturigine calidae manant aquae mortalium morbis salubres, ibique terna sunt
balinea, paribus divisa labris atque siphunculis egregioque opere
concamerata. In medio autem lacu insula est manu facta, superiacta[s] moles congestis caespitibus, et protracto in linguae similitudinem lapideo ad continentem isthmo, ut per viam silice constratam Neptuni templum, quod in ea perantiquum est, vel pedibus
adiretur. Infinitam fulicarum multitudinem lacus alit ab immo
herbidus, et ob id ad pinguem ac nobilem pastionem aves alliciens.

7   Itaque laxatis et depressis angustiis, plures cumbae ab attiguo
mari in lacum scutulis atque hominum umeris impelluntur. Armata perticis iuventus et canes palustribus assueti venationibus
ripas corona obsident. Nos cum feminis cumbas conscendimus,
atque item complures instructi arcibus, quibus argillaceae pilae ad
certos ictus excutiuntur. Excitatae fulicae huc et illuc provolant.
Ab omni parte infestos hostes inveniunt, undique cum plausu et
mutua gratulatione dissipantur et creberrimis pilis impetuntur. Eo
modo natando et revolando fessae, debilitatae ictibus varioque
periculo terrefactae, ad densissimos iuncos totis ripis se recipiunt.
Neque enim, ut nimium obesae inertes et timidae egregio conatu,

open in the north, the hills provide deep channels for the outflow of waters, and from there, as if from a mighty gate, one can gaze out far and wide upon the seas. On the left are verdant meadows, which with their curved, open spaces spread out from the pleasant shores of the lake to the gently rising hills themselves. All the edges have been adorned and marked off either with hedges consisting of reeds and mastic trees or with crowded myrtle groves. In the south begin the tallest mountains, hollowed out at their peak. At their base, next to the lake, a salubrious spring pours forth hot waters that are healing to human ailments. Here one finds three baths, separated by basins and siphons, and vaulted by a splendid structure. In midlake, moreover, is an artificial island. A mound of earth was piled over with grassy turf, and a stone isthmus like a tongue extended to the mainland, so that the temple of Neptune, which is the most ancient thing on the island, can be approached on foot via a road paved with lava stone. The lake bed is quite grassy, feeding an infinite multitude of waterfowl and enticing them to fine, rich pasturage.

And so, once the narrows had been opened and deepened, a 7 number of boats were conveyed on skids and men's backs from the adjacent sea into the lake. Young men armed with poles and dogs trained in swamp hunting formed a blockade along the shores. We, along with the womenfolk, boarded the boats, as did many men equipped with bows with which they shot clay missiles with precision. The startled waterfowl flew out this way and that, encountering the enemy in every direction. The birds were scattered and attacked on every side by a constant rain of missiles accompanied by applause and mutual congratulations. Thus exhausted by swimming and flying round and round, disabled by blows, and terrified by the ever-changing danger, they retreated from the entire shoreline into the dense reeds. Nor did they dare to fly out either into the hills or to the adjacent sea, since they were too fat, sluggish, and timid to make the extraordinary effort required.

vel in montes vel in mare proximum evolare audent. Ibi ergo varium et maxime cruentum instauratur proelium. Canes enim trepidis et sese occultantibus allatrare insultare capere mordicus; ipsi
venatores eas latebris extrudere, saxis[5] fustibusque necare, manu
comprehendere, aut in adversas cumbas unde pilarum procella
continenter effundebatur pavidas compellere; ita cum aliquamdiu
pugnassemus, tanta earum strages est edita ut interfectis aut captis
amplius trecentis dominarum cumbae complerentur.

8   At dum eo modo res gereretur, regia triremis ab alto ante
conspecta Antonium Musetium in proximum litus exposuit. Veni-
ebat is cum ab Senatu Neapolitano missus tum ab Ugone Mon-
cata prorege, qui Carolo Lanoio ad Aversam febre absumpto in
honore successerat, ut Davalum ad maturandam profectionem
hortaretur. Multa enim eum ab eo munere suscipiendo retarda-
bant, quoniam sibi ad seditiosum contumacem omnique scelere ac
licentia contaminatum exercitum, sine magna pecunia, minime re-
deundum esse iudicabat ne,[6] cum vitae periculo existimationisque
iactura, rem antea Romae[7] et a se et a Lanoio improspere tentatam
experiretur, quamquam militum animos ab se minime alienos esse
intellegeret, et per litteras a singulis Hispanorum et Germanorum
ordinibus vocaretur. Praelatus enim sibi a caesare fuerat Philibertus[8] Orangius Belga[9] nobilitate familiae, odio adversus Gallos, et
caesaris gratia insignis, ceterum primorum stipendiorum adulescens,[10] qui Borbonio interfecto exercitui cum imperio praeesset,
cum ipse, tot bellis totque periculis testata virtute, sese inique vel[11]

There the battle was renewed, in a different and exceedingly gory form. Even as the frightened birds were seeking cover, the dogs were barking, leaping upon them, and catching them in their teeth. The hunters themselves flushed them out from their coverts, killing them with stones and clubs or catching them by hand or driving them terrified toward the boats opposite, from which an unremitting shower of missiles was pouring. When we had fought this battle for some time, such a huge aviary massacre had occurred that the ladies' boats were filled with more than three hundred birds, dead or captured.

While the hunt was going on in this way, a royal warship, sighted earlier from on high, set Antonio Muscettola[14] ashore on the adjacent beach. Dispatched by both the Neapolitan senate and the imperial viceroy Hugo de Moncada,[15] who had succeeded to that post after Charles de Lannoy[16] had died from a fever at Aversa, Muscettola was coming to exhort d'Avalos to hasten his departure.[17] Many things were delaying d'Avalos from taking up that duty. He judged that, unless he took with him a great deal of money, by no means ought he to return to an army that was seditious, disobedient, and defiled by every crime and licentiousness. Nor would he attempt, with danger to life and sacrifice of reputation, what previously both he and Lannoy had tried at Rome with unfortunate results,[18] even though he understood that the minds of the soldiers were by no means estranged from him, and even though he was being summoned by letter from particular companies of Spaniards and Germans. Moreover, Philibert de Châlon, prince of Orange[19] — a Belgian distinguished by nobility of family, by his hatred of the French, and by the emperor's favor, but still a youth with precious little military experience — had been given precedence over d'Avalos by the emperor.[20] So when Bourbon had been killed,[21] Orange was given full command of the army, whereas d'Avalos himself, his prowess attested by so many wars and dangers, protested that he had been passed over unfairly, even

8

ingrate praetermissum esse quereretur; classis quoque Veneta, quae sese in Baianum intulit sinum, eum de Prochita Aenariaque sollicitum, et longe pulcherrimae carissimaeque mulieres, ne se in eo belli periculo desereret deprecantes,[12] haud invitum retinebant. Quibus de causis, cum induci atque expugnari Davalum haud facile posse putarent, Musetium ante alios miserant ut[13] in ipsa legatione non parum inesset dignitatis (nam ex senatorio ordine erat) et idoneum hominem familiaritate fide obsequiis Davalae domui coniunctissimum et vehementi facundia valentem adhiberent.

9   Itaque cum in pratis lacui proximis[14] aliquamdiu remotis arbitris disceptando deambulassent, me tertium e proxima ripa ad colloquium evocarunt[15] satietate quadam a persequendis fulicis temperantem. Cum autem appropinquarem, procurrens Musetius me quam artissime est complexus et, quae eius semper fuit humanitas, alacriter etiam gratulatus quod non modo me e tanta[16] caede cruciatibus pestilentia carcereque et liber et incolumis eripuissem, sed honorem etiam Nucerini episcopatus benignitate pontificis essem consecutus, ut fortunarum omnium iactura quam publica clade fecissem aliqua[17] ex parte sarciretur.

10   Tum ego ⟨IOVIUS⟩ inquam 'Museti, cur mihi non potius gratularis *Historias* salvas et[18] incolumis, qui eas augurari immortales futuras et tamquam dignas liberaliore saeculo laudare consuevisti? Namque eas dudum et laetus quidem, vel gravi redemptas pretio,[19] in hanc insulam feliciter asportavi; condideram eas, cum scyphis et tot[20] pateris meis erudita arte fabrefactis,[21] in praealtam maximi

ungratefully. Also, there was the Venetian fleet to consider: it had entered the Bay of Naples, and d'Avalos was concerned for Procida and Ischia. Finally, the women who were the most beautiful by far and the dearest to him were detaining him, albeit certainly not against his will, by their pleas that he not desert them in this dangerous time of war. For these reasons, the senators thought that d'Avalos could not easily be persuaded or won over. So they had sent Muscettola in preference to all others, so as to give sufficiently high prestige to the legation, since he held the rank of senator. Also, they wanted to employ someone well suited for the task, since he was both capable of impassioned eloquence and tightly bound to the house of d'Avalos by friendship, trust, and allegiance.

Once d'Avalos and Muscettola had walked in the meadows 9 next to the lake for a while in private conversation, and as I, having had my fill, was slackening in my pursuit of waterfowl, they called me over from the nearby shore to join the conversation as the third participant. As I drew near, Muscettola ran forward, embraced me as tightly as possible, and also — such has always been his humane disposition — congratulated me enthusiastically for having not only extricated myself, free and unharmed, from disaster, torments, plague, and imprisonment, but for having also acquired, through the pope's kindness, the bishopric of Nocera.[22] This was done so that I might to some extent be reimbursed for all the possessions I had lost in the public disaster.

Then, I [GIOVIO] asked, "Muscettola, why don't you instead 10 congratulate me that the *Histories* are safe and intact — you, who have repeatedly predicted that they will be immortal and have praised them as worthy of a more honorable century? For in fact, luckily, a short time ago I brought them to this island, happy indeed to have bought them back, even at an exorbitant price. I'd stashed them, along with my goblets and many dishes made with

altaris testudinem in Minervae templo. Sed frustra fuit eas adeo religiose numinibus iratis commendasse: namque Herrera Hispanus et Gamboa Cantaber cohortium praefecti, excruciatis sacerdotibus aedituis, occultos recessus omnes diligentissime perscrutati, et meam pariter[22] et sacratam altaribus suppellectilem donariaque omnia rapuerunt.

11 'Nulla enim umquam tota vita iucundior dies desideriis meis illuxit, cum *Historias*, velut postliminio redditas, eadem ferrata conclusas arcula recepi, clarissimis quibusdam ducum praeclare iuvantibus, qui gloriae cupidi plurimum interesse ad ipsorum famam intellegebant si ea scripta ab imperitis barbaris minime perderentur, sic ut beneficio deorum accidisse constet quod nequaquam ad Cimbrorum rabiem pervenerint, qui irati infestique litteris infinitam nobilium librorum multitudinem, et in Campo Florae et in omnibus triviis, voluptatis causa, Gothica insanaque libidine concremarunt.'

12 Ad haec MUSETIUS 'Recte' inquit 'Iovi, in deos refers, quod libri tui ab honestissimo quoque magnopere desiderati tum, cum omnia foedo atque terribili casu corruerent, in publicis ruinis minime interierint et tu ipse eodem beneficio sis conservatus, qui multo plura ac[23] etiam iucundiora gravissime et diligentissime sis conscripturus. Maxime enim cuperem ut bona pax, ab omnibus iam cum lacrimis exoptata, afflictis Europae rebus daretur, ut praeclara illa nec minus necessaria expeditio adversus Turcas, tot regum atque pontificum conciliis agitata et semper omissa impie et negligenter, aliquando susciperetur, ut haec aetas tot nostris

skilled craftsmanship, in the deep vault of the high altar in the Church of Santa Maria sopra Minerva.[23] But it was of no avail to have entrusted them thus reverently to angry gods: once the priests and sacristans had been tortured, the commanders, the Spaniards Herrera[24] and Gamboa,[25] conducted a thorough search of all the hidden chambers and made off with my possessions dedicated to the altars and all the other donatives.

"Really, in my entire life there has never dawned a day more 11 gratifying to my desires than when I recovered the *Histories*, enclosed in the same ironclad chest — restored as if from enemy hands[26] — with the brilliant assistance of certain distinguished commanders. Desirous of glory, they recognized that it greatly benefited their own reputations for these writings not to be destroyed by ignorant barbarians. It is clear that this played out as it did through the kindness of the gods: that is, that the *Histories* had not been exposed to the mad frenzy of the Germans. Angry and hostile toward literature, they had burned a countless multitude of famous books both in the Campo de' Fiori and in all the crossroads, and they did so just for fun, out of an insane and Gothic willfulness."

To this MUSCETTOLA replied, "Giovio, you're right to attribute 12 it to the gods that your books, which every gentleman longs to see, had not been destroyed in the communal disasters right at the time when all things were collapsing in a foul and terrible ruin. And you yourself, by the same kindness, were kept safe — you who, with exceptional seriousness and diligence, will compose far more things that are still more pleasing. I would wish most of all that a reliable peace, for which all men already have longed tearfully, be granted to Europe in her distress, that that splendid and no less necessary expedition against the Turks, set in motion by the plans of so many kings and popes yet always impiously and heedlessly allowed to fall by the wayside, now at last be undertaken. Thereby this age, famous for our many calamities, could be

cladibus insignis ab honestiore rerum gestarum memoria et aliorum et tuis maxime scriptis posset illustrari.

13 'Sed video fieri haud dubie providentia deorum, qui immania
flagitia nostra ulcisci pergunt, ut retro cuncta corruptis moribus,
neglecta religione extinctaque virtute referantur. Nusquam enim
est vel decoris cura vel dedecoris metus, nulla certa fides, nulla vera
pietas, nulla hominum caritas atque amicitia gratuita. Ipsi reges
gloriae nequaquam student, cum perpetuis bellis ac odiorum inveteratae libidini effuse[24] deserviant. Qui vero regibus studium atque
operam praestant saepius commodo et quaestu quam officio consilia moderantur, sic ut cunctos fere[25] in suscipiendis ac administrandis bellis alium profecto quam sibi animis destinarint consiliorum exitum[26] sensisse videamus. Et[27] hercle non dispudet adhuc
Fortunae conviciari, quae ab imperitis et[28] insanis dicitur cunctarum rerum esse dominatrix ac impotenter fatali cursu conatus hu-
manos abripere, cum virtutes ipsae cum civiles tum militares, negotio gerendo fautrices fidelissimae, ex omni prope principum
aula, urbibus cunctis, et provinciis[29] eiectae expulsaeque sint.

14 'Pietatem cuius est primus Christiani hominis respectus[30]
convulsam esse conspicimus, qua sublata et fides et iustitia huma-
nitasque omnis protinus evertuntur ita ut merito perbeatum et
maioribus etiam terminis atque victoriis dignum Turcarum imperium esse censeamus. Namque apud ipsos Ottomannos reges, qui
impie atque nefarie sanguinarii semper extiterunt, erga alienissi-
mos etiam deos admirabilis pietas viget; et antiquissimae Graecorum leges florent, quibus et praeclara facinora laude et praemiis

rendered illustrious by the memory of worthier exploits, both by others' writings and especially by yours.

"But I see that these calamities are certainly occurring through 13 the providence of the gods, who go on punishing our monstrous crimes: all are payback for corrupt morals, neglected religious observance, and the extinction of virtue. Nowhere is there either care for honor or fear of dishonor; there is no unwavering faith, true piety, love of humankind, or disinterested friendship. The kings themselves are by no means keen for glory, since they are enslaved to constant wars and unrestrained indulgence in vendettas. Moreover, those who render zealous service to the kings are shaping their counsels with an eye to interest and gain rather than duty. We see the result: in initiating and conducting wars nearly all have experienced an outcome of their plans that is unquestionably different from what they had intended. And, by God, they are still not ashamed to rail at Fortune—whom the ignorant and insane say rules all things and, in a rage, hastens human endeavors on a fatal course—even though the virtues themselves, both civil and military, which are the most reliable aids to the conduct of affairs, have been thrown out and banished from nearly every princely court, from all cities, and from the provinces.

"We see that piety, respect for which is the foremost attribute of 14 a Christian, has been subverted. Once piety has been removed, straightaway good faith, justice, and every human feeling are overthrown to such an extent that we might rightly reckon that the empire of the Turks is the most blessed and is worthy of even wider boundaries and greater victories. For in the courts of those very Ottoman rulers, who have always been impiously and heinously bloodthirsty, there thrives an admirable piety toward even the most foreign gods; and there flourish the exceedingly ancient laws of the Greeks by which splendid deeds are adorned with praise and rewards and, in like manner, crimes are avenged with

exornantur, et scelera pariter inexorabili severitate vindicantur. Selimus huius Solimani pater, Hierosolymas victor ingressus, Christianos sacerdotes non modo reliquit incolumes, sed perhumane in alimenta multorum dierum pecuniis etiam donavit. Idem paucos post dies, tertia etiam victoria superbior apud Memphim infantis Christi sacellum in Balsameto cupide est veneratus, qui neque patri neque fratribus eorumque filiis immanitate animi quin omnes ad unum necaret parcere nequiverat. Hic vero, qui modo nobis oscitantibus vel dissidentibus[31] excidium parat, Solimanus Rhodo capta nihil ex celeberrimi ac opulentissimi templi donariis omnino sustulit; Budaque nuper capta,[32] et regiam et templa religiosissime conservavit, contentus scilicet duabus aeneis statuis egregii operis, quae nutu ad insignis victoriae monumentum in medio foro Byzantii sunt collocatae.[33]

15   'Nos Romae non modo sacra omnia spoliata ac profanata, sed in Divi Petri et Pauli vetustissimo templo aram maximam, multis eorum cadaveribus qui frustra ad tutelares urbis divos[34] confugerant conseptam atque opertam inundante sanguine fuisse conspeximus. Nec adhuc[35] se non esse Christianos profitentur,[36] qui et haec et multo quidem immaniora scelera patraverunt adeo ut te, mi Davale, non modo prudentem ab exacto iudicio sed, sicut cunctis in proeliis, ita et tuis quoque consiliis felicem saepius[37] admirer, qui divina mente, ne tot familiae tuae decora totque proprias animi[38] corporisque virtutes penitus maculares et everteres, inauspicati sceleratique belli initia defugisti excessistique his castris, in quibus impia et[39] nefaria consilia contra publicam fidem

relentless severity. When Selim,[27] the father of this Süleyman[28] of ours, had entered Jerusalem in victory, he not only left Christian priests unharmed, but most humanely even provided the funds for many days' rations.[29] A few days later, glorying even more in a third victory near Cairo, this same man fervently venerated the Shrine of the Infant Christ of the Balsam[30]—yes, the very man whose bestial cruelty would not allow him to show mercy either to his father or to his brothers and their children, so that he killed every last one of them. Then there is Süleyman, who just now is readying destruction for us as we are yawning from weariness or disagreeing among ourselves. When he had captured Rhodes, he did not remove a single one of the votive offerings of its most famous and richest church;[31] and, recently, after capturing Buda, with the greatest care he preserved both the palace and the churches. Evidently he contented himself with two bronze statues of outstanding workmanship which, at his command, were placed in the central square of Byzantium as a monument of his distinguished victory.[32]

"But in Rome, we saw not only that all sacred things were pillaged and desecrated, but that in the ancient church of Saints Peter and Paul,[33] the high altar was hedged in by the many corpses of those who vainly had sought refuge before the guardian saints of the city, and it had been covered in their flowing blood. Yet those who have perpetrated both these crimes, and indeed far more monstrous ones, still fail to acknowledge that they are not Christians! And so, my friend d'Avalos, I often admire you not only as a man with prudence derived from scrupulous judgment but also as one of good fortune both in all your battles and in your counsels. You showed divine foresight in keeping clear of the initial phase of an ill-omened and criminal war and in withdrawing from those encampments in which wicked and criminal plans were being stirred up, contrary to an official guarantee.[34] Thus you entirely avoided sullying and subverting the many honors of your

15

agitarentur, ut magnam partem eius futurae invidiae gravi ac honestissimo discessu sustulisse viderere. Quae tum caesari, ut credi par est, vere pio et Christiano, ac[40] tum aequissima condicione indutias comprobanti, ab Borbonio nobis et sibi funestissimo duce parabatur.'

16   Ad ea DAVALUS 'Rectissime,' inquit, 'iudicas Museti. Nam me tam non paenitet quattuor[41] maximis bellis, quae totidem victoriis confecimus, haud mediocri cum laude interfuisse quam me iuvat tum abfuisse ab male sano concitatoque exercitu, cum nobilissimam et sanctissimam eorum quae sunt aut antea fuerunt urbem violatis divinis ac humanis rebus funditus evertit. Enimvero, cum postea Romam ad exercitum rediissem, ut perpetuae et[42] insatiabili militum crudelitati et cruciatorum civium miseriis modus imponeretur, perequitando Urbem lustravi oculis, adeo omni pristino honore atque ornatu spoliatam, tamque taetro ac horribili insepultorum cadaverum odore ceterarumque omnium rerum strage et miserabili foeditate deformatam ut nequiverim fletum tenere et cohibere lacrimas, vel torve respectantibus barbaris, qui saevitiam suam ac feritatem ab obvio quoque laetis vultibus excipi et comprobari debere iudicabant.

17   'Laetabar equidem felicitate caesaris sed non ea victoria, quae nullam spem pacis praeberet et toti Italiae diram vastitatem minaretur. Et[43] certe animus meus, iusta tactus religione ac[44] ex eius cumulatissimae felicitatis memoria valde commotus, capti pontificis custoditique senatus conspectum exhorruit. Nam tametsi ab eo publicam iniuriam cum summo meo periculo Mediolani fueram expertus, peculiari tamen benignitate eum[45] domui nostrae Piscarioque imprimis patrueli amicissimum fuisse recolebam, adeo ut ei gratias etiam nunc tacite referendas putemus, si tam grati

family and the many virtues of your own mind and person. Also, by your solemn and highly honorable departure, you appear to have obviated the lion's share of the infamy that was impending.[35] It is reasonable to believe that the emperor is truly pious and a Christian, and that he approved an armistice on the fairest of terms: the infamy that ensued was engendered for him by Bourbon, a commander most deadly to us and to himself."

To this D'AVALOS replied, "Quite right, Muscettola. I do not 16 regret having participated with distinction in four major wars, all of which we won; but I'm even more gratified to have been away from an insane and agitated army: once it had defiled things divine and human, it utterly destroyed the noblest and holiest city of all that are or have ever been. Thereafter, once I had returned to the army in Rome so that I might set a limit to both the insatiable cruelty of the soldiers and the miseries of the tormented citizens, I surveyed the city on horseback. It had been so robbed of every pristine honor and adornment and so disfigured by the revolting and horrible stench of unburied corpses, by the devastation of all other things, and by a miserable foulness, that I was unable to hold back my tears, even as the barbarians were glowering at me. They supposed that everyone they encountered ought to welcome and approve their cruelty and savagery with a cheery expression.

"For my part, I rejoiced in the emperor's good fortune, but not 17 in that victory, which offered no hope of peace and threatened all Italy with dreadful devastation. Certainly, my sensibility, albeit touched by his proper religiosity and deeply moved by the memory of his accumulated successes, nonetheless bristled at the sight of the pope held captive and the cardinals under guard. Even though I had experienced public injury at the emperor's hands amid grave personal danger at Milan,[36] I still recalled that he, with extraordinary kindness, had been well disposed toward our family, and especially toward my cousin Pescara.[37] So even now I think that I must thank him silently if I wish to be as grateful and de-

et pudentes in sentiendo beneficio atque aestimanda voluntate esse velimus quam magno et quam forti incorruptoque[46] animo in repudiando munere fuerimus. Nam [cum] ante hoc bellum, quod diis adversantibus postea suscepit ut adversus caesaris potentiam atque fortunam Italiae libertatis fundamenta moliretur, fratrem Piscarium et regno amplissimo et totius Italiae militari imperio dignum iudicavit. Quibus postea consiliis, non sine gravi dolore meo, et eum in has coniectum esse miserias et urbem Romam cum bona parte Italiae inusitata belli acerbitate vastatam esse conspicimus.

18   'Sed ut haec omittamus, et ad tuum, Museti, tantae gravitatis et sapientiae[47] sermonem revertamur, non est profecto cur diffitear (ut sentire videris) religionem ex mentibus hominum diuturnitate atque atrocitate maleficiorum convulsam esse, et Turcas, quos ut impios et immanes convitio potius quam armis persequimur, et in cultu deorum et in constanti virtutum omnium disciplina Christianis meliores evasisse dubitemus. Vita enim eorum et dignitas omnis in poena praemioque consistit, qua una re et tot finitima regna imperio antea virtute parto feliciter adiunxerunt; et nunc maxime, in omni consilio conatuque bellico, et deos mire propitios et secundam semper fortunam experiuntur. A[48] servili saepe illuvie[49] ad honores paratis et constitutis gradibus tantum[50] provehuntur quantum spectata virtus extulerit. Degeneres ac ignavi sordibus tenebris rusticisque laboribus mancipantur; praeclara ausos nobiliora militiae loca, opes, praefecturae statim excipiunt. Quod si quid contra fas et aequum obliti condicionis admiserint, ex eodem fastigio celeriter et graviore quidem casu praecipites dantur.

cent in appreciating his kindness and valuing his goodwill as I was great and brave and of unsullied mind in refusing this military duty. Before this war, which subsequently the pope[38] undertook (with the gods in opposition) to lay the foundations for the liberty of Italy against the emperor's power and good fortune, Caesar judged my cousin Pescara worthy of an expansive domain and the military command of all Italy. Subsequently, to my own great sorrow, we see that by his own policies the pope[39] has been hurled down into these miseries, and the city of Rome, along with a good part of Italy, devastated in a war of uncommon bitterness.

"But let us set these things aside, Muscettola, and return to what you were saying, which was so dignified and wise. There is certainly no reason for me to deny (as you might seem to think) that religion has been plucked from men's minds by the duration and savageness of their crimes. Nor should we doubt that the Turks, whom, though impious and brutal, we pursue with reproaches rather than with arms, have turned out better than Christians both in their worship of the gods and in their constant exercising of all the virtues. For their way of life and their whole system of rank consists in punishment and reward. By this alone they have successfully annexed so many neighboring kingdoms to an empire they had previously acquired by their courage; and especially now in every stratagem and martial endeavor they are always enjoying the marvelous support of the gods and good fortune. Insofar as a tested virtue has lifted them up, they are propelled out of servile filth toward honors by steps that are ready and well established. The inferior and cowardly are given over as slaves to filthy conditions, low station, and agricultural labor. The nobler army posts, the financial resources, and the governorships immediately fall to those who have shown outstanding courage. But if any, forgetful of their rank, commit something contrary to law and fairness, they are quickly toppled headlong from that same pinnacle and suffer a worse fate. 18

19   'Selimus orientis victor Bostangem generum suum necare et, ante curiae fores proiectum eius cadaver Byzantiis ostentare minime dubitavit quod ille gratiae ac affinitati frustra innixus superbe atque avare Lydiis Cariis[51] et Phrygibus imperasset. Hic etiam Solimanus, qui modo Pannonicum regnum, Ludovico rege cum proceribus acie caeso, celeriter evertit.[52] Sapherum[53] classis praefectum alioqui virum fortissimum,[54] quoniam in delectu remigum totoque negotio maritimo avarius ac acerbius se gessisse[55] convinceretur, in medio Bizantii foro, aurata indutum veste, furcae supplicio protinus affecit. In agnoscendis porro remunerandisque fortibus factis, tales omni tempore se praebuerunt[56] ut, cum novis hominibus ex merito amplissima praemia tribuant, iam nemo amplius fortunam desideret, ubi virtuti plenissime confidat.

20   'At nostri, cum diu laborando, pericula subeundo agendoque aliquam virtutis opinionem adepti fuerint, tum demum eis perdifficile cum fortuna simul ac invidia certamen relinquitur, adeo ut ignavi portentosa felicitate alienae operae fructum saepissime ferant, et strenuissimi quique belloque optimi ignominia taciti dedecoris onerentur. Sic enim pessimis artibus bella geri, sic delirare principes ac[57] eos sera plecti paenitentia, et cuncta foedissimis erroribus permisceri videmus, ut aliquando tales nobis reges exoptandos arbitremur quibus operam nostram alacriter probemus, quales mirifica virtus et religiosa disciplina ad certam spem

"Selim, the conqueror of the East, did not hesitate in the slight- 19
est to kill his own son-in-law, Bostanges, because he had ruled
haughtily and rapaciously over the Lydians, Carians, and Phry-
gians. Bostanges had relied upon the ruler's favor and upon being
related to him by marriage, but to no avail: Selim had his corpse
thrown out in front of the doors of the court and put on display to
the Byzantines.[40] Consider also Süleyman, who just now quickly
toppled the kingdom of Hungary once King Louis II along with
his nobles had been slaughtered in battle.[41] When Ja'fer Bey,[42] admiral of the fleet and an exceedingly courageous man besides, was
convicted of having acted quite greedily and harshly in the recruitment of rowers and in his entire maritime commission, Süleyman
at once subjected him, attired in gilded clothing, to the punishment of the fork in the central square of Byzantium. On the other
hand, in acknowledging and rewarding brave deeds, they have
shown themselves on every occasion such that, when they bestow
copious rewards upon new men on account of their merit, nobody
who relies entirely upon valor ever again feels the want of a greater
fortune.

"But once our men have won some reputation for valor by la- 20
boring for a long time, enduring dangers, and taking action, even
then an extremely difficult struggle with chance and envy awaits
them. This is so much the case that cowards by monstrous good
luck very often reap the fruit of others' efforts, whereas the ones
who are the most vigorous and the best in battle are burdened
with the disgrace of dishonor and neglect. For we see that wars are
being conducted by the very worst tactics, princes are out of their
minds and are punished because they repent too late, and all
things are thrown into confusion by the most shocking errors.
This is so much the case that sometimes we think we should long
for the kinds of rulers to whom we might quickly prove the
worth of our efforts: the kind that marvelous virtue and religious
training have molded most properly so that they inspire the sure

insignium praemiorum immanibus illis barbaris rectissime confor-
mavit.

21   'Sed cur tam repente et a subole exemplisque maiorum et ab
ipsa virtute desciverimus naturaque ipsa huic aetati maligna potius
noverca quam parens esse videatur, nequaquam animus meus deprehendit. Sunt enim qui haec ipsa mortalia sinistris et infelicibus
radiis planetarum adeo vehementer conturbata ad taetram et fu-
nestam rerum omnium confusionem arbitrentur, ut non animan-
tia[58] modo sed terras etiam denegatis frugibus a vetere ⟨perf⟩ec-
tione[59] deficere p⟨r⟩orsus appareat. Tot enim inusitati nec minus
prodigiosi quam admirabiles ⟨asp⟩ectus et coitus errantium siderum, qui triennio ante in unam caeli sedem et Februarium men-
sem ⟨stipaveran⟩t, ut ex disciplina promittebant nequaquam sera
fide, haec detrimenta mortalibus exsolvere iudicantur, ⟨. . .⟩i ex
divinis litteris veterascere mendum[60] existimant, hominis etiam
naturam sensim ⟨declinare et⟩ deficere constanter credunt, velut
quasi infinitis renascentium modis affecta et aliq⟨ua⟩[61] vehementer
fatigata iam tandem in seipsa pl⟨icata⟩.[62] Propterea vellem ut tu,
Museti, causas mihi et plerisque aliis occultas insoliti[63] effectus
uberiore tua facundia nobis explicares, postquam et locum per se
amoenum et omni molestia atque interpellatione vacuum nacti
sumus; et totius aucupii exitus nullo modo interrupta feminarum
voluptate videtur exspectandus.'

22   Ad ea MUSETIUS 'Satis importune,' inquit, 'Davale, aut certe
militariter facis, qui iureconsulto ex philosophia quaestionem
imponis Iovii ingenio facultateque dignissimam. Neque enim
salvo pudore suscipi potest id munus quod alteri iure optimo
debetur. Et tu recte feceris, Davale, si me isto onere levatum voles,

expectation of wresting glorious prizes from those monstrous barbarians.

"But I fail to understand why we have broken away so suddenly   21
both from the stock and the precedents of our ancestors and from
virtue itself. Nor do I know why nature herself seems to be a
spiteful stepmother to this age rather than a mother. There are
those who think that the adverse and ill-fated rays of the planets
have so violently thrown these mortal affairs into a foul and deadly
universal confusion that not only living creatures but even the soil,
denied crops, appears indeed to fall short of its ancient perfection.
For the great number of unaccustomed and no less portentous
than wondrous aspects and conjunctions of the planets, which in
the month of February three years ago crowded together into one
seat in the heavens, are judged to be unleashing these hardships on
mortals, as they predicted with ready assurance, on the basis of
their 'discipline.' [. . .] Others[43] think on the basis of Scripture that
the defect is growing with age, that the nature of man is gradually
and constantly declining and weakening. It is as if nature, broken
and somehow immensely exhausted by the infinite ways things
come back to life, is now at last coiling into itself. Therefore I
should wish, Muscettola, that you, with your more abundant eloquence, might explain to us the causes of this strange outcome,
which have been hidden to me and to many others, now that we
have reached a place that is both pleasing in itself and free from
every annoyance and interruption; and I think we need not wait
for the end of the entire bird hunt, since there is a break in the
women's entertainment."

To this MUSCETTOLA replied, "D'Avalos, you are acting inap-   22
propriately, or at least in a military manner, in putting to a lawyer
a question from the realm of philosophy best suited to the talent
and skill of Giovio. Nor, indeed, can one undertake with modesty
intact a task which properly belongs to another. You would do
well, d'Avalos, if you will be willing for me to be relieved of this

et Iovio ad dicendum excitato, me plane auditorem esse patieris. Nam tametsi aliquos ex philosophia flores, animi causa, ab ineunte aetate decerpserim, et in orandis causis dicendisque sententiis multo plura quam iureconsulto sit necesse, scire sim visus ex iis disciplinis quae alienae a forensibus negotiis reputantur, tamen in magna rerum naturae caligine semper sum versatus, cum animadverto nihil tam certum in philosophia videri de quo non diversa atque pugnantia opinentur, qui eius scientiae studiosi dici volunt et eandem etiam sectam profitentur, adeo ut saepe, cum altiora et naturae abditissima[64] quaeque perscrutarer, dubiisque eorum et convolutis rationibus vehementer essem implicatus, ad sacras litteras tamquam ad statuam salutis ac libertatis confugerem, ne quid animo meo solidam pietatem ex divinae legis placitis respectanti ad exitium penitus insideret.'

23   Tum ego ⟨IOVIUS⟩ inquam 'Museti,[65] astute pariter et verecunde egisse videris, cum onus pergrave atque difficile umeris excussisti tuis, ut illud alienis imponeres.'

24   Ad id DAVALUS 'Uter,' inquit, 'incipiat non refert. Nam cum uterque vestrum eximiam habeat cum eloquentiae tum ingenii in explicandis huiusmodi rebus facultatem, non putabo id esse in alium sarcinam excutere, sed benigne ad allevandum pondus in partem oneris subire.'

25   Tum ego ⟨IOVIUS⟩ 'Si ita est,' inquam, 'et[66] bona fide Musetius repromittat, incipere non gravabor, quando nihil ei umquam de facilitate et comitate sim concessurus.[67] Sed de natura rerum ac animorum[68] divinaque potestate disceptare ex praeceptis Peripateticorum homini Christiano periculosum esse censemus. Nam sicut ea quae in hoc inferiore mundo perpetua elementorum dimicatione tantaque humanarum cogitationum atque operum varietate

burden of yours and, once Giovio has been called upon to speak, you allow me merely to listen. For although I may, for relaxation's sake, have culled some flowers from philosophy in my youth, and in pleading cases and giving legal opinions I have seemed to know many more things from those disciplines considered unsuited to the practice of law than a jurist requires, nonetheless I have always been completely in the dark regarding the nature of the universe. I notice that nothing in philosophy appears so certain but that those who wish to be called learned in that science, and even those who are members of the same school, hold conflicting and opposing views. As a result, when I was studying carefully all the loftier and most recondite aspects of nature and when I was firmly entangled in their uncertainties and involved calculations, I often had recourse to sacred texts as to a statue that provides safety and liberty, lest, as my mind looked to solid piety based upon the tenets of divine law, something worm its way into it and destroy me."

Then I [GIOVIO] replied: "You would seem to have acted both   23
astutely and modestly, Muscettola, since you have shaken a heavy and unwieldy burden from your shoulders in order to place it on those of another."

To this D'AVALOS said: "It makes no difference which of you   24
begins. Since each of you has an outstanding faculty both of eloquence and a talent for explicating things of this sort, I won't suppose that this is a case of throwing a burden onto another but a kind offer to lighten the weight by sharing it."

Then I [GIOVIO] said: "If that is so and Muscettola should agree   25
in good faith, I don't mind beginning, since I would always want to match his good nature and courtesy. But we reckon that it is dangerous for a Christian to discuss the nature of the universe and of souls and of divine power in accordance with the teachings of the Peripatetics. For just as it seems to befit a mistaken and stupid philosopher to have ascribed emphatically, to a very certain reckoning of a divine plan, those things which in this lower world are

semper agitantur, ad certissimam divini consilii rationem asseveranter retulisse[69] aberrantis insulsique philosophi esse videtur, ita valde impium est, contra id quod firmissime credas, exposcere rationes quae ex[70] ambiguis arbitrariisque philosophiae principiis emanarint. Quamquam ea, quae tam anxie de animorum immortalitate, de motore atque anima caeli eiusque motuum inextricabili ratione ab ipso Aristotele philosophiae magistro, adeo obscure perastuteque tradantur ut gentiles isti atque tumidi sapientes illi convicium facere nequeant[71] qui, ut graviter eruditus Christianus, simul et philosophus esse voluerit.[72] Ceterum[73] dabitis veniam, ut pio homini[74] antistiti etiam sacerdoti propediem futuro, si ab iis quos in gymnasiis enixe coluerim[75] philosophis aliqua ex parte dissensero, ut haec vestra quaestio quae quorundam sapientium animos diu torsit, clarius explicetur.

26   'Igitur[76] naturam hominis[77] ab ea quae superioribus saeculis exstiterit, nequaquam extenuatam aut debilitatam esse existimandum est, si corporis robur pariter ipsiusque animi vires consideratius aestimemus, et ceterorum animantium genera uno perfectionis perpetuo tenore propagata cum humana specie conferantur.[78] Infinitis siquidem rotationibus et certo perennique motu circumagitur caelum, eadem sempiterna siderum potestate terrae globum circumplectens, sic ut elementarem materiam alternis agitationibus evariet et cuncta certa atque utili proportione permisceat, nec umquam tamen animis nostris dominetur, quos primus opifex Deus et liberos et immortales effinxit.[79]

27   'Itaque terrena haec ex contrariis composita elementis, cum vim ipsam caelestis luminis et irrequieti motus necessario sentiant, necesse est ut diverso coitu et successivo[80] errore planetarum, solis

always set in motion by the constant struggle of the elements and by such a great variety of human thoughts and efforts, so in turn it is exceedingly impious to demand explanations, contrary to what you believe most firmly, that have derived from the ambiguous and arbitrary principles of philosophy. Although those points about the immortality of souls, about the mover and life force of the heavens, and about the tangled pattern of its movements are handed down from Aristotle himself, the master of philosophy, they are conveyed so cryptically and cleverly that those miserable pagans and presumptuous 'wise' men cannot make a mockery of a deeply learned Christian who has at the same time wanted to be a philosopher. But you will forgive me — a pious man, who before long will be a bishop and also a priest — if I dissent to some degree from those philosophers to whom I devoted myself assiduously in the schools, in order that I may more clearly give an account of this question of yours, which has for a long time tormented the minds of certain wise men.

"We must, then, judge that the nature of man has not been at all diminished or impaired from what it was in previous centuries, if we estimate carefully the strength of the body and likewise of the mind itself, and if the kinds of other living creatures, produced in one sustained course of bringing-to-completion, are compared with the human race. The heavens are turned about in infinite rotations and with a fixed and perennial motion, embracing the earth by the same eternal power of the stars in such a way that they vary the elemental material by their alternating movements and mix all things together in a sure and advantageous proportion. But they never have control of our souls, which God, the First Creator, has made free and immortal.

"And so these earthly things, compounded of opposing elements, since they are inevitably affected by the very power of heavenly light and unceasing movement, must be greatly varied by differing conjunctions and successive wanderings of the planets, by

26

27

lunaeque deliquiis, et reliquo occultiore fixarum stellarum influxu
magnopere varientur et alias atque alias quadam naturae vicissitu-
dine facies ostendant. Universa tamen rerum moles, infinitis naturae vinculis colligata, ut in se ipsa perfecta[81] et immutabilis, perpetuo continetur, ordoque rerum et ipse praesertim intellectus
semper remanet incorruptus; nam sicut elementa inter se tota in
universum neque a summa naturali potestate deduci[82] neque deleri
possunt, sempiterno caeli vigore custodita, ita animi caelitus de-
lapsi communem quandam cum caelo firmitatem atque[83] praestan-
tiam sortiuntur. Caelum enim elementari temperatura minime
constat. Verum[84] ex alia quidem nobiliore materia tornatum abso-
lutumque est, sic ut purum translucidum et gratissimo[85] colore,
distinctis stellarum ignibus perpictum, oculis nostris offeratur.[86]
Neque ullis externis affectionibus ac iniuriis vitiari foedarive, neque ullo umquam tempore senescere aut in rotatione retardari vel
incitari[87] queat, nisi infinitus ille mundi artifex et sapientissimus
rerum omnium arbiter adnuerit.

28   'Simili ratione, animae nostrae perpetuo vivent ergastulo corporis exsolutae, verum cum eas et liberas et appetitionum omnium
moderatrices cuncti prope philosophi esse[88] fateantur, plerumque
accidit ut a voluptate sensibusque deceptae imperio uti nesciant;
et, ultro vitiatae sceleribus oblitaeque praestantissimae libertatis,
in servitutem pessimis hostibus dedantur, ita ut non humano, sed
ferino quidem more in ipsis versentur corporibus.

29   'Quamobrem saluberrima atque divina remedia legibus sunt
constituta, ut depravatus animus in officio posset contineri homi-
nesque ratione pro libidine ut assuescerent, atque ut ita facerent ad
parendum poena et praemio monerentur. Sociabile enim docile-

eclipses of the sun and moon, and by the remaining, more hidden influence of the fixed stars; and by a sort of mutation of nature, they display different aspects at one time or another. Still, the entire mass of things, fettered by the infinite chains of nature, is complete and unchangeable, and is perennially self-contained. The order of things, and especially the intellect itself, always remains uncorrupted. For just as all the elements, guarded by the eternal vigor of the heavens, can neither suffer diminishment of their full natural power nor be destroyed, so too the souls, having descended from heaven, are allotted a certain strength and excellence shared with it. Indeed, heaven does not in the least consist in the blending of elements. Instead, it has been smoothed and perfected out of some noble material in such a way that it is displayed to our eyes as pure, transparent, and pleasing in color, painted throughout with the distinctive fires of the stars. It can be neither corrupted nor dimmed by any outside influences and injuries, nor can it ever decay or be either slowed or hastened in its rotation, unless that infinite Creator of the world, the perfectly wise Judge of all things, permits it.

"By similar reasoning, our souls, once liberated from the prison 28 house of the body, will live forever. Nearly all the philosophers acknowledge that our souls are free and that they control all the appetites. Nonetheless, it often happens that, deceived by pleasure and by the senses, souls fail to understand how to use their power of command: corrupted of their own accord by wicked deeds, and forgetful of their excellent liberty, they surrender themselves as slaves to their worst enemies, so that they dwell in those very bodies in a manner not human but bestial.

"For this reason, salutary and divine remedies were established 29 by laws, so that a corrupted soul might be held to its duty, and so that people might become habituated to reason instead of to lust — and in order that they might do this, it was established that they be prompted to obey by punishment and reward. For the

que[89] est hominis ingenium, facileque id ad decus, ad honestatem, et ad praealta quaeque contendit, si bonis moribus excolatur; at boni mores sine legibus esse non possunt, quae tum optimae atque utiles exsistunt cum a conditoribus ipsisque principibus observantur. Namque principes et reges tum crimine tum ipso maxime exemplo peccant, quoniam vita, eorum omnium proposita oculis, sensum multitudinis ad aemulandum excitare consuevit. Sic factum puto ut illud tum[90] florens et beatum saeculum esse diceretur, cum sapientissimi fortissimique viri aut res publicas aut regna gubernarent, talesque se bello paceque gererent ut neque vis hostium timeri neque ordo civilium rerum ulla hominum audacia et temeritate conturbari posse videretur.

30   'Neque proinde caelestes causas, quae certis saeculorum periodis terras mariaque agitant, simili ratione mortalium animos[91] afficere commovereque arbitramur, ut a virtute abhorreant, quam antea in honore habuerint, et damnata ante vitia nova insanaque cupidine complectantur. Sicut videmus insulas aliquando repente enatas, alias porro esse demersas; Circaeos continenti adiectos, abscisam ab Italia Siciliam; ipsum aggeribus Gessoriacis cessisse oceanum, qui alibi submersas inundet urbes; flumina cursum avertere, ut sibi novos alveos parent.[92] Quin et alia[93] subito exarescere[94] siccarique,[95] alia repente scaturrire,[96] non alia ratione quam cum[97] montes absorbentur. Hiant terrae, erumpunt novi ignes; veteres, ut in hac insula et in Aetna modo ipsa, penitus exstinguuntur. Has quondam ferunt operuisse terras aestuantia maria, et quae mersae erant siccatas ac[98] habitabiles reddidisse. Haec enim ad ornatum[99] universi pertinere putamus, ut quae clades senserint,

nature of man is sociable and teachable, and it willingly strives toward honor, integrity, and all the most elevated things if only it is cultivated with good morals. But good morals cannot exist without laws, which are best and advantageous when they are observed by the ones instituting them and by the princes themselves. For princes and kings sin not just in committing a crime, but above all in the example they thereby set, since the manner of life they display to the eyes of all their people generally stirs the minds of the multitude to emulate it. This is why I think we would call prosperous and blessed that age when exceedingly wise and courageous men were ruling either republics or kingdoms, and were acting in both war and peace in such a way that they would neither be seen to fear the strength of enemies, nor could any human audacity or impetuosity be seen to upset the order of civic affairs.

"Correspondingly, we do not suppose that celestial causes, which 30 act upon lands and seas at fixed periods, likewise influence and stir up the minds of mortals so that they shrink from a virtue they had previously held in honor and with new and insane desire embrace vices they had previously condemned. We see that islands have at times suddenly arisen; others, in turn, have been submerged: the Circeans were added to the mainland, but Sicily was cut off from Italy. The ocean itself yielded to the breakwater at Gessoriac, although elsewhere it submerges and inundates cities. Rivers have changed course so that they furnish themselves with new beds. Some are suddenly parched and dry up, but others unexpectedly gush forth in the same way as when mountains are submerged. The ground opens up and new fires erupt; but old fires are entirely extinguished, as on this island and just now in the case of Mt. Etna itself. They say that the boiling seas once covered these lands, and later the lands that had been submerged dried out and were made habitable. We think that all these things pertain to the cosmic order: since nature manages all things well, those lands

alternis vitibus, recte cuncta dispensante natura, a nova fertilitate
decorentur,[100] et multis intermissam saeculis antiquam frequentiae[101] recipiant dignitatem.

31   'Ceterum de ingeniis moribusque hominum paria credidisse
eius esse videtur qui depravato[102] vel abiecto animo in corpus
sensusque suos[103] imperium amiserit. Actionum enim[104] humanarum procul dubio animus et arbiter et imperator exsistit, neque
umquam illa officiunt quin suo plenissimo iure ac imperio potia-
tur, quod temperaturas corporum vis caelestis et impotentia sidera
plerumque dissolvant, coaequalemque illam exagitent umorum
proportionem, qua homines a diversa ingeniorum potestate ac
immoderatis morum excessibus, constantes aut imbecilli, feroces
aut mansueti, turbidi aut lenes et dociles reddantur.[105] Hanc enim
corporum intemperiem, quam stellae nobis insinuant, animi vitiis
plerumque fovemus, et sponte nostra alimus insaniam, quam ante
omnia alienatis et perditis sensibus consectamur. Effingimus profecto nobis mores quos volumus, et ad id una maxime consuetudine pertrahimur.

32   'Vos Neapoli in universum[106] erecto corpore et obstipa[107] cervice
inceditis, et composita gravitate loquimini, ut Hispanorum personam effingatis. Contra, nos[108] transpadanos[109] vultus et sermonis
alacritas liberique corporis motus, repraesentato ubique simplicis
animi candore, plurimum delectant, quae omnia velut Gallica consuetudine inducta, sicut vos damnare soletis, ita et nos eum totum
intenti[110] habitus conatum saepissime deridemus.

33   'Itali milites, ante externarum gentium adventum, sic arma
tractabant bellaque gerebant ut ab amplissimis saepe victoriis

that have undergone calamities in their turn enjoy new fertility and recover their former suitability for habitation, which had lapsed for many centuries.

"But to believe that the same is true of men's characters seems 31 to be the mark of someone whose mind is depraved or debased and who has lost control of his body and his emotions. Indeed, the mind is surely both the judge and the commander of human actions: celestial causes[44] never prevent it from being master of the full range of its rights and authority. And this is the case even though the force of the heavens and the intemperate stars may often upset bodily constitutions and stir up the proportional balance among the humors. It is this proportionality whereby, in accordance with the differing strength of characters and immoderate excesses of behavior, men are made steadfast or weak, aggressive or mild, unruly or gentle and teachable. Thus, by reason of mental defect, quite often we foster this bodily intemperateness which the stars instill in us, and of our own accord we nourish madness, which we seek above all other things once our senses have become estranged and lost. Certainly we mold for ourselves the morals that we want, and we are drawn on toward that end mostly by habit alone.

"You Neapolitans as a rule strut with body erect and head 32 cocked to one side, and you speak with a studied solemnity, so as to imitate the manner of the Spaniards. We northern Italians, on the other hand, take delight in liveliness of facial expression and of speech, in the uninhibited movement of the body, and in a purity of unaffected character that is evident everywhere. Just as you generally condemn all those things that have been introduced according to the French custom, as it were, so we often mock your entire affectation of an earnest demeanor.

"Before the coming of foreigners, Italian soldiers used to wield 33 weapons and wage wars in such a way that from the most distinguished victories they often brought back unbloodied swords be-

incruentos gladios reportarent, quod satis mulctatos eos existimabant quos vivos cepissent ac subinde[111] armis vexillis castris exuis-
sent. Illi in hibernis numquam rapto vivere, numquam bello nisi ex
hostico praedari, semper sociorum frugibus parcere, amore denique et studio potius quam metu[112] cuncta quae usui essent ab in-
colis promereri, tecta vel[113] apud hostes nusquam exurere, abstinere a templis, et nihil crudelius evastare consueverant.

34 'At postquam insana ambitione principum, evocatis in Italiam
externis gentibus,[114] antiquum decus et opes et libertatem amisimus, tales evasere Itali milites ut multo[115] superbiores[116] Gallis,
rapaciores Hispanis,[117] et denique Germanis in omni genere inferendae vastitatis[118] immaniores esse videantur. In tanta siquidem
temporum iniquitate et corpora pariter ac[119] animos imitatione
barbarorum penitus efferarunt, et cunctae fere civitates eorum
crudelissimo dominatu illos antiquos mores pristinamque vitam,
modestia, simplicitate, munditiis religioneque plenissimam, relin-
quere sunt coactae. Foede tantum ac[120] insulse prodigi esse, fre-
quentibusque epulis et vino praesertim diligenter studere didicimus. Feminarum amisimus pudicitiam, sublatisque[121] litterarum
studiis liberorum nostrorum ingenia perdidimus, impiique demum, vel desperatione rerum nostrarum vel exemplo immanissimorum[122] militum, omnis penitus obliti virtutis, per[123] inusitata
facinora debacchamur.

35 'Pietate[124] igitur aequitate[125] constantiaque animi effingi bonos
mores, optimis vero moribus conciliari haud dubie Fortunam et
virtutem peti, manifestum est; qua demum ad summum bonum

cause they thought those men sufficiently punished whom they had captured alive and then stripped of arms, banners, and camps. The Italian soldiers of old never made a habit of living in their winter quarters upon what they had pillaged or of plundering during war at all, except from enemy territory. Instead, they always spared allies' crops and in the end obtained all that they needed from the inhabitants through affection and zeal rather than fear. At no time did they make a practice of burning down houses, even among the enemy. They kept away from churches and practiced no wanton destruction.[45]

"But after our princes out of insane ambition had summoned 34 foreign armies into Italy, we lost our former dignity, resources, and freedom. Italian soldiers have turned out to be such that they seem far more arrogant than the French, more rapacious than the Spaniards, and more monstrous even than the Germans in every mode of inflicting devastation. Accordingly, amid the great iniquity of the times, in imitation of the barbarians they have become utterly bestial both physically and mentally. Almost all Italian cities have been compelled by the cruelest domination of the barbarians to relinquish those ancient morals and the pristine way of life characterized by modesty, simplicity, tasteful elegance, and religious observance. We have learned, so very foully and stupidly, to be wasteful and to devote ourselves to frequent banquets and especially to wine. Women are no longer chaste; and since the study of literature has been eliminated, we have ruined our children's minds; and finally, being irreligious and wholly forgetful of every virtue, either out of despair over our circumstances or in imitation of the example of savage soldiers, we celebrate an orgy of outlandish wickedness.

"It is clear, then, that good morals are formed by piety, fairness, 35 and constancy of mind, and that we win over Fortune and strive after virtue by means of good character. In this manner, we are most assuredly carried forward at last to the supreme good, and to

ipsamque tam diu in humanis frustra quaesitam felicitatem certis-
sime[126] provehimur. Propterea valde improbe[127] sidera convicio
suggillamus, et Fortunam exsecramur, quasi infestissimis eorum
radiis inique flagellati et ab hac omnino deserti simus, ut reluctari
in tantis malis[128] et virtutis lucem aspicere nequeamus. Est enim
haec scientia sideralis tam aerumnoso cassoque labore a curiosis
quaesita potius quam inventa, si sani esse velimus et vere philosophi, inter fallacissimas artes redigenda. Occupavit profecto multorum animos dulcedo illa incredibilis futura praenoscendi, ut
humani ingenii vanitas in toto vitae arcano divinis mentibus ae-
quaretur. Nec mirum ut credulos magis egregie deciperet; ex professo validas stirpes et praeclaram originem a certissimis mathe-
maticorum disciplinis ostendit, quarum nobili pariter et gravi
lenocinio ad fallendum Chaldaeorum commentis insignis auctoritas adderetur.

36   'Sed profecto nihil est haec astrologia divinatrix, quae genituras
hominum primordiaque[129] imperiorum et[130] urbium[131] impudentissime perscrutatur ut tot casuum eventa contra Fatorum imperium, cum inani laetitia aut vano[132] metu credentium, aperiat.
Quod si aliquid est haec ars omnino ludicra et spuria quadam
adoptione disciplina, eam certe in intimis[133] recessibus ac arbitrio
divinae mentis abditam putamus. Necesse est enim ut[134] intellectus noster ad praealta illa caelestium causarum momenta penitus
caliget, cum in reputandis terrae miraculis, dum nihil certum repe-
rit,[135] vehementer etiam obstupescat.

that very happiness in human affairs which has for so long been sought in vain. And so it is highly presumptuous for us to castigate the stars as if we have been unfairly lashed by their hostile rays, and to curse Fortune as if we have been entirely forsaken by her, so that amid such great ills we are unable to resist or to gaze upon the light of virtue. In fact, if we wish to be of sound mind and truly be philosophers, we must relegate this astrology to the ranks of the most deceitful arts. Rather than simply being discovered, it has been the object of much troublesome and fruitless inquiry on the part of the curious. That incredible allure of having advance knowledge of future events has certainly possessed the minds of many, who hope that the foolishness of human ingenuity might be made equal to divine minds in all the arcana of life. Nor is it surprising that astrology would practice extraordinary deception upon the credulous. It boasts professedly a sound lineage and a distinguished derivation from the unerring methods of mathematicians, in order that, for purposes of deceit, their authority might, by a seduction at once noble and influential, be augmented by the fabrications of the Chaldeans.

"But this art of astrology has, of course, no power of divination. 36 With utter shamelessness it scrutinizes people's horoscopes and the beginnings of empires and cities, so that it brings to light many outcomes of chance events that go against the command of the Fates, and it prompts foolish joy or empty fear in the minds of those who believe in it. But if this quite ridiculous art—which is a discipline only by some spurious adoption—amounts to anything, that, we believe, has certainly been hidden away in the innermost recesses and judgment of the divine mind. In fact, our intellect must be entirely shrouded in darkness regarding those most elevated influences of celestial proceedings, given that it is also utterly struck dumb when it finds nothing certain in reflecting on wondrous earthly events.

41

37   'Me, hercle, ab ineunte aetate, huic arti cum exquisito apparatu instrumentorum atque voluminum vehementer incumbentem, multorum insignium virorum exitus, contrarii[136] penitus disciplinae placitis, saepius eluserunt atque ita fefellerunt ut ingenuo pudore convictum et propterea stomachantem a fallacissimis studiis averterent. Quis[137] umquam astrologus M. Antonio Columnae, qui tormento discerptus interiit, cum advocatis undique professoribus genesim in manibus teneret, aliud quam amplissimum militiae imperium victorias triumphos ac placidum demum in exacta aetate vitae exitum promisit? Quis item Alfonsum Petrucium Cardinalem, cum in ipso aetatis flore, obscuro in carcere delicatas cervices strangulanti Aethiopi daturus esset, cunctis fortunae bonis ac honoribus fulgentem ad senectutem perventurum minime praedicavit?

38   'Decubuit ipse[138] Leo Pontifex, cum firmissima valetudine, aetate integra et temperatura praecellenti favebatur,[139] ut humana ac divina cuncta mox cum ipso conciderent.[140] Cum ei quasi triennio ante vitae periculum vitasset, astrologi omnes, ex amplissimo et prorsus liberali Alchocoden, multos et iucundos vitae annos pollicerentur. Quis modo Franciscum regem vinci acie, vivum capi, captivum in Hispaniam perduci, ut in Galliam se ipso melior et sapientior[141] rediret umquam praedixit? Quis Ludovici Pannoniae regis genituram, quando in themate nullus esset siderum aspectus vel[142] funestus vel malignus, adeo diligenter contemplatus est ut illum diceret, cum universa gentis nobilitate, Turcarum[143] gladio periturum? Excussimus profecto nos ipsi has regum geneses curiose admodum et diligenter, sed responsa prudentum quam astrologorum multo veriora deprehendimus.

"My God, when as a youth I used to apply myself rigorously to 37
this art with a fine apparatus of instruments and books, the deaths
of many famous men, turning out quite contrary to the tenets of
the discipline, very often baffled me and proved me wrong in such
a way that they drove me away from these fallacious studies when
I had been truly shamed and consequently was boiling with rage.
Consider the case of Marcantonio Colonna.[46] What astrologer
ever guaranteed to him anything other than an eminent command
in the field, victories, triumphs, and finally a calm death at an advanced age? Although he had in his possession a horoscope cast by
the 'experts' he had consulted, he died after being mangled by an
artillery shot. And who did not likewise predict that Cardinal Alfonso Petrucci, shining forth with all the goods and honors of
fortune, would reach a ripe old age? Yet in the very flower of
youth, he soon gave over his delicate neck to be strangled by an
Ethiopian in a dark dungeon.[47]

"Pope Leo himself passed away when he was favored with ro- 38
bust health and unimpaired by age and possessed an outstanding
physical constitution; things human and divine soon collapsed
with him. Although he had escaped an assassination attempt[48]
around three years before, all the astrologers had guaranteed him
many pleasant years of life on the basis of an exceedingly large and
absolutely generous Alchocoden.[49] And just recently, who ever
predicted that King Francis would be conquered in battle, captured alive, and taken as a captive to Spain, with the result that he
returned to France better and wiser than he had been before?
Who studied the horoscope of King Louis of Hungary so diligently, at a time when there was no appearance of stars either fatal
or malign, that he said that the king, along with all the nobility of
his people, would perish by the sword of the Turks? Certainly we
ourselves scrutinized these horoscopes of kings with immense care
and diligence, but we received far truer answers from sensible men
than from the astrologers.

39   'Sed quid dico "prudentum," cum insanus vir Senensis ex atrio
       Vaticanae curiae praetereuntibus cardinalibus totique populo Ro-
       manam cladem clarissima voce praedixerit? Porro quid magis per-
       tinet ad explodendos[144] huius artis ficticiae professores quam
       eorum vanitas impense deridenda qui, anno a partu Virginis mille-
       simo quingentesimo et vicesimo quarto, ex coitu multiplici plane-
       tarum in signo aqueo, tantam aquarum molem terris denunciarunt
       ut noti cives et in ipsa etiam urbe Roma, ubi per insaniam potius
       quam per imprudentiam homines peccant, cum alterum Deucalio-
       nis cataclysmon timerent, in altissimis editorum locorum turribus
       cubilia referta cibariis fabricarunt? Quamquam plerique philoso-
       phi non deessent adversus astrologos et imprimis Nyphius Suessa-
       nus, qui disceptando et scribendo imperitos populos hac inani
       sollicitudine muliebrique timore liberarent.'

40   Ad ea MUSETIUS 'Apud nos etiam,' inquit, 'haec opinio mul-
       tum valuit, adeo ut plerique tam anxia[145] summi periculi exspecta-
       tione vehementissime torquerentur. Sed tantum abfuit ut, sublatis
       caeli cataractis, aquae desuper terrarum orbem inundarent, ut per
       id tempus, ridendo certe sed miserabili eventu, in Africa Hispania
       Sicilia Apulia, exustis siti frugibus, inusitata siccitate sit labora-
       tum. Sed ille profecto mirificus siderum concursus, nequaquam
       ipsis exceptis astrologis, homines fefellit, quando postea ab Alpi-
       bus non fluminum diluvia, sed legionum externarum, torrentium
       more cuncta vastantium, perpessi fuerimus.'

41   Tum vero inquam ⟨IOVIUS⟩ 'De astris[146] recte existimas, Mu-
       seti, nam caeli signis nihil firmius,[147] cum nihil, ex adverso, homi-
       nis coniectura sit incertius, quod te saepius re ipsa deprehendisse

"But why do I say 'sensible' when a Sienese lunatic[50] prophesied   39
the conquest of Rome at the top of his lungs, from the entryway
of the Vatican, as the cardinals and the entire populace were passing by? And what helps us more in hissing off the stage the 'experts' of this counterfeit art than does the foolishness of those who
foretold a great flood for the year 1524, based upon the manifold
conjunction of the planets under Aquarius?[51] This has to give us a
good laugh. Thanks to their predictions, even in the city of Rome
itself, where people sin through insanity rather than through a
lack of foresight, well-known citizens built lairs jam-packed with
provisions in the tallest towers on the highest ground; they were
fearing another deluge of Deucalion.[52] To be sure, a good many
philosophers, especially Agostino Nifo of Sessa Aurunca, were not
remiss in their opposition to the astrologers: by debating and writing they freed ignorant peoples from this foolish and womanly
anxiety."[53]

To these things MUSCETTOLA added, "Among us too this be-   40
lief was so very influential that many people were violently tormented by an anxious expectation of extreme danger. But instead
of waters inundating the world once the floodgates of heaven had
been raised, at precisely that time it happened that, after the crops
had been ruined by lack of water, the world was plagued by unaccustomed drought in Africa, Spain, Sicily, and Apulia. The outcome was dreadful, but it was funny too. In fact that marvelous
concourse of the stars played a trick on human beings, not excepting the astrologers themselves, in that afterward we did experience
'floods' from the Alps — not of rivers, but of foreign troops, devastating all things in the manner of rushing streams."[54]

Then I [GIOVIO] said, "You are right about the stars, Muscet-   41
tola. Nothing is steadier than the signs of the heavens, whereas,
from the opposite perspective, nothing is more uncertain than the
prophecy of a human being. I divine that you have often discerned

coniecto[r] cum Pontani libris, in quibus de stellarum significatione luculenter agitur, plurimum inhaereres.'

42   At ille ⟨MUSETIUS⟩: 'Ita est,' inquit 'Iovi,[148] caelestia Pontani ab adulescentia[149] valde me delectarunt. Summi etenim viri et cui neminem adhuc video parem auctoritate commotus,[150] non modo scire sed praescire etiam res humanas alacriter et curiose contendebam. Ceterum[151] ut honesto cum rubore verum non infitiar, ea divinandi praecepta aliquanto elegantius quam verius traduntur, ita ut Pontanum appareat in excolenda adeo salebrosa materia praestantis eloquentiae laudem, potius quam ab eius divinae artis scientia gloriam, quaesivisse. Sed liquido iam astrologos mortalium mendacissimos aestimemus, et ad Fortunam revertamur, de cuius potestate, aliqua tibi, Iovi, perstricte sunt referenda.'

43   'Sane,' inquam ⟨IOVIUS⟩, 'et hanc in iudicium devocabo, ut refutatis eius praestigiis atque fallaciis, ex hoc humanae vitae theatro redargutam et traductam protinus exsibilemus. Quam misere, edepol, decepti sunt, qui eam in tota vitae ratione boni et mali, tamquam expensi pariter ac accepti, utramque paginam implere crediderunt. Monstrum profecto est chimaerae simile ad alendam illorum insaniam repertum qui, ubi pessime res cedant, vel ignavi animi vel naturae praecipitis culpam infestae Fortunae nomine praetexunt. Est enim ad hanc praeclaram et fictilem deam non ignobilis receptus miseris omnibus, qui sive turbidi sive hebetes ingenio fuerint in transverso et foedo[152] consiliorum exitu, se tamen imprudentes esse numquam fatentur. Quis enim ingenium sensum iudicium alteri umquam invidit, cum fortunam tantum invideat? Quae profecto ex concursatione rerum et casuum ac

this in actual fact, since you were so absorbed in the books of Pontano,[55] in which he brilliantly treats the signification of the stars."

"So it is, Giovio," he [MUSCETTOLA] conceded. "Since my 42 youth, the celestial writings of Pontano have delighted me immensely. Prompted by the influence of that eminent man, whose equal I have yet to see, I labored with eagerness and care not only to know human affairs, but also to have foreknowledge of them. But to confess the truth with an honorable blush: those precepts of divining are handed down somewhat more elegantly than accurately. And so it seems that in treating such a thorny subject, Pontano sought praise for outstanding eloquence rather than glory from knowledge of that divine art. But let us now reckon unequivocally that astrologers are the most deceitful of all mortals, and let us return to Fortune. Giovio, you really must touch briefly on her power."

"Of course," I [GIOVIO] said, "and I will summon her into court 43 so that once we have refuted her dodges and deceptions, we may at once hiss her out of this theater of human life as one convicted and exposed to scorn. By God, how pitifully deceived are those who have trusted her to fill out each of the two columns in the entire reckoning of the good and ill of life, just as in the case of debits and credits! A monster like the chimera has certainly been found for nourishing the delusion of those who, when things turn out for the worst, have cloaked the fault of either a sluggish mind or an impetuous nature with the name of hostile Fortune. For recourse to this 'splendid' clay goddess is a respectable refuge for all the wretches whose confusion or dimwittedness has caused their plans to be thwarted and turn out disgracefully, yet who still never admit their imprudence. After all, who ever envies another's talent, good sense, and discernment when he might only envy his good fortune? Certainly Fortune, born from the convergence of circumstances, accidents, and the vain drawing of lots, has always had as

inani sorte edita, tam multos imperitos cultores semper habuit quam philosophos irrisores.

44   'Quod si eae[153] rationes aliquos[154] non movent quae ab usu rerum ipsaque veterum disciplina deducuntur,[155] exempla certe superiorum aetatum absque ulla dubitatione permovebunt, ut nostra potius pravitate et transalpinarum gentium iniuria[156] felicitati nostrae invidentium quam occultis astrorum influxibus vel senescentis naturae vitiis hanc aetatem pristino honore dignissimorum hominum orbatam esse intellegatis. Nam si longissime quoad possumus praeteritorum saeculorum clades ex monumentis litterarum recordari velimus, liquido constabit post inclinatam atque extinctam Romani nominis gloriam et bonas artes et litteras frequentibus barbarorum irruptionibus interiisse.

45   'Ex illa enim luctuosissima imperii translatione, Constantinus Imperator ab eius impii facti memoria detestandus, Italiam cum urbe Roma, omni exutam dignitate praesidiisque nudatam, barbaris occupandam evastandamque reliquit. Ita eam non multo post Heruli et Trualongi feroces populi tenuere, quos demum Gothus numerosus et furens armis expulit, ornamentaque omnia Romanae magnitudinis funditus evertit. Nec Gothi suffecerant ad delendum omne Romanum nomen, nisi Hunnos et totam demum Scythicam rabiem Italia opportuna omnium iniuriis accepisset. Tunc enim plane victa et superata, manus dedit quae paullo ante cunctis quas sol aspicit gentibus imperarat. Subsecutae quoque sunt aliae gentes, velut coniuratione facta, ut veteres iniurias vindicarent: Vandali Visigothi Burgundii et Longobardi qui, diversa

many unskilled worshippers as she has philosophers who have mocked her.

"But if these reasons, which are derived from practical experi- 44 ence and from our ancestors' teaching, fail to move some, examples from earlier ages will surely and without a doubt carry conviction, so that you may understand that this age has been deprived of the pristine honor of worthy men by our own wickedness and the injustice of Transalpine peoples who envied our happiness, rather than by the hidden influence of the stars or by flaws arising from nature's decline. For if we wish to recall from as far back as possible the calamities of past centuries, gleaned from the monuments of literature, it will become clear that after the glory of the Roman nation had been brought low and extinguished, both the fine arts and literature perished on account of the frequent invasions of barbarians.

"From the time of that utterly calamitous transfer of empire,[56] 45 the Emperor Constantine—who must be accursed on account of the memory of that impious deed—abandoned Italy along with the city of Rome. Rome was divested of every dignity and stripped of protection and left to be occupied and devastated by the barbarians. Not long after that, the Herulians and the †Trualongi†,[57] savage peoples, occupied Italy. In the end, innumerable raging Goths expelled them by arms and completely effaced all the monuments of Roman grandeur. Nor would the Goths have had sufficient strength to destroy the Roman nation had not Italy, lying open to the injuries of all, let in the Huns and in the end the savagery of all the Scythians. Then indeed, utterly conquered and vanquished, Rome surrendered—a city which, a little earlier, had ruled over all the nations upon which the sun shines. Other peoples too followed closely behind, as though they had formed a conspiracy to avenge old injuries: the Vandals, Visigoths, Burgundians, and Lombards, who, with different desires and varied

libidine varioque eventu, aut cuncta rapuerunt aut, pulsis indige-
nis, colonias in terris ab se occupatis posuerunt.

46   'Porro Italia, secundum eam tempestatem, multa a Gallis sed
multo maxima a Germanis detrimenta suscepit. Angli et ipsi Bri-
tannica gens et Normanni et Britones ab Aremorico litore, cum
aliquamdiu mercenaria arma in Italia exercuissent, certas sibi sedes
et imperia paraverunt. Quibus perpetuis et gravibus incommodis
Italia omnis adeo enervata convulsaque est ut, cum aliis atque aliis
semper oppressa cladibus respirare nequiret, in squalore et lacrimis
servire cogeretur.

47   'Factum est decem fere saeculis, ut et nativi sermonis nitor varias ex omni barbaria sordes acceperit, mores ad virtutis effigiem
legibus instituti penitus exsoleverint, evanuerint exquisitae artes,[157]
gymnasia conticuerint, et denique disciplinae Musae cunctaeque
litterae penitus exularint. Nam cum Odoacer omnibus iniurius[158]
leges everteret, ab Alarico statuae signa tabulae conflarentur aut
frangerentur, Radagasius et Totila immanitate ruinis et cladibus
exsultarent,[159] et Hunnus Attila, non modo ornamenta quaeque
gloriosi saeculi sed libros omnes cremabundus, furiosa crudelitate
persequeretur, neque honestati locus amplius fuit, neque suus honos artibus est relictus. Quando nemo industriae, nemo probitati,
nemo studiis litterarum faveret, ut haec ad decus vitaeque ornatum
retinere necessariisque subsidiis tueri possent, cum, late vagantibus
barbaris et in obvia quaeque grassantibus, virtutes ipsae fugatae
dispalataeque ad extremum ubique terrarum obsessae tenerentur,

results, either made off with everything or, once they had driven out the natives, founded colonies in the lands they had seized.

"Next, after that violent storm Italy sustained many defeats at the hands of the Gauls, but by far the most at those of the Germans; also the Angles, themselves a British people, and the Normans and Bretons from the Armorican coast[58] obtained for themselves secure settlements and dominions after they had for some time fielded mercenary armies in Italy. By these uninterrupted and severe misfortunes all Italy was so weakened and shattered that, being always oppressed with some calamity or other, it could not catch its breath and was forced into servitude amid squalor and tears. 46

"Over the course of nearly ten centuries, it came about that the splendor of our native speech had absorbed various kinds of filth from every barbarian people. The customs that had been instituted by laws in the image of virtue fell completely into desuetude; the choice arts faded away; the schools fell silent; and finally learning, the Muses, and all literature were driven completely into exile. For when Odoacer,[59] more baneful than all others, was overturning the laws; when the statues, flags, and paintings were dashed to pieces or put to the torch by Alaric;[60] when Radagasius[61] and Totila[62] were running riot with brutality, destruction, and slaughter; when Attila the Hun, destined to burn not only each and every adornment of a glorious age but also all the books, was repeatedly attacking with raging cruelty—then neither was there further scope for honorable action, nor did the arts have their own honor left to them. No one was supporting industry, uprightness, and literary study in order that they might be able to hold fast to those things for the dignity and adornment of life and protect them with necessary aid; the barbarians, roving far and wide, were attacking everything in their path; and the virtues themselves, which had been put to flight and had gone away, were being pinned down under siege in the remotest corners of the earth. Thus, for the 47

servivit itaque Italia magna ex parte externis gentibus, qui in ea aut regnabant aut stipendia faciebant, usque ad Galeatium Vicecomitem qui principum in Italia longe opulentissimus atque fortissimus "Comes Virtutum" est appellatus.

48 'Is peracres et decoris avidos complures nactus duces, militiam apud Italos paene exstinctam et ab alienigenis usurpatam cum magna gloria reparavit, ita ut de Gallis atque Germanis, qui vetere eorum consuetudine in Italiam irruperant, incomparabiles victorias reportarit brevique effecerit ut nullus omnino nisi mercennarius[160] externus miles in Italia relinqueretur. Is optimis artibus mire favit, et Musas squalore obsitas ab exilio reduxit, instituto Ticini celeberrimo gymnasio et bibliotheca perinsigni ad usum ingeniorum ingenti sumptu publicata, adeo ut cuncta ad antiquam amplitudinem ac dignitatem Italici nominis magnificentissime revocaret.

49 'Ab hoc principe, qui certe longiore vita dignus fuit, cuncti Italiae reguli et liberae civitates summique item pontifices, et ante alios Nicolaus Quintus, magnificentiae, litteris, militiae, et decori incredibili quadam alacritate studere coeperunt; et cum alius alium amplissimis operibus aemulari, et praeclaro certamine superare contenderet, brevi tempore tantus splendor est invectus tantaque saeculi felicitas est consecuta ut nullam fere ex antiquis artibus quisquam desideraret ad absolutam operum speciem morum elegantiam et rerum omnium dignitatem.

50 'Haec aetas Albericum Balbianum Italicae militiae magistrum, et duo fulmina belli, Sfortiam et Braccium, haud magnis tulit intervallis. Protulit Etruria Dantem, Petrarcham, atque Boccacium,

most part, Italy was enslaved to foreign peoples who were either
ruling or engaged in military service there, all the way down to
Giangaleazzo Visconti,[63] the richest and most courageous by far of
the princes in Italy, who was called 'the Count of the Virtues.'

"Having obtained the support of many commanders who were   48
eager for distinction, with great glory Giangaleazzo restored among
the Italians a military organization that had been nearly extinguished and taken over by foreigners.[64] And he did so in such a
way that he won incomparable victories over the French and Germans, who by longstanding custom had invaded Italy, and in a
brief time he brought it about that no foreign soldier at all was left
in Italy except for the mercenaries. He marvelously favored the
noblest arts, and once the famous school at Pavia had been established and an illustrious library had been opened at great expense
to encourage intellectual pursuits, he brought back the Muses,
who had been enveloped in darkness, from their exile. Thus he
magnificently restored all things to their ancient grandeur and
prestige and redeemed the dignity of the Italian nation.

"Beginning with this prince, who surely merited a longer life, all   49
the petty kings of Italy, the free cities, and likewise the supreme
pontiffs — above all Nicholas V[65] — began with a certain incredible
rapidity to cultivate magnificence, literature, military science, and
elegance. And when men were striving to emulate one another in
exceedingly distinguished works and to surpass one another in an
illustrious contest, in a short time such splendor was introduced
and so much good fortune of the age followed that no one felt a
lack of practically any of the ancient arts to achieve perfect beauty
of workmanship, elegance of character, and the dignity of all
things.

"That age brought forth, in rapid succession, Alberico da Bar-   50
biano,[66] the commander of an army composed of Italians, and
the two thunderbolts of war, Francesco Sforza[67] and Braccio da
Montone.[68] Tuscany produced Dante, Petrarch, and Boccaccio,

qui primi ex tenebris optimas agnovere litteras, et[161] ab his Hercu-
leo quodam labore, situm omnem atque robiginem deterserunt.
Emersere item iureconsulti, si non plane Latini, longe tamen acutissimi, Bartholus et Baldus, Raphaelesque duo, Comensis atque
Fulgosius, et alii admodum illustres qui postea sunt secuti. Astro-
nomiae et ceteris mathematicis splendorem et famam dedit Blas-
sius Pelacanius Parmensis. Exculta quoque est medicina subtilius a
Trusiano et Gentile Fulginate.

51   'Giottus sub Cimabove praeceptore atque aemulo dignitatem
picturae restituit. Pippus Brunelescus summus in admiratione[162]
omnium fuit architectus. Pisanus procerum effigies aereis in no-
mismatibus praecellenter expressit. Donatellum in statuariis operibus incomparabilis fama subsecuta est. Ab his initiis atque his
auctoribus immortali laude dignissimis, perpetuo quodam tenore
per centum annos, sine ullo umquam externi hostis metu, in glorioso[163] semper virtutum omnium certamine floruimus. Sicut et
nunc quoque luculentius atque beatius floreremus, nisi Ludovicus
Sfortia, eius Galeatii qui auream aetatem condidit pronepos, Alfonsi regis immani superbia exagitatus, et Veneti ambitiosius quam
liberam gentem deceret, itemque Alexander Pontifex hominum
deterrimus, rebus omnibus pestifera confusione perturbatis hunc
nobis luctum atque has miserias peperissent.'

52   Tum MUSETIUS, 'Quamquam,' inquit,[164] 'reputatione malorum, quae inciderunt et imminent, admodum tristis videri possit,
haec tua tamen periucunda fuit a proposita oratione digressio, et
medius fidius necesse est ut illam superiorem aetatem avorum
scilicet patrumque nostrorum eximiis laudibus in caelum efferamus.

who were the first from out of the shadows to have recognized the best literature, and by a Herculean labor, so to speak, they cleaned away all the mold and rust from it. There appeared also jurists who, though inferior Latinists, were nonetheless extremely acute: Bartolus[69] and Baldus,[70] and the two Raphaels, Comensis[71] and Fulgosio;[72] and there were other quite illustrious men who followed afterward. Biagio Pelacani[73] of Parma gave splendor and fame to astronomy and the other mathematical arts. Medicine also was developed with more precision by Torrigiano[74] and by Gentile da Foligno.[75]

"Giotto,[76] under the supervision of his teacher and rival, Cimabue,[77] restored the dignity of painting. Filippo Brunelleschi[78] was the best architect, enjoying the admiration of all. Pisano[79] outstandingly portrayed in bronze relief the likenesses of the foremost men.[80] An incomparable reputation in statuary followed after Donatello.[81] From these beginnings and these authorities, worthy of immortal praise, by a certain steady course through a hundred years, without ever any fear of a foreign enemy, we continuously flourished in a glorious competition of all the excellences. In a like manner we would be flourishing brilliantly and blessedly now too, had not all things been disrupted with deadly disorder and the following people brought forth for us this present sorrow and these miseries: Ludovico Sforza[82]—great-grandson of that Giangaleazzo Visconti who founded the golden age—who was provoked by the monstrous arrogance of King Alfonso;[83] the Venetians, more ambitious than was befitting a free people; and likewise Pope Alexander VI,[84] the worst of men." 51

Then MUSCETTOLA said, "Even though this digression of yours from the set topic of discussion could appear quite gloomy in its reflection on the ills which have come about and are impending, it has nonetheless been most welcome. And so help me God, we must exalt to the heavens with extraordinary praises that earlier era, namely that of our grandfathers and our fathers. To be sure, 52

Enimvero tunc primum aenea tormenta reperta sunt, quae demum mirificis artibus additis sequentium industria paullatim absolvit, eorum siquidem inventione nihil ipsa specie stupendius, nihil usu vel efficacius vel violentius umquam fuit. Unde mirus profecto ille fuerit talium inventor et machinator nec omnino detestandus, nisi ea ad excidium humani generis verterentur. Tormentorum enim inusitato horrisonoque strepitu inferorum et superum iras ac potestatem, ut poetae dicunt,[165] exaequamus, quando inferi, cum saeviunt, non plus quam terremotu, nec superi magis quam fulgetris et fragore ictuque fulminum bella gerant, cum mortalibus exitium minantur.

53 'Quid vero de librariorum arte dicemus? Qua brevi facilique labore et nullo prope impendio, infinita volumina, plumbeis litterarum formis atramento perlitis, excuduntur ad certam scilicet et sempiternam bonarum artium propagationem atque custodiam! Numquam enim interiissent tot priscorum ingeniorum monumenta sicut foede perierunt, si vel Graecia exquisitarum artium inventrix, vel Roma ipsa in his augendis et poliendis omni Graecia fecundior, eo prorsus nobilissimo artificii genere minime caruissent. Hoc autem munus tum[166] gloriae tum utilitatis infinitae uni Germaniae posteritas omnis debebit quae ab hinc nonaginta annis hoc invenerit, sicut et antea mirabili casu tormenta repererat.

54 'Sed praeter haec duo inventa omnium fortasse clarissima nihil hoc saeculum, ut mihi videtur, aeque feliciter nobilitavit quam novus terrarum orbis ad occiduum oceanum, auspice Columbo Ligure, Hispanorum armis et classibus peragratus. Nempe hoc insano sed felici ausu Columbus dum a Gadibus provehitur, dum ignotum antea sulcat oceanum, dum alterius caeli sidera

back then bronze firearms were first invented.[85] The industry of those who followed gradually perfected them with marvelous workmanship, for there has never been anything more astonishing in very appearance than this invention, and nothing in practice either more effective or more violent.[86] Hence the inventor and engineer of such weapons surely would be admirable and should not be cursed, unless they are turned to the destruction of the human race. Indeed, as the poets say,[87] with the unaccustomed and dreadful din of firearms we match the anger and power of the gods above and below—since, when the gods below rage, threatening mortals with destruction, their greatest weapon is an earthquake, while for the gods above it is lightning and the roar and crash of thunderbolts.

"But what shall we say about the bookseller's art? With what 53 little and easy effort and nearly no expense, once the leaden forms of the letters have been smeared all over with ink, countless books are printed, evidently for the sure and eternal propagation and protection of liberal studies! Nor would so many writings of ancient intellects ever have been lost—as, in fact, they were, shamefully—had not both Greece, the inventor of the choice arts, and Rome itself, more fruitful than all Greece in augmenting and refining them, entirely lacked that most noble art. But all posterity will be indebted to Germany alone for this gift, both glorious and infinitely useful, which was invented ninety years ago; just as earlier, by a remarkable accident, she had devised firearms as well.[88]

"But besides these two inventions—perhaps the most famous of 54 all—nothing, it seems to me, has made this age so renowned for its good fortune as this: that the New World in the western ocean has been scoured by the armies and fleets of the Spaniards—and Columbus,[89] a Ligurian, led the way. By this insane but successful venture, Columbus first sailed out from Cadiz, then plowed across a previously unknown ocean, and then contemplated the stars of

contemplatur, non modo Herculis tam prope columnas velut terrarum orbis terminos statuentis gloriam superavit, sed Romanis
etiam gentium victoribus ostendit ad navigandum in haec regna
aurifera caeli temperie perbeata aut peritiam tamquam magnetis
usus et[167] rei navalis rudibus, aut animos tamquam uno tantum
orbe contentis omnino defuisse.'

55   Tum vero DAVALUS, ad Musetium conversus, 'Magna' inquit
'haec sunt et inter inventa humani ingenii omnium maxime celebranda, quibus haud dubie superior aetas facta est admodum
insignis, sicut et aliis quoque rebus ac moribus eximiis luculenter
effloruit. Ceterum valde sapienter et accurate Iovius malorum omnium quae nobis inciderunt causas enarravit, Fortunam et sidera
ab humanis actionibus procul excludens, et illud ante alia praeclare
affirmans: cuncta quae bello paceque gerantur uno animi nostri
imperio et dicione penitus contineri, talemque esse ac in poste-
rum[168] fore temporum condicionem qualem sibi mortalium mores
vigente semper libera voluntate fabricarint, ita ut amplius minime
dubitem quin existimare oporteat, postquam nullum his aerumnis
finem videmus, nos ad veteres servitutis sordes celeriter esse redi-
turos. Neque enim sperandum est, cum[169] factionibus serviamus,
rerum omnium inopia premamur, et in summa consilii difficultate
laboremus, ut aliquo egregio et salutari omnium consensu in libertatem vindicemur. Et iam plane intellego nos omnes non modo ab
his quos superiores et feliciores aetates tulerunt, sed ab ipsis etiam
patribus nostris et eorum aequalibus, qui modo naturae concesserunt, manifeste degenerare. Unde nequaquam multum abesse,
quem plerique divini vates Italiae denuntiarunt, foedissimum

another sky. Not only did he outdo the glory of Hercules when that hero established the Pillars so near us as the bounds of the world, but Columbus also showed the Romans, the conquerors of nations, that they completely lacked either the expertise (as for example in the use of the compass) and were too unskilled in nautical science for navigating toward those gold-yielding kingdoms, which are blessed with temperateness of climate, or the spirit to do so, since they were content with only one world."

Then D'AVALOS turned to Muscettola and said: "These are 55 great things and among the inventions of human ingenuity that should be most celebrated. Undoubtedly, an earlier age was made famous by them, just as it also flourished splendidly in other respects and in extraordinary character. But Giovio has explained wisely and accurately the causes of all the ills which have befallen us — while isolating human actions from the effects of Fortune and the distant stars. Above all, he has affirmed splendidly that all things achieved in war and in peace are contained entirely in the authority and dominion of our minds alone; and that the condition of the times is and in future surely shall be such as mortals' characters have always constructed for themselves, provided that free will is flourishing. So I no longer harbor the least doubt that, once we understand there is no end to these calamities, we will return quickly to the old squalors of servitude. Since we are slaves to factions, oppressed by want of all things, and are suffering amid an acute shortage of good counsel, we must not hope that we may be liberated by some unusual and salutary outbreak of universal harmony. I now fully understand that we all are plainly degenerating, not only from those whom earlier and more fortunate ages brought forth, but even from these very fathers of ours and from their contemporaries who have just now passed. And so, since we rejoice in base and shameful deeds and think it absurd to be praised on account of virtue, I reckon that an extremely foul end

rerum omnium finem arbitramur, postquam improbis et turpibus laetamur factis, et a virtute laudari ineptum putamus.'

56   Ad ea MUSETIUS inquit, 'Tu profecto videris, Davale, si qui hodie arma tractatis ab his quos proximo bello aut in vestris aut in adversis partibus apprime novisti a vetere disciplina degeneretis. Neque enim togatos decet de armatis agere censuram et famam singulorum excutere, ne qui ad districtos gladios provocationem habent, inepto et liberiore iudicio nostro fortassis irritentur. Tu enim, qui neque tela neque etiam tormenta timere consuevisti, et quantum quisque virtute valeat in acie saepius expertus es, optime de militari munere totoque imperatoris officio non tantum in remotiore colloquio sed ad populum disserere potes, et te iam, ut id diligenter et prolixe persequaris, vehementer obsecramus. Nos quoque pariter de optimis litterarum studiis agemus, si tibi videbitur. Nam ubi securiore in otio fas est animum relaxare, te non minus cupide Palladis quam Martis studia complecti conspicimus.'

57   Hic DAVALUS 'Non tam ipsae,' inquit, 'victoriae, quarum dulcedo mihi semper incredibilis fuit, in medio[170] belli ardore me delectant quam peramoena vestrarum litterarum studia requiescentem in hibernis alliciunt, adeo ut aliquando nihil potius quam pacem exoptem, quamquam eius nomen militum auribus non modo ingratum sit, verum etiam exsecrandum. Animadverto enim non plane illum posse perfici qui ampliorem militiae gloriam quaerat, nisi rerum ubique gestarum scientia priscorumque exemplis ac praeceptis abunde[171] sit instructus, ut in quoscumque eum casus belli Fortunaeque varietas adduxerint, praesenti consilio, tamquam nihil omnino novum vel inusitatum offeratur, auxilia pariter atque animum expedire queat.

of all things, which many divine prophets have foretold for Italy, is by no means far distant."

To this MUSCETTOLA replied: "You will know best, d'Avalos, 56 if you men who bear arms today fall short of the old discipline and fail to measure up to those whom you knew very well in the recent war, whether on your own side or the enemy's. For it is inappropriate for civilians to sit in judgment over armed men and to investigate the reputations of individuals, lest perhaps those who have the power to challenge us with swords drawn should be annoyed by our foolish and unlicensed judgment. In fact, you who have become accustomed to be unafraid either of swords or even of firearms and who have often experienced in battle just how brave each man is are best able to hold forth about military duty and the entire charge of the commander, not only in a private conversation but to the populace at large. So now we ardently beseech you to pursue this subject carefully and at length. We shall in like manner discuss literary studies, if you approve, since we see that when it is permissible to relax the mind in secure leisure, you embrace the studies of Athena no less eagerly than those of Mars."

Here D'AVALOS said, "Those very victories which have always 57 charmed me immensely do not gladden me amid the heat of battle so much as the delightful studies of your literature entice me when I am relaxing in winter encampment — so much so that sometimes I long for nothing more than for peace, even though its name is not only unwelcome but even anathema to soldiers' ears. In fact, I observe that he who seeks the more abundant glory of military service cannot attain it completely unless he has been amply equipped with knowledge of exploits performed everywhere and with the examples and precepts of the ancients. Thus, with whatever dangers the vicissitudes of war and of Fortune may have confronted him, he can prepare his troops and his mind with a ready plan on the grounds that nothing new or unusual is presenting itself.[90]

58   'Itaque perpulchrum profecto fuerit eorum qui in Italia cum
laude vivunt, singulas expendisse virtutes, et cum superioribus aetatibus contulisse. Et hercle, ut opinor, non iniquam omnino truti-
nam subibunt. Nam sicut his disciplinis atque artibus quae libero
homine sunt dignae uterque vestrum[172] cumulate quidem ornatus
est, ita de litteris exacte atque praeclare iudicaturos existimo. Ego
certe postquam primum excellentiae locum, et iure quidem optimo, militiae tribuistis, quid in castris didicerim, et nunc maxime
iudicem, de nostrae tempestatis ducibus libero ore proferam; nec
verebor quorundam offensiones si eorum existimationi[173] aliquid
falsae laudis fortasse detraxero, cum ab iis quos minime probem
nec amari quidem velim. Improbi enim est ingenii, dum vivis adu-
lari properas, bonis mortuis suam gloriam invidere.

59   'Sed an haec terra Italia, quondam omni prope aetate magnorum
atque felicium imperatorum ferax, velut effeta nunc primum steri-
lescere incipiat, an potius corrupti saeculi vitio ignaviaque nostra
et principum supina pravitate id accidat, non facile dixerim; quamquam ea, quae superius de animi nostri libertate disputastis, veritati peregregie[174] consentire videantur.

60   'Ego enim totam negotii militaris disciplinam optima regum
aut gentium liberarum institutione feliciter coalescere et ad perfectum decus pervenire semper existimavi. Quid enim Persarum reges, quorum arma non modo finitimis orientis gentibus, sed toti
Graeciae et Romanis denique ipsis terrori saepius fuerunt,
ad insignem famam magis extulit quam Cyri invicti regis disciplina? Neque ipsi quoque Macedones et Magnus Alexander,
in quorum virtutis titulo censetur terrarum orbis amplissimis

"And so, it would certainly be a splendid thing to measure the   58
individual virtues of those men of good reputation who are living
in Italy and to compare them with earlier ages. And by God, in my
view, when they are weighed on the scales, they will surely turn
out to be evenly matched. For just as each of you two is equipped
with the education and skills worthy of a free man, so I think you
will pass judgment on literature with accuracy and flair. For my
part, since you have very properly awarded the first place for excellence to the art of war, I will testify frankly as to what I have
learned in the field and what I now conclude concerning the commanders of our era. Nor shall I shrink from giving offense to certain persons if perhaps I have removed some bit of false praise
from their reputation, since I would not want even to be liked by
those of whom I do not in the least approve. It is the mark of an
unsound character to begrudge the honorable dead the glory that
is their due while being quick to toady to the living.

"But I could not easily say whether the land of Italy, which for-   59
merly in almost every age produced great and successful commanders, is now worn out, as it were, and for the first time starting to become barren, or whether this has happened instead owing
to the fault of a corrupt generation, to our cowardice, and to the
languid viciousness of princes. But those things you were contending earlier about the freedom of our will appear to be absolutely
consistent with the truth.

"I have always thought that the entire science of military affairs   60
is happily synthesized from the best teachings of kings or free
peoples and thus arrives at perfect glory. What elevated the Persian kings to outstanding reputation, whose arms terrorized not
only neighboring peoples of the East but all of Greece and finally
the Romans themselves, more than did the military system of the
invincible King Cyrus?[91] And also consider the Macedonians
themselves and Alexander the Great[92]: in the accounts of their
prowess, the entire earth is reckoned to have been traversed with

victoriis peragratus, tantum belli gloria valuissent, nisi eis Philippus dux acutissimus rem militarem divinis praeceptis et legibus
egregie constitutam opportune reliquisset. Quid magis etiam Romanos et rerum dominos et gentium omnium victores effecit quam
excellens rei bellicae disciplina, in omnes aetatum processus diligenter atque severe custodita, cum ea sensim eximiis regum et
consulum ingeniis amplificata ad summam cum potentiae tum
laudis opinionem[175] salubriter excrevisset? Hinc enim, quando
omnia belli munera certo ordine et firmissimis legibus tenerentur,
provenere mirificae legiones, invicta equitum robora, et frequentes
ac praestantissimi duces cum ad perpetuas victorias tum ad gloriam et triumphos vera virtute destinati.

61   'Siquidem vel ignavos et rudes brevi strenuos bonosque milites
efficit disciplina, aequabili poenae pariter[176] et praemiorum ordina-
tione stabilita, e quibus simili ratione, si labore ingenioque ad virtutem contenderint, incluti centuriones et tribuni vel alarum praefecti et primorum ordinum ductores evadunt. Ex horum autem
nobili grege tamquam e fecundissimo seminario generosi imperatores educuntur, ita ut neque egregiis ducibus ad officium gerendarum rerum prompti atque exercitati milites, neque militibus operam naviter praestare cupientibus singularis peritiae atque fortunae
duces umquam defuerint. Labante vero disciplina, et ea sicut hodie videmus foedissime dissoluta, frustra quis vel a milite obsequium requiret vel a duce auctoritatem ac industriam exspectabit.

62   'Perierunt enim cuncta verae militiae iura, et quae eius sunt
praecipua fundamenta, parendi voluntas et gloriae honestaeque

distinguished victories. They would never have enjoyed exceptional martial glory had not Philip,[93] a very shrewd commander, conveniently bequeathed to them a military system that was outstandingly established with excellent instruction and laws. And what made the Romans both lords of the world and victors over all peoples more than their excellent training in military science, a discipline diligently and strictly maintained through all the cycles of the ages? Once that training had been gradually enlarged by the extraordinary talents of kings and consuls, it grew beneficially to a pinnacle both of power and of praise. For from the fact that all the duties of warfare were held in place by a sure ordering and by the strictest of rules, they produced amazing legions, invincible cavalry, and a steady supply of exceptional commanders who were destined by genuine prowess both to perpetual victories and to glory and triumphal processions.

"Since in a short time discipline makes even sluggish and untrained men vigorous and competent soldiers, once a uniform system of punishment and rewards has been firmly established, if they strive for prowess with hard work and talent, they end up as centurions, tribunes, captains of light cavalry, and commanders of the front ranks. From the noble band of these men, just as from the most fertile nursery of seedlings, distinguished commanders are reared. The upshot is that outstanding commanders have never lacked soldiers who are ready and prepared for carrying out their duty, nor have soldiers who desire to perform their task diligently lacked commanders of singular skill and good fortune. But with discipline tottering—and as we see today, having become dreadfully slack—in vain will anyone either seek obedience from a soldier, or expect leadership and diligence from a commander.

"Indeed, all the laws of genuine military service have perished. Those character traits which are its particular foundations—the will to obey, and regard for glory and for honorable praise—have

laudis respectus, funditus sunt eversa, quoniam bella hac maxime
tempestate gerantur mercenario milite ex pessima ac ignobili hominum sorte raptim collecto, ita ut difficile sit abiectae vel perditae
vitae homines omnibus coopertos flagitiis et diversis de causis mi-
litantes, et propterea inter se parum notos, in agmine ductare,
digerere in ordines et, cum facto opus sit, opportune componere
vel explicare, nisi cruentum adhibeas gladium, et temere dicto nequaquam audientes plus quam hostiliter caedas, et furenti manu
etiam transfodias: quod tam hodie mihi et ceteris ducibus necessarium est quam inhumanum. Ius enim imperii cito clementia leni-
tateque resolvitur, peritque facile illa rerum omnium praeclara gu-
bernatrix auctoritas, nisi contumaces et protervi, per mortes et
saeva vulnera, parere doceantur.'

63   Ad ea MUSETIUS 'Quam vellem,' inquit, 'Davale, ut haec tua
singularis auctoritas, qua apud legiones tantopere polles, a reverentia pudoreque militum potius quam ab acerbitate atque saevitia
tua duceretur, quamquam sciam tua liberalitate incredibili eximiaque humanitate praeclare tibi omnium animos esse devinctos. Vereor enim ne in eo liberius peccare videare in quo et Piscarius ipse
aliquando atrocius quam eius natura promitteret, peccasse apparet; nam ⟨eum⟩ multos milites, cum agmine atque acie temere
exirent, sua manu confodisse audivimus, quae fama ab imperitis
fortasse obtrectatoribus maligne adaucta eum vehementer crudelitatis nota[177] conspersit.

64   'Agnosco equidem quam mite, quam excelsum, et quam remo-
tum sit ab inhumana crudelitate ingenium tuum, neque id propterea vellem huius tuae nimis expeditae et numquam leviter ferien-
tis dextrae saevitia defoedari, quasi in castris et ad id quidem
conducti satellites[178] desint, quorum ministerio sontes ac improbi,

been totally overturned, since especially at this time wars are being waged by a mercenary soldiery hurriedly assembled from lowborn and common men.[94] So you are dealing with men of a debased or depraved manner of life, covered with all sorts of crimes, serving for various motives and therefore too little known to one another. As a result, it is difficult to lead them in battle formation and organize them into ranks and, when necessary, to contract or expand their formation, unless you brandish a bloody sword and ferociously cut down and with raging hand stab the rashly disobedient. For me and other commanders, this thing is as necessary today as it is inhumane. The right of command is quickly dissolved by clemency and mildness; and authority, that outstanding helmsman of all affairs, easily disappears unless the insolent and shameless are taught obedience by means of deaths and savage wounds."

To this MUSCETTOLA replied, "How I would wish, d'Avalos, 63 that this remarkable authority of yours, by which you have such influence with the legions, would derive from the deference and modesty of the soldiers rather than from your harshness and cruelty, even though I know that you have splendidly bound the minds of all to you by your incredible liberality and extraordinary humaneness. Indeed, I fear that you appear to err rather freely in that quality in which Pescara himself also seems sometimes to have acted more cruelly than his nature might augur: for we heard that he fatally wounded many soldiers by his own hand when they were straying recklessly from the column and the line of battle. Once this reputation had been spitefully increased, perhaps by ignorant detractors, it indelibly stained him with the infamy of cruelty.

"I, for one, acknowledge how mild, lofty, and remote from inhu- 64 man cruelty your nature is, and I would not want it to be defiled by the brutality of this right hand of yours—excessively free and striking no gentle blow—as if a military camp lacked minions to punish the guilty severely, not in a flare-up of anger, but with utter

nequaquam exardente ira sed animo maxime pacato, severissime puniantur. Quis enim magni nominis Romanus imperator in ullo vel repentini proelii momento gladium, quem in adversum hostem distringeret, civis vel militis sui cruore pertinxit, cum aequissimi moris esset vel seditiosos, vel locum in acie deserentes, et aliis criminibus convictos aut ad vitem[179] aut ad virgas securesque lictorum omnino delegare?'

65   Hoc loco DAVALUS 'Cave,' inquit, 'existimes, Museti, militem, quo passim utimur, sola ac inani quadam imperii maiestate in officio posse contineri! Furendum enim saepe est, et in sceleratos ac[180] petulantes districto gladio propere saeviendum, si ducis nomen retinere volueris, quoniam obedientia, quae militis prima est laus, praesentibus[181] poenis potius exigitur quam[182] capitalis iudicii metu; facilius enim atque licentius delinquunt qui in tarditate atque apparatu supplicii intercessione amicorum et praefectorum ab duce veniam non desperant. Quod si repente fervida manu ducis crimina[183] vindicentur, insignis illa severitas omnium proposita oculis pluribus simul morbis egregie medebitur, cum poena ad paucos (exemplum autem) et certissimi terroris atrocitas, ad universos omnino pertineat.[184] Praestat enim in paucos crudelem et sanguinarium appellari quam exitiabili lenitate totius exercitus esse proditorem.

66   'Sed cur eum ducem "saevum" vocabimus qui, dum improbos tollit, disciplinam instaurat qua salus publica in tantis periculorum momentis rectissime custoditur? Maximilianus Caesar, quo nemo principum animi magnitudine ac lenitate superior fuit, Soncinii[185] apud Abduam flumen[186] notum Germanum militem consternatas ad arma cohortes tympani sonitu concitantem sua manu contorta tragula transfigere minime dubitavit. Itaque desinant vel me vel

calmness. Did any famous Roman general, in any moment of sudden battle, take the sword which he drew against an enemy and soak it with the blood of a citizen or his own soldier? Certainly not, since the most impartial practice was to put the seditious, those deserting their place in the battle line, and those convicted of other crimes into the charge of the centurion's staff, or of the rods and axes of the lictors."

At this point D'AVALOS said, "Do not fancy, Muscettola, that   65
the soldiery whom we make use of here and there can be kept in line by a mere empty majesty of command! If you want to retain the reputation of a commander, you must often, with sword drawn, rage violently and take quick and savage action against criminal and unruly elements. Obedience, which is the chief excellence of the soldier, is achieved by prompt punishments more than by the fear of a death sentence. In fact, those men actually misbehave more readily and boldly who, because of a delay in inflicting punishment, do not despair of the commander's forgiveness, obtained through the intercession of friends and officers. But if crimes are punished instantly by the angry hand of the commander, that memorable severity, displayed before the eyes of all, will at once provide a splendid cure for a number of maladies, since punishment against the few (but as an example) and the dreadfulness of a most certain death surely have an impact on all. It is better to be called cruel and bloodthirsty toward a few than by your fatal leniency to be the betrayer of an entire army.

"But why will we call that commander 'savage' who, while elimi-   66
nating criminals, restores the discipline by which the public safety is most properly guarded in such moments of danger? No prince has surpassed Emperor Maximilian[95] in greatness of soul and in mildness. But he did not in the least hesitate to hurl a spear with his own hand and pierce a notorious German soldier at the Adda River in Soncino—a soldier who was rousing his shattered cohorts to arms with the sound of the drum. So people should stop

Piscarium immitem et cruentum in suos appellare, quando id fecisse oportuit, ut tot et tantae victoriae cum caesari tum ipsis militibus pararentur.

67 'Sed hoc est quod falso de tempestate nostra conquerimur, quoniam huius aetatis duces nequaquam antiquis animi virtute pares esse videantur. Nam si disciplinam amisimus ac eadem quoque socordia suboles virorum et ducum optimorum interiit, quomodo militaris officii dignitatem ad priscorum specimen proferre vel omnino tueri poterimus? Nemini vero dubium esse debet haec sensim accepta fuisse incommoda, propter imminutas vehementerque attenuatas totius Italiae facultates, quoniam iustos exercitus, dum funestis factionibus servimus, alere nequeamus; qua de causa milites, ubi primum Martis laboribus atque periculis assuescere coeperint, propter impensae gravitatem celerrime dimittantur,[187] quod Romanis velut maxime opulentis facere non erat necesse, utpote quibus terrarum orbis imperium affectantibus numquam armorum causae, numquam bellandi materia deessent.

68 'Proinde nequaquam mirum esse debet si Itali saepius ab externis gentibus in acie superentur. Utuntur enim tirone semper milite ex subitario delectu, audentque cum exercitatissimis dimicare qui in Italia inveterati cunctis stolide dissidentibus miserrimae servitutis iugum imposuerunt. Verum eos tot opimae victoriae, tot opes in praedam actae adeo corruperunt, cum urbes et regna victoriis parta hostiliter evastarent, ut dicto audientes esse desierint, et nihil miseris sociis praeter brevem vitae usuram, nihil caesari praeter inane nomen imperii reliquerint. Quibus luctuosis Italiae

calling either me or Pescara pitiless and cruel toward our own men, since we had to act as we did in order to acquire so many great victories, both for the emperor and for the soldiers themselves.

"But this is what we mistakenly complain about concerning our 67 times when we suppose that the commanders of this era seem unequal to the ancients in courage. If we have let military discipline slip away, and if also, thanks to the same sluggishness, the offspring of the best men and commanders has died off, how will we be able to advance the dignity of military service after the model of our ancestors or preserve it at all? But nobody should doubt that these setbacks have been sustained gradually owing to the impaired and much diminished capabilities of all Italy, since being in thrall to destructive factions, we cannot maintain proper armies. So as soon as the soldiers have begun to get used to the hardships and dangers of war, they are very quickly discharged on account of the heavy expense. The Romans, wealthy as they were, had no need to do that, since, as they were aspiring to rule over the entire world, they never lacked either occasions for battle or the materials for making war.

"So it ought not to be the least bit surprising if Italians are de- 68 feated in battle quite often by foreign peoples. They always make use of a novice soldiery from a spur-of-the-moment recruitment. And they venture to contend in battle against highly experienced troops already established in Italy, who have placed the yoke of the most miserable servitude on all those who are stupid enough to oppose them. But when in the manner of an enemy these troops devastated cities and kingdoms they had acquired by conquests, so many victories full of spoils and so many resources seized for plunder corrupted them to such an extent that they ceased to obey orders. And so they left behind to their miserable allies nothing except for brief enjoyment of life; and to Caesar nothing except for the empty name of 'empire.' These grievous losses for Italy have

detrimentis effectum est ut non modo militum probatorum sed
insignium etiam belli ducum gravissima lacrimabilique penuria laboremus.'

69   Tum vero ego ⟨IOVIUS⟩ inquam, 'Davale, multarum rerum causas subtiliter et generose quidem protulisti. Ceterum dictorum
tuorum fides in ipsa veritatis luce resplendeat, quam rei bellicae
periti viderint. Mihi certe huius aetatis duces ab industria singula-
rique virtute non modo satis gloriosi verum etiam admirabiles
videntur, si inusitatos armorum motus et novas bellandi artes et
rerum denique omnium condiciones cum superioribus aetatibus
conferamus.[188] Eos tamen ante omnia ab his nostris puto segre-
gandos quos veterum historiae celebrarunt neque enim sum adeo
impudens vel insanus, ut hos cum Marcello vel Scipionibus ipsove
Mario et C. Caesare comparari posse contendam. Vivant scilicet
illi ut divini heroes ac aeterna verae virtutis laude perfruantur, eo
posteris suis beatiores quod Romana res, amplitudine opum vix se
ipsam capiens, uberiorem ipsorum industriae et triumphis materiam continue praebuerit. Relinquitur ergo ut qui patrum avorum-
que nostrorum memoria maximorum ducum nomen et titulos
sunt consecuti cum iis comparentur qui nunc vivunt et conspicui
ante alios florent aut, paullo ante fato exstincti, primos honores
militiae meruerunt.

70   'Quod si ita est, non video quare huius aetatis imperatores iusto
honore vel certe debita laude spoliemus. Si enim Bracciani Sfortiadae Picinnini et Coleones,[189] quorum res gestas maiores nostri
magnopere sunt admirati, in haec tempora exacerbati Martis
incidissent, profecto nostros aequales neque iudicii magnitudine

brought it about that we are oppressed with a severe and pitiful scarcity not only of tested soldiers but also of outstanding military commanders."

Then for my part I [GIOVIO] said, "D'Avalos, you certainly 69 have set out, with nuance and nobility, the causes of many things. Let the credibility of your words shine brightly with the very light of truth, which those expert in the business of war will perceive. To me at any rate the commanders of this era appear not only sufficiently glorious on account of their industry and singular excellence, but even admirable, if we should compare with earlier eras the unusual disturbances of wars, the new technologies of making war, and, in short, the circumstances of all things. Before all else, however, I think that those commanders whom the histories of the ancients have celebrated must be set apart from these of our time. I am not so brazen or insane that I would contend that the latter can be compared with Marcellus, the Scipios, or Marius himself and Julius Caesar. Let those men live on as divine heroes, and let them enjoy the everlasting praise of true excellence as more blessed than their descendants to this extent, that the Roman state, scarcely containing itself in the abundance of its resources, provided without interruption to those very men rich material for diligence and for triumphs. It remains, then, for those who have attained the reputation and accolades of the greatest commanders in the memory of our fathers and grandfathers to be compared to those who are now living and flourish visibly above others, or to those who died recently and earned the highest honors for their military service.

"But if that is the case, I fail to see why we should strip the 70 commanders of this age of their rightful honor, or at least of due praise. After all, what if the Braccios, Sforzas, Piccininos, and Colleonis,[96] whose exploits our forebears greatly admired, had happened to live in these times of aggravated warfare? Surely they could not have surpassed or even equaled our contemporaries,

neque vigore corporis et[190] animi neque rerum asperrimarum insigni tolerantia superare vel etiam aequare potuissent.

71 'Illis namque temporibus vel acerrimi belli pericula prope minora erant quam ea quae in ludis hastatorumque spectaculis subirentur. Tum enim contra hostes excavatis ac inanibus hastis res gerebatur; nulla erant in usu tormenta nisi quibus turres ac moenia ferirent; sclopettariis hostibus captis manus praecidebant, ut ceteros ab eo usu velut[191] mortiferi teli genere deterrerent. Victoriae namque in fuga potius quam caede hostium censebantur, siquidem memorabilis illa pugna, qua Venetus exercitus ad Caravagium a Francisco Sfortia, capto Gentile Leonissano imperatore, profligatus est, non plurium quam septem omnino militum morte constitisse fertur, e quibus etiam duos non vulneribus confossos sed in fuga ab equitatu[192] protritos apparuit.

72 'Sed quid veteres pugnas inepte commemoro, cum in Bononiensi ad Ricardinam a Coleone et Federico Urbinate, quod protracta in serum diei esset, pugna ex condicto praetentis utrimque ab universo armigerorum puerorum ordine funalibus sit dimicatum? Quo proelio etiam, ridendum visu atque auditu, sese utrimque armati duces praeclare atque benigne consalutarunt, et denique cum nimis cruente ab Illyriis, qui rumpiis ingentibus equorum crura succidebant, res geri nuntiaretur, mutuo consensu et nequaquam diiudicata proelii fortuna, receptui cecinerunt.

73 'At quae nunc pericula, quas rerum et laborum difficultates bonum et non ignobilem ducem, ut dignitatem tueatur in oculis exercitus, adire oportet? Sternuntur enim saepe integrae legiones horribili procella tormentorum et, ut quisque bello maxime cruente

either in greatness of judgment, or in strength of body and spirit, or in impressive endurance of the harshest circumstances.

"In those times, the dangers of even the most violent of wars 71 were little more significant, really, than the perils encountered in games and jousts. Back then, they waged war against enemies with thin, hollowed-out spears, and used no artillery except for bombarding towers and town walls. They used to sever the hands of captured enemy arquebusiers to deter others from using, as it were, a kind of deadly weapon.[97] Certainly they reckoned victories by the flight of enemies, rather than by their slaughter. Consider that famous Battle of Caravaggio,[98] at which, once the captain Gentile da Leonessa[99] had been captured, the Venetian army was utterly crushed by Francesco Sforza.[100] It is said that the battle cost the deaths of no more than seven soldiers in all, and that two of those clearly had been fatally wounded not by weapons, but by being trodden under foot by cavalry during flight.[101]

"But why do I foolishly recall old battles when there is the Bat- 72 tle of Riccardina in the Bolognese[102] fought between Colleoni and Duke Federico of Urbino?[103] Once it had been prolonged into twilight, by agreement the combat was settled by the entire corps of young esquires between ropes extending from both sides. Also in that battle—and this must have been amusing to see and hear—the armed commanders on both sides greeted each other with chivalrous courtesy. And when it was finally announced that the Albanians were too bloodthirsty in their fighting, since they were felling horses by targeting their legs with enormous spears, then by mutual consent they gave the signal to retreat, even though the outcome of the battle was by no means decided.

"But now, what dangers, harsh conditions and ordeals must a 73 good and noble commander undergo in order to retain his standing in the eyes of the army? Often, indeed, entire legions are utterly defeated by a monstrous storm of shots from artillery, and the more bloodthirstily a man has acted, the more bravely he is

egerit, ille rem gessisse fortissime iudicatur. Vos aeris inclemen-
tiam atque omnes vel irati caeli iniurias egregie contemnitis; nivosa
hieme non secus ac aestate florida, exercitus huc et illuc raptatis,
nec cum hostibus solum, verum etiam cum ipsa repugnantis naturae duritie asperitateque contenditis. Neque hercle in Italia solum,
sed in ipsis etiam provinciis bellandi mos ille pervetustus exolevit,
ita ut nisi fortissimis viris huius saevioris militiae munus susci-
piendum esse videatur. Consalvus Ferdinandus, quo nemo externorum ducum in Italia vel generosius vel felicius arma tractavit,
cum in asperis Bruttiorum saltibus et in siticulosis Apuliae campis
et ad Lirim in Minturnensium paludibus cum Gallis de Regno
dimicaret, Bellum Betricum, in quo ipse tantus imperator evase-
rat, sibi prope ludum fuisse praedicabat, si Mauri iaculatores atque
illa barbarorum linteata sonantiaque agmina cum robore et specie
catafractorum Gallorum conferrentur.'

74   Haec cum dixissem, 'Obruisti me,' inquit ⟨DAVALUS⟩, 'Iovi, ipsorum annalium memoria exemplorumque multitudine, ita ut iam
qui hodie militant optima ratione sibi ipsis placere plurimum possint. Verum non quanti simus quorundam veterum collatione, sed
quantum industria vigore disciplinaque valemus, aequiore libra
perpendere debemus. Anhelandum enim est ad summam gloriam
antiquissimorum ducum nomini aut parem aut propinquam, quam
nemo mediocribus factis atque ausibus umquam paravit. An propterea se alterum Herculem vel Liberum patrem, qui mortalium
imperatorum laudes ingentibus factis excesserunt, seipsum esse

judged to have fought. You pay no attention to the harshness of the weather and to all the suffering inflicted by the heavens, even when they are angry. You drag along armies hither and thither, in the snow of winter no differently than in flowery summer, and you contend not only with enemies but also with the bitterness and harshness of recalcitrant nature herself. And, by God, that ancient manner of making war has died out not only in Italy but also in the provinces themselves, so that it appears that only the most courageous men should undertake this more savage military service. None of the foreign commanders in Italy managed armies either more nobly or more successfully than Gonzalo Fernández de Córdoba.[104] When he was fighting over the kingdom of Naples against the French in the harsh mountain ranges of Calabria, the desiccated plains of Apulia, and at the Garigliano River in the swamps of Minturno, he used to say that the Battle of Granada,[105] in which he himself had made his name as a great captain, had been practically a game to him if the Moorish javelin throwers and those linen-clad and noisy battle lines of the barbarians were compared with the strength and appearance of the mail-clad French."

When I had said these things, he [D'AVALOS] said: "You have overwhelmed me, Giovio, with your recollection of these historical events themselves and multitude of examples—so much so that by now those who serve as soldiers today can with very good reason be immensely pleased with themselves. But we ought to weigh with a more even scale, not how great we are in comparison with certain ancients, but how strong we are in hard work, vigor, and discipline. In fact, we must exert ourselves strenuously toward a glory either equal or near to the highest renown of the most ancient commanders, a glory that no man has ever acquired by ordinary deeds and ventures. Will Hernán Cortés[106] think that he's a second Hercules and Bacchus, gods who surpassed the excellence of mortal commanders, on the grounds that he brought the Far

74

putabit Ferdinandus ille Curtesius, quod, extremo occidente in potestatem redacto, multa milia Indorum inermium exigua manu trucidarit? Est ille quidem egregie cordatus et fortis, et incogniti ab se reperti orbis titulo celebrandus; verum non adeo fuerit ineptus ut a caesare summum militaris imperii munus in Italia sibi demandari una tot victoriarum Indicarum commendatione insolenter expostulet. Explorant equidem dura atque aspera fortes animos, et hostes longe acerrimi ducum et militum famam impense nobilitant, si res gestae certa militum casuum et locorum qualitate comparentur.

75 'Galli paucis ante annis Italorum ordines, nulla tum rei bellicae disciplina stabilitos, impetu suo facile protrivere. Contra mox Gallus vim Helvetiae phalangis sustinere non potuit. Hispani vero coniuncti cum Germanis,[193] exquisitis belli artibus, Helvetios pariter et Gallos ubi confligere licuit, adeo late cecidere ut iam erepta ceteris omnibus belli gloria Macedonibus ipsisque Romanis orbis victoribus exaequandi videantur.'

76 Tum vero MUSETIUS 'Non patiar,' inquit, 'Italos, quamquam exitiali[194] stultitia, dum modo iis modo illis favemus, in has servitutis miserias praecipitatos, omni vetere armorum honore spoliari; nam si quid fortiter atque feliciter ab Hispanis gestum videtur, id profecto vel nostrorum ducum auspiciis atque opibus vel nostrarum cohortium alarumque subsidiis ad eas victorias perventum esse manifeste perspicimus, quando veteranus Italus miles, neque ingenio neque viribus neque ulla in re, vel patientia vel promptitudine, ulli externo militi, sive equo sive pedibus mereret, primum

West under his control and with a small band of troops killed many thousands of defenseless Indians?[107] That man is without doubt outstandingly intelligent and brave and deserves to be celebrated for having discovered an unknown world. But he should not be so foolish as to demand arrogantly, based solely upon the recommendation of so many victories over Indians, that the emperor should entrust to him the highest post of military command in Italy. In truth, difficult and harsh conditions put brave hearts to the test; and if exploits are to be compared with reference to a fixed quality of soldiers, dangers, and places, it is the bitterest enemies by far who emphatically ennoble the reputations of commanders and of soldiers.

"A few years ago, the French easily ground down by their on- 75 slaught the Italians' ranks, which had not at that time been strengthened by any military training. But soon the French were unable to keep in check the force of the Swiss pikemen. The Spaniards, however, conjoined with the Germans, by their superb military skills cut down the Swiss and the French wherever they could join battle. They have by now done so over such a wide field that they have snatched martial glory from all others and appear poised to equal the Macedonians and the Romans themselves as world conquerors."

But then MUSCETTOLA said, "I shall not, in spite of their fatal 76 stupidity, allow the Italians, who have supported now one group, now another, and have fallen into wretched slavery, to be despoiled of all our old reputation for military prowess. For if something seems to have been accomplished bravely and successfully by the Spaniards, we see clearly that these victories have been achieved either under the auspices of our commanders and with their resources, or with the assistance of our companies and auxiliary troops. The veteran Italian soldier, whether he serves in the cavalry or on foot, has never yielded first place to any foreign soldier, whether in tactical brilliance, strength, or anything else,

laudis locum umquam concesserit. Habent certe, nec id infitiabor, Hispani qui in Italia inveteraverunt corpora atque animos ad promerendam in omni genere rei militaris laudem magnopere paratos ac idoneos. Sed illi de adventiciis ab Hispania, tamquam ineptis tironibus per iocum et contemptum saepius obloquuntur, ita ut haec inusitatae virtutis opinio in una exercitatione posita censeatur, cui ab initio horum bellorum Italos, incuria et malignitate quorundam principum, nequaquam opportune deditos videmus; et certe ante alios, Piscarius noster Hispanis in Italia natus quam Italis ad excolendam disciplinam favere maluit.

77   'Nunc vero tot sunt in armis Italorum cohortes ut si unus omnibus ad parandam libertatem animorum esset consensus, frustra esset vel Gallorum vim vel Hispanorum artes vel robora Germanorum in defensione omnium salutis pertimere.[195] Docuerunt enim Itali, cum vel mercede conducti ultra Alpes tetendere, quantum momenti esset in nullo uxorum et liberorum et propriae domus respectu. Ablegatis enim vel ultro in alienas terras, nulla res magis praesidio fuit quam coeundi persistendique necessitas, quae modo, ut videtis, Hispanos non tantum[196] ab communi omnium odio conservavit, sed paene[197] rerum Italicarum dominos nobis cunctantibus effecit.'

78   Ad ea DAVALUS 'Non permittam,' inquit, 'ut hoc onere iniqui iudicii tacendo praegraver. Nam sic Hispanorum qui meo ductu militarunt virtutem semper aestimavi ut magni facere Italicas cohortes ac eas in honore praecipuo habere consueverim. Cum enim regem Gallorum proelio superatum cepimus, ab Italo pedite, totius

whether in patience or in promptitude. Of course, I shall not deny it, the Spaniards who have established themselves in Italy have bodies and minds ideally prepared and suited to merit commendation in every kind of military endeavor. But quite often those commanders speak ill about foreigners from Spain, laughing and ridiculing them as if they were inept beginners. And so this supposition of their own extraordinary excellence is assessed on the basis of training alone—to which, from the beginning of these wars, we see that the Italians most inappropriately have not been exposed at all, on account of the neglect and malice of certain princes. And yet admittedly, more than anyone else, our friend Pescara, born in Italy, preferred to show favor to Spaniards over Italians for the purpose of developing military skill.

"But now so many companies of Italians are in arms that if 77 there were to be a single consensus of minds to obtain liberty for all, it would be mistaken, in defending the safety of all, to be terrified of either the number of the French, the skills of the Spaniards, or the strength of the Germans. The Italians have taught us, when they marched as mercenaries beyond the Alps, just how important was their lack of thought for their wives and children and their own home. For those sent away on a mission even farther into foreign lands, there has been no more effective protection than the necessity of banding together and continuing to do so—a necessity which just now, as you see, has not only preserved the Spaniards from the shared hatred of all, but has almost made them, while we dithered, the lords of Italy."

To this D'AVALOS said, "I shall not silently bear the burden of 78 this unfair judgment. For although I've always valued the prowess of the Spaniards who have served under my command, I have generally esteemed the companies of Italians and held them in particular honor. When we captured the French king, who had been defeated in combat, it is a fact that by far the bravest fighters in the battle were the Italian infantry, for with admirable stead-

equitatus Gallici et Helvetiae phalangis et tormentorum impetum admirabili constantia sustinente, longe fortissime dimicatum esse constat. Nec alibi umquam caesarem eos nobis[198] coniunctos habuisse paenituit. Neque hodie plus spei mihi puto reponendum in Hispanis, exaequato numero, quam in his septem tricenariis cohortibus quas, ex totius Italiae veteranis coactas, nobiscum ducit Fabritius Maramaldus.

79 'Ceterum de ducibus potius quam de toto militum grege disceptandum videtur. Quamobrem unde commodum discessi, opportune revertar, affirmaboque in Italia maiorem quam aetate nostra viderimus probatorum ducum esse penuriam. Non enim arbitror, ut antea dixisse me recolo, eum ducem satis magnum ac illustrem esse qui mediocri laude sit contentus, vel qui una tantum aut altera belli virtute spectabilis evadere contendat. Ad praealtam enim et cumulatam militiae dignitatem, insatiabili cupiditate per omnes disciplinae numeros egregiis viris est[199] enitendum. Et hercle Pyrrhus ipse in fama hominum nequaquam tantus exstitisset si, qui primus tutissima ratione castra metari docuit, cetera belli munia remissius attigisset. Hannibal quoque, quo nemo diligentius agmen duxit et callidius insidias hostibus tetendit, nequaquam in universo belli negotio ulli muneri defuisse putandus est. Fuit aliquando cunctator Caesar, qui felici celeritate cuncta perdomuit, et Fabium legimus, qui a singulari patientia bello Punico cunctatoris nomen adeptus est, alias ut prudentem et impigrum decebat ducem acerrime dimicasse. Itaque eos numquam impense laudaverim qui uni tantum virtuti sunt innixi. Cum diversa enim in bellicis casibus peragenda occurrant, necesse erit ut ab duce consilii egeno haerenti ac implicito imperite cuncta administrentur.'

fastness they sustained the assault of the entire French cavalry, the Swiss pikes, and the artillery. The emperor never regretted having them on our side. Nor do I think today, if the numbers are equal, I need to repose greater hope in the Spaniards than in those seven 300-man companies assembled from veteran soldiers of all Italy which Fabrizio Maramaldo[108] commands along with us.

"But our debate needs to be about commanders rather than about the entire rank and file. And so, as required, I will return to that point from which I just strayed and will affirm that now, in this age, there is a greater dearth of excellent leaders than we have ever seen in our time.[109] I remember I said earlier that I do not think a commander who is satisfied with moderate praise, or who strives to emerge as noteworthy in just one or another excellence of war, is sufficiently great and illustrious: to attain to the most lofty and exalted rank of military leadership, outstanding men must strive, with insatiable desire, through all the stages of training. By God, even Pyrrhus himself, who was the first to teach how to lay out a camp in the most secure way, certainly would not have stood out as so great in the opinion of men had he carelessly handled all his other military duties. No man has led a marching column more circumspectly or laid ambushes for enemies more skillfully than Hannibal; but we must not imagine that he was unequal to any duty involved in the whole business of war. Caesar, who completely subdued all enemies with propitious speed, temporized on occasion; and we read that Fabius, who from his singular patience in the Punic War obtained the epithet 'The Delayer,' on other occasions had fought very fiercely, as was befitting a deliberate and energetic commander. So I would never bestow lavish praise upon those who have relied upon just a single talent. Since diverse things arise that need to be accomplished in war, it necessarily follows that a commander who is without a strategy, perplexed, and unable to act will manage all things unskillfully."

80   Tum vero MUSETIUS 'Perpulchra,' inquit, 'narrasti Davale, sed
quae in bene[200] sanis hominibus, ut arbitror, non tam accendere
militiae studium quam restinguere posse videantur. Magna enim
difficultas hac praesertim tempestate proponitur, si ad primos honores fortibus factis sit evolandum. Quo fit ut[201] amplius minime
dubitem[202] an ex omnibus humanis rebus valde arduum et longe
maximum sit perfecti imperatoris munus, quando ante alia omnia
huius saeculi disciplina valde corrupta egregiae virtuti plurimum
officiat.'

81   Tum DAVALUS 'Ita est,' inquit, 'ut rectissime sentis, Museti,
unde admodum vereor ne si nostros hodie militaribus factis florentes singulos enumerando cum superioribus conferre voluero, cum
ignominia nostra omnis illustris laus non antiquis modo sed his
ipsis, qui me militante sunt defuncti, absque ulla dubitatione relinquatur. Et hercle, ut hinc incipiam, neminem ex Romano sanguine
militem intueor in quo eximia[203] maximi ducis auctoritas[204] eniteat, cum Roma peculiari felicis caeli fecunditate duces insignes
atque fortissimos omnibus fere terris ac populis semper dederit. Et
ut ipsas quoque familias inter se comparemus, quinam erunt ex
Columnia domo qui se Fabritio et Prospero conferre audeant, aut
M. Antonii et Mutii, quos in medio vitae cursu crudeli fato bellum
absumpsit, vim studium ac ardorem se aequaturos[205] confidant?
Hoc enim mihi vel liberali cum pudore vel ingenua pietate de parentibus eorum facile concedent Vespasianus et Ascanius, quamquam in utroque eorum diversae illae atque dissimiles paternae
virtutes eluceant. Nam quis hodie vel maturiore prudentia, vel
accuratiore disciplina, vel firmiore et clariore auctoritate quam

Hereupon MUSCETTOLA commented: "You have set out some 80 fine ideas, d'Avalos, but ones that, I think, appear able not so much to inflame zeal for the military in sufficiently sound men, as they are able to extinguish it. Indeed, a great difficulty is in store, especially in these turbulent times, if one has to rush upward by brave deeds to the foremost honors. On this account, I no longer doubt that the charge of the perfect commander is very difficult, and by far the greatest out of all human affairs, since above everything else, the exceedingly corrupt training of this century is an immense obstacle to outstanding excellence."

D'AVALOS replied: "You are right on target, Muscettola. For 81 the reasons you have identified, I fear very much that if I want to count up the number of our commanders flourishing today in military deeds and compare them with our predecessors, there is absolutely no doubt that they must relinquish all military glory, to our great shame, not only to the ancients, but to those very men who have died while I've been active as a soldier. And by God, let me start off from this consideration: I see that there is no military man of Roman blood in whom the exceptional authority of a great commander shines forth. And this is the case even though, by a special fruitfulness of the auspicious heavens, Rome has always given distinguished and very brave commanders to nearly all lands and peoples. And so that we may make comparisons within families, I ask you: Who among the Colonnas might dare to compare themselves to Fabrizio[110] and Prospero,[111] or might be confident that they will soon equal the strength, ardor, and passion of Marcantonio[112] and Muzio,[113] who by a cruel fate were killed in wars in the midst of life's journey? Vespasiano[114] and Ascanio[115] will readily grant what I say of their parents, either through the modesty befitting a free man or through an honorable filial duty, even though in each of them his father's distinctive virtues shine forth. For who today has carefully examined matters of war and peace with either more mature prudence, more meticulous train-

Prosper belli pacisque negotia usque ad gloriosum vitae exitum pertractavit? At quem exaequari Fabritio posse putabimus, quando vir ille candore ingenii vitaeque splendore cunctos proceres antecessit? Et duces omnes flagranti illo corporis atque animi vigore, et in suscipiendis repente consiliis, et rebus fortissime peragendis, felici sollertia et celeritate superavit.

82 ʻQuamquam Vespasiano prudentia insit pace et bello ex paterna illustri disciplina singularis, et studium armorum etiam valde eximium adeo ut, quamquam altero crure debilitatus ad Frusinonem, ab ulla militari cura vel nocturna etiam exercitatione minime conquierit. In Ascanio autem nec hoc edepol tam arctae cognationi nostrae sit datum. Fateor me aliqua praeclara vehementer admirari: ingenium scilicet peramoenis excultum litteris itemque etiam pergrave et acutum, a quo consilia generosa militaris atque civilis plena prudentiae firmis ducta rationibus emanare videntur; quae etiam adeo distincta et dulci nec ea umquam affectata facundia proferre consuevit ut in conciliis et disceptationibus tot ducum seniorumque procerum, dum de arduis rebus deliberatur, neminem eo rectius aut melius sententiam dicere et futura divinius praesentire praedicemus. Porro cum in eo Fabritii patris habitum ac oris lineamenta et plerasque eius viri virtutes intuear, aliquarum etiam rerum moderationem in filio laudamus, quae nonnumquam patri deerat fervidis cupiditatibus liberius servienti.

83 ʻHoc autem bello per Lanoium ad Frusinonem imperite gesto, vel ut pontificii luctuose conqueruntur, insidiosa pace confecto, cum explorata prope esset de adventante hoste victoria, solus

ing, or more steadfast and famous leadership, all the way to the glorious end of his life, than Prospero? On the other hand, who will we think can match Fabrizio, given that he outstripped all the nobles in brilliance of intellect and in the distinction of his manner of living? With both successful resourcefulness and swiftness, he also surpassed all other commanders in his ardent vigor of body and mind, both in undertaking policies on the spur of the moment and in very bravely following them through to the end.

"Although from his father's training Vespasiano has singular 82 good judgment in peace and in war, he also has exceptional enthusiasm for arms — so much so that at Frosinone, although one of his legs was injured, he didn't take the least time off from any military responsibility or even from nocturnal training. But by God, I can't say the same of Ascanio, despite our very close relationship. I admit that I intensely admire in him some outstanding qualities: I mean, of course, an intellect that is steeped in the most delightful literature and is deeply thoughtful and keen, from which are seen to flow noble-minded counsels full of military and civic wisdom that have been developed by powerful reasoning. He has often expressed these ideas with an eloquence that is so lucid and delightful, without ever being affected, that we declare that when lofty topics are discussed in the councils and debates of commanders and senior nobles, no one either speaks his mind more suitably or better or foresees the future with greater clarity. Moreover, while I admire in him the character, facial features, and many of the virtues of his father Fabrizio, in the son we praise in addition a restraint in some matters that was sometimes lacking in his father, who was more openly in thrall to impetuous passions.

"And then there is this recent battle fecklessly conducted 83 by Lannoy at Frosinone — a battle concluded, as the pope's men sadly lament, with a treacherous peace.[116] When victory had been almost certain over an enemy who was drawing near,

Ascanius quid agendum esset opportune providit: solus impar hostibus, gladium destrinxit[206] cum primae aciei praeesset, et Lanoium ne proelium committere dubitaret, frustra hortaretur, ita ut confessione omnium ostenderit Lanoio imperatori non sibi vel consilium vel animum in eo negotio defuisse. Sed iam eum procul dubio omni ex parte ducem egregium haberemus, nisi ad primum Gallicum bellum, ut erat adulescens et magister equitum, tanto ardore atque apparatu contendentem, in itinere adversa valetudo deprehendisset: nam in tanta rerum castrensium et renovati totiens belli varietate, multis ad parandam laudem occasionibus minime defuisset, sicut postea non defuit, ceteris rebus omnibus postpositis, cum de caesaris imperio ac dignitate conspirantibus pro libertate Italiae cunctis principibus ageretur.

84   'Nec Iulius atque Marcellus iam plane senes, qui sunt Pompei Cardinalis fratres, summae[207] defunctorum quattuor affinium gloriae nomen exaequare potuerunt. Nam Iulius, quamquam laboriosus et militiae intellegens et hac clariore apud Senas eruptione atque victoria nobilitatus ut coeperat adulescens,[208] se nequaquam postea maioribus[209] bellis exercuit. Nec Marcellus eam spem quam iuvenis Neapolitano bello insigni cum laude tulerat provecta demum aetate implere visus est. Sed is nuper Hieronymum filium, ut mihi videtur, ab optimis militiae initiis ad amplissimum decus sese alacriter efferentem nuper amisit, qui non modo Columniae gentis dignitatem egregie tueri, verum etiam insigni virtute latius extendere potuisset. Prosperum vero Iuniorem, cognomento Rubrobarbum, totum id animi virilis robur quod iuvenis cum Fabritio patruo foris ardenter ostenderat, ad quietis et venationis studium contulisse videmus. Sed is est quibusdam in rebus gentilibus

Ascanio alone foresaw opportunely what needed to be done. Unequal to the enemy on his own, when he was commanding the front rank and vainly exhorting Lannoy not to hesitate to join battle, he unsheathed his sword so that, as everyone admitted, he made clear to his captain that in that situation he had not lacked either sound judgment or courage. But by now we would undoubtedly regard him as an outstanding commander in every respect had he not been stricken with illness as he was marching in haste, young man and cavalry commander that he was, with so much ardor and display to engage in the first French War:[117] for in such great variability of military campaigns and of a war so often renewed, he would by no means have lacked many opportunities to acquire praise. This was the case later on, when the princes set aside all other matters and conspired together to free Italy, and the sway and standing of the emperor were at stake.

"Nor could Giulio[118] and Marcello,[119] Cardinal Pompeo's[120]   84 brothers, who are now quite elderly, equal the glorious reputation of their four deceased kinsmen. Although Giulio was industrious and knowledgeable about warfare, and was ennobled by that very distinguished sortie and victory at Senigallia when he had begun his career as a young man, thereafter he failed to take part in major wars. Nor was Marcello upon reaching maturity seen to fulfill that promise which he had shown with conspicuous praise as a young man in the Neapolitan war. But he recently lost his son Girolamo,[121] who, I believe, from the very outset of his military career was rising briskly toward the most eminent glory. Girolamo would have been able not only to preserve outstandingly the dignity of the Colonna family but also to enlarge it more widely with distinguished excellence. We see, however, that Prospero the Younger,[122] nicknamed 'Barbarossa,' has applied to leisure and hunting all that strength of manly spirit which as a young man he had ardently shown abroad along with his paternal uncle Fabrizio. But in certain of his familial responsibilities, he is perhaps more

suis fortasse prudentior, et ob id maxime, quod pontificio bello
nequaquam sumptis armis, a tota ea velut impia vel parum decora
contentione abesse voluerit. Neque Sarram ex paelice natum, qui
cum Ascanii fratris ala equitum in bello Gallico et in obsidione
Cremonensi et Roma capienda[210] strenue versatus est, et nunc in
Umbria Guelfos omni belli clade persequitur, tantos spiritus gerere
puto, ut se umquam tribus fato exstinctis Columnis virtute et
fama parem futurum existimet.

85   'In Stephano Columna Praenestino, aetate mihi aequali, qui
domi et foris sub Prospero militavit pedestrique munere maxime
delectatur, aliqua video non dubia signa bellicae gravitatis constantiae fortitudinis, sed necesse foret ut maiora auspicia quam capti
pontificis[211] sequeretur. Incredibile enim dictu est quantum crescenti virtuti noceant intermissa militiae studia; militando enim
iugiter, sive in bona sive in damnata belli causa, industria omnis
vel mediocris cum bono nomine protinus efflorescit. At sedendo et
parem votis rerum exitum exspectando, quicquid decoris antea
partum fuerit, et[212] tuo languore pariter[213] et aliena oblivione paullatim exstinguitur.

86   'Porro haec tam frequens Ursinorum iuventus, quam hactenus
de se uberioris frugis spem praebuit, ut suorum virtutes aemula-
tura videatur? Quis enim eorum Magni Virginii dignitatem splendorem disciplinam, quis Petiliani grave iudicium patientiam robur,
vel tiro vel vetus etiam miles ostendit? Quem etiam Liviano, vel
animi promptitudine, vel corporis labore, vel in gerendis rebus celeritate similem videmus? Nisi Rentium Ceritem Anguillarium
his aequare velitis; quem, sicut valde industrium et impigrum et

prudent, and especially on this account: by no means did he take up arms in the papal war, wishing to keep clear of that entire, as he thought, impious or disreputable quarrel. Then there is Sciarra,[123] son of a mistress, who has engaged vigorously with the light cavalry of his brother Ascanio in the French War, the siege of Cremona,[124] the capture of Rome, and is now harrying the Guelfs in Umbria with every kind of military disaster. But I do not think that he displays such great courage that he will ever be able to think himself equal in prowess and fame to the three[125] deceased Colonnas.

"Then there is my coeval Stefano Colonna of Palestrina,[126] who   85
fought under Prospero at home and abroad and takes special delight in infantry service. I see some solid evidence of warlike seriousness, steadfastness, and bravery in him, but he would need to aspire to greater commands than guarding a captured pope. It's remarkable how injurious it is to the development of excellence for one's military activity to be interrupted. When one is fighting continuously, whether in a good or hateful cause, every diligent action, even one that is undistinguished, instantly blossoms with good repute. But while one sits in camp and awaits the hoped-for outcome of events, whatever honor was previously acquired is gradually extinguished, both on account of your idleness and, in equal measure, because of others' forgetfulness.

"Next let us consider these numerous young men of the Orsini   86
family: what hope of a fruitful maturity have they so far presented that they may appear destined to rival the virtues of their line? Who, indeed, matches the dignity, splendor, and discipline of Virginio the Great?[127] Who, whether a beginner or a long-experienced soldier, shows the eminent good judgment, patience, and strength of the count of Pitigliano?[128] Whom, besides, do we see like d'Alviano,[129] either in promptness of mind or exertion of body or speed in action? Unless, that is, you should wish to compare Renzo da Ceri[130] to them. We concede that he is very diligent

denique, si sic Romanos iuvat, munitionum peritum omnisque periculi contemptorem fatemur, ita profecto cum ab suis perpetuis exercitationibus magnum esse diceremus, nisi hac fatali et suprema infelicitate non modo suae sed cunctorum gentium florentissimae patriae, ut caderet, dux admodum funestus exstitisset.'

87   Hic cum ego anxius astricta fronte suspirassem, 'Dic obsecro Iovi,' inquit DAVALUS, 'qui tam alte suspiria sustulisti, quidnam Clementem Pontificem, tanta modo prudentiae opinione bello paceque versatum, adeo sinistre impulit ut cunctis his rebus ac hominibus quibus nihil umquam ipse[214] confidisset adeo temere crederet, hisque demum qui aliquando ipsius inimici capitales exstitissent in gravissimo summi periculi momento suam pariter ac omnium salutem committeret? Irrisimus profecto, cum Roma capta ad exercitum venissem, illum oblongum muri tractum, ipsis fere hortorum maceriis debiliorem, et vitium eius ineptae munitionis, quae a Porta Vaticana in summum Ianiculum erat exporrecta, ita ut vos plane insanos fuisse diceremus, quod tutiora consilia, aut recessus intra urbem abruptis pontibus, aut temporariae fugae ad paratas triremes minime cepissetis. Et subinde nequaquam miraremur quod expediti[215] veterani ab omnibus muri partibus puncto temporis in urbem sine ullo prope vulnere penetrassent.'

88   Tum ego ⟨IOVIUS⟩ 'Parce,' inquam, 'Davale huic dolori meo, quem acerbissimarum rerum memoria renovavit, neque a me porro ea exigas precor quae salva officii mei verecundia proferri nequeunt. Neque enim propterea quod saepe liberiore iudicio aliqua damnaverim quae toto hoc exitiali bello praepostere consuli, aut certe parum strenue administrari, ad hunc luctuosum exitum

and energetic and (if it so pleases the Romans!) is both expert in fortifications and a despiser of every danger. And so we would undoubtedly say that he is great on account of his continuous campaigns, had he not been the calamitous commander in this fatal and supreme misfortune and downfall of his own flourishing homeland and that of all peoples."

At this point when I, feeling uneasy, furrowed my brow and heaved a sigh, D'AVALOS said: "Please tell us, Giovio, you who have sighed so deeply: what cause so unluckily pushed Pope Clement, who enjoyed so great a reputation for prudence in war and peace, to put his faith rashly in all these things and people whom he himself had never trusted and, in the gravest moment of extreme danger, to entrust his own safety and likewise that of all men precisely to those who in the past had shown themselves to be his own mortal enemies? After Rome had been captured, when I had come to the army, we derided that oblong stretch of city wall — weaker, almost, than the very walls of gardens, and a flaw of that inept fortification which had been extended from the Vatican Gate to the top of the Janiculum Hill. And so, we called you people manifestly insane in failing to adopt safer strategies — either withdrawing inside the city after destroying the bridges or having ships at the ready for a timely escape. After that, we weren't in the least surprised that light-armed veterans had, in an instant, penetrated into the city from all sections of the wall, practically without suffering a wound." 87

Then I [GIOVIO] said, "D'Avalos, show some consideration for my grief, which the recollection of the bitterest events has renewed, and do not demand of me things I can't mention while preserving the deference befitting my office. Though during this entire deadly war I often outspokenly condemned some points of wrongheaded counsel or lax administration that I foresaw would lead to this lamentable outcome, I do not on that account think that the pope's plans, which were generally very reasonable, ought 88

providebam, aequissimis in universum maximi pontificis consiliis
obtrectandum puto. Quis enim non erit impudens si ab eventu
tam tristi foedissimarum rerum sanorum[216] hominum egregie
consulta reprehenderit? Nam tametsi homines tum falso atque
improbe de Fortuna conquerantur cum, diu impetu atque libidine
pro ratione usi, illa ipsa cunctorum casuum domina eorum coeptis
non arridet, tamen neque pontificem neque aliquos eius consiliorum arbitros graviore invidia onerandos arbitramur. Nam si fides et virtus et decoris cura in iis fuissent in quibus summa esse
debuerant, ut nunc sumus foede victi et misere subacti minime
lugeremus.

89   'Enimvero si prudentia, quae divinus habitus potius est quam
virtus, a consilii gravitate, sollertia ingenii, et a multiplici rerum
humanarum cognitione proficiscitur, non video quem hodie
magnorum principum prudentiorem Clemente pontifice nomine-
mus. Quis enim eo graviora negotia constantius tractavit? Quis
suas et alias rationes accuratius perpendit? Quis denique in omni
bellico vel politico genere praestantis actionis, fines rerum ac origines vel respexit aptius vel divinius prospexit? Cognatum est enim
naturae ipsius, maximis simul atque tenuibus in rebus, considerare
subtiliter, mature diiudicare, excessus omnes aptissime moderari et
denique, quod paucis est datum, ad aequitatem ad decus cuncta
consilia terminare.

90   'Quod si eas etiam artes spectemus sine quibus nemo umquam
fuerit perfectus imperator, eum abunde omnibus disciplinae praesidiis instructum esse fatebimur. Nemo siquidem eo in statuendis
arcibus muniendisque urbibus in exquisita etiam architecturae
norma peritior, nemo in toto fusilium tormentorum artificio
ingeniosior, nemo in avertendis corrivandisque amnibus ⟨et⟩

to be disparaged. Only a brazen man would criticize the excellent counsels of sound men on the basis of so baleful an outcome of horrible circumstances. To be sure, people complain about Fortune mistakenly and shamelessly when, after they've spent a long time relying on impetuousness and whimsy rather than reason, that very mistress of all affairs fails to smile on their projects. Nonetheless we think that neither the pope nor his advisors should be burdened with deep hatred. After all, if there had been good faith and virtue and a concern for honor in those men who ought to have had them in the highest degree, we certainly would not be in mourning, foully conquered and miserably subdued, as we now are.

"Moreover, if prudence, which is a divine condition rather than 89 a virtue, proceeds from weightiness of counsel, shrewdness of intellect, and a nuanced understanding of human affairs, I fail to see which of today's great princes we should cite as more prudent than Pope Clement. For who has managed severe troubles more steadily than he? Who has weighed his own plans and those of others more meticulously? And lastly, who, in every type of military or political activity has either taken account of the origins of things more suitably or foreseen their ends more prophetically? It is proper to that very man's nature, in matters both great and small, to meditate with subtlety, to settle things at the right time, to keep all digressions appropriately in check, and finally — an attribute that has been given to few — to refer all plans to the criteria of justice and honor.

"But if we should look also to those skills without which no 90 man ever has been a perfect commander, we will acknowledge that he has been furnished abundantly with all the bulwarks of the art of war. No one is more expert than he in erecting fortresses and fortifying cities and in the meticulous discipline of architecture; no one is cleverer or more skillful in the use of cast-metal firearms; and no one is better versed and more effective in diverting and

95

pontibus construendis[217] paratior et efficacior; nec mirum eo disceptante architecti silent, fabri conflatores conticescunt, aquileges cum tacita indignatione singularem eius ingenii captum admirantur. Quid dicam de navali negotio, de picturae[218] sculptoriae et plastices arte deque secretis agri culturae thesauris? In quibus ipse tantus et tam copiosus ab ineunte aetate semper fuit ut ipse unus tot singulares artium magistros anteire videatur. His adminiculis procul dubio ad supremum rerum fastigium est evectus.

91   'Qui tamen priusquam caelestem hanc lucem aspiceret, occiso patre, in maternis visceribus infelix fuit. Priusquam pubesceret, patria et domo pulsus, exulavit. Priusquam se sacris initiaturum putaret, atrocissimas pestes fugam errores morbos egestatem vehementer sensit: atque ita sensit et pertulit, ut postea inimicorum vim insidias conatus, singulari patientia et fortitudine potius quam ullo Fortunae beneficio superarit. Sed fatale est verae virtuti, quae in universum astris et Fortunae libidini[219] dominatur, ut quandoque[220] velut semivicta[221] humanis casibus succumbat, scilicet ut eam mox videamus fortiter erectam et "sublimi vertice sidera ferientem." Fata enim eum certe pronuntiant carcere evolaturum, pro solacio[222] mortem visurum[223] inimicorum fere omnium, et dissidentium regum animos firmissima pace parta coniuncturum[224] et extremo quodam voto,[225] et pontificiae maiestatis Christianique imperii ac Italiae[226] dignitatem admirandis consiliis feliciter aucturum.

92   'An non in clarissimo exemplo censebitur Andreas Grittus? Veneti senatus princeps atque ille praecipuus rerum omnium

channeling rivers and in the construction of bridges. So it's no wonder that when he is giving his opinion, architects are silent, builders and metal-casters grow quiet, and water managers marvel with mute indignation at his uniquely capacious mind. What should I say about marine warfare, about painting, sculpture, and the plastic arts, and about the arcane principles of agriculture? From an early age, this very man has always been so great and so eloquent on these subjects that he himself alone is seen to surpass the special masters of the arts. It was with these supports, undoubtedly, that he ascended to the highest summit.

"But before he espied that celestial light, while still in his 91 mother's womb, he was unlucky: his father was murdered.[131] Before he reached maturity, driven out of house and homeland, he went into exile. Before he thought he would devote himself to sacred rites, he experienced the most horrible disasters, exile, wanderings, disease, and poverty—and he experienced and endured them in such a way that thereafter he overcame his enemies' violence, intrigues, and attempts on his life with singular perseverance and fortitude rather than by any favor of Fortune. But true virtue, which in general is governed by the stars and the caprice of Fortune, is fated at one time or another, half-conquered, as it were, to succumb to human misfortunes—only for us to see it soon afterward bravely raised up and 'striking the stars with uplifted head.'[132] Indeed, the Fates are giving notice that he will soon escape from prison and by way of consolation will see the deaths of nearly all his enemies and, once a rock-solid peace has been effected, he will harmonize the minds of quarreling kings and, as a kind of last wish, by means of marvelous policies, he will succeed in magnifying the dignity of the pontifical majesty, of the Christian empire, and of Italy.

"Will not Andrea Gritti[133] be reckoned as a very famous case in 92 point? That man, the leader of the Venetian senate and the chief director of all its affairs, deserved that position on account of an

moderator praeclara sapientiae opinione eum locum meritus. Nemini certe mortalium fortuna intemperantius illusit, nemini acerbiores contumelias inflixit, nemini consilia plena prudentiae impudentius fefellit, siquidem post perpessas tam diu barbaras catenas in quibus, cum discrimine capitis Byzantii fuit, cum demum in exercitu legatum ageret, ad Abduam stratas et foede caesas legiones, fugientem equitatum,[227] castra et tormenta capta conspexit. De Veneto imperio ab ea clade actum intellexit. Contemplatus est non multo post, iam captus, saevitiam barbarorum cum se duce male defensa Brixia deleretur. Inhumani mox carceris in Gallia paedorem sensit, nec multum inde se spectante et fuga salutem per saltus Ligurum quaerente, Gallorum sociorum exercitus ante Novariae moenia ab Helvetiis est trucidatus. Porro quales eius fuere gemitus, quae lacrimae, cum fuso exercitu, caeso collega, tot ducibus interfectis, ex fuga in Vicentiae murum ne caperetur extractus est. Quae denique rerum desperatio fortissimum eius animum repente occupavit, cum Mediolani intra suburbanas munitiones Hispani duce Piscario provolassent, et ipse nocturna fuga res perditas Laudensibus nuntiatum ire properaret.

93 'Sunt tamen in ipsius eximiae virtutis[228] togati imperatoris titulo, tot urbes de manibus hostium receptae et res publica in pristinum amplitudinis statum[229] fortissime restituta ac demum, quod ad privatum pertinet decus, in eo senatu partus amplissimae dignitatis principatus. Quae eo maiora videri possunt et augustiora, quoniam nihil ab his laudis, ex professo iam infesta Fortuna vindicavit, quando eam liquido constat pertinaci vividaeque[230] virtuti suam ex merito gloriam reliquisse.'

outstanding reputation for wisdom. Surely Fortune has mocked no mortal more intemperately, inflicted harsher abuses on no one, and cheated no man's abundantly prudent plans more brazenly. When he was in Byzantium, in mortal danger, he endured foreign chains for a long time. Then when at last he was acting as a legate in the army at the Adda River, he saw his legions utterly defeated and shamefully killed, the cavalry in retreat, and his camp and artillery captured. He understood that as a result of that defeat the Venetian Empire was undone. Not much later, when he had been captured, he observed the savagery of barbarians when Brescia, which had been poorly defended under his command, was destroyed. Then in France he experienced the filth of a harsh prison. Soon after, as he was looking on, the army of his French allies was massacred by the Swiss in front of the walls of Novara.[134] Thereupon he sought safety by flight through the Ligurian countryside. Another time, what groans and tears were his when, after the army had been scattered, a colleague struck down, and so many commanders killed, he fled and was hauled up over the walls of Vicenza to avoid capture.[135] Finally, what despair suddenly took hold of his brave spirit when the Spaniards under Pescara's command had rushed forward into the outlying fortifications of Milan, and he himself was hastening to flee by night and tell the men of Lodi that the battle had been lost.

"But numerous cities recaptured from the hands of enemies, and a republic boldly restored to its ancient condition of greatness, form part of this citizen-commander's claim to exceptional excellence;[136] and finally, as for his personal honor, he acquired the dogeship, the highest office in the Venetian senate. These things may appear all the greater and more august because Fortune, even though by that time overtly hostile, could arrogate no praise for these achievements: for it is crystal clear that she rightly abandoned her own claim to glory to his steadfast and spirited excellence."

94   Tum vero DAVALUS 'Cumulate,' inquit, 'Iovi, de Fortuna et
de[231] virtute duorum, ut arbitror, summorum[232] in Italia virorum
disseruisti. Sed Grittum cum omnibus Italis tum[233] maxime Venetis
admirandum relinquamus,[234] et ad Clementem revertamur qui, si
est, ut affabre nobis expressisti, non minus maximarum virtutum
dote quam sacri imperii maiestate conspicuus, necesse est ut eum,
remota etiam sacrorum et religionis causa, fateamur tanta calamitate indignum exstitisse. Deest tamen, sicut audimus,[235] ad tantarum laudum[236] cumulum ut vir[237] perfectissimus ac optimus princeps[238] evadat, illa virtus illustris, quae in vita summam apud
omnes gratiam et dignitatem parat, et post Fata ex dulci hominum
recordatione scriptorumque memoria[239] gloriam effusissime largi-
tur. Ea est multorum vitiorum occultatrix egregia, quae bonae famae ianuam alacriter pandit, obtrectatoribus atque maledicis eripit
venenum,[240] et inimicorum facile[241] redimit voluntates.'

95   Hic ego ⟨IOVIUS⟩ inquam, 'Agnosco plane hanc virtutem cogna-
tam magnis regibus, qua modo comite Leo Pontifex[242] in caelum
evolavit, ita ut iudicem si Clementi cum Leone fratre virtutes in
unum commiscere datum fuisset, eo quidem singulari temperamento, velut exaequatis morum ponderibus, utrumque talem evasurum fuisse qualem adhuc neminem ulla hominum vel litterarum
memoria veneretur. Sed certe Clementi bona fortuna defuit, quam
huius lucidissimae virtutis parentem sapientes esse statuerunt.
Quid enim praestare potuit amicis et litteratis perpetua bellorum
lue consumptus, et coniectus in has rerum difficultates ab initio
pontificatus in quibus non modo ei sed opulentissimo cuique regi
fuerit decoquendum?'[243]

96   Haec cum dixissem, 'Iovi, edepol,' inquit MUSETIUS, 'dum prudentiae nomen contra Fortunam tueris, egregie etiam pontificem

Then D'AVALOS said, "Giovio, you've fully discussed the for- 94
tune and virtue of, in my view, the two best men in Italy. But let us
move beyond Gritti, whom all Italians and especially the Venetians
have to admire, and return to Clement. If, as you have skillfully
portrayed him to us, he is no less illustrious in endowment of the
greatest virtues than in sovereignty of holy authority, then we
must acknowledge that, even if we put aside considerations of holiness and religion, he was unworthy of such a great calamity. But
as we have heard it, this perfect man and best prince lacks a noble
virtue that is necessary for attaining the summit of such praises:
namely, that virtue[137] which provides in life the highest favor and
esteem among all men and which, after death, confers glory lavishly from men's sweet recollection and from writers' historical accounts. It is an outstanding concealer of many vices. It quickly
opens the door to good reputation, snatches away the poison from
detractors and slanderers, and easily purchases the support of enemies."

At this point I [GIOVIO] said: "Of course I recognize that vir- 95
tue, proper to great kings, with which Pope Leo recently flew up to
heaven. And so, I judge that if it had been given to Clement along
with his cousin Leo to compound the virtues into one, then by
that special blending, as if the weights of character had been made
level, each of the two would have turned out to be of such a kind
as to be honored in a way that no one else has been up to now in
human memory or in written accounts.[138] But certainly Clement
lacked good fortune, which the wise have decided is the parent of
that very shining virtue. For what has he been able to do for
friends and literati, when he has been exhausted by the continuous
calamity of wars and, from the outset of his pontificate, has been
hurled into those straitened circumstances in which not only he
but every very powerful king must be brought to bankruptcy?"

When I had finished speaking, MUSCETTOLA commented, "By 96
God, Giovio, while you are protecting the good name of prudence

et Grittum ab omni eius enormis beluae contumelia defendis ita ut, quod est in veteri[244] proverbio, visus sis duos parietes una fidelia dealbare. Et recte quidem contendisti. Nam id certe commune vitium videtur imperitae multitudinis, ut eos ab eventu maxime condemnent quem maxime exagitatum a Fortuna conspiciant. Sed harum rerum et consiliorum causas puto a te in *Historiis* plenissime fuisse pertractatas. Igitur tu, Davale, potius haec omittes, et muneri tuo et nostrae pariter exspectationi satisfeceris. Video enim te, dum singulos duces recensendos putas, in vastissimum velut illud Aegypti harenarum aequor pedibus esse ingressum, in quo multum ac diu sit aberrandum, nisi singulari memoria tua fretus tamquam navali magnete ad certa sidera cursum omnino direxeris.'

97   At ille ⟨DAVALUS⟩ 'Non est,' inquit, 'cur tantopere solliciti sitis de imbecillitate virium mearum. Nam tametsi, quod saepe iuvat, aliquando fuerim obliviosus, hoc tamen vel delatum vel sponte susceptum munus enucleate et diligenter absolvam, quandoquidem ii admodum sunt pauci qui ampliore cum praeconio laudum bellicarum numerandi esse videantur. Quamobrem, priusquam superiorem repetam sermonem, scire velim, Iovi, an in occultam vim urgentium Fatorum hos improvisos rerum eventus aliqua ex parte contuleris, dum hac tua tam eximia pietate praeclaroque studio eundem et sacrorum principem et dominum tuum adversus ignarae multitudinis iudicium defendis. Ab iis enim philosophis e quorum secta te esse profiteris, et Fatum et Fortunam tolli penitus et explodi manifeste didicimus, rem vero civilem et bellicam consilio et ratione penitus gubernari, ita ut tibi magnopere sit cavendum ne, cum errata graviora excusare contendas, aut ineptus difficillimae causae defensor aut malus omnino philosophus esse videare.'

against Fortune, you also admirably defend the pope and Gritti from every affront of that enormous beast in such a way that you have seemed to whitewash two walls with one bucket,[139] as the saying goes. And indeed, you've argued well. For surely this common failing appears to belong to the ignorant rabble: that they blame those men exceedingly on account of a result which they see was instigated above all by Fortune. But I think you have treated the causes of these situations and plans in detail in the *Histories*. Therefore, d'Avalos, you should instead let these things drop and fulfill your task and satisfy our expectation. In fact, I see that since you suppose that particular commanders need to be surveyed, you have set foot in that vast, as it were, desert of Egypt, in which you have to wander far and long unless, relying upon your singular memory as on a compass, you steer a course entirely according to the fixed stars."

But D'AVALOS replied, "This is not the reason you are so anxious about the feebleness of my powers. For even if I am sometimes forgetful — which is often a boon — I will nonetheless finish that task precisely and with care, whether it has been assigned to me or I have taken it on willingly, since those men are quite few who, it seems, must be accorded a superior reputation for military prowess. Therefore, before I review our previous discussion, I would like to know, Giovio, whether you assign these unexpected events in some degree to the hidden power of the Fates closing in,[140] since with your exceptional piety and outstanding devotion you are defending the pope your master against the judgment of the ignorant rabble. We have learned from those philosophers to whose school you claim to belong that both Fate and Fortune are utterly eliminated and clearly discredited, but that civil and military affairs are entirely governed by deliberation and reason. So you need to take great care that, while at pains to make excuses for quite serious errors, you do not appear either the foolish defender of a difficult case or a bad philosopher."

97

98   Tum ego ⟨iovius⟩ inquam, 'Davale, neque Fato neque item Fortunae vel casibus nostras actiones adscribendas putavi, utpote qui iam pridem supremam humanarum rerum potestatem in trino numine Immortalis Dei vigere crediderim. Dii enim cuncta rectissime provident atque decernunt aequissimoque iudicio vel ad scelerum poenam vel ad virtutis praemium quibus decet, et mentem dare et pariter eripere consueverunt; ideoque numina[245] vel sanis et graviter examinatis mortalium consiliis potentiora videri, cum nobis superbe atque impie terrena molientibus adesse nolint. Quibus etiam adversis et infestis irascimur, tamquam generis humani desertoribus, nec mirum quando eorum patientiam supina et procaci neglegentia nostra[246] iam pridem abrupimus.'

99   Haec cum dixissem, 'Mirifice,' inquit musetius, 'me delectant haec amoena deverticula quibus instituti sermones nostri, non secus ac in pictis tabulis videmus, in quibus non tam ipsae grandiores imagines ex decreto pictoris eleganter expressae commendantur, quam illa parerga in remotis recessibus ad prospectus rationem successive deminuta,[247] ut sunt venationes silvae flumina pastorales casae et evagantium nubium simulacra, quae extemporanea quadam lascivia manus eruditae ad detinendos spectantium oculos cum iucunda dissimulatione depinguntur. Ceterum, Davale, iam aequum est ut ad Romanos redeas, a quibus paullo ante devertisti.[248] Vellem enim ut inde celeriter te ipsum explicares et Neapolim progredereris, ubi in tanto regulorum numero aliquamdiu tibi singulos aestimanti omnino erit immorandum.'

100   Ad id arridens davalus 'Quin tu,' inquit, 'Museti, me potius Romae etiam commorari iubes? Nam simul ac Neapolim applicuero, cuncta celerrime transigentur. Cum enim duces quaeramus

Then I [GIOVIO] replied: "D'Avalos, I did not suppose that our 98
actions ought to be ascribed to either Fate, Fortune, or accidents,
inasmuch as I have for a long time believed that the highest power
over human affairs abounds in the triune majesty of Immortal
God. For the gods foresee all things rightly and with absolutely
impartial judgment determine for whom either punishment for
crime or reward for virtue is appropriate; they grant understanding
and likewise take it away. Divine influence seems more powerful
than the deliberations of mortals, even when these are sensible and
well thought out, for the reason that the gods refuse to assist us as
we are undertaking arrogant and wicked actions on earth. And
when they are hostile and unfavorable, we even get angry with
them, accusing them of abandoning humankind; but it is no wonder that they act that way, since by our lazy and brash negligence
we wore out their patience long ago."

When I [GIOVIO] had said this, MUSCETTOLA said: "These 99
charming digressions with which our discussions have begun delight me exceedingly, exactly as we see in the case of paintings.
There, the larger images that the painter has chosen to portray
elegantly receive less praise than do those subordinate details in
remote corners which are made successively smaller for the sake of
perspective—things such as hunts, woods, rivers, pastoral cot-
tages, and images of drifting clouds. With a certain improvised
playfulness of a skilled hand, these are painted with agreeable dissimulation so as to detain the eyes of observers. But it's right,
d'Avalos, for you now to return to the Romans, from whom a little
while ago you made a detour. I wish you would quickly extricate
yourself from there and go on to Naples, where, as you evaluate
each one among so great a number of Neapolitan princes, you will
definitely have to tarry for some time."

To that D'AVALOS replied with a laugh: "Muscettola, why do 100
you not rather ask me to linger in Rome? For as soon as I move on
to Naples, all things will quickly be wrapped up. Indeed, when we

militares, in illa tanta multitudine procerum fere neminem conspicimus[249] adeo vel nova virtute vel antiqua laude conspicuum, ut ei
iustus exercitus recte committi posse videatur.

101 'Igitur ut ad Ursinos redeamus, si quid apud eos est maturae
virtutis ac industriae, id fere totum spectatur in Ioanne Antonio
Gravina et Camillo Nomentano. Ii enim a pueris equestria stipendia meruerunt, et nonnullis asperis in proeliis strenue versati sunt.
In Ludovico Petiliani filio robur erat et constantia militaris, sed is,
dum cum Senensi populo, ulturus avum ab Suanensibus agrestibus crudeliter interfectum,[250] de finibus certat, in rusticano[251] bello
consenuit. Valerium porro imberbem fere iuvenem, cum, Latino
bello tam foede et turpiter utrimque gesto, alam equitum ductaret,
saepius ante alios impigre et fortiter dimicavit, adeo ut Ursinorum
clarissimus sit evasurus. Virginius autem ipse Magni Virginii ne-
pos, quamquam animo sit alacer et ore toto plenioreque habitu
avum referat et bellicae laudis valde sit appetens, tamen Fortuna
nuper ad Senas adverso exitu prima eius imperii insignia[252] defoe-
davit. Huic patruelis est ipse Neapolio[253] Farfareus Abbas,[254] qui
si, ut est ingenio acri vario feroci, a sacris quibus est initiatus aliquando discesserit, profecto partium dux impiger ac intrepidus
evadet. De[255] Mario quoque Valerii fratre nihil dicam qui, si quicquam pensi habuisset, numquam pro[256] caesarianis et Columniis
Ursinae familiae viris hostibus[257] adversus pontificem militasset.[258]
In Paulo etiam Rentii filio, bellicus ardor et audacia, fervore aetatis
ad omne patrandum facinus incitata, conspicitur.[259]

are seeking military commanders in that great multitude of leading men, we catch sight of almost no one sufficiently distinguished either by fresh prowess or by longstanding reputation that we can justifiably entrust him with a regular army.

"So let us return to the Orsini. If there is among them some 101 degree of mature virtue and diligence, it is nearly all visible in Gian-antonio[141] of the Gravina branch and in Camillo,[142] the lord of Mentana. From boyhood on they have served in the cavalry and participated vigorously in some fierce battles. The Count of Pitigli-ano's son, Ludovico,[143] has displayed physical strength and military steadfastness. But while he is fighting against the Sienese over boundaries in order to avenge his grandfather,[144] who was cruelly killed by Sovanian peasants, he has wasted away in a rural war. Next I mention Valerio,[145] almost a beardless youth. After the war in Latium had been waged foully and shamelessly on both sides, Valerio led a squadron of light cavalry and quite often fought more energetically and bravely than the others, and so he is on his way to being the most famous of the Orsini. Virginio,[146] himself the grandson of Virginio the Great, has a quick mind and resembles his grandfather in his entire countenance and stout body. He is very eager for military fame. But Fortune has just defiled the first distinctions of his command by the defeat at Senigallia. His cousin is none other than Napoleone, the Abbot of Farfa.[147] As he has a shrewd, many-sided, and fierce temperament, if Napoleone ever leaves his abbatial duties, he will surely prove to be a tireless and intrepid commander of military forces. I shall say nothing either about Valerio's brother, Mario,[148] since if he'd had any scruples, he would never have made war against the pope on behalf of the im-perialists and the Colonnas, enemies of the Orsini family. And in Giampaolo,[149] Renzo's son, we see warlike ardor and boldness stirred by the passion of youth to perpetrate every outrage.

102   'In Sabella vero domo, in qua modo quinque simul fortissimi[260] viri claruerunt—Lucas, Sylvius, Troilus, Anthimus,[261] atque Iacobus—unus ante alios emergit: egregius adulescens Baptista Iacobi filius, in quo manifesta signa paternae prudentiae et domestici decoris Latino bello enituerunt. In Grappellia etiam comitum familia, in qua perpetua serie bini semper clari duces exstiterunt, vix Baptista adulescens familiae atque militiae nomen tuetur.

103   'Farnesii unum habent Ranucium, praeclara indole iuvenem, nomen et virtutem patrui, qui Tarrensi proelio cecidit, referentem. Is huius Aloisii frater est ex eodem patre Alexandro Cardinale quem, ex iracundia impie contra patrem concepta, Borbonio adhaesisse et adversus pontificem Romamque patriam arma tulisse vidistis. Igitur, ut vos ipsi manifeste perspicitis, ii nostri Romani non modo[262] illis antiquis heroibus nequaquam exaequantur, sed nec his etiam[263] quos diximus, bonis mortuis, quibus tu praesertim Iovi, dum *Historias* conderes, familiaris exstitisti.

104   'Neapoli quoque, cum Aragoniis regibus belli decora magna ex parte exstincta videmus; nam cum vetus quisque dux bello clarus naturae concesserit, translato demum ad externos imperio,[264] defuere domi reges qui militum et ducum subolem perpetua liberalitate tuerentur. Honoribus enim et frequentibus ab illustri gratia beneficiis eos etiam provehi animadverto, qui vel tenuem virtutis speciem ante praetulerint, ita ut nequaquam mirum esse debet, si externi in Italia quam Itali[265] erepta quodammodo e manibus nostris arma felicius exercent, cum illis sui reges impense[266] faveant, et

"In the Savelli household, five men recently began to distinguish themselves at the same time: Luca,[150] Silvio,[151] Troilo,[152] Antimo,[153] and Giacomo.[154] But another kinsman is rising beyond the others: the exceptional young Gianbattista,[155] Giacomo's son, in whom clear signs of his father's discretion and of the family's honor shone forth in the war in Latium. And in the Grappelli family of counts,[156] in which a succession of distinguished commanders has always appeared in twos, the young Battista can scarcely maintain his family's good military reputation. 102

"The Farnese have only Ranuccio,[157] a young man of outstanding natural ability. In his name and his prowess he recalls his uncle who was slain in the Battle of Fornovo.[158] Pier Luigi[159] is his brother by the same father, Cardinal Alessandro; you have seen him, raging wickedly against his father, cling to Bourbon and fight against the pope and his own Roman homeland. So, as you yourselves clearly perceive, these Romans of ours not only fail to measure up to those ancient heroes, but even to these recently deceased good men whom we have mentioned, with whom you, Giovio, were especially close while you were composing your *Histories*. 103

"At Naples too we see that for the most part martial glories have been wiped out along with the Aragonese kings. Once every elderly commander of military distinction had succumbed to nature, and rule had finally been transferred to foreigners, at home there were no kings to protect the children of soldiers and commanders with uninterrupted liberality. In fact, I notice that even those men who displayed a thin veneer of virtue are promoted with honors and regular favors from noble preference. And so it should not be at all surprising if foreigners in Italy wield better than Italians the weapons that have somehow been snatched out of our hands: since the Italians' own princes, at great expense, support those foreigners, and on that account the marvelous natural ability of 104

ob id mirifica nostrorum indoles in obscuro segnique otio vel belli tempore relinquatur.

105   'Quis enim ⟨dubitet⟩ de Sanseverinis duobus regulis, Ferdinando Salernitano eximiis corporis ac animi dotibus ornatissimo adulescente, et Pyrrho Antonio Besenniano iuvene promptitudine simul atque prudentia praestanti, quin,[267] si educantur, et dignus innatae virtuti pateat locus, patres ipsorum referant et clarioribus etiam factis exsuperent. Nonne Alfonsum Picolomineum Amalfium sororium meum ab his virilis alacritatis et constantiae initiis, quibus ad Frusinonem inclaruit, in praestantem evasurum ducem omnino putabimus si, ut est diu expetitus et evocatus, Senensium vexilla ad tuendam eorum libertatem acceperit, vel hoc bello, quod a Gallis renovatur, caesari operam praestiterit. Probatur vero mihi maxime Sergianus Caracciolus Melfictae princeps: est enim honestis litteris et moribus expolitus, itemque egregie cordatus et fortis, quibus innixus praesidiis, alendo equites et privato sumptu turmam[268] tuendo, ex occasione ad ampliorem aspirat laudem.

106   'Fuere aliquamdiu nobiles et robusti alarum ductores duo Pinnatelli: Hector scilicet[269] ille moderatus Siciliae praefectus,[270] et Troilus, qui apud Venetos militavit. Duo item Capuanae familiae, Iulius et Franciscus, longo usu bellicarum rerum aliquamdiu[271] magnopere valuerunt.[272] Sed ante alios, duo Feramuscae Campani fratres insigni gloria florent: Guido et Caesar, qui multa domi suae decora militiae parta ostentant, cum ipsius Raynaldi patris, qui in oppugnatione Caietae tormento ictus interiit, et Rosseti avi

our own soldiers is left in obscure and lazy leisure, even in a time of war.

"As to the two Sanseverino princes, Ferrante of Salerno,[160] a youth excellently adorned with choice gifts of body and mind, and Pietrantonio,[161] prince of Bisignano, a young man outstanding in nimbleness and likewise in discretion: who would doubt that, if only they should receive training and if an opportunity worthy of their innate talent should be available, they would resemble their fathers and even surpass them with more illustrious deeds? Then there is my brother-in-law, Alfonso Piccolomini of Amalfi.[162] Surely we will think that, starting out from the beginnings of manly vigor and steadfastness for which he became famous at Frosinone, he will turn out to be an outstanding commander — if, as he has for a long time been asked and summoned to do, he takes up the command to secure the liberty of the Sienese;[163] or if, in this war which is being renewed by the French, he discharges his service to the emperor. I think most highly of Sergianni Caracciolo, the prince of Melfi.[164] He is refined in honorable learning and in character, and also is outstandingly judicious and brave. Relying upon these strong points, and by providing livelihood for the cavalry and maintaining a squadron at his own expense, he aspires to enhance his reputation when the opportunity presents itself.

"For some time, two of the Pignatelli have been noble and strong leaders of light cavalry: Ettore,[165] that moderate governor of Sicily, and Troilo,[166] who has done military service for Venice. Two men of a Capuan family, Giulio[167] and Francesco,[168] also have lengthy military experience and have been highly effective for quite a while now. But more than anyone else, two brothers of the Fieramosca family from Campania, Guidone[169] and Cesare,[170] are abounding in distinguished glory. They are said to display the many military virtues of their house: those of their father, that very Rinaldo[171] who died of a gunshot wound during the siege of Gaeta; their grandfather Rossetto,[172] a distinguished commander;

clarissimi ducis, tum fratris Hectoris, qui devictis apud Quadratam Apuliae tredecim Gallis equitibus, cum ex[273] totidem Italis unus admodum conspicuus fuisset[274] tredecim, postea torques pro insigni ad incomparabilis eius victoriae memoriam tulit. Sed Caesar, virtute corporis ac ingenii et militarium morum elegantia, talem apud caesarem gratiae et familiaritatis locum promeruit qualem nemo adhuc Italorum apud externos reges adeptus est.'

107　　Tum ego ⟨IOVIVS⟩ 'Agnosco nimis,' inquam, 'hunc Caesarem. Est enim ille qui funesta de pace mandata a Carolo[275] caesare ad pontificem detulit, quibus omnes egregie decepti, cum ipsa urbe Roma periimus.'

108　　Hic DAVALUS 'Ne putato,' inquit, 'eum perfidiosis artibus instructum ab Hispania venisse, ut vos opprimeret. Egit enim sincera fide quantum valuit, et certe eius auctoritas, tametsi opinione vestra minor erat, plurimum valuisset, nisi Borbonius contra caesaris voluntatem[276] studio evertendae vestrae libertatis inflammatus, sponte sua, incitatos milites ad exscindendam urbem propulisset.'

109　　Ad id ego ⟨IOVIVS⟩ 'Ignoscam Feramuscae,' inquam, 'si dii perfidiae ultores, qui Borbonium perfidiose nobiscum de pace legatos mittentem[277] in ipso victoriae limine[278] mactaverunt, aliis quoque impiis deceptoribus omnino pepercerint. Video enim caelitus comprobari eas diras quas pontifex in carcere crudelissimis hostibus est imprecatus, cum in illa[279] pestilentiae contagione eum[280] suppliciter pro salute deprecantem arce educere[281] et periculo eximere noluissent. Cecidit enim triduo pestilentia exstinctus Nagereus, omnium in exercitu consiliorum[282] moderator. Cecidit et prorex ipse[283] Lanoius qui, cum foedus feriret, se numquam pontifici defuturum iuraverat. Neque umquam postea, cum Romam venisset,[284] ulla

and also their brother Ettore.[173] In the Challenge of Barletta, in Apulia, when thirteen French cavalrymen had been trounced, out of the same number of Italians, Ettore alone had been distinguished.[174] Afterward, he wore a collar as a mark of honor to commemorate that incomparable victory. But Cesare, with an excellent body and mind and by refined military conduct, has earned the kind of position of favor and intimacy at the emperor's court that no other Italian has won in the courts of foreign kings."

Then I [GIOVIO] said: "I recognize this Cesare only too well: 107 he's the one who brought to the pope from the Emperor Charles the calamitous terms for peace.[175] Outrageously deceived by them, we all were ruined, along with the city of Rome itself."

Here D'AVALOS said: "Do not fancy that he came from Spain 108 equipped with those treacherous tactics for crushing you. In fact, insofar as he had the power to do so, he negotiated in good faith. And surely his[176] influence would have prevailed—even though it was less than you think—had not Bourbon, contrary to the emperor's will, inflamed by a desire for overturning your liberty, of his own accord, driven on the excitable soldiers[177] to destroy the city."

To this I [GIOVIO] said: "I would forgive Fieramosca if the 109 gods—avengers of treachery who killed Bourbon when he treacherously sent legates to make peace with us as he was on the very threshold of victory—had spared the other impious deceivers as well. For I see that the dreadful curses the imprisoned pope called down upon the cruelest of enemies have divine sanction. He did so when, in the midst of that plague, he begged them for his safety to lead him out of the Castel Sant' Angelo and remove him from danger, but they refused. Within three days, Nájera,[178] the director of all the army's counsels, died of the plague. Then the viceroy Lannoy himself also died.[179] When making the treaty, Lannoy had sworn that he would never fail in his duty to the pontiff; but after he had come to Rome, he could not ever be induced by

pietatis vel humanitatis ratione induci potuit, ut[285] omnibus
inediae[286] miseriis et pestibus[287] circumventum pontificem inviseret, aut cibariorum[288] munusculis recrearet.[289] Sed haec in alium
sermonem reservemus; nam haec tanta iucunditas tristissimarum
rerum amaritie et felle minime[290] videtur[291] esse perfundenda. Tu
vero, Davale, ad tuos ductores redi.'

110   At ille ⟨DAVALUS⟩ 'Non agam,' inquit, 'eorum causam qui, cum
caesari gratum facere studerent, summam illi imprimis invidiam
conflaverunt, cum gravissimas iniurias diis ac hominibus intulerint
ut ipsi ditarentur;[292] nec evastare Italiam cessent, cuius firmis et
paratis opibus caesar indigeat[293] si, ut pie optat, adversus Turcas
animum intendit, ut gloriosum et longe iustissimum bellum contra
vero⟨s⟩[294] hostes geratur.[295] Igitur redibo ad me ipsum, ut vobis
obtemperem.

111   'Sunt enim[296] plerique alii fortes et splendidi equites qui, cum
aliquando turmis aut cohortibus praefuerint et foris domique cum
laude sint versati, nomen suum crescenti famae commendarunt.
Sed cum egregium ducem quaeramus, alio iam, Museti, nobis[297]
erit properandum. Non enim ab indole tantum praeclara et maxima
pollicenti, sed a probata maturaque virtute laudatur et quaeritur
imperator. Nam ut Sergius Catilina in contione militum pronunti-
avit, tanta est unius cuiusque virtus quanta in bello patere solet.
Propterea nonnullos videmus Gaspari Sanseverino, cui ab immoderata fortitudine Fracasso cognomen fuit, omnino similes evasisse, qui, cum iuvenis animi ac virium ferocia supra ceteros in acie
terribilis emineret, eius demum flos virtutis, ut nimium praecox et
redundans, ad frugem pervenire non potuit atque ita sensim pro-
clinantibus[298] annis penitus exaruit.

112   'Igitur non adibo iam civitates et ceteras Italiae regiones, sed
in castra percurram cum nostrorum tum eorum qui, ut Italiae

appeals to his piety and humanity to visit the pope, who was beset
by starvation and disease, or to revive him with little gifts of food.
But let us save these points for another conversation; we need not
soak this pleasant occasion with the bitter gall of gloomy topics.
So, d'Avalos, do return to your commanders."

Then D'AVALOS said: "I will not plead the cases of those men,   110
who, though they were eager to oblige the emperor, ignited deepest animosity toward him when, to enrich themselves, they inflicted the severest injuries on gods and men. And they keep on
devastating Italy, even though the emperor needs its substantial
and ready resources if, as he piously wishes, he is to turn his attention to prosecuting a glorious and infinitely just war against our
real enemies, the Turks. I shall return to my topic, then, to humor
you.

"There are in fact a good many other brave and noble cavalry   111
officers who, since they have at some point commanded squadrons
or cohorts with distinction both at home and abroad, have won
growing fame. But, Muscettola, since we are searching for an outstanding commander, we will need to move quickly in another direction. A commander is sought out and praised not so much for
his excellent natural talent and promise as for a tested and mature
prowess. As Sergius Catilina put it, when addressing an assembly
of soldiers, each man's prowess is just so great as it is wont to show
itself in battle.[180] We see, moreover, that some have proven to be
entirely like Gaspare Sanseverino.[181] He was called 'Fracassa' on
account of his boundless courage, and as a young man, frightful in
the ferocity of his spirit and strength, he outshone the others in
battle. But in the end, his youthful flower of excellence, as it was
too precocious and excessive, was not able to come to fruition, and
thus as the years gradually progressed, it withered away.

"So, I will not any longer visit the cities and other regions of   112
Italy. I shall pass quickly over the military camps both of our

115

libertatem defendant, iam sibi duriora servitute incommoda contraxerunt. Nam optimum quemque, hoc nobili canente classico, ad
bellum domo excitum videmus. In his autem recensendis, nullum
fere aut aetatis aut familiae aut dignitatis ordinem sequemur; nam
eos satis existimatione pares puto quos ceteris reiectis honoribus[299]
clara militiae facinora omnium iudicio coaequarint.

113   'Ex iis itaque quos noverim ducibus, vetustissimus mihi videtur
Theodorus Trivultius, quem improvisa et admirabili illa irruptione
Mediolani Piscarius noster[300] vivum[301] cepit. Is inveteratae disciplinae atque prudentiae dux semper est habitus, quoniam pluribus
quam quisquam[302] alius ex his qui supersunt in Italia, proeliis interfuit. Nam cum ab adventu Gallorum terdeciens collatis signis
sit dimicatum, se alae equitum praefectum iusta acie septiens
pugnasse referebat. Verum multis suis fortasse periculis cautior
factus: consilii tantum[303] maturitatem et bellicarum rerum notitiam ostendit, traditis ad usum praeceptis, quae promptiores disci-
puli fortiter exsequantur,[304] cum nulla in eo vis ardens, quod est
effetae vitium aetatis, et nulla prope vehementia militaris emi-
neat.'

114   Haec cum Davalus cursim explicaret, erigens sese MUSETIUS
'Patere,' inquit, 'Davale tantisper institutum sermonis tui cursum
interrumpi, et recense obsecro quibusnam in locis quibusve ducibus in Italia terdeciens iusto proelio sit decertatum. Nam neminem adhuc ducem talia ordine narrantem audivi; et profecto haec
animum mire delectant, et non modo ad usum bellicarum verum
etiam civilium rerum et ad senatoriam prudentiam haud mediocriter conferre existimantur.'

115   'Morem, ut libet, geram[305] Museti' DAVALUS respondit, 'sed ea
cursim attingam et quam brevissime, quoniam ad reliquos duces et

people and of those who, in seeking to protect the liberty of Italy, have already incurred for themselves hardships more severe than slavery. We see that when the noble call to arms is sounding, every good man is summoned from home off to war. In reviewing them, we will follow practically no order of age, family, or rank; for I think that those men are sufficiently well matched in reputation whom, after they had rejected other honors, their famous military exploits have made equal in the estimation of all.

"Of those commanders whom I know, the oldest, I believe, is 113 Teodoro Trivulzio,[182] whom our Pescara captured alive in that un-expected and surprising assault at Milan.[183] He has always been held to be a commander of practiced discipline and discernment since he has taken part in more battles than anyone in Italy who is still alive. After the coming of the French, there were thirteen pitched battles. Trivulzio used to say that he had fought in seven of them as a captain of light cavalry in the regular battle line. But perhaps the many dangers he has hazarded have made him too cautious. All he displays now is his maturity of judgment and knowledge of military affairs, handing out his precepts for the brighter among his students to carry out bravely. No intensity burns in him, a failing typical in worn-out old men, and he displays practically no energy for fighting."

While d'Avalos was offering these cursory explanations, MU- 114 SCETTOLA, raising himself straight, said: "Just for a moment, d'Avalos, please allow the discourse you have begun to be inter-rupted and review in which places or by which commanders these thirteen pitched battles were fought. For I've never yet heard any commander narrate such things; and certainly they wonderfully delight the mind and are thought to contribute substantially not only to military practice but to that of civil affairs and to the wis-dom of senators."

D'AVALOS replied, "I shall indulge you, Muscettola, but by 115 touching on these things cursorily and as briefly as possible,

mihi et Iovio festinandum videtur. Nam cum sol iam ad occasum vergat, dum sedulo probabiliores enumero, alii multo plures, qui ad primum ambiunt locum, memoria profecto excident, aut necessario praetermissi ad aliud iudicium relinquentur.'

116   Haec cum dixisset, Davalus et paullulum interquievisset: 'In Brutiis' inquit 'ad Seminariam primum Ferdinandus Iunior Aragonius cum Obegnino Gallorum duce improspere dimicavit, qua pugna, cum neque Itali pedites muniti potius armis quam iustis lanceis instructi Helvetiam phalangem, neque Hispani clipeati equites et rudes Siculi catafractorum Gallorum vim sustinuissent, Ferdinandus victus miraculo quodam ad uberiorem victoriam festinavit; nam eum[306] ex fuga Neapolim vacuis etiam milite[307] navibus provectum, cives tamquam victorem eiectis Gallis singulari studio receperunt. Quo casu manifeste apparuit ad exemplum in[308] principe amore et studio populari nihil esse validius.

117   'Paucis inde diebus, rex Carolus ad Tarrum, cum mutua caede atque ignominia nostra, quo voluit ad salutem via ferro patefacta penetravit. Quo proelio didicimus non esse temere ad pugnam procurrendum, nisi loco ante explorato et subitariis agrestium[309] aut militum operis probe purgato et complanato. Animadversum quoque est scutatum peditatum cum hastatis Germanorum ordinibus minime esse conserendum, et equites catafractos minutis divisos turmis in maiora et conglobata hostium agmina numquam immittendos. Trucidati enim sunt facile per partes turmatim a Gallis qui, conferti in unam praedensam aciem, deleri minime potuissent.

because both Giovio and I think we must hurry on to the remaining commanders. The sun is already inclined toward setting, and so, while I diligently enumerate the ones who are a bit above average, many others who vie for first place will actually slip my mind or, passed over out of necessity, will be left for another judging."

Once d'Avalos had said this and paused briefly, he began: "In the first battle, at Seminara di Reggio Calabria,[184] Ferdinand the Younger of Aragon[185] fought against the French commander d'Aubigny,[186] but with unfortunate results. In that battle, the Italian foot soldiers, furnished with defensive arms rather than with regular lances, failed to hold the Swiss phalanx in check; nor did the Spanish cavalrymen, armed with shields, along with the unskilled Sicilians, check the strength of the armored French. But by a kind of miracle, even though Ferdinand had been conquered, he hastened to a quite fruitful 'victory': for even though he had sailed from the rout to Naples in ships empty of soldiers, once the citizens had driven out the French, they welcomed him with remarkable enthusiasm as if he were the victor. From this outcome it has been made clear by example that, for a prince, nothing is more efficacious than the love and devotion of the people.

"A few days later, amid heavy casualties on both sides and to our disgrace, King Charles VIII[187] penetrated as far as the Taro River, after clearing with the sword his desired route to safety. In that battle[188] we learned that one must not dash forward rashly into the fray unless the site has been reconnoitered, thoroughly cleared, and leveled by the work of peasants conscripted ad hoc or soldiers. We realized too that infantry carrying shields must not engage with German troops armed with spears, and that armored cavalrymen split up in small squadrons must never be sent against a large block of enemy infantry. For they were easily killed in stages, squadron by squadron, by the French who, packed shoulder-to-shoulder into one extremely dense battle line, could not possibly have been destroyed.

116

117

118   'Tertia ad Ebulium in Picentinis pugna fuit, qua Persivus[310] Gallus, qui etiam ad Seminariam[311] cum Obegnino fuerat, Aragonias copias imperitia Matalonii ducis sine ullo suorum incommodo debellavit, cum equitatus noster, in plures divisus ordines, interpositos pedites suos foedissima strage edita perturbasset. Relinquenda enim sunt inter acies iusta spatia ad explicandas vires, quando nemo umquam sapiens imperator, ex equite simul ac pedite alternis[312] permixtis et digestis ordinibus, speciosa illa et multum inutili[313] diversitate aciem instruxit.

119   'Ad Petracem[314] autem fluvium non longe a Seminaria aliquot[315] post annos, ipse Obegninus ab Hispanis Ugonis Cardonii virtute superatus est, cum forte Gallicus equitatus caeco impetu vehementius in hostes illatus, peditatum suum longius in tergo reliquisset, ita ut postea neque victori equiti pedes neque mox circumvento pediti victor equitatus subsidio esse potuerint.[316]

120   'Porro post septimum ab hac pugna diem in Apulia ad Cerenniolam, Gallorum copiae a Magno Consalvo funditus sunt deletae. Quo proelio Ludovicus Namursius dux Gallorum est interfectus, et duo Columnae eximiam peritiae militaris laudem tulerunt: Fabritius ut erat strenuus et vehemens, quod tanta arte levem armaturam equestrem,[317] cui ea die praeerat, certo semper intervallo productam Gallis opposuerit, ut ab his[318] subsequentium legionum agmina conspici et obliquum earum iter explorari nequiverint; Prosper vero, quod opportuno in loco, munitis repente castris, fossam contra Gallorum impetum obiecerit; quae duae res ad summam victoriam Consalvi testimonio maxime contulerunt.

"The third battle was at Eboli, in the Picentine Mountains, 118
where the Frenchman Précy[189] (who had previously been at Seminara with d'Aubigny) defeated our Aragonese army.[190] The French
troops emerged unscathed thanks to the inexperience of the
Count of Maddaloni.[191] Our cavalry was broken up into many
separate units, and this threw our infantry into confusion. They
were caught in the middle and a horrible slaughter ensued. Thus
we see that regular spaces must be left between the ranks so as to
spread out one's strength, since no wise captain ever deployed a
battle line consisting of horsemen combined and alternating with
infantry, an outwardly impressive but utterly useless variation.

"Several years later, at the Petrace River not far from Seminara, 119
d'Aubigny was himself vanquished by the Spaniards through the
prowess of Hugo de Cardona.[192] The French cavalry had vehe-
mently attacked the enemy in a night assault; they had left the
infantry far behind, so that afterward neither the victorious cavalry
nor the soon-encircled infantry was able to be of any help to the
other.[193]

"Seven days after this battle, troops of the French were to- 120
tally annihilated in Apulia at Cerignola di Foggia by Gonsalvo
'the Great.'[194] At that battle the French commander, Louis
d'Armagnac,[195] the duke of Nemours, was killed, and two Colonnas won choice praise for their military skill. Fabrizio, energetic
and vigorous, adroitly blocked the path of the French with the
light-armed cavalry which he commanded that day. He led them
forth, always at a fixed interval, so that the French could not catch
a glimpse of the columns of legions following, nor could they re-
connoiter the legions' slanting path. As for Prospero, once our
camp had been quickly fortified, he had a trench dug in a suitable
place as a defense against a French assault. These two actions, according to Gonsalvo, contributed the most to that crucial victory.

121   'Sexta ad Lyrim de Gallis pugna, vel ut mihi potius videtur, de
semivivis inediaque confectis strages, edita est insigni Gallorum
ducum avaritia simul atque vecordia qui, dum quaestui crudelius
ac impudentius studerent et superba aemulatione inter se essent
discordes, eam sibi ultro singularem calamitatem contraxerunt.
Hinc liquido nihil damnosius esse conspicitur quam cum plures,
natura voluntateque disiuncti, pari prope imperio copiis praefi-
ciuntur.

122   'Septimum et illud maxime cruentum ad Abduam est depugnatum, cum externi reges adversus Venetos in unum omnes coniuras-
sent et Ludovicus Gallorum rex primas sibi inferendi belli de-
sumpsisset. Ea die, quae fuit Italis longe luctuosissima, manifeste[319]
periculosum esse apparuit propinquo hoste movere castra cum,
nisi ex aequissimo loco lacessitus, minime pugnare decreveris.
Nam Petilianus cunctator egregius et Livianus acerrimus bellator,
cum neuter suum propositum teneret, et Grittus legatus adversa
eorum ingenia exaequare nequivisset, mutuis impediti vitiis, nec in
munito loco consistere nec in agmine ad occursum hostis aciem
explicare potuerunt.

123   'Secundum id proelium, pugna illa ad Ravennam secuta est, inter multas funestas, admodum memorabilis, scilicet caesis utrimque omnibus fere ductoribus et flore militum maioribus tormentis crudeliter interfecto. Quam cladem pertinacia sua Navarrus
peperisse est visus, qui, depresso considens loco et vana suorum
carrorum quos venabulis in temone[320] praefixis instruxerat opinione

"The sixth battle involving the French—or rather, in my view, a   121
massacre of men who were half-alive and weakened by starvation—took place at the Garigliano River.[196] This one was caused
by the extraordinary greed and senselessness of the French commanders. They were cruelly and shamelessly zealous for gain and
were at variance among themselves with overbearing rivalry, and so
they brought that singular calamity upon themselves all on their
own. From this example, we see clearly that nothing is more damaging than when several commanders who are divided in nature
and in purpose are put in charge of troops with virtually equal
authority.[197]

"The seventh battle, an especially gory one, was fought at the   122
Adda River when all foreign kings to a man had conspired against
Venice. King Louis XII of France had arrogated supreme command to himself.[198] On that day, which was by far the most sorrowful for the Italians, it was obviously dangerous to move camp
when the enemy was close by and when you have decided not to
offer battle unless attacked on a level field. Here our leaders were
Niccolò Orsini, the count of Pitigliano, outstanding at a strategy
of delay;[199] and Bartolomeo d'Alviano, an exceedingly fierce warrior.[200] After the legate Gritti[201] had been unable to even out their
diametrically opposed temperaments, although neither of the two
was sticking to his intention, they were still hampered by their opposite shortcomings. So they could neither encamp in a well-
protected spot nor on the march arrange themselves in formation
to meet the enemy.[202]

"Following this conflict, there ensued that famous battle at   123
Ravenna.[203] Among the many bloody battles, this one was altogether remarkable: nearly all the commanders on both sides were
felled, and the flower of the soldiery was savagely killed by the
artillery. Navarro[204] was seen to have caused that disaster by his
obstinacy: encamped in a low-lying position and puffed up with
groundless pride in his wagons, which he had equipped with

inflatus, cum universis potius quam cum paucis amnem trans-
euntibus pugnare voluerat, frustra reclamante Fabritio, qui in amnis alveo haerentes et impeditos adoriendos esse praedicabat.
Utcumque praeclara certe tametsi admodum cruenta Gallis parta
erat victoria, nisi Gasto Fusius iuvenis imperator, immoderata de-
lendi hostis cupiditate inflammatus et propterea confossus, ab extremis eam penitus corrupisset.

124   'Eo etiam anno qui secutus est, Helvetiorum exigua manus ad
Novariam validum Gallorum exercitum incredibili virtute superavit, cum Trivultius atque Tramulius, maximae auctoritatis[321] et
summae etiam fortunae duces, eam agrestium multitudinem sine
ullo tormentorum apparatu vel equitum subsidio numquam tale
facinus ausuram putavissent. Ex quorum infelicitate didicimus ad
perpetuum militiae documentum, castra semper fossa atque aggere
esse munienda, illosque minime sanos esse imperatores qui vel genus vel numerum vel etiam fortunam hostium in ulla locorum aut
temporum condicione despiciant.

125   'Paucis porro ab hac insigni pugna mensibus, Livianus Veneti
dux exercitus, cum apud Vicentiam caesarianos abeuntes plenioris
spe victoriae inductus intemperantius sequeretur, cum magna Piscarii nostri gloria, puncto temporis intellexit, quid necessitas, acerrimus virtutis stimulus, valeret, et quam parum in subitariis Italorum delectibus adversus Hispanos atque Germanos veteranos
fuerit confidendum.

126   'Biennio post, Franciscus Gallorum rex Helvetias legiones
apud Mediolanum difficili periculosoque certamine per noctem et
diem continuato late cecidit. Quo proelio contemptor mortis
Helvetius immoderatae ferociae suae poenas dedit cum in vallata

hunting spears fastened in front on the yoke beam, he had wanted to fight the whole enemy force rather than the few crossing the river, though Fabrizio[205] vainly protested, who had declared that they should attack the men who were held up and hindered in the riverbed. In any event, the victory — which was certainly brilliant, albeit very bloody — would have been a splendid one for the French, had not the young captain Gaston de Foix[206] completely ruined it at the end: since he was inflamed by an inordinate desire to destroy the enemy, he ended up getting stabbed.[207]

"In the following year at Novara,[208] with remarkable prowess a   124 small company of Swiss overcame a strong army of Frenchmen, since Trivulzio[209] and Trémoille,[210] commanders of the highest reputation and also the greatest success, never could have imagined that that rabble of peasants would dare such a deed without any artillery or cavalry support. From their misfortune we have learned, as a perennial object lesson for the army, that we must always fortify a camp with a ditch and a rampart, and that the least sound captains are those who, in any place or at any time, show contempt for either the type or the number or even the good luck of their enemies.

"A few months after this extraordinary battle, at Vicenza, the   125 commander of the Venetian army, d'Alviano, induced by hope of a more complete victory, was impetuously pursuing the imperialists as they were withdrawing.[211] But then, to the great glory of our Pescara, he grasped in an instant how effective necessity is as a sharp spur to excellence, and how little one must put one's trust in emergency recruits of Italians when they are up against Spanish and German veterans.[212]

"Two years later, King Francis of France slaughtered the Swiss   126 legions at Milan[213] in a difficult and dangerous battle that was prolonged through night and day over a large area. In that battle, the Swiss, who scoffed at death, paid the penalty for their excessive ferocity when, without cavalry and without a fixed commander,

castra et perpetua tormentorum cincta custodia, sine equite et sine certo duce, irrumpere minime dubitasset.

127 'Aliam nos ipsi de eadem gente atque iisdem fere ducibus prope Mediolanum[322] ad Bicocam vicum, cum pro Gallis sub ipso Pallicia atque Lotrechio militarent, victoriam sumus consecuti, stratis atque repulsis minorum tormentorum procella eorum legionibus quae ad invadenda castra pari temeritate convolarant. Novissime autem, cum Francisco rege ad Ticinum conflximus, quo capto deletoque eius exercitu, tantos ex ea victoria spiritus desumpsimus, ut neminem iam in terris esse gentem arbitremur quae se nobis bellica virtute aut gloria conferendam putet.'

128 Haec cum dixisset, et Musetius singularem ex eius brevi et pleno tamen sermone voluptatem cepisse videretur, ego ⟨iovius⟩ inquam, 'Davale non quam diserte distincteque egeris te laudaverim, sed quam acute et sapienter de summa ingentium proeliorum iudicaveris, ut maxime admirer est necesse. Expressisti enim adeo excellenti memoria atque adeo gravi perstrictoque iudicio ducum vitia pariter atque[323] virtutes, tamquam ipsorum eventuum certissimas causas, ut si nequaquam ingenio[324] sumus[325] valde obtuso, eximia te bellicae artis documenta tradidisse fateamur. Quod vero non plures quam tredecim pugnas enumeraveris, id te consulto fecisse putamus,[326] quoniam eas minime nobiles exstitisse ducas in quibus non multa hominum milia ceciderint.

129 'Audivi tamen pugnam egregie fuisse depugnatam a Vitellocio Tiphernatae apud Surianum, fusis Alexandri Pontificis copiis et capto imperatore Guidone Baldo Feltrio, unde certam spem Itali duces ex eventu conceperint, pedestris militiae disciplinam Italis,

they had not hesitated to rush in against a camp that was fortified and was encircled by a perpetual sentry of artillery.

"At the village of Bicocca near Milan, we ourselves acquired another victory[214] over that same people and mostly the same commanders when they were fighting on behalf of the French under Lautrec[215] and de la Palice himself.[216] With equal rashness, the French legions had assembled rapidly to attack the camp, but we overwhelmed them and drove them back with a hail of small-artillery fire. Most recently, however, when we clashed with King Francis at Pavia,[217] once he had been captured and his army destroyed, we became so elated by that victory that now we reckon there is no nation on earth that thinks itself comparable to us in military excellence or glory."

When d'Avalos had said these things and Muscettola appeared to have taken special pleasure in his brief, yet comprehensive narration, I [GIOVIO] said: "D'Avalos, I have to praise you, not for how eloquently and clearly you have made your case, but instead for how keenly and wisely you have evaluated the gist of momentous battles, so that I must greatly marvel. You have described the failings and the virtues of the commanders as the definitive causes of the events themselves, with excellent memory and with such weighty yet restrained judgment that if we are not dimwitted, we ought to declare that you have taught us outstanding lessons of the art of war. We think, however, that you have deliberately recounted no more than thirteen battles because you have considered insufficiently notable those in which there have not been many thousands of deaths.

"I have heard, however, that Vitellozzo Vitelli[218] of Città di Castello fought outstandingly at the Battle of Soriano[219] once the troops of Pope Alexander had been routed and their general Guidobaldo da Montefeltro[220] captured. And from the outcome of that battle, I gather, Italian commanders have drawn a sure expectation that infantry training can be given to Italians, or even to

127

128

129

vel etiam agrestibus, tradi posse: nam e Tiphernatium agris deductos rudes paullo antea belli homines, aciem, phalange facta, more Germanorum omnibus modis circumvertere[327] docuerat, atque adeo perite tum[328] in aciem produxit ut Germani hostes numero fere pares et validus equitatus eos sustinere nequiverint, ob id maxime, quod Tiphernates lanceis cubito longioribus uterentur, et ordines miro silentio conservarent.

130 'Magna etiam sed incondita Germanorum multitudo in Carnicis Alpibus ad Cadoriam a Liviano inter sinuosos saltus est trucidata, quo congressu apparuit Germanos, inaequalitate ac asperitate loci dissipatos nec locum aut ordinem tenere valentes, non eam habere virtutis opinionem quam ipsi plano in campo in unum conglobati, et in sua praedensa phalange insuperabiles, omnibus bellis sint consecuti. Contra vero Italum militem, ut promptum ingenio corpore atque armis expeditum, extra ordinem in subitaria et varia dimicatione evadere meliorem, qui nondum in acie multis ordinibus stabilita contra Germanos pugnare didicerit.

131 'Sed prosequere,' inquam ⟨IOVIUS⟩, 'Davale, et ex tot minutis et mancis ductoribus, praegrandes et integros duces nobis excerne, eorumque mores et totius naturae effigiem sollerti tuo peracrique ingenio, ut pictor eruditus in singulis tabellis, delineato, res vero gestas eorumque facinora sat erit, si ad apicem levi et parca quidem[329] manu tetigeris.'

132 At ille ⟨DAVALUS⟩ 'Prosequar,' inquit, 'ut iubes, et valde perstricte: nam omnia fere quae de natura ac ingenio ducum rebusque eorum bello gestis sunt dicenda video a te in *Historiis* plenissime fuisse pertractata. Ab Alfonso igitur Atestino incipiam principe

peasants. Vitelli gave instruction to men from the fields of Città di Castello, who shortly before had been inexperienced at war. Once they'd made a phalanx, he taught them to turn around the battle line in all directions in the German manner.[221] Then he led it expertly into the fray in such a way that the enemy Germans, almost equal in number and strong in cavalry, were unable to hold them in check, especially because the people of Città di Castello were using pikes that were a cubit longer and were maintaining their ranks with a surprising absence of fuss.[222]

"Also, a large but disorganized multitude of German troops was   130 slaughtered by d'Alviano amid the winding woodland paths at Cadore in the Carnic Alps.[223] From this encounter, it was evident that the Germans, scattered by the unevenness and harshness of the terrain and not strong enough to maintain their position or order, did not retain that reputation of excellence which they themselves had aimed at in all wars: when massed into one in the field, their extremely dense phalanxes had been invincible. The Italian soldiery, on the other hand, had not yet learned to fight against the Germans in a battle formation steadied by many ranks. Yet since the Italians were ready in spirit and agile in body and with weapons, they turned out to be superior in guerrilla fighting and in unplanned and variable encounters.

"But go on, d'Avalos," I [GIOVIO] said, "and sift out for us, from   131 so many petty and defective captains, the exceedingly great and sound ones. Sketch out their character with your ingenious and penetrating brilliance, and what they are like overall, as a skilled painter does on individual panels. As for their accomplishments and deeds, it will be enough if you touch upon the high points of these with a light and economical hand."

He [D'AVALOS] replied: "I will continue, as you ask, but only   132 very briefly, because I see that in your *Histories* you have already treated comprehensively nearly all the things that need to be said about the nature, talent, and military accomplishments of

Ferrariensi, in quo et prudentia excellens et constantia singularis et efficax bellica virtus vigere existimantur. Nam validas et periculosas admodum belli tempestates fortissime sustinuit, cum duo pontifices, Iulius et Leo, eum a segni pacis otio ad gloriosos militiae labores excitassent. Venetam enim classem iam constituto ab hostibus in citeriore Padi ripa insigni propugnaculo, ipsis prope Ferrariae moenibus imminentem, incredibili peritia coaptatis ad aggerem maioribus tormentis ita afflixit, et cum miserabili nauticorum hominum interitu strenue cepit ut una tantum praetoria triremis effugerit.

133   'Nec multo post, ad Fossam Giliolam, Pado subitario ponte constrato, pontificias copias improviso adortus, late cecidit sic ut neque acrius neque celerius rem geri et confici potuisse hostium duces existimarint. In Ravennate autem pugna primae aciei adeo scienter et strenue praefuit ut, tormentis obliquo et maiore spatio ad latera hostium circumductis, ipse unus ad eam victoriam maxime contulisse iudicetur.

134   'Novissime vero, cum inepte vel certe parum sapienter repudiaretur ab hostibus nostris, scilicet, ut illum nobis ad ipsorum perniciem applicarent, urbes suas Regium et Mutinam[330] feliciter[331] recepit, et a caesare in imperio copiarum Borbonio est suffectus, in quo honore refutando mihi longe sapientissimus videtur, cum imperare aliis quam sibi a seditioso consternatoque exercitu imperari malit.

135   'Vultu acer est, sed ingenio cum severitate perhumanus, et in cultu domestico pergravis et moderatus, et imprimis nobilium

commanders. Let me begin, then, with Alfonso d'Este,[224] the duke of Ferrara, in whom outstanding discernment, singular steadfastness, and effective military prowess are believed to flourish. He endured very bravely the mighty and highly dangerous storms of war when two popes, Julius II and Leo X, had provoked him from the lazy tranquility of peace to undertake glorious labors on the battlefield. For when a Venetian fleet was almost menacing the very town walls of Ferrara and had established a prominent redoubt on the nearer shore of the Po River, once Alfonso had with incredible expertise positioned the larger artillery along the riverbank, he damaged and quickly captured the fleet with pitiable loss of sailors, so that only the commander's flagship escaped.[225]

"Not much later, at Fossa Giliola,[226] after throwing a makeshift bridge over the Po, Alfonso unexpectedly attacked the pope's forces. He slaughtered them across a wide field in such a way that the enemies' commanders had been of the opinion that it couldn't have been carried out more vigorously or completed more quickly. Then in the Battle of Ravenna he commanded the front line so expertly and forcefully that when he'd had the artillery wheeled around to the enemies' flanks, set at an angle and spaced more widely,[227] he was judged to have made a unique and substantial contribution to that victory.

"And most recently, when he was being scorned foolishly (or at least, unwisely) by our enemies—so that, naturally, they drove him over to our side, to their very own destruction—he successfully recaptured the cities of Reggio and Modena, and the emperor offered him command of his troops in succession to Bourbon. In rejecting that honor, it seems to me, he showed his exceptional wisdom, in that he prefers to command rather than to be himself commanded by a seditious and disorderly army.

"He is harsh in features, but in disposition very kindly with an admixture of severity, and both very serious and restrained in the care of his household, and an especially generous admirer of the

133

134

135

artium munificus aestimator. In apparatu vero tormentorum, eum adeo copiosum diligentem ac sumptuosum vidi ut nequaquam etiam admirer quod horum ingeniosissimus conflator et artifex usque ad fabrilem illuviem et contemptum dignitatis exsistat. Cui negotio architecturam etiam militarem in exstruendis munitionum molibus et constituendis propugnaculis apte atque subtiliter addidisse conspicimus. Quo fit ut putem,[332] si conti⟨n⟩gat eum[333] aliquanto[334] maioribus auspiciis quam suis extra fines ad bellum proficisci, fortem et strenuam omnino operam maturi et statarii ducis esse navaturum.

136 'Hunc dignitate consequitur Franciscus Maria Feltrius princeps Urbinas, qui nunc adversus nos bellum gerit Veneti exercitus imperator. Is varia saepe fortuna diversis bellis arma tractavit, et adversis potius inclaruit quam secundis. Cum magnos enim ab adulescentia exercitus regeret, semper severus ferox excelsus in utraque perstitit fortuna, et ab eo maxime tempore quo Alidosium scelestum Cardinalem virili manu Ravennae trucidavit.

137 'Nunc vero disciplinam in castris poena et praemio constantissime tuetur, iustitiam colit, cuncta militiae munera cautis et firma ratione exaggeratis consiliis tractat et absolvit. Et quae praecipua eius est laus, peregregie castra metatur, ducta ut arbitror disciplina[335] a Federico avo materno, qui senex bellando factus, nullam umquam ab adverso Marte iniuriam sensit. Sed nec Franciscus eloquentia ipsi avo concedit. Nemo enim in frequentibus consiliis vel de universi[336] belli summa vel de proeliorum[337] occasione rerumque omnium momento, consideratius, tutius atque sollertius umquam[338] disceptavit.[339]

noble arts. Moreover, I have seen that in the equipping of artillery, he is so lavish, exacting and extravagant that I am not at all surprised that he shows himself to be an exceedingly talented metalcaster and artist, right down to the metalsmith's dirt and disdain for status. We observe that in building up the massive structures of fortifications and in erecting ramparts, he has added military architecture to this activity and has done so suitably and with precision. And so it is the case, I think, that if he should happen to set out to war beyond his borders with a somewhat greater position of leadership than he now has, he will surely devote himself to the brave and energetic work of a mature and steady commander.

"Next to Duke Alfonso in distinction is Francesco Maria della   136
Rovere, the duke of Urbino, who as the commander of the Venetian army is now prosecuting the war against us.[228] He has wielded arms in different wars, often with varied results, and he has gained renown more for his defeats than for his successes. Since youth he has commanded great armies. He is always ruthless, fierce, and lofty, steadfast in good fortune and bad—and especially so at that time when at Ravenna, with his own manly hand, he murdered the villainous Cardinal Alidosi.[229]

"Now, however, he maintains discipline in camp by the consis-   137
tent use of punishments and rewards. He attends to justice and conducts and completes all his military duties with decisions that are cautious and enhanced by sound reasoning. He particularly excels at laying out camps. I think he learned that skill from his mother's father, Federico da Montefeltro;[230] though he grew old under arms, Federico never suffered any injury in an unsuccessful campaign. But neither is Francesco inferior to his grandfather in eloquence. In crowded councils of war, no man has ever debated more cautiously, prudently, and skillfully than he does, whether on the overall topic of war or regarding the favorable conditions for battles and the importance of all the circumstances.

138   'At Cremona proxime expugnata, eam meo iudicio laudem est
adeptus qualem nullus ante eum aetate nostra dux Italus omnino
meruerit. Nam cum ea urbs a veterano nostrorum praesidio acerrime defenderetur, incredibili labore, vi[340] aperta ac inusitato quodam oppugnationis artificio, deditionem atque victoriam ab obsti-
natis hostibus feliciter expressit. Nam quamquam asperius sit ac
admirabilius urbem manu capere, ut unus hac tempestate Piscarius noster expugnata Genua fieri posse docuit, multo tamen utilius atque praeclarius videtur ad aequitatis et continentiae laudem
civitatem eiectis hostibus conservasse.

139   'Porro quantum postea laudis[341] tulerit, cum lente cunctaretur,
et nostri in eius oculis apud Bononiam[342] agros crudeliter evastarent et ad excindendam urbem Romam properarent, non facile
iudicaverim. Nam puto eum alienas caute aestimantem vires, aut
salubri adductum consilio aut senatus imperio coercitum, spectatorem potius quam partium defensorem esse voluisse, ne una forte
adversa dimicatione, quod iam fato quodam imminet, Italiae corruenti miserabile iugum imponeret.

140   'In Federico Gonzaga principe Mantuano, mirificae virtutes primis stipendiis enituerunt, quibus iam profecto ad exoptatum decus strenui[343] atque optimi ducis pervenisset, nisi gravissimae
et multiplices causae eum proximis bellis a toto susceptae militiae officio retardassent. Cum enim urbis Mantuae dominatum
beneficiario iure ab antiquis caesaribus obtineat, pontifici et

"But recently, after Cremona had been taken by storm,[231] in my 138 view he absolutely earned a reputation which no Italian commander in our era had gained before him. When that city was being defended very keenly by an experienced garrison of our men, della Rovere, through a combination of incredible effort, open force, and an uncommon sort of cleverness in mounting an assault, successfully wrested surrender and victory from those determined enemy forces. Although it may be harder and more admirable to capture a city by force—as our Pescara alone showed could be done in our time by taking Genoa by storm—nonetheless, it appears far more profitable and more noble for one's reputation for justice and self-control to have saved a city by throwing out enemy troops.

"On the other hand, I could not readily say how much praise 139 della Rovere will receive from here on, now that he has delayed taking action both as our men were, within his field of vision, cruelly devastating the fields near Bologna and as they were hastening to destroy the city of Rome. I think that, by a cautious assessment of the enemy's strengths or led on by good counsel or coerced by a command from the Venetian senate, he wanted to be an onlooker rather than the champion of a particular faction, lest perhaps by one unsuccessful battle—a thing which, by a kind of fate, was now impending—he should place the yoke of misery upon Italy as it was collapsing.

"Then there is Federico Gonzaga, the duke of Mantua.[232] Since 140 his first military campaigns he has displayed marvelous virtues, thanks to which he would already have attained the desired distinction of being a vigorous and excellent commander had not weighty and complex considerations hindered him in the recent wars from discharging all the obligations of military service he had assumed. The problem was that, since he held the lordship of the city of Mantua as a privilege granted by earlier emperors, he felt that in this war he simply could not perform service for the pope

Florentinis, quorum erat imperator, hoc bello ne caesari noceret, operam minime praestandam esse iudicavit. Sed magnam profecto laudem Ticino urbe adversus Gallos et Venetos egregie defenso consecutus est; et praeclara semper, ubi facto opus fuit, vividae virtutis signa edidit.

141 'Ipse domi, ablegatis ad officium copiis, patriam adversus barbaricos terrores inexpugnabilem reddit, conditis novis moenibus qua paludes reced⟨a⟩nt,[344] et stupendis passim eductis propugnaculis, in quibus et artem incredibilem et ingentes sumptus admiramur. Sed nec privatae magnificentiae interim deesse videtur, nam praeter ⟨Marmir⟩olum[345] suburbanum pulcherrimis operibus adauctum, etiam ad stabula illa regiae opulentiae, quae sunt extra Sebastianam Portam, luculentissimas aedes adiunxit, eruditis picturis exornatas, itemque hortos raris arboribus nobiles, quos liquidissimae piscinae dirimentibus euripis ab attiguis aedibus disiungunt. Quae omnia pertinent ad cohonestandum insigne illud hippodromum, quod praeter vestibulum directis ad lineam viae marginibus in longitudinem duodecim stadiorum extenditur. Equorum enim studio hereditaria liberalitate delectatur, nam in militaribus semper aut certe militiae propinquis exercitationibus iuventam agit. Ceterum ingenio suavis[346] alacer munificus hospitalis, id certe unus quod nemini contigit feliciter est adeptus, ut ab externis et Turcarum denique[347] regibus ceterisque publice gentibus[348] omnibus ametur ac enixe etiam percolatur.

142 'Secundum hunc, si dignitatem nominis sequamur, Michael eminet Salutius Regulus qui, ut est Subalpinus, Gallorum partes semper[349] est secutus. Is multum bellici[350] vigoris agendo et dimicando superioribus bellis ostendit, essetque procul dubio, alacritate pugnandi, et castrensi munificentia et nobili quadam comitate, Ludovici patris nomen excessurus nisi tantam indolem nimia aleae

and the Florentines (whom he was serving as a captain) lest he do injury to the emperor. But unquestionably he covered himself with great praise for skillfully defending the city of Pavia against the French and the Venetians; and whenever action has been required, he has always shown splendid signs of spirited valor.[233]

"At home, after the troops have been dispatched to their duties, 141 Duke Federico makes his homeland impregnable against barbarian threats. Where the swamplands give way, he has had new town walls built. Far and wide, he has extended stupendous battlements, marvelous for their unbelievable technical skill and huge expense. But at the same time, he does not neglect private magnificence. For besides augmenting the suburban villa at Marmirolo[234] with beautiful annexes, he has attached the most splendid buildings to those regally opulent stables that are outside the Porta Sebastiana. These he has decorated with skillful paintings, and likewise, noble gardens with rare trees. The most limpid fishponds, divided by canals, separate the gardens from the adjacent buildings. All these things contribute to decorating that outstanding hippodrome which extends a mile and a half beyond the entrance with its length running parallel to the road. Indeed, with a liberality he has inherited, he delights in horsemanship, for he always leads the young men in military, or quasi-military, exercises. But he is pleasant in disposition, eager, generous, and hospitable. He alone has successfully attained a status enjoyed by no one else: he is not only liked but also earnestly cultivated by foreign peoples, both the Turkish kings and all others in official dealings.

"After him, if we should proceed according to dignity of name, 142 Michele Antonio del Vasto, the marquis of Saluzzo, stands out.[235] As he is Piedmontese, he has always followed the lead of the French factions. In earlier wars, he displayed much martial vigor in leading and in fighting. He would undoubtedly have surpassed the reputation of his father Ludovico in eagerness for combat, generosity toward his troops, and in a sort of noble graciousness, had he

cupiditate corrupisset. Nihil enim puto in imperatore pestilentius quam aleae studio distineri, cum in bellicis muneribus obeundis, naturam ipsam vel necessariis desideriis fraudandam diligentissime duces arbitrentur. Frangit enim hoc exitiabile studium ante omnia existimationem apud hostes, avaritiae et rapinis aditum praebet, et denique[351] liberalitatis nervos elidit, nisi modus in summa temporis atque pecuniae prorsus adhibeatur. Pacis vero tempore vel in hibernis, cum arma et classica conquiescunt, tam turpe existimo ab honesta talorum et pictarum chartularum collusione penitus abstinere quam in medio belli ardore huic damnosae voluptati perpetuas horas impendisse. Sed hoc vitium in gregario milite non minus erit detestandum quam in duce. Nam saepe ad primum vel alterum talorum iactum, menstrui stipendii pecuniae deperduntur, ita ut milites ira et desperatione praecipites disciplinam celerrime dissolvant. Quamobrem a multis gravibus ducibus Henricum Britanniae regem magnopere fuisse commendatum accepimus, qui, cum in Morinos traiecisset et Gallos equites[352] ad Tervannam[353] ingenti et, quod pulchrius fuit, incruento proelio profligasset, severa lege edixit militi fore capitale si talis vel chartulis in castris collusisset.

143   'Porro[354] Vitellium[355] Tiphernatem continuatus multis bellis labor et domestica excellens disciplina patrisque et patruorum fortissimorum ducum, quamquam funesta insignis tamen memoria, clarissimum reddunt, sed consilio tamen quam manu promptior habetur. Nam et usus bellicarum rerum et illa parum illustris ex alieno periculo facta prudentia sic eum erudiverunt ut numquam fore lacessendam infidi Martis fortunam putet. Ipse alioqui castrorum atque urbium defensor et copiarum conservator egregius,

not ruined his fine disposition by an excessive passion for gambling.[236] In fact, I think that nothing is more disastrous in a captain than to be distracted by enthusiasm for gambling, since in undertaking military service commanders reckon that nature herself must be utterly cheated of even necessary desires.[237] Unless you impose a limit on your outlay of time and money, this destructive pastime shatters your reputation among your enemies, provides an opening for greed and plunder, and in the end destroys the sinews of liberality. I think it a disgrace to abstain completely from honorable gambling of dice and playing-cards in peacetime or in winter quarters, when weapons and trumpet-calls fall silent. But I think it every bit as disgraceful to have committed uninterrupted hours to this damaging pleasure amid the heat of war. And this vice is no less abhorrent in a common soldier than in a commander: often, on the first or second toss of the dice, a month's salary is completely lost, and so the soldiers, rash in their anger and desperation, very quickly lose discipline. We've heard that many of the most important commanders speak highly of King Henry VIII of England on account of the fact that, once he had crossed over into Picardy and had crushed the French cavalry at Thérouanne in a battle that was massive and, what is nobler, bloodless,[238] he decreed the harsh law that it would be a capital offense if any soldier in the camp gambled with dice or cards.

"We come next to Vitello Vitelli[239] of Città di Castello. Uninterrupted work in many wars and excellent training at home from his father and uncles, who were very courageous commanders (their history, although sorrowful, is nonetheless distinguished), have made him very famous; but all the same, he is held to be readier to make a plan than to take action. His military experience, along with that ignoble caution which is based on the dangers others have encountered, has trained him to think that the hazards of war, treacherous as it is, ought never to be chanced. In other respects, he is outstanding as a defender of camps and cities 143

semper id maxime contendit, ne[356] proelio vinceretur. Sic studio
⟨et⟩ vigilantia[357] nulli militiae muneri umquam deest, ut in consu-
lendo atque agendo nullum paenitentiae locum relinquat, quamquam illud meo iudicio maxime sit paenitendum, cum exploratam
e manibus victoriam timida cunctatione prorsus emiseris. Constat
enim multorum opinione eum, cum eodem collega Rentio Cerite,
Hispanos in Umbria, isto duce Feltrio[358] Urbinate, in vadis Me-
tauri Amnis haerentes, et nuper Frusinone obsidione liberata, per-
turbatum et terga dantem Lanoii exercitum omnino delere nesci-
visse.'[359]

144   Haec cum dixisset, 'Cur,' inquit MUSETIUS,[360] 'Franciscum
Sfortiam, quem nuper Mediolano[361] detraxistis, inter alios Italiae
regulos adiecta peculiari laude minime numerasti? Cuperem enim
abs te, Davale, aliqua de natura eius ac moribus audire; nam de eo
homine varia omnino feruntur iudicia, et certe is est pro cuius dignitate atque salute hoc gravissimum bellum vehementi conspiratione principum adversus[362] nos repente excitatum esse conspicimus.'

145   Tum DAVALUS 'Nequaquam,' inquit, 'Museti, eum putato oblivione fuisse praetermissum, cum de bellicosis agerem ducibus;
nam[363] militaris ille vigor qui in avo mirabiliter enituit in eo nequaquam elucet. Est enim Ludovico patri similior, qui sapientia
tam diu ceteros principes antecessit quam diu consilia eius, quaecumque ea fuerint, infensa et volubilis Fortuna minime fefellit, ita
ut hic Franciscus iisdem prope miseriis quibus pater oppressus
interiit, implicatus esse videatur, nisi Galli et Veneti qui exitio patri fuerunt, ei salutem afferant principatumque recuperent, aut
caesar ipse, quod magis est credendum, admirabili naturae suae

and protector of troops: his prime aim has always been to be undefeated in battle. Thus in respect of zeal and vigilance he falls
short in no military duty, so that he leaves no place for regret in
his planning and his actions—although, in my view, it is most re-
grettable to let certain victory slip from one's hand by timid delay.
For it is the fixed opinion of many that, along with his colleague
Renzo da Ceri, he failed to destroy the Spaniards when they, under that Feltrian Duke of Urbino, were stuck in the shallows of
the Metro River in Umbria;[240] and recently, after Frosinone had
been liberated from siege,[241] they were unable to finish off Lannoy's army, though it was fleeing in disorder."

Once he [d'Avalos] had said this, MUSCETTOLA asked: "Why   144
have you failed to include Francesco Sforza,[242] whom you not long
ago took away from Milan, among the other princes of Italy
singled out for special praise? I would like to hear from you,
d'Avalos, something about his nature and character, for quite di-
vergent views about him are in circulation. And certainly we see
that it is for the sake of his standing and safety that this very serious war has been suddenly stirred up against us by a mighty conspiracy of princes."

Then D'AVALOS said: "Do not fancy, Muscettola, that when I   145
was discussing warlike commanders I passed over him out of forgetfulness; for in him that military vigor, which shone marvelously
in his grandfather,[243] fails to shine forth at all. He is more like his
father Ludovico, who surpassed other princes in wisdom so long
as his policies, whatever they were, were not thwarted by a hostile and changeable Fortune. As a result, this Francesco appears to be involved in almost the same troubles as the ones by
which his father was overwhelmed and met his end—unless the
French and Venetians, who were the cause of his father's ruin,
bring him safety and win back sovereignty for him; or unless
(which is more likely) the emperor himself, by the admirable

clementia et lenitate id totum ingrati vel consternati animi crimen[364] Italiae precibus indulserit.

146 'Agnosco enim caesaris spiritus qui semper alta et speciosa re-
spicient, nisi eos ad verum decus inflammatos aliena malignitas
obtuderit.[365] Ego certe hominem, qualiscumque adversus eum sit
caesaris animus, tanta calamitate indignum puto. Nam certe gravissimas causas habuit a caesaris praefectis desciscendi, et est ingenio[366] moderatus aequus religiosus; valet litteris et multarum
rerum notitia et, super haec, explicata lenique facundia, ac ea praesertim rerum suarum difficultatibus accommodata. Nulla in eo
crudelitas, nullae dirae libidines, nullus gravior fastus, nulla verborum acerbitas vel ab inimicis eius notantur. Liberalem certe plerique eum esse desiderant, cum tamen in tanta rerum difficultate[367]
semper cum ratione munificus exstiterit. Aliqui etiam inepte quidem eum, tot saevissimis obnoxium morbis, et maxime strenuum
et acerrimum bellatorem vellent, quasi virium felicitas non a naturae benignitate et munere deorum immortalium, sed ab uno tantum animi voto deducatur. Fortem certe eum et valde constantem[368] tolerata septem menses[369] obsidio nuper ostendit, cum foeda
animalia pro opiparis ferculis illi fuerint. Neque prius deditionem
fecerit quam eum, atroci morbo etiam conflictatum, alimenta
cuncta penitus[370] defecerint.

147 'Ceterum res adversae praeclarae etiam virtutis opinionem celeriter elevant, amicorum benevolentiam tollunt, contemptum parant, et paullatim multitudinis[371] studia restinguunt. Illud quoque
de eo minime tacuerim: me nequaquam paenitere, quod eum dedita[372] arce excedentem in eo lugubri et summo salutis[373] metu,[374]
ab omni iniuria fuerim tutatus, cum Borbonius, qui ad eius imperium vehementer anhelabat, eum tollere cuperet; et tacite

clemency and leniency of his nature, accedes to the prayers of Italy and forgives that entire crime of an ungrateful and timorous spirit.

"I recognize the emperor's disposition, which will always be   146 oriented toward the noble and the beautiful unless, in its passion for true glory, it is assaulted by another's malice. Whatever the emperor's attitude is toward him, I for one think Sforza unworthy of so great a calamity. Surely he had very substantial reasons for defecting from the emperor's prefects, and he is balanced, fair-minded, and reverent in character; he excels in literature and in the knowledge of many subjects and, beyond these things, in clear and smooth eloquence — especially in that eloquence which is suited to his adverse circumstances. Not even his enemies observe in him any cruelty, dreadful lusts, excessive pride, or harsh language. Many find him, to be sure, tightfisted, though in great adversity he has always proven generous when he had good reason. Indeed, some foolishly would also wish that he, who has been exposed to so many raging diseases, should also prove a vigorous and ferocious warrior, as though a fortunate endowment of strength derives, not from the bounty of nature and the favor of the immortal gods, but from the mind's will alone. Surely by withstanding a siege of seven months on a diet of vile animals in place of sumptuous dishes he was recently proven to be brave and steadfast. Nor, even while afflicted with a frightful disease, did he surrender until all provisions completely ran out.

"But adverse circumstances quickly lessen a reputation for even   147 noble virtue, put an end to the goodwill of friends, elicit contempt, and little by little extinguish the devotion of the many. I would not suppress this matter concerning him: I do not at all regret that, upon surrender of the fortress, as he was withdrawing from the place, amid that doleful and intense fear for his safety, I preserved him from every injury when Bourbon, who was striving mightily for his position of command, was eager to kill him. Silently

minabundus eam liberandi metu animi occasionem opperiretur,[375] et Hispani Germanique milites[376] ei pluribus[377] de causis essent infensi. Sed ea fuit militum omnium modestia ac reverentia ut, cum[378] lateri meo haereret[379] et per medias cohortes transiremus,[380] ei etiam tamquam incolumi principatus fortuna nudatis benigne capitibus assurgerent. Quo beneficio accepto, propter singularem ac eximiam fidem in custodienda ipsius salute meam fidem,[381] et tum et postea non destitit me vitae[382] suae conservatorem appellare.

148 'Ceterum, ut ad militares viros redeamus, Vitellio, quem dixi, comes fuit a primis militiae rudimentis Guido Rangonus; tantulae staturae dux, ceterum providus acutus memor plenus rationis atque consilii. Hunc ante alios, cum oppugnaremur, meliora contra nos excogitasse cognovimus decora et aspera factu facinora meditantem et ultro se fortiter propositis[383] offerentem periculis, adeo ut plerique existiment hoc bellum quod gessimus longe alios eventus fuisse habiturum, nisi alii duces consideratum expediti hominis impetum segnioribus consiliis hebetassent. Sed ita saepe[384] accidit ut virtus frustra adsit, ubi ei[385] locus opportune minime sit patefactus. Nam saepe publicam sentimus infamiam cum, etiam inviti et reluctantes, imperitorum male auspicata[386] consilia subsequimur. Et iniqua certe lege, ex adverso, gloriari vel ignavissimis licet, cum manu consilioque optimi victoriam sibi pariter ac illis communem[387] omnino pepererint.

149 'At plerique hodie sunt qui non modo parem verum superiorem Vitellio et Rangono iudicent Federicum alterum Gonzagam, cognomento Bozolum, qui in Gallorum militat castris.[388] Eum certe[389] laboriosum industrium et pugnacem existimamus. In providendis

menacing, Bourbon was awaiting the chance to set his mind at rest; and the Spanish and German soldiers were hostile to Sforza for many reasons. But there was such restraint and respect among all the soldiers that, as we passed through the midst of the troops, him clinging to my side, they even rose out of respect for him, with heads courteously uncovered, as if the good fortune of his rule were intact.[244] After having received this favor through my particular and special good faith in guarding his safety, both then and since, he has not stopped referring to me as the one who saved his life.

"But let us return to our men of arms. From his earliest military training, Guido Rangoni[245] was a companion of Vitelli, whom I have mentioned. As commanders go, Rangoni is very short, but leaving that aside, he is prudent, shrewd, has a good memory, and is full of good sense and wise counsel. When we were under attack, we got to know that he, before the others, had thought out a better course of action against us: he planned to undertake noble and difficult deeds and bravely volunteered for the dangerous mission that he had proposed. Hence, a good many think that the battle we were fighting would have had far different results had not other commanders, by their sluggish strategies, blunted this ready man's well-considered plan of attack. But it often happens that, when excellence has no scope for action at the appropriate time, it stands by in vain. We often experience public disgrace when we follow, albeit unwilling and resisting, the ill-omened policies of the inexperienced. On the other hand, by an unfair rule, even utter cowards have license to boast when the best men, by their fighting and strategy, have wholly produced a victory shared by those men and themselves.

"But there are many today who think that the other Federico Gonzaga—the ruler of Bozzolo, who is serving in the camp of the French—not only equals but surpasses Vitelli and Rangoni.[246] We think he is at any rate energetic, industrious, and eager to fight. In

enim et conficiendis rebus, robusta[390] eius ingenio et corpori vis
inest, ita ut in dicendis sententiis nihil umquam[391] bello factu difficile fortibus viris arbitretur. Venit enim proxime in conspectum
Romanae arcis, ut pontificem de libertate et fuga cogitantem[392]
pietate commotus exciperet,[393] atque inde, deceptis vel repulsis
Hispanorum excubitoribus, in proxima castra deduceret. Sed Fata
et tam pio ipsius officio et felicitati pontificis inviderunt; nam dum
in propinquo loco facinori patrando[394] sese accingit, labente equo
atque eo desuper[395] revoluto, ita afflictus est ut milites eum pro
exanimi in castra retulerint. In eo praeterea est singularis militiae
nostratis et externae cognitio, in regendis maxime pedestribus copiis, adeo ut eum in difficillimis belli negotiis, vel hac ratione,
prorsus accommodatum putem: quoniam inspectis alienis vitiis
atque virtutibus ac his in unum egregie permixtis, extrema salubriter temperasse videatur.

150 'Huic succedit Malatesta Baleonus Pauli filius,[396] ex Liviani disciplina inter aequales suos longe promptissimus, quem nulla umquam pericula nullique labores umquam deterruerunt quominus,
quod hercle difficile videtur, acrem simul et providum se gereret in
omni parte militiae. Nam pari semper eximiae virtutis opinione, et
levi armaturae equestri et catafractorum turmis praefuit, et cohortes rexit, et in negotio atque apparatu ⟨to⟩rmentorum scientissime
versatus est. Sed eum ab his muneribus vehementissime retardat
morbus prope tabificus ex Gallica lue conceptus, tam forti homine
certe indignus, sic ut monitos velim insignes viros his documentis,
ne corporis speciem ac robur, quod est donum naturae pulcherrimum, dum intemperanter ubique venerem exsolvunt, libidini cor-
rumpenda vastandaque proiciant. Supersunt etiam complures stre-

devising and carrying out operations, he has such mental and physical vigor that when he speaks his mind, he takes the view that nothing in war is ever difficult for brave men to do. In fact, just recently he came into sight of the Castel Sant' Angelo in order that, out of piety, he might rescue the pope, who was contemplating an escape to freedom. His plan was that, once the Spanish sentries had been tricked or fended off, he would lead the pontiff to a nearby encampment. But the Fates grudged both this man's pious service and the pope's good fortune: while Federico was nearby, arming himself to perform the deed, his horse fell and rolled on top of him, injuring him so badly that the soldiers brought him back to camp as good as dead.[247] He has a singular understanding of military affairs, domestic and foreign, especially in commanding infantry. I think that he is exceedingly well suited to the most difficult military operations, perhaps because once he has investigated the weaknesses and strengths of others and excellently blended the latter into one, he appears to have achieved a healthy balance of extremes.

"After him comes Malatesta Baglioni,[248] Gian Paolo's son. He is 150 by far the most enterprising among his contemporaries who were trained by d'Alviano. No dangers or hardships have ever deterred him from showing himself at once keen and cautious in every military role—a thing which, by God, is not easy. He has always, with equal distinction, presided over light-armed cavalry and squadrons of mail-clad men, commanded cohorts, and engaged expertly in the operations and equipping of artillery. But a wasting disease, which he contracted from the French pestilence[249]—a thing surely unworthy of so brave a man!—powerfully inhibits him from these military duties. I want such examples to serve as a warning to outstanding men lest by intemperately satisfying their sexual appetite everywhere, they throw away their good looks and strength, the most beautiful gift of nature, letting them be ruined and laid waste by lust. A fair number of vigorous young noblemen

nui nobilesque iuvenes, et nonnulli qui fortibus factis et nomen et claritatem meruerunt, quos, si nominare velimus, minime in hanc classem referemus.'

151   Tum MUSETIUS, cognoscendi admodum cupidus: 'Perge obsecro, Davale, et praestantiores saltem enumera, qui imperatoriam indolem prae se ferre videantur. Nam postquam isti quos modo nominasti a conficiendis bellis conserendisque manibus plurimum abhorreant, necesse est ut minorum ducum labore atque audacia bellum geratur; et certe eos esse intellego qui levis armaturae equitatu maxime delectantur, et in eam operam, ubi frequentius virtus enitescit, omne suum studium reponunt.'

152   'Ita est profecto,' ait DAVALUS. 'Nam ii qui agendo saepeque pugnando vires atque animos ostentare et famam ex periculis adipisci percupiunt, cum expeditis alis equitum exercentur. Nam qui catafractis praeest equitibus numquam fere, nisi totis concurratur copiis, in acie conspicitur, quod, dum sero quis exspectare perseverat, plerumque fit ut toto integro bello intra castra segnis et inglorius consenescat. Quis enim, ut hoc ad exemplum minime subticeam, Mercurii Epirotae sortem non miseratur atque deridet, qui nunc in ipsa catafractorum equitum praefectura imbellis et inglorius iacet, cum antea levis armaturae ductor insignis atque terribilis per triginta annos cum illustri gloria militarit. Porro, qui praefecturas cohortium ambitiosius quaerunt, ii saepius quaestum quam decus respicere iudicantur, cum falsum militum numerum quaestoribus referant et, turpi perniciosoque flagitio ad fallendum, alii ab aliis vicissim centurionibus integros militum manipulos mutuentur. Plerique vero, ut inane ducis nomen praesumant, cohortes[397] exsecrabili disciplina imbutas[398] sine stipendiis ducunt, et

live on, and some who have won a good reputation for their brave deeds; but if we should list them, we will definitely not assign them to the top class."

Then MUSCETTOLA, keen to find out who these are, said: 151 "Please go on, d'Avalos, and name at least the more outstanding ones who appear to display the natural endowment of a commander. For since those men whom you have just named are averse to directing wars and engaging in the fighting, war must be waged by the exertion and daring of lesser commanders; and certainly I understand that there are those who delight immensely in the light-armed cavalry and devote all their energy to that occupation, where excellence frequently shines forth."

"It is surely so," said D'AVALOS. "Those who are eager to show 152 strength and courage by taking action and fighting frequently, and to win fame from braving dangers, serve in the light cavalry. For he who commands heavily armed horsemen is almost never seen in battle unless the whole army is engaged. When someone waits too long, quite often he ends up in camp through the entire war, wasting away sluggish and inglorious. And lest I pass over this example in silence, who indeed does not pity and ridicule the lot of Mercurio Bua[250] from the Peloponnese? Now he is laid low, unfit for war and without glory, in that very office of captain of heavy-armed cavalry, although previously he had served for thirty years with lustrous renown as a distinguished and terrifying commander of light-armed horse.[251] But those who ambitiously seek command of cohorts are judged to have their eyes more often on profit than on honor, since they report a false number of soldiers to the paymaster and, so as to deceive by a foul and baneful crime, the centurions take turns borrowing entire companies of soldiers from each other. On the other hand, in order to assume the empty title of 'commander,' many lead without pay cohorts that have been steeped in detestable military discipline; and, with the bitterness of an enemy, they plunder the fields and homes of their allies.

sociorum agros et domos hostili acerbitate depraedantur. Quorum
ingenio nihil immanius et truculentius reperitur.

153   'Ceterum ex his qui equestri maxime gloriae student, Robertum
Sanseverinum Calatinum regulum, qui referre avum Robertum
videtur cum robore virium tum magnitudine animi, et totius
equestris disciplinae peritia ceteris omnibus praestare existimate.
Secundum eum Caesar Fregosius, eius Iani filius qui Genuae tenuit principatum, prospera fama militiam exercet; est enim valido
ingenio et robusto corpore iuvenis. Petrus quoque Maria Russius
alacer et pugnae avidus adulescens et contemptor omnis periculi
exsistit. In Alexandro Vitellio Pauli filio paterna vis et fortitudo[399]
et, supra haec, animus ad ampliorem laudem paratus conspiciuntur.[400]

154   'In[401] Gonzaga familia, quae multis fortibus viris floret, insigni
bellicae virtutis laude ceteros antecellunt duo Aloisii: quorum alter
Federicum Bozolum patruum admirabili robore lacertorum et specie corporis excelsa[402] et vehementia militari saepe dubiis in proeliis[403] spectata, et quod in milite rarissimum est,[404] amoenissimarum[405] etiam litterarum elegantia et studio carminum[406] plurimum
excedit; alter quoque bello[407] vehementer exercitatus ingenio acri
erudito[408] constanti Rodulfum patrem, qui Tarrensi in pugna egregie cecidit, alacriter aemulatur.

155   'Sed Ferdinandum Federici principis fratrem, a praeclara indole
quam a Borbonio[409] gravis armaturae equitibus praefectus nuper[410]
ostendit, magnum et intrepidum ducem evasurum existimo. Elucet enim in eo liberalitas alacri ratione dispensata, quae est praecipua ad gloriam tendentis animi laus; et in hoc miserabili urbis

There is nothing more monstrous and savage than the character of such men.

"But you really must judge, of those who are the most eager for fame in cavalry, that Roberto Sanseverino, the ruler of Caiazzo,[252] stands out above the others. He appears to recall his grandfather Roberto[253] both in robust strength and in greatness of spirit, and he surpasses all others by his expertise in the training of cavalry. After him, Cesare Fregoso,[254] son of that Giano who ruled Genoa, has a favorable reputation for running a military campaign. A young man, he has both a powerful mind and a strong body. Pietro Maria de' Rossi[255] is also emerging as a youth who is lively, eager for a fight, and a despiser of every danger. And Alessandro di Paolo Vitelli[256] displays his father's strength and courage and in addition a spirit ready to win greater commendation. 153

"In the Gonzaga family, which is adorned by many brave men, two named Luigi exceed the rest in conspicuous praise for military excellence. The first of these[257] surpasses his uncle, Federico Gonzaga, prince of Bozzolo, in his remarkable muscles, his height, and in the military intensity that is often put to the test in battles where the outcome hangs in the balance. In addition — something really rare in a soldier — he also excels to the greatest extent in the most delightful literary elegance and in his enthusiasm for poetry. The other Luigi,[258] likewise immensely proficient in war, is endowed with a shrewd, well-instructed, and trustworthy character. He eagerly emulates his father, Rodolfo, who died with distinction in the Battle of Fornovo.[259] 154

"But then there is Ferrante, the brother of Prince Federico.[260] In my view, thanks to his outstanding natural ability, which he displayed recently after Bourbon put him in charge of the heavy cavalry, Ferrante will turn out to be a great and intrepid commander. There shines forth in him a generosity, dispensed with quick reckoning, which is the chief excellence of a mind inclined toward glory; and in this miserable destruction of Rome, he seems to me 155

excidio, mihi maxime pius et abstinentissimus videtur, et in miseros afflictosque[411] Romanos magnopere liberalis. In ingenio item Alexandri cognomento Novellarii, qui sub caesarianis militat signis, supra Martium vigorem eximia Palladis ornamenta saepius admiramur. Nec ullis gentilibus suis virtutis indole Caninius cedit prioris Aloisii frater. Ab ipso Federico Bozolo patruo militiae continenter educatus, in cuius exactissima iuvenilis corporis proceritate et venusti oris decora specie, ad colligendam ab omnibus gratiam quidam vigor militaris dignitatis efflorescit.[412]

156 'Sunt etiam a Perusia Baleoni Braccius et Sfortia viri fortes, et ante hos Horatius Malatestae frater, qui superioribus mensibus totam Campaniae oram urbemque Neapolim occupato Salerno atque eo fortiter defenso admota classe territavit. Sed est, ut ferunt, valde impius et sanguinarius; nam eius iussu patruum Gentilem nuper cum tribus consanguineis in cubiculo trucidatum fuisse audivimus. Bene etiam atque[413] fortissime domi et foris se gesserunt honesti equites Romani Hieronymus Mattheus et Simo[414] Tebaldius. Militant non obscura cum laude Guido Vainus e Flaminia, e Latio Philetinus Caesar, e Neapoli Io⟨annes⟩ Baptista Castallius noster et, qui supra hos confessione omnium eminet, Paulus Luzascus Mantuani equitum praefectus; eo enim nemo peritius, nemo acrius, nemo felicius id munus implevit.

157 'In toto siquidem equestri negotio hac tempestate vis omnis ad levem armaturam, commutata rei bellicae ratione, redacta est, cuius rei scientia, cum multa exercitatione tum mirifica Graecanicae disciplinae, cognitione continetur. Graeci enim et Epirotae equorum agilitate et levitate armorum et incredibili nocturni

to be especially pious and restrained and very generous toward the miserable, ruined Romans. Similarly, in the character of Alessandro Gonzaga, called 'Novellara,'[261] who fights under the imperialist banner, we admire the choice gifts of Athena more often than the vigor of Mars. Nor is "Cagnino" Gonzaga,[262] brother of the first Luigi,[263] inferior to anyone in his family in natural capacity for virtue. He was trained continuously by his uncle, Federico di Bozzolo himself. In the fully mature height of his young body and the noble appearance of his charming face, there blossoms forth a certain vigor of martial excellence that gains all men's favor.

"Braccio and Sforza Baglioni[264] from Perugia are also brave   156
men, and Malatesta's brother, Orazio,[265] is even more so. In recent months, once Orazio had occupied Salerno and fortified it solidly, having brought his fleet nearby, he struck fear into the entire coast of Campania and the city of Naples. But he is, as they say, exceedingly unscrupulous and bloodthirsty: we have heard that he recently ordered that his uncle, Gentile, along with three relatives, be killed in his bedroom.[266] The honorable Roman knights Girolamo Mattei[267] and Simone Tebaldi[268] have conducted themselves well and very bravely at home and abroad. Others who serve in the military with conspicuous praiseworthiness include Guido Vaina[269] from Pentapoli, Cesare Filettino[270] from Latium, our own Giambattista Castaldo[271] from Naples, and Paolo Luzzasco,[272] commander of the cavalry at Mantua, whom everyone acknowledges to stand out above these men. In fact, no man has discharged his duty more expertly, keenly, or successfully than he.

"By a change in the method of warfare, cavalry operations have   157
been entirely altered, and in our time cavalry forces have been dominated by light-armed horse.[273] Skill in this consists both in abundant practice and in an awe-inspiring understanding of Greek training. For the Greeks and the Epirots, who were soundly defeating the cavalry of other peoples by mobility of horses and

diurnique laboris patientia aliarum gentium equites egregie supe-
rantes, huius artis praecepta Italis amplificanda et temperanda
tradiderunt. Quibus per continuas excursiones, vel iniquissimis
anni temporibus bellando, insidias tendere, expedire commeatus,
ludificari gravem armaturam ac eam circumvenire didicimus. In
hoc autem munere obeundo, sollertia potius divinoque iudicio
quam vera vi ipsoque impetu opus est. Naturam camporum et
fluminum primo aspectu deprehendisse singularis est laus, itemque conspectorum e longinquo hostium consilia, animos,[415] equorum genus, ex alacritate tristitiaque agminis ac[416] incedentium fes-
tinatione, respectu concursatione petulantia ipsisque etiam
hastarum motibus[417] praesensisse magnas attulit utilitates. Quibus
haud obscuris rerum significationibus, a perito duce pernotatis,
insignes plerumque victoriae de hostibus parantur, adeo ut iam
catafracti propter equorum magnitudinem et tarditatem ac armorum barbarorumque pondera contemni ludibrioque haberi coeperint, ab Italis praesertim, qui in hoc genere equestris militiae instructius atque peritius exercentur.

158   'A Graecis enim, ut dixi, laboriosam disciplinam, a Turcis vali-
dos et pernices equos clavasque ferreas, a Gallis ferrata ephippia, a
Germanis habilem singulis artubus[418] armaturam accepimus; quibus rebus accurate ac industrie modum perfectae rationis addidi-
mus, ita ut ipsi Graeci, a nostris thoraces et galeas et crassiores
lanceas salubri consilio mutuantes, suas demum Graeculas hastas
et peltas pileosque dimiserint.

159   'Ex iis vero qui graviore militiae studio catafractorum alas
ductant, et in consiliis sententias dicunt, et castella oppugnare

lightness of arms and through incredible endurance of hardship by night and by day, bequeathed to the Italians the precepts of this art, which needed to be elaborated upon and modified. From these precepts, through continued expeditions and from fighting in even the most inclement times of the year, we have learned to set ambushes, to supply provisions, and to make sport of heavy-armed troops and surround them. Moreover, in engaging in this task, cleverness and excellent judgment are more essential than actual strength and force itself. It is especially praiseworthy to be able to grasp on first view the nature of fields and rivers. Likewise, you get major benefits by gleaning at a distance early knowledge of the strategies, attitude, and type of cavalry of an enemy seen from afar — from the eager or gloomy demeanor of his army, from the haste, backward glances, jostling, and rowdiness of those on the march, and even from the motion of their lances. By these clear indicators, well known to a skilled commander, distinguished victories over the enemy are often achieved. And as a result, because of the great size and slowness of their horses and the weight of the barbarians' armaments, the mailed cavalry have by now begun to be despised and mocked — especially by Italians, who have been better trained and have better experience in this kind of equestrian warfare.

"So from the Greeks, as I have said, we have received rigorous 158 training; from the Turks, powerful and swift horses and iron clubs;[274] from the French, armored saddles; and from the Germans, armor tailored to fit particular men's limbs.[275] To these things we have meticulously and laboriously added a type of perfected system, with the result that the Greeks themselves, fruitfully borrowing from us our breastplates and helmets and thicker lances, have at last let go of their puny Greek spears and their light shields and javelins.

"As to those men who command squadrons of mailed infantry 159 with serious enthusiasm for war and express their ideas in coun-

tuerique,[419] et ad motus hostium ascitis sibi maioribus copiis difficiles et frumentarias expeditiones suscipere solent, et denique ad
imperatoris nomen et laudem feliciter aspirant[420] non tam magnus
hodie est numerus, quam nuper fuit. Proelia namque multos[421]
absumpserunt, multos efferati Martis pericula deterruere,[422] nonnulli etiam ad securum otium honestis de causis transiverunt,
siquidem incredibile est dictu quam multi nostra tempestate praeclaram bellicae virtutis indolem contumaci superbia vanitateque
perdiderint. Fit enim plerumque, ut nobiliores minime decorum[423]
arbitrentur si humili loco natis, quamquam ab insigni virtute dignissimis, omnino pareant; et contra,[424] viri fortes militiaeque
assueti saepius indignentur, cum imperitis ac ignavis ab una tantum familiarum claritate illustribus praefecturas militares ac[425] imperia demandari conspiciant, ita ut totum militiae deserant studium.

160   'Nemo est enim adeo iners miles aut feroculus tiro, cum semel
gladium cruore pertinxerit et luculenter, ut impius, diis et deabus
nominatim maledixerit,[426] qui⟨n⟩[427] sibi alium superiorem ferat
ab[428] primis statim stipendiis;[429] aut vexillum ferre aut turmis et
cohortibus[430] praeesse volunt. Quibus vitiis laborantes Italos saepe
animadvertimus ceteris gentibus in acie pares esse nequivisse,
quando ingenui, et qui dedecoris metu nihil nomine indignum
admittere solent, cum pedibus merere deberent, alas demum et[431]
legiones supplendas, opificibus servis atque lenonibus relinquant.
Neque ullum video finem tam exitiabili corruptelae, nisi aliquis

cils, who are accustomed to besiege and defend fortresses and, once they have commandeered more troops for themselves, to undertake difficult expeditions against enemies' maneuvers and to make runs for provisions, and who in the end aspire successfully to the name and reputation of 'captain': their number is not so great today as it was not so long ago. For in fact, battles have carried off many; the dangers of savage Mars have deterred many others; some too have for honorable reasons made the transition to carefree retirement — even if it is remarkable how many in our era, through their insubordinate haughtiness and vanity, have squandered an outstanding natural capacity for military prowess. It frequently happens that those who have some degree of nobility think it quite disgraceful if they have to obey men of humble birth, even though those men are exceedingly worthy on account of their extraordinary prowess. And conversely, men who are brave and accustomed to wars often take offense when they observe that military prefectures and positions of command are being entrusted to inexperienced and lazy men who are famous only on account of the distinction of their relatives; and so these brave men abandon the pursuit of a military career.

"No man, whether he be a soldier or a braggart novice, is so   160
unskillful that, once he has drenched his sword in blood and has flamboyantly cursed the gods and goddesses by name like a pagan, he fails to acquire for himself a higher commission immediately after the first one. These men want either to carry the flag or to command squadrons and cohorts. Often we observe that the Italians, struggling with these failings, have been unable to equal other peoples in battle, since 'gentlemen' — I mean those who, out of fear of a disgraceful defeat, are in the habit of doing nothing unworthy of their good name — although they ought to be serving in the infantry, abandon to artisans, slaves, and pimps the squadrons and legions that need to be brought up to full strength. And I see no end to such deadly corruption unless someone surpass-

summi animi ac[432] ingentis opulentiae, divinus heros, caelo demittatur, quem nos omnes tamquam magistrum optimum et senescentis militiae reductorem concordibus animis consequamur.'[433]

161   Tum vero ego [IOVIUS] inquam 'Haec[434] vera sunt, Davale, sed aliqui etiam non desunt qui, cum[435] ab adulescentia cum laude militiae, saepius animi vigorem ostenderint gravi demum consilio; damnata huius temporis disciplina, et pessima hac bellorum causa, domi in otio conquiescunt, ut est Sinibaldus Fliscus Ligur opulentissimus. Hic interrogatus cur a Marte ad Palladem defecisset: "Quid mihi" inquit "gloria opus est militiae parta, si ea cum ignominia et dira clade Italiae externis regibus militando quaerenda est? Quid item mihi divitiis opus est, si per excidia miserarum urbium et vastationes agrorum alienae opes mihi sint rapiendae? Sed nec pro Italia, Fatorum iniquitate corruenti, pessima condicione pugnaverim, quando praestet in otio nefarii belli agere spectatorem quam turpissime vinci."'

162   Ad id DAVALUS 'Trahitur' inquit 'quisque iudicio suo potius quam alieno; nos enim sic militamus, ut post victoriam, constitutis[436] minoribus imperiis, Italiam secura pace florentem videamus. Quid enim nisi felix et faustum exspectare poterimus, si cuncta uni Carolo caesari, ut Romano quondam Augusto, devicta[437] pacataque paruerint? Audimus enim eum[438] religioso temperatoque esse animo et ad iustitiam, aequitatem atque[439] concordiam maxime proclinato ita ut[440] Summum Pontificem brevi carcere emissum ipsius iussu me visurum sperem. Quod si ab Hispania ipse tandem in Italiam venerit, non diffido quin salutarem opem afflictis et perditis[441] rebus sit allaturus.

ingly high-minded and immensely wealthy—a divine hero—should be dropped from heaven for us all to follow with one accord, as being the best teacher and restorer of a military that is growing feeble."

Then I [GIOVIO] replied, "This is true, d'Avalos. But there are 161 also some who from youth have frequently shown vigor of spirit, with praiseworthy military service and certainly with thoughtful counsel. But since the military discipline of this era is odious and the justifications offered for wars are reprehensible, these men remain inactive, at leisure, at home. Such is the case of the exceedingly wealthy Ligurian, Sinibaldo Fieschi.[276] Upon being asked why he had abandoned Mars for Athena, he replied: 'Why do I need the glory acquired from military service if it must be sought by fighting for foreign kings, with the shameful and cruel defeat of Italy? Why likewise do I need wealth, if I'm required to seize someone else's riches by sacking wretched cities and laying waste to fields? No, on these direst of terms, I would not fight on behalf of Italy while the unfairness of the Fates is ruining it. For it is better to play at leisure the part of spectator in a criminal war than to be yourself most foully conquered.'"

To this D'AVALOS said: "Everyone is led by his own judgment 162 rather than by another's. In fact, we are making war so that after victory, once smaller dominions have been set up, we may see Italy flourishing in a secure peace. What will we be able to look forward to that is not happy and auspicious, if all Italy is decisively conquered and pacified and obeys the emperor Charles alone, as it once obeyed the Roman emperor Augustus? We hear that his mind is religious and temperate and is exceedingly inclined toward justice, equity, and concord; and so I would hope to see the pope soon freed from prison by that very man's order. If Charles himself should at last come from Spain into Italy, I am confident that he will bring salutary assistance to our ruined and calamitous situation.

163   'Sed ut revertamur ad huius secundae classis duces quos diximus, ut quidam in otiosa militia senescentes minime nominentur. Ugonem Pepulum ceteris omnibus antepono: est enim prudentiae insignis et promptitudinis eximiae et variae exercitationis alarius ductor. In Ioanne Saxatello, cuius filium praeclarae indolis Vicentino proelio occidimus, corporis pariter atque animi robur viget, cum[442] prudentia multis bellis atque periculis quaesita. Paulum etiam Camillum Trivultium[443] a nobilitate imprimis et a multis stipendiis testatisque operibus laudandum[444] puto. Sed militaribus studiis abunde mihi instructus videtur Ludovicus Balbianus, ardenti vir ingenio, qui a Gallis ad nos transivit.[445] Is[446] atavum Albericum refert; hic[447] Ioannis Galeatii magister equitum fuit, et ab inclutis[448] rebus gestis magni cognomen adeptus est. In Philippo Torniello strenuo iuvene mira est praestandae bello operae cupiditas, prosperis saepe belli successibus amplificata. Consenuit in armis, dum caesari faveret, usque ad miserabilem Ticini patriae suae interitum. Mattheus Beccaria, recto et liberali ingenio vir, nobisque Davalis hospitii iure coniunctissimus.[449] Vigent[450] adhuc nec a militari munere requiescunt fortis Mamfronius cautus Landrianus, et laboriosus Longena.'

164   Tum ego ⟨iovius⟩ 'Impone,' inquam, 'Davale, finem huic tam prolixo[451] catalogo: stomachum enim mihi tam multi alarii ductores[452] moverunt, et certe non putabam te umquam ad Mamfron⟨i⟩os[453] et Longenas esse descensurum. Quin etiam vereor si cupide[454] petenti Musetio nimium[455] indulseris, ne tibi sint centuriones omnes, qui vel semel serio tubarum cantum audierint,[456] ex quaestoris indice[457] recitandi.'

"But let us return to the commanders of this second class whom   163
we have discussed, since certain men who are growing old idly in
military service ought not to be mentioned at all. Before all the
others, I place Ugo de' Pepoli,[277] a light cavalry commander of
outstanding prudence, choice promptitude, and varied experience.
In Giovanni Sassatelli[278]—whose son, a man of conspicuous natural ability, we killed in the Battle of Vicenza[279]—there flourishes
strength both physical and mental, along with a prudence obtained
from many wars and dangers. I also think that Paolo Camillo Trivulzio[280] must be praised especially for his nobility and for his
many commissions and well-attested achievements. But Ludovico
da Barbiano,[281] a man of passionate character who changed allegiance from the French to us, seems to me amply equipped in the
military arts. He brings to mind his ancestor Alberico: that man
was a cavalry commander for Giangaleazzo Visconti and even obtained the epithet 'the Great' on account of his glorious deeds.[282]
Filippo Tornielli,[283] a dashing young man, has a marvelous passion
for discharging his military duties that has often been enhanced by
success in war. Matteo Beccaria[284] grew old in arms while he was
siding with the emperor, down to the wretched extinction of his
homeland at Pavia. A man of upright and liberal character, he is
intimately connected by ties of hospitality to us in the d'Avalos
family. The brave Manfron,[285] the cautious Landriano,[286] and the
industrious Longhena[287] are still flourishing and have yet to retire
from military duty."

Then I [GIOVIO] said, "D'Avalos, bring this lengthy catalog to   164
a close: for so many light cavalry captains have put me in an ill-
temper. I certainly did not imagine you would ever sink to the
level of Manfron and Longhena. And what is more, I fear that if
you yield too much to Muscettola's eager petitioning, all the centurions who have earnestly responded even once to the call of the
trumpet must be read off from the paymaster's roll."

165   At ille ⟨DAVALUS⟩ 'Apage,' inquit, 'Iovi, et aequo animo patere
me in hac censura fuisse prolixum; nam cum optimos quosque
requiratis summamque eorum esse inopiam conqueramur, necesse
fuit tamquam in pompa et hos quoque vel obscuri nominis praefectos traduxisse,[458] ut non tantum quam pauci sint, qui imperare
aliis egregie possint, noscatis, sed etiam quam rari exsistant, qui
probabiles et periti vel vobis etiam imperitis esse videantur. Et
mehercle, hoc vitium commune est militibus cunctis: ut nemo se
tam inertem vel[459] male fortunatum putet quin se aliquando in
praestantem evasurum ducem constanter credat, quoniam[460] nemo
est qui alteri viribus pariter ac[461] ingenio concedere[462] velit; nam si
quid proprio iudicio[463] desit, id totum Fortunae petulanter ascribi-
tur. Inde plerumque accidit ut quisque alienas virtutes maligne
aestimando elevet verbis, ut supra aequum et verum attolat suas.

166   'Sed tantum abest ut horum vel fama vel indole vel rebus gestis
probatiores[464] illis maioribus et statariis quos amisimus ducibus
aequare velim, ut nec cum Ioanne Medice, qui nuper, irrumpentibus ad Mincium Germanis, tormento ictus cecidit, conferendos
putem. Is enim dux effrenatus et acer nimis ⟨non⟩ nisi decora alta
atque aspera factu facinora inflammato animo agitabat, adeo ut
vim eius ardorem atque impetum vix strenuissimi hostes ferrent.
Sive pedes enim[465] sive eques ingentibus lacertis oreque terribili[466]
pugnam cieret, cum animo tum arte etiam[467] ac viribus semper
erat invictus, et metum hostibus et pudorem suis afferebat.

167   'Sed cum iam in eo et iuvenilis inconsultus furor et immanis
iracundia et immoderatae libidines aliqua ex parte refrixissent,

But he [D'AVALOS] said, "Back off, Giovio. Be patient, and let 165
me range widely in this census; for since you are searching for all
the best men, and since we are deploring the acute dearth of them,
I have had to march past, as if in a parade, the captains of undistinguished reputation as well. That way, you may find out not only
how few there are who can command others outstandingly, but
also how rare are the ones who appear, even to you who are inexperienced, to be commendable and skillful. And by God, this failing is common to all soldiers: no one thinks himself so incompetent or so unlucky that he does not firmly believe that some day he
will turn into an outstanding commander. This is the case because
no one would be willing to concede superiority in strength and
character to another man; if someone lacks judgment, he will inso-
lently attribute that entire failing to Fortune. Hence it frequently
happens that each person denigrates anothers' merits so as to elevate his own above what is just and true.

"But it is very far from the case that I could wish to put the 166
more acceptable of these men on the same level, whether in reputation, natural ability, or accomplishments, as those greater, steadfast commanders whom we have lost. For instance, I would not
think them comparable to Giovanni de' Medici,[288] who died recently after being struck by a gunshot as the Germans were storm-
ing toward the Mincio River. For that commander, headstrong and
keen to a fault, performed with ardent spirit only deeds that were
glorious, elevated, and difficult—so much so that the most vigorous enemies scarcely endured his strength, passion, and drive.
Whether as an infantry- or cavalryman, he spurred on the battle
with his huge muscles and terrifying facial expression. In mind,
skill, and strength, he was always unmatched, and he was accustomed to inspire both fear in his enemies and self-respect in his
own men.

"But then, when his rash and youthful passion, monstrous tem- 167
per, and outsized lusts had already cooled to some degree, and

essetque in spe admodum propinqua regendi magni exercitus, in cursu cecidit, pontificis ac[468] Italiae fato potius quam suo, nam profecto si paucas superfuisset horas, aut nobilissimam de Germanis victoriam retulisset, aut ipse[469] superatus victores magna caede extenuatos aliis exercitibus et[470] paganis debellandos omnino reliquisset. Sed quaecumque eius fortissimi viri vel acerbissima necis sors fuit, dum locum promovendis castris cum paucis explorat, fatali malo potius, ut dixi, quod omnibus imminebat, quam ullo ictu fortuito emissi in incertum tormenti, crudeliter est extinctus, ita ut plerique hostium, quibus viri virtus erat notissima, Italiam ea die suam dexteram amisisse praedicarint.[471]

168   'De pedestri vero militia, quae hodie ad summum usum summumque honorem haud dubie revocatur, id tantum dicam: neminem esse adeo clarum qui non multos habeat et fere innumerabiles exercitatione et factis inclutis pares. Et profecto Itali pedites nullam adhuc eximiae spectataeque virtutis opinionem meruerunt, cum in his coalescere stabilis disciplina nequaquam possit, quoniam pedites sub signis, propter intolerabiles sumptus, longo tempore retineri inveterarique nequeant, ita ut non difficile fuerit eos[472] tot proeliis a Germanis et Hispanis veteranis superari. Qui vero[473] hodie in Italia sunt Hispani atque Germani, nequaquam iusto nomine milites appellari debent,[474] quando nulla certa[475] stipendia, nulla iam[476] imperia, nulla auspicia sequantur. Aluntur[477] enim[478] uno tantum sanguine provinciarum, crudelitati[479] et sceleri[480] tamquam ducibus parent, et nihil humani nihilque[481] divini iuris agnoscunt, ita ut caesari tantorum scelerum ignaro, quod Italiam numquam viderit nec miserorum gemitus exaudiverit, singularem invidiam parent,[482] ac eum[483] alieno scelere invisum

when he had the imminent prospect of commanding a great army, he fell as he was leading an advance. This was more to the ruin of the pope and Italy than it was to him. For certainly, if he had survived a few hours, either he would have claimed an exceedingly noble victory over the Germans or, if he himself were conquered, he would have left the victors, weakened by a great slaughter, to be conquered by other armies and by peasants. But whatever was the bitter lot of death that befell this bravest of men, while he was reconnoitering with a few men a place for moving the camp, he was blotted out, as I said, by a fatal evil that was threatening all rather than by any random gunshot fired at an indistinct target — so much so that many of the enemy to whom the man's prowess was well known, declared that on that day Italy had lost its right hand.

"As for the infantry, which today is undoubtedly being called 168 back to the greatest utility and the highest honor, I will say only this: no one is so famous that he does not have many — almost countless — equals in experience and illustrious deeds. And the reason that Italian foot soldiers have as yet merited no reputation for special, tested excellence is surely that solid discipline has been unable to take root among them because, on account of the unsustainable expense, foot soldiers cannot long be retained or become established under their standards; and so it was not difficult for German and Spanish veterans to vanquish them in so many battles. Mind you, the Spaniards and Germans who are in Italy today ought not properly to be called 'soldiers' at all in that they no longer follow any fixed contracts, authorities, or commands. They feed only on the blood of the provinces; they obey cruelty and crime as their commanders; and they recognize no law, human or divine. Thus, they are creating singular ill-will for the emperor — who is ignorant of these great crimes because he has never seen Italy or heard the groans of the miserable — and by means of a crime that he did not commit, they are making him detestable to

Italis omnibus reddant. Sed haec compresso gemitu feramus,[484] postquam sic non iniqua Fata, sed ipsi principes Itali perversis agitati consiliis omnino[485] voluerunt.'

169   Hoc loco MUSETIUS 'Desinamus,' inquit, 'Davale, hanc communem libertatem ut iam conclamatam inanibus querelis prosequi; nobis vero, qui hoc indignum ferimus iugum, pro solatio sint taeterrimi vitae exitus illorum qui, cum has aerumnas et[486] pestes nobis pararent, iustiore quadam deorum immortalium vindicta, temeritatis ac insaniae[487] poenas persolverunt. Alfonsum enim iuniorem regno pulsum vidimus et, in conversa belli fortuna, regnum a filio frustra repetentem, qui cum diram illam regnandi libidinem[488] simulata religione comprimere velareque[489] contenderet, ex rege sacerdos factus, animi potius dolore quam morbo excruciatus in exilio Messanae[490] periit. Nec Ludovico Sfortiae ultrices Furiae pepercerunt quem, ab Helvetiis militibus suis Gallo regi de manu traditum, ita ferratus carcer excepit, ut ibi ad graviorem etiam miseriam erepto calami solacio tam diu torqueretur, quoad ab affecto curis pectore, illum dirum spiritum efflaret,[491] quo Gallos insana libidine ad turbandam pacem in Italiam evocarat.

170   'Quid vero ab divina ultione Alexandri Sexti Pontificis foeda morte praeclarius? Qui cum, per omnia scelera graviter efferatus,[492] opulentos senatores ad coenam vocatos veneno tollere percuperet, fallente servolo qui a poculis ministrabat, eodem aconito se ipsum necavit. Sensit subinde et suas[493] meritas clades Venetus senatus qui, ut ambitiose fines imperii prolataret, Gallos itidem in Italiam ducere minime dubitarat. Ab illa siquidem[494] insigni externorum regum conspiratione sic est afflictus ut caesis exercitibus,

all Italians. But let us endure these things with our groans held in check, since not the adverse Fates but the Italian princes themselves, driven on by misguided counsels, entirely willed them so."

At this point, MUSCETTOLA said: "Let us leave off, D'Avalos, 169 escorting the cortège of our common Italian liberty, as we have already bewailed its loss with vain laments. To us who bear this unworthy yoke, may there serve as a solace the hideous deaths of those who plotted these afflictions and plagues for us: by a certain just vengeance of the immortal gods, they have paid the penalty for their temerity and madness.[289] We have seen Alfonso the Younger banished from his kingdom and, in a reversal of the fortunes of war, in vain demanding back the kingdom from his son.[290] When, changing himself from a king into a priest, he hastened to conceal with feigned religiosity that ill-omened desire of ruling, he died in exile in Messina, tormented by mental anguish rather than disease. Nor did the avenging Furies spare Ludovico Sforza. Handed over to the French king directly by his own Swiss troops, he was put in an ironclad prison. There, once they had taken away the solace of writing so as to make his misery even more oppressive, he was tormented for a long time. In the end, mentally afflicted, he breathed his last breath—that same ill-omened breath with which, with insane caprice, he had summoned the French into Italy to upset the peace.

"And what is more notorious than the foul death of Pope Alex- 170 ander VI at the hand of divine vengeance? After he had run the gamut of savage crimes, he was keen to poison some rich cardinals he had invited to dinner. When the serving boy in charge of the drinks made a mistake, Alexander did himself in with that same poison. Shortly thereafter, the Venetian senate experienced the disasters it deserved: in order that it might ambitiously extend the bounds of its empire, it too had not hesitated to bring the French into Italy. But as a result of the extraordinary plotting of foreign kings, Venice has been so afflicted that it is reeling: its armies

urbibus amissis, agris evastatis, exhaustis opibus, imperium illud, a stirpe fere convulsum, vehementissime nutarit. Istis enim quattuor praecipuis auctoribus, et turbatum opulentae pacis otium et barbaricas[495] compedes Italiae importatas constat, unde non immerito infelices et proditi populi eorum nomina cum exsecrabili devotione persequantur.[496]

171 'Sed nos forti[497] animo hanc fortunae acerbitatem feramus, et a virtute optimisque studiis certa praesidia desumamus, quibus ab omni eius iniuria praeclare vindicemur. Vivendum enim nobis est, ut opinor, cautorum et frugi servorum more, qui infracto callidoque ingenio ita condicionem dissimulant, ut non tristi sed alacri cum patientia maturam libertatem exspectent.'

172 Tum vero ego ⟨IOVIUS⟩ 'Museti,' inquam, 'recte nos mones, et ex Stoica quidem disciplina, ut huius importunae tempestatis fluctus, qui mihi modo visi sunt esse decimani, si non adversa prora proscindere, saltem versatili remigio declinare velimus. Sed quousque hunc laborem[498] in perenni aestu[499] lacerti nostri iam prope exsangues ferent? Quando immanis hic Boreas efflare cessabit? Quando irati spumosique aequoris undae residebunt ut, tamquam alcyones, qui ⟨non⟩ nisi in certa serenitate nidificant,[500] rem nostram cogitationes consilia spesque ipsas sistere stabilireque possimus? Affulgere quidem nobis potest hilarior dies, quae has tenebras repente discutiat et cuncta salutari lumine protinus serenet, ut sperandum est, ex divina maxime iustitia optimi caesaris et eius clementia singulari;[501] quod, ut perquam mature affulgeat, solemni voto suscepto diis immortalibus supplicemus. Tu vero Davale,[502] si quid est in militia reliquum, nobis explicare non graveris.'[503]

were cut to pieces, towns lost, fields devastated, and resources exhausted, its empire nearly ripped up by the roots. Indeed, it is evident that with these despicable four as the chief instigators, the leisure of a prosperous peace was disturbed, and barbarian fetters were inflicted upon Italy. Hence — and with good reason — the wretched, betrayed peoples assail their hateful names with curses.

"But let us endure this bitterness of fortune with stalwart 171 minds, and let us choose reliable defenses derived from virtue and the best studies, which may protect us excellently from every harm of fortune. In fact, I think we need to live in the manner of wary and honest slaves who, with a humble and cunning ingenuity, disguise their status in such a way that, with a submissiveness that is not sullen but eager, they await liberty in good time."

Then I [GIOVIO] said: "Muscettola, you are advising us well, 172 and indeed in accordance with the Stoics' teaching, that with respect to the waves of this oppressive storm — which just now have seemed to me to be outsized — we should wish, if not to cut through them prow-first, then at least to parry them with a revolving oar. But how much longer will our muscles, already nearly exhausted, endure the labor in this perpetually swelling sea? When will this beastly north wind cease to blow? When will the angry and foaming waves of the sea subside in order that like halcyons, which build a nest only in reliably fair weather, we may be able to set right and stabilize our property, thoughts, plans, and our very hopes? A cheerier day can shine upon us, such as would all of a sudden dissipate these shadows and brighten all things with the light of salvation, springing (as must be hoped) from our noble emperor's divine justice and singular clemency. We should make a solemn vow and should humbly beseech the immortal gods that this light may in time shine forth. But, d'Avalos, if something in military affairs has been left unmentioned, do not grudge us an explanation."

173   Tum ille ⟨DAVALUS⟩ 'Non gravabor' inquit. 'Quid enim iucundius esse potest quam vobis praeclara cupientibus obtemperare?
Reliqua igitur[504] militiae pars in maritimo negotio versatur, in
quo[505] veteres summum studium[506] omni tempore posuerunt, quoniam maximam vim propter varias et rerum et locorum opportu-
nitates in parandis etiam terrestribus victoriis habere existimabant.
Eius rei apparatum, quo antea plurimum pollere solebant, Genuenses[507] ipsique Pisani et novissime Neapolitani reges, cum misera essent[508] oppressi servitute, ita deseruerunt, ut soli sint hodie[509] Veneti, qui eam sumptuose et peregregie tueantur.

174   'Nam cum in convehendis mercibus onerariae,[510] quae quadratis
aguntur[511] velis, ad longinquos maritimos cursus maxime valeant,
triremibus prope solis et remigio insignibus[512] rostratis bella ge-
runtur, quando iis imperent navarchi[513] adversus omnes ventorum
contumelias, et onerariae contra, incertissimae ventorum libidini
semper oboediant;[514] et si illi concidant[515] vel inflare plenius cessent, in alto immobiles ac opportunae triremium iniuriis saepissime, ut in segni[516] malacia relinquantur.

175   'Hac navali gloria unus maxime nunc floret: Andreas Auria
Genuensis, qui sub pontifice dudum merebat. Is[517] servis iure belli
captis catenatisque noxiis[518] remigibus utitur. Vir acutus, et sine
arrogantia gravis, idem unicus et divinus maris ac nubium spectator, et in omnibus expeditionibus et pugnis, semper strenuus et
felix. Sed eius virtuti imprimis contra praedones Barbaros fortuna
mirifice respondit, captis supra sexaginta Punicis biremibus et infinitis prope Christianis hominibus libertati restitutis, adeo ut in
patria[519] sacellum Deiparae Virgini Fautrici in media portus mole
quadrato exstructum saxo, ex[520] Punicis manubiis cum insigni victoriarum titulo dedicarit, et nunc oppressis caesaris triremibus, et

Then he [D'AVALOS] said: "I shall not. For what can be more 173
pleasant than to humor you when you are requesting excellent
things? The remainder of military affairs, then, consists of the
navy. Past generations in every era have devoted intense study to
this subject, since they supposed that on account of the varied opportunities both of circumstances and of locations the navy has an
immense capacity for producing victories even on land. The Genoese and the Pisans themselves and most recently the kings of Naples, overwhelmed by miserable servitude, have given up a navy,
the former basis of their power, so that the Venetians alone maintain this lavishly and outstandingly.

"Although cargo ships propelled by square sails are especially 174
effective in conveying merchandise on lengthy maritime voyages,
wars are waged almost exclusively by triremes, and those with
beaked prows, notable for their oarsmen, since captains can control them in the face of battering winds. Cargo ships, on the other
hand, are always subject to the most inconstant caprice of the
winds, and if the winds die down or completely cease to blow, very
often they are motionless in the open sea and exposed to attacks
from triremes; hence they are abandoned in the dead calm.

"There is one man in particular who now flourishes in naval 175
fame: Andrea Doria of Genoa, who served for a long time under
the pope. He uses war captives and chained criminals as oarsmen.
Shrewd and authoritative without arrogance, this man is an unparalleled and prescient observer of the sea and the clouds and is
always vigorous and successful in all his expeditions and battles.
But especially against the Barbary pirates his fortune wonderfully
measured up to his prowess: he captured over sixty Moorish
biremes and restored countless Christians to liberty. From his
Moorish spoils he has built in his native city a chapel on a square
rock on the mound in the middle of the harbor. Containing a
great list of his victories, it was dedicated to his patron, the Virgin
Mother of God. And, now that the emperor's triremes have been

recepta subinde Genua, ut libertatis maxime cupidus et assertor, "pater patriae" decreto publico sit appellatus.

176 'E Venetis autem nemo clarioribus factis est inclutus, quando omnes fere patricii scientiae navalis opinione pares aestimentur. Nam postquam cum Ottomannis regibus in parta pace, mari contendere desierunt, sublata est facultas ostendendae virtutis et tuendae maxime disciplinae. Nuper tamen cum laude Paulus Iustinianus, mari multum versatus, ut est alacri et prompto vir ingenio, in Caroli Lanoii classem flagranter invectus est, cum Armerius Venetae classis praefectus cum parte triremium ignava cunctatione in proelium ire dubitasset.

177 'Verum ut ad eos paucos, qui nostri operis sunt, duces[521] revertamur, quosque[522] supra sincero iudicio numeravi,[523] illos hercle[524] ceteris omnibus bello meliores[525] esse contendo. Sed tamen eos ita probo, ut a nemine perfectam imperatoriam laudem exspectem. Nam id totum quod est praefuisse copiis, quadratum vexillum sceptrum speciososque ceteros supremi militaris imperii titulos praetulisse et[526] magnificum in castris praetorium cum largissimis mensis[527] erexisse, ad opinionem potius quam ad solidam existimationem imperatoriae virtutis pertinere videtur. Vidi ego nonnullos proximis bellis qui, cum numquam alicui insigni proelio interfuissent, hos honores tamen meruerunt. Qua ergo animi fortitudine is tum se egregium ducem[528] geret, cum fuerit confligendum, qui concurrentes exercitus numquam viderit?

178 'Nihil profecto atrocius,[529] nihil terribilius conserto proelio vel mente[530] concipi, vel ipsis excipi auribus vel oculis offerri posse putatote; non pilis iam et sagittis et fundis ab initio, ut rudiore

defeated and Genoa thereupon recovered, Doria, who is especially
eager for liberty and a great defender of it, has been designated by
public decree as the 'Father of his Country.'

"Of the Venetians, however, no man is celebrated for distin- 176
guished deeds, because nearly all the patricians are considered
equals in their reputation for naval expertise. For after they had
done with fighting at sea with the Ottoman rulers and peace had
been procured, the opportunity of displaying naval prowess and
especially of maintaining naval training was lost. But Paolo Giustinian, a man experienced at sea and of a lively and quick mind,
recently garnered praise by ardently attacking the fleet of Lannoy
when Alban d'Armer, the admiral of the Venetian fleet, had hesitated—out of cowardice, it is said—to go into battle with a portion of the triremes.[291]

"But let us return to those few commanders in my line of 177
work,[292] each of whom I listed earlier with a candid evaluation: by
God, I submit that they are better in warfare than all the others.
But still, I esteem them with the reservation that I expect from
none of them the perfect excellence of a commanding officer. For
that whole business of commanding troops, carrying a square banner, a scepter and other fair trappings of supreme military command, and setting up camp in a splendid headquarters with lavish
tables seems to pertain to a captain's reputation for virtue rather
than to a reliable appraisal of that virtue. In the most recent wars
I have seen some who received such honors even though they had
never taken part in any notable battle. Well then, with what fortitude will such a man then conduct himself as an outstanding commander when he has to fight a battle and yet has never seen armies
clashing?

"You really must believe that nothing can be heard, seen, or 178
conceived that is more appalling or frightening than a pitched
battle. Nowadays, right from the start, we do not fight using
spears, arrows, and slings, as was the norm in a less 'civilized' age,

saeculo erat solitum,[531] sed maioribus tormentis res geritur. Imperatori in fumo et tenebris, ne quid temere fiat, providendum; et cum terra tremit[532] et fragore caelum crepitat,[533] surdis et caecis[534] militibus imperandum pugnandumque omnibus pari sorte adversus tormenta, quae passim integras cohortes et turmas crudeli morte prosternunt,[535] ita ut urbes atque oppida vel tueri vel expugnare, quae tam[536] aspera et difficilia existimantur, si ipsam excitati proelii procellam vimque illam repentini turbinis animo[537] reputemus, mihi paene ludus esse videatur. Sed sic res se habent et haec tempora sic ferunt, ut satis multis virtutibus is instructus esse putetur, qui cunctari patienter sciat, caute et explorato ducat agmen, permunite castra metetur, nihil casibus committat, nihil devocet ad Fortunam.

179   'Ii etenim[538] ducum mores res publicas magnopere delectant et liberis[539] civitatibus mire placent, utpote quae[540] vehementes regum impetus eorum oppugnantium libertatem, cauta et sollerti cunctatione[541] retardari, quam repelli acrius et refringi penitus malint, quoniam ferociora ducum ingenia reformidant, qui incaute atque praepropere[542] confligendo magnas saepe clades importarunt. Quam infelix enim audacia, quam funesta temeritas Liviani pugnacissimi ducis Venetis exstiterit, omnes intellegunt. Nam bis unius horae momento, cum et spes adauctae et res iam in tuto essent, illorum rem publicam amissis foede copiis in summum discrimen adduxit.[543]

180   'Neque propterea tamen[544] aliquos negaverim pristina sua consuetudine strenuos et pugnaces naturam omnino velut necessitate imposita mutavisse, ut disciplinam civitatum ingeniis et temporibus accommodatam aliena secuti arbitria vel indecoro etiam

but instead with massive artillery. Amid smoke and shadows, a captain needs to exercise forethought to prevent reckless action; and when the ground trembles and the air crackles with crashes, he must command soldiers who are deaf and blind; and all have to fight in similar circumstances against the artillery, which is everywhere flattening entire cohorts and squadrons with cruel death. And so, if we should think over that very storm of vigorous battle and that force of a sudden whirlwind, it seems to me to be mere child's play either to protect cities and towns or to assault them — things that are regarded as grievous and difficult. But as circumstances stand and as these times allow, that man is thought to have been equipped with sufficient virtues who knows how to delay patiently, who leads an army column cautiously and safely, who lays out camp with thorough fortifications, who leaves nothing to chance, and who by no means summons the help of Fortune.

"And as a matter of fact, this conduct of commanders delights 179 republics and wonderfully pleases free cities, since they prefer that the violent impulses of kings who are besieging their liberty be kept in check by cautious and clever delay, instead of being more vigorously driven back or entirely destroyed. This is so because they shrink from the fiercer temperament of commanders who have often incurred great disasters by going into battle recklessly and hastily. All men recognize the extent of the unfortunate audacity and fatal rashness of the exceedingly aggressive Venetian commander, d'Alviano. Twice in the space of one hour, when hopes had increased and the situation was already on a sure footing, he disgracefully lost troops and brought the republic into the greatest jeopardy.

"But I would not on that account deny that some vigorous and 180 combative men wholly changed their nature from what it was before, as though a necessity had been imposed, so that, having followed others' decisions with a compliance that is perhaps even inglorious, they diligently accommodated their military training to

obsequio diligenter applicarent. Quamquam illis suae nimiae cunc-
tationis et tarditatis, quae ignaviae calumniam saepe recipiunt,
minime paenitendum esse putem, si vires ipsae,[545] si sociorum
mores, si tempora, si denique[546] remotae spes utrimque iusta quadam aestimatione conferantur. Quo fit ut Urbinatem et ceteros
hostium duces, quos imperiti togatique vituperant, a salutari prudentia saepe laudemus, qui profecto nobis hos labores atque molestias minuissent, si cum tirone exercitu adversus veteranas copias,
aut in Aemilia aut in Apennino, vel demum Roma capta ad munitiones nostras dimicassent. Ceterum cum haec ante alias virtus illis
desit quae in toto militari negotio praeclarissima iudicatur, aequo
animo ferent si dicam ex vivis me neminem videre absolutae disciplinae perfectum ducem.

181   'Tria enim semper ante alia in imperatore desideravi: scilicet[547]
consilium expeditum, integram auctoritatem, et promptum in ex-
sequendis officiis corporis atque animi vigorem. Consilium stabile
definitum[548] efficiunt, longus bellicarum rerum usus, et innata
animo considerata celeritas. Tum enim id vari[a]e[549] atque feliciter
ad ipsos vel repentinos[550] casus et cuncta[551] rerum momenta con-
vertitur.

182   'Auctoritas autem praeclara semper atque firmissima quattuor
rebus maxime[552] comparatur. Primo nominis dignitate, ut in Ludovici et Francisci Galliae Regum Maximilianique item Caesaris
castris vidimus, qui facillime vel diversissimas gentes una regali
existimatione et solis prope nutibus regebant. Secundo publica
quadam provectae et in armis exactae aetatis reverentia, qua
Petilianum, Trivultium et Prosperum Columnam valuisse constat,
nam eos non secus ac patres venerari milites solebant. Tertio

the character of states and to the times. Yet I should think that those men do not in the least need to regret their excessive delay and tardiness — which often invite a false accusation of coward-ice — if strength itself, the character of allies, the times, and finally the distant prospects of both sides should be compared on the basis of a well-founded evaluation. Thus it happens that we often praise for their saving prudence the Duke of Urbino and other enemy commanders whom inexperienced and civilian men criti-cize, supposing that surely those commanders would have lessened these sufferings and troubles for us if they had fought with a nov-ice army against veteran troops either in Emilia or in the Apen-nines or, finally, near our fortifications, once Rome had been cap-tured. But since they lack that virtue which is judged to be the most splendid above others in the entire business of war, they will accept it with calmness if I say that I see no man living who is an ideal commander of perfected discipline.

"I have always longed for three things above all others in a cap- 181 tain: prompt decisiveness, complete authority, and a ready vigor of body and mind in discharging duties. Long experience of military affairs and an innate, reflective quickness produce steadfast, precise policy. Then this is directed variously and successfully to deal with those sudden contingencies themselves and with all changes of circumstance.

"Illustrious and rock-solid authority is always achieved chiefly 182 by means of four things. In the first place, distinction of name, as we have seen in the armies of Kings Louis and Francis of France and likewise in those of the Emperor Maximilian. These men ruled quite diverse peoples without difficulty simply by their royal status and almost by their nods of assent alone. Second, authority is achieved by a certain common respect for advanced age, and es-pecially for a lifetime spent in arms. Everyone knows that the Count of Pitigliano,[293] Trivulzio,[294] and Prospero Colonna[295] pre-vailed because their soldiers were accustomed to venerate them like

severitate commixta comitati, quo temperamento Franciscus Gonzaga Mantuanus princeps, cum longe maximos exercitus contra
Carolum ductaret, varias nationes in officio disciplinaque conti-
nuit, quando partim metu ad parendum partim benevolentia ducerentur. Quarto autem eximii ducis auctoritas felicitate eventuum
mirifice sustinetur, ut in Magno Gonsalvo nuper enituit, et in ipso
Navarro humillimae sortis homine, cum primis tribus Punicis expeditionibus singularem famam summi ducis, nondum eam ver-
tente Fortuna, fuisset adeptus.

183   'Sed haec auctoritas in qua tantum momenti reponimus nonnumquam in magnis victoriis amittitur, cum in duce concepta
laetitia severitatem facillime dissolvat. In adversissimis vero casibus, quis eam vel dux ferox constanter[553] retinuit, cum in fugam
coniecti milites non imperium sed salutem omnino respiciant?
Porro ille corporis atque animi vigor ubique praesens et volucris
naturae potius est munus et deorum immortalium, quam virtus
humana quaesita facultate. Propterea haec praecipua res maxime
est admirabilis, nam in ipsis praesertim proeliis versatur quibus
bellum in summa saepissime concluditur atque conficitur, unde
pulcherrimae ac[554] ingentes victoriae deletis hostibus referuntur.
At gravis et cauta cunctatrixque prudentia extrahere bellum egregie quidem potest, pericula devitare, atterere atque extenuare alienas opes, et ex longinquo prosperum belli finem, exclusis proeliorum casibus prospectare.

184   'Quae omnia sicut iniuriam sustinentibus, si ipsi sint copiosi
atque opulenti, propria videntur, ita bellum inferentibus impor-
tuna et maxime perniciosa esse conspicimus. Haec enim in hostibus nostris imbellis et inefficax et tarda prudentia, si regiones incendiis evastatas et urbes miserabilem in modum a praesidiis

fathers. Third, authority is established by severity united with courtesy. With this blend, Francesco Gonzaga, marquis of Mantua, kept together various peoples in duty and discipline when he was commanding massive armies against Charles VIII;[296] in part by fear and in part by kindness, he led them to comply. And fourth, the authority of an excellent commander is wonderfully sustained by successful results, as recently shone forth in Gonsalvo the Great, and in Navarro himself—a man of very humble circumstances—when, in the first three campaigns against the Moors he obtained the remarkable reputation of a top commander (a reputation that Fortune as yet is not subverting).

"But this authority on which we place so much importance is 183 sometimes let slip in the midst of a great victory, since the exuberance generated in the commander's mind very easily does away with sternness. On the other hand, in disastrous outcomes, what leader—even a fierce one—has consistently maintained authority when the soldiers, put to flight, look not to the supreme command but entirely to their own safety? Moreover, that vigor of body and mind that is present in all circumstances is fleeting and is a gift of nature and the immortal gods rather than a virtue obtained by human skill. That is why it is particularly admirable: for it is especially a factor in the very battles that often bring an entire war to completion—those from which, once you have crushed the enemy, you carry off the most splendid and momentous victories. But a measured, cautious, and dilatory prudence can in fact admirably prolong a war, obviate dangers, thin out and exhaust the other side's resources, and espy from afar the war's favorable outcome without one's having to face the hazards of battle.

"All these things appear to apply in particular to those who 184 are being attacked unjustly, if they should be well supplied and wealthy, but we see that they also are highly destructive to those who are attacking. If we should place before our eyes the regions destroyed by fires, the cities brought to such miserable ruin by our

afflictas nostris, et gravissimum Romanae urbis excidium ante oculos proponamus, certe[555] funestior fuit omnibus proeliorum periculis; quae subiisse vel adverso Marte satius fuisset, quam ipsos imperatores ac milites[556] et sanos et incolumes, tantis Italiae[557] cladibus ac ignominiis superstites exstitisse. Ergo illi in exitu quidem belli, ut libet, famam suam ac existimationem[558] reponant modo nostros hactenus vel vividae virtutis vel, si ita etiam[559] appellent, furiosae[560] temeritatis minime paeniteat.

185 'Idcirco ex hoc numero ducum, cum eorum sit maxima penuria, neminem video in quo eae tres simul virtutes (ut alias prope innumerabiles optimo cuique requisitas[561] omittamus) non modo summae sed ne mediocres quidem appareant, cum se ipsos in universum contrariis vitiorum[562] excessibus exsuperent, adeo[563] ut[564] perdifficile videatur perfectum imperatorem, qualem afflicta et[565] oppressa malis Italia desideret, cogitatione ac[566] animo vobis effigiasse, si praecipuas peculiaresque virtutes ex uno quoque duce decerptas detractis subinde[567] omnibus vitiis in unum hominem[568] conferre velimus.

186 'Exemplo quodam Zeuxidis[569] pictoris qui, cum apud Crotoniates ut Helenam[570] pingeret pretio esset conductus, non unam tantum quae formae dignitate praecelleret, sed plures longe pulcherrimas virgines ex omnibus acri iudicio delectas ad aemulandum sibi tradi postulavit, quoniam vir acutus et sapiens facile intellegebat naturam, cum ratione et quadam singulari aequitate liberalem in concedendo nobilissimo munere, nequaquam omnia uni, quae summa essent et venustissima, tribuisse. Alia siquidem oris venustate praestabat, aliam capillus vel natura aureus vel laeta arte compositus honestabat; alia placebat oculis radiosis[571] paetis[572]

troops, and the most grievous destruction of Rome, then this 'prudence' of our enemies — unwarlike, ineffectual, and sluggish — was surely more deadly than all the dangers of battles. It would have been better for them to have faced these dangers, even if Mars was averse, than for captains and troops to have survived, safe and sound, the great disasters and disgraces that befell Italy. Accordingly, let those men make their reputation and their good name, if they please, depending on the outcome of the war, but let not our men in any way regret now their spirited prowess or frenzied rashness (if such they would call it).

"Therefore, of these commanders, since there is a great dearth   185 of them, I see no one in whom these three virtues together (to leave aside the almost innumerable others that any outstanding man needs) appear not only in the highest but even in a moderate degree, since on the whole they outdo themselves with counterbalancing excesses of vice. Hence it appears very difficult to fashion theoretically for you a perfect captain of the sort afflicted and oppressed Italy longs for, if we should wish to confer upon one individual the foremost and special virtues culled from every single commander, once we have removed all the vices.

"This follows the particular example of the painter Zeuxis. In   186 Croton, when he had been hired to paint Helen, he required that not just one exceedingly beautiful woman be delivered to him as a model, but several young girls who had been marked out as a result of keen judgment to be by far the most beautiful of all.[297] The acute and wise man did this because he readily recognized that Nature, by reason and remarkable fairness generous in granting every noble gift, has by no means bestowed all the best and most attractive charms upon a single woman. If one woman was preeminent in attractiveness of face, another was dignified by hair either naturally golden or arranged with pleasing skill. If one gave pleasure with cheerful, radiant eyes that had a cast to them, another did so with a dazzling and glistening vitality. If one was

hilaribus, alia candido et nitenti suco; alia periucundo gestu,[573] alia scite commensuratis atque teretibus membris erat insignis.

187 'Ita est profecto de ducibus nostris, qui ab una tantum aut altera insigni laude[574] sunt illustres: neminem enim singulis virtutibus ad admirationem exornatum videmus, quandoquidem, ut dixi, natura in multos potius quam in unum benigna, nihil in simplici genere omni ex parte perfectum edere consuescat. Neque hoc de nostris tantum Italis intellegi volo; neminem enim ex Hispanis vel Germanis et Gallis qui in Italia militarint, agnosco vel conspicuum vel omnino probabilem ducem; quamquam multos longe fortissimos, quorum vita omnis in armis constiterit, enumerare possimus.

188 'Ugonem enim ante alios Moncatam. Etsi is[575] natura peracutus decorisque avidus et promptissimus etiam bellator ab omnibus, et a caesare qui illum ditavit, prorsus aestimetur, non puto pro summo duce a sanis hominibus esse deligendum, quoniam fatali quadam infelicitate terra marique Fortunam fere semper improspere sit expertus. Et profecto credendum est bene fortunatum omni alio[576] prudenti et bellica virtute cumulato imperatore, etiamsi sit ignavus, esse potiorem. Alarco etiam vetus equitum praefectus, cuius diligentiae capti pontificis sicut antea Francisci regis custodiam demandatam videtis: dignus potius cui imperetur quam ipse aliis imperet existimatur, ita ut Ioannis Dorbini, apud meas legiones castrorum magistri, ingenium robur vigorem patientiam, magni ducis officio proximas virtutes, potius commendem; et vix ei Navarrum arbi⟨tror⟩[577] praeferendum, quem apud Lotrechium universis pedestribus copiis praesse audivistis.'

outstanding in her delightful bearing, another was so in her taste-fully symmetrical and shapely limbs.

"So it surely is in the case of our commanders, who are illustri- 187 ous as a result of only one or another outstanding quality. For we see no one furnished with every single virtue to the point of being admirable, inasmuch as nature—which is, as I have said, generous toward many rather than toward one—is not accustomed to pro-duce in a simple kind anything that is perfect in every detail. Nor do I want this to be understood only in respect to our Italians, for I recognize none of the Spaniards or Germans and French who have fought in Italy to be either entirely distinguished or entirely commendable as a commander—although we might be able to list many whose whole life has been spent in arms, who are by far the most courageous.

"Hugo de Moncada precedes the others. Although he is ac- 188 counted by all—including the emperor, who made him rich—shrewd by nature, keen for glory, and an exceedingly brave warrior, I think that sensible men should not choose him as the consum-mate commander, since he has by a certain deadly ill fortune on land and at sea nearly always put Fortune to the test with unfa-vorable results. Surely we must believe that a lucky commander, even if he should be cowardly, is preferable to any other captain, even if the latter is prudent and has many military skills. Consider also Alarcón,[298] an aged cavalry commander to whose care we see that the custody of the captive pope has been handed over,[299] just as that of King Francis was before. He is thought worthy to be given orders rather than to give them to others. And so, I com-mend rather the talent, strength, vigor, and endurance of Juan de Urbina,[300] the camp master among my legions. These are the vir-tues closest to the function of a great commander. I hardly think that Navarro, who you have heard was in command of all the in-fantry for Lautrec, should be preferred to him."

189   Hoc loco MUSETIUS 'Huius Navarri virtus,' inquit, 'ni fallor, ab illa vetere belli gloria multum elanguit, animusque eius, qui tanta ac tam inusitata cogitationibus agitabat, vehementer etiam refrixit. Nam cum arma adversus suae gentis homines ferre conatus est, inefficax et infelix semper ac, ut ita dicam, "Navarrogallus" apparuit.'

190   Ad id arridens DAVALUS 'In arte,' inquit, 'bellica Museti ultimus vitae simul et gloriae dies indicat de omnibus; nam a postremis operibus imperatorum decora censeri conspicimus.'

191   Tum ego ⟨IOVIUS⟩ 'Non valde' inquam[578] 'longum erit eius vitae exitum opperiri, ut de eo suprema censura finiatur[579] qui hactenus tantundem bonae famae meruit quam malae. Nam eum[580] ex paedore diuturni carceris ad letalem tabem adeo consumptum vidi, cum Romam venisset et ab eo perhumaniter disserenti Punicarum rerum notitiam haurirem, ut non diu in armis se posse iactare videatur. Sed dic obsecro, Davale, postquam hucusque sermonem protulisti, n⟨u⟩m alii duces sint in Hispania bellicis operibus insignes.'

192   Tum ille ⟨DAVALUS⟩ 'Complures' inquit 'si ingenia pariter ac studia regulorum ad bellum proclinata potius quam spectata militiae facinora velimus aestimare. Pax enim illa admodum diuturna post Punicum nomen ab Hispania pulsum, innatae gentis virtuti, quin late floreret, plurimum offecit. Enimvero post illud[581] otium tanto labore partum, ilico defuit campus ad serium[582] certamen, in quo[583] praeclarae corporis ac animi vires spectarentur.

193   'Ceterum duo sunt iam plane senes qui in Italia nominis memoriam reliquerunt ab eo tempore quo Magnus ille Consalvus

At this point MUSCETTOLA said, "The prowess of this Navarro, 189
unless I am mistaken, has slackened greatly from its former military glory; and his mind, which used to ponder in its deliberations
great and original ideas, has also grown exceedingly dull. For when
he has attempted to take up arms against men of his own nation,
he has always shown himself to be feckless and unsuccessful and,
so to speak, a 'Gallo-Navarran.'"[301]

Laughing at this, D'AVALOS said: "In the art of war, Muscettola, 190
the final day of life, like that of glory, discloses all; for we observe
that the reputations of captains are judged by their last achievements."

Then I [GIOVIO] added: "The end of his life will not be long 191
awaited, so that the final judgment may be determined concerning
a man who so far has won just as much good as bad repute. For
when he had come to Rome and I was drinking in news of Moorish affairs from him, as he discussed them with great kindness, I
saw that he was so wasted away to the point of mortal illness from
the filth of his long incarceration that it appeared he could not
engage in warfare for long. But d'Avalos, now that you've advanced
the discussion to this point, please say whether there are other
commanders in Spain who are distinguished in military service."

Then D'AVALOS replied: "There are several, if we should wish 192
to consider natural abilities and likewise the devotion of princes to
war, rather than deeds tested on the battlefield. Indeed, after the
Moors had been driven out from Spain, the long-lasting peace that
followed was highly detrimental to a widespread development of
that people's innate abilities.[302] After great effort had brought about
that tranquility, immediately there was no field of action for serious combat in which outstanding strength of body and mind
might be put to the test.

"But there are two men, by now quite elderly, whose good name 193
has lived on in Italian memory since that time when Gonsalvo

Gallos Neapolitano Bello superavit: Ferdinandus scilicet Andrada de Obegnino in Brutiis victor et triumphator, qui etiam praefectus classis Hadrianum Pontificem Romam devexit; et Didacus Mendocius, cuius alacritatem cum laude aliquot in pugnis enituisse cognovimus. Sed longe omnibus excelsi animi virtute et[584] nobilium morum gravitate praestantem audio Indicum[585] Vellascum totius Hispaniae equitum magistrum, et Menricum Amirantem pusillo quidem corpore sed ingenio longe omnium altissimo[586] qui, paribus auspiciis, Gallorum copias, per occasionem tumultuantis Hispaniae ad Iberum usque penetrantes, non longe a Grunio deleverunt. Ceterum si in Italia et in Insubria praesertim bellum sit gerendum, non video quem Antonio Levae parem ponamus. Ingenio etenim[587] plane Punico et militari, sic bellum gerit ac sustinet ut, quamquam Mediolanum et ceterae proximae urbes inhumana eius et[588] nostrorum militum[589] acerbitate sint deletae, non magnopere vel Gallorum vel foederatorum impetum timeamus.

194   'Porro quantum pertinet ad Germanos Georgium Franispergum, qui pluribus quam quisquam[590] alius dux Germanus felicibus proeliis interfuit. Non tam ingenio sollertem sobrium[591] vigilantem esse crediderim, quam intrepidum constantem et strenuum ducem in asperis militiae rebus. Cuius etiam classis atque ordinis putantur Marcus Sithius et Guillermus ⟨. . .⟩[592] Rogandolfius, viri fortissimi, sed qui tamen sua pedestri gloria, atque ea numquam ad summi militaris imperii decus provecta sunt contenti.

195   'Multum enim interest, nisi rerum vocabula confundantur, inter "ducis" et "ductoris" nomen, quando enim innumerabiles prope artes callere et caeleste quoddam acumen ingenii ab astris ducere sit

the Great vanquished the French in the Neapolitan War: there's
Fernão Pires de Andrade,[303] the victor and conqueror of d'Aubigny
in Calabria,[304] who also as admiral of the fleet conveyed Pope Adrian
VI to Rome. Then there is Diego Hurtado de Mendoza,[305] whose
briskness of action, we have learned, shone forth with distinction
in several battles. But I hear that Iñigo de Velasco,[306] master of the
cavalry of all Spain, is far superior to all others in the excellence of
his lofty mind and in the dignity of his noble character. And there
is Juan de Manriquez:[307] granted, he has a puny body, but he possesses an intelligence by far the highest of all. On the occasion of
Spain's being in an uproar, these men, in joint command, annihilated not far from Logrogno the French troops who were penetrating all the way to the Ebro River.[308] But if war must be waged in
Italy, and especially in Insubria, I don't see whom we should put
on a par with Antonio de Leyva:[309] for with a distinctly Moorish
and military brilliance he wages and sustains war in such a way
that, although Milan and other nearby cities have been destroyed
by his bestial harshness and that of our soldiers, we have little fear
of an attack from either the French or the federated troops.

"Next, insofar as the Germans are concerned, there is Georg   194
von Frundsberg,[310] who has taken part in more victories than any
other German commander. I would not think that he is as clever,
temperate, and vigilant in nature as he is intrepid, steady, and vigorous as a commander in the harsh conditions of military service.
Marc Sittich von Hohenems[311] and Wilhelm von Rogendorf,[312]
courageous men, are also thought to be of his class and rank. But
all the same, they have been satisfied with their fame as infantry-
men, a fame that has never risen to the glory of the highest military command.

"If there is not to be a confusion in the words for things, there   195
is a great difference between the category of 'commander' (*dux*)
and that of 'officer in command' (*ductor*), since the man who plays
the role of outstanding captain exceptionally well must have expe-

necesse, qui imperatoris personam egregie sustineat; ductores vero satis sit esse manu promptos, dicto parentes, laboriosos, diligentes, ut fere sunt qui hodie ceteros honoribus antecellunt. Propterea Franciscum Sfortiam superiorem,[593] qui fuit felicis atque divinae virtutis imperator, dicere solitum accepimus: se quidem milites et praefectos, qui optimi essent evasuri, ab ipso statim oris habitu moribusque naturae scire, deligere, illum vero minime qui insignis dux esset futurus. Quoniam illam vim occultam inusitatae virtutis, quae genesim potius quam ipsam corporis temperaturam orisque indolem consequatur, in nemine ab aspectu et lineamentis facile deprehendamus: nam ea tum eminet cum spectata bello facinora crescenti famae et nominis celebritati ianuam aperiunt.

196 'Nec iam plane scio an ipse Odectus F⟨usii⟩ cognomento[594] Lotrechius, qui nuper e Gallia Bosco oppido et Alexandria Ticinoque urbibus manu captis, Antonio Levae nostrisque praesidiis exitium minatur, perfectus imperator sit appellandus. Nam tametsi ex omnibus Galliae proceribus maxime belli gloria multo rerum usu variisque periculis impigre parta sit illustris, bellaque gerat ingenio valde constanti et a⟨n⟩imo vel in adversa fortuna semper invicto, in eo tamen viri militares ad absolutae virtutis opinionem aliqua desiderant quae, nisi adsint, tanta ea claritudo cum felicitate rerum gestarum minime possit esse diuturna.

197 'Ferunt enim eum adeo elato pertinacique animo, quod neminem praeter se de belli summa recte iudicare posse existimet, aliorum ducum consilia despicere, ut cuncta, vel in maximis rerum difficultatibus, ex una tantum sententia sui captus obeunda et

rience in almost innumerable arts, and must draw on, as it were, supernatural keenness of intelligence from the stars; but for an 'officer in command,' it may suffice to be keen in battle, obedient to orders, hardworking, and diligent—as those men typically are who today surpass others in honors. We have heard that Francesco Sforza the Elder, who was a captain of successful and divine excellence, used to say that he could choose at once, based on their face and natural character, which soldiers and officers would turn out to be the best, but not the man who would be an illustrious commander. This is so because in no one do we readily grasp from the expression of the eyes and face the hidden strength of extraordinary excellence that follows one's horoscope rather than accords with one's physical constitution and countenance. That hidden strength reveals itself when deeds proven in war open the door to a rising reputation and renown.

"Then there is Odet de Foix, called 'Lautrec.'[313] Coming from 196 France, after having taken the town of Bosco Marengo and the cities of Alessandria and Pavia by force of arms, he is menacing Antonio de Leyva and our garrisons. But I am not yet quite sure whether he should be called a perfect captain. Of all the leaders of France, he is especially illustrious in the martial glory that is acquired energetically by much campaigning experience and by various dangers, and he wages wars with a very steady temperament and a spirit unconquered even in adverse fortune. But despite all that, army men find wanting in him some things that pertain to a reputation for perfect excellence, without which such great fame accompanied by successful military exploits cannot be long lasting.

"In fact, they say that he is so stubborn and haughty that he 197 despises the counsels of other commanders because he believes that no one except him can judge correctly about the sum total of war. And he is deeply convinced that even in the most difficult situations, all things should be undertaken and carried out on the

peragenda penitus arbitraretur, quasi errare malit propriis innixus pervicacis animi decretis, quam cum ceteris ducibus communicando ac disceptando ad certum prosperumque exitum imminentium negotiorum consultationes explicare. Quod unum maxime vitium in imperatore cum exitiosum[595] ac inexpiabile tum inanis caecaeque superbiae plenum videtur. Quis enim vere sanus et victoriae maxime cupidus imperator, cum facto opus fuerit, a singulis praefectis veteranisque militibus sententias non exquisivit, sensusque suos in dubio consilio aliorum rationibus et placitis minime ponderavit et inflexit? Quod si Lotrechii conatus talem forte exitum habuerint qualem sibi ipse despondet, ii profecto eventus multorum iudicio Fortunae libidini potius quam virtuti prudentiaeque ducis ascribentur.'

198   Ad ea vero MUSETIUS 'Pergat' inquit 'vel ire Neapolim, ut Fata vocant, ipse Lotrechius, ex eventu aut sapientiae aut temeritatis famam habiturus. Tu vero, Davale, nobis ea signa explices obnixe postulamus, quibus ille Franciscus Sfortia exactissimus militiae magister adduci erat solitus, ut oblatos milites statim probaret, ut ad bonam militiae frugem omnino perventuros.'

199   Tu⟨m⟩ DAVALUS 'Peditem' inquit 'eum fore optimum putabat, qui esset procerus robustus lacertosus, par ferendis armorum ponderibus, ut fere sunt gravioris operae opifices et qui spe praedae ab rure ac ipsis aratris evocantur. Equitem autem volebat non ignobilem expeditum acrem elatum, equis et armorum insignibus maxime conspicuum. In universum vero mire placebant ora hominum: torva ferocia sanguineo rubore perfusa, et denique paratam bilem celeremque iracundiam gestu atque oculis prae se ferentia, sed qui

basis of his judgment alone, as if he would rather err in reliance on his own headstrong mind's decisions than engage in consultations with other commanders by communicating and debating so as to achieve an assured and successful outcome of the task at hand. This one vice in a captain appears both destructive and unpardonable, not to mention full of hollow and blind arrogance. For what captain who is really sound and intensely desirous of victory has not sought opinions from every single officer and experienced soldier when it was necessary to do so and has failed to weigh and modify his own judgments in an uncertain decision in light of the reasoning and judgment of others? But if Lautrec's initiatives should perhaps have the kind of outcome that he is promising himself, those results will surely be attributed, in the view of many, to Fortune's caprice rather than to the prowess and prudence of the commander."

To these things, MUSCETTOLA added, "Let Lautrec himself 198 continue on his way to Naples, as the Fates summon him, and from the outcome he will shortly have a reputation either for wisdom or for recklessness. But we insist, d'Avalos, that you explain to us those signs by which Francesco Sforza, a very exacting military commander, had been regularly led to approve of the soldiers placed before him as destined to be militarily useful."

Then D'AVALOS replied, "He thought that that man would be 199 the best foot soldier who was tall, robust, muscular, and equal to bearing the weight of arms (as are, as a rule, workmen whose crafts are physically demanding and those who are lured by the hope of spoils from the fields and the very plows). In contrast, he wanted a cavalryman who was noble, agile, shrewd, proud, and above all distinguished in horsemanship and in military honors. On the whole, the things he found uncommonly pleasing in the faces of men were a grim ferocity, a ruddy complexion, and of course signs visible in their bearing and their eyes of swift anger and a quick temper. But nonetheless, they needed to be calm when

tamen pacati inter socios versarentur, et vehementes[596] illos impetus ad congressus hostium ipsaque proelia reservarent. Squalentes autem tristi quodam pallore vel obesos et segni pituita redundantes reicere erat solitus. Verum illis ab eo militari habitu delectis, prudenti quoddam instituto, praeficiebat senes natura cautos consilio et moribus temperatos, quorum gravi iudicio et tarditate, fervida iuvenum ingenia velut certis habenis recta vel, ut res posceret, incitata calcaribus in aciem ducerentur. Omnium vero pessimos milites dicebat esse lenones et urbanos gladiatores, quoniam in contuberniis inquieti ac seditiosi, in agmine inertes, in acie vero fugaces et timidi esse consuevissent.

200   'Sed ut ad Gallos revertamur: non tam multi hodie in Gallia sunt duces ut paullo ante uberiore quodam proventu exstitisse cognovimus,[597] clade siquidem illa Ticinensi admodum[598] funesta Galliam cunctis fere clarissimis viris orbatam et penitus[599] exhaustam fuisse constat. Nam qui nunc iure optimo conferri poterunt cum[600] Tramulio vetere illo et totiens[601] triumphali imperatore, vel cum Palicia, quem nullae umquam hostium acies terruerunt, vel cum Admirante[602] Bonivetto,[603] qui iam cunctarum gentium bellicas artes et exactam disciplinam didicerat, ut ceteros Gallos omnes anteiret? At quis etiam maiore virtutis indole quam Lescutus Fusius Lotrechii frater in omnibus belli periculis ad summi ducis nomen properavit?[604] Cecidere etenim ii omnes adversis vulneribus et decore quidem ut tum decuit in tanto sui regis periculo, sed

spending time among allies, reserving their violent impulses for encounters with enemies and for the battles themselves. On the other hand, he had been in the habit of rejecting those men who were unkempt and had a certain gloomy pallor or who were fat and oversupplied with sluggish phlegm. But once he had chosen his men for their military physique, he adopted the prudent practice of putting in charge of them elderly men who were cautious by nature and moderate in counsel and character. By their dignified good judgment and deliberate way of proceeding, they would lead these hotblooded young men into battle, keeping them on a tight rein, so to speak, or, as the situation required, driving them on by spurs. He used to say, however, that the worst soldiers of all were pimps and street fighters,[314] because they were regularly restless and quarrelsome with fellow soldiers, sluggish in the midst of battle, and timid and apt to flee from combat.

"But to return to the French: there are not so many command- 200
ers in France today compared to the rich harvest of such men that we witnessed not long ago, since it is clear that by that utterly calamitous Battle of Pavia, France was deprived and entirely depleted of nearly all illustrious men. For who now could justifiably be compared with Louis de la Trémoille,[315] that veteran captain who was so many times triumphant; or with de la Palice,[316] whom no battle lines of enemies ever deterred; or with Bonnivet,[317] the admiral of France, who had already learned the military tactics and the precise training of all peoples in such a way that he surpassed all other Frenchmen? But also there is Thomas de Foix,[318] Lautrec's brother: in all dangers of war, who has moved quickly to the title of top commander with greater natural capacity for prowess than he? And as a matter of fact, all these men fell by blows as they faced the enemy—and indeed, nobly so, as was then fitting, since their king was in great danger—but so help me God, they

medius fidius aliquanto maiore cum laude, si felicius ut[605] in ipsa[606] victoria cadere licuisset.

201 'Igitur secundum Lotrechium Galliae spes omnes sitae sunt in uno[607] Ioanne Stuardo, Albaniae regulo, cuius vim atque iudicium peritiamque multo belli[608] usu quaesitam plerique suspiciunt. Est enim in eo animi robur cum[609] summa perseverantia,[610] promptitudo cum gravitate, impetus sine vecordia. Huic proximi accedunt Claudius Guisiae regulus, Antonii Lotharingiae principis et Ioannis Cardinalis frater, in magnis proeliis atque victoriis domi et foris clarissime versatus, cuius nomen virtutis ac munificentiae causa, cum mercenario milite opus est, cupidissime[611] Germanorum legiones sequuntur (hic est ille non modo summae virtutis sed eximiae pietatis imperator, qui parva manu innumerabilem Germanorum Lutheranae factionis multitudinem in finibus Argentinensium duobus tumultuariis proeliis ad satietatem cecidit); et Ioannes[612] Sancti Pauli regulus, Vandomii procerum Galliae nobilissimi et Ludovici item Cardinalis frater, qui Italicis bellis ab adulescentia plurimum insuevit et in illa luctuosa Ticinensi pugna, cum diu peregregie dimicasset ut erat Borboniae familiae nomine dignum, inter suorum ac hostium cadavera semianimis est repertus.

202 'Verum si licet ab initiis fortissimorum operum aliquid de nascenti eximia virtute coniectari, Ludovicum Valdemontium Guisiae fratrem ad militaris opinionis fastigium celeriter evolaturum arbitramur. Sunt enim in eo iuvene spiritus liberales bellicae laudis ardentissimi[613] et perhumani item mores ex domestica disciplina ad studium armorum egregie conformati, atque ipsa demum heroica proceritas: eo regno digna quod nuper haud obscuro familiae

would have won somewhat greater praise if they had been luckier and had been able to die in an actual victory.

"So next after Lautrec, all the hopes of France have depended 201 solely upon John Stuart, the duke of Albany,[319] whose strength, good judgment, and expertise, acquired by much experience of war, many admire. He has toughness of mind as well as the greatest perseverance, promptitude with dignity, and drive without frenzy. After him come two others: Claude, the duke of Guise,[320] and François,[321] the count of St. Pol. The former, who is the brother of Duke Antoine of Lorraine[322] and of Cardinal Jean de Guise,[323] has taken part with much distinction in great battles and victories at home and abroad. On account of his excellence and generosity, when there is need of mercenaries, the legions of Germans eagerly follow him. He is a captain not only of the greatest prowess but also of exceptional piety who with a small company had his fill of slaughtering a countless hoard of Germans of the Lutheran sect in two makeshift battles in the territory of Strasbourg. François, the count of St. Pol, is the brother of the exceedingly noble Vendôme, one of the leading men of France,[324] and Cardinal Louis de Bourbon.[325] From his youth he had gained experience in the Italian Wars. In that sorrowful Battle of Pavia, after he had fought outstandingly for a long time in a manner worthy of the Bourbon family name, he was found half-alive amid the corpses of his own troops and of the enemy.[326]

"But if we are allowed to infer something about the exceptional 202 virtue that originates from the beginnings of very brave deeds, we think that Louis, count of Vaudémont,[327] who is the Duke of Guise's brother, will quickly soar to a high military reputation. That young man has an honorable, intensely burning eagerness for military praise, a most humane character outstandingly shaped from his upbringing to complement the study of arms, and finally that heroic tallness itself: a thing worthy of that duchy which, induced by the clear claims of his family upon it and with papal

iure inductus favente pontifice, felici ausu, potius apprehendit quam tenuit. Sunt[614] etiam in Memorantio, qui est maximus regiae aulae magister, ingenium militaris gloriae avidum, memoria cum belli notitia singularis, et consilium nequaquam fervidis rationibus definitum. Ipsum porro Philippum Brionium, quem a supremo maris imperio "Magnum Admirantem" vocamus, mire commendant alacritas iudicio virili copulata, promptitudo in armis flagrantissima, splendor mensarum domi prope regius, et eloquentia condita comitate iucundissima. Nec mirum si hic et ille, propter naturae suavitatem et obsequium ab ineunte aetate diuturnum, primum semper dignitatis et gratiae locum apud regem meruerunt.

203   'Ceterum ut ad intermissum sermonem aliquando redeamus.[615] Necesse est ut ingenue fateamur bonos mortuos nobis ipsis omnino fuisse meliores, et neminem ex his quos in albo ducum posuimus, nequaquam ulla industria talem evasurum, ut ex bellica laude aspirare ad Piscarium nostrum possit. In eo enim summa omnia deprehendi, cum sub eius disciplina militarem, et nunc maxime agnosco, cum ad aliorum errata saepius obstupescam. Et quamquam tu, Iovi, eo saepe et in castris et in otio Romae familiariter usus fueris,[616] resque eius bello gestas, et ipsius et aliorum[617] sermonibus exceptas, scripseris admodum fideliter et luculenter; et tu quoque, Museti, totum hominem ab intimis moribus atque consiliis novisse videare, nequaquam tamen putatote[618] praeclarum eius atque divinum ingenium penitus vobis[619] patuisse.

204   'Multas enim in eo varius bellorum successus cum[620] admirabiles tum[621] inexspectatas virtutes aperuit, quas ii tantum intellegebant, qui ipsis gerendarum rerum momentis intererant, in omni

support, he recently seized with successful daring rather than held. Anne de Montmorency,[328] the grand master of the royal court, also has a natural zeal for military glory, a memory unique in its knowledge of warfare, and advice on policy that is quite free of impetuous plans of action. Next, there is Philippe de Chabot[329] himself, whom we call the 'Great Admiral' on account of his supreme command of the sea. His energy coupled with manly judiciousness wonderfully recommend him, as do an intensely burning promptitude in arms, the almost regal splendor of the dinners at his house, and a most delightful eloquence seasoned with courtesy. Nor is it surprising if de Chabot and Montmorency, on account of their charm of character and their allegiance, which has been constant from an early age, have always merited the first place of dignity and prestige in the king's court.

"But to return at last to the interrupted topic: we must candidly   203
admit that the good men who have died were entirely better than we ourselves are, and that no man out of those whom we have recorded in our register of commanders, no matter how hard he works at it, will by any means turn out to be so great that he can rival our Pescara in military prowess. Indeed, when I was fighting under his command, I recognized in him all the supreme qualities of discernment — and especially now I recognize them, since quite often I am dumbfounded by the mistakes of others. You, Giovio, often enjoyed his friendship both in camp and in peacetime at Rome, and have written up his martial exploits quite faithfully and brilliantly, taken down from his own conversation and that of others. And you, too, Muscettola, might seem to know the whole man with respect to his innermost character and plans. But do not either of you fancy that his splendid and godlike nature was completely accessible to you!

"In fact, varying success revealed in him many virtues both ad-   204
mirable and unexpected. Only those who were present at those critical moments of action recognized these things, since in every

siquidem difficili periculosoque negotio, semper in eo vigebat stabilis iudicii mira conservatio; in praesentiendis vero hostium consiliis rerumque omnium eventis, divinatio singularis. Tantam ei
apud milites auctoritatem pepererant, ut nemo iam quaereret quo
duceretur, si quod nocturnum facinus sublatis repente signis patrandum esse censuisset, quoniam[622] ad certam praedam explora-
tamque[623] victoriam duci viderentur.

205   ʽEnimvero magna saepe pericula adierat in oculis exercitus et,
cum subiti casus poscerent, gregariis immixtus non ad dubiam
saepe mortem cum hoste concurrerat: animus namque ille tot virtutum praesidio munitus et cupido gloriae immoderata omnis eum
periculi contemptorem vel reclamantibus nobis effecerant; qua
praecipua laude[624] auctoritatem certam parari[625] diximus: nam
nemo tam ignavus est miles qui fortia et aspera[626] audentem ducem non sequatur. Nec ex adverso[627] quisquam[628] est adeo[629] strenuus et alacer, qui parum pugnaci et cauto ad alienam aleam fortia
imperanti parendum putet. Ad exemplum enim ducis quisque est
egregius probri aut decoris mortisque[630] pariter et salutis aestimator. Propterea dicere[631] erat solitus Alexandrum Macedonem et
Caesarem dictatorem, quos ante alios omnes admirabatur, cum
corpora sua ex occasione ingentibus periculis opposuissent, non
modo sibi devicto orbe peperisse incredibiles victorias sed, quod
posteris eorum etiam profuit, milites singulari institutione prorsus
insuperabiles reddidisse, quandoquidem mutuis exemplis egregiae
fortitudinis et milites ducem, et dux ipse milites nobilitarent atque
perficerent.[632]

difficult and dangerous situation he maintained a remarkable abundance of steady judgment, and he had an unparalleled foresight in divining enemies' stratagems and the outcomes of events. These things yielded him such great authority among the soldiers that no one any longer inquired where he was being led if Pescara decided that some deed must be done at night, with camp quickly struck, since they thought they were being led toward sure plunder and certain victory.

"Moreover, he had often met great dangers within the sight of 205 the army and, when unexpected contingencies demanded, having joined in with the common soldiers, he had clashed with the enemy, often at significant risk to his life: for in fact that spirit, strengthened by the support of so many virtues and by a limitless desire for glory, made him a despiser of every danger, though we tried to dissuade him. We have said that secure authority is acquired by this particular excellence: for no soldier is so cowardly that he fails to follow a commander who dares to undertake actions that are courageous and arduous. Nor, conversely, is there anyone so vigorous and energetic that he thinks he has to obey someone who is himself unwarlike and cautious when he is ordering brave action to be undertaken at another's risk. If his commander is taken as an example, each man is an exceptional evaluator of the shameful and the honorable, and likewise of death and personal safety. Thus, Pescara had been in the habit of citing the examples of Alexander the Great and Julius Caesar, whom he admired beyond all other commanders. Once they had exposed their own persons to massive dangers at key moments, not only had they acquired incredible victories for themselves in conquering the world, they had also accomplished something that has benefited their descendants: they made their troops completely invincible by their unique training; by being examples of outstanding bravery to each other, the soldiers ennobled and perfected the commander and vice versa.

206 'Sed non tantum[633] in iusto proelio et in ipsis minutorum certa-
minum congressibus vitae pericula cum ignobili milite libenter
adaequabat, verum etiam, cum ab imminente numeroso hoste receptus necessitas imponeretur, tanta enim constantia, tanta alacritate, atque peritia ordinatim agmina praemittebat, ut novissimus
ipse in postremis curaret; neque tum in equo pernici sed in stri-
gosa mula vel ignobili cantherio[634] conspiceretur. Quo suis metum
demeret et hostibus, ut omni timore vacuus, fiduciam ostentaret,
sic ut nullus umquam saucius aut aeger miles, nullum umquam
tormentum, vel militis impedimentum maturandi aviditate relinqueretur. Incredibilis enim labor et magna semper fuit in his casibus difficultas, et certe periculum prope par consertae pugnae
abeuntibus proponitur (nam neque opportunius neque facilius
fundi potest exercitus quam cum terga dat et discessu festinato
salutem quaerit) quando ad dignitatem ducis et totius exercitus
omnino pertineat egregie praestitisse, ne quid fugae simile iter habere videatur. Referebat enim se multo ampliorem gloriam aequabili militiae peritorum iudicio fuisse consecutum, cum ab Ollii
fluminis ripis, urgente Lotrechio, extra tormentorum insidias
castra reduxit et a Massilia raptato exercitu per asperas cautes in
Italiam contra Gallos est reversus, quam cum, postea Mediolanum
cum una peditum centuria fugatis hostibus cepit, vel cum Ticini
captis regibus tanta felicitate dimicavit. Quamquam ego, si aetatem spectes, multo nobilius prudentiae bellicae facinus putem quo
ipse, plane adulescens, apud Lendenariam sese e manibus explicuit
Liviani ducis acerrimi, cum ille Rodigii deleto Hispanorum

"But Pescara not only gladly shared equally with his lowly   206
troops the mortal dangers of pitched battle and of minor skir-
mishes, but also, when he had to retreat from a threatening enemy
that was superior in numbers, he used to send the troops on in
advance in orderly formation—and he did so with such great self-
possession, briskness, and skill that he himself, last of all, took
charge in the rearguard. Nor then was he spotted on a swift horse,
but instead on a scrawny mule or a disreputable hack. By this device he relieved his men from fear, and by his own complete lack
of anxiety he displayed his confidence to the enemy, so much so
that no wounded or sick soldier, no artillery piece or soldier's bag-
gage was ever left behind on account of eagerness for making
haste. These occasions always involved incredible exertion and
great difficulty, since it is important for the esteem of a commander and of the entire army that their march seem to bear no
resemblance to flight. (And certainly those retreating are threatened with a danger almost equal to that of a joined battle, as an
army cannot be put to rout more expeditiously or easily than
when it takes flight and seeks safety by a hasty departure.) Indeed,
Pescara used to say that he had acquired far greater glory in the
fair judgment of those expert in warfare when, under pressure
from Lautrec, he removed his encampment from the shores of the
Oglio River, beyond the range of the artillery—and when, after
hurrying his army away from Marseille, he returned into Italy over
harsh crags to face the French—than he acquired afterward when
he captured Milan with one century of infantry after the enemy
troops had been put to flight, or when he fought with such great
success at Pavia after the members of the royal family[330] had been
captured. Admittedly, if you take age into account, I might reckon
as far nobler that deed of martial prudence by which he himself as
quite a young man escaped the clutches of the keen commander
d'Alviano at Lendinara, when, after the Spanish cavalry had been

equitatu, incredibili celeritate ad eum opprimendum frustra convolasset.

207   'Sed quid ego fortia eius facinora singillatim enumero, cum nullus in tota superiore Italia sit locus in quo ipse virtutis egregiae monumentum non reliquerit, nulla res fortiter sit gesta, quae aut consilio eius excogitata, aut manu confecta non fuerit. Nam tametsi plerumque titulus ac imago militaris imperii penes eos esse videretur, qui aut aetatis honore aut regum insigni gratia ceteros anteirent, ipse unus tamen consilio manuque, iura atque auspicia summi ducis exercebat.

208   'Constat enim ad Vincentiam, cum Cardonius itineri intentus, in receptu legiones antecederet, a Piscario in novissima acie conversis signis esse dimicatum; et sine vulnere eam[635] partam esse victoriam, quae mox omnium animos admiratione terroreque complevit. Ad Bicocam certe, paene prius Helvetiorum agmina prostravit quam, in tam repentino et diverso hostium adventu, praeclarus alter imperator quid facto opus esset expedite praeciperet; prius Laudem Pompeiam admotis repente scalis, territis ac oppressis Gallis hostibus cepit quam eum ceteri duces, qui in tergo erant, in conspectum urbis pervenisse existimarent. Tum vero Genuam inter primos per strata hostium cadavera armatus ingressus est, cum ceteri maiores duces, cum miseris et iam captis civibus, in diversa murorum parte de condicionibus agitarent.

209   'Ceterum numquam[636] adeo afflictae res aut spes perditae fuerunt in repentinis adversorum casuum momentis, quin ipse, ceteris fere omnibus mente perculsis et haesitantibus, celeritate consilii opportuna subsidia minime reperiret. Nullus umquam tam vehemens et inopinatus hostium incursus ita eum exterruit, ut vel

destroyed at Rovigo, d'Alviano had with incredible swiftness swooped down to crush him—in vain.

"But why do I count up his brave deeds one by one, when in all 207 northern Italy there is no place in which he himself has not left behind a reminder of his outstanding prowess? There is no brave exploit which has not been either contrived by his planning or accomplished by his hand. For even if for the most part the title and image of military command were to appear to belong to those who surpassed others either in the respect given to age or in the singular gratitude of kings, still, this one man himself was exercising in thought and deed the prerogatives and authority of the best commander.

"Indeed, it is well known that at Vicenza, when de Cardona, 208 intent on the march, was leading the legions in retreat, Pescara, having turned his troops around in a new battle line, engaged the enemy.[331] And without any wound, he brought about that victory, which soon filled the minds of all with admiration and terror.[332] At Bicocca at any rate, amid the sudden and varied arrival of enemy troops, he laid low the battle lines of the Swiss almost before the other famous captain[333] could give the orders for the necessary countermeasures. By rapidly moving up the scaling ladders, he captured Lodi from the terrified and overwhelmed French enemy before the other commanders, who were toward the rear, thought he had come into view of the city. Then again, in heavy armor, he was among the first to enter Genoa through the midst of the enemies' strewn corpses when the other senior commanders, in a different section of the walls, were treating for peace with the miserable citizens who were already captured.

"But never were the circumstances so dire or hopes so dashed in 209 sudden crises but that he himself did not find timely resources through quick planning, even as nearly all the others had been beaten down in spirit and were at a loss. No enemy attack was ever so violent and unexpected that it terrified him in such a way that

puncto temporis vim illam expeditae rationis eriperet, cum alii nonnulli summae opinionis duces ad improvisa pericula adeo mente oculisque rigerent, ut vitalia ex pavore deficere viderentur. Ex hac disciplina, nimirum, evasere tot acerrimi centuriones atque signiferi, quorum terga nulli hostes umquam viderunt. Neminem enim ex iis, quos amici vel necessarii duces producerent vel a principibus essent commendati, cohortibus praeficere erat solitus, nisi ipse eos acriter pugnantes aliquando conspexisset.

210 'Hos etiam regia prope liberalitate et, ob id, ad grave dispensatoris supercilium, sic speciariis donis honestabat, ut ceteros ab occulto livore etiam accenderet. Quibus cum se praeclare foenerari sine crimine praedicabat, quando eorum virtute urbes et castra hostium capere consuevisset, unde omnes ex opima praeda ditarentur. Erat obiter alienae virtutis et infimorum etiam militum laudator eximius; suae autem vel in epistolis, quas ad caesarem perscribebat, valde parcissimus. Tanto itaque studio attollendos ornandosque vel gregarios milites arbitrabatur, ut neminem in castris satis nobilem esse putaret, nisi qui saepius militaribus factis inclaruisset.

211 'Unde saepenumero Franciscum Gallorum regem magnopere commendabat quod, in illo ancipiti et maxime cruento proelio quo Helvetiorum ferociam contudit, a nullo alio potius quam a Baiardo equestri dignitate donari voluisset, quamquam totius Galliae proceres essent in conspectu tale munus ex dignitate sibi omnino deberi existimantes. Illum enim omnium longe dignissimum putavit, a quo, ipse tantus eques, virtutis ergo militariter ornaretur, quem

it took away even for an instant that strength of nimble reasoning—even though some other commanders of the highest reputation were so paralyzed in mind and eyes in the face of sudden dangers that their vital organs seemed to fail out of panic. From his training emerged many very brave centurions and standard-bearers, whose backs in flight no enemy ever saw. His practice was to place in command of cohorts none of those men whom either his friends or closely affiliated commanders were promoting, or whom princes had recommended, unless at some time or another he himself witnessed them fighting vigorously.

"Also, with almost regal generosity—and on that account to the great disgust of his paymaster—he honored his men with special bonuses so as to incite others, who were inwardly jealous, to similar action. He used to say that they yielded a splendid and blameless return, since by their prowess he had been wont to capture the enemies' cities and camps; hence they were all getting rich out of the plentiful spoils. He was at the same time exceptional in praising the prowess of others, even the humblest soldiers. But in the detailed dispatches which he wrote to the emperor, he was parsimonious in praising his own prowess. So zealously did he reckon that even ordinary soldiers should be praised and honored that he thought no man in camp had been sufficiently celebrated unless he had often been recognized for his military accomplishments. 210

"On many occasions, accordingly, Pescara commended Francis I, because in that extremely gory Battle of Marignano, where the outcome hung in the balance, in which he crushed the fighting spirit of the Swiss, the king had wished that knighthood be conferred upon himself by the Chevalier de Bayard[334] alone—in spite of the fact that the leading men of all France were present and believed that such an assignment was owed to themselves on grounds of rank. King Francis thought Bayard by far the worthiest of men, a man by whom he—himself a great knight—might be decorated 211

in media hostium phalange fortissime dimicantem fuisset admiratus. Et certe Baiardo ipsi multo speciosius atque nobilius fuit Francisco super regii fastigii maiestatem equestria insignia cruento gladio contulisse, quam si eum amplissimae tot procerum et ducum fortunae tum opibus mediocrem amplissimi regis liberalitas adaequasset.'

212   Haec cum diceret,[637] ego et Musetius ita quae dicta laudavimus[638] ut eum etiam[639] certatim atque enixe precaremur, ut coeptum nobis imperatorem cunctis militiae numeris absolutum perficere, et de Piscario enumeratis castrensis vitae laudibus iudicium suum proferre vellet; nam nobis vehemens desiderium incesserat ea de Piscario audiendi, quae ipse paucis admodum comperta esse dixisset. Et profecto intellegebamus neminem praeter eum vel fidelius vel[640] uberius esse dicturum, quoniam per sex annos continuatis semper bellis numquam ab eius praetorio discessisset.

213   Itaque ad ea inquit DAVALUS 'Obtemperabo aliqua ex parte postulatis vestris, nam sine pudore sineque ullo adulationis convicio ingenue possum proferre, quae de Piscario audire concupitis; constanti namque omnium opinione tot partis ingentibus victoriis aequalium suorum militiae palmam tulit, tantumque abest ut ampliora veris de hoc homine[641] praedicentur, ut ex infinitis prope virtutibus clariores quasdam sim relicturus, quae alio tempore proferentur, si Iovius vitam eius litterarum memoriae mandare voluerit.

214   'Sanguine enim mihi patruelis, amore vero germanus, et in tradenda disciplina idem et benignus parens et accuratissimus magister fuit, ita ut eius invicti viri simulacrum numquam sine lacrimis

for military valor. He had admired Bayard when the latter had fought bravely in the midst of the enemy line. And certainly it was far more prestigious for Bayard himself that, with a blood-drenched sword, he had bestowed knightly insignia upon Francis to add to the majesty of his regal rank than if the liberality of an exceedingly great king had placed him, then middling in means, at the same elevated level of fortune as so many leading men and commanders."

When d'Avalos had said this, Muscettola and I praised his 212 words and competed strenuously with each other in our request that he be willing to put the finishing touches to the description he had begun of the perfect captain for all aspects of military affairs, as well as to express his own opinion about Pescara, now that the exploits of his military career had been detailed. For we were smitten by a strong desire to hear about Pescara the things which d'Avalos himself had said were known to exceedingly few men. And certainly we understood that no man would speak either more faithfully or more fully than d'Avalos, since over the course of six years of continuous warfare he had never departed from Pescara's headquarters.

To this, then, D'AVALOS replied: "I will comply to some extent 213 with your requests, because unashamedly and without incurring any reproach for flattery, I can tell you candidly the things that you are eager to hear about Pescara. For in fact, in the consistent opinion of all, once he had acquired so many massive victories, he won the prize for military prowess among his contemporaries. I am so far removed from embroidering the facts about this man that, out of his nearly infinite virtues, I shall leave out certain illustrious ones which may be set out at another time, if Giovio should be willing to write his biography.[335]

"By blood he was my cousin, but in actual affection he was a 214 brother; and in passing on his military training, he was at the same time both a kindhearted parent and a very meticulous teacher, so that I never recall the likeness of that invincible man

ad memoriam revocem, quod profecto tale oculis offertur meis, quale illius fuit, cum novissimam instrueret aciem et, me primas cohortes educentem,[642] pro laude ad subeunda asperi Martis pericula gravi laetoque sermone et flagrantibus oculis hortaretur. Is enim vir, et tum et alias semper cum induta galea districtoque gladio illum militarem ductum oris et rubentem barbam igneosque oculos contorqueret, nemo erat qui se illi parem certamine singulari arbitraretur. Habilem namque corporis staturam, non suco effluido,[643] sed valido nervorum nexu, firmissimam insuefecerat pedestribus cunctis et equestribus disciplinis. Nam omnis exercitatio et agitatio vitae, cum primum incedere et loqui coepit, in militaribus studiis semper fuit, ita ut saepe tacito quodam pudore subrideam, cum me et strenuum et armorum appellant peritissimum, qui profecto, si illi comparer, omnino desidiosissimus videar.

215   'Tanta vero gravitas in vultu, quem susceptae cicatrices militariter honestabant; tantum pondus in verbis atque sententiis, cum nihil vel in iocis non consideratum exiret ex ore; tanta denique, cum vellet, facundia inerat, ut si in consilio disceptaret, quod ipse iudicasset,[644] id ut optimum ab omnibus probaretur. Si vero seditiosus exercitus foret alloquendus, nemo iam erat qui dubitaret quin omnium animos mitigatos, et rursus inflammatos quo vellet, esset impulsurus. Saepe fremitum exortae seditionis inopinato audacique accursu protinus restinxit;[645] saepe consternatos ad arma atque irate merita stipendia flagitantes oratione pacavit atque permulsit. Sed ea die maxime[646] divinus et felix fuit, cum Laudi Pompeiae[647] adversus Gallorum regem moturus castra, equites pariter et pedites dicto nequaquam audientes severissime castigavit; nam adeo praeclare contumaces animos flexit, ut ab tota concione

without tears: it presents itself to my eyes as it was when he drew up his final line of battle: with a grave and joyful speech and with glowing eyes he would exhort me, as I was leading out the first cohorts, to undertake the dangers of harsh Mars for the sake of glory. Both then and always at other times, when, with helmet donned and sword drawn, he turned his soldierly countenance, red beard, and fiery eyes this way and that, there was no one who thought himself an equal to him in one-on-one combat. For in fact he had habituated his strong body, of appropriate height, which was characterized by no flab but a strong interlacing of muscles, to all infantry and cavalry training. As soon as he began to walk and to talk, his every exercise and activity of life consisted in military studies. Often I smile with a certain silent bashfulness when people call me both vigorous and highly skilled at arms, since if I should be compared to him, I would really seem utterly sluggish.

"Moreover, he possessed such great dignity in his face, which 215 was adorned in military mode by battle scars; such great weightiness in his words and thoughts, since nothing escaped from his mouth, even in jest, that was not well considered; and finally, he possessed, when he wanted it, such great eloquence that if he were arguing in council for what he himself had decided upon, it would be approved by all as the best course. If a mutinous army needed to be addressed, there was no one who would doubt that he would soften the hearts of all and then enflame them and make them do what he wanted. Often by an unforeseen and bold attack he instantly quelled mutterings of sedition that had arisen; and often with his words he pacified and soothed those who had been stirred to revolt and were angrily demanding their earned pay. But he was especially godlike and successful on that day when, at Lodi, as he was about to advance camp against the French king, he severely upbraided the cavalrymen and foot soldiers who were disobeying orders. He moved their defiant minds so excellently that he drew

lacrimas exciverit,[648] et eos haud dubia spe ingentis victoriae conci-
tatos, extemplo sequi signa compulerit.

216   'Sed incredibile est, cum belli tempore semper esset a voluptatum blanditiis incorruptus, quanta patientia assiduitate vigilantia
fortitudine[649] cuncta militiae munera obiret, ut non mirum sit
quod numquam vel tenuissimae valetudini parcendum putaret. Si
mors immatura medium vitae cursum, velut consummatis summae[650] gloriae atque virtutis operibus, interrupit, plurimum tamen
Fortunam, quae ei bellicis in rebus semper favit, meritis eius invi-
disse videmus: nam spes tantis rationibus conceptas apud caesarem elusit, et cum egregio imperatori nihil praeter laudem, neque
ex hostibus neque ex sociis, reportandum esse existimaret. Post
tantas victorias me laborum potius quam divitiarum, difficili im-
plicitum bello et multo etiam cum aere alieno reliquit heredem.'

217   Haec cum diceret, exsurrexit, iam enim nos ad reditum hortabatur Quintius insulae praetor; quem collectis fulicis cumbas in
mare reduxisse, et praeter balnea equos etiam deduci iusisse videbamus. Itaque terrestri itinere rediimus, ut feminas comitaremur:
nam eae, ut sunt admodum delicatae, cum ex levi etiam iactatione
maritima nauseam subversionesque timerent, equis vehi quam na-
vigare maluerant. Nec multo post, ingressi arcem, praedam omnem detulimus ad Victoriam Columnam, quod ea sibi indicto
perpetuo luctu propter ingens desiderium clarissimi coniugis, non
modo publica abstinebat luce, sed atratis conclusa cubiculis nihil
ad afflictum dolore[651] animum praeter graves lectiones aut sanctis-
simos sermones admittebat.

tears from the entire assembly, and immediately he spurred them on to follow the banners, galvanized by the sure expectation of a massive victory.

"But even though in time of war he had always been uncor- 216 rupted by the allurements of pleasures, it is incredible with how much patience, persistence, vigilance, and fortitude he undertook all military duties, so it is not surprising that he never thought he needed to go easy on his very feeble health. If premature death cut short his life in midcourse, as if his feats of exceeding glory and prowess were complete, we see that Fortune, who always favored him in military matters, nonetheless intensely envied his merits. For she foiled the hopes that with such good reason he had placed in the emperor, since she judged that the outstanding captain must bring back, whether from his enemies or from his allies, nothing except praise.[336] After such great victories, he has left me as the heir to labors rather than to riches, as I am enmeshed in an unwieldy war and also in a great deal of debt."

When d'Avalos had said these things, he got to his feet, for al- 217 ready Quinzio,[337] the chief magistrate of the island, was urging us to return. We saw that, after the waterfowl had been gathered up, he had returned the skiffs to the sea and had ordered that the horses be led over next to the baths. And so we made our return by a path on land in order that we might escort the ladies: for as they are very delicate, since they feared nausea and capsizing from even a slight disturbance of the sea, they had preferred to be conveyed by horse rather than by boat. And soon thereafter, once we had entered the fortress, we offered the entire catch to Vittoria Colonna—because she, having imposed constant mourning upon herself owing to her grief at the loss of her illustrious husband, was not only keeping herself from the public light but, enclosed in darkened bedchambers, allowed nothing into her grief-stricken mind except for solemn readings and holy sermons.

⟨DIALOGUS SECUNDUS⟩[1]

1 ⟨IOVIVS⟩'. . . omnibus capitalis odii telis armatus aperte persequitur, quae est liberi et efficacis animi clarissima laus, et hac maxime[2]
tempestate, in qua nihil incertius, nihil insidiosius hominum voluntatibus experimur.[3] Colui ego eum semper, dum pontifici plane
hostis non fuit, quod liberali[4] ac excelso animo ingeniis faveret,
quod clientium defensor esset acerrimus, quod ad res bello paceque gerendas natus esse videretur, quod denique, commutata voluntate, illis turbulentissimis comitiis erga Iulium Medicem supre-
mae eius dignitatis praeclarus auctor exstitisset, et nunc maxime
ad officium sit reversus, adeo ut pontifex in tanta calamitate luc-
tuosissimisque temporibus eum aliquanto amiciorem quam in felici fortuna atrocem hostem invenerit. Et dii faxint ut qui priora ac
summa beneficia maximis iniuriis nuper evertit et exstinxit, ea demum qua pollet apud barbaros auctoritate cuncta restituat. Audivimus enim eum, postquam tam lugubri nostro eventu et partium
libidini et odiorum insaniae satis indulserit, in arcem venisse ad
genuaque sordidati pontificis provolutum multas et dignas Romano cive et Christiano cardinale lacrimas effudisse, eoque animo
discessisse a complexu ut et vehemens studium et singularem operam in maturanda ipsius pontificis ac senatus libertate praesta-
turus esse videatur.

2 'De quibusdam aliis autem cardinalibus, qui procul ab urbe nihil harum calamitatum privatim senserunt, nihil attinet dicere,

DIALOGUE TWO

[GIOVIO:][1] ". . . [upon whom], armed with all the arrows of mortal enmity, he [Pompeo Colonna] seeks vengeance openly, a splendid source of glory for an independent and capable mind, especially at this time when we're finding out that nothing is more doubtful, nothing more treacherous than men's loyalties. As long as he wasn't plainly the pope's enemy, I cultivated him, because he supported men of literary talent with a generous and lofty spirit; because he was thought a most vigilant defender of his adherents; because he appeared to be a born leader in war and in peace; and lastly because, in those tumultuous days of the conclave, he'd changed his mind and become a conspicuous proponent of getting Giulio de' Medici elected to that supreme position. I'm especially well disposed toward him now because he's returned to the service of the pope, who has found him more a friend in these calamitous, grief-stricken times than he was a fierce enemy when the pope was enjoying good fortune. Recently, by exceptionally lawless actions, he subverted and nullified the privileges he'd previously had. But may heaven bring it about that in the end he will recover them all by the influence he enjoys among the barbarians. In fact, we've heard that amid our lamentable misfortune, after he'd sufficiently indulged his partisans' wantonness and their hateful madness, he came into the Castel Sant' Angelo and, having fallen prostrate before the pope, who'd been desecrated, he wept copiously—as befitted a Roman citizen and Christian cardinal—and he left the pope's embrace prepared to display intense zeal and special effort in hastening his liberation and that of the cardinals.

"It is not fitting, however, to speak about certain other cardinals far from Rome who personally experienced nothing of these calamities, since the late hour of the day admonishes us to return to

quoniam serum diei nos admonet ut ad bonos et studiosos redeamus. Sed aliquos vel ob id diis maxime probatos esse existimetis
velim, quod multum antea tantis ereptis malis perbeato in otio et
caesaris voluntatis respectum et Gallici belli exitum exspectant.'

3   Tum vero DAVALUS 'Quam strenuum,' inquit, 'et quam studio-
sum etiam defensorem ac laudatorem cardinales habent ipsorum
existimationis ac dignitatis! Et quo etiam et quam singulari temperamento usus es, Iovi, qui sic a veris laudibus singulos extulisti
ut neminem omnino laeseris, adeo ut ipse Armellinus, quem ab
omnibus pessime audire credebamus, non iam omnium deterrimus
sed nobis plane probabilis sacerdos esse videatur.

4   'Sed tu, Museti, prosequere intermissum antea sermonem et de
reliquis insignibus viris edissere, qui cum exiguo vel nullo quaestu
sed multo maxima cum laude humanioribus studiis delectantur; ii
namque, ut opinor, certius et honestius ad immortalitatem contendunt, et ipsi praesertim poetae ante alios, quos famam nobilitate
carminum illustrem et maxime diuturnam ab infinitis prope saeculis produxisse videmus, secus ac nonnullos reges armis imperio atque fortuna potentissimos qui, perbrevi temporis curriculo ab-
sumpti, vix nomen posteris reliquerint.'

5   Ad id MUSETIUS 'Obtemperabo et quidem perlibenter, nam
mihi antea hanc materiam sermonis ut peramoenam cogitatione
praesumpseram. Utar autem ea distinguendi ratione ut, cum nobiliores in hoc genere studiorum ab aliis segregentur, poetae primum
obtineant locum, quod ipso naturae habitu prope divino absque
ullis fere studiorum auxiliis ea canant quae doctissimi saepe viri
vehementer admirentur. Et certe aliquanto facilius esse putamus
magnum et sibi omni ex parte constantem oratorem quam absolutum et dignum insigni gloria poetam evasisse; nam plerosque assidua imitatione pertinacique industria stilo pedestri valere arbitror,

the good and studious men. But I wish that you would regard
some of them to be especially favored by heaven, at least on this
account: that since their great troubles had been taken away long
ago, in blessed leisure they are awaiting the consideration of the
emperor's favor and the end of the war with France."

Then D'AVALOS said, "How energetic and zealous an advocate   3
the cardinals have for their reputation and dignity! And also, what
singular restraint you've exercised, Giovio. You've extolled individuals with authentic praises in such a way that you've offended nobody. We used to believe everybody thought very ill of Cardinal
Armellini; now, it appears to us that he's no longer the worst of all,
but plainly is even a commendable priest.[2]

"But you, Muscettola: continue the discussion that was broken   4
off earlier, and describe in detail the other noteworthy men who,
with little or no financial profit but with much the greatest honor,
delight in the liberal arts, for they, I believe, strive more surely and
more nobly for immortality. This is especially true of poets who,
by the quality of their verse, have enjoyed an illustrious and enduring reputation, stretching back for almost countless centuries —
quite differently from some kings, who, despite the greatness of
their military exploits, temporal power, and fortune, disappeared
in a very short time and left barely their name to posterity."

To this MUSCETTOLA said, "I shall comply, and most gladly,   5
for I'd already thought of this topic of conversation as a very pleasant one for me. But I'll organize the discussion in such a way that
when the nobler sorts of studies are set apart from others, poets
may have primacy, since by an almost divine nature and with virtually no assistance from study, they sing of things which the most
learned men often passionately admire. And certainly I reckon
that it's somewhat easier to be a great and thoroughly steadfast
orator than to become a poet who attains perfection and is worthy
of great fame. I think that while most, through careful imitation and tenacious effort, manage to achieve a plain prose style,

cum excellentissimi poetae rari admodum appareant et vix singulos
illustres singulae aetates protulisse videantur, siquidem soluta oratione scribentem, etiamsi id non summa fiat eloquentia, sua tamen
et ea quasi certissima sequitur laus; mediocribus autem poetis neque honorem vivis neque vitam eorum carminibus vel dii vel homines umquam concesserunt, quando nulla nisi summis vatibus
sit gratia nullaque praeclara auctoritas nisi iis qui sublimius evecti
sanos a scribendo carmine deterruerunt, quamquam eos non omnino vituperem qui malint in secundis et tertiis theatri gradibus
considere quam genium fraudare suis flammis suoque naturali
impetu et ea demum spe tota quae, concepta fervidius, valida ingenia numquam destituit.

6   'Sed tantum abest ut quempiam a studio carminum propter
summas difficultates laudis assequendae deterrere velimus, ut insulsis etiam poematibus plurimum oblectemur, ab insulso enim
poeta singularis cum[5] suavissimo risu voluptas exprimitur. Quis
enim est vel a natura vel a curis tam tristis qui effuse non rideat
cum Latina Cantalicii et[6] vernacula Cassii gemmati poemata evol-
vit? Sed nec eos etiam e[7] collegio poetarum exturbaverim qui erudite et facetissime sciunt ineptire; video enim Leonicum, tantae
gravitatis philosophum, aliquanto latius sui[8] nominis famam ex-
tendisse cum iuvenis fortunam miseram cecinisset.[9]

7   'Verum ut ab insulsis ad sapidissimos poetas veniamus, duplex
eorum est ordo et uterque admodum numerosus, Etruscorum
scilicet et Latinorum; sed Latini utrumque munus plerumque
feliciter absolvunt, cum ipsi saepe vernaculi sine litteris cultioribus
ab ingenii acuitate commendationem accipiant. Horum sicut[10]
plures simul pari gratia de loco summo certare conspicimus, ita illorum Bembus facile princeps evadit. Is, nobili fretus ingenio et

extraordinary poets appear very rarely: it seems that each era has produced scarcely one illustrious poet apiece. Praise comes in due course to a writer of prose. Even if what he writes is not of the highest eloquence, nonetheless that praise is his own, and it is almost guaranteed. But neither heaven nor earth has ever allowed honor to poets of average quality during their lifetimes or immortality to their writings, since no favor is shown but to the best poets, and no outstanding recognition is accorded except to those who by their sublime achievements have deterred sensible men from writing verse. To be sure, I wouldn't fault those who would rather sit in the second or third tier of the theater than cheat inspiration of its passion, natural vigor, and indeed of that entire hope which, fostered with greater intensity, never forsakes powerful talents.

"But far be it from me to deter someone from writing poetry on 6 account of the immense difficulty of obtaining praise, for we may derive the greatest delight even from insipid poems. In fact, an inept poet elicits singular pleasure along with very sweet laughter. Indeed, who is so depressed either by nature or by worries that he doesn't laugh uproariously when he reads the Latin verse of Cantalicio[3] and the vernacular poetry of the bejeweled Girolamo Casio de' Medici?[4] Nor would I drive out of the society of poets those who know how to play the fool with learning and great wit. For I see that Leonico,[5] a philosopher of high seriousness, somewhat broadened his appeal after he composed as a young man his poem on ill fortune.

"But to pass from the insipid poets to the choicest, there are 7 two groups of them, each very numerous: the 'Tuscans' and the Latins. The Latin poets generally achieve success in both fields, whereas the vernacular writers, lacking knowledge of good letters, often receive praise just for their keen natural talent. Just as we observe that a number of the latter enjoy equal popularity and vie with one another for the top position, so Bembo[6] easily emerges at

multis reconditis instructus disciplinis, ut veteranus et ambidexter utroque stilo feliciter pugnat, adeo ut in eadem harena cum Syncero Actio[11] certamen non detrectet, quem tamen sibi sicut aetate, ita etiam heroico carmine superiorem esse liberali quodam pudore profitetur. In hoc enim Latino poemate quod *De partu Virginis deiparae* nuper est editum, nihil castius, nihil splendidius, nihil denique divinius esse potest. *Piscatoriae* vero et peramoena tituli novitate et varietate maritimarum rerum et suavitate carminum adeo sunt admirabiles ut multorum iudicio nullis vel antiquorum operibus cedant. Quamobrem si gravia religiosius spectes et lusus teneros cum[12] Latina cum vernacula lingua conscriptos benigne legas totiusque vitae munditias contempleris, necesse est ut Actium vere Syncerum et excelsum et prorsus equestris ordinis poetam esse fateare.

8   'Porro Bembus, qui accurata exercitatione ad bene sanum ac vividum pedestris eloquentiae habitum pervenerat, ad Etrusca ingenium deflexit cum certam ac summam ab his studiis dignitatem petere quam a Latinis dubio eventu speratam gloriam consectari mallet. Nam certe hac perpetua laude florebit, quod nimiam scribentium licentiam peregrinamque luxuriem publicato ad Etruscae veteris eloquentiae normam exactissimo opere castigarit. Spero tamen eum prudenti iudicio ad dialogos Latinos, quos iam pridem scribere coepit in honorem Guidonis Baldi principis Urbinatis, esse rediturum et pontificias breves epistolas ab omni barbariae suspicione repurgatas editurum, ut posteri castum ipsius simul et succulentum dicendi genus ad imitandum admirentur.'[13]

9   'Sed cur est,' DAVALUS inquit, 'Museti, quod plerique Latinis et Graecis eruditi litteris hac aetate se totos ad vernaculae linguae studia contulerunt, secus ac superiores fecerint qui aut non attigere

the head of the former. Relying on outstanding talent and versed in many profound disciplines, he is a successful veteran fighter, equally skilled in either idiom, not shrinking from a contest in the same arena with Sannazaro,[7] whom he nonetheless acknowledges with generous modesty as surpassing him not only in age but also in hexameters. There can be nothing purer, more splendid, in short, more divine than Sannazaro's recently published Latin poem *The Virgin Birth*; while the *Piscatory Eclogues*, with the appealing novelty of their title, the variety of maritime themes, and the charm of their verses, are so admirable that in the judgment of many they are inferior to no works of the ancients. So, if you scrutinize his serious works more devoutly, and if you read indulgently his lighter verse composed in Latin and the vernacular, and survey the elegant compositions of his entire career, you must acknowledge that Sannazaro is truly excellent and absolutely a poet of the first class.

"Bembo, however, who by careful practice had attained to a very 8 sound and lively prose style, redirected his skill to focus on Tuscan, wishing through these efforts to solicit a sure and exalted reputation rather than, through his Latin writings, to chase after the fame he longed for, with uncertain results. For his future glory is assured from the exceedingly precise published work in which, following the standards of classic Tuscan speech, he has corrected the excesses and foreign extravagances of those writing in that tongue.[8] I do hope, however, that guided by sound judgment, he will return to the Latin dialogues which he began in honor of Duke Guidobaldo of Urbino[9] and that he will produce papal briefs cleansed of any trace of barbarity, so that future generations may strive in admiration to imitate his manner of expression, which is at once pure and lush."

"But why is it, Muscettola," asked D'AVALOS, "that most of 9 those schooled in Latin and Greek literature have in this age turned their attention entirely to the vernacular tongue, departing from

Etrusca aut ab his tamquam a parum honestis Musarum illecebris celeriter sese receperunt? Ut in Pontano videmus, qui nullam Etruscis rhythmis operam insumpsit, et in ipso Politiano qui, cum Mediceum illud nobile certamen equestre ludicrum singulari patriae linguae felicitate celebrasset, totum id studium repente deseruit — sed tamen, ut mihi videtur, aliquanto[14] maiore pudore quam iudicio, cum in Latina *Manto* et *Ambra* et *Rustico* subiratas postea aut certe duriores Musas invenerit — ita ut astute et sapienter agere credatur Balthasar Castellio, vir honestissimorum studiorum cumulata laude conspicuus, qui nobilem suum equitem, ab incunabulis omni bellica civilique virtute exornatum ut regali aula sit dignus, vernaculo potius quam Latino sermone perfecit. Prudentes enim et vere litterati quo naturae genius ducat cito provident et nihil umquam, tametsi quid saepe grandius specieque nobilius videant, invita Minerva moliuntur; quoniam Musae, quamquam omnibus et faciles et amabiles appareant, vim sibi tamen a protervis procis inferri nolunt quae saepius simplicitate ingenuisque blanditiis quam ullo exquisiti lenocinii artificio ad osculum evocantur.'

10   'Sic est profecto, Davale,' inquit MUSETIUS. 'Nihil a renitente vel prorsus invita Minerva improbitate iudicii videtur extorquendum. Verum alias quoque causas subesse perspicimus quare in summa ingeniorum libertate Latinarum litterarum studia ut vernaculis serviamus saepissime deserantur. Nam ante omnia communi vel Etrusca lingua scribenti pulcherrimis antiquorum et recentium etiam Latinorum inventionibus et sententiis inniti commodissimum videtur ad locupletanda vel exornanda scripta quae blandius atque facilius vernaculis sermonibus excuduntur. Potest enim is pudore incolumi peramoenos locos a politioribus

the usage of their predecessors, who either had no contact with things Tuscan or quickly retreated from them as from less than honorable enticements of the Muses? We see this in Pontano, who wasted no effort on Tuscan measures, and in Poliziano[10] himself who, once he'd celebrated, with such outstanding felicity in the Tuscan language, that famous joust of the Medici,[11] suddenly abandoned that entire pursuit. (But still, I think, he did so more out of embarrassment than good judgment, since, in the Latin *Manto* and *Ambra* and *Rusticus*, he found the Muses to be out of sorts with him, or at any rate less accommodating.)[12] So too Baldassare Castiglione, a man of the noblest pursuits who is visibly brimming with honors, is thought to be clever and wise, having fashioned his noble courtier — adorned from the cradle with every martial and civic virtue that he might be worthy of a royal court — in the vernacular rather than in Latin.[13] The reason is that wise and truly learned men soon perceive in what direction their natural talent is leading them, and no matter how grand and impressive something looks, they expend no labor against Minerva's will.[14] After all, no matter how compliant and friendly the Muses seem to all, they don't want to suffer violence at the hands of impudent suitors. They are enticed to give a kiss by candor and frank compliments more often than by any contrivance of flattery."

"It is certainly so, d'Avalos," said MUSCETTOLA. "Evidently, if 10 Minerva resists or is utterly unwilling, it would show a shameful lack of judgment to attempt to wrest anything from her. But we discern other, underlying reasons why, when talents are most at liberty, Latin letters are quite often forsaken in favor of the vernacular. First of all, it appears extremely convenient for someone writing in the common or Tuscan tongue to use the finest inventions and ideas of the ancient and even modern Latin authors to enrich and embellish his compositions which, being written in the vernacular, can be hammered out more smoothly and with less difficulty. For he can unashamedly borrow very pleasant passages

philosophis mutuari, poetarum consectari lumina sales argutias et totius denique Latinae linguae conspicuos flores ludenti et vaga manu impune decerpere. Quae omnia, mox dulcissime translata et opportunis in sedibus egregie collocata, instar lucidissimorum emblematum inter teneras vernaculae linguae lascivias sic refulgent tantamque excitant admirationem ut Etrusca Latinis iucundiora simul et grandiora nonnullis videantur, et iis praesertim qui ad recondita optimarum litterarum studia vel occupationibus vel ingeniorum imbecillitate minime penetrarunt.

11 'Cuius rei condicionem in iis qui Latine scribunt multo maxime diversam esse manifeste conspicimus. Neminem certe Latine scribentem tanta insania prorsus invaserit ut sibi pro libidine cuncta rapiendi mutuandi transferendique potestatem sine risu concessam putet. Fieri enim nequit nisi impudentissime vel ineptissime ut quis in eadem lingua optimorum auctorum verba, sententias ac integros etiam versus stulta libertate suffuretur, aut illorum sensus et divinas cogitationes, elocutione commutata, se melius atque felicius expressurum esse confidat. Verum haec tum explicare poterimus, et magis quidem opportune, cum singulos poetas Latinos Iovius absolverit.'

12 Tum ego ⟨IOVIUS⟩ inquam: 'Id per se celeriter fiet. Sunt enim poetae admodum pauci quos vigiliis suis viri doctissimi superfuturos opinentur, et ego etiam idcirco, ne vos morer, aliquanto[15] festinantius recensendos putabo; animus namque meus, in hac re hactenus ambiguus, veriores causas huius inusitatae ingeniorum defectionis audire concupiscit.

13 'Igitur ex iis qui se totos Latinorum carminum gravitati dediderunt omnium facile principem et vatibus antiquis maxime propinquum Cremonensem Hieronymum Vidam statuimus; est enim

from more polished philosophers, imitate the brilliant turns of phrase, witticisms, and subtleties of the poets, and pluck for pleasure and at will the flowers he sees anywhere in the entirety of the Latin language. Once all these things have been sweetly translated and prominently and suitably arranged in the manner of the most luminous mosaics, they so shine among the tender amusements of the vernacular tongue and stir up such admiration that to some they seem more delightful and impressive in Tuscan than in Latin — particularly to those who, either because of other preoccupations or from lack of ability, have not gained entrance to the profound learning of classical literature.

"We observe plainly that, in the case of those who write in 11 Latin, the manner of this borrowing varies greatly. Certainly no one writing in Latin would be possessed by such insanity that he would believe he had the ability to pluck out, borrow, and transplant anything he desired without becoming a laughingstock. For only out of the most brazen impertinence would anyone writing in the same language pilfer with licentious folly the words, ideas, and even entire lines from the best authors, or dare to think that by putting differently their ideas and inspired thoughts he is going to express them better and more felicitously. But we will be able to elaborate on these things, and certainly more conveniently, when Giovio has finished discussing the Latin poets individually."

Then I [GIOVIO] said: "That will happen quickly on its own, 12 for the most learned men think there are precious few poets whose work will give them life after death; and so, in order not to detain you, I'll consider a rather hasty accounting of them to be sufficient. For my mind continues to waver in this matter, longing to hear the truer causes of this extraordinary defection of talented minds.

"So I have determined that of all those devoted entirely to the 13 dignity of Latin poetry, Marco Girolamo Vida[15] of Cremona is easily the foremost and the nearest to the ancient poets. In fact, he

adeo praeclarus et verecundus Maronis imitator ut, si quid forte suspensa manu surripuit, id totum a sollerti ac erudita commutatione proprium esse vel oculatissimis videatur. Verum meo iudicio eius carmina, cum a lectis et illustribus verbis tum ab exquisitis maxime comparationibus, mirabilem felicitatem accipiunt, quae etiam incomparabili quadam modorum et numerorum rotunditate decorantur. Eius erant apud chalchographos imprimendae formis cum Roma caperetur *Eclogae* plures et *De arte poetica* libri tres, item *Bombices* et in alveo lusorio latrunculorum pugna lepidissime descripta, ut haec in publicum interim evolarent dum[16] historia *De nece Christi*, grandibus et religiosissimis heroicis decantata, acriore lima poliretur. Huius divinum ingenium admirans Gibertus in lucem produxit excudendisque tam multis operibus honestissimum et pingue otium domi et in Tusculanis montibus paravit.

14 'In M. Antonio Flaminio, pio iuvene et poeta castissimo, quem urbs antiqua Utinum protulit, praeclara ingenii signa elucent ad consummatam carminum laudem; est enim eruditus tener splendidus canorus. Tulere et proximae Alpes e Belluno Pierium Valerianum, qui Hyacinthum et Violam adamata nomina, dum ferveret amor, suavibus elegis celebravit. At nunc totis illis ignibus penitus exstinctis solutam orationem repudiato carmine suscepit et *Hieroglyphicas* notas quibus Aegyptii reges obeliscos pro litteris inscribebant erudite et diligenter interpretatus est. In Nicolao Archio nobili regulo, qui nunc domi procul a strepitu corruentis Italiae in subalpinis silvis supra Benacum tranquille cum Musis exercetur, iam pridem enituit indoles exactissimi vatis, cum me Ticini

is so splendid and restrained an imitator of Vergil that if he has chanced to steal something with a deft touch, even the most keen-sighted would think that through adept and erudite variation he has made it his own. Truly, in my view, both from the clarity of their diction and from their especially striking figures, his verses achieve a marvelous felicity; they are also graced with unparalleled smoothness in their meters and prosody. At the time when Rome was captured, several of his eclogues, his three books *On the Art of Poetry*, as well as *On the Silkworm* and a book in which the battle of chessmen on a board is most charmingly described, were at the printers' ready to be published,[16] while his narrative poem on the Passion of Christ, *The Christiad*, which he'd composed in dignified and very pious hexameters, was undergoing a thorough revision.[17] Giberti, admiring this man's inspired genius, has brought it to people's attention and has furnished for him a most honorable and comfortable retreat at a villa in the Tusculan hills for hammering out all his many works.

"In Marcantonio Flaminio,[18] a devout young man and faultless   14 poet from the ancient city of Udine,[19] there shine forth distin-guished signs of brilliance that will bring him great praise for his poetry, for he is learned, delicate, noble, and melodious. Also, out of Belluno, the nearby Alps have produced Pierio Valeriano[20] who, as long as his love was ablaze, celebrated in sweet elegies the be-loved names of Hyacinth and Viola. But once all those fires had been entirely put out, he rejected verse and took up prose, now producing learned and painstaking explanations of the hiero-glyphic symbols with which, in place of letters, the kings of Egypt inscribed their obelisks.[21] The noble prince Nicolò d'Arco[22] is at home now, in the subalpine forests overlooking Lake Garda. There, far from the din of Italy's collapse, he is kept peacefully oc-cupied with the Muses. His natural capacity of innate skill as a painstaking poet was evident long ago: when I was at Pavia, fever-ish with the passion of youth and, at the same time, writing

aestuantem iuveniliter ac irate obiter *Anterotica* conscribentem, ut
saevas amici flammas pie miseratus, salutaribus elegis delinivit.

15 'Latinis valet elegis atque iis admodum venustis Etruscisque
maxime rhythmis Marius Molsa Mutinensis, poeta eruditus perurbanus comis, quem saepe saevis amoribus perditum ac exulan-
tem sinu suo molliores Musae benignissimae receperunt. Is amicae
Furniae crines adeo teneris versibus Latine celebrat et in amatorio
carmine Etrusco tantam praefert dignitatem tantumque excitat risum in facetissimis fabulis quas ad imitationem Boccaccii iucunde
conscripsit ut in summa naturae ipsius comitate summi vatis gravitatem minime desideres.

16 'In maxima nunc hominum eruditorum admiratione floret Andreae Maronis Brixiani ingenium incredibile ⟨et⟩ portentosum, qui
ex tempore ad quam iusseris quaestionem Latinos versus variis
modis ac numeris fundere consuevit — audax profecto negotium ac
munus impudentiae vel temeritatis plenum, nisi id a natura impetu prope divino mira felicitas sequeretur. Fidibus et cantu Musas evocat, et cum semel coniectam in numeros mentem alacriore
spiritu inflaverit, tanta vi in torrentis morem concitatus fertur ut
fortuita et subitariis tractibus ducta multum ante provisa et medi-
tata carmina videantur. Canenti defixi exardent oculi, sudores manant, venae contumescunt, et quod mirum est, eruditae aures
tamquam alienae ac intentae omnem impetum profluentium numerorum exactissima ratione moderantur. Eum Leo Pontifex mirifica facundia magnopere delectatus sacerdotio, quod concupiverat,
liberaliter honestavit, ac demum Gibertus inter carissimos habuit
familiares, apud quem ampliora profecto esset consecutus nisi in
hac clade ipsius ac omnium spes et fortunae concidissent.

angrily my *Anterotica*, he took affectionate pity on the fierce passions of a friend, calming me with healing elegies.[23]

"Francesco Maria Molza[24] of Modena, a poet of learning, so- 15
phistication, and gentleness, excels in the most charming Latin elegies, and especially in Tuscan rhymes; the gentler, most obliging Muses have taken him to their bosom as one whom cruel passion has often reduced to ruin and exile. He celebrates his beloved Furnia's hair in Latin verses so tender, in his Tuscan love poetry displays so much distinction, and in his humorous tales, delightfully composed after the manner of Boccaccio, provokes so much laughter, that in his utterly gentle nature you don't feel the need of the seriousness characteristic of a supreme poet.

"These days the incredible, astonishing brilliance of Andrea 16
Marone[25] of Brescia enjoys the utmost admiration of the learned, for he is accustomed to pour out Latin verses on the spot in a variety of meters and rhythms on whatever subject you name—a bold undertaking, to be sure, and an impudent and reckless occupation if wondrous success did not follow naturally and through a nearly divine impulse. He summons the Muses with lyre and song, and once he has set his mind to verse and inspired it with a heightened excitement, like a torrent he is carried along with such force that his poems, though composed on the spur of the moment and without premeditation, seem the result of long advance planning and prior reflection. As he recites, his fiery eyes are fixed, his sweat pours, his veins swell; and—what is wondrous—as the verses flow forth, his trained ears, as though not his own, intently and precisely regulate every beat. Pope Leo, greatly pleased with this wonderful eloquence, generously bestowed on him the priesthood that he wanted, and in the end Giberti counted him among the most cherished members of his household. There, he would certainly have accomplished greater things, had not the hopes and fortunes of him and of all perished in this disaster.

17   'Vivit in agro Brixiano Quintianus, poeta naturali furore pernobilis, verum in multa et subagresti litterarum notitia confragosus.
Hunc plura quam quisquam[17] alius non insanus scripsisse ferunt,
variis poematibus cuncta quae caelo continentur immenso captu
vastaque memoria complectentem. Is summam in contumaci syllabarum censura gloriam ponit et, iusta quadam iactantia, in his
splendidioribus poetis errata puerilis inscitiae se deprehendisse
profitetur. Ceterum qui tam severus est, ridiculis festivioribusque
titulis plerumque delectat, ut in iis libris quos de concubitu Martis
et Veneris intemperanti sed erudita stili lascivia ad Elephantidis
imitationem lucubravit.

18   'Marius Cattaneus Novariensis, vir Graece Latineque doctissimus, qui iam pridem C. Plinii Caecilii epistolas luculentis com-
mentationibus illustravit, ingravescente aetate ad studia carminum
provehitur et alacriter Gottifredum canit, deletis Syrorum et Par-
thorum copiis Hierosolymarum regnum Christiano nomini vendi-
cantem. Odas scribunt graves et elegantes Lampridius Cremonen-
sis et Fabius Vigil Spoletanus, ille vehementer Graecis deditus
litteris, hic linguarum prope omnium et antiquitatis admodum
studiosus.

19   'Carolum Capellium nobilem Venetum, qui Graece etiam profecit, generosum poetam evadere perspicimus. Et Bernardus Ma-
mertinus sacerdos cucullatus, idem philosophus et poeta insignis,
in caesaris aula celebratur. Antonius quoque Tilesius Cosentinus,[18]
cuius peramoenus est liber *De coronis*, lepide et suaviter versus facit, adeo ut aliquando *Zonarium* illius *reticulum* et *Fabrefactam fictilem lucernam* et *Noctu volantem cicindelam*[19] malim quam Modesti
nostri totam legere *Venetiadem*, quamquam in multo tractu lucu-
lentam et admirabilem; inepte enim fit si poemata versuum

"In the Brescian countryside lives Quintianus Stoa,[26] a poet en-   17
nobled by natural inspiration, but harsh in many respects and
rather rustic as regards his acquaintance with literature. It is said
that this man, with limitless grasp and prodigious memory, has
written about more things than anyone who isn't insane, embracing in poems of all sorts everything that the heavens contain. He
supposes his highest glory is being an arrogant watchdog of prosody, and he is able to boast with some justice that in those poets
who are more illustrious, he has found ignorant and childish errors. Still, even one so strict affords a great deal of enjoyment with
the playful and quite humorous titles of his books, as for example
those at which he labored long into the night on the coupling of
Mars and Venus, composed in the openly racy but learned style of
Elephantis.[27]

"Then there is Giovanni Maria Cattaneo[28] of Novara, a man   18
most learned in Greek and in Latin, who long ago wrote lucid
commentaries on the letters of Pliny the Younger.[29] In his old age
he is drawn to poetic pursuits, and vigorously sings of Godfrey's
conquest of the kingdom of Jerusalem for the name of Christ after
the armies of Syria and Parthia had been destroyed.[30] Lampridio[31]
of Cremona and Fabio Vigili[32] of Spoleto write dignified, elegant
odes: Lampridio is a great devotee of Greek literature, while Vigili
is very much a scholar of nearly all languages and of antiquity.

"In my view Carlo Cappello,[33] a Venetian patrician who is like-   19
wise accomplished in Greek, is emerging as an excellent poet. And
Bernardino from Oppido Mamertina,[34] the hooded priest who is
eminent in both philosophy and poetry, is celebrated in the emperor's court. Also Antonio Telesio[35] of Cosenza, author of the
beautiful *On Crowns*,[36] composes verses so elegant and sweet that
now and then I would rather read his *Mesh Purse* and *Crafted Pottery Oil-lamp*[37] and *Night-Flying Firefly*[38] than the entire *Venetiad* of
our Modesti,[39] although Modesti's work is brilliant and admirable
in its abundant expansiveness. It's absurd that poems should be

numero quam pondere potius aestimentur. Quis enim umquam artificem a labore multo vel ipso gravis operae sudore potius quam a docta atque habili digitorum argutia laudavit? Probo tamen ipsius Modesti sanctissimi hominis ingenuum[20] laborem, cum in navalibus praesertim exprimendis felicissime laborarit.

20   'Sed ita est profecto ut aliquot quos legi versus *De morbo Gallico* Fracastorii Veronensis medici fecisse malim quam Aurelii Augurelli operosam illam *Chrysopeiam*, qua etiam egentes quomodo repente et sine aliena quidem iniuria ditari possint luculentissime doceantur. Ludit enim saepe versibus et iis quidem in omne aevum duraturis Fracastorius, in philosophia tam graviter et eleganter doctus quam in medicina probe fortunatus et sapiens.[21]

21   'Ex iis vero qui epigrammata cum lepore conscribant, ceteros omnes antecellit M. Antonius Casanova, Comense patre Romae genitus. Is est districtis admodum sententiis expeditus, infinite mordax, et flexuose in sensu et verbis circumductus; numeris autem et argutiis asperior urbanis hominibus videtur, qui peregrinam acutioris stili salsedinem in Romano carmine vituperant, quasi ille Martiali[22] similis esse malit quam Catulli et quorundam veterum imitari candorem illamque simplicem, et sine aculeis puram lenitatem, quam externi aut urbis inquilini poetae numquam attigerint.'

22   Ad ea MUSETIUS 'Agnosco' inquit 'quid illi velint emunctissimae naris eruditi qui Martialem ut plane barbarum cum facetis tum virulentis etiam cachinnis insectantur. Horum enim hominum sectam iam pridem ortam audivimus qui quotannis permulta undique collecta Martialis volumina, stato sollemni die ad declarandam vindictae libidinem, Vulcano consecrare consueverunt, quasi eius velut parum Latini poetae monumenta deleturi, nisi consensu et plausu aetatum omnium recepta iam nunc infinita ac

prized more for the number of their verses than for their significance. For who has ever praised a craftsman for his lengthy labor or his exertions instead of for his skill and dexterity? Still, I commend the noble effort of the saintly Modesti, since he has labored with immense success, especially in describing naval warfare.

"But that's how it is—indeed, so much so that I would rather 20 have authored some of the verses which I have read in the *Syphilis* of the Veronese doctor Fracastoro[40] than that elaborate *Chrysopeia* of Giovanni Aurelio Augurelli[41] in which, supposedly, even the poor are instructed splendidly how to become rich quickly and without doing harm to anyone. For Fracastoro, who is as deeply and elegantly learned in philosophy as he is wholly successful and wise in medicine, often amuses himself with verse that will in fact endure for all time.

"But Marco Antonio Casanova,[42] born at Rome of a father 21 from Como, surpasses all others who compose witty epigrams. He's quite adept in producing pointed aphorisms. Both in words and in sense, he's relentlessly caustic and tortuously expansive. To Roman critics, however, his verse seems unrefined in meter and coarse in terms of wit. In a poem on Rome, they find distasteful the foreign flavor of his sharper style, claiming that he would rather be like Martial than imitate that mildness and pure smoothness, free of affectation and barbs—things typical of Catullus and certain of the ancients—which foreign poets or those merely residing in Rome never have attained."

To this MUSCETTOLA said, "I understand what those hyper- 22 refined men are after who attack Martial as quite barbarous on account of his guffawing and venomous humor. I've heard that a sect of these people arose long ago who every year have a solemn day dedicated to exposing lustful behavior to punishment, on which they are accustomed to commit to Vulcan's flames the numerous volumes of Martial they have collected from all over; they would destroy the literary works of this poet of, in their opinion, inferior

immortali formarum tutela servarentur. Ego medius fidius Martialem ut iucundissimum vatem semper sum admiratus: nec valde ineptum puto fuiss⟨e⟩ Hadrianum Caesarem, qui et Martialem suum Maronem app⟨ellabat⟩.[23] Verum[24] si benigno ac pio alicui poetae liceret eius libros verecunda manu defecare,[25] arbitrarer profecto eum ab arguta hilaritate longe optimum et suavissimum, postquam in illo genere, et in tanto praesertim aevo, neminem adhuc eo meliorem invenimus.'

23   His ego ⟨IOVIUS⟩, 'Benigne' inquam 'iudicas, Museti. Sed quis hominum vel deorum etiam, nisi sit ipse Vulcanus, tam lutulentum vatem ab olidis sordibus satis laute repurgabit?'

24   Tum ille ⟨MUSETIUS⟩, 'Nimium profecto nasuti estis qui in Romana academia dedistis nomen. Nam cum aliquorum poetarum ter maximi sitis admiratores, ceterorum demum omnium cum bile quadam non ferenda acerrimi hostes et vituperatores esse consuevistis. Vixere equidem vel ingenio mediocres, Statius, Flaccus, Silius atque Lucanus, qui animos lecto Marone desponderant, sicut etiam clarissime vivent qui[26] vestrum Vidam nostrumque Actium longo etiam intervallo subsecuuntur.

25   'Sed ut ad Martialem redeamus,[27] tantum abest ut Casanovae ingenio Bilbilitanam notam indigne inustam esse conqueramur, ut ille summo etiam voto a Musis exoptet ut omnibus numeris Martiali simillimus evadat, quamquam non plane intellegam quidnam purius et candidius illo epigrammate desiderare possimus quod De Virgilii tumulo lepidissime conscriptum, dum Romae superiore anno legatus essem, mihi ipse benigne recitavit. Cuius et verba et numeros cum teneam, ipsum auditote:

Latinity were these not now saved, after the consent and approval of all eras, by the everlasting safeguard of printing. So help me, I have always admired Martial as a most delightful poet; nor, to be sure, do I think it foolish of the Emperor Hadrian even to call Martial his 'Vergil.' But if it were to be allowed to some kindly and pious poet to purify Martial's books with a respectful hand, I would certainly judge him, thanks to his clever wit, by far the best and most charming, since we have yet to find anyone better in his chosen genre, and especially in so great an era."

To these things I [GIOVIO] said, "You are a kindly judge, 23 Muscettola. But who on earth — or even in heaven, unless it should be Vulcan himself — will adequately purge so sordid a poet of his fetid filth?"

Then MUSCETTOLA replied, "Clearly, you members of the Ro- 24 man Academy are too satirical. For while you are thrice-great admirers of some poets, with a gall that is intolerable you're habitually the bitterest enemies and censurers of all the others. To be sure, poets of moderate talent have survived too: Statius, Valerius Flaccus, Silius, and Lucan, even though they had despaired of achieving fame once they'd read Vergil. In the same way, those who follow after your Vida or our Sannazaro, even at a considerable distance, will live on illustriously.

"But to return to Martial: I am not going to lament that his 25 stigma has been undeservedly branded upon Casanova. Far from it, for Casanova is actually begging the Muses, even with solemn vows, that he might prove to be just like Martial in all his verse. Yet I don't quite understand what in the world we can wish for that is purer and more deft than his charming epigram on the tomb of Vergil. While I was in Rome on a diplomatic mission last year, he kindly recited it to me; since I can recall both its words and its meters, listen to it, if you will:

Dicite, qui Minci ripas coluistis olores,
  Vobiscum exorta est gloria Virgilii?
Dic mihi Parthenope (sic sis, pulcherrima, semper),
  Virgiliusne tuo decidit in gremio?
Et meruit, cui contigerat nasci inter olores,
  Inter Sirenum decubuisse choros.

26   Ad haec ego ⟨IOVIUS⟩ inquam, 'Museti, gratias tibi ago perin-
gentes quod civis et sodalis mei, purissimique hominis ingenium
probes, dum Martiali favere videris nec dubitaverim quin de hoc
tuo propensiore studio atque iudicio quas ipse tibi habeo ille suavissimis versiculis aliquando referat, si id rescierit et in hac modo
clade sit servatus, sicut eum[28] nuper carcere inclusum et convictum
Clemens admirabili lenitate conservavit, cum imprudenter potius
quam maligne sacrosancti eius numinis maiestatem probroso carmine lacerasset. Levi enim persuasione inductus se gratum facturum crediderat Pompeio Columnae domino, qui tum flagrantis-
simas simultates cum pontifice promotis armis exercebat. Sed
postquam Maronis sepulchrum tam laeto carmine depictum omnibus placet, audite et hos versus, quos eodem spiritu de Homero
mollissime decantavit:

An Smyrna est quae te nascentem excepit, Homere?
  Anne fuit vatem quae tumulavit Ios?
Altera habet nomen violae, tenet altera myrrhae:
  Fata tuum his decorant ortum obitumque simul.
Quid magis est, quod te, divine, deceret Homere,
  Quam nasci in myrrha, decidere in viola?

Say to us, swans, who dwelt on the banks of the Mincio,
    did the glory of Vergil come forth in your midst?
Tell me, Parthenope (may you be beautiful always!),
    does Publius Maro repose in your arms?
That Mantuan whom it befell to be born among swans
    is worthy to sleep among choirs of Sirens forever.

To this I [GIOVIO] said, "Muscettola, I'm deeply grateful that 26
in your apparent liking for Martial, you commend the talent of an
exceedingly virtuous man who is my fellow citizen and friend. Nor
would I doubt that with charming little verses he will eventually
make good my gratitude for your kindly zeal and favorable estimation—if only he learns of it and is saved from the present disaster,
in just the way that happened recently with the pope. With admirable leniency, Clement recently protected him when he was
thrown in jail and convicted, since it was from foolishness rather
than spite that he had insulted the majesty of His Holiness in a
scandalous poem. For he had thought, misled by frivolity, that it
would ingratiate him with his patron, Pompeo Colonna, who,
with his armies advancing, was then engaged in a vehement feud
with the pope.[43] But since you all enjoyed his beautiful poem describing Vergil's tomb, listen to these lines of the same inspiration
tenderly celebrating Homer:

Was Smyrna, O Homer, the site that was graced with your
    birth?
    And were you, O bard, on the island of Ios interred?
One bears the name of the violet, the other of myrrh;
    with these do the Fates at once honor your birth and your
    death.
What fate that's more suitable could be conceived, divine
    Homer,
    than that you, who were born in the myrrh, should die
    among violets?

27   Haec cum Davalus et Musetius mirum in modum extulissent,
'Ne putatote,' ego ⟨IOVIUS⟩ inquam, 'eum in ceteris minus aequabilem poetam exstitisse. Servant enim illam notam ingenii cum
austeritate dulcissimi reliqua poemata quae circumferuntur, adeo
praeclare ut uno leporis tenore integrum librum scribere nequaquam difficile ei fuisse appareat. Neque Casanovam propterea solum nominatum velim, quoniam solus in eo carminum genere cum
gloria versetur. Nam et[29] alii[30] protinus occurrent qui epigrammatis scitissime ludant, nec ipsos omittam qui modo Romae florebant, et ante alios[31] Blosium Palladium ab epistolis Summi Pontificis, cuius ingenio ad cuncta vel solutae orationis munera praeclare
habili nihil paratius, nihil amoenius umquam fuit, ut illo maxime
panegyrico enituit in honorem Leonis Decimi habito, cum
S.P.Q.R. optimo pontifici marmoream statuam in Capitolio posuisset;[32] Colotium item Esinum, ab eruditi iudicii absoluto candore perspicuum Curtiumque Hernicum, cuius Musa modestior a
subrustico pudore commendatur, in eo praesertim poemate quo
Romanae civitatis excidium gravissime nec plane quidem siccatis
adhuc lacrimis[33] deflevit; et Thomam Petrasanctam, salsae comita-
tis et doctae liberrimaeque censurae poetam; et ipsum Petrum
Mellinum, natalibus ac ingenii suavitate Romanae principem iuventutis, qui est periucundus Catullianae puritatis imitator. Cecinere etiam vixdum pubescentes hilari quodam furore Marcellus
Pallonius Romanus et Ianus Vitalis Siculus: hic monstrum quod[34]
has clades portendit, ille autem Ravennatem Pugnam tot mutuis
ducum funeribus insignem. Qui profecto ut adulescentes aliquanto
maiores quam iuvenes, clariorem ingenii famam postea essent
consecuti nisi, ut quibusdam videtur, intra ipsas gloriosi tirocinii
laudes conquiescere voluissent.'

When d'Avalos and Muscettola had extolled these lines to the 27 skies, I [GIOVIO] said, "Nor should you think that the rest of his verse fell short of this. His other poems in circulation preserve the same distinction of restrained sweetness, and with such excellence that for him it appears effortless to write an entire book that is uninterruptedly charming. Nor should I wish that Casanova alone be named, as if he were the only one who practices that genre of poetry with success. Others too come readily to mind who dabble in epigrams with the utmost cleverness; and I shall not omit those who until recently were flourishing in Rome. And before the rest, there is the papal secretary, Blosio Palladio:[44] his ability to discharge all his duties, including prose composition, with readiness and elegance has never been surpassed — as was most abundantly clear in that panegyric delivered in honor of Leo X after the Senate and People of Rome had placed a marble statue of that great pontiff on the Capitol.[45] I may also mention Angelo Colocci[46] from Jesi, distinguished by the unqualified sincerity of his learned judgment; and Pietro Corsi[47] of Latium, whose plainer poetic style is commended by a somewhat rustic sense of modesty, especially where he sang touchingly and tearfully of the destruction of the city of Rome;[48] and Tommaso Pietrasanta,[49] a poet of witty and learned congeniality and of very outspoken opinion; and Pietro Mellini[50] himself, first among Roman youth in distinction of lineage and gentleness of character, who delightfully imitates the pure style of Catullus. Also Marcello Palonio of Rome and Giano Vitale from Sicily, when both were scarcely of age, were poets of a lively passion. Vitale sang of the monster that presaged the present disasters,[51] while Palonio sang of the Battle of Ravenna,[52] famous for the deaths of so many commanders on both sides. In some measure better as youths than when they got older, they certainly would have attained greater fame for their talents had they not been content (as it seems to certain men) to rest on the laurels of a glorious debut."

28   Tum vero ad haec renidenti fronte MUSETIUS: 'Cur est,' inquit,
'Iovi, quod poetarum ingenium praecox rarissime pervenit ad frugem? An forte est quoniam vena illa uberior et exsultans quae in-
tempestive prosilit, cum a perennibus et plenissimis naturae fontibus minime deducatur, velut mox consumpto profluentis impetu
celeriter exarescat?'

29   Ad id, ego ⟨IOVIUS⟩ inquam: 'Hoc equidem in causa esse potest. Nam a natura, quae interiores labes futurosque defectus prae-
sagire consuevit, cum vehementi et supremo sensuum omnium
conatu saepissime mirabiles impetus effunduntur, ut in aegris
iamiam vita migraturis contingere videmus qui repente collectis
viribus ad inanem spem dubiae victoriae enixe cum ipsa morte
colluctantur. Sed nihil meo iudicio magis adulescentium poetarum
ingenia perdit vel exterit quam adulantium circumfusa multitudo.
Eorum enim primitias paedagogi imprimis ita vehementer extollunt, ita stupide parentes admirantur, ut post[35] teneri et inflari faciles eorum animi, nequaquam vera laude subnixi, omne studium
graviorum litterarum penitus intermittant et caducis tantum nas-
centis gloriolae floribus inanissime nutriantur. Ita processu aetatis,
absque ullo doctrinae suco, ieiuna admodum et inani pedum volubilitate profusa carmina neminem amplius vel adulantium etiam
delectant. Nonnulli etiam certam vim ingenii occultiore mensura
praefinitam a primordiis pueritiae statim ostendunt, quam vel accuratis exercitationibus provehere ac extendere aut frustra aut difficile semper fuit, quando id vitium naturae quadam infelicitate
sortiantur, ut in Menicocio nuptiali claroque tibicinae vidimus qui,
cum Romae per triginta annos aliquid ab elegantioribus musicae
artis praeceptis ad tibias addere saepissime cupivisset, desperato
semper successu in illis semel conceptis veteris[36] choreae modulis
consenuit.'

To this, MUSCETTOLA, with cheerful countenance, said, "Why   28
is it, Giovio, that the precocious talent of poets has so rarely borne
fruit? Is it perhaps because that bursting and riotous vein which
rises prematurely quickly dries up when it doesn't draw from the
perennial and abundant springs of nature—the force of the initial
burst, as it were, soon having been exhausted?"

To this, I [GIOVIO] responded, "This can surely be a reason.   29
For nature, which usually foresees inner defects and future failings,
very often releases remarkable forces along with a powerful, supreme effort of all the senses, as we see happens in the sick who
are just on the point of dying; all of a sudden, gathering all their
powers in the vain hope of a doubtful victory, they are locked in a
strenuous struggle with death itself. But in my opinion nothing
corrupts or wears away the talents of young poets more than being
surrounded by a crowd of flatterers. Their teachers, especially, re-
soundingly praise their first offerings, and their parents show foolish amazement—and because they're young, they're easily suscep-
tible to flattery. As a result, they afterward neglect entirely any
more serious literary pursuit: lacking any real merit, they point-
lessly subsist upon the transitory flowers of a slight glory that
doesn't mature beyond its infancy. Thus, as they grow older and
are lacking the vital juices of learning, their poems, feeble and
flooded with metrical inconsistencies, no longer please anybody,
even among their flatterers. Some display from boyhood on a definite talent that is predetermined by some inner measure, but always find it either impossible or very difficult to advance or expand
that talent, even after assiduous practice, when through nature's
unkindness they possess that fatal flaw—as we saw in the case
of Menicocius,[53] the famed wedding flautist, whom we witnessed
seeking again and again during his thirty years in Rome to intro-
duce to the instrument some of the more refined musical principles, but who always gave up, and grew old playing the same
strains as he had the first time."

30   Hic arridens MUSETIUS 'Hoc,' inquit, 'edepol verissimum esse
videtur. Nam certos quosdam humani captus terminos in singulis
prope artificibus esse deprehendimus, qui numquam vel laboriose
et sollerter enitendo facile superantur. Quis enim Perusino, qui
nunc etiam octogenarius satis constanti manu sed inglorius pingit
cum aetate floreret maiore concursu vel claritate picturam exercuit? Favere siquidem illi (aliquamdiu et ambitiose quidem) omnes
Italiae principes, cum ille passim dignissima ut tum videbantur
artis monumenta deponeret. Nemo enim illo divorum vultus et
ora praesertim angelorum blandius et suavius exprimebat, vel testimonio Xysti Pontificis, qui ei palmam detulit cum in pingendo
domestico templo nobilissimi artifices quaestuosa contentione de-
certassent.

31   'At postquam illa perfectae artis praeclara lumina—Vincius,
Michael Angelus atque Raphael—ab illis saeculi tenebris repente
orta illius famam et nomen admirandis operibus obruerunt, frustra Perusinus meliora aemulando atque observando partam dignitatem retinere conatus est, cum semper ad suos bellulos vultus
quibus iuvenis haeserat sterilitate ingenii recidere cogeretur, sic ut
prae pudore vix ignominiam animo sustineret quando illi augusta-
rum imaginum nudatos artus et conitentis naturae potestates in
multiplici rerum omnium genere stupenda varietate figurarent.'

32   Tum vero ego ⟨IOVIUS⟩ inquam, 'Museti, lepido valde exemplo
sententiam meam confirmasti. Sed de hoc certiora philosophis
coniectanda relinquamus, ut ad ceteros poetas aliquando revertamur et ad vestros praesertim Neapolitanos, apud quos magnus
semper numerus effloruit. Nam, ut opinor, et Sirenum tumuli et
Virgilii Maronis sepulchrum, quod praeter Pausilipi dorsum via

Now MUSCETTOLA said, with a laugh, "This, by God, seems to   30
be a fact. For we observe definite limits to the human capacity of
nearly all artists, which not even hard labor and keen striving can
ever exceed. For who ever executed a painting with greater acclaim
and renown than Perugino did when he was in the prime of life?
Now, some eighty years old,[54] he still paints with a steady enough
hand, but receives no honor for it. Mind you, as long as he turned
out everywhere what then seemed admirable works of art, all the
princes of Italy favored him with patronage, even for a while seeking him out with much solicitation. Indeed, no one rendered more
charmingly and more beautifully than he the features of saints and
especially the faces of angels—as is attested by Pope Sixtus IV,
who awarded him the palm when the most famous artists had
contended for the lucrative commission of painting the Sistine
Chapel.[55]

"But then there emerged unexpectedly from the darkness of   31
that age those luminaries of perfect art—Leonardo da Vinci, Michelangelo, and Raphael—and their wondrous works overshadowed Perugino's reputation and name. By observing and copying
them, he tried to hold onto the distinction he had acquired—but
in vain, since, lacking the talent, he was compelled always to fall
back upon those pretty faces to which as a young man he had been
attached. As a result, his heart could scarcely endure the shame of
his disgrace as, in an astonishing variety of genres and subjects,
those artists created majestic portraits of naked muscularity and
gave form to the powers of struggling Nature."

Then I [GIOVIO] said, "Muscettola, your very amusing exam-   32
ple corroborates my view. But let's leave this subject to the surer
theories of the philosophers, and return at last to the other poets—especially your Neapolitan ones, who have always flourished
in great number. For in my view the tombs of the Sirens as well
as that of Vergil beyond the ridge of Posillipo on the road to
Pozzuoli—which was a much-venerated shrine before the severe

Puteolana religiosissime colebatur, antequam dirae Gothorum iniuriae nobilissimi operis vestigia delevissent, vel angustiores animos ad praeclare canendum semper excitarunt, ut in quota parte divinae benignitatis Baianas etiam aquas et Averni lacus antra Sibyllinis carminibus incluta minime computemus. Quae omnia, non secus ac ipse quondam in Graecia Parnasus cum Aganippes et Heliconis fontibus ac densissimis illis ad decerpendas coronas lauretis, Musas ac Apollinem conciliare existimantur, in tam laeto praesertim virentium collium recessu et tam opportuna semper vernantis et piscosi litoris amoenitate.

33   'E Neapolitanis enim, ut omnes ex hac extrema Italiae parte uno nomine complectamur, perpulchra aliqua publicarunt Petrus Gravina, nitidissimus idem et doctissimus senex, cum etiam uberiorem gloriam ab heroicis, quos verecundius domi continet, exspectare facile possit, et Hieronymus Carbo, Pontani amicitia clarus.[37] Hieronymum etiam Angerianum genere Lucanum amatoria iudiciis hominum[38] famae commendata celebrem fecerunt. Est etiam foris clarus Anisius sacerdos honestissimus, cuius sunt praeter lyrica *Satyrae* plures Horatiana simplicitate compositae. Valet heroico Antonius Minturnus Graece et Etrusce pariter eruditus, et in duabus praesertim *Silvis* Statio paene par, quarum altera clades Italiae deplorantur, altera Columniorum procerum genus ab Alcide deducitur. Iactabatur paullo ante fortunae fluctibus Pomponius Gauricus Picentinus, ipsius Lucae celebris astrologi frater, qui adeo studiose Graecis se dedit ut si quorundam iudicium sequamur a Romanis plane defecisse videatur.'

34   Hoc loco perblande ridens MUSETIUS 'Ita est,' inquit, 'Iovi. Plerique adeo ambitiose Graecas litteras et, cum paullo fervidius

damages inflicted by the Goths destroyed what was left of that celebrated monument—always inspired even slighter talents to excellent poetry. And that's not to mention, among so many divine blessings, the waters of Baia and the grottoes of Lake Avernus, made famous by the Sibyl's prophecies. All these places are held to attract the Muses and Apollo no less than Mount Parnassus and the fountains of Aganippe and Helicon and those laurel groves, so leafy for the gathering of wreaths, at one time did in Greece. And this is particularly the case because of the delightful seclusion of the verdant hills nearby and the lovely convenience of a seashore where it is always springtime and the fish are abundant.

"Of the Neapolitans (for let us include all those from this far- 33 thest region of Italy under one name) Pietro Gravina,[56] an elderly man exceptional for both his elegance and his learning, and Giro-lamo Carbone,[57] known for his friendship with Pontano, have published some very beautiful poems—although Gravina could easily expect more abundant glory from the epic verses which he shyly declines to release. Girolamo Angeriano,[58] a Lucanian[59] by birth, is celebrated for love poems which the public has judged worthy of fame. There's also Anisio,[60] an exceedingly honorable priest who is famous abroad. Besides his lyric poems, he has com-posed many satires in a pure Horatian style. Antonio Minturno,[61] equally learned in Greek and Tuscan, excels in epic poetry. Espe-cially in his two works called *Silvae*, he is nearly the equal of Sta-tius: in the one he mourns the disasters of Italy; in the other he traces the lineage of the leading men of the Colonna family back to Hercules.[62] A short time ago a Picentine, Pomponio Gaurico,[63] brother of the famous astrologer Luca, was tossed about on the seas of fortune. He gave himself so devotedly to Greek letters that in the opinion of some he is considered to have forsaken Latin completely."

Then MUSCETTOLA laughed agreeably, saying, "So it is, Gio- 34 vio. The majority of those who embrace Greek and, when their

243

ebullit ingenium, etiam Hebraicas amplectuntur ut Latinas plane
deserant atque despiciant, quoniam gloriosius putent ignota lingua
in coronis publice loqui quam si communi concinne et eleganter
utantur et scribant. Ego enim Graeca, ut Pontanus dicere solebat,
quatenus et lucem et ornamenta Latinis afferunt studiis sedulo
perdiscenda arbitror, non ut ab his peculiarem laudem ubique
Graecissantes tamquam Athenis nati petere videamur, ut hic ipse
Pomponius qui Neapoli, cum Recasentiam puellam semigraeca
oratione in funere laudaret, nobis qui pullati eramus pro lacrimis
risum extorsit.[39] Satis namque studiosis in cottidianam operam
aerumnosi laboris propositum esse animadvertimus, si Latinos
auctores medullitus inspicere et vim priscae elocutionis observare
velimus.'

35   Ad id ego ⟨IOVIUS⟩ inquam, 'Rectissime sentis, Museti. Nam
nos Romae Antonium Marosticum novimus hominem doctum et
plane candidum qui, cum Graecis litteris mirabundus aetatem fere
omnem insumpsisset, ad extremum Latinarum paene[40] oblitus in
ea quae est *Pro Ctesiphonte* Demosthenis oratione consenuit. Verum
iis omnino necesse est Graece scire qui, cum philosophiae et subtilioribus disciplinis vacent, aliquid purius et castius non ex rivis
lutulentis sed ex vivo et liquido fonte haurire praecipiunt.[41] He-
braica vero consectantes non improbo, modo ea ad instrumenti
veteris enarrationem pia curiositate potius quaesita quam ad ostentationem ridiculae blaterantis gutturis arcessita videantur.

36   'Sunt etiam in aliis Italiae urbibus poetae celebres, ut apud
Parmenses Georgius Anselmus, varia[42] ingenii[43] fecunditate pernobilis,[44] et Dardanus, urbana facilitate insignis, et Carpesianus, qui
ad unam aram Apollinem et Aesculapium colit. Crotum in honore
habent Rhaegienses, in versu cum gravitate peracutum. Laudatur a
Perusinis Bartolinus, qui Austrianorum principum et Maximiliani

intellects boil a little hotter, even Hebrew, are so ambitious that they completely desert and scorn Latin letters, in the belief that speaking before the public in an unknown tongue confers greater glory than the common idiom expressed and written with skill and refinement. I think that, as Pontano used to say, we should be diligent scholars of Greek to the degree that it adds clarity and beauty to our Latin studies, and not Hellenize on every occasion as if we were native Athenians, appearing to seek from it personal glory; the latter is what this Pomponio Gaurico did at Naples when, delivering a half-Greek eulogy at the funeral of a girl of the Requesenz family, he wrested from us mourners laughter instead of tears. For we scholars recognize that the daily and difficult labor of our work is challenge enough, if a searching scrutiny of the Latin authors and a proper attention to their ancient style of expression are things we value."

I [GIOVIO] said in reply, "You're right, Muscettola. In Rome I 35 became acquainted with Antonio Marostica,[64] a learned and quite upright man. After he'd spent almost his entire life in the admiring study of Greek literature, he nearly forgot the study of Latin and grew old with that oration of Demosthenes, *On the Crown*. Surely, knowing Greek is altogether necessary for those who have time for philosophy and the finer disciplines and know how to take purer and less tainted drafts, not from muddy streams, but from a clear and flowing spring. Nor do I disapprove of those who study Hebrew, provided that they are pursuing it out of devout interest, in order to interpret the Old Testament, not importing it to make a display of ridiculous, guttural bleating.

"Also in other cities of Italy there are famous poets; Parma, for 36 example, has Giorgio Anselmi,[65] renowned for his rich and varied creativity; Bernardino Dardano,[66] marked by his sophisticated ease; and Carpesani,[67] who honors Apollo and Aesculapius at the same altar. Reggio honors Crotti,[68] whose verse is serious but precise. Perugia esteems Bartolini, who narrated in forceful verse the

praesertim Augusti victorias robusto carmine prosecutus est. Nihil etiam Mariangeli Accursii ab Aquila Furconensium Musa iucundius, qui Ausonium subtiliter interpretatur. Et iam pridem facetissimo dialogo edito quorundam obscure et rancide scribentium, expressis personis atque iis in scenam ad excitandum risum introductis, foeda vitia bellissime castigavit.

37 'Ceterum Andreas Naugerius in duobus quae per lusum fecit epigrammatis tantam in iis priscae venustatis gratiam est consecutus ut plerosque sanos et nequaquam temporariam spectantes laudem a proposito et tota spe meliora aut paria consequendi omnino deiecerit. Quid enim hoc epigrammate quod est ad auras dictum simplicius, lenius atque suavius esse potest? Ipsos quaeso numeros verba pedes aequis auribus perpenditote:

Aurae quae levibus percurritis aera pennis
    Et strepitis blando per nemora alta sono,
Serta dat haec vobis, vobis haec rusticus Idmon;
    Spargit odorato plena canistra croco.
Vos lenite aestum et paleas seiungite inanes,
    Dum medio fruges ventilat ille die.

38 'Mira est hercule,' inquit MUSETIUS, 'haec Romana simplicitas; non retortis enim et turbidis argutiis, sed florentibus et liquidis sensibus aures implet ac animos vel languentes exhilarat, ut est et illud eiusdem de frigido ac umbroso fonte, propter divinam suavitatem latius evulgatum:

Et gelidus fons est, et nulla salubrior unda,
    Et molli circum gramine terra viret.

victories of the Austrian princes and especially of the Emperor
Maximilian.[69] There's nothing more delightful than the poetry of
Mariangelo Accursio[70] from Aquila, who interprets Ausonius with
precision.[71] In a very witty dialogue published long ago he brought
clearly delineated characters to the stage, both for laughter's sake
and to correct the unseemly faults of those whose writing was
obscure and distasteful.[72]

"On the other hand, Andrea Navagero,[73] in two epigrams he   37
composed for fun, attained such graceful, ancient charm that he
completely dislodged men of sound judgment, who sought a more
permanent fame, from their aim and their whole hope of achieving equal or greater things. For what can be simpler, smoother,
or more pleasant than the following epigram, addressed to the
breezes? I ask you to listen and evaluate fairly its cadences, words,
and meter:

> O breezes that wing your way through the air with your light
>> feathers
>> and rustle so charmingly through the tall trees,
> It's Idmon the peasant who gives you these wreaths; upon you
>> full baskets he sprinkles of sweet-smelling saffron.
> O lessen the heat, and cast off the unusable chaff,
>> as he winnows the grain in the midst of the day.

"Heavens," said MUSCETTOLA, "what a wonder is this Roman   38
simplicity! For it fills the ears not with clever twists and turns,
but with flowering and delicate sounds, cheering even spirits that
are weary. So too does that poem of his, more widely known on
account of its sublime delightfulness, about a cool and shady
spring:

> Here is an icy-cold spring: there's no stream that's more
>> healthful;
>> Green is the earth with soft grasses that grow all around.

Et ramis arcent soles frondentibus alni,
   Et levis in nullo crebrior aura loco
Et medio Titan nunc ardentissimus orbe est,
   Exustusque gravi sidere fervet ager.
Siste, viator, iter; medio iam torridus aestu es.
   Iam nequeunt lassi longius ire pedes.
Accubitu lang⟨u⟩orem, aestum umbra auraque recenti,
   Exiguo poteris fonte levare sitim.

Tum vero ego ⟨IOVIUS⟩ inquam, 'Hoc ipsum edepol Catullum deceret auctorem; nec crediderim[45] veteres ipsos qui interierunt ut Stella,[46] ut Calvus, vel Pedo, et Marsus in huiusmodi carmine tenerius atque limpidius umquam lusisse. Verum sicut librum scripsisse integrum perdifficile semper fuit, ita certis incitati ingenii flatibus quisque mediocri exercitatione unum atque alterum aliquando epigramma felici eventu poterit decantare.[47] Hinc fiebat[48] ut paullo ante urbem funditus eversam, frequenti et permolesta poetarum multitudine premeremur, cum Romae certissimis litteratis omnibus esset receptus, et inepti saepe atque ridiculi, ubi quaternos versus Coritianis statuis affixissent, per iocum corona laurea donarentur. Itaque horum nomina nequaquam citabo; nam ea satis sunt illustrata iucundo poemate quod mihi *De poetis urbanis* nuncupavit Arsilius Senogalliensis, idem medicus et poeta insignis. Sed tu, Museti, recte' inquam 'feceris, si, ut paullo ante promisisti, reliquas causas nobis singillatim explicaveris, quibus huiusce aetatis ingenia ad amorem Etruscarum potius quam Latinarum Musarum proclinata et traducta penitus esse videantur.'

Here are the alders, with branches whose leaves block the
    sunlight;
    Light breezes in greater abundance can nowhere be found.
Now is the sun god ablaze in the midst of his journey;
    The soil's now hot: by Titan's hard light it's been baked.
Wayfarer, rest from your travels:
    Already you're parched from the heat of midday;
      So tired, you cannot continue on feet that have ached.
Recline, and relieve your exhaustion:
    Be cooled and refreshed by the shade and the breeze,
      and by this small spring may you find that your thirst
      has been slaked.

At this point I [GIOVIO] said, "By God, this would be worthy of
the pen of Catullus himself, nor would I believe that those ancients whose works are lost, such as Stella,[74] Calvus,[75] Pedo,[76] and
Marsus,[77] ever made poetry of this kind that was purer and more
tender. But, while it has always been very difficult to write an
entire book of poems, with momentary fits of inspiration and
moderate practice anyone can croon one or two epigrams now
and then with success. For this reason, a little before Rome was
sacked, back when the city was a refuge for all the devoted savants,
we were overwhelmed by a throng of disagreeable poets; and often, incompetent and laughable scribblers who fastened quatrains
to Goritz's statues were given in jest a poet's crown.[78] I shall therefore refrain from naming them; they were adequately memorial-
ized in the charming poem *De poetis urbanis* dedicated to me by
Arsilli of Senigallia, who is both a physician and a noted poet.[79]
But I shall be grateful to you, Muscettola, if you will explain to us,
as you promised a little earlier, each of the remaining reasons why
it seems the talents of our age have entirely turned and transferred
their affection from the Latin to the Tuscan Muses."

39   'Explicabo,' ille ⟨MUSETIUS⟩ inquit, 'facillime, et certe ante[49] alias in promptu causa est, quoniam studendum sit ei linguae quae, tametsi hodie sit popularis atque vernacula, tamen cum ex grammaticae praeceptis ab aequabili norma receperit dignitatem aliquando apud posteros sit futura fortasse[50] nobilior ipsa Latina. Namque eam non negabimus vere maternam atque domesticam antiquitus exstitisse, siquidem idiotae rusticanique homines, cum Latine vulgo loquerentur, Graecum idioma ut litteratum auribusque alienum, quod non a nutrice sed a doctoribus cum labore peteretur, suspicere admirarique solebant, ut nunc huiusmodi litterarum ignari ceteros Latina eleganti lingua loquentes, dum nihil fere intellegant, penitus admirantur. Evastata enim totiens Italia, post raptum a barbaris imperii nomen, a victoribus sermonem accepit permixtum et confusum ex variis linguis, sicut etiam magis ac magis accipiet, quando vecordia nostra accipiendis in iugum externis gentibus nullus finis futurus esse videatur.

40   'Ferent itaque tantam ingenii et felicis industriae gloriam Petrarcha, Dantes, atque Bocacius in hac vernacula, quam Etruscam honoris causa libet appellare, quantam in rudiore Latinae linguae saeculo[51] meruerint vel ipse Ennius vel Cato Portius et M⟨arcus⟩ Varro, qui verborum delectu habito et ad normam elocutione constituta Romanae eloquentiae fundamenta iecisse existimantur. Nec dubitandum est quin Etruscae litterae paucis temporum curriculis omnino Latinis in communem mortalium usum sint successurae, quando iam Latina in ore nobilium sensim obsolescant et neglecta etiam intereant, sic ut Latine eruditi in ea aliquando sint futuri existimatione qua nunc sunt qui Graece sciunt et pretio

MUSCETTOLA responded: "I'll be happy to explain. Certainly   39
the one cause above all others is right in front of us. Even if Tuscan is the language of the common people today, nonetheless it
must be an object of study; for once it has attained to a degree of
authority through a uniform, grammatically ordered system, our
descendants may someday regard it as more noble than Latin itself. Surely we must not deny that in ancient times Latin was a true
mother language and native idiom. Uneducated people and those
in the countryside who spoke it as a common tongue would usually regard a Greek expression with respect and wonder, as something literary and foreign to their ears, to be learned, not from a
nurse, but from scholars, and with drudgery. Just so, persons who
nowadays are ignorant of Latin literature show profound amazement at the rest who speak in elegant Latin, but they understand
almost nothing. Indeed Italy, which was devastated so many times
and saw the glory of its empire snatched away by barbarians, received from its conquerors a language that is a confused hodge-
podge of many different tongues; and this will happen more and
more since, as a result of our madness, it seems that there's no end
in sight to this insane willingness of ours to bow to foreign nations.

"Accordingly, in this vernacular which out of respect we are   40
pleased to call 'Tuscan,' Petrarch, Dante, and Boccaccio will win as
much honor for their talent and hard work as Ennius himself and
Cato the Elder and Marcus Terentius Varro deserved: men who,
in a more primitive period of Latin, are considered, by their choice
of words and the standards of expression which they established,
to have laid the foundations of Roman eloquence. Nor should we
have any doubt that, within a few years, writing in Tuscan will
entirely take the place of Latin in everyday use, since already Latin
is slowly fading from the speech of distinguished men and even
perishing from neglect. Thus those learned in Latin will one day
be thought of like those who know Greek nowadays and who take

Homerum et Lucianum curiosis et studiosioribus adulescentulis interpretantur. Ergo complures iuvat Etruscis assidue vehementerque vacare, scilicet invitatos benignitate facultatis quae in omni scribendi materia decorem invenit et loca etiam ubique praetenera, in quibus stilus ipse passim perquam[52] hilariter efflorescat. Qua maxime ratione alacria ingenia ad spem vel aeternitatis vel non obscurae laudis eriguntur, cum ad mediocres vigiliarum labores amplissimos fructus propositos esse conspiciant.

41   'Erit certe Bembus, ab illo subtili luculentoque volumine quo voces vernaculae ad exactam regulam religiose revocantur, aliquando novus Aristarchus et ut grammaticae conditor inter Italos alter Priscianus, et ceteri pariter qui eleganter et accurate conscripserunt nobilium auctorum gloriam sortientur. Iam enim videmus translatas in maternum sermonem Graecas Latinasque historias ab idiotis ac mulieribus legi memoriterque teneri, et passim Venetiisque praesertim vulgari lingua lites et iudicia exerceri, publicas tabulas confici, orari causas et rationes omnes quibus utitur populus vulgarium litterarum memoriae demandari. Nec mirum eadem lingua municipales gravissimae leges foederaque et societatum iura conscribuntur, ita ut uni prope Ligures Latinae linguae consuetudinem in publicis et privatis rationibus servent, cum aliter corruptissimi sermonis patrii sonum tam paucis elementis exprimere nequeant.

42   'Alia quoque causa est, nec ea omnino contemnenda, quoniam si hilariter atque praeclare scribere velimus, eas quas ab uberibus matrum exuximus voces ad quasque sensuum ingeniique motiones excipiendas atque enunciandas facilius quis⟨que⟩ admoverit et inflexerit quam verba assiduis comparata lectionibus, velut ea potius

money to explain the writings of Homer and Lucian to those boys who are curious and more interested. That is why composing in Tuscan is an activity to which many see fit to devote substantial time and energy, attracted as they are by its generous capacity to attain charm in any written material, and also to devise exceptionally delicate passages in all contexts, wherein the pen itself may flourish throughout with the utmost delight. That is the chief reason eager talents are moved to hope for immortal praise, or at least to escape obscurity, when they note the plentiful rewards promised to brief and unremarkable labors.

"For his subtle and brilliant volume that challenges and inspires 41 the vernacular to attain a precise standard, no doubt Bembo will someday be regarded as a new Aristarchus and, as a founder of grammar among the Italians, another Priscian[80] ; and likewise others who have written elegantly and accurately will share in the glory of noble authors. Indeed, we already see women and the uneducated reading and remembering Greek and Latin histories translated into our mother tongue. Everywhere, especially in Venice, lawsuits and trials are conducted, public records kept, and legal cases pled in the local tongue, and all transactions useful to the people are preserved in writing in the vernacular. Not surprisingly, the most important municipal laws, treaties, and statutes of associations are recorded in the same language. The Ligurians are almost alone in maintaining the use of Latin in public and private transactions, since they would otherwise be unable to render the sense concisely in the exceedingly debased language of their native region.

"There is also another cause, and one not at all to be despised. 42 If we wish to write with ease and distinction, every one of us will apply and articulate that speech which we sucked in with our mothers' milk. Thus we can capture and express all the movements of the senses and intellect more easily than if we use the words we have collected by assiduous reading (words, as it were, gathered

studio ac industria passim deligente quam ad celerem usum offe-
rente natura, ita ut nobis hodie multo difficilius et gravius et (si
dicere fas sit) etiam ad laudem gloriosius esse censeatur perornate
et luculenter Latina conscripsisse quam ipsis antiquioribus fuerit
Romanis, cum editissimam illam arcem nativae patriaeque eloquentiae tenentibus ullae aliae civitates ullique populi in dicendo
vel scribendo pares esse nequivissent. Et nos profecto scimus quantis vigiliis quantisque laboribus vel mediocres ad scribendum facultates in tanta etiam librorum copia et tot praeclaris adhibitis
doctoribus hac aetate nostra comparentur, quod certe vel uno eo
argumento liquidissime constabit: si eos quos velut disciplinis omnibus et rerum maximarum doctrina refertissimos in umbra loquentes admiramur, stilo demum et scripto enixe vacantes severius
aestimare expendereque velimus?

43   'Quem enim Hermolao, Merula, Politiano omnis generis eruditione locupletiorem aut iustorum operum gloria superiorem hodie
videmus? Qui tamen vel divinis ipsorum ingeniis vel acutissimis
aliorum iudiciis puritate orationis stilique splendore satisfacere
plenissime nequiverunt, quoniam perfecta eloquentia summam ac
diuturnam studii consuetudinem, vim multam praestantis excel-
saeque naturae et ferreum quoddam stabilis ingenii robur omnino
deposcere videatur, ut quae repente fieri non potest molli et cotti-
diano usu sensim coalescat et ad altitudinem animi praeclara me-
ditantis efferre sese celeriter possit, et demum ut ipse studiosus et
ingenuus continui laboris ac desperationis, quae molliorum spiritus saepius frangit, tota illa graviora fastidia fortissime ferat.

44   'Neque hercle dubium est an eruditionem et cumulatam rerum omnium notitiam accurata et pertinaci multorum voluminum lectione atque uno firmae memoriae beneficio saepissime

from far and wide by diligent application rather than those made available by nature for ready utility). The result is that it is considered much more difficult, burdensome, and (if I may say so) ostentatious for us to write elaborate and splendid Latin than it was for the Romans of old, for as long as they occupied that soaring citadel of native, hereditary eloquence, no other Italian city or citizenry had been able to equal them in speaking and writing. Certainly we also know what long and intensive labors are required in this day and age, even with so many books and distinguished scholars on hand, to acquire even modest skills at writing, something that the following deduction alone makes plain as day: if we admire these writers for their profusion of knowledge and their learning about all the most important subjects when they are speaking in the seclusion of their studies, should we want to judge and evaluate more strictly those having leisure time to devote assiduously to the pen and to writing?[81]

"To wit: do we see anyone today more richly endowed with all 43 manner of learning than Ermolao,[82] Merula,[83] or Poliziano,[84] or more renowned for the correctness of their works? Yet in their purity of expression and excellence of style, they could not fully match either their own immortal talents or satisfy the penetrating criticism of others, inasmuch as perfect eloquence seems altogether to demand the habit of long and profound study, the strength of a noble and dignified nature, and the iron toughness of a steadfast intellect. In this way, what cannot be attained all at once becomes solid gradually, by easy daily practice, and is able to rise up quickly to the contemplation of what is best; and only then can the virtuous scholar valiantly resist the many strong aversions to continuous labor, and the despair which too often breaks weaker spirits.

"Nor, by God, am I inclined to think that the exacting and 44 persistent reading of many volumes and the gift of a sound memory alone very often bring erudition and universal knowledge to

consequantur qui nec ad perpetuam ac indefessam oculorum atque aurium operam acumen et subtilitatem ingenii nobilioris attulerint. Multos equidem videmus ex illo ornatissimo globo hominum multiplicis doctrinae auctoritate florentium qui, cum integras vires ad scribendum applicarent, nequaquam parem exspectationi laudem sunt consecuti, aut totum hoc scribendi desiderium tamquam intempestivam periclitandi ingenii atque appetendae gloriae libidinem penitus abiecerunt, nec tamen ut perosi ingenuum laborem ac inerti otio defluentes, quando ea de vigilantissimis ⟨non⟩ nisi maligne dici possint. Sed profecto eos incredibilis eius rei difficultas omnino deterruit, cum ingenii laudem praesenti tantum famae dedicare quam eam permittere uberiori iudicio posterorum atque immortalitati consecrare malle videantur. Neque etiam ex litteratis aliqui desunt qui adeo moroso et fastidienti sunt stomacho ut, cum sua non probent neque obiter aliena possint degustare, cuncta quae offerantur repente reiciant — quod est vitium infelicitatis inexpiabilis ac omnino deridendae.'

45   Tum ego ⟨IOVIUS⟩ 'Vera,' inquam, 'dicis, Museti; nimia prudentia plerosque timidos atque degeneres facit. Multi enim viri eruditissimi collectam in umbra studiorum auctoritatem in sole demum, ut deceret, periclitari numquam volunt, nec facile dixerim an id aliquanto cautius fiat quam honestius. Quis enim umquam optimarum litterarum, disciplinarum, rerum atque linguarum maiores opes ingenio memoriaque congessit Aleandro nostro? A quo neque nos quicquam extorquere umquam potuimus neque ipse Gibertus umquam vel subsicivas adnotationes cottidianis etiam conviciis impetravit, qui tamen et insatiabili liberalitate et Bibliothecam Vaticanam et opes et legationum honores et Brundusinum demum archiepiscopatum de manu sua tradiderat.

those who have not applied to the ceaseless, tireless effort of eyes and ears a keen, refined, and ennobled intelligence. Indeed, we see honored for their vast and varied learning many of that ever-so-distinguished throng of men who, although they devoted all their strength to writing, have fallen short of expectations or thoroughly renounced all inclination to write, regarding it as an unseasonable desire to put their talent to the test and chase after glory. This has not come about through an abhorrence of honest labor or from slothful dissipation (such things can only be said in order to spite those who are the most industrious). But certainly the incredible difficulty of the undertaking has entirely deterred them, since it seems they would rather win present fame for their talent than expose themselves to the riper judgment of posterity and consecrate that fame to immortality. Nor do we lack learned men who are so churlish and finicky that, unable to approve of their own productions or to sample others' when they encounter them, they immediately reject anything that is offered them — a grievous failing that springs from an accursed infelicity of temperament that should absolutely be held up to ridicule."

Then I [GIOVIO] said, "What you say is true, Muscettola; too 45 much caution makes a good many cowardly and dishonorable. For many men of great learning never wish to expose to the light of day, as they should, the prestige they've acquired in the darkness of their secluded studies; and it would be hard to say whether they do so more from prudence than from good taste. For whose powers of mind and memory have ever gained a greater command of the best literature, learning, history, and language, than our own Aleandro?[85] I've been unable to wrest anything from him; and Giberti himself, even with daily reproaches, has never gotten even so much as incidental annotations out of him, even though he'd conferred on him personally and with inexhaustible generosity the post of Vatican librarian, riches, diplomatic missions, and most recently the archbishopric of Brindisi.

46 'Sed perge,' ⟨IOVIUS⟩ inquam, 'Museti, et alias propiores[53] causas enumerato ut haec quaestio, superius agitata, liberrimis omnium sententiis explicetur.'

47 Tum ille ⟨MUSETIUS⟩: 'Ea quoque de causa plerique viri ornatissimi ad Etruscas litteras studium suum contulerunt, quoniam
eae Latinis ipsis ad amplissimum humanarum rerum usum aliquanto paratiores atque utiliores esse intellegantur. Sunt enim et
gratae senibus et suaves[54] et commodae iuventuti et feminarum
ingeniis optabiles et periucundae, ita ut quisque vel egregie Graecis
et Latinis excultus litteris ab omnibus contemnatur velut insulsus,
agrestis, ab humanitate penitus alienus et, quod turpissimum est,
in hac civili luce excludatur etiam ab his vestris elegantissimorum
hominum et feminarum coronis, nisi Etruscae linguae leporem et
suavitatem omnino degustarit.

48 'Siquidem eae molliores facetissimaeque fabulae et delicati versi-
culi cupidinis flammas singulis modulis spirantes magna et luculenta sunt instrumenta amorum atque libidinum, quibus servivisse
sicut et dulce et pergratum iuventuti, ita et earum meminisse pro-
vectis et senibus laetum ac iucundum semper fuit, et insignes
etiam ante alios principes clarioris Fortunae amatoriis dediti vani-
tatibus praesenti gratia atque muneribus ingenia provocant, ut affectionum aestus atque illae totas exurentes medullas curae dulcis-
simis numeris exprimantur. Quarum rerum mollitudinem atque
hilaritatem subtilissimis conceptam sensibus atque infinitis et lascivis coloribus exornatam aliquanto tenerius et acutius Etrusci
quam Latini nostri versibus comprehenderunt.

49 ⟨IOVIUS:⟩[55] 'Qua in parte perurbani muneris te, Museti, ut semper amoribus deditum, neque propterea tamen dedecorantem aut
vitam aut senatorii ordinis dignitatem, egregium valde et perpolitum artificem agnovimus. Et in te quoque, Davale, inaestimabilem

"But go on, Muscettola," I [GIOVIO] said, "list the other causes   46
that hit closer to home, so that this inquiry we started upon may
be settled by everyone freely giving his opinion."

Then he [MUSCETTOLA] continued, "Another reason why a   47
good many of the most distinguished men have devoted their efforts to Tuscan letters is that they consider these somewhat more
adaptable and useful than Latin for their wide application to human affairs. Since Tuscan is dear to the elderly, pleasant and convenient to the young, and desirable and delightful to the dispositions of women, everyone well versed in Greek and Latin is
universally despised as a dullard, a rustic, and as someone entirely
cut off from the human race. And what's worst of all, in civic life a
person is an outcast even from your gatherings of the most refined
men and women unless he has experienced all the charm and delight of the Tuscan language.

"These quite tender and extremely clever tales, and delicate lit-   48
tle poems which exude the flames of desire with each and every
measure, are manifestly powerful tools of passion and longing,
which youth has always found it sweet and delightful to serve. The
recollection of them has always cheered and entertained those
too who are older and well on in years. And so, famous princes
of more eminent fortune, devoted even more than others to the
vanities of love, by ready favor and appointments encourage the
talented to express in the most charming meters these waves of
emotion and all-consuming pangs. Somewhat more tenderly and
poignantly than our Latin authors, the Tuscans have captured
with the utmost sensitivity the lightness and gaiety of these things
in their verses and have embellished them with numerous and
playful figures.

[GIOVIO:] "In this role of courtly service, we acknowledge that   49
you, Muscettola, are an exceptional and highly skilled practitioner
who, although always devoted to love, did not on that account
dishonor his life or the dignity of his senatorial rank. And most

horum numerorum facultatem proxime adeo sum admiratus ut,
cum non modo peracer et strenuus dux sed poeta etiam mollis atque levissimus[56] e castris rediisses, te hac Apollinea simul et triumphali laurea dignum esse diceremus. Quare si non omnino perini-
qui sodales estis, enumerate, obsecro, Etruscos vates rependitoteque
operam diserte et luculenter quam a me satis ieiunam et frigidam
in recensendis Latinis dudum recepistis. Nam inepte edepol et
quidem intemperanter de alieno munere disseruisse sum visus
dum liberalius vestrae obsequerer voluntati, quando versibus pan-
gendis ne poeta malus evaderem numquam toto aetatis tempore
sim[57] delectatus, et profecto eam bene a vobis audiendo mercedem
referam quam ineptissime dicendo promereri nequiverim: nam is
et bene et eleganter semper dicit qui docte et egregie facere consuevit.'

50   Tum DAVALUS 'Totam,' inquit, 'hanc laudem ipsi Musetio concessam velim. Neque enim ita est, Iovi, ut de me benigne admodum dixisti et nonnulli etiam alii[58] praedicant adulantes; nam vim
Etruscae linguae tantis involutam difficultatibus, quam longa observatione infinitisque praeceptis, ut Bembus docet, vix otiosi homines consecuntur, in castris agnoscere nequivi, neque carmina
quae perfectis iudiciis placere possent umquam conscripsi cum
mihi tantum uni et meis amoribus ludendum putarem. Et meher-
cule si proficeremus et blandius invocatae Musae meis lusibus arri-
derent, hoc tamen poetae nomen ut importunum subirate quidem
et cum stomacho repudiandum arbitrarer; praeclare enim mecum
cum barbaris legionibus ageretur si, cum in contione de virtute,
fide, tolerantia, stipendiis ac disciplina foret disserendum, ut sunt
nequissimi atque salsissimi veterani me pro triumphali imperatore
laureatum poetam subitis acclamationibus appellarent. Quare obsecro, Museti, totam hanc tibi uni habeto gloriam, et pro me etiam

recently, d'Avalos, I also admired your incalculable skill in this verse — so much so that, when you'd emerged again from military service as not only a surpassingly brave and spirited commander but also a poet of sensitivity and great delicacy, I said that you were worthy of Apollo's laurel crown together with a triumphal one. For this reason — if you, my companions, are not wholly opposed — kindly provide a catalog of the Tuscan poets, and thus repay with skill and clarity the fairly paltry and feeble service which I've just given you in my survey of the Latin poets. For by God, I think it was foolish and certainly intemperate for me, too generously complying with your request, to have held forth about the profession of others, when in my whole lifetime it never pleased me to compose verses for fear of turning out to be a bad poet. I assure you that by listening well, I shall pay you the dues which I've failed to earn by my utterly inadequate words; for he who is accustomed to act with skill and distinction always speaks properly and with polish."

Then D'AVALOS said, "I'd like to hand over all of this honor to 50 Muscettola. Your generous words, Giovio, and the praises of some other flatterers, are undeserved. As a soldier, I couldn't understand the complex and intricate sense of the Tuscan language which, according to Bembo, those with the time for long study and unlimited instruction scarcely grasp. Nor did I ever compose poetry which could satisfy mature appraisals, since I was thinking only of my own amusement and that of my lovers. And God knows, if I should make headway, and if my prayers should be answered and the Muses look upon my trifles with more favor, even so, I'd think that to be called a poet would irritate and distress me, and I'd reject the title as unsuitable. After all, I'd be in quite a fix before my foreign contingents if, during my address to them about their bravery, endurance, campaigns, and discipline, the veteran soldiers with their wicked humor suddenly acclaimed me a laurel-crowned poet instead of a victorious general. So, Muscettola, kindly keep

de vernaculis poetis te cumulate atque verissime dicturum reci-
pito.'

51 Ita MUSETIUS 'Obtemperabo,' inquit, 'vobis iusta petentibus, et
eum quidem in his enumerandis ordinem tenebo, ut non ii semper
ante alios de industria nominentur qui ceteris sint praestantiores,
sed ii prorsus quos mihi veteres amicos memoria repetenti confuse
rerum imagines obtulerint, ut qui desiderari a vobis prudentiam
meam in hac censura, si id celeriter expediteque perfecero, quam
facilitatem malim. Quin etiam magno et gravi profecto invidiae
onere suspicioneque levabor, si hos omnes, tamquam ex tumultua-
rio indice subitarioque delectu inordinatos, nec plane militiae more
diligenter de censu, de moribus atque stipendiis interrogatos ad
signa transmittemus. Nullus enim ex hac poetarum multitudine
sic ante alios gloriam occupat, ut ea inter omnes tamquam aequales minime dispensetur. Hinc est ut neque pauci neque multi nisi
inepte vel cum invidia possint numerari, nam in turba rari eminent
qui non in extremos pedum digitos erecti potius quam proceri videantur.[59]

52 'Igitur ab Acolto Aretino exordiar, qui non minus ab inclutis illustrium feminarum amoribus quam a nobilitate carminis Unici
cognomen adeptus est. Multa eius variis modis descripta carmina
circumferuntur, sed in eo maxime unicus et insignis semper fuit
cum Polyxenam ad aram pereuntem et quartum Virgilii librum de
Didonis amoribus ab se incomparabili felicitate translatum ad ly-
ram magnis principibus recitaret.'

53 Tum ego ⟨IOVIUS⟩ inquam: 'In quota ergo parte poetici census
numerantur reginarum amores, lyra lasciviens, principales aures
et ipsum etiam Unici cognomentum? Quod si non a familiari
et festiva assentatione sumptum videtur, sed ab acclamantibus

all this glory for yourself, speaking copiously on my behalf about the vernacular poets, and with strict adherence to the truth."

So MUSCETTOLA said, "What you are requesting is reasonable, 51 and I will comply; and in my accounting of them I'll maintain such an order that the ones I mention ahead of the others are not by my intention always the more distinguished, but rather those who from my memory of events appear to me in a confused fashion as I recall old friends. I'd prefer that you find my skill wanting rather than my liberality, if I bring my assessment to a swift and loose conclusion. In fact, I will be relieved from the great and certainly grievous burden and suspicion of envy if we dispatch them all to the field in disarray, as though levied all of a sudden and called up in haste, and certainly not vetting them carefully, as we do in the army with regard to their property, conduct, and past service. For there is none in this multitude of poets who so surpasses the others in renown that they should not all be treated as equals. Hence, only out of folly or with malice can they be said to number this many or that many. For those who are truly tall are few, as opposed to those who stand out in a crowd by raising themselves on tiptoe.

"So I'll begin with Bernardo Accolti of Arezzo, who got the 52 epithet 'Unico Aretino' as much from his love affairs with illustrious women as from his celebrity as a poet.[86] Many of his poems are in circulation, written down in various styles, but he was always at his most 'unique' and remarkable when, before great princes, he sang to the strains of the lute Polyxena's death on the altar and the fourth book of Vergil on the passions of Dido, rendered in his own incomparably felicitous translation."

"Then I [GIOVIO] said, "Come, now! Do the romances of 53 queens, the playful lute, the ears of princes, and for that matter the very appellation 'Unico' figure large in your census of poets? If this name 'Unico' appears not to have been assumed from the endearing flattery of his friends but has been conferred by the

poetis et plausu quodam theatrali delatum sit, nihil te moror, Museti, quin ille ut vere unicus in medio et propiore quidem orches-
trae loco aequissimo iure collocetur. Nec omnino refert si ceteri
poetae livore pariter et fame enecti primam illi sedem invideant,
cum illi etiam torques aureos et gemmas, purpuram, fundos, castella, sacerdotia ceu fortunae temere faventis munera iam pridem
inviderint.

54 'Sed perge, Museti. In praecipuo enim honore erunt qui in secundis et tertiis gradibus considebunt. Primus namque locus videtur invidiae multum expositus, et moderatos ac verecundos plenior
saepe laus et gloria consequitur. Pares enim nobis multos aequissime ferimus, qui unum prae ceteris superiorem libero animo pati
non possumus.'

55 Ad id vero DAVALUS perfacete 'Sinito, Iovi,' inquit, 'hunc Uni-
cum sua illa inveterata cognominis perfrui dignitate, quando eum
bene sani et ambitiosi etiam poetae quam quemquam alium sibi
principem malint.'

56 Ita cum subrisissemus MUSETIUS ad institutum sermonem
reversus 'Operosum est,' inquit, 'atque omni eruditione, lepore ac
urbanitate perornatum Ariosti poema, quo furentis Orlandi fabulosi herois admirabiles res gestas in gratiam non otiosarum modo
matronarum sed occupatorum etiam hominum iucundissime decantavit. Sunt et nonnullae eius *Satyrae* et *Suppositi* perfaceta co-
moedia, sed in exspectatione summa est ad prioris fabulae coroni-
dem alterum volumen iustum quo seipsum superare perhibetur.

57 'Vivit adhuc Florentiae atque etiam aeternum vivet Hieronymus Benivenius, sanctissimus senex qui poema nobile quod iuveni
et incauto impotentes amores extorserant paucis scitissime

acclamation of poets and the applause of the public, I have no objection, Muscettola, to placing him front and center in the orchestra seat that he deserves as one truly 'unico.' And it matters not at all if the other poets, tormented by envy as well as by greed, begrudge him the first position, since for a long time they have also begrudged him gold necklaces and gems, purple cloth, lands, castles, and ecclesiastical offices, as if these were the gifts of impetuous Fortune.

"But continue, Muscettola. Indeed, those who sit in the second   54
and third tiers will be held in special honor, for the first position seems much exposed to envy, and often, more abundant praise and glory come to those who are modest and unpretentious. We can bear with the greatest equanimity having many persons equal to ourselves, but a noble spirit can't tolerate it when a single individual is given preference."

But D'AVALOS replied very roguishly, "Giovio, let this Unico   55
enjoy fully the enduring dignity of his nickname, since poets with their wits about them — and the ambitious ones, too — would rather have him as their leader than anyone else."

We smiled, and MUSCETTOLA, thus returning to the line of   56
conversation he had started, said, "There is Ariosto's poem, a work of painstaking composition and adorned with all refinement, charm, and elegance, in which he most delightfully recounted the wonderful exploits of the legendary hero Orlando Furioso, winning the favor of not only ladies of leisure but also men of affairs. There are as well his *Satires*, and *The Pretenders*, a hilarious comedy, but there is immense anticipation of a second volume — in which, it's said, he outdoes himself — that will bring the earlier tale to a suitable conclusion.[87]

"Still living in Florence and also sure to live forever, is Giro-   57
lamo Benivieni,[88] a very holy old man. After his character had at last matured, he took a noble poem which immoderate passions had wrested from him as an incautious youth and, by making deft

commutatis ad divinas laudes Mariae Virginis maturiore demum ingenio convertit, et hoc uno etiam maxime gloriosus quod alterum eius poema grave et iucundum ille Picus Mirandula, in sacris et subtilioribus litteris hactenus phoenix, eruditissime fuerit interpretatus. In Amanio Cremensi pressum et floridum dicendi genus commendamus, et in eo maxime carmine, quod *Turbidus Padus* inscribitur, in quo maiorem certe famam esset consecutus si, cum optimi viri ac in studiosos omnes beneficentissimi maiestatem sugillaret, aliquam modestiam cum ingenii libertate coniunxisset. Laudatur in Veriteii Veronensis carmine nitidissimus candor atque is in omnem semper partem diffusus et aequabilis. Hieronymus autem Citadinus Insuber poemata sua odoratis atque veneriis floribus mollissime conspergit. Florent Venetiis pulcherrimorum carminum laude illustris ac elaboratus Teupulus, iucundus atque alacer[60] Delfinus et Valerius cum in versu tum in amatoriis dissertationibus elegans, acutus, salsus.[61]

58   'Scripsere tragoedias viri nobiles[62] optimis exculti litteris Vicentinus Georgius[63] Trisinus et Alexander[64] Paccius Florentinus, hic, *Hyphigeniam*[65] ille vero *Sophonisbam*, et ambo inventore tamen Trisino[66] repetitas in fine syllabas, ut rem exprimendis sensibus importunam ac inutili nec multum decora lascivia ab antiquioribus conquisitam, e toto carmine sustulerunt. Sed Trisinus etiam reconditas artes, ut nihil ab illitterato vulgo desideretur, in Etruscum vertit novasque item litterarum notas ut alter Palamedes adinvenit quarum potestate scripta omnia naturali vocum et accentuum sono certius exprimuntur, quod inventum ut nimis superstitiose eruditum, quibusdam morosis et in discendis novis elementis repuerascere nolentibus fortasse displicuit.[67]

alterations, turned it into divine praises of the Virgin Mary. And he is especially proud of the fact that another poem of his, a sober and appealing one, was very learnedly interpreted by Pico della Mirandola, hitherto a phoenix in sacred and humane letters.[89] I recommend the compact and florid style of speech of Niccolò Amanio[90] of Crema, especially in that poem entitled *The Roiling Po River*. Surely he would have attained to greater fame by it if, when insulting the dignity of one of the best of men — and one who has been most generous to all the learned — he had added some restraint to his creative license.[91] The poetry of Girolamo Verità[92] of Verona is esteemed for brilliance and purity that is always in every respect pervasive and uniform, whereas Girolamo Cittadini[93] the Insubrian very tenderly festoons his poems with fragrant and seductive flowers. Famous in Venice for their exceedingly fine poetry are the celebrated and painstaking Niccolò Tiepolo,[94] the appealing and lively Niccolò Delfino,[95] and Giovanni Francesco Valerio,[96] who is elegant, shrewd, and witty both in verse and in treatises about love.

"Two noblemen of the greatest learning have written trage- 58 dies: Gian Giorgio Trissino[97] of Vicenza, the *Sophonisba*; and Alessandro de' Pazzi[98] of Florence, the *Iphigenia*. Moreover, with Trissino having led the way, they both removed from an entire poem the rhyming of final syllables,[99] on the grounds that it was unsuitable for expressing the emotions and that it had been taken over from the older writers with an unprofitable and rather unseemly lack of discipline. But Trissino also translated arcane knowledge into Tuscan so that the unlettered masses would lack nothing, and, as another Palamedes,[100] also devised new letterforms by which everything that is written is pronounced with greater certainty, using the natural sound of its tones and accents.[101] This invention was perhaps displeasing, as too pedantically learned, to certain disagreeable men who did not want to learn new letters and become boys again.

59   'Macevellus et rei militaris et Florentinorum annalium vernacu-
lus scriptor cui amoenum ingenium abunde superest, cum Fortunae desint, lepidissime[68] lusit ad effigiem comoediae veteris Aristo-
phanem imitatus, cuius etiam circumfertur *Nicia* ridiculus senex in
scenam introductus, qui suscipiendae prolis tam stolide quam sinistre cupidus a pruriente iuvencula uxore in currucam facetissime
transmutatur.[69] Item Mantuano Iacobo Calandrae qui est arcis
custos fide, litteris et vitae modestia insignis[70] Ferrariensique Pis-
tophilo a libellis Alphonsi principis molliores Musae delicata ubera
praebuerunt. Laudatur et a curtis et imparibus modulis, quos a
mandra pastorali vocabulo "mandriales" vocant, Barennianus e
Brixia ut circumscriptus, suavis et floridus. Retinet adhuc Saxus
Pamphilus Mutinensis pristinum illum volucris et exsultantis ingenii furorem, et in hac exacta aetate Latinis etiam et Etruscis epigrammatis cum florentissimis iuvenibus colludit.

60   'Apud Neapolitanos nostros in praeclara sunt opinione — post
Actium Syncerum, cuius ingenium extra aleam omnis invidiae
positum volo — Antonius Epicurus, sicut optimis instructus litteris et iucundissimis moribus conditus, ita in scribendo sine inani
tumore excelsus et absque nervorum nimia mollitie delicatus; et
Balthasar Marchesius, in nitore heroici carminis et numero peramoenus et grandis; et Severinus Antonius quem tu, Iovi, Romae
cognitum,[71] a civili modestia et a stili suavitate mihi magnopere
commendasti.

61   'Sunt etiam clari apud Ligures, quibus Etrusce loqui difficillimum semper fuit, evulgatis fecundi ingenii monumentis Gavius
Lucas et Paulus Pansa.[72] Sed hic velut ab ioco ad studia Latinorum carminum, in quibus serius atque felicius se exercet, ingenium

"Machiavelli, a vernacular writer both on military subjects and 59
Florentine history, still has a superabundance of pleasant ingenuity, although Fortune has abandoned him.[102] He has composed
amusements very elegantly in the manner of ancient comedy, imitating Aristophanes. Also popular is his *Mandragola*,[103] in which a
ridiculous old man is introduced to the stage who longs both foolishly and perversely to father a child, and whom his voluptuous
young wife hilariously turns into a cuckold. Likewise Giangiacomo
Calandra[104] of Mantua, who is a castellan known for his loyalty,
learning, and modest way of living, and Bonaventura Pistofilo[105] of
Ferrara, secretary to Prince Alfonso, have both drunk from the
tender breasts of the gentler Muses. For his brief and uneven measures which are called *mandriales* ('pastoral') from the *mandra* of
shepherds, Barignano[106] of Brescia also is praised as succinct,
pleasant, and colorful. Panfilo Sasso[107] of Modena still retains that
pristine inspiration of a soaring and exuberant mind, and even at
an advanced age trades epigrams in Latin as well as Tuscan with
the most vigorous youths.

"Those who have an outstanding reputation among my fellow 60
Neapolitans—behind Sannazaro, whose brilliance I intend to be
placed beyond all competition—include Antonio Epicuro,[108] Baldassar Marchese,[109] and Severo Varini.[110] Not only is Epicuro
deeply learned in the classics and adorned with a most agreeable
character; he also writes in a lofty style free of pomposity, and his
poetry displays tenderness without being too enervated. Marchese
writes heroic verse that is beautiful and sublime for its grace and
measure. You, Giovio, met Varini in Rome, and you've zealously
commended him to me for his unassuming modesty and sweetness
of style.

"Among the Ligurians, too—for whom it has always been very 61
difficult to speak Tuscan—Lucas Gavius[111] and Paolo Pansa[112] are
known for published works of abundant talent, but the latter has
turned his talents from playful works, as it were, to Latin poetry,

traduxit.[73] Et quonam theatri loco quave laude dignum esse putabimus hunc quem in muscoso cautis gradu prae modestia conti-
centem conspicitis, Hippolitum Quintium huius insulae praetorem, gravissimum iureconsultum, quo Latini populi Alatrumque
patria maxime gaudent? Eius enim carmina, cum Latina tum
Etrusca, et decoris sensibus et gravibus argutiis et florentibus
numeris concluduntur. Huic similem quoque videmus Claudium
Ptolomaeum Senensem in eadem iuris scientia plane eruditum,
qui pereleganter Latine et Etrusce Musas excolere[74] consuevit.

62   'In Iulio Camillo Foroiuliense varia eruditione liberaliter exornato, iudicium acre profundum incomparabile suspiciunt, qui
Etruscae elocutionis[75] proprietates, modos exactissimasque regu-
las, si puriter et generose scribendum sit omnino perdiscenda sanis
hominibus arbitrantur. Leander quoque nobilis Perusinus equestri
quodam et luxurianti stilo luculenter exsultat.[76] Mire etiam placent Sempronii Amaranthi Spoletani lyricae illae sextanae cantio-
nes ad ostendendam vim subtilioris artificii, paribus repetitorum
finium modis, in seipsas difficillima ratione triplicatae. Caesiani
quoque Pisani admirabile videtur ingenium in agnoscenda atque
observanda linguae proprietate et antiquorum poetarum sensibus
enodandis; qua laude Tryphonem Venetum iam pridem sibi eximiam in Etruscis auctoritatem comparasse constat.

63   'Hos fere omnes scitote esse ex ordine veteranorum, in quem et
conferri Brittonium nostrum aequo animo patiemini, vel ea saltem
ratione, quod[77] *Davaliadem* scripserit et veteres vigilias Victoriae
nostrae Columnae dedicarit. Ceteros in secunda classe relinque-
mus, quamquam in iis plerosque valentes ac ingenuos tirones
agnoscam qui ad frugem et ad certam gloriam, ut hic qui ad
laudem adulescit, Rotilius noster, iam felix Epicuri praeceptoris

to which he applies himself with more seriousness and success. And what section of the theater and what praise will we suppose that Ippolito Quinzio[113] merits, whom you observe on the mossy step of a rock, keeping silent out of modesty? He is the governor of this island, a venerable jurist, the pride of Latium and especially of his native Alatri. His poems, both in Latin and in Tuscan, are finished with dignity of sentiment, subtle gravity, and metrical excellence. We see his like, too, in Claudio Tolomei[114] of Siena, a man quite learned in the same field of law, who is accustomed to honor the Muses very elegantly both in Latin and in Tuscan.

"Then there is Giulio Camillo[115] of Friuli, who is liberally sup- 62 plied with all manner of learning. Those who consider the characteristics, manners, and precise rules of Tuscan oratory necessary for sensible people to learn thoroughly, if their writing is to be pure and of quality, admire his perceptive, penetrating, and incomparable judgment. In addition, Leandro,[116] a noble Perugian, revels colorfully in a courtly and effusive style. There is wonderful appeal in those lyrical sestinas by Sempronio Amaranti[117] of Spoleto, who employed a quite challenging threefold repetition of even measures at the ends of lines in order to display the power of his finer art. Cesano of Pisa,[118] too, appears remarkable for his ability to recognize and respect the properties of language and to make the meaning of the ancient poets plain. The distinction with which Trifone[119] of Venice long ago acquired a special authority in Tuscan letters is well known.

"Take note that nearly all these are of the veteran rank; you will 63 indulge me if I include also our Britonio,[120] if for no other reason than his *Davaliad* and the earlier long labors which he dedicated to our Vittoria Colonna. The others I will consign to the second rank, although I will acknowledge that there are several young recruits of energy and character among them—such as this Rota[121] of ours, who's already an outstanding imitator of his teacher Epicuro[122] and is maturing toward honor—who are marching with

imitator, plenis passibus contendunt; cum illis etiam reliquos omnes aggregabimus quorum carmina ad Puteolanas aquas numquam pervenerint.

64 'Sed certe mihi ac omnibus Neapolitanis nuper triste sui desiderium reliquit Draconettus, poeta divinae inventionis et iuvenum ingenii iucunditate florentissimus (proh dolor!) ex equi lapsu acerbissima morte surreptus; sicut etiam per hos dies, apud Caesarem Feramuscam in Campania, Martellium Florentinum in ipso aetatis flore occidisse audivimus, quo nemo in amatoriis lusibus blandius atque subtilius lascivi[v]it, nemo heroica attigit generosius atque limpidius.'

65 Haec cum dixisset, tum DAVALUS 'Quam disertus es,' inquit, 'et callidus, Museti, qui ab initio sermonis velut ex improviso lacessitus, visus es maluisse veniam deprecari quam culpa vacare, quasi haec omnia haud plane excogitata atque in ordinem scitissime digesta amplo illo[78] et docto pectore minime contineres. Magnum est hoc enim et praeclarum cum exactae eruditionis tuae tum in hoc munere poetico perfectae facultatis argumentum, quod nobis tot poetarum ingenia tamquam vultus ipsos et veras effigies ex lineamentis et ductibus eorum operum ut eximius artifex elegantissime depinxisti, adeo ut te iam amplius minime miremur, ex summo iureconsulto summum etiam poetam evasisse velut quem, domi toga deposita, quosque novos non modo excutientem libellos, sed curiose etiam ipsa opera atque ingenia poetarum penitissime terebrantem deprehenderimus.'

66 'Utinam' inquit MUSETIUS 'haec tanta laus tumultuariis et subrepticiis lucubrationibus meis obveniret; esset mihi profecto magnopere laetandum si et hanc quoque secundam lauream Etruscae Musae capiti meo se imposituras esse promittere viderentur, quibus certe semper sum oblectatus et nunc maxime etiam delector cum e clamoso foro atque e senatu molestis fatigatum muneribus

full stride toward success and sure glory. I will gather along with them all the rest whose poems have never reached as far as the hot springs of Pozzuoli.

"But surely Dragonetto,[123] a poet of divine inventiveness and 64 the most excellent of youths for his agreeable nature, recently left me and all Neapolitans in grief when alas! he died miserably of a fall from a horse. So, too, in the course of these days I've heard that the Florentine Martelli,[124] serving under Cesare Fieramosca in Campania, died in the very flower of his youth. Nobody indulged in playful love poems with more delicate charm or applied himself to heroic verse with more honor and clarity than he."

When Muscettola had spoken, D'AVALOS said, "How eloquent 65 and shrewd you are, Muscettola, for you have presumed from the beginning of your discourse, as if answering an unforeseen challenge, to prefer to seek our pardon rather than to be blameless, as if you just couldn't keep all this inside your ample and vastly learned mind because it hadn't been thought out and expertly set in order. It's a great and crystal clear proof of your precise erudition as well as the excellence of your gift for poetry that, from the features and outlines of the works of so many poets, you've created for us a most elegant portrait of their abilities, just as an exceptional artist would create a faithful likeness of their physical features. Hence we no longer marvel that you have developed from an expert jurist into a supreme poet as well, as we have discovered that, laying aside your toga at home, as it were, you do not simply scour all the latest publications but carefully penetrate deep into the poets' works themselves and into their minds."

MUSCETTOLA answered, "If only great praise such as this might 66 accrue to my stolen vigils and scrappy, late-night studies! I'd be very glad indeed if the Tuscan Muses seemed resolved to place this other laurel crown too upon my head. Certainly they've always given me pleasure, and I delight in them now more than ever when, from the din of public affairs, wearied by troublesome

meme recipere vel in Nidiam[79] porticum vel tenerioris officii causa
ad illustres dominas evolare contingit. Sed cur potius, Davale, hos
sermones non tandem omittimus et Iovium cohortamur ut aliquid
de soluta oratione pronuntiet, et in ea clarissimos quosque vel digito saltem nobis ostendat? Neminem enim ex his qui in parando
stilo non ignobiliter desudant[80] eo vel liberius vel fortasse doctius
iudicare posse existimaverim, quippe quem ab ineunte aetate pedestri exercitationi deditum impigre semper eluctantem atque an-
helantem ad arduum paene illud eloquentiae iugum pervenisse
videmus cum a nobis ornatissimae eius historiae lectitantur. Enimvero aestimetur hic ipse Iovius ab aliis, ut libet,[81] et absolutus
philosophus et medicus quoque illustris atque etiam fortunatus;
ego certe istis omnibus eximiis artibus eloquentiae dotes antepono.
Quid enim in ingenuo atque erudito homine aut rarius aut excel-
lentius aut denique etiam utilius esse potest ad utriusque vitae ornamentum ac illustrem famam splendida atque magnifica dicendi
facultate? Cuius uno praesidio nos ipsi, qui minima saepe victus
intemperie aut cert[a]e naturae nutu quam ocissime perimus, et a
mortis iniuria vindicamur et, si quae sunt vel ad usum vel ad elegantiam totius humanae vitae liberalibus studiis aut casibus adinventa, ea demum nobilissime ad posterorum notitiam transmit-
tuntur.'

67   Tum ego ⟨IOVIUS⟩ ad Musetium conversus: 'Parce, obsecro, ab
his et falsis et intempestivis laudibus; non enim aures fero adeo
impudentes ut tantum abs te benevolentiae erga me tuae tribui
velim ut tu,[82] qui alioqui exactissimus iudex ad tribunal esse dice-
ris, improbo vel crassiore iudicio videare, cum me ad summum
paene eloquentiae iugum pervenisse arbitreris. Memento te in Ae-
naria esse et iuxta Pontani statuam loqui, quae hispido, ut vides,
supercilio sermones vel ludicros revocat ad stateram, secus ac vos
Neapoli soletis in Campana vel ipsa maxime Nidia[83] porticu, in

responsibilities, I chance to retreat to the Nidian portico[125] or, out of a more tender duty, rush to the sides of noble ladies. But d'Avalos, why don't we finally put aside these discussions, and instead encourage Giovio to relate something about prose style and at least point us to each of its most illustrious practitioners? In my view, none of these who toil with any distinction to develop a writing style can pass a freer or more learned judgment than he, inasmuch as he has been devoted to the practice of prose from an early age. Every time we read his exceedingly elegant *Histories* we see that, struggling and panting but never tiring, he has almost reached that steep summit of eloquence. Others, indeed, may wish to recognize Giovio himself as both a complete philosopher and as a celebrated, even successful physician. I at any rate prefer his gifts of eloquence to all those extraordinary skills. For what can be more fine and rare in a noble and learned man, what in the end is more useful for embellishing and winning fame in both kinds of life[126] than the power of grand and sumptuous eloquence? This is the single safeguard whereby we, who often perish quickly from a slight distemper in our regimen or just because of Nature's decision, are delivered even from an unjust death, and whatever we have discovered by our liberal studies or by experience for the practical use or refinement of human life, eloquence in the end hands down in the noblest way for the edification of posterity."

I [GIOVIO] then turned to Muscettola and said, "Please put an end to these erroneous and untimely praises! I'm not so shameless as to wish to hear so much kindness from you that your judgment while on the bench — which is considered very precise in other respects — may be thought to have been tainted or crude when you determine that I've nearly arrived at the highest peak of eloquence. Remember that you are on Ischia, speaking next to the statue of Pontano, whose bristling eyebrow, as you see, calls back even playful conversations to the goldsmith's scales — not, as is your habit in Naples, in the Campanian portico and especially in the Nidian

67

qua aversos et adversos, ut libet, peregrinos pariter et cives modo adulanter unguentatis illis vestris eloquentiae fluminibus proluitis, modo etiam hostiliter haustis ex sentina liquoribus foedissime conspurcatis.

68   'Sic enim me natura genuit et usus rerum ac amicorum varietas erudiverunt ut, sicut malevolorum periniqua et peracerba iudicia ingenti animo nunc maxime contemno, ita minus veris vel ineptis laudibus nequaquam permovear atque eas libero fastidio repudiandas putem. Et haec una quidem est via admodum salubris ad discendum, si te ipsum nihil inani persuasione sustuleris, etiamsi tua tibi atque rarissimis amicorum placere videantur. Tunc enim cum in gravioribus studiis, tum in hac difficillima scribendi arte aliquid profecimus, cum nihil exacte atque memoriter[84] scire, nihil expedite ornateque scribere posse crederemus, quando quidem pudore simul ac dolore pertinacique aemulatione libera ingenia admotis velut facibus accendantur, et tum profecto iuvat neque oculis neque toti valetudini pepercisse, cum novas continue fruges recondendo atque avide cumulando e refertissimis demum horreis et penuariis cellis recognito atque alacriter prolato tantarum rerum apparatu, laboris ac diligentiae tuae fructum sentis et ex frugi timidoque agricola te nobilem repente factum et maxime opulentum contempleris.

69   'Quod tamen mihi adhuc minime contingit experiri, velut parum fertilem et male subactum agrum multo laboriosius quam felicius excolere contendenti, ita ut uni praesertim Sadoleto tantam messem tantamque ubertatem invideam. In eius enim dialogo qui *Hortensius* inscribitur, quamvis eum nondum absolverit, et in duabus orationibus quas pro Carpenthoractensi colonia adversus Iudaeos faeneratores suggillata Armellini Cardinalis avaritia

portico itself. There, at one moment you bathe citizens and foreigners together, either to their faces or behind their backs, as suits you, with those perfumed streams of your fawning eloquence, and the next moment you turn enemy and spatter them with foul-smelling bilgewater.

"For nature has formed me, and the experience of things and 68 the fickleness of friends have taught me, especially at this moment, to despise intensely unjust and harsh judgments from the malicious; so by the same token I'm completely unaffected by praise that is lacking in aptness and truth, and I think it must be refused with frank disdain. And this indeed is the one entirely wholesome path to learning: not in any way to exalt yourself by paying heed to empty flattery, even if your own writings appear to please only you and a very few of your friends. I made some progress both in more serious pursuits and in this surpassingly difficult art of writing just when I believed myself unable to know anything precisely and accurately, or to write anything on the spot and elegantly. This is so because noble minds are set afire by shame, suffering, and stubborn rivalry, which act like torches, so to speak; when later you experience the return for your labor and care, you are glad that you did not spare your eyes or overall health at an earlier time. For by continually storing fresh harvests, as it were, and eagerly building them up, you can review and quickly bring forth a wealth of material from your packed granaries and storerooms, and you will find that you've suddenly been transformed from a frugal and cautious farmer into an illustrious one—and a very rich one too.

"Up to now, however, I have not had the chance to experience 69 this, as I strive with much more labor than luck to cultivate an infertile and poorly worked field. I'm especially jealous of the plentiful harvest enjoyed by Sadoleto[127] in particular. For in his dialogue entitled *Hortensius* (although he hasn't yet finished it) and in two orations which he wrote on behalf of the provincial town of Carpentras against the Jewish moneylenders, chastising Cardinal

perscripsit, elocutionem admiramur emendatam ac plane illustrem et generosam quam non modo ab exquisita ratione atque scientia sed a natura singulari atque divina et quadam optima consuetudine ductam esse conspicimus.

70 'Andreas quoque Naugerius splendidum et perpolitum scribendi genus[85] est consecutus, ut ex duabus praesertim orationibus deprehendi potest quas in Liviani Veneti imperatoris, et Lauredani senatus principis funeribus habuit. In his enim est verborum copia delectorum et sententiarum candor eximius et in toto orationis fluxu mira lenitas, in qua nervi quidem validiores absque ulla austeritatis suspicione potius apparent quam emineant. Eum puto Venetae historiae a fine M. Sabellici conscribendae munus quod sibi publico decreto atque stipendio demandatum fuit egregie absoluturum, si a gravissimis susceptae apud caesarem legationis occupationibus ad requisitam otii tranquillitatem se contulerit. Quem pacatum vitae statum liberalitate regia consecutum videmus Paulum Aemilium, stili ubertate fecundissimum senem qui Lutetiae Gallicam historiam ab initiis reciperatae[86] libertatis ad haec usque tempora castigata serie perducit, sicut et Polydorus Virgilius Urbinas qui res Britannicas liberaliter invitatus Latine perscribit.[87]

71 'Ceterum I.[88] Sanga Romanus ab epistolis Giberti et consiliorum Pontificis Maximi ab illustri fide particeps, ut plane existimo, supra aetatem profecit: est enim in optima imitatione prudens, sedulus, aequabilis, venustus, ita ut credam eum eloquentiae laude Romanorum principem futurum. In Laurentio Granio Signino antistite designato, huius aequali, spiritus quidam inest cum varia excellentique doctrina coniunctus qui stilum altius attollit, et actio arte singulari cum voce tremula auribus lugentium

Armellini for his greed,[128] I admire the pure, clear, and dignified expression which is evidently drawn not only from the discriminating use of his reason and expertise but also from a uniquely inspired nature as well as from habitual practice of the best kind.

"Andrea Navagero,[129] too, has achieved a splendid and highly 70 refined style of writing, as can be discovered especially from two orations which he gave for the funeral rites of the Venetian commander d'Alviano and of Doge Loredan.[130] For these feature an abundance of carefully chosen words, an exquisite clarity of ideas, and a wonderful gentleness in the entire flow of the speech, which is rather vigorous and muscular but with no hint of stiffness; the sinews are evident without standing out. I think he will complete magnificently the task of writing the history of Venice from the point where Marcantonio Sabellico[131] left off—a task entrusted to him by public decree and with a stipend[132]—if he will turn from the burdensome responsibilities of being an envoy to the emperor, to the peace and leisure that he requires. Paolo Emili,[133] whom we see has attained this undisturbed state of life through royal generosity, in his old age is the prolific practitioner of an exuberant style. Living in Paris, he is tracing the history of France from the initial recovery of liberty all the way up to the present, correcting the sequence of events. Likewise, Polydore Vergil[134] of Urbino has been induced by generous rewards to chronicle in Latin the affairs of Britain.[135]

"For the rest, I certainly believe that the Roman, Giovanni Bat- 71 tista Sanga,[136] Giberti's secretary and thanks to his illustrious loyalty a participant in the pope's counsels, has excelled beyond his years. In his imitation of the best, he is skillful, diligent, impartial, and charming, so I think his eloquence will lead the Romans in honor. In Lorenzo Grana,[137] the bishop-designate of Segni, who is Sanga's age, there is a certain inspiration, united with varied and excellent learning that further elevates his style, and a tremulous delivery adapted by singular skill to the ears of mourners; for he

accommodata (nam is defunctos principes in funere luculentissime laudare consuevit)—ipsi Vincentio Pimpinello, cum poetae laureato tum oratori canoro et suavi, quibusdam in rebus priscae actionis minime contemnendis haud dubie superior, qui, in eo munere aliquamdiu celeberrime versatus, ad archiepiscopatum Rosanense[89] pervenit. Marius etiam Montanus antistes Sipontinus, quem una cum Giberto atque aliis pro obside Germanis traditum audivistis, ab innato quodam calore virili eleganter orationes dictat et diserte etiam pronuntiat.

72   'Sed nunc frustra oculis cogitationeque requirimus oratorem cuius oratio nitidissima pronuntiatione resplendeat ex perfecta antiquorum elocutione actioneque deducta, qua una virtute constare auctoritatem cunctis oratoribus[90] cum Graeci tum Latini rhetores iudicabant. Interiit enim paene tota vetus illa disciplina recte ac temperate Latinas voces exprimendi et rotunda facundia orationes et carmina recitandi postquam T. Phaedrus et Portius Camillus, praeclara Academiae Romanae lumina fato exstincta, optimas litteras felicioris eloquentiae luce orbatas reliquerunt. Sonus namque eorum pro suggestu Latine dicentium adeo clarus erat et cum iucunda articulorum suavitate moderatus ut nihil paullo tumidius aut asperius segniusve pronuntiatum tamquam insolens vel putidum e peregrinitate quae sese infudit, et e vetere Gothorum barbaria conceptum, penitus excideret quod teretes et vere Romanas aures offendere posse videretur. Litterae vero singulae ac item verborum accentus adeo exquisito iudicio proferebantur ut illae neque confragosius expressae neque oppressae languidius, ii autem cum dulci ac hilari gravitate passim excitati cum voluptate aurium pariter ac invidia sentirentur. Quorum laudem, ut in arte difficili ab aliis desperatam, unus ante alios Romanus iuvenis

makes a practice of delivering splendid eulogies over deceased princes.[138] In his use of certain elements of ancient delivery that are not to be disdained, without a doubt he is superior to Vicenzo Pimpinella[139] himself, the poet laureate and a delightfully melodious orator; having served famously in that capacity for some time, he became archbishop of Rossano. Also, there's Gian Maria del Monte,[140] the bishop of Siponto, who, as you've heard, has been given to the Germans as a hostage, along with Giberti and others.[141] With an inborn ardent passion, he elegantly composes orations and also skillfully delivers them.

"But these days our eyes and minds search in vain for a speaker   72
whose lustrous expression is resplendent with the perfect enunciation and delivery of the ancients—the one virtue upon which, as the Greek and Latin rhetoricians thought, the authority of every orator rests. For nearly that entire ancient discipline of expressing Latin words with proper measure and of reciting orations and poems with polished eloquence vanished once death extinguished the brightest luminaries of the Roman Academy, 'Fedra' Inghirami[142] and Camillo Porcari.[143] This left the best literature bereft of the light of a happier eloquence. For truly the sound of them speaking Latin at the front of a platform was so clear and so moderated by the appealing evenness of their clauses that no utterance escaped from deep inside them that was the least bit inflated, harsh, or sluggish, or that could possibly offend the sophisticated ears of true Romans—as does the inappropriate and offensive foreign affectation which, born from Gothic barbarism, has seeped into the pronunciation of words. What's more, they enunciated individual sounds as well as the accents of words with such judicious care that the former neither erupted raucously nor were weakly articulated out of laziness, and the latter were everywhere animated by a gravity that was sweet and cheerful, to both the delight and the envy of their listeners. More than anyone else, the Roman youth Giacomo Gottifredi[144] has worked passionately

Jacobus Gottifredus elaborata frequentique actione adipisci arden-
tissime contendit.

73 'Unde profecto id verum et constantissimum esse videtur quod
Pomponius Laetus, qui primus Romae ab ignobili saeculo Latinas
litteras scitissime docuit, dicere solebat: humanorum scilicet studiorum decus et dignitatem tribus omnino facultatibus atque praesidiis sustentari — suco videlicet uberiore, validis ac explicatis ner-
vis et, vivido suavique colore — ut in humani[91] corporis temperato
et bene sano habitu concurrere videmus. Eleganter enim ille copio-
sam eruditionem sucum appellabat, robustum atque volubilem
stilum nervos ipsos, laetum vero colorem illam de qua dicimus
politam ac admirabilem actionem, quae duas res inter se coniuga-
tas necessario comprehendit, vocem et gestum cum verbis atque
sententiis ad commovendos animos congruentes. In quibus tantam
vim vel unius Demosthenis gravi testimonio inesse constat ut ipse
tantus orator illam contra naturae vitium, calculis ore susceptis,
duxerit temperandam; hunc autem Cicero noster, comoedo Roscio
docente, diligenter percipere non erubuerit.

74 'Sed trium illarum rerum Pomponius, vir arguto sapientique
iudicio, primam sibi vindicasse transpadanos, in secunda Neapolitanos eminere, tertiam vero, quae esset omnium iucundissima,
nullibi magis quam in Romanis labris sessitare atque florere testabatur, ita ut ea singulari facetaque sententia summae laudis homines Hermolaum et Pontanum, tum maxime florentes persalse[92]
nec obscure perstringeret, quando Hermolaus in translato a se
Themistio durior et, ut ita dicam, strigosior esse videretur,[93] et
Pontanus ad omne genus eloquentiae natus, ab agresti ac inepto

through painstaking and frequent performance to obtain honor in these things, something that others despaired of in a difficult art.

"Thus what Pomponio Leto,[145] the first after a shameful expanse of time to teach Latin letters in Rome with great skill, used to say appears to be perfectly true and utterly invariable: that the glory and dignity of humane studies relies entirely upon three powers and protections, namely, an abundance of vital juice, sinews that are strong but supple, and a vivid, healthy complexion — things that we can see coexist in the physical constitution of a regulated and sound human body. It was Pomponio's clever idea to use the term 'succulent' for extensive learning, and to call a muscular but flexible style the 'sinews,' and that polished and respectable delivery of which we speak a 'joyful complexion.' This last-named inevitably embraces a combination of two things, voice and gesture, which act in harmony with words and content to make an impression upon the minds of the listeners. The case of Demosthenes alone offers enough testimony to the power of voice and gesture, so much so that even an orator of his greatness thought he had to temper his delivery by placing pebbles in his mouth to counter his defect of nature. And our own Cicero, as instructed by the comic actor Roscius,[146] was not ashamed to follow Demosthenes' example scrupulously.

"But Pomponio, a man of shrewd and wise judgment, declared that of these three things, those living north of the Po had claimed the first for themselves; the Neapolitans were prominent in the second; and the third, which gave the most delight of all, resided and prospered nowhere more than on the lips of the Romans. With this one clever observation, he very wittily and openly slighted the men of highest honor who were then in their prime, Ermolao[147] and Pontano — since he thought that Ermolao, in his translation of Themistius,[148] was rather wooden and what I might call dry, while Pontano, naturally suited for every genre of eloquence, scarcely dared recite his own works to friends or to speak

73

74

ore vix sua amicis recitare et Latine loqui cum externis[94] legatis auderet. Neque tamen propterea Pomponius se ipsum qui optime pronuntiaret Romae principem statuebat, pudore adductus propter haesitantiam linguae qua ridicule admodum in vernaculis sermonibus per totum vitae spatium irrita spe remedii laboravit, quamquam (quod valde mirandum est), cum pro suggestu intenta voce et pleno oris hiatu Latine esset orandum, discusso repente omni linguae vitio et tota ea deformi titubatione depulsa velut alieno ore et quidem facundissimo loqueretur.'

75 Tum vero MUSETIUS 'Iovi,' inquit, 'prosequere, nam me hoc amoeniore sermonum deverticulo plurimum refecisti. Quid enim suavius esse potuit quam aliquid de pronuntiatione, nec sine eloquentissimorum hominum e feracioris aetatis memoria, perurbane disseruisse? Sed cur hodie doctorum ora aut conticescant aut satis inepte veterum vocem, gestum ac totam huius subtilioris artificii rationem aemulentur ut diligenter explices postulamus.'

76 Ad haec ego ⟨IOVIUS⟩ inquam, 'Ut coniectura facile assequimur, id duabus de causis arbitror evenisse. Primo, quoniam iucundissima illa studia theatralium recitationum veterumque praesertim comoediarum quae per ingenuos et patricios adulescentes nuper agebantur apud Romanam iuventutem penitus fuerint intermissa, irrumpentibus in scaenam vernaculis histrionibus in gratiam, ut putamus, feminarum ac indoctae multitudinis, quae, cum Latina obesis auribus non attingant, Etrusca demum scurrarum et sannionum[95] scommata Terentianis et Plautinis salibus anteponunt, a quibus priscae puritatis auctoribus adolescentes tamquam ab incunabulis tenerioris eloquentiae expedita et salutari quadam disciplina ad pleniorem et grandiorem Latini oratoris habitum celeriter

Latin with foreign ambassadors because of his unsophisticated and awkward manner of speaking. But Pomponio didn't on that account judge that he himself had the best manner of delivery in Rome, for he was ashamed of a stammer which in everyday conversations in the vernacular afflicted him for his entire life, prompting laughter, and which he tried to cure without hope of remedy. And yet—what is quite wonderful—when he had to speak in Latin before an assemblage, projecting his voice and fully opening his mouth, then every defect of the tongue was suddenly dispelled and all that inelegant stumbling driven away; he spoke as if with another man's mouth, and a very eloquent one at that."

Then MUSCETTOLA added, "Go on, Giovio; your pleasant di- 75
gression from our main subject has greatly refreshed me. Indeed, what could have been more agreeable than your elegant remarks about oratorical delivery, and also your recollections of the most eloquent men of a more fruitful age? But please explain in detail why the mouths of the learned today either fall silent or strive ineptly to equal the voice, gesture, and entire method of this exceedingly subtle art."

To this I [GIOVIO] said, "I think that, as we may easily surmise, 76
this has come about for two reasons. In the first place, it's happened because those delightful exercises of theatrical recitation, especially of the ancient comedies, which were until recently performed by young noblemen and patricians, have been entirely forsaken among the youth of Rome. Vernacular actors are invading the stage to the delight, I think, of women and the illiterate multitude. Since their dull ears do not admit any Latin, they actually prefer the Tuscan insults of jesters and buffoons to the wit of Terence and Plautus. By reading those authors of ancient purity from the cradle, as it were, with an expedient and profitable method of instruction, young men once progressed quickly from a fledgling eloquence to the fuller and grander demeanor of a Latin orator. Recall what admiration from among the people

evadebant. Quantam enim paucis ante annis ii[96] quos modo nominavi, Blossius et Granius, hominum admirationem excitarunt cum ludis Capitolinis novo Leonis X pontificatu Plautinus *Poenulus* in honorem Iuliani fratris, qui cum civitate donabatur, est actitatus! Tanta enim id munus cum dignitate ad priscae artis[97] elegantiam peregere ut, tum[98] Romanus populus Roscios, Aesopos et[99] Latinos a maioribus olim suis cum admiratione audiri solitos minime desideraret. Porro quae tum Latina poemata vel suavitate lyrica vel pastorali simplicitate vel heroica granditate a nobilissimis[100] fuere decantata! Protulit enim tum Roma supremo et fatali quodam conatu quicquid veteris artis magnificentiae decorisque receperat, velut e tanta festae pacis hilaritate ominata⟨e⟩ clades quibus modo dementia nostra invectis incredibili atque inopinato[101] casu cuncta misere corruerunt.

77 'Altera autem causa haec omnino videtur, quod non ea ut[102] paullo ante eleganter orantibus praemia proponuntur. Unde fit ut advocati nobiliores qui, dum publice senatus habetur, gravissimarum causarum actores esse consueverunt elaboratis et meditatis tantum praemiis sint contenti, quando cetera, quae ornate narrari, scite dividi, confutari acriter, copiose confirmari perorarique vehementer et gravissime, ac subinde ea statutas suas sedes respicere tenereque deberent, supina quadam temeritate penitus omittantur aut in unam turbidam verborum revoluta colluviem[103] interruptis ieiunisque[104] singultibus evomantur. Nec id valde mirum est, quando eadem praemia in hoc obtusiore saeculo bonae pariter ac malae dictionis operam sine discrimine subsequantur.

78 'Ubi vero aliquis senator, cardinalis vel princeps civis in funere venit laudandus, qui curandis exsequiis ex testamento praesunt

Blosio[149] and Grana, whom I've just named, inspired in the Capitoline games held not many years ago on the occasion of Leo X's ascent to the papacy, with their production of Plautus' *Poenulus* to honor Leo's brother Giuliano on his being granted citizenship.[150] Their fine performance of that play was so worthy of the artistry of old that the people of Rome felt they were in the presence of the likes of Roscius, Aesopus, and Latinus, whom their ancestors once used to hear with admiring ears. And remember, too, what Latin poetry was recited then by the noblest poets, be it sweetly lyrical or innocently pastoral or grandly heroic! For at that time, in a final, fateful effort, Rome strove to bring forward all that she had recovered of ancient art, grandeur, and beauty; it was as if such great and joyful celebrations of peace presaged the defeats which we in our folly have just brought upon ourselves, and which, through an incredible and sudden disaster, have caused the sad collapse of everything.

"But the second cause seems to consist in this: skilled orators 77 are not offered the rewards that they used to be offered a short time ago. For this reason the more noble advocates who, when the senate meets publicly, are accustomed to speak on the most important cases, have only been eager for rewards, which are the objects of their striving and intention, while their remaining responsibilities—an elegant narration, skillful analysis, sharp rebuttal, ample corroboration, and an impassioned and powerful conclusion, as well as respect for and understanding of how each of these features has its own established place—either are entirely ignored through careless brazenness or are merged into one murky sludge and disgorged with broken and meager gurgling. And there's nothing very surprising in this, since in our enfeebled era the same rewards are bestowed without distinction on bad as well as good oratorical efforts.

"Moreover, when some deceased senator, cardinal, or leading 78 citizen requires a funeral eulogy, those whom the will has put in

non optimum ac insignem tota urbe oratorem, quod ii ⟨non⟩ nisi
centenis aureis contionentur, sed adventicium quempiam et auda-
cem paedagogum qui vel adversa nomina fama clarescere velit
paucis obolis conducunt, quando nihil ad funeris dignitatem pertinere arbitrentur honeste et eleganter, an turpiter atque ridicule,
supremi officii ac humanitatis munus, ut iam nihil sentienti, bono
mortuo persolvatur, modo aliquis pullatus cynocephalus inter ne-
niarum sacra in suggestu post flebilis et rauci murmuris initia altius incipiat allatrare. Neque illis etiam sua manent praemia qui in
pontificiis sacris solemnibus fastorum memoriam pia Latinaque
oratione solent celebrare; nam eas partes sibi plurimum usurpa-
runt omnium ordinum cucullati qui, dum eloquentiam insolenti
quodam arbitrio ad insulsarum aurium iudicium accommodan-
dam putant, eam a splendido eruditoque genere ad tumultuarias
morum increpationes et eas quidem grave olentes et cynicas detor-
serunt. Solebant enim paucis ante annis qui ex eo loco erudite
luculenterque dixissent ad praesulatum aliosque sacros honores
commendatione senatus ac humanitate pontificum facile perduci.
Itaque sublatis praemiis nemo rem difficillimam industria atque
assiduitate consectatur, nemo huius artis peritus pueros exercet ut
longe omnium iucundissima facultas, quam sub Romano caelo facile suscipimus, per manus non interitura transmittatur ad posteros.

79   'Sed ut revertamur ad sacratos viros bonarum litterarum intel-
legentes, sunt et alii antistites in honore, et ante alios Nicolaus
Scombergus e Misna Germaniae Campanus archiepiscopus, qui
nunc, cum captus Pontifex Maximus, vel iubente pio Caesare,

charge of the funeral do not employ the best orator or someone eminent throughout the city, for such men charge at least a hundred gold ducats per speech; rather, for a paltry sum, they hire any presumptuous schoolteacher who happens to pass by and wants his name to shine forth, even if in notoriety. They think it matters nothing to the dignity of a funeral whether the final duty of humanity to the deceased is discharged honorably and elegantly, or basely and comically. In their view, the dear departed, who now perceives nothing of it, is fully served if amid the solemnities of ritual dirges, some baboon[151] in mourning attire stands before the assemblage and begins to howl above the soft, tearful whimpering of the mourners. Nor are there rewards anymore for those who are accustomed to honor feast days at pontifical masses with a pious Latin oration, for cowled representatives of all the orders have for the most part usurped that role for themselves. Thinking with willful insolence that they must tailor their speaking to the taste of mindless listeners, they have warped a splendid and learned genre into little more than haphazard moral rebukes, and these indeed have something fetid and hypocritical about them. Indeed, not many years ago, those who had given learned and polished orations from that position found easy admittance, with the commendation of cardinals and the benevolence of popes, to the episcopacy and other sacred offices. Now that such rewards have been taken away, no one works persistently to attain something so difficult; no expert in this art trains boys in a skill that is by far the most delightful of all, and one that we under the Roman sky readily embrace, in order that it not die out but be handed down imperishably to posterity.

"But to return to the churchmen who have a keen understand- 79 ing of fine writing, there are also some bishops who are well thought of, above all Nikolaus von Schönberg,[152] the archbishop of Capua, who is from Meissen in Germany. Since the pope remains imprisoned and has not been released even at the command

nequaquam adhuc carcere sit exsolutus, eius exsecrabilis facti
indignitatem apud Ugonem Moncatam assidue deprecatur. Est
enim animo plane generoso ac liberali atque iis litterarum studiis
praedito, quibus ad singularem personae dignitatem exornantur
qui in gravissimis legationum muneribus apud maximos reges operam praestant. Verum sicut firma iudicii gravitate et fidei constantia studioque praecellenti apud pontificem inclaruit, ita gratiam ab
omni prope mortalium genere ingenua quadam benignitate et suavissimis moribus collegit.

80   'Suspiciunt[105] etiam viri doctissimi Federicum Fregosium Saler-
nitanum archiepiscopum, in quo generis claritudo, utriusque linguae scientia pernobilis et infracti animi gravitas ac altitudo ad
perferendam exilii fortunam exaequantur.[106] Vigent etiam in celebri fama hominum Augustinus Iustinianus antistes Nebiensis,
cuius ingenio multoque labore sacram paginam Hebraicis Chaldaicisque[107] et Arabicis Graecisque litteris et characteribus translatam
et excusam[108] legimus,[109] et[110] Paulus Forosemproniensis summus
astronomus qui, si annum coaptare velimus, subtiliore[111] ratione
intercalandum esse demonstravit ne ab imperceptibili errore so-
lemnium fastorum[112] stata religio praevertatur. Est etiam in Petro
Bono⟨m⟩o[113] praesule Tergestino nobile ingenium, doctrina excellens et humanarum rerum peritia insignis.

81   'Sed unus omnes eruditissimorum studiorum laude superaret
Petrus Carafa, nisi eum assidue de contemnenda gloria cogitantem
incomparabilis pietas atque religio minime simulata ab humanis
laudibus longius abstraxisset. Abdicavit enim sese sponte duobus
opulentioribus sacerdotiis, Brundusino et Theatino, ut in altitudine sacrarum contemplationum expeditius atque beatius versaretur. Huic doctrina et pietate proximus accedit Philippus Saulius
Montanorum Ligurum et Segestae Tiguliorum episcopus, ceterum ingenio valde humanus et mitis ac procul a tristi severitate

of the pious Emperor, Schönberg is at present busy interceding with Hugo de Moncada to end the indignity of this execrable deed. He's quite noble minded, generous, and gifted in those literary pursuits which bring a singular distinction of character to those who serve mighty kings in important diplomatic positions. Truly, just as in papal service he became famous for his steadfast and serious judgment, immutable loyalty, and outstanding devotion, so too he has acquired the esteem of nearly every nation of mortals for a certain inborn liberality and for his very pleasant character.

"Men of great learning also admire Federigo Fregoso,[153] the 80 archbishop of Salerno; his noble birth, his renowned command of Latin and Greek, the dignity of his unbroken spirit and his profound readiness to endure the misfortune of exile stand out in equal measure. Also enjoying great popularity are Agostino Giustiniani,[154] the bishop of Nebbio, through whose genius and great labor we can read sacred writings that he has translated and had printed in Hebrew, Chaldean, Arabic, and Greek letters and characters; and the great astronomer Paul of Middelburg,[155] bishop of Fossombrone, who has shown that in order to correct the calendar we must add days with greater precision, or risk by an imperceptible error having the appointed rites of solemn feast days observed prematurely. Also notable for his intellect, learning, and experience of human affairs is Pietro Bonomo,[156] the bishop of Trieste.

"But one man, Gian Pietro Carafa,[157] would be honored more 81 than anyone else for his scholarship had not his incomparable piety and genuine devotion diverted him too much from the earthly glory that he has always been intent on spurning anyway. He resigned voluntarily from two rich benefices, Brindisi and Chieti, in order to live a less encumbered and more blessed life, deep in holy contemplation. Nearly his equal in doctrine and piety is Filippo Sauli,[158] who is the bishop of Brugnato and Sestri Levante. But his nature is kind and gentle, and free of the gloom of an overly

religiosioris vitae, nec abhorrens ab ea studiorum elegantium suavitate qua in actione humanarum rerum viri nobiles ac animo
maxime tranquilli cum laude honestaque voluptate delectantur.

82   'E minoribus etiam sacratis viris, robustus est et emendatus et
hilaris[114] in coronide suorum *Caesarum* et in *Racemationibus* amoe-
nus et diligens Baptista Egnatius, qui Venetiis iuventutem docet.
Est etiam casta facundia Gregorio Cortesio Mutinensi monacho,
ut ex iis apparet dissertationibus quas a Gregorio Nazanzeno in
Latinum nitidissime convertit. Huius civis est alter Gregorius
cognomine Lilius, quem amarulento stilo[115] de nostrae aetatis in-
gratis hominibus periculosissimum librum scripsisse cognovimus.
Laudatur Hieronymi Nigri Veneti ingenium in toto eloquentiae
studio sibi constans, fecundum atque habile praesertim ad praeclare imitandum, quae est laus studiosis omnibus vehementer ex-
petenda. Valde generoso spiritu rerum Bononiensium annales alte
repetita urbis origine scribere est exorsus Achilles Bochius equestris ordinis.[116]

83   'Sunt et alii admodum celebres qui politissimis epistolis et minutis operibus non spernendam gloriam sed eam tamen brevi interituram consequuntur. Verum ii mihi admodum similes videntur
delicatis et pinguibus et numquam salutem in discrimen pro laude
vel commodo devocantibus qui, cum aliquo terrarum magna adhi-
bita festinandi diligentia sit properandum, a porta viae Flaminiae
ad sextam et septimam usque mansionem, mutatis ad celeritatem
iumentis, alacri animo et valentibus quidem membris provehuntur; at si continuatis ac longe extentis itineribus aut in Gallias aut
in ulteriorem Hispaniam sit evolandum, totum id periculosissimi
laboris officium reformidant cum iactationem solem pulverem sitim nequaquam patienter ferre queant, fatiscentibus scilicet convul-
sisque artubus ad insolitum ac vehementissimum laborem.'

84   In hac comparatione MUSETIUS, cum effuse rideret, testatus
est 'Pontanum ipsum, qui fuisset in coronis elegantium hominum

austere religious life; nor does he shrink from the sweetness of refined studies in which, amid the business of life, men of excellence
and great serenity take delight with praise and honest pleasure.

"Even among the lesser religious figures there's Battista Eg-   82
nazio,[159] who is a lecturer in Venice. He is solid, faultless, and
joyful in the completion[160] of his *Caesars*,[161] and is charming and
accurate in his *Gleanings*.[162] The monk Gregorio Cortese[163] of
Modena also possesses a pure eloquence, as is evident from those
disquisitions of Gregory of Nazianzus which he translated into
magnificent Latin. A fellow citizen of his is a second Gregorio,
named Lilio, whom we understand has written at very great risk to
himself a most dangerous book in an acrimonious style about in-
grates of our times.[164] Girolamo Negri[165] of Venice is praised for
his talent: in the entire pursuit of eloquence it is harmonious,
prolific, and open to distinguished imitation — an honor very much
to be desired by all the learned. Achille Bocchi,[166] a man of very
generous spirit who is of the highest rank, has begun to chronicle
the history of Bologna from the distant origins of the city.

"There are others, too, of great distinction whose highly refined   83
correspondence and short works win a fame that is not inconsider-
able, but nonetheless short-lived. But to me those authors very
much resemble the spoiled and well fed who never jeopardize their
safety in the pursuit of praise or profit: when they must hurry to
some place with deliberate haste, they ride with eagerness and indeed vigor from the gate of the Via Flaminia all the way to the
sixth or seventh station, changing horses for speed; but if it is demanded that they make continuous and protracted journeys into
France or the farther reaches of Spain, they shrink from taking on
the task of a very dangerous labor, since they are unable to endure
the jolts, sun, dust, and thirst, their joints wearying and strained
from the unaccustomed and grueling hardship."

At this comparison MUSCETTOLA laughed heartily and affirmed   84
that "Pontano himself, who in the assemblies of elegant men

cum severitate perurbanus, huiusmodi eruditos homines stili laborem mollissime detrectantes palam carpere festiveque deludere
consuevisse, quando pari prope exemplo his similes esse diceret
feroces illos urbanos gladiatores qui vel ab inani verborum contumelia nudi nudos ad singulare certamen pares provocant, intrepide
plagas suscipiunt et victi paeneque iugulati nec vocem quidem in-
dignam ferocia ad impetrandam salutem emittere volunt; quos, si
dantes nomina cum bellum ingruit ad legiones rescripseris, eos
demum castrensibus et longis impares laboribus experiare. Nam
tametsi in ipso proelii momento strenue et alacriter pugnent, brevi
tamen ut inutiles ac ignavi milites ignominia notabuntur, quoniam
facere opus, obire vigilias, humi et sub divo saepius cubare, inediam
aestum nives ventos tempestates nequeant tolerare, ut qui umbratili militiae assueti in agmine ac itinere insolito ferrei thoracis et
galeae pondere fatigentur.'

85   Haec cum dixisset, 'Recte' inquit DAVALUS 'et periucunde delicata ingenia lepidis comparationibus expressistis, et hercle neminem fere video e nostris qui iustum de gravibus ac honestis rebus
volumen ediderit, nisi inter magna viventium opera *Polyantheam* et
Margaritam poetarum et *Oceaneas Decades* omnino computemus.
Proinde, ⟨Iovi⟩, (quae tua est facilitas) nobis edissere quonam
benigno sidere sublevatus et adiutus tot libros *Historiarum* elucu-
brare potueris, praesertim peculiaribus occupatus studiis et nonnumquam ad laboriosos quaestus inopia cogente revocatus. In earum enim voluminibus, ut vim perpetuumque tenorem splendidae
orationis te praesente minime laudemus, id mihi difficile atque arduum semper est visum cunctis urbibus, fluviis et regionibus, tam
late quam Mars ipse arma concusserit, Latina et vetusta nomina

mingled severity with his wit, was given to criticize openly and mock wittily such men of learning who in a most cowardly way were recoiling from the hard labor of the pen: for he would draw a close parallel between them and those fierce urban gladiators who even for a petty insult challenge their fellows to unarmed one-on-one combat, are undaunted by blows and, when defeated and nearly killed, will not utter so much as a word unworthy of their fighting spirit to beg for their lives; but if, at the onset of war, you enroll them into the legions as enlisted men, you may find in the end that they are unequal to the protracted hardships of the military life. For even if in the hour of battle they fight with eager energy, nonetheless as soldiers they will soon be ignominiously marked out as unreliable and listless, for they cannot build fortifications, keep watches, sleep on the ground outdoors (as is quite often required), or endure hunger, heat, snow, wind, and storms. Used to civilian soldiering, so to speak, and unaccustomed to the march of the column, they are worn out by the weight of an iron breastplate and a helmet."

To this D'AVALOS said, "With your clever comparisons you've 85 given us a portrait both accurate and enjoyable of these effete men of learning; and by God, I see almost nobody from among our people who has published a complete book on serious and worthy matters, unless indeed we include among the greatest works of living poets the *Polyanthea*, the *Margarita*, and the *Oceanian Decades*.[167] So then, Giovio, obliging by nature as you are, reveal to us what favorable constellation encouraged and enabled you to devote long hours to so many books of your *Histories*, particularly since you were occupied in your own studies and sometimes, compelled by poverty, had to return to gainful employment. In regard to those volumes — I'll avoid praising in your presence the vigor and continuity of their splendid eloquence — it has always seemed to me a demanding task to call by their ancient Latin names all the cities, rivers, and territories in that vast expanse where Mars himself has

reddidisse quarum rerum vocabula singillatim, sicut et ducum centurionumque omnium qui a triginta annis militarint aspera cognomina cum tota serie rerum gestarum memoriter recitare sis solitus, ita ut te magno occultiore aliquo ad excolendam memoriam artificio uti credamus, postquam ista commentariorum et indicum minutorum subsidia religiose ab aliis usitata semper et admodum superbe[117] contempseris; quorum iacturam plerique Romanorum in hac eversae urbis clade sic lugent ut, si studiorum dignitatem recuperatam velint, repuerascere omnino sibi ipsis necesse esse fateantur.'

86   Tum ego ⟨IOVIUS⟩ inquam 'Museti, ne putato me tam stolidum ut oleis ac medicamentis memoriae vires fovendas atque augendas putem ut ex ancipiti remedio et bene memor et pariter etiam insanus evadam, ut M. Petreio Cassiati evenire singulari nostro cum dolore conspeximus, cui misero assiduis inunctionibus[118] exoticisque remediis, ne obliviosus esset, pituitae redundantiam exsiccare contendenti fons ille commensurati humoris ad alendam memoriam a natura praeparatus calidarum rerum intemperie paucis diebus exaruit.

87   'Neque item existimatote me loca, simulacra, numeros et rerum imagines exquisita industria sensibus habere constitutas quas Latro Portius, stupendae memoriae rhetor, quaesivisse dicitur et Ciceronem designasse potius quam ad usum posterorum aperuisse deprehenditis. Ea enim ars ad contextus orationum perdiscendos magis quam ad rerum aut nominum memoriam, quae in Cynaea et Carneade, ac Hortensio et Lucullo summa fuit, conferre iudicatur,[119] quoniam in ea adeo longus et inextricabilis labor exigitur ut recta et trita via sine compendio[120] subtilissimis illis deverticulis et

wielded his weapons. Yet it's been your practice to recite their names one by one from memory, as well as the difficult surname of every commander and captain who has served during the last thirty years, and everything he has done in his career. We think you must be using some great and secret system for improving the memory, having always and with utter contempt disdained to rely upon those exhaustive commentaries and indices that others use religiously. Their loss in this disastrous sack of the city is mourned by a good many Romans, to the point where they admit that they will have to return to schoolboy exercises to recover their former level of scholarship."

Then I [GIOVIO] said, "Muscettola, don't think me so senseless   86 as to believe in the use of ointments and potions to sustain and increase the power of memory, when from some doubled-edged remedy I could end up preserving my memory but losing my mind, as I was aggrieved to see happen in particular to my friend M. Petreius Cassiatus.[168] By constantly smearing on ointment and by diligent applications of exotic remedies the wretched man intended to dry up the excess of phlegm so as to prevent forgetfulness; but from too much exposure to warmth he caused that source of the opposite humor[169] which nature supplies for nourishing the memory to dry up in a few days.

"Likewise, my friends, don't suppose that by a studied effort the   87 locations, forms, dimensions, and appearances of things are arranged in my mind—something Porcius Latro, a rhetorician with an astonishing memory, is said to have devised, and which, you may observe, Cicero described but did not explain for the benefit of future generations. For that art is judged more useful for memorizing how to organize speeches than for the recollection of things or their names (which was supreme in Cynaea and Carneades as well as in Hortensius and Lucullus), since it is so long and so tortuous an undertaking that the straight and well-worn road, with no shortcuts, seems easier and more convenient than

ambagibus commodior et facilior esse videatur. Pauca tamen inde sumpsi quibus aliquando in asperis utor nominibus; nec arcanum artis arbitrariae nunc proferam, ne ea quae tanto mihi usui semper fuerunt a vobis ut insulsa et puerilia rideantur. Quae igitur in me est et ea quidem valde mediocris memoria naturali quodam vigore a patre, ut arbitror, deducto sustentatur atque perficitur, cuius aciem assiduis lectionibus et pervicacia quadam reminiscendi sic acuimus ut inter multos obliviosos non immemoris nomen nobis contigisse potuerit. Cum quid enim volebam egregie meminisse, id schediis et commentariis minime mandare eram solitus, quoniam usum litterarum vehementer memoriae obstare auctoritate Platonis arbitrabar et certe quae scriptis reponuntur velut in summa securitate custodire desinimus.

88 'Quantum autem ad *Historias* pertinet, earum famam neque inepte elevo neque etiam intemperanter extollo; id enim posteri viderint, quibus potius ut minus invidis quam viventibus hunc ingenuum laborem vetere quodam animi decreto commendavi. Sciebam enim conscribendae historiae gravissimum semper munus vel divinis ingeniis exstitisse, quoniam tanta res invidiae exposita et praeparatum otium et non exiguum tempus et singularem prudentiam cum eloquentia coniunctam requirere videretur. Quarum rerum facultates mihi numquam affuturas putavi nec etiam speravit ipse Benedictus Iovius frater, vir (nisi amor iudicium fallit) linguarum peritia et rerum omnium memoria nemini secundus. Is enim, qui in me puero erudiendo optimi patris et praeceptoris officium impleverat, cum me tandem in patriam revectum duplicis laureae honore insignem suscepisset, peramanter hortabatur ut conquiescerem in iis studiis in quibus meliores annos insumpsissem et

those exceedingly narrow side paths and detours. Still, I've adopted a few of those techniques, which I use on occasion in the case of difficult names; but I won't now reveal the mystery of that uncertain art, lest the things which I have always found so useful should appear to you laughably senseless and jejune. Well then, the quite ordinary memory that I possess is sustained and perfected by a certain innate vigor inherited, I believe, from my father. By constant reading and a stubborn will to retain memories, I have sharpened its edge so that, amid the many who do not remember, I've managed to acquire the reputation of one who doesn't forget. When I wanted to remember something impressive, I avoided committing it to scraps of paper and notebooks since, on the authority of Plato,[170] I judged that the use of writing hindered the memory; and surely we do cease to retain those things which are set down in writing, thinking that they are completely secure.

"But as for the *Histories*, I'm not so foolish as to discount or 88 exaggerate their reputation; let future generations see to that. I made my mind up long ago to entrust this candid work to them rather than to those now living, since posterity will be less envious. Indeed, I was aware that even for inspired intellects, writing history always was the most burdensome of tasks, because an undertaking of such magnitude, exposed to envy, seemed to require the procurement of leisure in advance, a significant amount of time, and a special kind of practical wisdom, joined with eloquence. I never thought I'd have enough of these resources; nor did my brother, Benedetto Giovio,[171] have such hopes although, unless love clouds my judgment, he was without equal in his knowledge of languages and in the comprehensiveness of his memory. In raising me, he served as the ideal father and teacher, and when he welcomed me home at last, honored with my double laureate, he urged me with great affection to settle down to the studies in which I had spent my better years, and to make good the expenses I had incurred by pursuing with distinction the more

sumptus quos feceram utiliores artes cum laude consequendo ante
exspectatis proventibus resarcirem.

89   'At ego eum *Patriam historiam* et librum de bellis et moribus
Helvetiorum elegantissime conscribentem honesta commotus invidia aemulari ex occulto non desinebam. Itaque non multo post,
Comensibus pestilentia afflictis Romam profectus cum ab eo dis-
cessissem, sordidam illam utilitatis rationem liberalis genius pervi-
cit quo naturali cupiditate ad scribendas res gestas vehementissime
concitabar; adeoque tanta virium ac animi obstinatione rem difficillimam sum aggressus ut neque occupata in gymnasiis opera neque animo diurnis actionibus impedito eam me suscepisse plerique
viri insignes existimarent. Nam tametsi antiquissimi scriptores me
saepius desperatis praeclarae imitationis successibus ab arduo in-
cepto deterrebant, una tamen spe et ea prope certissima sustenta-
bar: quod eos qui eloquentia valerent vel occupatos esse vel parum
idoneos ad colligendam tantarum rerum materiam videbamus, eos
vero qui in castris atque consiliis versati essent et rerum gestarum
memoriam tenere dicerentur nequaquam tantas bonarum artium
facultates quantas in nostris praesidiis haberemus ad scribendum
allaturos arbitraremur.

90   'Ceterum in ea luce Romana et nationum omnium domicilio
versanti, amicitiae illustres magnorum ducum facile quaesitae, ut
oportuit, in cognoscenda rerum et consiliorum veritate desiderium
inflammatae mentis expleverunt. Nec defuere sub eo caelo ad im-
bibendam perficiendamque eloquentiam maxime opportuno homines eruditi, antiquitatis peritissimi sanoque iudicio magnopere
pollentes, qui me peregrinum satisque iuvenem in Q. Curtii et
Taciti topiatis[121] scaenis lateque luxuriantibus umbraculis extra

useful arts beforehand, given the proceeds that could be expected from them.

"But while he composed with exquisite style a history of our 89 home town and a treatise on the warfare and customs of the Swiss, I, stirred by honorable emulation, did not cease to compete with him secretly. Thus I soon left plague-stricken Como and headed to Rome. Once I had bidden farewell to him, those base considerations of practicality were completely overcome by a noble spirit which roused in me an extremely intense, natural enthusiasm to write history. And I applied so much physical and mental determination to that arduous task that quite a few distinguished men supposed I'd undertaken it because I had no teaching commitments and was unencumbered by daily duties. Even if the most ancient writers quite frequently dashed my hopes of producing an excellent imitation and discouraged me from this difficult undertaking, nonetheless I was sustained by one hope, which was almost a confident expectation. This sprang from my observation that those who excelled in eloquence had been either otherwise engaged or unequal to gathering the evidence of great events. As for those who'd spent time in battle and had been involved in planning military strategy, and who reportedly remembered what had occurred, I judged that they would not bring to the work anything like the rich stores of learning that I had at my command.

"Moreover, basking in the splendor of Rome, where all nations 90 are at home, my mind's impassioned longing to learn the truth of events and policies was satisfied, as was only proper, by distinguished friendships with great leaders to whom I had ready access. Nor in that spot so suited to the partaking and perfecting of eloquence was there any shortage of learned men well versed in the ancients and preeminent in soundness of judgment to guide me as I, a foreigner and quite young, wandered heedlessly on the imaginative stage sets of Quintus Curtius and Tacitus, and through the shady bowers growing luxuriantly everywhere just outside the

Romana moenia incaute divagantem monerent et subinde, singulari humanitatis officio, in Sallustianos hortos in illasque praeclaras curiae Caesaris testudines et Livianum porticum tamquam ad liquidissimi aeris et saluberrimae lucis umbram reducerent.

91   'Inde me iam satis notum ipse Leo Pontifex optimus verae virtutis aestimator, cum forte octavum *Historiarum* librum benignissime perlegisset, liberalitate sua dignum putavit et de manu sua tradidit Iulio patrueli, qui tum erat cardinalium longe amplissimus. Eum itaque ad pontificatum pleno vadentem passu tantis auspiciis secuti perpetuos decem annos conspicuo semper loco, quae eius est humanitas, tot et tanta domi et foris bello paceque et quidem in utraque eius fortuna cognovimus, ut iam *Historias* umquam interituras minime dubitemus, etiamsi nullus ad producendam vitam eloquentiae spiritus accesserit. Scriptorem enim maior et illustrior laus ex incorrupta rerum fide quam ex orationis facundia consequetur, et hercle non multum interest an eruditiores hanc ut ieiunam minime probent, modo illam ut sinceram qui scribenda fecerunt minime refellant. Vivunt enim qui haec gessere et, cum de se conscripta volumina saepius legant, ex consiliorum suorum conscientia externarum[122] etiam rerum fidem metiuntur.

92   'Verum iam multo plures libros nobilissimarum rerum legeretis si hic pontificatus spes meas, quamquam etiam mediocres optima ratione conceptas, minime fefellisset et me Gibertus ipse qui subinde animo consternatum privatis copiis refovebat sua felici dextra sublevare potuisset. Enimvero satis mihi laudis ex iusti iam operis labore comparatum ratus, alio ingenium indignabundus traduxi, postquam nonnullis qui decori ac immortalitati studere debuissent

Roman walls. Then, with singular kindness, they would lead me back into the gardens of Sallust, those storied, vaulted ceilings of Caesar's *curia* and the portico of Livy, as into the coolness of purest air and most-salutary light.

"Later, when I had become sufficiently well known, Pope Leo 91 himself, an excellent judge of true worth, once he had the chance to give a very favorable reading to Book Eight of my *Histories*,[172] thought me worthy of his generosity. From his own hand he delivered me personally to his cousin Giulio,[173] who was then by far the most distinguished of the cardinals. Thus I spent ten continuous years in Giulio's service, always in a prominent post (such is his kindness), while he was advancing swiftly and with excellent prospects toward the papacy. In so doing I've learned a great many things about affairs domestic and foreign, war and peace, in good and bad fortune. So I'm certain my *Histories* will never be forgotten, even if no inspired eloquence were added to prolong their life. For greater and more illustrious honors will attend an author for his adherence to the truth than for his fluent oratory. And, by God, it matters little whether learned men dismiss it as unprofitable, so long as those whose deeds are recorded don't refute its integrity. For those who performed these deeds are still living, and since they quite often read the volumes composed about them, they gauge their accuracy in the reporting even of foreign affairs from consciousness of their own intentions.

"But by now you'd be reading many more books of the noblest 92 events if my expectations, even the modest ones which I had good reason to harbor, hadn't been disappointed by this papacy; and if Giberti himself, who again and again drew upon his own resources to alleviate my panic, had been able to sustain me with his own prosperous hand. Believing that I'd already derived sufficient honor from the labor of a work now complete, I naturally took my talent elsewhere, filled with indignation, since the most worthy labors of myself and others seemed to become contemptible to

ut in praealto neglegentiae veterno consopitis honestissimae nostrae aliorumque vigiliae sordescere viderentur.'

93   Ad haec MUSETIUS inquit, 'Misere edepol et flagitiose etiam insaniunt huius saeculi principes et quicumque alii vitam pro laude belli periculis obiectantes, cum Musarum obsequia superbe repudient vel stomachose fastidiant quasi per ea neque ab interitu neque ab omni posteritatis oblivione vindicentur. Intellexit hercle ille terrarum orbis domitor Alexander, cum Achilli invicto heroi Homerum vatem penitus invideret, quantum ad diuturnam ac illustrem famam bellicae gloriae conferrent praeclara ingenia, quorum vi atque mirifica potestate quae caduca forent perpetuo vitae munere donarentur. Scipionem etiam Africanum se ipso admirabiliorem atque feliciorem posteris evasisse quis nescit propensiore studio T. Livii, cum ille in Scipionum penates liberaliter benigneque receptus auctusque fortunis gloriam illius divini hominis lectissimis eloquentiae floribus exornandam et augustiore spiritu ad posteros transmittendam esse iudicasset?

94   'Quo fit ut a sapientissimis Graeciae civitatibus summa cum ratione institutum antiquitus fuisse existimem, ut in theatris atque porticibus publicisque omnibus locis in quibus spectacula edi populis solerent una et eadem ara Herculi et Musis dicaretur, quoniam indicare volebant praestantissimam etiam virtutem et rerum praeclare gestarum gloriam brevi curriculo prorsus interituram, nisi ea Musarum beneficio velut posterorum famae consecrata adversus omnem temporum invidiam venturis saeculis traderetur. Ceterum cum facile intellegam te vel a Fortuna vehementer

some who should have been eager for honor and immortality, but had fallen asleep as in a profound torpor of neglect."

To this MUSCETTOLA said, "Truly the princes of this age and 93 all others who endanger themselves in battle for honor's sake have lamentably, and in fact disgracefully, lost their senses, in that they arrogantly repudiate and churlishly despise the services of the Muses, on the grounds that literature cannot deliver them either from death or from utter oblivion in the future. Heaven knows, Alexander the Great, the conqueror of the world, deeply envied the unconquered[174] hero Achilles his bard Homer, understanding as he did how much great intellects contributed to an enduring and illustrious reputation for glory in war: for it was by their strength and marvelous power that things that would have passed away were endowed with the gift of everlasting life. Who doesn't also know that the character of Scipio Africanus stood out for posterity in a more admirable and favorable light because of the more positive disposition of Livy, after he was welcomed with kindness and courtesy into the circle of the Scipios, than because of Africanus' own acts? Once his own fortunes had improved, Livy determined to embellish the glory of that godlike man with the choicest flowers of eloquence and to transmit it to posterity with a more majestic spirit.

"That is why, I believe, the wisest cities of Greece for excellent 94 reasons ordained from ancient times that in theaters, porticoes, and all public venues where popular spectacles were staged, a single altar should be consecrated to both Hercules and the Muses. By this they intended to show that even the most exceptional valor and the glory of magnificent deeds would be wholly forgotten in a short space of time unless they were consecrated (so to speak) to the judgment of posterity and, with the Muses' help, recorded for generations to come, securing them against oblivion. But since I readily understand that you could not desist from your accustomed work as a writer even when Fortune actively hindered you,

impeditum[123] a solito scribendi munere vacare minime potuisse, quid interea vel male feriatus excuderis nobis edissere.'

95   Tum ego ⟨IOVIUS⟩ 'Recte,' inquam, 'existimas, Museti, nam me neque ullae curae neque itinera neque commota etiam valetudo quin aliquid ioco vel serio dictarem aut commentarer umquam interpellarunt. Verum ante alia Ludovico a Corduba regulo Suessano liberaliter invitante Magni Consalvi eius soceri vitam diffusissime conscripsi. Confecimus etiam eodem cursu librum *De piscibus* eruditum pariter atque festivum, nec multo post *Leonis* etiam *vita* ad finem fere perducta est cum a Cosmo proavo Mediceae familiae decora latissime repetissem et ad id me plurimum hortaretur Felix Trofinus antistes Theatinus, cuius humanitati et desideratissimi pontificis memoriae hoc quoque vigiliarum munus persolvendum arbitrabar. Ad eundem etiam Felicem libellum cum utilem tum iucundum *De optima victus ratione* perscripsi, et Franciscus Cheregatus antistes Aprutinus, amicorum suavissimus, libellum mihi extorsit et publicavit quem de regione et moribus Moscovitarum ad Rufum archiepiscopum Cosentinum composueram. Et profecto in iis omnino constitissem, nisi me incredibilis Urbis clades ad magnitudinem scelerati facinoris posteris tradendam et Victoria Columna liberali benignitate ad intermissum *Historiarum* munus omnino revocassent.

96   'Quod totum consilii mei propositum postquam ita postulastis explicare non erubui, ut sciretis me *Historias* illas, quae ne mihi quidem ipsi plane probantur, si non felici at certe multo liberali cum labore conscripsisse ut iis tribus et triginta annis maximarum rerum toto orbe gestarum memoriam vigiliis nostris maxime diuturnam redderemus, si viri doctissimi tam honestum munus ut periculosum aut inane suscipere recusassent. Non facile enim

reveal to us what you've produced in the meantime, even in this enforced idleness."

Then I [GIOVIO] responded, "You're right, Muscettola; neither   95
cares nor journeys nor even ill health has ever hindered me from dictating or making notes on something, whether seriously or in jest. But above all, at the generous invitation of the duke of Sessa,[175] I composed an extensive *Life* of his father-in-law, Gonsalvo the Great, while at the same time I also wrote a book *On Fish*,[176] as learned as it is diverting. Not much later, I brought close to completion my *Life of Leo the Tenth*, having retraced at length the great deeds of the Medici family starting from Cosimo the Elder. I received much encouragement in this from Felice Trofino, the archbishop of Chieti, and so I decided that this product of my labors must repay his kindness as well as honoring the memory of the much-missed Pope Leo.[177] To this same Felice, I wrote a book both useful and pleasant *On the Best Diet*; and Francesco Chieregati, bishop of Teramo, the most charming of friends, extorted from me for publication a small book which I'd composed for Giovanni Ruffo, the archbishop of Cosenza, on the land and customs of the Muscovites.[178] And certainly I would have altogether stopped at these, had not the incredible devastation in Rome absolutely called me back to record for posterity the magnitude of this wicked outrage, and had not Vittoria Colonna, in her gracious generosity, bade me resume my interrupted work on the *Histories*.

"Following your request, I haven't blushed to explain the whole   96
of the plan I intended. This I did so that you might know that I've composed these *Histories* — which clearly not even I find wholly acceptable — with much honorable effort, certainly, if not success, in order to render by my labors a most durable record of the great events in the history of the entire globe during those thirty-three years, seeing that exceedingly learned men had declined to undertake so honorable a task as something dangerous or useless. For although the memory of this time will always be a source of

patior huius aetatis memoriam, quamquam miserae Italiae luctuo-
sam semper futuram, vel interire vel ab ineptis et maligne contra
rerum fidem falsa narrantibus litteris demandari, ut quosdam impudenter fecisse absque ullo sensu impendentis ignominiae cum
multo nostro risu conspicimus, quorum opera nihil magis obruet
quam constans hominum fama ac simul illa ipsa quam ingenui
venerantur vivacissima atque firmissima veritas iugulabit. De iis
autem nihil dico qui, cum arcana scribant quae occultari velint,
otio atque oleo intemperanter abutuntur, quorum princeps est
Massainus, senex erudite et salse maledicus qui luculentos invecti-
varum libros, quibus aliquorum pontificum et cardinalium aetatis
suae famam capitalissime proscidit, in ipso suo funere publicandos
reservat.

97   'Sed profecto multos summae eruditionis summique iudicii homines a iuvanda vel oblectanda posteritate et ab extendenda nominis dignitate cum variae res tum obscuriores ac honestissimae
causae retardant et impediunt, multos angusta res domi ad alienam utilioremque operam traduxit, multos ultro quaesita servitus
occupavit. Plures saeva tempora, domestici casus, incommoda
valetudo perturbarunt; nonnullos toga frequens, ambitio, lites a
toto consilio pulcherrimorum operum deiecere. Multos obtrivere
ignavae voluptates, qui omnium maxime hoc turpissimo nomine
desidiam suam excusant, quod acria nimis atque perversa maledi-
centissimi saeculi iudicia sanis hominibus minime subeunda arbitrentur. Quos perblande interrogatos velim an praeclare et recte
secum agere videantur si, cum in perennibus studiis totam aetatem
agitarint, prae inani demum et incerto metu solidam spem verae
laudis et eam quidem ad aeternitatem prope certissimam abiiciant,
quasi parem tantis vigiliarum laboribus mercedem referant si

sorrow for unfortunate Italy, I cannot lightly let it be lost completely, or hand it over to be written by fools and malicious liars who will distort what happened — as we see certain men have done with no sense of shame or, to our great amusement, to their imminent disgrace. Nothing will more effectively put their works out of sight than an unwavering verdict of public opinion and, at the same time, nothing will better silence them than that very truth, most vigorous and unshakable, which honest men revere. But I will keep silent about those who extravagantly waste time and lamplight writing secrets which they intend to keep hidden. Chief among these is the old man Massaini,[179] a learned and witty slanderer. At great risk to his life, he has defamed certain popes and cardinals of his time in his splendid books of invectives, which he is holding back for posthumous publication.[180]

"Certainly many men of immense learning and discretion are   97
detained and prevented from providing benefits and pleasure to future times, and from increasing the glory of their own reputation. This comes about from changing circumstances, as well as from causes less conspicuous but no less honorable. Many have been driven by limited means to work more profitably for others, and many are bound by a servitude that they willingly sought. More have been troubled by the violence of the times, domestic misfortunes, and adverse health. Some, by numerous public duties, office seeking, and legal strife, have been prevented from any consideration of the most noble labors. Many are disgraced by slothful pleasures and offer the most shameful of excuses for their idleness: namely, that they think sensible men should not be subjected to the overly caustic and wicked judgments of an exceedingly malicious age. I should like to ask them very amiably whether they think they are behaving nobly and properly if, having devoted their whole lives to continual study, they spurn the firm hope of genuine honor — and one almost certain to last forever — on account of a vague and ultimately empty fear, as if the rewards they

aliquot tantum dies in momentanea existimatione caducisque hominum linguis his evanidis et tepidissimis laudibus perfruantur.
Quae enim non grandia exornata sempiterna scripturos atque edi-
turos nonnullos putamus, quos honoris causa libet nominare, si
vires agnoscere, si gloriam inde respicere, si movere ingenii lacertos
velint itemque liberaliter proferre veteres vigiliarum opes, atque his
maxime ad audendum gravissimorum amicorum cohortationibus
accendantur?

98   'Nihil enim vel aspectu arduum vel re ipsa difficile vel magnitudine immensum morari posse existimo Lactantium Ptolemeum
Senensem, cum familiae atque opum dignitate tum reconditis artibus atque animi virtute nobilissimum. Quod erit in litteris munus
tam asperum aut tantis saeptum atque implicatum difficultatibus
quod et aggredi audacter et prospere perficere nequeat Romulus
Amasaeus, qui Bononiae optimas litteras profitetur? Quo non
evadet acumineque vividioris ingenii minime penetrabit Theocre-
nus Ligur, qui Francisci regis liberos apud caesarem obsides eximiis imbuit disciplinis? Quid non ad perfectam suscepti laboris
laudem praestarent Lazarus Bassianus, discendo atque docendo
senex factus,[124] qui Alexandrum Campegii Cardinalis filium, Bo-
noniensem antistitem, et Hieronymus Borgia, qui Ranuccium Farnesii pariter cardinalis filium, militia gaudentem, summae sed
diversae indolis adulescentes in praeclaram famae lucem provexe-
runt? Quid non adsequerentur et Caelius Calcaninus et Franciscus Conternius et Hieronymus Fondulius et Petrus Crassus,[125]
litterarum copia ac ingenii suavitate praediti singulari? Quid

would get for such long hours of effort would be matched by just a few days' enjoyment of transient and indifferent praise in the ephemeral esteem and the fleeting chatter of the public. What grand, elegant, and everlasting works will not some men write and publish, I believe—and I'm pleased to give their names to show them honor—if, that is, they choose to acknowledge their powers, give thought to fame, flex the muscles of their genius, and also heartily demonstrate their former capacity for long labors; and especially if they are roused to the greatest daring by the encouragement of their most respected friends?

"I think there's no task either difficult in appearance, hard in reality, or vast in extent that can hold back Lattanzio Tolomei[181] of Siena, a man famous both for his family's rank and wealth and for his own subtle learning and excellent mind. What literary work will be so troublesome or encircled and enveloped by such difficulties that Romolo Amaseo,[182] a professor of fine letters in Bologna, cannot undertake and complete it successfully? Consider the Ligurian Tagliacarne,[183] who instructs in the noblest disciplines King Francis' children, who are the emperor's hostages. To what will he not turn, and what will he not penetrate with the perceptiveness of his quite lively intellect? What of Lazzaro Bonamico,[184] who has grown old from teaching and learning, and what of Girolamo Borgia?[185] Each of them led a young man of distinguished gifts into the splendor of great renown—the former, Cardinal Campeggio's son Alessandro, the bishop of Bologna;[186] the latter, Ranuccio Farnese,[187] likewise a cardinal's son but of quite different temperament, who delighted in soldiering. How would these teachers not win unmatched praise for their undertaking? What would Celio Calcagnini,[188] Francesco Conterni,[189] Girolamo Fondulo,[190] and Pietro Grassi[191] not achieve, all of them endowed as they are with a wealth of learning and a remarkably pleasant nature? And what, finally, wouldn't some others

98

denique et nonnulli alii, quorum nomina necesse est ut memoria dilabantur, Latine et perornate non absolverent?

99   'Non desunt profecto huic aetati nostrae magna excelsaque ingenia quae etiam absque ulla dubitatione praeclariora forent atque etiam sempiterna nisi, ut diximus, aut metu parum virili debilitata aut voluptatibus intestinaque segnitie corrupta atque evastata penitus perderentur. Pares certe et, si dicere licet, fortasse meliores Pontanis, Sabellicis, Politianis, Merulis atque Hermolais haberemus nisi ea nos[126] sponte contracta vitia nimium hebetarent, et avari vel occupati principes algenti desertaeque virtuti viliora etiam praemia sustulissent. Quamobrem optimae litterae a paucis annis, quod in Italia aliquanto illiberalius quam solerent habitae viderentur, ultra Alpes ad externas gentes coeperint proficisci, apud quas et suscipi cum honore et humanissime tractari soleant.'

100   Tum MUSETIUS 'Ita est,' inquit,' Iovi, ut dicis: emigrare iam litterae incipiunt et latissime quidem peregrinantur. Verum non eum secum ferunt elegantiae nitorem, ut quam maxime resplendeant, quem nos Latini consectamur atque ante alia omnia adipisci concupimus. Iis enim quoddam simile accidere videtur quod Idumaeis palmis quae, si translatae in Italiam fuerint ut ad Flumentanum portam in aede Mariae Virginis Popularis videmus, coalescunt quidem et generose diffunduntur, et dactylos etiam crassiores ferunt sed qui non plane maturescant, et nullam fere ab illo spadiceo atque translucido suco vel saporis vel pulchritudinis commendationem accipiant, utpote quae nativi soli et benignioris caeli temperiem sentire non possint. Enimvero neminem adhuc ex ipsis quamquam litteratissimis externis vidi qui eloquentiam antiquorum feliciter sit imitatus, neque ullum hodie esse audio qui velut ab alto latissimoque pelago omnifariae doctrinae in propositum

accomplish, writing the most elegant Latin, even if their names must have escaped my memory?

"Certainly this age of ours is not without great and noble intel- 99 lects. Doubtless they would be still more illustrious and even immortal were it not the case, as I said, that they were being entirely squandered, either because they were disabled by unbecoming timidity or because they were corrupted and ruined by pleasures and inner sluggishness. Surely we would have writers the equal of, and (if I may say so) perhaps better than, the likes of Pontano, Sabellico, Poliziano, Merula, and Ermolao, had not our faults, willingly acquired, so blunted our faculties; and had not rulers, out of greed or distraction, taken away even the paltriest rewards for learning, leaving it deserted, out in the cold. On account of the fact that the best scholarship is treated with somewhat less respect in Italy than it used to be, for a few years now it has begun to travel beyond the Alps to foreign peoples, where it may expect to be welcomed with honor and treated with the utmost kindness."

Then MUSCETTOLA said, "It's just as you say, Giovio: learning 100 is already beginning to emigrate and indeed is traveling abroad, far and wide. But it doesn't take with it, to shine its brightest, that dazzling elegance which we Latins strive for and long to acquire above all else. For something seems to happen to them there, resembling what happens to palm trees from the Holy Land. When these are transported into Italy, as we see for example by the Porta Flaminia at the church of Santa Maria del Popolo, they take root and branch out splendidly, and even bear dates that are fatter, but they don't ripen fully, and they lack almost entirely that brownish, shiny juice that enhances taste and beauty, missing as they do the warmth of their native soil and the milder climate. Certainly thus far I've seen no one in a foreign land, however erudite, who is able to imitate the eloquence of the ancients with success; nor do I hear of anyone today who is traveling at full sail, out of the deep and vast ocean of every kind of learning, straight into that

atque exoptatum portum perfectae orationis inflatis velis rectis-
simo cursu deferatur, ut alias de Longolio Gallo immatura morte
surrepto amicissime atque verissime praedicantem te polliceri audivimus.'

101   Tum vero inquam ⟨iovius⟩, 'Recte sentis, Museti, et certe
Longolius avido volucrique ingenio aliqua elegantissime conscripsit
quae idcirco doctissimis placebant, quoniam id iam iter feliciter
esset ingressus quo haud dubie ad consummatam eloquentiae laudem erat profecturus, nisi tam propere stomachi vitio concidis-
set.[127] Verum hoc ipso Longolio nostro, ut bene sanis censoribus
videtur, in scribendo multo felicior fuit Rodulfus Agricola, in extremis Frisiorum litoribus natus et in Italia educatus, atque ita
quidem felicior ut a mille annis nemo mortalium Romano stilo et
in agresti quidem materia, ut est eius *Dialectice*, melius eo scripsisse
iudicetur.

102   'Sed[128] recte sentis,' inquam, 'Museti, qui eos ad summum expo-
litae facundiae splendorem nequaquam pervenisse arbitraris, tametsi ab eruditione et a varietate litterarum singularem excellentiae
ceperint opinionem. Verum et id quoque necesse est ut ingenue
fateamur neminem adhuc ex nostris esse qui optimum scribendi
genus sit assecutus, nec illud quidem intellegi volo quod ut asse-
queretur Cicero longe omnium maxime laboravit. Quis enim non
insani atque arrogantis ingenii fuerit qui ulli industriae ullisque
vigiliis adeo felicem eventum promittat ut excelsissimum perfectae
orationis apicem se aliquando tenere posse audacter speret? Satis
etenim pulchrum atque decorum vel ardentissimis ingeniis esse
putandum est si exacte atque eleganter faciem unius ex probatis
antiquis scriptoribus aemulentur; vel, si id nequeant quod perfecte
imitari atque ad amussim delineare sit difficillimum, saltem certos

port of perfect eloquence he intended and longed to reach, as on another occasion we heard you promise, speaking in a most heart-felt and truthful manner of the Frenchman Longueil;[192] but he was snatched away by an untimely death."

And so I [GIOVIO] said, "You're right, Muscettola; and surely 101 Longueil, with his ardent and swift genius, composed with sur-passing elegance some things that pleased those of great learning, who considered that he had already begun auspiciously on that road by which undoubtedly he was destined to attain the highest measure of praise for his eloquence, had he not fallen victim so quickly to a stomach disorder. But a far more successful author than this Longueil of ours, according to critics who have their wits about them, was Rudolf Agricola,[193] born on the far shores of Frisia and educated in Italy; indeed, he was so much more success-ful that nobody over the last thousand years is judged a better writer in the Roman style — even on an unrefined subject, as is his *Three Books on Dialectical Invention*.

"But you're right, Muscettola," I said, "to suppose that those 102 men have by no means arrived at the splendid height of refined eloquence, even if the erudition and variety of their writings have given them a remarkable reputation for excellence. Still, we must also admit frankly that so far there is no one from our own ranks who has been able to equal the best class of writing. By this, I do not mean what Cicero labored to attain, far beyond all others; and indeed what person not insane or arrogant would promise so fe-licitous an outcome to his diligence and labors of any kind, so as to presume that he could one day occupy the most exalted summit of perfect eloquence? Truly, even the most impassioned intellects ought to consider it sufficiently glorious and noble if they imitate accurately and elegantly the outward appearance of just one of the approved ancient writers. Or, if they are unable to do that — since it's extremely difficult to imitate perfectly and to trace the outlines with precision — then at least let them pick with a skilled hand

ex omnibus erudita manu flores decerpant et coronas ex iis decenter contexant, quibus severi et nasuti homines ab iucundis exquisi-
tisque nexibus et a nova ac admirabili confragrantium florum suavitate delectentur, cui rei perficiendae si mens ipsa, oculi atque
aures paullo acutius atque fervidius intendantur, tales stilo celeriter
evadimus quales vultu et totius oris lineamentis sumus, hoc est, a
ceteris omnibus omnino dissimiles.

103 'Nam sicut iisdem parentibus conceptos partuque editos alii atque alii vultus et varii maxime oculorum et genarum habitus
consequuntur, ita nobis etiam insunt occultae quaedam et perennes animae motiones spiritusque mensurae, quibus ipsa uniuscuius-
que natura, tamquam peculiaribus et definitis utitur instrumentis
ad exprimendas res omnes quae cogitatione ac internis sensibus
agitantur, ita ut quae in singulorum sermone atque oratione tam
varia esse videmus, tractus sonos intervalla periodos commissuras,
a propriis vique caelesti congenitis animae numeris deducta esse
atque inde profluere iudicentur. Neque tamen negaverim ab accurata arte ac diligentia magna elocutioni ornamenta comparari, in-
ductis passim et prudenter coaptatis numerorum modulis, quibus
sic puto serviendum, sicut Cicero docuit, ut dissimulanter obser-
ventur, et nihil ad lenocinii nomen mulcendis auribus dedita opera
quaesitum esse videatur.

104 'Sed huiusce rei felicitatem naturae potius quam arti et studiis
adscripserim quoniam nonnullis et pedum et harum subtilitatum
penitus ignaris oratio naturali profluat cursu plerumque numerosa,
iucunda, delectabilis, porro aliis curiose atque anxie nimis ea
sectantibus ieiuna inaequalis luxataque proveniat. Sonorum enim

certain proven flowers from them all, and tastefully weave garlands from them, in order that stern and censorious people may take pleasure from their agreeable and careful entwinings and from the fresh and wonderful sweetness of commingled floral bouquets. If the mind itself, the eyes, and the ears are directed a bit more keenly and intensely to accomplish this, we quickly develop in our style as we do in our looks and in the features of our whole face: that is, we turn out completely unlike all others.[194]

"For just as children conceived and born to the same parents 103 acquire different looks and various qualities, especially in the eyes and cheeks, so too we have in us certain hidden and perennial movements of the passions and spiritual capacities which each person's unique nature employs as its designated implements to express everything that is thought and felt. The result is that the features we perceive in the language and speech of individuals — quantities, tone, pauses, periods, and juxtapositions — are so varied that they are judged to have originated in the heaven-born harmonies of their own particular souls and to emanate from them. But I wouldn't deny that eloquence is much embellished by skilled craftsmanship and diligence, and by the introduction and sensible application of measured rhythms throughout; one must, I think, abide by these, just as Cicero taught, in such a way that their observance is not noticed, and that there's nothing that would be seen as meriting the charge of deliberately pandering to the ears with sweet sounds.

"But I would give credit for success in this matter to nature 104 rather than to skill and study, seeing that, in some who are completely ignorant of meter and like subtleties, their style of speaking is harmonious, agreeable, and delightful, and frequently flows out in a natural course, while in others who expend too much care and worry on such technicalities, their style turns out dry, uneven, and disjointed. A sonorous, melodious, and graceful manner of speaking preceded and was much more ancient than any observance of

numerosum atque elegans dicendi genus omni rhetorum ac poetarum observatione prius et antiquius fuit, nam numerorum modos
qui ab eloquentium ore naturali volubilitate manabant primo acuti
auditores id admirati feliciter exceperunt. Inde popularis imitatio
eos ad normam artemque transtulit et subtiliora demum ad delec-
tationem aurium ab iis sunt excogitata, qui totam orationem suavissimis numeris astringendam esse iudicarunt.'

105   Tum vero MUSETIUS 'Perquam apposite,' inquit, 'Iovi, de numeris orationis iudicium tuum protulisti, cum eos neque omnino
ieiuna aure negligendos putes neque ita religiose atque affectate
passim asciscendos ut fortasse propius sint fastidio liberis auribus
quam voluptati, quae fere semper temperamento potius quodam
quam immoderatis rerum excessibus exprimitur. Sed vellem ut ea
nobis etiam aperires quae tuo iudicio in paranda florentis atque
dilucidi stili facultate maximam vim ac utilitatem afferre existi-
mentur, nisi ea sint occulta quaedam mysteria quae vos ipsi, qui
nobiliori[129] eloquentia famam quaerere videmini, velut coniurati
ceteris ad eandem gloriam anhelantibus omnino suppressa atque
occultata esse velitis.'

106   Tum ego ⟨IOVIUS⟩ 'Apage,' inquam, 'Museti! Nullae inter ingenuos et vere studiosos coniurationes esse possunt, nullaque habentur huius apertae artis abstrusiora mysteria. Nam si quae sunt ad
compendia facultatis ab acutioribus ingeniis excogitata, ea demum
si prolata erunt arcana minime videbuntur. Sunt enim indices cum
verborum tum elocutionum ex intimis medullis probatorum librorum diligenter inspectis arbitrio studentium excerpti, quos equidem probo, modo[130] non tam avide tamque insatiabiliter eae copiae
cogantur, ut illi qui haec colligunt in ipso delectu atque apparatu
misere vel ridicule consenescant. Remittitur enim memoria cum

rules by rhetoricians and poets; for in the beginning, those listening attentively to the rhythmic measures which poured forth with a natural fluency from the lips of the eloquent embraced them with admiration. Afterward, popular imitation converted them into norms and a prescribed art; and at length more exquisite methods of delighting the ears were devised by those who judged that all speech had to be bound up in the most euphonious cadences."

At this point MUSCETTOLA said, "It is exceedingly fitting, 105 Giovio, that you've made your opinion on the cadences of oratory known, which is that one must neither be entirely deaf to them nor apply them everywhere with such scrupulousness and affectation that, for unbiased listeners, they may perhaps occasion disgust rather than pleasure—pleasure being nearly always derived from a certain right proportion rather than from unbridled extravagance. But I would also like to learn from you what you consider to be the most potent and useful tools in developing the capacity for vigorous and vivid writing—provided that there aren't some occult rites which you yourselves, who appear interested in the glory gained from more noble eloquence, want entirely suppressed and concealed from others who strive after the same glory, as though conspiring against the rest."

Then I [GIOVIO] said, "Come now, Muscettola! There can be 106 no conspiracies among high-minded and genuine scholars, and no overly obscure mystic rites are conducted in this art, which is accessible and open to all. For if any shortcuts to facility have been devised by keener intellects, they will not seem mysterious when revealed. Certainly there are lists of both words and expressions plucked on the authority of scholars from deep inside books that they have carefully examined. For my part I approve of the practice, provided that these riches are not assembled so eagerly and insatiably that their collectors turn into wretched old fools while choosing and organizing them. Indeed the memory slackens when

nimium chartarum fidei atque iis numerosis indicibus credimus, aliturque ignavia stili exercendi in iis qui ignobili labore tot coactis opibus supra aequum temere confidunt.

107 'Ceterum ante omnia ad id quod quaeritis vehementissime conferre arbitror optimorum praeceptorum institutiones: quibus vel etiam turbida obtusaque ingenia et aciem et lumen haud magno cum labore paullatim recipere videmus, rectae siquidem et salutaris disciplinae praecipuum semper fuit nobilissimorum auctorum delecta volumina e manibus numquam dimisisse, et illustriora ex iis memoriter didicisse; quorum assidua lectione tria et ea quidem maxima ad praeclare scribendum emolumenta sentiuntur: primo statim grammaticae artis proprietates legitimo ac illustri antiquorum usu comprehensas nequaquam ambiguis exemplis agnoscimus et observamus; secundo solemnis ille delectus habetur verborum insignium, quorum postea erudita atque hilari positura mirum in modum splendescit oratio; tertio variarum elocutionum figurae— spatia, ductus ornamentaque omnia—accuratis quaesita legibus clarissime deprehenduntur.

108 'Verum haec tot et tanta meditantem dignissimorumque scriptorum fibras sedulo rimantem ante vigesimum aetatis annum calamum arripere et scribendo ingenii vires periclitari illi ipsi vetabant qui hac via et his praeceptis mirifice profecissent. Adhibenda enim est cura cupidis et alacribus ingeniis ne ut implumes aviculae non plane siccatis alis festinantius provolent, sicut in dispari sed non omnino dissimili facultate carioribus discipulis praecipere erat solitus Leonardus Vincius, qui picturam aetate nostra, veterum eius artis arcana sollertissime detegendo, ad amplissimam dignitatem provexit. Illis namque intra vigesimum, ut diximus, aetatis annum

we rely too much on written records and those numerous indices, and the disinclination to practice writing is nourished in those who, in their undistinguished labor, place too much blind trust in such rich compilations.

"But above all else, I consider that the precepts of the best 107 teachers have the greatest bearing upon what you seek. From these we see that little by little, with hardly any effort, even those confused and blunted intellects acquire light and eyes to see. Indeed, it has always been a preëminent feature of true and beneficial learning never to let go of the choicest works of the most celebrated authors and to learn their more famous passages by heart. By reading them continually, one discerns three advantages, and indeed very important ones for excellence in writing. Right away, in the first place, we notice and observe unambiguous examples of the grammatical properties embraced by the authentic and honorable usage of the ancients. Secondly, we acquire the custom of choosing extraordinary words, whose learned and lively placement imparts afterward a wondrous splendor to our own speech. Thirdly, we very clearly discern various rhetorical figures — their extent, their treatment, and their embellishments — chosen in accordance with precise principles.

"But those very men who achieved marvelous proficiency from 108 this path and these precepts prohibited anyone who gave thought to so many great things and eagerly probed the innermost fibers of the most worthy authors from taking hold of the pen before his twentieth year and endangering his talents by writing. Avid and eager intellects must take care not to venture out too hastily, like unfledged nestlings whose wings are not quite dry. In a different but not entirely dissimilar craft, Leonardo da Vinci — who by most ingeniously revealing the secrets of its ancient practitioners has raised the art of painting in our age to its greatest glory — used to instruct his more valued students in just this way. For he entirely forbade them brushes and paints before their twentieth year (as

penicillis et coloribus penitus interdicebat, cum iuberet ut plumbeo graphio tantum vacarent priscorum operum egregia monumenta diligenter excerpendo et simplicissimis tractibus imitando naturae vim et corporum lineamenta quae sub tanta motuum varietate oculis nostris offeruntur; quin etiam volebat ut humana cadavera dissecarent ut tororum atque ossium flexus et origines et chordarum adiumenta considerate perspicerent; quibus de rebus ipse subtilissimum volumen adiectis singulorum artuum picturis confecerat, ne quid praeter naturam in officina sua pingeretur, scilicet ut non prius avida iuvenum ingenia penicillorum illecebris et colorum amoenitate traherentur quam ab exercitatione longe fructuosissima commensuratas rerum omnium effigies recte et procul ab exemplaribus exprimere didicissent. Hoc itaque directo tramite, quamquam fastidioso atque difficili, ad verum scribendi laborem, qui in fine iucundissimus efficitur, studiosis erit procedendum ne aliquando, si haec in ipsis probatae antiquitatis auctoribus indagasse atque observasse[131] piguerit, te demum nimis cito scribere ausum fuisse paeniteat.

109 'Ceterum postea cottidianus stili usus sine controversia rectissimus atque optimus bene scribendi magister existimatur, sicut in aliis quoque artibus id verum esse liquido perspicimus. Ferunt Donatellum Florentinum, cuius est cum insigni artis gloria in foro Patavino statua Catamellatae aenea equestris, cum de summa discendae artis ratione ex arcano sententiam rogaretur, respondere solitum "facere saepius atque reficere in arte proficere est." Porro nisi plenum et turgidum variis disciplinis sit pectus, ut feliciter iis accidit qui liquores omnes ex Aristotele praesertim et Platone insatiabiliter hauserunt, nulla umquam vel pertinaci stili exercitatione oratio succulenta, decora admirabilisve proveniet.[132]

I've just said), telling them to devote their time, using the lead pencil alone, to selecting carefully the outstanding monuments of ancient works, and to copying with the simplest strokes the natural power and the bodily features which we can discern underlying so great a variety of movements. He even wished them to dissect human cadavers in order to examine carefully the curves and sources of muscles and bones and the supports for the guts; he himself had prepared a highly perceptive volume on this topic, with pictures added of each joint and limb, so that nothing contrary to nature would be portrayed in his workshop. His purpose was to prevent the ardent talents of young men from being enticed by the attraction of brushes and the charm of colors before they had learned through practice—by far the most fruitful of activities—to create proportionate likenesses of all things, properly and without models. Hence scholars must walk this straight, albeit painstaking and difficult, path to the genuine labor of writing (which proves in the end most agreeable), so that, even if you disliked investigating and heeding these precepts in the accepted ancient authors, you never end up sorry for having dared to write too soon.

"That said, thereafter, daily practice of the pen is regarded as 109 unquestionably the best, most suitable teacher of good writing, as we see clearly is the case in other arts, too. There's a story about Donatello of Florence, whose bronze equestrian statue of Gattamelata, a work of immense renown, stands in the main square of Padua. It's said that when asked in confidence for his opinion about the best method to study art, he used to respond: 'make something often, then make it again—that's how to make progress in your art.' Moreover, unless one's mind is filled to overflowing with all manner of learning, as is the happy lot of those who have drunk greedily all the libations from Aristotle especially as well as from Plato, no exercise of the pen, howsoever persistent, will ever make one's style of speaking lush, elegant, or admirable.

110 'Sed ut ad imitationem de qua dicebamus aliquando revertamur, eos hercle perbeatos et diis immortalibus longe gratissimos esse puto qui antiquiores perfecte et in iusto quidem opere sciant imitari. Quis enim tantis vel naturalis ingenii vel humanae industriae muneribus erit exornatus, qui perspicuum illum divi Caesaris candorem excipere aut ad florentem copiam indefessi Ciceronis accedere, imitari sobriam et dulcem Sallustii brevitatem, et denique ex lacteo Livianae ubertatis flumine aliquid haurire se posse confidat?

111 'At eos autem arbitror fortunatos qui tanta ingenii fecunditate sollertia firmitate perfruuntur ut honestas ac stabiles ad scribendum facultates habeant comparatas quibus ut libet sine pudore atque invidia tamquam bene partis opibus uti possint, sic ut emineant in toto contextu orationis peculiares artificum notae, ac item[133] ingeniorum officinae e quibus illa prodierint apertissime deprehendantur, sicut inspecta nobiliore tabula penicillum et manum artificis statim agnoscimus: nam summas in singulis virtutes proprii et necessarii quidam n⟨a⟩evi tradente natura comitantur.

112 'Habent Michaelis Angeli figurae profundiores umbras et recessus admirabiles, ut clarius illuminatae magis extent et emineant; in humanis vultibus quos egregie Sebastianus exprimit suaves et liquidos tractus blandissimis coloribus convelatos intuemur; in Titiano laetae rerum facies austeris distinctae lineolis et obliquitates exquisitae laudem ferunt; Doxium imagines rigidae vivaces convolutae effumidis adumbratae coloribus mire delectant quae, tametsi in eadem re certius exprimenda, et specie varia sint et dissimilia. Summam tamen omnes alius alio modo ut genii iudiciaque tulerunt, excellentis industriae commendationem accipiunt. Quo exemplo facile adducor ut habenas immittendas atque laxandas

"But to return at last to imitation, about which we were speak- 110
ing: I certainly think those men most fortunate and by far most
pleasing to the immortal gods who know how to imitate the ancients perfectly and indeed in a proper work. For who will ever be
so endowed with gifts of natural talent and human diligence as to
trust that he can capture the clear simplicity of the divine Caesar,
or come near to the splendid riches of the indefatigable Cicero,
imitate the sober and sweet concision of Sallust, or, finally, take a
drink from the milky stream[195] of Livy's fullness?

"Still, however, I consider fortunate those who enjoy such fruit- 111
ful, skillful, and powerful talents that they have the worthy and
steadfast resources suited to writing. Without shame or envy, they
can use at will those resources that they have honestly acquired, so
that throughout the construction of a speech the special peculiarities of the artists stand out. And likewise the workshops of the
masters which produced these works are perfectly evident—just
as, upon examining a well-known painting, we immediately discern the brush and hand of the artist. For nature betrays them,
and certain characteristic and inevitable blemishes accompany the
most excellent traits in each.

"The images of Michelangelo have deeper shadows and remark- 112
able recesses, so that when they are more brightly illuminated
these stand out more prominently. In Sebastiano del Piombo's superb portrayals of human faces we discern sweetly fluid strokes
concealed in the most charming colors. In Titian, the rich shapes
of things, distinguished by austere little lines and exquisite
obliques, receive honor. The Dossi brothers'[196] paintings—severe,
vigorous, involved, and shaded with smoky colors—give extraordinary pleasure; even if quite clearly portraying the same thing, yet
they are both different and distinctive in appearance. Still they all,
each one in his own manner as inspiration and judgment have
led him, are esteemed highly for the excellence of their work. By
this illustration I'm readily persuaded that the reins should be

putem egregiis ingeniis eloquentiae studio flagrantibus ut, si divinum antiquorum stilum perfecte imitari nequeant, aliquam saltem tolerabilem nec invenustam dicendi formam proprio quodam delectu et suapte natura consequantur. Quod an externi scriptores eleganter adepti sint, non populari trutinae sed absolutis artificum[134] iudiciis examinandum relinquimus.

113   'Magis enim est ingenuum vel mediocriter a propria naturalis ingenii vena stilum deducere[135] quam impudenter et operoso vilique labore conficere centones et ridendas illas ex Cicerone rhapsodias infeliciter ostentare, ut modo accidit Alcyonio, alioqui luculenter docto et memori, cum Genesius Hispanica sedulitate excussis eius operibus integra passim atque transposita clausularum furta edito libro publicasset illeque propterea miserabili pudore adductus universos Genesii libros per singulas Italiae tabernas conquirere emptosque cremare cogeretur.

114   'Sed unum[136] id non tacebo cavendum esse ne, dum tritam semitam fastidimus et per lubricos margines militarium viarum aspretaque deverticula pergere concupimus, foedo casu aut in sentes aut in caenosas fossas delabamur, ut Pio doctissimo homini accidit omnem semper ab optima imitatione laudem velut servili opere quaesitam obstinate repudianti qui, cum obscure et[137] loqui et scribere gloriosum putaret sicut solus[138] in tam[139] novo et lutulento genere, ita plerisque delicatis stomachosus et ridiculus evasit. Sed ille, ut est voluntate atque iudicio et apertus et pervicax, monenti mihi aliquando perblande et familiariter ut imitari aliorum

slackened for the exceptionally talented who burn with a zeal for eloquence. Even if they are not able to imitate perfectly the heavenly style of the ancients, at least according to a certain personal choice and their very own nature they will attain some passable and not unattractive kind of eloquence. But as to the question of whether foreign writers have correctly acquired this level of eloquence, I leave that to be weighed not on the scales of popular opinion, but in the final judgment of experts.

"It is more noble to draw even an unremarkable style from one's 113 own vein of natural talent than to be shameless enough to assemble a patchwork of borrowed passages with laborious and worthless effort, or to put on a pitiful display of well-turned phrases appropriated from Cicero with laughable clumsiness. This recently happened to Alcionio,[197] otherwise brilliantly learned and endowed with a fine memory, when Juan Ginés de Sepúlveda,[198] with the zeal of a Spaniard, sifted through his works for the clauses which Alcionio everywhere stole intact. Of these, Sepúlveda made a published edition. For this reason Alcionio was wretchedly humiliated and felt compelled to search every shop in Italy for those books of Sepúlveda and to purchase and burn them.[199]

"But I won't pass over the one thing we must guard against, that 114 in spurning the well-worn path and seeking to follow the slippery verges of military roads and uneven byways, through a shameful misstep we become entangled in brambles or mired in ditches. This happened to the massively learned Pio,[200] who always stubbornly spurned any honor derived from excellent imitation as he thought it was servile work: and, thinking it glorious to speak and write obscurely, as if he were the lone practitioner of some new and mud-stained genre, he thus became for most people of taste a cantankerous buffoon. But he is so blunt and stubborn about what he thinks and wants that once when, in friendship, I made the gentle suggestion that by imitating the style of others he would

cultum vellet ut civilius expoliretur perfacete respondit: "Nolo" inquit, "mi Iovi, ex isto tuo nobili consilio in manifestum famae pariter ac vitae periculum devocari quos tu enim ut praeclaros laudas
Ciceronis imitatores, ego eos agnosco ut simias togatas et centona-
rios fures, quibuscum, si ego memoria mea fretus furti agere ad
praetorem velim, magna et ea quidem convicta et condemnata
poetarum et scriptorum turba publici carceres singulis in urbibus
complerentur.'"

115   Haec cum dicerem, in liberum sese exsolvens cachinnum MUSE-
TIUS 'Facetissime,' inquit, 'et verissime hunc Pium tuum video
dixisse. Namque omnia immanibus furibus plena esse conspicio et
nonnulli etiam Etrusci poetae, quod minus tolerandum videtur,
aliena et viventium quidem atque florentium auctorum integra
poemata non modo illustribus matronis, sed in porticibus etiam
apud subtiles et peracutas aures pro suis soleant[140] recitare. Fit
enim in hac ingeniorum perversitate ut plerique fures esse, postquam tam certa proponitur impunitas, quam pannosi, olidi atque
agrestes in hac cultioris vitae luce videri malint.

116   'Sed propterea nolim ingenuum poetam furti a severioribus cri-
ticis condemnari, si quid ab optimo vate non inepte atque impudenter sed scite modesteque surripiat; non ferenda siquidem videtur invidiosa severitas, cum libet adeo curiose alienas excutere
vigilias ut occultissima demum et exigua quaeque[141] malevole re-
prehendas et obiectes. Nam si non puduit summum vatem Virgi-
lium integrum carmen a Catullo aequali suo mutuari cum dixit
"Invitus, regina, tuo de littore cessi," profecto non erubescet quis-
piam nostrorum temporum poeta liberaliter institutus si aliqua ad
praesentem usum verecunde sumpta atque ingeniose collocata sustulerit.

become more refined and polished, he gave this very witty reply: 'Giovio,' he said, 'I don't want to call down from that noble assembly of yours, with manifest peril to my life and reputation, any of those whom you, indeed, esteem as worthy imitators of Cicero, but whom I know to be toga-clad apes and patch-dealing thieves. If I trusted my memory and wanted to charge them before the magistrate for theft, there would be a huge crowd of poets and writers, all of them convicted and condemned, filling up the public jails in every city.'"

As I spoke, MUSCETTOLA dissolved in unrestrained laughter, 115 saying, "It seems to me this Pio of yours spoke with surpassing wit, and surpassing accuracy; for all around us I see an abundance of horrible thieves. And some poets — even the Tuscan ones, which seems harder to bear — are accustomed to recite as their own whole poems of others, of authors who in fact are living and active. And they do this not only for noblewomen, but also in porticoes before exacting and very discriminating listeners. Evidently, since impunity is assured, most would rather be thieves in this corrupt use of their talents than be seen ragged, stinking bumpkins in the daylight of a more refined circle.

"But I wouldn't therefore want an honest poet to be condemned 116 for theft by overly harsh critics if he appropriates something from an outstanding poet not artlessly and shamelessly, but with skill and moderation. An odious severity truly seems intolerable when one is pleased to sift through others' labors so intrusively as to expose and reprove spitefully everything they've taken, however obscure and minute. For if Vergil, the greatest of poets, wasn't ashamed to borrow intact a passage from his contemporary Catullus when he said, 'Unwillingly, queen, did I leave your shore,'[201] certainly no liberally educated poet of our times will blush to have lifted things for present use when he has taken them with humility and positioned them with ingenuity.

117   'Sed perge, obsecro, Iovi, et de externis nominatim aliqua disse-
rito; nam tametsi nihil ab Italia ultra Alpes sit evagandum, ut
propositum nostrum teneamus, tamen et mihi et, ut video, ipsi
etiam Davalo singularem afferes voluptatem si quae in provinciis
ingenia floreant vel nuda tantum nomenclatura nobis indicaveris.
Video enim externos valde esse fecundos[142] et fertilitate varietate-
que[143] operum nostros omnes anteire, quibus si stilus accesserit
grandior, temperatior et in acuitate paullo suavior, non erit cur
diutius reluctemur et scientiarum simul ac eloquentiae gloriam illis
minime concedamus, sicut illi impigre audendo atque agendo invicta antea Romana arma nobis oscitantibus extorserunt.'

118   'Non gravabor' ego ⟨IOVIUS⟩ inquam, 'Museti, hoc perlevi
onere, quoniam id valde moderatum imponitis. Nam, si qui sunt
praestantissimis scientiis illustres, ut a Gallis exordiar, persequi
velim, dies profecto ante deficiet quam vel principes ipsos attingam. Innumerabiles enim disciplinarum omnium doctores in fre-
quentissimis provinciarum gymnasiis esse referuntur quos nec
fama quidem noverim; eos igitur tantum referam qui in Italiam ad
petendas vel certe ad expoliendas litteras concesserunt, aut scribendo ingenii nomen latius extenderunt, e quibus, ut et hoc arti
vestrae, Museti, honoris causa tribuatur, longe omnium doctissimus existimatur Budeus iureconsultus, qui in iure civili commentationes edidit admodum subtiles et generosas et librum *De asse* ab
infinita reconditarum rerum observatione luculentum.

119   'E nostris vero medicis Ruellius, qui Dioscoridem vertit in Latinum, mihi admodum eruditus et in doctrina ac stilo compositus
videtur. Coppum quoque, ipsius Francisci regis medicum, egregie
medendo et vertendo Graeca Latinis, ut industria atque ingenio ita

"But please go on, Giovio, and say something about literary 117
men outside of Italy, one by one; even if, to keep to our purpose,
there's no need to wander out of Italy and over the Alps, nonetheless you will give singular satisfaction to me as well, I think, as to
d'Avalos if you just name for us briefly the talented writers who
enjoy success in the provinces. In my view, foreigners are quite
prolific and surpass all of our writers in the fruitfulness and variety
of their works. If they acquire a style that is grander, better proportioned, and a little sweeter in its subtlety, there will no longer
be any reason to oppose them, or to refuse to concede to them the
honor of eloquence as well as learning—just as they, by their vigorous daring and drive, wrested from us, as we were half asleep,
the previously undefeated arms of Rome."

"I won't be weighed down, Muscettola," I [GIOVIO] said, "by 118
this slight burden, since it is a very limited one that you place upon
me. Beginning from the French, if I wish to discuss those whose
profound expertise distinguishes them, no doubt I'll run out of
daylight before I mention briefly even those of the first rank: for
it's said that in the numerous schools of the provinces there are
countless teachers in all the disciplines, whom I don't know even
by reputation. So I'll mention only those who have come to Italy
to seek out literary learning or at least to refine it, or who by writing have made their talents more widely known. Of these—to pay
also this tribute of honor to your craft, Muscettola—the jurist
Budé[202] is considered by far the most learned of all. He has published treatises on civil law that are surpassingly precise and respected, and a book *On Coins*, distinctive in its limitless concern
for esoteric subjects.[203]

"Of our doctors, Jean Ruel,[204] who has translated Dioscorides 119
into Latin, seems to me highly learned and practiced in science
and style. I also admire Guillaume Cop,[205] King Francis' own physician, as an outstanding healer and as a translator from Greek
into Latin. He is as renowned for his wealth and charm as for his

fortunis et gratia nobilem suspicimus. Faber Stapulensis, quem propter eius singularem temperantiam adhuc vivere putamus, multa in philosophia, astronomia et theologia eleganter appositeque conscripsit. Lazarus Baephius, qui lepidum *De re vestiaria* librum confecit, cum Graecis tum Latinis litteris exornatus est. Brissonem Romae vidimus mathematicum ingenio maxime sobrio et veloci profundissimae artis omnes subtilitates explicantem.

120   'Delectantur autem optimarum litterarum studiis plerique viri insignes et in iis cardinales duo, Ludovicus Borbonius cui librum *De piscibus* dicavimus, et Ioannes Lothoringus ad quem nostra exstat longior epistola de Hamochrysi lapidis viribus admirandis. Exculti quoque sunt humanioribus litteris antistites vitae modestia singulari Poncherius Parisiensis et Brissonettus Maclodiensis, et Ioannes Bellaius Baionensis qui versibus scitissime ludit. Antonius etiam Pratus, epistolarum magister in quem maximarum rerum cura incumbit, oblectari litteris politioribus atque iis favere liberaliter fertur. Sed unum ante alios Galli omnes in honore habent Io⟨annem⟩ Glorierium virum quaestorium, qui liberali animi virtute flagrantique studio seipsum ac domum suam amoenioribus litteris et priscae elegantiae artium monumentis exornavit. Quarum rerum admirabili eruditione pollet ipse Franciscus ad cohonestandam regii fastigii dignitatem, quem ingenii mira benignitas extrusa foribus avaritia humano generi conciliavit et saevior fortuna dum illum vinceret invictum fecit et longe clarissimum, cum iam id totum quod in summa felicitate et tantarum virtutum concursu timendum fuit timere desierit.

121   'In Britannia autem eruditione et stili gravitate ceteris omnibus antecellit Thomas Linacrus qui Galeni aliquot libros et Procli

diligence and intelligence. Jacques Lefèvre d'Étaples,[206] who I think is still living thanks to his singular self-discipline, has written many elegant and suitable compositions in philosophy, astronomy, and theology. Lazare de Baïf,[207] who has completed a charming book *About Clothing*, is master of both Greek and Latin learning. In Rome I saw the mathematician Brisson[208] unravel all the minutiae of that exceedingly profound art with a swift and sober intellect.

"But most of their eminent men delight in the cultivation of classical literature, and among them are two cardinals: Louis de Bourbon de Vendôme,[209] to whom I dedicated my book *On Fish*, and Jean de Lorraine,[210] whom I sent my long letter about the miraculous powers of the Hamochrysus stone.[211] There are also bishops ennobled by more liberal learning whose lives are known for their moderation: François de Ponchier[212] of Paris and Briçonnet[213] of Meaux, as well as Jean du Bellay,[214] the bishop of Bayonne, who composes very skillful verse. Antoine du Prat,[215] the chancellor of France who is burdened by the most momentous concerns, is also said to appreciate elegant letters and to patronize them generously. But all the French honor one man alone above others: the treasurer Jean Grolier,[216] who by his noble excellence of mind and ardent zeal has brought distinction to himself and his homeland with writings of the more charming kind and with books that testify to the ancient eloquence of the arts. Francis I himself commands remarkable learning in these matters, bringing honor to the majesty of his kingship. Greed has been driven from his door, the wondrous kindness of his character has endeared him to the human race, and although a terrible misfortune conquered him,[217] it has rendered him invincible and renowned far and wide; for he has now ceased to fear all that, at the height of prosperity and in the union of such powers, he needed to fear.

"In England Thomas Linacre[218] surpasses all others in his erudition and sophisticated style; he translated some books of Galen

120

121

Sphaeram in Latinum cultissime transtulit, et in Thoma quoque Moro peramoenum floret ingenium cuius est *Utopia* politici generis pressa et festiva oratione conscripta. Sed in utraque lingua impense doctissimus videtur Ricardus Paceus, ut ex Plutarchi et Luciani quibusdam dialogis coniectari licet et ex iis maxime commentariis quos de bello Scotico ad locupletandas historias ad me transmisit. Eum nunc tantis legationum honoribus perfunctum et tantis litterarum et divitiarum auctum facultatibus atra bile vexari incredibili cum dolore audivimus. Est etiam in Polo regiae stirpis iuvene mirifica indoles eloquentiae candidioris, qui Patavii optimis studiis operam dedit ita ut eum. . . .'

and the *Sphere* of Proclus into very elegant Latin.[219] Also, Thomas More[220] is celebrated for his great charm and intellect: his *Utopia*, a work on politics, was composed in a restrained and playful style. But Richard Pace[221] seems to be by far the most learned in Latin and Greek, as may be inferred from certain dialogues of Plutarch and Lucian, and especially from those notes about the war in Scotland which he sent me to enrich my *Histories*. I've heard that now, having discharged his responsibilities as an ambassador, and endowed with such great resources of learning and wealth, he is tormented by melancholy and by incredible anguish. Reginald Pole,[222] a young man of royal lineage, also has a marvelous disposition for quite lucid eloquence. In Padua he has so exerted himself in liberal studies that . . ."

[END OF EXTANT MANUSCRIPT]

DE FEMINIS ILLUSTRIBUS
DIALOGUS TERTIUS

1 Postero die cum nos Davalus oblectandi animi[1] causa ad reginarum scopulos deduxisset, subiit eius animum iucunda admodum
recordatio nobilissimarum feminarum quae, incolumi et florente
Aragoniorum imperio, ea loca ad suavioris otii tranquillitatem
frequentare consuevissent. 'Videtis' inquit 'hos scopulos, qui numero et situ et propinqui litoris amoenitate Hesperidum insulas
referre dicebantur: non erant paullo antea inculti et deformes, aut
hac incondita arbustorum luxurie praepediti. Eos enim reginarum
studio sic excultos et cunctis hortensibus deliciis exornatos vidimus, ut nulla esset tam glabra tamque horrida cautes quae exaggeratis ubique caespitibus et odoratis atque fructiferis arboribus importatis toto dorso ad miram voluptatem non silvesceret. Scaenae[2]
etiam eminebant et fornicatae[3] et fastigiatae, serpentibus in eas
Iulianarum vitium palmitibus, et iasminorum[4] et[5] violarum sequa-
ces thyrsi sic in medias testudines evadebant ut tota aestate opacae
deambulationes caducis earum floribus spargerentur. Hinc vero
atque inde harundineae transennae incumbentia rosaria adeo apte
specioseque sustentabant ut, cum frondosa virgulta ad lineam arcerentur, rosae tantum sic summa capita singulis clatrorum[6] intervallis exsererent ut avide conspici et delicatis puellarum digitis decerpi[7] cupere viderentur.

2 'Insularum maxima continenti litori ligneo exemptili ponticulo
iungebatur. Transcendentes areola complanato saxo statim excipie-
bat. Inde coclea concisis sinuosisque gradibus in summum

DIALOGUE THREE
ON FAMOUS WOMEN

On the following day, d'Avalos led us as a pleasant distraction to what were called the Queens' Rocks, where he began to reminisce happily about the noblewomen who used to gather there, when the Aragonese dominion was still safe and flourishing, to enjoy the tranquility and pleasant relaxation. "Do you see," said D'AVALOS, "those rocks, which were said to resemble the islands of the Hesperides in their number and position and in their relationship to the charm of the nearby shore? Not long ago they were neither neglected and disfigured as they are now nor obstructed by that haphazard overgrowth of shrubs. Rather, owing to the queens' diligent supervision, they were cultivated and adorned with every possible garden delight. Once the topsoil had been built up and fragrant fruit trees introduced, no rock was so stark or rugged that it did not put out thick growth along its entire ridge, becoming a source of marvelous pleasure. There were trellises, with both round and pointed arches supporting branches of Julian vines that crept into them; shoots both of jasmine and of violets wove themselves inside the arbors in such a way that for the entire summer, the shaded walkways were strewn with their dropping blossoms. Here and there, trellises propped the leaning roses upright so neatly and gracefully that with the leaves of the bushes held back in a straight line, the highest heads of the flowers stuck out so far from each lattice opening that they seemed to be begging to be admired and to be plucked off by the delicate fingers of girls.

"The largest of the islands was linked to the nearby shore by a little removable wooden bridge, and a small courtyard of polished stone welcomed at once whoever crossed over. From here, a spiral staircase led by small and winding steps to the topmost

hortulum perducebat, qui ad tuendum puellarum pudorem et
muro saeptus et firmis foribus munitus erat. Ex hac in proximam,
et ab ea in alias pari prope inter se spatio distantes, iniectis pontibus[8] facile poterat transiliri.

3   'Huc Ioanna regina, eadem et amita et uxor Ferdinandi Iunioris
qui Regnum Alfonsi patris superbia foede amissum, felici virtute
postea recepit venire erat solita cum delecto nobilissimarum virgi-
num comitatu, cum aestas Neapoli paullo fervidior tenera corpora
mollesque animos ad opaciorem liberioremque secessum invitaret.
Regina autem singulas insulas[9] totidem puellis attribuerat excolen-
das, quae sicut[10] maximam ab eius Hispaniensi cognomine infantiam appellarat, ita illae[11] sua nomina ceteris indiderant. Fuere
enim, cum ea, genere et forma admodum illustres: Sancia Scylla-
cea, quae postea Alexandri Pontificis nurus fuit, et Hippolita Davala, huius Constantiae amitae meae soror, Camillaque Sangria
Hispana. Item Xysta, et ab Epiro Angela Castriota, et Violantilla
Crapinia Alipharum regulo desponsata, quae pulchritudine et morum elegantia humanae admirationis modum excessisse ferebantur.
Itaque illae flagranter inter se studio diligentia sumptibusque cer-
tabant ut ornamenta, quae in infantiam[12] collata erant, exquisitis
amoenitatum deverticulis exaequarent.

4   'Namque ut in hoc obiecto Crapiniae latere derasis cautibus in-
cisum id nomen conspicitis, ita et in aliis pleraque manufacta et
voluptatis regiae vestigia, si circumvehamur lembis, passim videbi-
mus. Quin etiam hos insulis interiectos minores scopulos in varias
rerum ac animantium effigies et cementitio et topiario opere

garden, which had been both protected by a wall and fortified by a solid doorway to safeguard the modesty of the maidens. From this island to the next, and from there to the others—each of which was roughly equidistant from its neighbors—the crossing was easy, once bridges had been laid down for that purpose.

"Queen Giovanna[1] had been accustomed to come to this place, along with a chosen retinue of the noblest young women, when the summer's heat in Naples inclined delicate bodies and sensitive spirits toward a more sheltered and leisured retreat. The queen was both the paternal aunt and the wife of King Ferrante II, who through successful valor had recaptured the kingdom of Naples, disgracefully lost through the arrogance of his father Alfonso II.[2] The cultivation of each island had been allotted by the queen to a particular maiden. So just as she had named the largest one *Infanta* from her Spanish title, her maidens in turn had bestowed their own names upon the others. With the queen were the following ladies, each illustrious in lineage and in beauty: Sancia d'Aragona,[3] who would later become the daughter-in-law of Pope Alexander VI; Ippolita d'Avalos, the sister of my aunt Costanza;[4] and, from Spain, Camilla di Sangro.[5] In addition, there were Sista[6] and, from Epirus, Angela Castriota,[7] and Violantilla Grappini, the promised bride of the prince of the Alifians.[8] All these women were said to have surpassed the bounds of human admiration in beauty and in elegance, and all were contending ardently among themselves with zeal, diligence, and lavish expenditure to equal in the exquisite amenities of their garden paths the ornaments bestowed by the queen upon the island called *Infanta*. 3

"For just as you see that name cut into the smoothed stone on the side facing *Grappini*, so too in other places, if we travel around by boat, we can see many artifacts and vestiges of the queen's pleasure. In fact, using both stonework and topiary effects, they had shaped these smaller rocks lying between the islands into likenesses of various things and animals. This one next to *Infanta*, be- 4

conformarant. Hic qui infantiae proximus est, ut oblongus, Niloti-
cum crocodillum exprimebat. Ad Sanciam autem Indicam testudinem dorso prominente et capite semiexerto adnatare crederes.
Crapinia coniunctam sibi petram tanta arte composuerat ut balena
ingens fluctibus expugnata et in litus eiecta videretur. Sangria par-
vulum nacta scopulum in striatam verterat concham.

5   'Davala vero propinquum informe saxum quod erat erectius,
atque illud introrsus allidentes maris undae penitus excavarant, in
Aethnae ardentis similitudinem effigiarat, ita ut subditis ab immo
ignibus flammas demum a cacumine per hiatus abruptos eructaret.
A Xista etiam haec prominula et nuda cautes quam saepe subso-
lani fluctus abluebant, in caput ingentis phocae redacta, vitreis
oculis in hos quos videtis orbes eleganter inclusis, terribilem adna-
tantis beluae faciem reddebat. At Castriota planiorem sortita scopulum, et lentiscis et nativa myrto et importatis minoribus plantis,
Cretensem labyrinthum adeo decenter expressit ut convolutis topiarii operis[13] ambagibus per inextricabiles vias ignarae atque ad-
mirantes puellae ducerentur.

6   'In mediis autem insularum spatiis atque inter scopulorum imagines, velut concluso in mari, et regina et pulcherrimae virgines
saepissime lavabantur. At vetulae interim et matronae puellarum
custodes stationem in his quos videtis[14] collium speculis obtine-
bant, cum viri pariter famulantes pluribus phasellis ab alto maria
custodirent, ne tot insignes puellae cum regina Nereidum more
perspicuo in mari lascivientes alicunde procacibus oculis spectarentur.

7   'Sed haec omnia quam brevi temporis curriculo eversa penitus
atque exstincta esse videmus! Ipsa domus Aragonia a stirpe interiit adeo ut nulla regia prole superstite reparari queat, cum modo
numerosa iuventute floreret ad summam spem certissimae

ing oblong, used to portray an Egyptian crocodile. Near *Sancia* was an Indian turtle with its back protruding and its head halfway stretched out, so you would think it was actually swimming toward you. Grappini had modified a rock near to her islet with such craftsmanship that it appeared to be a giant whale, overcome by the waves and tossed up onto the beach. Di Sangro, having alighted upon a very small rock, had turned it into a fluted conch.

"On the other hand, near Costanza d'Avalos' isle was a higher, 5 shapeless rock. Because the sea's waves, dashing against it, had totally hollowed it out, she fashioned it into the likeness of Mt. Etna erupting, so that when fires were laid underneath it belched flames from its peak through steep open jaws. That other rock, slightly protruding and bare, bathed by easterly waves, was transformed by Sista into the head of a huge seal. When glass eyes had been elegantly inserted into those sockets which you can see, it resembled the frightful countenance of a sea monster swimming toward you. But Castriota, allotted a flatter rock, becomingly portrayed the Cretan labyrinth, both with small evergreens and the native myrtle tree and with smaller imported young plants, so that the girls, unfamiliar with the maze and wondering at it, would be led along intricate paths by the twists and turns of the topiary.

"Between the islands and the rocky figures—in an enclosed sea, 6 as it were—the queen and her beautiful girls often went swimming. On these occasions, elderly women and matrons, who were the girls' chaperones, were posted upon those lookout points of the hills which you see, while serving-men in small boats likewise guarded the side toward the open sea lest insolent eyes espy from some vantage point so many beautiful girls and their queen, frolicking in the waters like so many Nereids.

"Yet in how brief a time we've seen all these things overthrown 7 and wiped out! The House of Aragon itself, although just recently flourishing with numerous youths giving the greatest promise of a secure line of succession, has withered away to the very root with

successionis, tot vero puellae ut a fortuna destitutae aetatem silentio transmiserunt. Nec pulcherrimis scopulorum operibus maria
pepercere, cum nemo esset qui, publicis rebus foede collapsis, iis
demum deliciis collocandam operam putaret.

8   'Nam Isabella Baucia Federici regis uxor, et Beatrix quae Mat-
thiae Pannonio optimo atque fortissimo regi nupserat, et altera
item Isabella Galeatio Mediolanensi principe marito orbata, vel
haec Constantia amita mea cum Alphonsum ac[15] etiam Roderi-
cum fratres Gallico bello amisisset: ut in gravissimo luctu non
modo haec ⟨non⟩ videre[16] concupiverant, sed nec pedem quidem
vel sacrorum sollemnium causa arcis limine umquam extulerant,
cum in hanc insulam secunda illa lugubri Gallorum irruptione
amisso Regno profugissent.

9   'Erant eae atque illae superiores, ut audimus,[17] cum formae atque natalium dignitate tum elegantissimorum ac illustrium morum praestantia longe clarissimae, ita ut nunc similes tota Italia
desiderare debeamus. Nam feminas multis in urbibus maximam
optimarum rerum quae sexum decerent iacturam fecisse plerique
seniores opinantur easque in universum et indolem ingenuae venustatis et temperiem victus et pudici cultus munditias et linguae
atque oculorum pudorem amisisse praedicant. Quibus, si fas esset
credere, omnino fatendum foret eandem siderum iniuriam sensisse
mulieres quam et viri pertulerint, ut ex bellicis et litterariis operibus superiore disputatione abunde demonstratum fuit.

10   'Verum, ut arbitror, illi plurimum iudicio aberrant; obsoletis
enim oculis senes huius aetatis feminas contuentur, nec iam
ut exsangues affectique vitiis id admirari queunt quo vividi ac
ardentes iuvenum oculi capiuntur, cum unam tantum in hac
vitae satietate antiquae voluptatis memoriam retinere videantur.

no surviving royal progeny to revive it, while many young women, now made destitute by misfortune, have been passing their lives in obscurity. Nor did the seas spare the beautiful crafting of the rocks, since, once affairs of state had shamefully collapsed, no one thought that effort ought to be expended for these luxuries.

"Take for instance Isabella del Balzo, the wife of King Federico 8 IV;[9] and Beatrice,[10] who had married Matthias Corvinus, the exceedingly fine and strong king of Hungary; likewise, the other Isabella, robbed by death of her husband Galeazzo, prince of Milan;[11] or my Aunt Costanza, when she had lost her brothers Alfonso and Rodrigo in the French war. When the kingdom was lost in the disaster of the second French invasion, they fled for safety to this island. In deep mourning, they not only lost the desire to see these things; they didn't even set foot outside the citadel, even to attend religious services.

"So distinguished were these women and their predecessors, as 9 we hear, both in excellence of beauty and parentage and in preeminence of elegant and illustrious character, that now we are bound to feel the absence of their like throughout all Italy. For most older men believe that the women in many cities have jettisoned the best adornments of their sex. Overall, they charge, women have lost their capacity for natural charm, a temperate lifestyle, the refinements of modesty, and restraint of tongue and eyes. And if it were right to believe these men, surely it would have to be conceded that women have experienced the same harsh treatment of the stars which men have had to endure, as was abundantly demonstrated by our earlier discussions of martial and literary achievements.[12]

"But I think these judgments are highly erroneous: for old men 10 scrutinize the women of this era with eyes impaired by age. Feeble now and weakened by physical failings, they can no longer admire what captivates the lively and ardent eyes of youth. Sated with life, they cling solely to memories of far-off pleasures.

Delectabilium enim rerum imagines, tenerioribus quondam sensibus impressae, adhuc in animis eorum vigent, et conspecta olim flagrantissimeque adamata rerum obiecta recentibus spectris et persimili iucunditate repraesentant. Quo fit ut mirum esse non debeat si nihil iam earum rerum probent quod hodie conspiciunt et nos ipsi magnopere et rectissima quidem aestimatione laudamus, quoniam ad subtilitatem pulcherrimorum[18] naturae operum hebetatis luminibus et contusis acutorum[19] sensuum instrumentis pervenire non possunt.'

II   Tum ego ⟨IOVIUS⟩ inquam, 'Ita est, Davale, medius fidius. Verum senes praeterquam quod nihil perspicue[20] nihilque subtiliter videant, etiam iunioribus praesentium rerum copiam et iucundioris vitae fructum invidere existimantur; antiquos enim semper mores mirificis extollunt laudibus, et praesentes severe condemnant, ut iunioribus meliores et feliciores fuisse[21] appareant. Ceterum si aliquid seniorum iudiciis condonare velimus ac illos feminarum decus peregrinis et parum honestis moribus obscuratum esse dicere patiamur, unum[22] certe nobis concedent, manifestis convicti exemplis, scilicet[23] superiora tempora nequaquam pulchriores ac ingenio nobiliores feminas protulisse. Nam si naturalem vultus formam et totam membrorum speciem cum venustate eruditis moribus atque munditiis quaesita non insulse computemus, ac earum quae nunc florent ingenia honestissimis litteris et subtilioribus disciplinis exornata ab aequissimis hominibus aestimentur, necesse erit confiteri mulieres nostrae tempestatis omnes alias superiorum aetatum cum ipsius formae tum etiam ingenii clarissimis dotibus anteire. Et ne longissime vel procul a domo rarissimarum virtutum exempla petantur; quid his nostris heroidibus quae summa in arce concluduntur ulla Italiae in parte aut stirpis claritate nobilius, aut tota specie formosius, aut eruditi

For images of alluring things, earlier imprinted upon more impressionable senses, still flourish in their minds: they look at what they now see in light of objects that they saw long ago and fervently loved, and do so on the basis of what they found delightful then. This being the case, it's no wonder if they fail to approve of things on which they fix their eyes today—things which we ourselves praise greatly, and indeed accurately—since, with eyes dimmed and the keener senses blunted, they cannot arrive at a refined judgment of the most beautiful works of nature."

Then I [GIOVIO] interjected, "By God, that's right, d'Avalos. 11 Apart from the fact that old men see nothing clearly or in fine detail, they also seem to envy younger men their present abundance and the fruits of a more rewarding life, for they are always extolling bygone mores with incredible praise and harshly condemning today's, hoping to make it look as if they had been better and happier than younger men. But even if we wish to grant a little something to the opinions of the elderly, and likewise allow them to contend that the glory of women has been dimmed by foreign and improper behavior, an abundance of manifest examples should force them to grant us at least one thing: by no means did earlier times produce women more beautiful and more noble in nature. For if we do not judge amiss the natural facial beauty and gracefully shaped limbs along with the acquired charm of elegant mores and manners, and if the natural abilities of those women who are now flourishing—abilities adorned by honorable literary activities and refined studies—are assessed by fair-minded judges, we'll have to admit that the women of our age surpass those of all previous eras in their illustrious endowments both of beauty itself and of natural talent. And let not instances of the rarest virtues be sought for at a great distance or far from home, for what could be found in any part of Italy either nobler in distinction of lineage, more beautiful in appearance, more polished in the graciousness of erudite thought, or purer in morals and

ingenii suavitate conditius, aut castitate et religione[24] sanctius poterit reperiri?

12 'Neque tibi, Davale, mortalium beatissime, haec de tuis cum sanguine tum omni humanae societatis vinculo atque officio coniunctissimis prolixius affirmarem, nisi te praeclaro iudicio longe ampliora in illis ac multo quidem pretiosiora animi pariter atque fortunae munera altius conspexisse et me etiam arbitrari ab omni adulationis suspicione vacare crederemus. Alias quoque et praesertim principes Italiae civitates multis mulieribus forma atque virtute clarissimis videmus exornatas, quas vegeto et excellenti ingenio viri superioribus anteferendas putant, qui et periucundo harum hodie florentium conspectu et illarum quae consenuerunt aut obierunt, grata et dulci memoria delectantur. Nam, ut dixi, feminae nobilitate et pulchritudine praestantes, ab his quamquam miseris eruditis tamen temporibus, magnum ingenii lumen magnaque et valde splendida ad omnem morum elegantiam ornamenta recipiunt, secus ac aviae et proaviae nostrae quae totas muliebris sexus virtutes in una tantum fecunditate reponebant, cum essent in omni vitae commercio subagrestes, sermone et moribus ineptae, litterarum penitus rudes, et ab exiguo denique animo domi et foris prope[25] ridiculae.

13 'Ubi haec nostra cultioris vitae lautitia spectaretur, in qua profecto perbeate viveremus, si communem libertatem, socordia ac insania principum nostrorum turpiter amissam, contra barbarorum libidinem teneremus.† Sed multis et exsecrandis, medius fidius, peccatis et erroribus nostris effectum est ut cum inusitata servitus perfectae vitae bona et cuncta prope commoda sustulerit,[26] etiam mulierum decus, quod in optima quiete et pace

religion, than these heroines of ours, guarded by the fortress high above us?

"Nor, d'Avalos, most fortunate of mortals, would I assert these 12 things at length about women intimately related to you both by blood and by every bond and duty of human society unless we believed that you, with outstanding judgment, had already beheld more deeply in these women far more abundant and precious gifts of mind and fortune alike; and unless we were to believe that I too reckon myself free from every suspicion of flattery. We see other cities as well, and especially the chief ones of Italy, that have been adorned by many women highly illustrious in beauty and virtue whom men of lively and outstanding intellect suppose ought to be ranked above their predecessors — and these are men who are delighted both by the charming sight of those women flourishing today and by the pleasant and sweet memory of those who have grown old or died. For as I've said, in these times which, although miserable, are nonetheless learned, women outstanding in nobility and beauty are gifted with the great light of genius and adorned most splendidly with every elegance of character. And this is unlike our grandmothers and great-grandmothers, who placed all the virtues of the female sex just in fertility alone, when they were unrefined in all social interactions, awkward in speech and manners, entirely ignorant of learned writings, and indeed nearly ridiculous at home and in public life on account of an inadequate mind.

"When we hold in view that luxurious and cultivated life of 13 ours, which we would certainly [still] be living rapturously, if we had maintained against the rapacity of barbarians our common liberty, which has been shamefully lost through the sluggishness and madness of our princes [. . .].[13] But our many errors and (so help me God) detestable sins have brought it about that, once unaccustomed servitude had destroyed nearly all the privileges and goods of a fully realized life, so too it violently outraged — or at

cumulatius futurum erat ac[27] illustrius, vehementer laeserit, aut certe non mediocriter obscurarit.'

14   Haec cum dixissem, MUSETIUS ad Davalum conversus, 'Non casu aliquo videris,' inquit, 'aut certa spatiandi consuetudine sed de industria nos ipsos in hunc intimum curvati amoenique litoris recessum perduxisse ut hos scopulos, reginarum domicilio et delectabilium operum varietate et poetarum carminibus inclutos, mente atque oculis intueremur, et iucundiores subinde sermones ex pulcherrimarum rerum memoria duceremus; postquam et ad lacum ubi cruento proelio terra marique cum fulicis fuit depugnatum, opportune atque divine de perfecti imperatoris officio disputasti, et in Pontano iuxta fontem in umbrosa scaena, ubi Iovianus ipse sine ceris et pugillaribus numquam fuit, de ingeniorum praestantia et liberalium studiorum laudibus subtiliore sermone disseruimus. Haec enim umbrosior et pendula et propemodum pensilis silva, quae ab imminentibus et subter excavatis rupibus sinum hunc beati litoris opacat totum et, decidente sole, ad subiectos scopulos umbram protendit. Itemque haec muscoso e tofo concisa sedilia nos admonent ut tenerius atque facetius de feminarum excellentia colloquamur. Nam et tempus discessus valde absurdum, et hac molli solitudine nihil aptius atque iucundius videtur.'

15   Tum DAVALUS 'Recte' inquit 'ac opportune nos admones, Museti, ut paullo molliora ac urbaniora tractemus; nam et unumquemque nostrum de suavissimis rebus cum aliqua liberius proferre, tum multa ab aliis dulciter audire, plurimum iuvabit; et mihi

least in no slight degree eclipsed—the honor of women, which would have been more abundant and more illustrious in the profound calm of peace."

After I had made this speech, MUSCETTOLA turned to d'Avalos 14 and said: "You seem to have led us into this innermost recess of a curved and charming beach by no accident nor out of your regular habit of taking a walk. Instead, you did this by design, so that with our minds and eyes we might gaze upon the rocks—famous both on account of a variety of delightful works of art and the verses of poets, and for their being the dwelling place of the queens—and that we might hereupon weave pleasant conversations from the memory of those surpassingly beautiful things. First, you argued your case about the responsibilities of a perfect commander, fittingly and as if by inspiration, next to the lake where the gory battle with waterfowl had been fought on land and sea. And next, we conversed in more refined words about the excellence of intellects and the merits of liberal studies in the Pontanian Garden next to the spring, in the shady scenery where Pontano himself was never without wax tablets and notebooks. Now, here, there is denser foliage, both dangling from the overhanging cliffs and almost floating up from the hollowed-out rock face below, which shades this whole expanse of pleasant shore and, as the sun is declining, stretches forth a shadow toward the exposed rocks. And besides, these benches, carved out of mossy tufa, remind us that we ought to be talking in tender and witty ways about the excellence of women. For this seems a highly inappropriate time to depart: nothing appears more suitable and more pleasing than this peaceful solitude."

Then D'AVALOS said, "Your advice is correct and convenient, 15 Muscettola: we should discuss things that are a bit more gentle and elegant. Certainly it will benefit every single one of us immensely both to speak more freely about aspects of the most charming matters, and to listen pleasantly to many such things

haec hilarior animi relaxatio, velut exquisita quaedam medicina adversus ingruentem morbum, praesumenda est. Nam cras Neapoli cum Ugone in Senatu erimus, unde necesse erit aures domum referre molestissimis sermonibus admodum fatigatas, quale illud in primis erit exercitum crudelitate atque licentia corruptum, numquam nisi persolutis ad obolum stipendiis dicto audientem futurum. Interim urbem Romam eorum saevitia et immanitate funditus everti, incredibilem Neapoli esse rei nummariae difficultatem, nullam ab Hispania opem, nulla a caesare tamquam ab his oris et curis remotissimo haberi terminata consilia; de sacrosancto autem pontifice capto agitari sententias graves varias ancipites, quem sicut nefas atque impium custodiri, ita summa iniuria et calamitate exacerbatum dimitti periculosum esse videatur.

16 'Quae res explicatu difficiles multo molestius ac acerbius animo meo negotium intendunt quam ullae voces quae de Gallorum irruptione prosperisque Lotrechii successibus[28] a rerum novarum cupidis efferuntur; nam si nobis pro iure imperii[29] seditiosi exercitus uti virtute licuerit, nullae profecto classes, nullae hostium manus exploratam totiens victoriam morabuntur. Quod si turpi hac et fortasse ipsis demum letali insania legiones diutius obdurescant, postquam humana ratione consilioque res geri non poterit, fors ipsa et fortuna caesaris ut saepe alias insperato et felici eventu cuncta gubernabit.'

17 Ad id ego ⟨IOVIUS⟩ inquam, 'Noli, Davale, hanc praeclaram rerum omnium, ut videtur, dominam, quae caesari semper indulserit, adeo sublimiter efferre laudibus; nam eam nos non aluimus

from the others. And for me, this cheerful relaxation of the mind is like a certain choice medicine to be taken in advance against an impending illness. For tomorrow we will be in the senate in Naples along with Hugo de Moncada, whence it will be necessary to bring home ears wearied to the limit by extremely distressing words, especially of this sort: that the army, corrupted by cruelty and lawlessness, is never going to obey unless the stipends have been paid out to the last coin; that meanwhile, the city of Rome is being knocked down to its foundations by the troops' savagery and barbarity; and that in Naples there's a severe shortage of cash. And Moncada will say that Spain provides no assistance and the emperor no settled counsels, being far away from these shores and cares; but on the other hand that various conflicting, important proposals are being hammered out regarding the pontiff, the holy prisoner. Just as it is forbidden and impious to hold the pope under guard, so it seems dangerous to set him free, enraged as he is by defeat and injustice.

"And these matters, which are difficult to resolve, affect me 16 more keenly and painfully than any words that are being uttered by men thirsting for rebellion on account of the French incursion and the propitious successes of Lautrec. For if we shall be allowed to make use of the prowess of the mutinous army on behalf of imperial law, certainly no enemy fleets or forces will prevent a victory that we have so often striven for. But if the legions should persist in this foul insanity, which may perhaps ultimately be lethal to themselves, once human reason and deliberation have failed to guide affairs, luck itself and the good fortune[14] of the emperor will guide all things, as they've often done on other occasions, with an unexpected and favorable outcome."

To this I [GIOVIO] responded, "D'Avalos, don't exalt so very 17 loftily with your praises that famous mistress of all things (as Fortune appears to be) who has always looked favorably upon Caesar! For we not only promoted her interests, but often by our

modo, sed praeposteris ac importunis saepe consiliis sic extulimus ut bellorum ad nutum moderatrix esse crederetur. Quod si quorundam qui ab ingenui iudicii libertate ad arduas res tractandas parum subtiles vel[30] parum idonei videbantur, recta ac aperta consilia valuissent, et aliquorum etiam quorum animus exitiali avaritia iam pridem erat effeminatus apud prudentissimum sed distractum pontificem aliquanto minor auctoritas exstitisset, vidissetis profecto illam in toto eius scaenae ioco longe alia facie cum suo caesare colludentem. Sed profecto[31] Deus ipse[32] omni fortuna superior rationis facultatem nobis praeripuit, ut superbiam luxuriem et tot egregia summae dementiae monstra bellissime castigaret.'

18   At MUSETIUS 'Desinite,' inquit, 'ea commemorare de quibus dii atque homines, ut in Fatis fuit, omnino transegerunt. Nam te, Iovi, refricata vulnera quae nulla iam vel salutari manu feliciter obduci queunt, multo amariorem efficiant necesse est quam mos tuus ferat ad hilaritatem naturaliter institutus. Et te quoque, Davale, quae impendent bellicae difficultates, dum ad animum in hanc curam excubantem subito revocantur, non possunt nisi maxime et vehementer commovere. Quare obsecro huic iam coepto sermoni mentem omni alia cogitatione vacuam adhibetote ut, cum[33] omnes Italiae urbes adiveritis studio spectandi et virorum ac feminarum illustrium mores abunde noveritis, digna praesertim hoc loco Nymphis et reginarum memoriae consecrato urbana iucunditate[34] proferantur. Nam tametsi disputationem omnino difficilem atque impeditam ingressi sumus — quoniam de forma, de moribus, de cultu, et de ipsis denique pudoris et elegantiae finibus sit iudicandum — tamen haec omnia facile coniecto[r] tum

preposterous and inopportune judgments raised her up to such an extent that her nod is believed to control the outcome of wars. But if the correct and candid counsels had prevailed of certain men who, for speaking their minds freely, were thought insufficiently perceptive or too little suited to treat difficult matters — and also if the authority of others, whose spirit had long ago been rendered unmanly by fatal avarice, had carried less weight with our very in-telligent but distracted pontiff — then in this entire spectacle you would certainly have seen Fortune, playing her part along with 'her' emperor, wearing a very different expression. But undoubt-edly God Himself, greater than all fortune, snatched away from us the faculty of reason so that He might in the most suitable way correct haughtiness, extravagance, and so many utterly mad and monstrous acts."

But then MUSCETTOLA said, "Stop talking of things which   18 gods and men have completely settled, as the Fates allowed. Surely, Giovio, it's inevitable that reopened wounds — which perhaps no hand, not even a healing one, can stanch successfully — make you much more bitter than your naturally cheerful disposition might allow. And you, too, d'Avalos: when impending military troubles suddenly occur to you, you cannot but be greatly and violently upset, vigilant as you are with respect to your responsibilities. For this reason, I implore you, clear your minds of everything else and turn them to this discussion that has already begun. That way, once you've visited all the cities of Italy in your zealous search and have examined in every detail the character of illustrious men and women, then with an urbane pleasantness you can bring forth evi-dence that especially befits this place, consecrated as it is to the nymphs and to the memory of the queens. Granted, we've entered upon a discussion that is assuredly difficult and confusing, inas-much as we need to pass judgment about beauty, character, re-finement, and finally the ends themselves of modesty and elegance. Nonetheless, I judge that by your talents all these things will be

commoda tum[35] expedita ingeniis vestris fore, quoniam nihil tam obscurum, nihil tam subtile, nihilque[36] tam reconditum esse potest in tota vita quam in clarissima semper hominum luce traduxistis, quod aut ingenium vestrum decipere, aut diligentiam frustrari, aut memoriam omnino subterfugere posse videatur.'

19   'Igitur,' ego ⟨IOVIUS⟩ inquam, 'Davale, hunc nobis tam belle et molliter adulantem praeeundo tandem excitemus. Postquam, ut opinor, totum hunc sermonem eruditis condimentis perfusurus; id a nobis tantum exspectat ut dicere incipiamus. Sed unde potissimum de feminarum laudibus exordiri possimus non video, quando earum genus tamquam inefficax et importunum si fecunditas ipsa tolleretur, apud antiquissimas gentes in honore paullo clariore numquam exstiterit. Cunctae enim fere barbarae nationes, ut Aristoteles gravissimus et morum et rerum omnium[37] perscrutator scripsit,[38] mulieres servorum loco habebant,[39] utpote quae suscipiendae ac alendae tantum proli ceterisque vilioribus ministeriis deservirent.

20   'Graeci etiam fere omnes eas ab omni reipublicae munere segregarunt, naturae levitatem et inconstantiam veriti, ne parum fida et ob id periculosa earum ingenia cum sensus iuvenum tum seniorum consilia, et quietem denique constitutae civitatis[40] perturbarent. Tantam[41] enim vim impotentibus earum animis ac illecebris inesse compererant, ut virorum robora mollire, consilia flectere, atque inde cuncta pro libidine moderari posse censerentur[42] — vel ipso quidem exemplo Lacedaemoniorum qui, quamquam singulari vitae duritia et perpetuis laboribus edomita durataque corpora, uni armorum gloriae devovissent, sic tamen uxorii muliebribus[43] devicti obsequiis et patriae[44] educationi dissimiles evasere ut mox

both pleasant and easy to achieve, since in the entire course of life there can be nothing so obscure, nothing so subtle, and nothing so abstruse that you haven't always displayed it in broad daylight to all men. It seems true that nothing can escape the notice of your talents, thwart your dedication, or in any degree slip from your memory."

"Well then, d'Avalos," I [GIOVIO] said, "let me go first, and   19
eventually stir to action this man who is so beautifully and gently
flattering us, since in my opinion he will sprinkle erudite season-
ings on our whole conversation. He awaits this one thing from us:
that we start in. But I don't see exactly where we could begin to
praise women, since their sex never was singled out by the ancients
for anything more than slight honor, as though women were weak
and worthless apart from their ability to bear children. Indeed,
Aristotle, a most venerable man and an investigator of customs
and of all things, wrote that nearly all barbarous nations used to
regard women as slaves, since it was supposed that they served
only for the bearing and nursing of offspring and for other tasks
held in rather low esteem.

"In addition, nearly all the Greeks, fearing the fickleness and   20
inconstancy of women's nature, excluded them from every civic
responsibility, lest their undependable (and on that account dangerous) natures should disturb both the senses of young men and
the counsels of their elders and ultimately the peace of an ordered
city-state. They had learned that there was such great power in
women's charms and intemperate passion that these could sap
men's strength, sidetrack deliberations, and then arrange all things
in accordance with their desires. So it was, for instance, in the
case of even the Spartans. It is said that they dedicated their bodies, subdued and hardened by a special austerity of life and
by perpetual labors, solely to the glory of arms. But they turned
out to be so uxoriously bound to the service of women, and became so alienated from the aims of their civic training,[15] that soon

feminae ex arbitrio totam prope rem publicam per vicarios viros gubernarent. Aristotele miseram fortissimae civitatis condicionem irridente, in qua, cum viri toti Graeciae bellica virtute terribiles dominatum tenerent, mulieres tamen, quae vetere eorum decreto a rerum publicarum consiliis arcerentur, ipsis dominatoribus contusa illa animorum fortitudine gloriosius imperarent. Quo pudendo amittendae libertatis atque virtutis discrimine adductos Celtarum populos qui plurimum armis valebant, feminarum amores formidasse et mares turpiter adamasse, idem Aristoteles scribit.

21 ʻPorro et ipse Plato, qui semper aequitate animi et sapientia divinus apparuit, adeo contemptim et supine in illa *Republica* de feminis statuisse est visus, cum tamen dimidia generis humani portio censerentur,[45] ut eas virorum omnium libidini prostituat, tamquam vilia mancipia et ad unam tantum edendam prolem ac explendam venerem virorumque servitium naturaliter instituta. Qui mos ab humanitate aequabilique iustitia penitus alienus, improbantibus cunctis et acuto praesertim explodente discipulo, sicut nullibi receptus est, ita materiam admodum festivam irridendi Platonis calumniatoribus eius aequalibus praebuit. Quae enim, medius fidius, ad pulcherrimarum toros contentiones, quae nocturnae rixae, quae in dividendis liberis cruentae seditiones, cum alii nobilitatem generis, alii opes aut florem aetatis, nonnulli vim ipsam ab iniquo rivalium certamine allaturi fuissent, ut dignissimarum feminarum amoribus potirentur!

22 ʻSed certe Socratem optimae[46] partis philosophiae conditorem mulieres suscipere debent, quod eas non modo benigne ac

the women were governing nearly the entire state arbitrarily through men suborned to the task. Aristotle laughed at the miserable condition of this exceedingly strong city-state. Although the men, terrifying to all Greece through their warlike virtue, held the power in Sparta, nevertheless the women, who were prohibited from the counsels of state by an ancient decree of Spartan men, controlled their very masters in a quite arrogant fashion, since their menfolk's fortitude of spirit had been crushed. The same Aristotle writes that the disgraceful risk of losing their freedom and manliness led the Celtic peoples, who were great warriors, to fear the love of women and to lust shamefully after men.[16]

"And what's more, Plato himself, who always appeared divine in 21 equanimity and wisdom, in that famous *Republic* of his seemed to judge women so contemptuously and thoughtlessly — even though they were counted as half of the human race — that he prostituted them to the lustfulness of all men, like lowly slaves who were designed by nature for the sole purpose of bearing children and for satisfying men's sexual appetite and for serving them. Plato's moral attitude, completely foreign as it is to human feeling and to equal justice, was taken up nowhere — for everyone disapproved of it, and his shrewd disciple Aristotle especially condemned it — and thus it supplied Plato's detractors with hilarious material for poking fun at him. And indeed, so help me God, what competitions over the marriage beds of the most beautiful women there would have been! What nocturnal squabbles, what gory insurrections in the matter of dividing up the children![17] Some would have brought to an unequal struggle of rivals the nobility of their own lineage; others, wealth or the fact that they themselves were in the flower of their youth; and still others, mere violence — all so that they might obtain the love of the worthiest women!

"But surely women ought to embrace Socrates, founder of the 22 best portion of philosophy,[18] not only because he judged that they should be regarded with kindness and honor, but also because in

liberaliter habendas iudicarit, verum[47] in constituenda republica viris etiam adaequarit, cum eis tradenda arma esse censeret, quibus civitatis moenia tuerentur asciscendasque eas in disciplinam et gravissimarum etiam curarum societatem; et in publicas illas comissationes, ut Graecorum moris erat, adducendas[48] arbitraretur, quoniam neque viribus earum quamquam imbecillis, si se fortiter exercuissent, neque ingeniis, si virilibus exemplis essent excitatae, vir omnium prudentissimus umquam ⟨diffisus esset⟩.[49] Neque hoc a Socrate in gratiam potius feminarum quam ad salutem ac utilitatem civitatis excogitatum interpretari fas esse putamus, cum ille et praeclaro totius vitae exemplo et illo Alcibiadis sui cachinno, quo physiognomon lepide refutatum ait Cicero, numquam mulierosus exstiterit.

23   'Sed quamquam ea quae a Socrate de moribus ad excolendam vitam inventa divinitus et salubriter instituta fuerant famam tantum ex Platonis ac Aristotelis libris habuisse videantur, sanctissimi tamen Senis memoria tam diu viguit et floruit quam diu stetere incolumes Athenae,[50] patria eadem crudelis et ingrata, quae optimum civem et divinum vitae magistrum nefaria crudelitate sustulerat. Vir enim ille ad invidiam saevissimae atque levissimae gentis pro unis Athenis, totam mox Graeciam ac universas[51] orbis nationes quas egregiis moribus erudiret immortalis factus invenit. Siquidem saluberrimis eius praeceptis cum aequalium tum[52] posterorum leges mirifice locupletatas et civitates exornatas esse conspicimus.

24   'Et haec quae de mulierum disciplina ac honoribus praedicavit, quamquam Aristoteles ingenii sui more libenter aliena placita

designing his commonwealth he treated them as equal to men: he decreed that arms must be given them to guard the walls of the city-state, and that they should be admitted to military training and even into a share of the weightiest responsibilities. Also, Socrates thought that they were to be brought along to those public revelries, as was the custom of the Greeks, since he, the most intelligent of all men, never lacked confidence in their strength (although weak by nature) once they had done vigorous exercises, nor in their natural abilities once they had been inspired by manly examples. Nor do we suppose it right to conclude that this was thought up by Socrates in order to win the favor of women rather than for the safety and the carefully considered advantage of the city-state, since he never had the reputation of being addicted to women. This is evidenced both by the distinguished example of his entire life and by his friend Alcibiades' loud guffaw which, according to Cicero, wittily refuted a physiognomist's allegation.[19]

"Although the moral teachings Socrates discovered through divine inspiration and laid down for our welfare seem to have acquired fame only from the books of Plato and Aristotle, nonetheless the memory of that entirely blameless old man thrived and flourished as long as Athens remained safe and sound—that very same cruel and ungrateful fatherland which by nefarious cruelty had destroyed its finest citizen and a divine teacher of the good life. For the man who for the benefit of Athens alone had endured the envy of an extremely fickle and savage people was soon immortalized in literature; he found that he could instruct all of Greece and entire nations of the world in outstanding morals. Accordingly, we observe that by means of his highly beneficial instructions, the laws both of his contemporaries and of subsequent generations have been marvelously enriched, and their city-states ennobled.

"Also the things he recommended concerning the instruction and moral status of women—although Aristotle, as was his habit, 24

convellentis abrogare contenderit, apud barbaras gentes etiam hodie[53] benignius observantur. In Perside enim Mediaque et Assyria in summo honore sunt uxores, quae equitandi et sagittandi omniumque armorum admodum peritae una cum viris ad bella proficisci consueverunt. Eas enim et laboris et gloriae comites atque participes neque ullae expeditionum difficultates frangunt neque pondera galearum et loricarum retardant neque acierum et proeliorum pericula commovent, quoniam omnes casus atque discrimina in utramque vitae fortunam ex aequo partienda cum viris arbitrantur. Constat enim ut ab iis qui interfuere didicimus, et in *Historiis* suo loco retulimus, complures feminas more catafractorum equitum armatas ea in pugna cecidisse qua Selimus Turcarum imperator et Sophos Hysmael rex Persarum in Calderanis campis ad Araxem collatis signis dimicarunt. Reperta enim sunt in legendis spoliis mirifica corpora feminarum, fulgentibus protecta armis et minoribus tormentis maxime traiecta, quas Selimus alias in victoria superbus et immitis, tamquam de patria, de viris, et de infirmissimo sexu optime meritas, cum virorum cadavera avibus et feris lanianda relinqueret, omni honore cumulatas adiecta non obscura laude tumulavit.'

25   Tum vero MUSETIUS 'Recte,' inquit, 'Iovi, et praeclare admodum coepisti, nam et ego quoque saepissime sum admiratus mulieres tam inique tamque contemptim et illiberaliter fuisse tractatas tum a Graecis tum etiam a Romanis, qui, sine controversia cum prudentius et gloriosius rempublicam gubernarent, etiam res domesticas aliquanto elegantius ac humanius tuebantur. Nam sicut praeclarus ille vester Aristoteles, Platonis et Socratis ac Lycurgi etiam perpetuus insectator, dum *Politica* et *Oeconomica* scriberet,

gleefully tore apart the views held by others and strove to overturn them—are regarded in a kindlier way among barbarous peoples even today. In Persia and Media and Assyria, wives are highly esteemed. Expert in horsemanship, archery, and all defensive arms, they have made it their practice to embark upon wars together with their men. None of the hardships of military expeditions exhaust them, partners both in work and in glory, nor do the burdens of helmets and breastplates slow them down, nor do the dangers of battlefields and combat trouble them, because they judge that all misfortunes and crises, in good or bad fortune, should be shared on equal terms with men. As I've learned from those who were there, and as I've recorded at the appropriate place in my *Histories*, it's an established fact that a fair number of women, armed in the manner of horsemen clad in mail, fell in that battle in which Selim, emperor of the Turks, and Ismail the Wise, king of the Persians, engaged in close combat in the fields of Chaldiran at the Aras River.[20] For when the spoils were gathered, there were found wondrous corpses of women that were covered with shining armor which had been pierced through by small arms fire. Although Selim was at other times haughty and pitiless in victory and left the men's corpses to be torn apart by birds and wild animals, he delivered a eulogy over the women and then buried them with every honor, because they'd nobly served their fatherland, their menfolk, and their 'very feeble' sex."

Then MUSCETTOLA said, "Giovio, you've begun properly and splendidly, for I too have frequently marveled that women were treated so unequally, contemptuously, and ignobly both by the Greeks and also by the Romans. Although the latter doubtlessly governed their state with wisdom and glory, they also looked after their domestic affairs with humanity and good taste. For instance, in his *Politics* and *Economics*, that outstanding man, your Aristotle—a constant attacker of Plato and Socrates and even of Lycurgus—placed women inside the home. He restricted them to

25

intra domum feminas ita coniecit atque conclusit ut eas tantum ad
liberorum alendorum molestias et sordidos labores totius penu⟨s⟩
curandaeque supellectilis ablegaret. Eas enim de publicis rebus
aliquid sentire aut omnino loqui vetabat, cum nihil eas quod virile
esset cogitare fas esse censeret, parere viris ac proli tantum studere
servireque demum omnibus in rebus eas iure optimo debere existi-
mabat.

26   'Nihilo setius, et Romani in omni humaniore disciplina facile
principes eas, ut credo, propter animi et rationis imbecillitatem ab
omni publico munere et gravioribus consiliis removerunt, et ho-
nori earum minimum, ut in tanta fortuna licuisset, tribuerunt,
sicut[54] apparet ex censoriis legibus, quibus vel moderatas earum
cupiditates iniquus et in severitate contumax senatus imminuit et
elusit. Sed haec fortasse iniuria aequiore animo ferenda, nisi illa
gravior de repudiis totius sexus dignitatem convellisset, cuius enim
erat impudentiae, cuius temeritatis atque nequitiae probam fecun-
damque uxorem exigua suspicione aut satietate aut cupiditate no-
vae libidinis domo exturbare, quae mox maritalia iura in inimico
saepe cubili resolveret, et arcana cuncta ad ignominiam repudiantis
viri incitata dolore atque iracundia propalaret. Sensit tales aculeos
iratae atque eiectae uxoris Terentiae Marcus Cicero, cum et senex
et morosus plane effectus suam tanti nominis famam C. Sallustii
peracuto et vehementi stilo lacerandam obiecisset. Sed de M. Ca-
tone philosopho imprimis et Stoico, qui avita hereditate potius ac
ingenii severitate quam honore censorius, tamquam improbissimus
leno Martiam uxorem probatissimam feminam alienae libidini ea

the tiresome and menial tasks of raising children, provisioning the household and attending to its furnishings. He forbade them to have an opinion about public affairs or to say anything about them at all, because he judged that it was an impiety for them to think about anything that was a male responsibility. He thought it was absolutely right for them to obey men and to be subservient to them in all matters, devoting themselves only to their children.

"To no less a degree the Romans—easily the leaders in every 26 humane discipline—also banished them from every public office and from the weightier decisions, as I believe, on the grounds of feebleness of spirit and reasoning capacity. They paid very little regard to women's status, though they might have done so given the great prosperity they enjoyed. This is clear, for example, from the censorial laws by which the senate, inequitable and unyielding in its severity, diminished and frustrated even their moderate desires. But perhaps that injustice could have been borne with more equanimity had not a more serious injustice concerning divorces wrenched away the dignity of the entire sex. Indeed, how shameless it was, how rash and wanton, to drive out of the household an upright and fecund wife on account of mere suspicion, or a feeling of satiety, or desire for a new object of lust. As a result, soon she would be discharging her conjugal obligations in a hostile bed and, spurred on by anguish and fury, would make public all the couple's intimate secrets, to the disgrace of the man divorcing her. Cicero felt such stings from his angry and discarded wife Terentia when he, having become a cranky old man, had exposed his huge reputation to be ripped apart by the sharp-witted and vehement pen of Sallust. Then there's Cato the Younger, chiefly a philosopher and a Stoic, who was 'censorious' more from the traits he had inherited from his grandfather and from his own austere nature than from holding the office of censor. Like an extremely unprincipled pimp, he handed over his wife Marcia, a woman of estimable reputation, to the lust of another man on condition that he might reclaim her

lege concessit ut fecundiorem et longe melius subactam aliquando
repeteret.

27   'Itaque feminas viliores contemptus facit, quoniam virorum
consensu et quadam velut conspiratione ad id vitae genus adigan-
tur quod obscurorum tantum ac humilium officiorum finibus
continetur. Quod si exercendis earum ingeniis ac viribus debita
atque ampliora spatia praeberemus, is sexus qui adeo mollis videtur ac imbecillus ad virilem profecto gloriam niteretur, ac omnino
foret manifestum in iis ad praeclarae virtutis decus amplectendum
non naturam defecisse sed curam. Siquidem iniuria potius nostra
quam sua infirmitate earum mores ad mollitiam[55] collapsos videmus, nec erigimus, quasi viris praestet impotenter illis imperare
quam eas ipsas, quae non obscure vili condicione deserviunt, habere consortes bonorum omnium et commodorum quae disciplina
et magnitudine animi et ceteris humanae vitae laboribus compa-
rantur.

28   'Neque hic est necesse ut omnium annalium memoriam evolva-
mus, ut illae mulieres ante alias numerentur[56] quae vel altitudine
ingenii vel animi constantia vel fortissimis factis vel operum et rerum gestarum magnitudine sempiternam laudem sunt consecutae,
cum nationes omnes cunctae urbes omnesque etiam aetates clarissimis insignium feminarum exemplis illustrentur. Nonnullae enim
ingentes exercitus ductando de pugnacissimis hostibus memorabiles sibi victorias peperere; aliquae maximas urbes cinxere moenibus admirandis; aliae divino spiritu praeclara[57] poemata cecinere;
aliae prudenter moderate feliciter imperio populos rexerunt; aliae
etiam pietatis ergo ac amore religionis augustissima templa condi-
derunt, cum infinitae etiam sint, quae[58] ab excelsi praesentisque

once she had at last been made more fertile and was much more experienced sexually.

"Thus scorn makes women more contemptible, since by the 27 consent of men and, as it were, by a kind of conspiracy, they are compelled to live the kind of life that is limited entirely within the bounds of humble and mean responsibilities. But if we were to provide the more ample space for exercising their talents and strength that they are due, that sex which appears so soft and feeble would at once aspire to manly glory,[21] and certainly it would be clear in their case that they had not lacked the natural abilities for attaining the honor of glorious virtue, but only the opportunity for doing so. For in fact we see that their morals have sunken into softness from our unjust treatment of them rather than from their weakness, and yet still we do not raise them up. It's as if men preferred having uncontrolled power over them to making those very women, who are serving them in no uncertain terms despite their obviously lowly circumstances, equal sharers of all the goods and advantages that are furnished by instruction and by nobility of mind, and by the other labors of a dignified life.

"We don't need to run through the history of all living creatures 28 in order to see how those women are counted before others who, whether by profundity of talent or constancy of mind, whether by brave deeds or by greatness of works and achievements, have attained eternal praise, since all nations, all cities, and even all eras are rendered illustrious by the most outstanding instances of distinguished women. Some, memorable for leading armies, have achieved massive victories over exceedingly aggressive enemies; others have surrounded very great cities with walls to be marveled at; some by a divine spirit have sung outstanding poetry; others have governed peoples with wisdom, moderation, and success; still others out of piety and love of religion have founded majestic churches. And then there are also countless women who

animi fortitudine famam et laudem[59] nullis umquam interituram saeculis omnino retulerint.

29   'Illarum scilicet virtutibus detegendis et ad omnem hominum memoriam extendendis neque saeva virorum imperia neque praereptae graviorum munerum facultates neque leges, interdictis nobilioribus officiis,[60] iniquissimae nocuerunt. Enimvero sese illae egregiis atque optimis moribus excoluerant qui nobis a natura nequaquam inseruntur,[61] quoniam mores ipsius artis esse constat atque humanae institutionis. Neque putandum est feminas earum rerum, quae captu marium comprehenduntur, minus esse capaces vel propterea ineptas ad id ac indociles videri quod minime pubescant, quod nos utero gestent et excludant, alant uberibus, et humi reptantes in hanc corporis atque fortunae amplitudinem[62] suis manibus perducant. Ingrati profecto sumus et nimium superbi qui, summas humanae excellentiae partes praesumendo, illis ipsis nostris parentibus, quae nos in lucem ad hunc vitae fructum[63] extulerint, commovendi ingenii exercendique liberius animi potestatem eripimus, cum vires earum mentis litterarum cogitationibus et arduarum rerum studiis pares esse pernegemus.

30   'Quae malum enim ratio est id tam impudenter existimare, quando iisdem artuum[64] ligamentis officiisque membrorum spiritu et sanguine ac ipsis denique[65] medullis feminarum pariter ac marium corpora constare manifestum sit et easdem esse animorum ac sensuum affectiones, eademque vitia morborum, desideria vitae, eiusque terminos, a natura definitos esse videamus? Quod si utrisque eadem sint ad cognoscendum nervorum fibrarum et spiritus instrumenta, ac animae, ut credi par est, divinitus infusae[66]

by the fortitude of a lofty and resolute mind have certainly carried
home fame and imperishable praise.

"To be sure, neither the cruel dominion of men, nor their hav-   29
ing snatched away from women the opportunity to hold the more
important public offices (the nobler offices having been forbidden
them), nor the most inequitable laws have prevented women's virtues from being revealed and perpetuated throughout history. Certainly those women had cultivated in themselves outstandingly
high moral habits, of a kind which are by no means innate, as it is
evident that such extraordinary moral habits are a matter of art
and human devising. Nor should one suppose women less capable
of those things which are thought to be the preserve of males, or
that they are inept and incapable of learning because they don't
remotely attain the physical maturity of males: indeed, it is they
who carry us in the womb and give birth to us, nourish us at the
breast, and, starting from the time we're crawling around on the
ground, they lead us by the hand into this physical maturity and
prosperity. Surely we are ungrateful and arrogant when, having
taken for ourselves preemptively the highest parts of human excellence, we have too freely snatched away from our own mothers
the opportunity for stimulating and exercising the intellect — even
though they have given birth to us that we might have the enjoyment of life — when we flatly deny that their strength of mind is
up to thinking about literature and studying difficult subjects.

"What the devil is the rationale for harboring such shameful   30
thoughts, when it's clear that the bodies of women and men alike
are composed of the same ligaments of the joints and functions of
the limbs, of the same breath and blood and of the very same marrow? We see that nature has ordained the same dispositions of
mind and sense, and the same diseases, the same longing for life,
and the same limits on its span. But if each of the two sexes has
the same tools for understanding, consisting of sinews, entrails,
and consciousness, and if women's souls, divinely infused (as it is

aequales et sempiternae sanis philosophis existimantur, necesse
erit feminas omnium earum rerum quae ratione attingi queant capaces esse confiteri et in iis bonorum omnium semina vigere,[67] si
ab incunabulis non ad labores textilium aut acu pictorum operum,
sed in spem optimarum artium ac insignium virtutum educen-
tur.[68]

31   'Non defuere siquidem[69] maiorum nostrorum temporibus, neque etiam desunt aut deerunt, mulieres prudentia graves vel consilio viriles vel[70] ingenio perspicaces et acutae, quae[71] ardua in omni
vitae fortuna gerendarum rerum munera susceperunt. Isabella ma-
terna caesaris avia, nonne Bethico bello eodem valde difficili et
maxime diuturno periculorum atque victoriarum comes fuit?
Nonne cum Ferdinando coniuge rege fortissimo eius aestuosae
provinciae soles et pulveres tulit, sub pellibus hiemavit? Mauro-
rum acies saepe pugnantes vidit ac vexillum de manu sua contra in
proelium euntibus[72] dedit, ut quae ulterioris Hispaniae dotale
Regnum Celtiberico adiecerat, in aliis parandis, adamato coniugi
et totidemque Hispaniae piam fortemque operam praestaret?

32   'Quis hodie in Margarita Maximiliani Caesaris filia moderationem temperantiam aequitatem prudentiam non admiratur? Quae
per viginti annos seditiosissimas Belgarum nationes pacis bellique
tempore sic rexit ut ii populi aliquando leves et infidi, cum totiens

proper to believe) are regarded by sensible philosophers as equals
to men's and eternal, then it will be necessary to concede that
women are capable of those things which can be arrived at by reason, and that the seeds of all good things thrive in them—if, that
is, they should be educated from the cradle, not for the production
of woven fabrics or of embroidery colored by the needle, but with
a view to their acquiring the best arts and extraordinary virtues.

"In any case, there was no shortage in the times of our ances- 31
tors, nor is there today nor will there be tomorrow, of women who
are authoritative for their practical wisdom, manly in counsel, or
penetrating and keen in natural talent. In every difficult circumstance of their lives, they've taken on the duties of conducting affairs of state. Consider Isabella, the emperor's maternal grand-
mother.[22] Did she not share in the dangers and the victories in the
war over Granada, which was certainly difficult and protracted?
Isn't it so that, along with her spouse, the immensely powerful
King Ferdinand, she endured the sun and dust of that sweltering
province? Did she not spend the winter in a tent? Didn't she often
look out over the Moors' battle lines as they were engaging in combat? And did she not personally hand over her military standard
to those going into battle against the enemy so that she, who had
given the Kingdom of Castile as her dowry to Ferdinand of Aragon, might provide brave and pious aid to her beloved husband
and by the same token to all of Spain, so that it might obtain still
other kingdoms?

"Who today does not admire Margaret,[23] the Emperor Maxi- 32
milian's daughter, for her moderation, temperance, equanimity,
and prudence? For twenty years she has ruled the exceedingly seditious peoples of the Low Countries, in times of war and of
peace, in such a way that those states, previously fickle in their allegiance and unfaithful, could not have been kept together in a
more fruitful or tranquil way, even though they'd been incited to

a Gallis atque Sugambris[73] solicitati ac[74] exagitati essent, salubrius et tranquillius[75] contineri nequiverint. Qua vero constantia, qua fortitudine, quo studio atque iudicio virilis infractique animi Ludovicam Francisci regis matrem tot asperrimarum rerum difficultatibus tot periculis tot funestis cladibus obviam fortiter ivisse modo conspeximus, cum, rege filio incredibili Caesaris felicitate ad Ticinum capto, occisis ducibus, strato nobili equitatu, deletis omnibus auxiliis, tuendae servandaeque Galliae et renovandi belli[76] redimendique regis tantas curas, nequaquam calamitate et fletu superata sustentavit? Quae nam huius filia atque eadem regis sorore Margarita forma virtuteque lectissima, vel probitate vel animi gravitate ornatior erit atque nobilior, quae in tanto luctu, ad caesarem in ulteriorem Hispaniam profecta longe impeditissimum difficillimae legationis negotium virili pietate suscepit? Sunt profecto eae tres feminae praeclaro prudentiae religionis constantiaeque lumine adeo conspicuae ut ab ipsarum potius studio industria[77] et felicitate pacem speremus, quam ulla regum aut consiliariorum industria, quando ii saepius dum privatis cupiditatibus student, spem pacis semper abruperint.[78]

33 'Vivit adhuc in exilium pulsa cum immortali inusitatae virtutis atque ferociae laude Maria Paceca Toleti antiquissima stirpe orta, quae cum rebellantibus Hispaniae populis adversus caesarem stetisset, eiusque vir Padillius dux partium proelio victus a caesarianis supplicio fuisset affectus, nihil crudeli coniugis morte conterrita, orbatae suo duce et metu[79] consternatae multitudinis vexillum

revolt and stirred up so many times by the French and the Germans. Have we not seen the steadfastness, courage, enthusiasm, and discernment of a manly and unbroken spirit in Louise,[24] the mother of King Francis I, when just recently she confronted bravely so many hardships in the most adverse circumstances, so many dangers, and so many disastrous defeats? At Pavia,[25] through the incredible good luck of the emperor, her son the king had been captured, his commanders killed, his famous cavalry struck down, and all his infantry wiped out. But she, by no means cast down by defeat and tears, shouldered the immense responsibilities of maintaining and protecting France, resuming the war, and ransoming the king.[26] Again, who could be nobler and more adorned with moral rectitude and seriousness of mind than the exceedingly beautiful and virtuous Marguerite de Navarre,[27] Louise's daughter and thus the king's sister? In the midst of great mourning she traveled to the emperor in Spain and undertook with a manly sense of duty what was by far the most intractable business of a difficult legation.[28] Without question, these three women are distinguished for the splendor of their prudence, piety, and constancy to such an extent that we have greater hope for peace out of the zeal, industry, and good fortune of these very women than we have from any efforts on the part of kings and their counselors — since those men too often are eager to satisfy their personal ambitions, and have always squandered the hope of peace.

"And María Pacheco, who is descended from a venerable lineage 33 in Toledo,[29] lives on in exile, as does immortal praise for her exceptional virtue and ferocity. When she had stood along with the peoples of Spain, who were rebelling against the emperor, and her husband, their commander Juan López de Padilla, who'd been defeated in the Battle of Villalar, had been tortured by the imperial troops and then executed, she wasn't in the least intimidated by the cruel death of her spouse.[30] She took up the standard of the common people, who'd been robbed of their commander and

cepit, et bellum priore asperius acerrime renovavit adeo[80] ut stupendis contionibus et facinoribus admirandis, dum et viri et ducis officia exsequeretur,[81] una ea mulier aliquamdiu morata sit felicissimi caesaris fortunam, quam et tunc et postea semper cuncti reges cunctaeque nationes facto saepius periculo formidarunt.

34   'Et ut ab externis recedamus, quo inepto[82] pudore adducti de hac nostra Columna Victoria silebimus, cuius ingenium cum sit in omni genere litterarum valde mirificum, etiam illud quod admodum difficile[83] semper fuit, in administrandis publicis rebus ut summum[84] vehementer admiramur? Nam ante alia Benevento seditiosissimae ac superbissimae Samnitium civitati sic praefuit a Clemente Pontifice praeposita dum vir eius Piscarius foris ingentia bella administraret, ut inquieta et sanguinaria iuventus et senatus illos[85] antiquos indomiti[86] Samnii spiritus gerens arma deponeret, factionum oblivisceretur, pacem optaret, et populus omnis gravissimi atque incorrupti animi[87] moderatione[88] permotus, pontifici per legatos gratias ageret, quod urbe⟨m⟩, cum suis flagitiis tum[89] superiorum praesidum acerbitate atque[90] avaritia collabentem, ad spem maturae salutis per eam feminam omni viro praeside meliorem, opportunissimo tempore conservasset.'

35   Tum vero DAVALUS 'Papae,'[91] inquit, 'Museti! Quam luculenter quam ornate mulierum causam actitasti? Magna tibi profecto non modo laus verum[92] et opima praemia contigissent, si haec audientibus feminis fuissent perorata. Neque enim opinor abs te ullam

thrown into confusion by fear, and with prodigious vigor she resumed the war more fiercely than before. Thus with stupendous inspirational speeches and marvelous accomplishments she took up the duties of that man who was both her husband and their leader. This one woman for some time checked the progress of the good fortune of that exceptionally successful emperor — the good fortune that both then and afterward all kings and nations feared, having put it repeatedly to the test.[31]

"And, to leave aside foreigners, what foolish sense of modesty 34 prevents us from mentioning our Vittoria Colonna?[32] We intensely admire her marvelous talent in every genre of literature and her supreme ability to manage public affairs, a task that has always been difficult. Before undertaking other duties, she ruled Benevento, an exceedingly seditious and proud city of the Sannio which had been entrusted to her by Pope Clement while her husband, the marquis of Pescara, was conducting massive wars abroad. She governed in such a way that the restless and violent youth on the one hand and the city council on the other, who were used to displaying the ancient mettle of unconquered Samnium, set down their weapons, forgot about factionalism, and decided upon peace. And the entire populace, deeply moved by the moderation of her highly authoritative and absolutely incorruptible character, gave thanks to the pontiff through ambassadors because at the most critical moment, through this woman, better than any male governor, he had saved the city just as it was collapsing both from its crimes and from the harshness and greed of earlier governors, and had brought it, just in time, toward the promise of a settled security."

But then D'AVALOS said, "I'm astonished, Muscettola. How 35 splendidly and elegantly you've pleaded the case of women! Certainly not only great praise but also rich rewards would have befallen you, had you given your closing statement at a time when the women were listening. Nor indeed do I think that any wife or

umquam mulierem vel viduam gravi lite laborantem tanto studio tantaque eloquentia in forensibus iudiciis esse defensam. Praeclara nempe quaedam ex reconditis et politioribus studiis, quae in foro dissimulare soles, alacrius protulisti adeo ut ea[93] indigna feminis et contumeliosa[94] esse confirmem. Sed[95] iam nulla novarum legum ope corrigi aut mutari queunt. Nequaquam[96] enim puto sanis et iustis hominibus de commovendo atque exagitando terrarum orbe fore cogitandum ut aequiores leges conscribantur, quibus feminarum iniurias vindicare atque eas restituere in ampliorem locum dignitatis velint, quandoquidem ea sine perniciosa rerum omnium confusione fieri nequeant,[97] postquam quemadmodum videtis publica saeculi fortuna sic leges contrivit et mores afflixit ut cuncta humana atque divina ut corrupta et iam plane ruinosa brevi concisura[98] esse videantur.

36   'Feramus igitur humaniter praesentes mores, temporibus obsequamur nostris, et feminas ab his virtutibus enixe laudemus quae earum ordinem satis honestum[99] reddunt et nequaquam obscure nobilitant.[100] Irritae namque spei ac alucinantis ingenii videtur ea velle expetere quae quidem[101] voto facilius imaginato concipi[102] possint quam in ipso rerum usu omnino[103] reperiri, si condicionem infirmissimi sexus et quibus opprimitur impotentium virorum iniurias animo reputemus.

37   'Ego illam[104] omni laude atque honore afficiendam esse mulierem[105] semper existimavi, in qua tria haec uno concursu moderata quadam et non iniqua temperie colligantur: generis claritudo, formae dignitas, et morum ac[106] ingenii cultus, ab institutione non ignobili personis locis horisque omnibus eleganter accommodatus.

even widow having difficulties in a serious legal case has ever been defended by you in public legal proceedings with such zeal and eloquence. You have certainly produced, and with enthusiasm, some fine arguments, relying on your hidden and more refined studies which you usually conceal in court, to the point where I myself would corroborate your view that there exist attitudes that are slanderous and unworthy of women. But as things now stand, these attitudes cannot be corrected or changed by new legislation. I don't in the slightest suppose that sane and just men should contemplate disrupting the whole world in order that more equitable laws may be written to make restitution for the injustices done to women and to restore them to a higher status. These things aren't possible without there being a destructive confusion in all affairs, now that, as you see, the general fortune of this age has so crushed the laws and battered down morals that all things human and divine, damaged and now plainly going to ruin, appear about to collapse in a short space of time.

"Let us therefore endure with compassion the morals of the   36 present and defer to our times, praising women assiduously on the basis of those virtues which make them respectable enough in their social rank and which ennoble them in a way that is by no means lacking in visibility. Surely it seems but the futile hope of a delirious mind to aspire to obtain things that are more easily pictured as a kind of imagined desire than they are to be found in the real physical world—that is, if we bear in mind the condition of that extremely frail sex and the injustices of the arrogant men by which it is oppressed.

"I've always supposed that one should endow with every mark   37 of praise and honor that woman in whom these three things are united in equal proportion into one well-tempered blend: fame of lineage, distinction of beauty, and refinement of intellect and character. The last of these, the result of a noble education, is properly adaptable for use among all people, in all places, and at all times.

Ab eruditis nutriciis et[107] a clara maxime[108] stirpe splendidi[109] mores oriuntur; decora facies, quae non minus a caelo quam a parentibus ducitur,[110] in virorum animos[111] imperium exercet; studia autem[112] litterata feminas[113] viris pares et[114] admirabiles reddunt. Quibus dotibus si castimonia corporis accesserit, tum demum humana specie augustiores et divinae penitus efficiuntur. Id enim singularis excellentiae condimentum semper fuit adeo ut natalibus obscurae facieque deformes, ac simul rudes litterarum et insulsae, satis se nobiles esse existiment, si consciae ipsius integri[115] pudoris, in aliis parum pudice viventibus haec praeclara tot dotium ornamenta condemnent et irrideant. Nihil enim iam praestat et forma conspicuas, et fortuna illustres, ac ingenio nobilissimas exstitisse, si pudicitiae decus plenis omnium sermonibus in dubium revocetur.

38   'Persimiles enim mihi videntur eae mulieres famosae[116] illi smaragdo quam senatus et populus Genuensis expugnata quondam Ptolemaide, tropaei nomine in patriam relatam et religiose[117] custoditam, nobilioribus advenis ostendere consuevit. Ea est in sexangulam pateram, productis utrimque ansulis conformata, fundo pulcherrimis orbiculis coronato ac eximia capacitate, a patulis item[118] labris mirabiliter[119] tota pellucens,[120] et extra atque intus egregie perpolita, adeo ut omnino regiae luxuriae sumptum ac omnem humanae indicaturae insaniam excedere videatur. Sed haec tam praeclara patera tantaeque admirationis gemma, quae una omnium opes exsuperare vulgo putatur, nullis umquam reipublicae difficultatibus subvenit; suspecta enim est pretiosissimae gemmae et pulcherrimi vasculi inusitata cunctorum[121] oculis amplitudo. Neque deleri ex hominum mentibus propter immensi pretii

Splendid character arises from skilled child rearing and especially from a renowned lineage; a beautiful appearance, which is drawn no less from heaven than from one's parents, wields power over men's minds; but literary studies make women equal to men and worthy of admiration. If purity of body is added to these endowments, then their majesty transcends their human form and they are completely divine. For chastity has always been a mark of such singular excellence that women of obscure birth and unattractive appearance who are unlettered and unrefined judge that they are noble enough if, in consciousness of their own purity, they can condemn and mock splendid and numerous accomplishments in other women who are less than pure in their way of life. It profits women nothing that they are outstanding in beauty, distinguished in social position, and possess the talents of an aristocrat if the glory of their chastity should be called into doubt by widespread gossip.

"Indeed, these notorious women seem to me very similar to that emerald which the Genoan state has been accustomed to show off to the noblest foreigners.[33] Brought back to the fatherland as a trophy after Ptolemais had been conquered, it has been scrupulously guarded. This gem has been fashioned into a hexagonal libation dish, with little carven handles on either side and the base crowned by the most beautiful rings, and it's extraordinarily large. Moreover, the whole gem, shining forth marvelously from its gaping lips, has been splendidly polished inside and out in such a way that it would appear to exceed the expense of every royal luxury and every mad extravagance of human valuation. But this splendid dish and much admired gem, which alone is commonly believed to exceed in value the means of all men everywhere, has never helped to relieve any of the republic's financial troubles, for it has been held suspect on account of its sheer size — no one has ever seen its like — of the surpassingly precious gem and its beautiful vessel. Nor, thanks to the exorbitant value attached to it, can the suspi-

38

gravitatem suspicio potest, quin pseudosmaragdus gemmaque fac-
ticia reputetur.[122] Ita reges eam emere non audent, publicani acci-
pere eam pignori oblatam recusant. Quis enim illam, ut ex[123]
pondere consideratius[124] examinaret, ad libitum tractavit? Quis ad
solis radios praetentam liquidius inspexit? Quis demum eius margines ferrea lima temptavit, cum e suggestu et ad tubae cantum et
funalibus accensis honoris causa, sacrato in loco, et ab infulato
quidem sacerdote semper ostendatur?

39 'Ergo sicut Ligures in re non multum[125] utili sed[126] ab vetere
fama praeclaraque[127] specie tantum gloriosa magnitudinem eximiam aequabilemque nitorem et figuram tot angulis accommodatam ad excipiendos frangendosque fulgentium colorum repercus-
sus plurimum admirantur, ita et mulierem frustra ab ipsis ingenii
et corporis ornamentis commendabimus, si pudor ipse, quo nihil
in mundo muliebri pretiosius esse potest, in dubium et certam
suspicionem clarioribus coniecturis fuerit devocatus.

40 'Sed in Gallia Cisalpina et imprimis Mediolani, hoc ipsum pudicitiae decus quod antea perillustre aut certe minus obscurum
fuerat, insignes, ut vidimus, maculas contraxit. In ea enim copio-
sissima et maxime luxuriosa[128] civitate quinque fere annos pace
et bello continuatos iuventam exercui, nec ullius puto de eius rei
opinione certius aut praeclarius testimonium fore quam meum.
Postquam enim ii populi externis gentibus servire coeperunt,
sicut fuit necesse et Neapoli etiam accidisse videmus, novi atque
insoliti mores cum viris tum ipsis maxime feminis sunt inserti.[129]
Galli primo invexere nepotinas cenas, vina iucundiora, multam

cion be erased from men's minds that it should be reckoned a fake emerald and an artificial gem. Thus kings don't dare buy it, and the tax collectors refuse to accept it when it has been tendered as collateral. Who indeed has been allowed to handle it freely in order to evaluate its weight more carefully? Who has examined it clearly, holding it up to the rays of the sun? Who, finally, has probed its edges with an iron file? No one, since it was always displayed on the platform, and to the sounding of a trumpet, and with torches lit to accord it honor, in a consecrated place and, what's more, by a priest adorned with a woolen headband.

"Therefore, just as the Ligurians, with respect to a thing that is 39 not very useful but only glorious from ancient repute and from a splendid outward appearance, greatly wonder at its outstanding size, its uniform luster, and the many-edged shape, suited to catching and breaking up the reflections of gleaming colors; so too it will be pointless for us to commend a woman on the basis of those very trappings of natural talent and of the body if chastity itself, the most precious thing in the world to a woman, has been called into doubt and is justifiably suspect on the basis of clear inferences.

"But in northwestern Italy and especially in Milan, as we have 40 seen, the glory of chastity, which previously had been well known or at least not hard to discern, has incurred conspicuous blemishes. I spent around five years of my youth, in war and in peace, in that immensely rich and luxurious city-state, and I don't think that anybody's testimony about this matter will be either surer or more perspicuous than mine. After those peoples began to be subservient to foreign nations, inevitably (and we've seen this happen in Naples as well), new and unaccustomed practices were imported both for men and especially for women. First the French introduced extravagant dinners, more pleasant wines, a great

sumptuosae vestis varietatem, et imprimis, quod familiarum fortunas evertit, sericum et purpuram insana animi petulantia circa limbos ex intervallis incidere, et argentum atque aurum textile ad elegantiam lacerare, et denique cuncta pretiosa[130] ludibrio habere docuerunt.

41   'Quin et[131] tripudia etiam lasciviora in multam noctem[132] perducere coepere[133] in quibus, certa lege, circumductis in orbem funalibus, a matronis oscula petebantur. Quae, tametsi[134] nihil sunt apud Gallos ad impetrandam venerem,[135] basia tamen[136] nos Itali sic aestimamus, ut cum quis matronam vel summis[137] labris suaviarit⟨ur⟩, eam semicorruptam esse et quasi expugnatam arbitremur, ita ut in *Politicis* Plato minime sit deridendus, qui strenuis bellatoribus praemii loco constituit ut pueros et puellas ut liberet osculari fas esset.[138]

42   'Igitur excrescente licentia et luxu in immensum exundante, et profligatis verecundiae custodibus, apertae libidines nobilissimas matronarum invasere adeo ut cum nonnullas Galli, homines repentini, liberales, et in amoribus plerumque violenti, florente eorum imperio pellexissent, in multarum demum cubilia Hispani nostri salaces et veteratores[139] importuni accuratioribus obsequiis ac insidiosis artibus penetrarint. Aliquae enim improbitate atque lascivia, nonnullae ingentibus pretiis, sed multo plurimae ambitione et metu atque obtrectatione alienae gratiae pudorem amisere. Nam ubi aliqua obstinate atque pudice neque animum neque aures probosis[140] sermonibus praebebat, nulla nobili equitum frequentia colebatur, et in villas eius et praedia, alae et cohortes ad excidium mittebantur, neque ullus expilandis possessionibus finis

variety of sumptuous clothing, and especially (a thing which has upended the fortunes of households), with insane wantonness of mind, they added silk and purple at intervals to the hems of dresses, cut up gold and silver fabric for the sake of elegance, and finally taught them to regard all precious materials as mere playthings.

"What is more, they began to prolong late into the night lascivious dances in which, by fixed rule, once they'd taken around torches to form a circle, kisses were requested from married women. Although, among the French, kisses are by no means intended as solicitations for sex, nonetheless we Italians esteem kisses in such a way that when someone has kissed a lady, even on the very tips of the lips, we judge her to be halfway ruined and her resistance overcome. Thus Plato is not in the least to be derided on the grounds that in the *Republic*[34] he decreed that warriors should be allowed to kiss whatever boys and girls they wanted as a reward.

"Therefore, with licentiousness on the rise, luxury overflowing into excess, and with the guardians of modesty cast aside, unrestrained sexual desire assailed the most noble of married women. Thus while the French held power, being impetuous, free, and frequently violent in their loves, they had seduced some of these matrons. Then our Spaniards, old hands at this, salacious and relentless in the more effective forms of courting women and in underhanded tactics, penetrated the boudoirs of many women. Some women lost modesty through depravity and lasciviousness, and not a few on account of exorbitant cash offerings. But by far the most did so because of self-interest, fear, and envy of the favor enjoyed by other women.[35] For whenever any woman stubbornly and chastely failed to surrender either her mind or her ears to shameful talk, no noble crowd of knights protected her, but squadrons and military detachments were dispatched into her villas and estates to destroy them. Nor was there any end to the looting

41

42

erat, nisi eas viri tantis incommodis fatigati uxorum noctibus rede-
missent, nullaque etiam ab avaritia militari domus erat incolumis
nisi domina, alicuius praefecti aut tribuni insignis amicitia, seques-
tra libidine niteretur.

43   'Luxuria vero ubique etiam hodie[141] tanta est ut cum praedio-
rum red[d]itus continua belli calamitate sint intercepti, vix eam
ullae privatae opes possint tolerare. Vehuntur quaternis equis in
curribus hebeno atque ebore tessellato fabrefactis et praetexto conciso[que][142] e serico coopertis. Sordidum autem ac ineptum putant
concolores equos non iunxisse, elegantiae vero summae ac eruditi
sumptus arbitrantur si affectionum suarum ac amorum argumenta
non vestium modo sed equorum etiam coloribus expresserint.[143]
Zebellinarum autem martarum,[144] quas Scythicae mittunt silvae,
pretiosis[145] exuviis non vestem modo sed femoralia furtorum veneris[146] conscia substernunt, manicae vero digitorum et manuum te-
gimenta peregrinis liquoribus[147] incoquuntur vaporariae lucernae
in quibus confarreata inter se indica unguenta in suffitus adolentur.[148] Nam si quid e rosa ceterisque floribus odoratis quod ex ipsa
domestica hortorum fecunditate facile paratur ad delicias pertinet,[149] id uti plebeium quiddam repente fastidiunt utpote quae
magnis ut ab incognito tantum oceano et iis quidem maxime[150]
fugacissimis sumptibus delectentur.

44   'Sed iam earum plane castigatam esse luxuriem audimus multis
et lugendis[151] huius belli detrimentis. Nam hoc tam gravi et tam
diuturno alendi exercitus nostri incommodo, non enervatam modo
sed eversis omnium fortunis penitus evastatam esse opulentam[152]
urbem ita ut pigeat eam umquam vidisse, credere debemus, quoniam obsessus ibi Antonius Leva nihil non peracerbe[153] sit facturus

unless husbands, weary from such great misfortunes, ransomed their plundered possessions with the nocturnal activities of their wives. And no home was safe from the greed of foreign soldiers unless a matron, by friendship with some well-known prefect or tribune, depended on his lust as surety.

"But today, there's so much extravagance everywhere that, once   43
the continuous calamity of war had deprived the estates of their yields, hardly any private resources could sustain it. These men are borne along by four-horse teams in chariots decorated by hand with ebony- and ivory mosaics and covered with fancy silk vestments. In addition, they suppose it a vulgar, tasteless thing not to have yoked together horses of matching colors: they judge it characteristic of the highest elegance and most erudite expenditure if they express the proofs of their inclinations and loves by the colors not only of the vestments but even of the horses. What's more, they line not just clothing in general, but especially that around their thighs, with precious sable fur from the Scythian forests to serve as accomplices to their illicit love.[36] And, their finger gloves and gauntlets are imbued with exotic liquids from a steamy oil lamp in which Indian perfumes, blended together as if in marriage, are vaporized to give off fragrant fumes. If a rose or other fragrant flower, easily procured from the abundance of their own gardens, could contribute to their indulgences, right away they disdain using it as something common, inasmuch as they delight most of all in the most exotic extravagances, as for example those coming only from an unknown ocean.

"But already we hear reports that the extravagance of those   44
women has clearly been chastened by the many sad losses of this war. For we must believe that not only has a wealthy city been weakened by the serious and ongoing inconvenience of provisioning our army, but, after the fortunes of all were overturned, it has been utterly devastated to such a degree that it pains one ever to have seen it. This is so because Antonio de Leyva, having been

ut cum excidio miserrimae civitatis constantiae suae famam quam diutissime tueatur.'

45   Tum ego ⟨IOVIUS⟩ inquam, 'Desine nos, Davale,[154] ad sensum maximi doloris revocare. Nescio enim quo pacto, contra id quod proposueramus, tam saepe ad eos sermones relabamur qui cum per se nobis plurimum sint molesti, eo etiam acerbiores videntur quod facetissimarum rerum iucunditatem interpellent, vel[155] eam certe minus gratam ac insuauiorem efficiant. Scio enim te, qui Mediolanensibus imprimis carus cum tua humanitate tum mutuis officiis ac meritis semper exstitisti, non posse non dolere tantae urbis interitum in qua, si aut pax impetrata aut victoria parta fore[n]t, tibi omnino esset velut in pergrato honoris ac voluptatis domicilio quiescendum. Et ego vix lacrimas possum continere cum patriam meam Comum[156] sex annos continuos a praesidiis vestris primo contra fidem publicam[157] crudelissime direptam ac demum penitus[158] eversam recolo, adeo ut[159] natalis soli et peramoeni[160] Larii facies ipsiusque Musei mei tam latorum hortorum litterati otii sedes, et frater amore atque virtute ante alia mihi iucundissimus, memoria perpetuo deponenda esse videantur.

46   'Proinde obsecro,[161] Davale, redeamus ad sermones nostros ut harum miseriarum obliviscamur, et quasnam Mediolani cognoveris paullo ⟨antea⟩ illustres forma et moribus mulieres nobis edissere. Nam eas quae tum florebant cum ego adolescens Mediolanum concessissem ut Demetrium Calchondylem et Parrhasium Cosentinum Graecas et Latinas litteras incredibili fama publice docentes

besieged there, will do nothing that is not very harsh, in order that, with the destruction of an exceedingly miserable city, he may keep safe for as long as possible his reputation for unbending resolution."[37]

Then I [GIOVIO] said, "D'Avalos, stop reminding us about   45
this painful subject. For somehow, contrary to what we've agreed, we keep slipping back to those topics which, although they have distressed us very much on their own account, seem all the more bitter because they interrupt the pleasantness of our elegant conversations, or at least they make that pleasantness less agreeable and more sour. For I know that you, who have always been especially prominent among those beloved of the Milanese thanks to your compassion, your official role, and your merits, could not but be grieved at the ruin of so great a city. There, if either peace should be achieved or victory accomplished, it would be entirely incumbent upon you to rest, so to speak, in the most agreeable abode of honor and of pleasure. And I can hardly hold back tears when I see that my homeland, Como, was first of all cruelly laid waste by your garrisons, contrary to public guarantees, and subsequently has been entirely ruined over the course of six years.[38] The destruction is so great that I have constantly to put from my mind the picture of my native and delightful Larian[39] soil, the recollection of my very own museum, of my erudite leisure, of my extensive gardens, as well as thoughts of my brother, most dear to me above all else because of his love and excellence.

"And so, please, d'Avalos, let's return to our subject in order   46
that we may forget these miseries, and tell us about the women whom you knew in Milan a little while ago who were illustrious in beauty and character. As a young man, I'd gone off to Milan so that I might study under Demetrius Chalcondyles[40] and Giano Parrasio,[41] who held publicly funded positions and were teaching Greek and Latin literature to incredible acclaim. But I have to believe that those women who were in their prime back then have

audirem, exuisse totius formae dignitatem et iam consenuisse credendum est. Matronarum enim tum princeps erat Damicella Tri-
vultia, huius Augustini Cardinalis soror qui superiore anno contra
Lanoium ad Frusinonem pontificiis in castris legatus fuit. In qua
cum insignis pulchritudo et clara nobilitas cum spectata castitate
essent coniuncta⟨e⟩, Latinarum etiam et Graecarum litterarum
studia ad rarissimam laudem eminebant.

47   'Secundum eam in honore erat Hippolyta Sfortia Alexandro
Bentivolio nupta, eadem nobilis perpulchra et Etruscis praesertim
rhythmis erudita. Quae adeo de pudore sollicita semper fuit ut
Cusanius nobilis medicus qui, ut invitam ad amorem pelliceret,
magicis carminibus mentem ei commovisse credebatur,[162] publico
sed iniquo quidem iudicio in quaestione[163] tortus et vexatus exstiterit. Novissime autem cum Mediolanum expulsis Gallis intrasse-
mus, et in Brecontianis aedibus Iulius Medices in exercitu legatus[164] hospitio fuisset exceptus, Claram vidi Galeatii Vicecomitis
filiam formae et morum venustate valde praestantem, cum illa ad
Dariam amitam tanto hospiti facile parem saepissime ventitaret.'

48   Haec cum dicerem, admotis ad oculos digitis, quasi lacrimalis
humor efflueret, DAVALUS 'Absiste,' inquit, 'Iovi, ab his meritis
laudibus congerendis. Nam haec Clara feminarum omnium humanitate ac elegantia vitae longe clarissima nuper interiit, ad cuius
elatae nuntium talem animo concepi dolorem ut is iam sit inter
hos sermones tuos cum incredibili vehementia renovatus. Nam
domus eius opulenta hospitalis elegantiarum omnium plena et
mihi et Piscario fratri semper patuit ita ut illam non patricii civis,
ut vir eius erat Petrus[165] Pusterula, sed alicuius magni regis nuptiis
dignam esse fateremur.[166]

already been deprived of the dignity of all beauty and have begun to go into decline. The doyenne among the matrons was Damigella Trivulzio,[42] the sister of that Cardinal Agostino Trivulzio[43] who last year was a legate in the papal armies against Lannoy in Frosinone. Once exceptional beauty, illustrious noble lineage, and tested chastity had been joined in her person, her studies in Latin and Greek literature were also outstanding, bringing her the rarest praise.[44]

"Next in honor after her was Ippolita Sforza,[45] Alessandro Bentivoglio's wife. Noble, very beautiful, and especially learned in Tuscan prose rhythms, she was always extremely scrupulous about chastity. As a result, the famous doctor Cusanius, who was believed to have influenced her mind with magical spells to entice the unwilling woman into making love, was tortured on the rack in public though unjust legal proceedings. Most recently, when we had returned to Milan after the French had been driven out, and Giulio de' Medici, a legate in the army, had been received as a guest in Bergonzio's[46] house, I saw Galeazzo Visconti's daughter, Chiara.[47] Exceptionally attractive in both beauty and character, she often used to make regular visits to her Aunt Daria,[48] who was herself the equal of her guest." 47

While I was saying this, D'AVALOS brought his fingers to his eyes as if a teardrop were escaping, and said: "Giovio, stop piling up these praises, justified though they may be. For that Chiara, by far the most illustrious of all women in cultivation and elegance of life, has just died. At the news of her burial, I suffered such anguish of mind that, with these words of yours, it has already returned with incredible intensity. Her home—sumptuous, hospitable, and filled with every refinement—always lay open both to me and to my cousin, Pescara, in such a way that we declared it worthy, not of the married estate of a patrician citizen (as was her husband, Pietro Pusterla), but of some great king. 48

49 'Ex iis vero quae supersunt incolumes, Hippolytam Castellioniam Hieronymi iurisconsulti eloquentissimi nurum familia nobili
et pervetusta[167] ortam et in eandem etiam nuptam ceteras omnes
arbitror anteire. Est enim aspectu imprimis liberali, perblandis
oculis, crine subcrispo, sermone molli, ac ingenio plane suavissimis
litteris ac moribus instituto.[168]

50 'Sed ante alias duae forma admodum insignes viduae, in summis educatae deliciis et a multis argutiis atque leporibus liberalis
ingenii praecellentes, essent hoc loco sub veris nominibus celebran-
dae, nisi verecundiae matronalis fines liberiore vita penitus exces-
sissent. Alia quoque inter formosas multorum iudicio singularis,
quae nupta est viro satis nobili sed in utramque aurem egregie
stertenti, tantam grata venustate ore incessu atque oculis modestiam refert ut quae sunt eius lasciviae propiores[169] pudico quodam
artificio facile recondantur. Verum haec, dum impotenti servit
adultero, summam ipsa nacta potentiam in ipsis patriae cineribus
triumphat.

51 'Quamobrem hinc propere discedam, ne, dum formosas nobiles
lepidasque consector (quando in his iam amissum sit aut certe vehementer adumbratum pudicitiae decus) aliae quae mox ex aliis
urbibus erunt nominandae de illiberali vel inepto iudicio nostro
conquerantur, si in earum ordinem, quae male audiunt[170] de pudore, conturbata pudicitiae ratione redigantur. Et hercle matronae
castimonia illustres hoc imprimis cavere debent: ne cum impuris

"Out of those who live on unscathed, however, I judge that Ip- 49
polita Castiglioni,[49] the daughter-in-law of the very eloquent jurist
Girolamo, a woman born into a noble and very ancient family who
also married into one, surpasses all the others. For she has a particularly honorable appearance, the most charming eyes, slightly
curly hair, tender speech, and natural talent that clearly has been
enhanced by her training in the most delightful literature and in
good moral conduct.

"But before the others there are two widows, very distinguished 50
in beauty, brought up in the utmost luxury, and standing out from
the many thanks to the wit and cleverness of their noble minds.
They would need to be celebrated at this point with their actual
names, had they not by a loose lifestyle utterly exceeded the
bounds of ladylike modesty. There is another too who in the judgment of many is unique among beautiful women. She's married to
a fairly noble man, but one who is snoring away, manifestly oblivi-
ous to her indiscretions.[50] She expresses such great modesty with
her pleasing charm, facial expression, gait, and eyes that those
lascivious acts of hers are easily concealed by a certain feigned decency. But this woman, who herself has obtained the greatest influence while serving a wanton adulterer, triumphs amid the very
ashes of the fatherland.

"I'll drop this subject quickly, lest in my hunt after beautiful, 51
noble, and charming women (seeing that the ones I've just mentioned have already lost the glory of their chastity, or at least had
it seriously obscured), other women from the other cities who are
next to be named should complain bitterly about our ungenerous
or inept judgment, should they be included among those with
a bad reputation for lacking modesty, as our accounting of chastity has been thrown into confusion. And, by God, ladies with
fine reputations should beware of this one thing above all: they
shouldn't consort with the impure, for their own cleaner souls

389

sedeant, quando ex earum foedo contactu illotisque sermonibus candidiores animae penitus inquinentur.

52 'Neque tamen negaverim complures Mediolani reperiri peramabili venustate nec absurdo quidem[171] ingenio ac honestissima stirpe satis claras, quae pudicitiae nomen constantissime tueantur. Sed nos in feminarum dote maius[172] quoddam quaerimus atque praeclarius; neque enim nisi formas summa raritate conspicuas admiramur, nullam nobilitatem nisi a praealta originis antiquitate repetitam agnoscimus, neque illud ipsum incorrupti pudoris nomen nisi a publica et constanti fama veneramur. Porro ingenia nequaquam suspicimus nisi in eis inusitatae quaedam et perennes amoenitates eluceant.

53 'Nec in Isabella Sfortia Pisaurense regulo genita desiderari quicquam[173] potest quod ad membrorum mensuram et totius oris speciem, vel ad animi cultum ex iucundioribus studiis in peramabili matrona pertineat. Ceteras nequaquam huius ordinis vel fortunae, si vitam spectes, multis de causis[174] non puto numerandas; nam longum certe opus atque difficile suscepisse videmur, si praeclaras insignium urbium mulieres expressis earum laudibus celebrare velimus. Quamobrem mi Iovi si ullae reliquae sunt ex illa vestra Gallia Cisalpina quae laudem mereantur eas protinus recense; nam et ego et Musetius quam primum abs te Venetias perduci magnopere desideramus, ubi mulieres esse dicuntur longe omnium delicatissimae atque pulcherrimae.'

54 Ad id ego ⟨IOVIUS⟩ inquam, 'Et in hac re vobis cumulate morem gessero, et mihi ipsi etiam singularem afferam voluptatem; nam in eius urbis opulentissimae atque admirabilis memoria recolenda plurimum oblectabor, utpote qui in ea omnium ingeniis maxime opportuna[175] saepissime et bonarum litterarum et, ut aetas ferebat, eruditarum quandoque voluptatum studia sim persecutus,

might be deeply polluted by the foul contagion and filthy words of those women.

"I wouldn't deny, however, that very many Milanese women are   52
distinguished enough for their adorable charm,[51] sensible ideas, and honorable lineage who are steadfastly protected by their reputation for chastity. But we seek in the endowment of women something greater and more illustrious. And indeed, we don't admire beauties unless they are extremely rare; we recognize no nobility unless it derives from a high, ancient origin; nor do we venerate a reputation for incorruptible chastity unless it is supported by invariable public report. Moreover, we don't admire talents at all unless certain unusual and constant charms shine forth in them.

"That adorable noblewoman, Isabella Sforza,[52] daughter of the   53
ruler of Pesaro, lacks nothing in the proportion of her limbs, the beauty of her entire countenance, or her mind, which is cultivated with the most pleasing studies. The remaining women, I think, are by no means of this rank or good fortune if you look at their life: for many reasons, they're not to be listed. If we should wish to celebrate the famous women of illustrious cities with explicit praises of each of them, we appear to have undertaken a task that is certainly long and arduous. On this account, my Giovio, if there are any remaining ones from your region of northwestern Italy who merit praise, list them right away: for both Muscettola and I are longing for you to lead us as soon as possible to Venice, where women are said to be by far the most refined and beautiful of all."

To this I [GIOVIO] acceded: "In this matter, I'll grant you plenty   54
of indulgence and also will give myself a singular pleasure, for in calling to mind the memory of that exceedingly rich and admirable city, I'll enjoy myself immensely. In that city, uniquely suited to talents of all kinds, I assiduously pursued studies in good literature and, as youth demanded, in more sophisticated pleasures, so that practically nowhere, I think, have I ever lived more happily.

ut paene[176] nullibi me umquam vixisse beatius putem. Et hercle in hac una semper ornatissima et maxime tranquilla civitate, quod reliquum est Italici nominis decus adversus infestarum gentium rabiem egregie tuemur; in qua nimirum rerum omnium quae in omnes usus exoptari queunt, copia singularis cum varietate laetissima semper efflorescit.

55 'Nullibi, siquidem viget, perducendae quietius et hilarius vitae aut iucundior aut securior libertas, quam incredibili navigandi commoditate, insularum adiacentium specie, eximiorum aedificiorum frequentia, et nobilium operum celebritate, exteri homines facile metiuntur. Quid enim, si pietatem spectes, tot templorum amplitudine et cultu religiosius? Quid Marciana curia magnificentius? Quid illa bicipiti Platea luculentius? Quid denique stupendis navalibus instructius ac opulentius toto terrarum orbe conspicies? Ad haec omnia per circumfluos singulis regionibus ac domibus euripos contecta cumba proveheris. Potes interea colloquia serere cum amicis, libris vacare et, si solus omnino sis, praeclara etiam commentari. Nullae diurnae vel nocturnae iniuri⟨ae⟩ ambulantem vel navigantem exagitant.

56 'Nulli denique bellorum strepitus qui animis officiant in eo felici admodum secessu sentiuntur. Nam senatus,[177] incredibili[178] severitate et moderatione, haec omnia continet et custodit in quo ad regendam rempublicam principes exsistunt. Grandaevi senes, vegetae mentis, eximiae prudentiae spectataeque virtutis, ii numquam in diversa studia scinduntur, cum id tantum quod publice rectum sit atque utile[179] respiciant. Nullae enim apud eos factiones; et si quae sunt novarum et veterum familiarum, eae

And my God, in this one city, always particularly distinguished and tranquil, we preserve admirably well, against the ferocity of hostile peoples, what remains of the good name of Italy. Without doubt, in this city there always flourishes a singular abundance as well as an exceedingly rich variety of all of the resources which can be desired for meeting all needs.

"Since the city is thriving, nowhere else is there more pleasant 55 or more secure freedom to live life peacefully and delightfully. Foreign peoples generally esteem this city highly on account of the incredible convenience of traveling by boat, the beauty of the adjacent islands, the abundance of exceptional buildings, and the reputation of noble works of art. For what, if you consider piety, is more devout than the size and adornment of their numerous churches? What is more magnificent than the court of St. Mark? What is more resplendent than that piazza, with its two famous columns? What, finally, will you see in the entire world that is better equipped and supplied than those admirable shipyards? A covered skiff conveys you to all these things through canals that flow around separate districts and homes. In the meantime you can engage in discussions with friends, find leisure for books and, if you should find yourself entirely alone, you can also occupy your mind with splendid things. No unlawful acts disturb the pedestrian or the boat passenger, either during the day or at night.

"Finally, no clamors of wars, which might impede one's spirit, 56 are felt at all in that fortunate retreat. For the Senate, with incredible strictness and exercise of control, holds all these things in check and keeps an eye on them. It is in the Senate that leading citizens come forward to rule the republic. These aged men, of vigorous mind, exceptional prudence, and tested virtue, are never riven by partisanship, since they turn their attention only to that which is appropriate and useful for the commonweal. There are no factions among them; and if there are some divisions between the new lineages and the old, these are hardly apparent and are the

subobscurae et comitiales tantum exsistunt, quae nulla animorum acerbitate sed solis suffragiis exercentur.

57 'Feminas in honore domi habent quarum pudorem dissimulanter potius quam aperte vel severe custodiunt, ad eas enim salutandas nulli nisi affines et propinqui ventitare solent. Ipsae, vel in festa sollemnium nuptiarum hilaritate cum tripudiis indulgent, cum personato vel ignoto nemine collocuntur. Quo fit ut non eas habeant eruditi sermonis illecebras quae in Mediolanensibus et circumpadanis[180] florent, quamquam non inept[a]e[181] suavitates quasdam rudibus[182] suis responsis atque colloquiis ferant, quae vel salsissimos homines allicere atque oblectare[183] possint. In universum, cultiores litteras non attingunt; comptui[184] elegantiae et munditiis plurimum student, capilloque maxime flavo et tepidis calamistris molliter inflexo. Atque item[185] sucosiore habitu magnopere delectantur, omnibus perblandi vultus, teneri sinus, lacteae cervices, adeo inter se certis finibus conformes ut Venetae, traductae in alias terras atque alieno cultu convestitae, a ceteris[186] facillime[187] dinoscantur. Porro quae stata sunt forma et genere minime nobiles tanta est earum[188] tota urbe multitudo ut[189] faciles et peramabiles munificis[190] amatoribus numquam desint.[191]

58 'Sed paucis ante annis ad sacratas[192] virgines incredibilis otiosorum et procacium iuvenum erat concursus, cum illae palam nullo metu dedecoris religionis et pudicitiae penitus oblitae lascivissime colerentur. Eae magna ex parte nobilissimis erant ortae familiis, quas parentes, insana dotium magnitudine deterriti, invitas sacris initiassent. Is tum enim mos inoluerat ut, cum quis patricius

business of public assemblies, which resolve them simply by voting, without animosity.

"The Venetians safeguard the honor of their women in the 57 home, and protect their decency discreetly rather than publicly or sternly. No men except kin and near relations are accustomed to come regularly to pay their respects. The women themselves, even when they indulge in dances in the festive cheer of wedding ceremonies, speak with nobody masked or unfamiliar. That's why they don't have the enticements that come from sophisticated conversation which flourish among the Milanese and those who live in the Po River valley. Still, not being completely naïve, they bring to their unsophisticated responses and conversation certain charms which may win over and entertain even the cleverest people. In general, they don't lay a finger on more refined literature; they're most eager for refinements of manners and for well-dressed hair, and especially blond hair that's been smoothly coiffed with warm curling irons. Likewise they delight greatly in a physique that evinces vitality: they all have charming faces, tender breasts, and milk-white necks. Indeed, Venetian women are so similar among themselves, within certain limits, that even when they are conveyed to foreign lands and dressed in exotic garb, they are easily distinguished from all the rest. Moreover, in the entire city, so great is the number of women with acknowledged beauty that even the ones who aren't at all noble by birth, being agreeable and entirely lovable, never lack magnanimous suitors.[53]

"But just a few years ago, there was an extraordinary crowd of 58 leisured and impudent young men consorting with nuns, when those women, plainly with no fear of disgrace and having entirely forgotten religion and any sense of shame, were being 'worshipped' in a very wanton way. For the most part, they had been born into very noble families. Their fathers, hindered by the insane size of dowries, had entered them against their will into religious orders. Indeed, this practice had then grown so that when any patrician

haud multum dives ternas aut quaternas filias suscepisset, primam splendidius ac ambitiosius collocaret, reliquae vero interceptis dotibus ad divinum cultum opulentis coenobiis conderentur.

59   'Quamobrem[193] illae, velut in tenera et simplici admodum aetate deceptae praetextuque[194] religionis, fraudatae nuptiarum deliciis, cum eam[195] contumeliam iniquissime ferrent, eam ulcisci[196] multa cum iracundia contumacique libidine properabant,[197] ubi per aetatem, et naturae stimulis et aliarum exemplis, humanae voluptatis sensum recepissent. Facile enim fiebat ut in illa vita umbratili et delicata, tot procis assidue depravantibus, omnes nervi religionis atque virtutis eliderentur. Nihil eis si ora corporaque spectares aut mollius aut venustius, nihil earum lectis et cubiculis apparatius atque munditius, nihil tota supellectile splendidius. Non deerant enim plerisque earum vasa argentea[198] aut puteolana ex Indicis figulinis itemque[199] tunicae interiores et vela suppara odoratis conspersa pulvisculis, cenae etiam[200] quae amatoribus parabantur[201] vere Saliares erant[202] et opiparae. Ipsarum porro ingenia erudita litteris, urbana facetiis, musicis vero artibus adeo instructa ad demulcendos commovendosque animos ut nemo tam saxeus esset qui tantis illecebris minime caperetur, si se in earum familiaritatem blandius insinuasset. Verum tum demum huic tam scelestae libidini severissimis senatus consultis obviam est itum, cum externi reges ad delendum Venetum imperium coniurati gravissimas calamitates intulissent.

60   'Ceterum[203] matronae[204] ex ordine patricio mihi admodum insignes quattuor ante alias sunt visae quae, ni fallor, acutorum omnium iudiciis etiam probantur. Vidi eas primum in Trivisanis

who was not immensely rich had to provide for three or four daughters, he'd be able to give the first in marriage with great splendor and ostentation, but the remaining ones, their dowries having been despoiled, he'd put away in rich convents to serve God.

"For this reason, duped at a tender and naïve age and cheated of 59 the pleasures of marriage under the pretext of religion, these women grew extremely indignant at that affront. Thus with great anger and defiant libido they hurried to exact retribution, since because of their youth, and spurred both by nature and by the example of others, they had recovered the sensation of human pleasure. For it easily happened in that sheltered and pampered life that, with so many suitors incessantly exerting a corrupting influence, religion and virtue lost all their powers. If you consider their faces and bodies, there's nothing either more tender or more charming than they, nothing better furnished and more elegant than their beds and bedrooms, nothing more splendid than all their furniture. Most of them had silver or Pozzuolian vases from Indian workshops, or undergarments and woven scarves sprinkled with scented powders; and the dinners which were prepared for lovers were truly sumptuous[54] and lavish. Moreover, the brilliance of these very women made them accomplished in letters, sophisticated in wit and, what's more, so skilled in musical arts of caressing and arousing the passions that there was no one so stone hearted that he would not be captivated by such great charms once he'd flattered his way into their friendship. But it was only after foreign kings, having conspired to destroy Venetian rule, had inflicted grievous defeats, that the Senate finally, by extremely severe decrees, took countermeasures against this wicked lust.

"However that may be, there are, in my view, four matrons from 60 the patrician rank who are most worthy of note, above the rest. Unless I'm mistaken, they are also approved of in the judgment of all intelligent people. I saw them first in the Trevisan palace,

397

aedibus, dum festo epulo et multis choreis invitatae supra sexaginta totius urbis longe pulcherrimae nuptias celebrarent. Quarum e numero postea decem arbitrio nostro nominatim delectas senatus incredibili benignitate concessit ad luculentiorem cenam invitandas, cum id Hieronymus Adurnus vir omni virtute ornatissimus, tum caesaris legatus humanissimis precibus expetisset. Inter has autem decem, illae etiam lectissimae quattuor ante alias convenere sic ut specimen summae venustatis prae se ferre absque ulla dubitatione viderentur.

61   'Prima erat Isabella[205] Iustiniana, Grimano Victori nupta, florenti aetate puella, cuius ori omnibus gratiarum numeris periucundo numquam deerat gelasinus. Nigris autem eius ocellis eminebat flamma, sic spectantium animos alliciens et accendens ut me ipsum ex ordine convivarum contra discumbentem, si non igne torrere, aliquo tamen vapore levi afflare potuerit, nisi repentinis amorum initiis, tanti mali non ignarus, pro virili reluctandum esse statuissem. Ea remotis mensis, choream duxit. Quam habili edepol corporis statura, quam composito quamque flexibili et alacri laterum motu in palla erat, solido ex auro ad cubitos fimbriata, cuius ab immo latior limbus zebellinarum tergoribus erat protectus. Torquem operoso ex auro, non a cervice, ut moris est, sed ab laevo umero suspenderat, in aliud latus decentissime revolutum. Corolla vero unionum insignium candidos et tumidulos sinus honestabat. Capillus ipse reticulo aureo adeo molliter erat collectus ut cum ad auras minime difflueret, illa tamen laxioribus eum maculis exsilire ac effulgere pateretur.

while over sixty women, the most beautiful by far in the entire
city, were celebrating a wedding with a festive banquet and many
dances. Afterward the Senate, with extraordinary kindness, allowed ten out of their number, chosen expressly by us, to be invited to an even finer dinner, since Girolamo Adorno,[55] a man
endowed with every virtue who at that time was an ambassador of
the emperor, had pleaded for it with the kindest entreaties. From
these ten, moreover, we selected a group of the four choicest
women, whom we saw beyond doubt were displaying the ideal of
the highest attractiveness.

"The first was Isabella Giustinian,[56] the wife of Vittore Gri- 61
mani,[57] a girl in the flower of youth from whose pleasant and end-
lessly charming face a smiling dimple was never absent. But standing out in relief against the backdrop of her dark eyes there was a
glow that attracted and inflamed the passions of those watching. If
she wasn't able to scorch me by their fires—I was in the row of
dinner guests sitting opposite to her—still, she might have been
able to breathe upon me some of their gentle warmth had I not
been aware of the potential for injury and decided that the sudden
shoots of love must be resisted to the best of my ability as a man.
Once the tables had been removed, she performed a dance—and,
oh my, with what a seemly and graceful posture! What a calm and
easy manner! And with what flexible, smooth, and lively movements of her limbs she wore her long outdoor dress, fringed with
solid gold up to the elbows, the wider hem of which had been
covered by the pelts of sables! She had an elaborate golden chain,
not suspended from her neck as is customary, but instead draped
in a half-circle over her shoulders in the most comely fashion.
Moreover, a small garland of extraordinary large pearls adorned
her white and slightly swelling breasts; and her hair had been
gathered gently in a golden net in such a way that, although hardly
any current of air disturbed it, it was allowed, gleaming and lively,
to slip through the wider gaps in the net.

399

62   'Secunda palma data est Lucretiae Veneriae cui omnes inesse
veneres plerique existimant: flaventes illi erant comae, colla can-
dida, papillae exstantes Phrygii operis fasciola castigatae. Tanta
etiam membris omnibus agilitas, decentiore saltandi arte comparata, ut nulla ad tibicinum cantum aut volubilius aut retortius aut
numerosius, dimensis ad modulos passibus ageretur.[206] His succedit L. Barbadica, eadem gravis et venusta, sucosiore sinu et mento,
et per totum nivea[207] fulgore mirabili, oculis decentibus sed ad
quendam subrusticum pudorem deiectis. In Benecta vero Gritta,
quae est ipsius magni Andreae principis neptis et fratri germano
Pisani Cardinalis nupta, sic totius oris lineamenta, et oculorum ac
cervicum habitus capillorumque nitor, et risus ac incessus modestia singularis ad absolvendam speciem concurrunt, ut longe omnium laude dignissima censeatur.

63   'Sunt et aliis suae partes eximii decoris. Sed quae ad paucorum
magis quam omnium animos respondeant, ut in Helisabeta Dedia
videmus quae, facta paullo habitior et naso etiam[208] resimior, gravitatis potius quam arridentis pristinae lasciviae retinet dignitatem.
Ioannes etiam Cornelius, cuius ingenio nihil humanius atque
splendidius Venetiis reperitur, Aryadnam[209] Pisanam uxorem domi
habet quae, cum sit stata potius forma quam excellenti, illam tamen sic attollunt et exornant excelsus mitisque animus, hilaritas
liberalis, suavissimi mores, et supra haec praeclara fecunditas ut si
has in unum tot occultarum rerum dotes computemus, merito inter superioris ordinis pulcherrimas numeretur.'

"The second prize was given to Lucrezia Venier.[58] Many hold   62
the opinion that she possesses every charm; golden hair, a white
neck, and protruding breasts made modest by a broad ribbon of
Phrygian workmanship. Also, once she'd learned the seemly art of
dancing, she had such great agility in all her limbs that no woman
ever moved better to the melody of flutes in her spins, turns, and
rhythmic movements, while her steps kept time to the music. After these women there followed Lucia Barbarigo,[59] dignified and
attractive, with a rather plump bosom and chin, and with a marvelous snowy-white brightness suffusing her whole body. Her eyes
were pretty, but downcast thanks to a certain rather unsophisticated modesty. There was also Benedetta Gritti,[60] granddaughter
of the great doge Andrea Gritti himself and the wife of a brother[61]
of Cardinal Pisani.[62] The lines of her entire face, the look of her
eyes and neck, the sheen of her hair, her smile, and what's more, a
singular modesty of gait united to put the finishing touches on her
beauty, so that she was considered by far the worthiest to win the
praise of all.

"Each of the other Venetian women has her own share of out-   63
standing beauty. But some answer to the passions of the elite few
rather than of all, as we see in Elisabetta Diedo,[63] who, having
grown a little stouter and having a thickset nose, possesses the
distinction of grave authority rather than that of an unalloyed,
pleasing sensuality. Then there is Giovanni Cornaro,[64] than whom
no one in Venice has a finer and more cultivated character, who
keeps his wife, Ariadne Pisani,[65] at home. Although she is of average rather than outstanding beauty, nonetheless a lofty and gentle
mind, urbane cheerfulness, a most charming character and, beyond these qualities, exceptional fertility adorn her to such an extent that if we were to take into account her many hidden endowments, we would count her as being deservedly among the most
beautiful women of the highest rank."

64   Tum vero DAVALUS 'Dispeream, Iovi' inquit, 'nisi eae ipsae super ceteras omnes mihi summopere placuerunt, quas tu singillatim
tamquam flores longe omnium pulcherrimos non acuto modo iudicio, verum etiam argutissimis manibus decerpsisti. Scis enim
cum Venetias sub id tempus spectandi studio cum delectis centurionibus venissem atque una de foedere ineundo, quod tum a vobis[210] enixe tractabatur, et de admirabili ea urbe apud Adurnum
ipsum essemus collocuti, me cuncta lustrasse oculis, et quod vos
me videre cupiebatis, thesauros Martianos non minus copia et
specie quam fama nobilissimos[211] considerate atque admiranter
inspexisse; quin etiam accessisse ad vestales parum pudicas[212] virgines, in quibus mores quidem plane eruditos, sed evanidam formae speciem deprehendi, cum iam earum tam luculenta suboles
paullatim interiret, nulla scilicet ingenua ex decreto publico senes-
centibus succedente, adeo ut in illis coenobiis omnia potius maero-
ris et querelarum quam hilaritatis atque lasciviae plena esse viderentur, cunctis scilicet[213] Lauredani principis memoriam ut ipsis
admodum lugubrem certatim exsecrantibus, qui tam severae et
peracerbae legis auctor exstitisset.

65   'Sed te qui, dum cupiditati nostrae obsequereris, nos adeo properanter Venetias perduxisti ut ceteras Cisalpinae Galliae civitates
nihil attigeris, valde obsecramus, ut quas memoria dignas arbitraris, enumerare velis priusquam tibi in Liguriam et Etruriam contendenti Apenninus ipse superetur.'

66   Tum vero ego ⟨IOVIUS⟩ inquam 'Ut vultis, morem vobis geram;
verum ea lege, ut nobiliores tantum urbes percurramus e quibus
etiam nobilissimae tantum feminae deligantur. Nam si cras
aut caurus aut septentriones perflaverint, ut ex illis nubeculis

Then, indeed, D'AVALOS said, "I'll be damned, Giovio, if these 64
very women didn't please me too, above all the rest whom you've
selected, like the most beautiful flowers of all, not only with your
shrewd judgment but also with extremely skilled hands. Remember when I'd come to Venice along with picked officers to do some
sightseeing and also at the same time to negotiate a treaty (and
you too were deeply involved in the negotiations). When we were
at the home of Adorno[66] himself, we discussed that admirable city.
You know that with my own eyes I'd scanned the entire city and
inspected carefully and admiringly the Treasury of San Marco,
which you wanted me to see. Its contents are most noble, and their
abundance and beauty equaled their fame. Yes, and I came near to
the not-so-chaste 'vestal virgins,' whose manners were clearly refined. And yet, I detected that their outward beauty was fading,
since already their excellent stock was dying off little by little. For
on account of a public decree, no noblewoman was coming along
to replace the aging ones, so that all things in those convents
seemed to be full of sadness and complaint rather than cheerfulness and playful sensuality. All of these women were rivaling one
another in cursing the memory of Doge Loredan,[67] who was the
author of that severe and distressing law, so sad in its impact upon
them.

"But in the process of yielding to our desire, Giovio, you've led 65
us to Venice so quickly that you haven't touched upon the remaining cities of northern Italy. We urgently request, before crossing
the Apennines on the way to Liguria and Tuscany, that you will
please enumerate those cities that you consider worthy of com-
memoration."

Then I [GIOVIO] said, "As you wish. I shall oblige you, but on 66
condition that we treat in succession only the more noble cities,
from which in turn only the most noble women shall be chosen.
For if tomorrow either the northwest or north wind is going to
blow strongly, as we may divine from those small clouds covering

ominamur quae celsissimum Nicollae montis cacumen integunt totum, ea Aeoli Neptunique iniuria pro beneficio ad otium non iniucundum uti poterimus, addemusque superioribus quartum sermonem, quo reliquarum feminarum secundae, ut dicimus, classis laudes celebrentur, quae certe in universum pudicitia saltem erunt clariores, si non haec vel affectatae formae vel superbae nobilitatis vel haec tanta laetioris[214] ingenii pudori saepe noxii praeclara[215] ornamenta secum attulerint. In quo genere feminarum, cum essem plane iuvenis et non moderatis etiam flammis circumventus, auream illam et beatam mediocritatem saepissime degustavi, omni procul dubio summae fortunae praestantia meliorem.'

67   Tum MUSETIUS perfacete 'Ergo,' inquit, 'haec secunda[216] classis Neptuni irascentis libidini permittetur? Nam ut puto, si ipse nobis fuerit benignus, illa minime navigabit, malacia cursum eius demorante, ut magnis accidit onerariis, quae, cum validis semper ventorum successibus delectentur, in summa alias pacati aequoris tranquillitate, erepto velorum usu, inertissimae[217] considant.'

68   Ad id ego ⟨IOVIUS⟩ inquam, 'Venti modo flare incipiant, vel adversi vel secundi, paullo pleniores. Nam tum otium nobis erit plane luculentum sive de feminis secundae classis sive de aliqua alia re humanius disceptare placuerit. Verum ut propositum nostrum teneamus: in Ticino urbe, cum gymnasium incredibili gentium omnium iuventute maxime floreret, Hippolita Floramunda Scaldasolio Malaspinae nupta non Italiam modo sed omnem prope terrarum orbem cum eximiae pulchritudinis fama tum principalium amorum celebritate replevit: quam te, Davale, quadragesimum fere agentem aetatis annum vidisse arbitror cum, Francisco

the topmost peak of Monte San Nicola, we'll be able to benefit from this injury inflicted on us by Aeolus and Neptune and enjoy further leisure — and we'll add on to the earlier ones a fourth discourse in which the praises of the second class (or fleet) of women may be celebrated. Surely in general they will be at least more illustrious in chastity, even if they won't have brought along with them those 'splendid' adornments either of affected beauty or of proud nobility, or those 'great' adornments of a pleasing nature that are often threats to their sense of shame. To be sure, when I was a young man and beset by uncontrolled passions, I sampled very often in this kind of women that golden and happy mean, which is without any doubt more excellent than the highest good fortune."

Then MUSCETTOLA said very wittily, "Is this second fleet 67 therefore to be entrusted to the lust of Neptune as he is flying into a rage? For if that god will be mild to us, I think the former fleet of women will certainly not sail forward, the dead calm hindering its progress, as happens to great freighters: although they always enjoy the powerful actions of the winds, at other times, in the great tranquility of a calm sea, they lose the use of their sails and settle in the water with great sluggishness."

To this I [GIOVIO] said: "May the winds presently begin to 68 blow just a little bit stronger, whether they be favorable or not. For then obviously, we will enjoy splendid leisure, whether it pleases us to converse about women of the second class or about some other more cultivated topic. But let's stick to our subject. In the city of Pavia, when the school there was flourishing to the highest degree with extraordinary youth from all nations, Ippolita Fioramonte,[68] the wife of Malaspina, the marquis of Scaldasole, filled not only Italy but nearly the entire world both with the stories of her outstanding beauty and with the renown of her distinguished suitors. When she was around forty, I think that you saw her, d'Avalos, when after King Francis had been captured, you took the

rege capto, Lescutum Gallum equitum magistrum[218] ex mortifero vulnere decumbentem in eius memorabilis matronae aedibus quae tua est etiam erga hostes singularis humanitas[219] aliquando visitasses.

69 'Sunt etiam e Brixia familiae Gambarae sorores duae — Veronica Corregiani reguli quondam uxor et Hisotta nubilis puella — quae ingenium cum formae et generis nobilitate coniunctum adeo feliciter extulerunt ut Veronica sexum supergressa elegantissime epistolas Etruscas et suaviora carmina conscribat, Hisotta vero Latinis in litteris tantum profecerit, ut vix dignum ea maritum reperiat. Frater eius Ubertus, pontificis in Britannia legatus, liberalibus studiis et vitae splendore inter clarissimos sacerdotes collocandus.

70 'Sunt et in eo Padi tractu in dextram recurvis sinibus decurrentis, aliquot illustres opulentis regulis nuptae. Et ante alias Russia, Vitellii Tiphernatis uxor, formae singularis ac ingenii admodum praestantis ad omnem elegantiam et gravitatem consilio et salibus exprimendam. Ludovici quoque Palavicini, omni bellica et civili virtute ornatissimi, filiam Virginiam, quae Brunoro Gambarae armis atque natalibus claro nupsit, ab illustri rarissimarum virtutum indole circumpadani omnes admirantur. Clarescit etiam in dies, quamquam provecta annis integra pudoris fama ad Palavicinae domus ornamentum, Ludovica virili admodum virtute et matronali specie mulier lectissima. Sed Margarita Pia, quae fuit Antonii Mariae Sanseverini uxor, splendoris vitae elegantia, ingenii fertilitate, ac regiis moribus, tantam de se, cum esset aetate tenerior, opinionem excellentiae praebuit ut etiam nunc inter primas amabiles Italiae matronas merito numeretur.[220]

occasion to visit Thomas de Foix,[69] the French cavalry captain lying abed from a fatal wound, in the house of that remarkable matron—for such is your singular humanity even toward enemies.

"Also from Brescia there are two sisters of the Gambara family: 69 Veronica,[70] wife of the ruler Giberto, the lord of Correggio, and Isotta,[71] a girl of marriageable age. So abundantly have they displayed brilliance conjoined with noble beauty and lineage that Veronica, having gone beyond her sex, with great eloquence composes Tuscan letters and charming poems; Isotta, on the other hand, has advanced so far in Latin letters that scarcely can she find a husband worthy of her.[72] Her brother Uberto,[73] the pope's legate in England, is to be ranked among the most distinguished of priests owing to his liberal studies and the splendor of his lifestyle.

"In that region of the Po, with its twisting curves flowing down 70 to the southeast, there are also some illustrious women married to wealthy rulers. Above all there is Angela de' Rossi,[74] the wife of Vitello Vitelli of Tivoli, a woman of singular beauty, exceptionally gifted in regard to her elegant wit and sound, authoritative judgment. Also there's Virginia,[75] the daughter of Ludovico Pallavicini, a man abundantly endowed with every military and civic virtue. She married Brunoro Gambara,[76] who is distinguished in arms and in origins. All people around the Po admire her on account of her illustrious innate disposition toward the rarest virtues. Also, Ludovica,[77] a woman very special in quite manly virtue and in matronly appearance, is becoming more and more famous. Although she has sailed ahead in years, her intact reputation for modesty is an adornment to the House of Pallavicini. But when Margherita Pio,[78] who was the wife of Antonio Maria Sanseverino, was younger, she occasioned so high a reputation for excellence by the elegance of the splendor of her life, by her fertility of talent, and by her regal character, that even now she is rightly counted among the most lovely matrons of Italy.

71   'Est etiam Mantuae Isabella Boscheta Calvisiani[221] uxor equitis
in Gonzagam familiam paternis meritis adoptati, quae una ab omnibus, et ab humanissimo principe Federico, supra ceteras omnes
laudatur et colitur. In qua plerique cum non omnia corporis et
morum eius plane bellissima esse iudicent, ea tamen cum incredibili venustate in unum copulata plurimum admirantur.

72   'Verum in Isabella, ipsius Federici principis matre, florentibus
paullo ante annis Italicarum heroidum longe pulcherrima, plures
et eae quidem clarissimae virtutes enitescunt, quae sunt velut here-
ditariae et dotales a regiis natalibus ductae. Ei nempe Aragonii
reges, quos materno genere arctius attingit, splendorem et regiam
gravitatem praebuere; ab Atestino vero patre Hercule prudentiam
hausit et moderationem et in toto vitae cursu aequabilem disciplinam, seu vel adverse ac[222] intemperanter flante fortuna, vel ea se-
cunde et molliter aspirante. Haec singillatim[223] tali temperamento
cum Gonzagae domus humanitate munificentia et comitate per-
miscuit ut nihil eo difficili diversarum rerum concursu aut melius
aut praeclarius esse videatur. Quae omnia, velut ad nutum summi
iudicii collecta in una, eius filia, Heleonora Francisci Mariae Feltrii
principis Urbinatis uxore, cum singularum etiam gratiarum et fe-
cunditatis accessione reflorescunt, ut illa et digna fortissimo castissimoque[224] viro et ille longe elegantissima et probatissima coniuge
dignus habeatur.

73   'Floret apud Veronenses altitudine eruditi et perelegantis ingenii
Laura Clioppa,[225] in qua etiam nunc formae decus, quamquam
multis inflexae aetatis iniuriis lacessitum, pertinacissime refulget.

"In Mantua there's also Isabella Boschetti di Calvisano, the wife   71
of a knight adopted into the Gonzaga family on account of his
father's merits.[79] She is praised and honored above everyone else
by all people, and in particular by the highly cultivated Prince
Federico.[80] Although many do not judge all her physical features
and her character to be exceptionally beautiful in an obvious way,
nonetheless they admire these things in her very much, along with
the incredible charm to which they have been joined.

"But in Isabella d'Este[81]—this Federico's mother and by far the   72
most beautiful of Italian heroines, who was in the prime of youth
a little while ago—there shine forth many virtues, and indeed the
most splendid ones, which are hereditary and given as a dowry, as
it were, from her royal origins. Of course the Aragonese kings, to
whom she is closely related on her mother's side,[82] have given her
splendor and regal dignity. But from her father, Ercole d'Este, she
has derived prudence, moderation, and decorous, orderly conduct
in the entire course of life, whether the winds of fortune are blow-
ing adversely and intemperately or favorably and gently. She has
married these qualities, one by one, to the humanity, generosity,
and graciousness of the House of Gonzaga, blending them in such
a way that nothing appears to be either better or more distinguished than this difficult union of diverse elements. All these
qualities, as though deliberately united by the nicest judgment, are
flourishing anew in one of her daughters: Eleonora,[83] the wife of
Francesco Maria della Rovere, the duke of Urbino, a woman who
possesses fertility and every grace. She is regarded as worthy of the
most powerful and virtuous of husbands, and he in turn is held
worthy of her who is by far the most elegant and upright of
spouses.

"There flourishes in Verona a woman of profound learning and   73
elegant wit, Laura Schioppi,[84] in whom even now the adornment
of beauty shines forth tenaciously, although it has been assailed by
the many injuries of bent old age. Diana d'Este,[85] scion of what is

Principatum venustatis eximiae apud Ferrarienses modo obtinuit
Diana Atestina, longe clarissima stirpe orta, cuius speciem, aetatis
et morborum vitiis temptatam, exquisitis heroicarum elegantiarum[226] moribus et suavi quadam[227] oris maiestate egregie etiam
nunc vigere[228] conspicimus.

74 'Bononiae vero, tam nobili tam opulenta et tam frequenti urbe,
vix unam aut alteram absolutae pulchritudinis atque virtutis feminam reperimus. Quod maxime videtur admirandum, cum florentissima ibi iuventus et proceritate corporum et vultuum decore et
suavitate morum et ingenua comitate ceteris finitimis antecellat, et
ibi quoque vigeant liberalium studia litterarum quibus vel pere-
grina ingenia facillime poliantur. Mulieres enim fere omnes sunt
admodum suculentae, ab nitida[229] cute perlucentes, femora illis
exstantia, cervices arvinosae, pleniores et[230] contusi vultus. Porro
ingenia earum haud tantum dedita[231] litteris quam liberrimae iucunditati,[232] corpora autem nocturnis potius quam diurnis illecebris accommodata, adeo ut Bononienses alterna sortitione cum
Mutinensibus egisse videantur, apud quos in universum, cum mulieres admodum formosae et peramabiles exsistant, ipsi contra
longe pulcherrima marium iuventute decorentur.[233]

75 'At Genuae, totius Liguriae urbe clarissima, alia est virorum ac
feminarum consuetudo, diversa penitus a Venetis moribus. Viri
enim inter se factiosi, ingenio valentes, negotiosi, diligentes, ⟨haud⟩
procul ab omni severitate, cum rei familiari et mercaturis maxime
studeant; certis tamen horis atque temporibus, voluptati liberius
indulgent, et ante alia feminarum amoribus oblectantur. Quarum
omnium disciplina valde est elegans delicata voluptaria liberalis —
siquidem observari palam, assidue coli, ac efflictim etiam adamari
matronae neque indecorum[234] neque inhonestum umquam fuit.

by far the most illustrious of lineages, has just recently secured
among the Ferrarese first place for her loveliness. We note with
admiration that her appearance, though afflicted by the debilitat-
ing effects of age and diseases, even now thrives outstandingly
with the exquisite character of heroic elegance and with a certain
agreeable majesty of countenance.

"In Bologna, however, a city so noble, rich, and populous, we   74
find barely one or two women of unqualified beauty and virtue.
This seems especially astonishing because it's said that the numerous young people there surpass those of neighboring cities in their
height and lovely countenances as well as in charm of character
and noble graciousness. And this is also surprising because the
liberal study of literature is thriving there, by which even foreigners' wits can readily be polished. Indeed, the women in Bologna
are generally brimming with vitality, with glowing skin, shapely
legs, plump necks, and rather full and somewhat snubbed facial
features. On the other hand, their minds are given not so much to
literature as to unrestrained pleasure, and their bodies are suited
more to nocturnal than to daytime allurements—so much so that
Bologna looks as if it took turns with Modena in a lottery, since
in general Bologna has beautiful and attractive women, whereas
Modena is striking for possessing the handsomest young men.

"But in Genoa, the most distinguished city of Liguria, the hab-   75
its of men and women are otherwise, and are entirely distinct from
Venetian customs. The men are given to faction, strong-minded,
businesslike, diligent, and not[86] unused to austerity since they devote themselves especially to their family businesses and to trade.
But at certain times and on certain occasions, they yield freely to
pleasure and are delighted above other things by love affairs with
women. The training of all of these women is certainly elegant,
refined, and pleasure loving—and honorable, if it's really possible
that it's never been either indecorous or shameful in that town for
a married woman to be openly ogled, fervently courted, or even to

Fit enim singulari quadam coniugum et propinquorum aequitate ac indulgentia, ut alterni saepe amores velut comparatis sorte quadam[235] inter se voluntatibus exerceantur.[236]

76   'Nec eam admirabilem laetissimae vitae iucunditatem aut pudori officere aut illustrem famam suspicionibus adumbrare posse putandum est, quoniam, in tanta adeundi et colloquendi publica facultate, occultis impudicisque congressibus aditus omnes eripi potius atque praecludi, quam parari saepius videmus. Et certe in tam tenera consuetudine conceptae libidines, susurris et fabulis longioribus exteruntur. Secus ac in valde custoditis accidit matronis quae, ubi primum remotis arbitris paullo blandius ad aurem emollitae et manu vel leviter attrectatae fuerint, inhumanum demum putant si cupidis amatoribus resistant, vel agrestius in re dulcissima reluctentur.

77   'Per[237] hiemem tota urbe pervigilationes nocturnae fovendis amoribus, supra quam[238] credibile sit, accommodatae vetere eorum consuetudine celebrantur. Nam ex unaquaque vicinia, cum minoris ordinis feminae nobiliores colant, frequentes conveniunt, consident ad lucernas velut consuendis linteis occupatae, ibique amatores et procos adapertis foribus exspectant. Ii, cucullatas et talares induti penulas, toto ori tenue sericum velum obtendunt, geminis orbiculis contuentur, cathedris assident, et ad benignas aures mollissimas cogitationes suas exponunt. Neque ulla est paullo clarior moribus ac venustate quae suum et celebrem quidem amatorem non habeat; nemo tam sordidus, tam senex, tam occupatus exsistit, qui mulierem aliquam non colat, vel ad spem libidinis vel ad

be the object of insane passion. In fact, it's the case that, out of a certain special sense of 'fair play' and indulgence on the part of spouses and kin, they often engage in lovemaking with different partners in a kind of random coupling.

"Nor must it be supposed that these wonderful pleasures of a 76 delightful life can either interfere with modesty or cast the shadow of suspicion on an illustrious reputation, because where there is such great opportunity of approaching and conversing with the opposite sex in public, we frequently see that all routes of access to secret and immodest interactions are blocked and taken away. And surely sexual desires conceived in such tender intimacy are worn down by extensive whispering and rumor spreading. It's quite different with ladies who have been strictly watched over: as soon as they are free of their watchers and their ears have been softened by a little flattery, once they've been touched even lightly by a hand, they suppose it actually to be cruel if they should resist lustful suitors or, even more boorishly, show reluctance in so sweet a matter.

"Throughout the city during wintertime, in accordance with 77 longstanding practice, nightly vigils suitable for nurturing love affairs are thronged to an almost unbelievable extent. When women of a lesser rank cultivate the attention of the more noble, they gather in throngs from every neighborhood, take up position in open doorways (being occupied ostensibly in stitching together pieces of linen by lamplight), and there they await lovers and suitors. The men, wrapped in hooded, ankle-length cloaks, their faces covered with fine silk veils, look intently with beady little eyes, sitting nearby on cushioned seats, and propound their amatory plans to well-disposed ears. Nor is there any woman of more illustrious character and charm who does not also have her own lover, even a notorious one. There's no man so poor, so old, or so busy that he doesn't pay court to some woman, either in prospect of satisfying

413

animi voluptatem et negotiorum curarumque omnium laxamentum.

78   'Aestate[239] elegantium villarum amoenitate perfruuntur, quas angustis in praediis et aspretis insatiabili studio insanisque sumptibus aedificant, et medicis citriisque[240] nemoribus et virentibus hortorum areolis mirum in modum exornant. Earum tanta est[241] intra quartum lapidem conferta multitudo ut navigantibus in portum et ab alto mari rectum omnino tenentibus cursum, unius continentis ac amplissimae urbis species[242] suis praecinctae moenibus[243] esse videatur. Est etiam ea urbs et ab excelsa arce conspicua, et tectorum sacrarumque turrium altitudine insignis, et ab recurvo operosae[244] molis obiectu valde speciosa laevoque promontorio, ab excussae arcis ruinis receptam libertatem ostentante, et toto denique vel elati portus vel exculti[245] litoris prospectu, adeo admirabilis ut non temere Genuam superbam appellarint, qui clarioribus Italiae urbibus propria et ex rebus nata cognomina, ludentes indiderunt. Mediolanum enim ingens, Venetias opulentas, Genuam superbam, Bononiam pinguem, Florentiam pulchram, peramoenam Neapolim, et Romam demum sacrosantam, ut Christianae religionis sedem, vocavere.

79   'Igitur mulieres perpetuis anni temporibus vel amatorias exercitationes vel honesti generis voluptates numquam intermittunt, nullis virorum obtrectationibus subiectae, nullis familiaribus implicatae fastidiis; cottidianarum namque rerum curae barbaris pedisequis ceterisque servitiis demandantur. Nullibi terrarum hercle degitur vel in molliore animi libertate vel in securiore solutae vitae licentia. Quin etiam illae ipsae ancillae, de Scythis et Numidis emptae, dominarum indulgentia festos dies amoribus impendunt; et lascivioribus in ludis et liberis choreis ad amatorium fontem et

lust or for the psychological pleasure of being released from all business matters and cares.

"In summer, they enjoy fully the charm of elegant villas, which   78 they build with enthusiasm and at insane cost on narrow properties and rough terrains, and they decorate them in an amazing manner with clover and citrus trees and small garden beds. Of these villas there is such a multitude packed together within a four-mile radius that, when you sail into the port, holding a straight course from the high seas, the outward appearance is of one unbroken and immense city surrounded by its walls. That city is also conspicuous on account of a tall fortress, and notable for the height of its roofs and steeples. The curving protection of the elaborate pier, the promontory on the left (which shows by the scattered ruins of the citadel that liberty has been recovered), and finally the entire view either of the lofty harbor or of the cultivated shoreline, stir admiration for the city. Not without cause has Genoa been called 'proud' by those who for amusement have assigned to the more distinguished cities of Italy nicknames that are suitable and that originate in their circumstances. Thus, they have termed Milan 'gigantic,' Venice 'opulent,' Genoa 'proud,' Bologna 'luxuriant,' Florence 'beautiful,' Naples 'very charming,' and finally Rome, the seat of the Christian religion, 'sacrosanct.'

"Well, then: through every season of the year Genoese women   79 engage continually in love affairs and the pleasures of the wellborn, being free of any disparagement from men as well as from the bother of keeping house—quotidian concerns are handed over to foreign attendants and to other servants. By God, nowhere in the entire world do people enjoy a more luxurious freedom of mind or carefree style of life. In fact, through the leniency of the ladies of the house, even the very slave girls, bought from Scythians and Numidians, devote their holidays to lovemaking. They occupy themselves both in licentious games and in unrestrained dances near the fount[87] of lovers and on the verdant shores of the Bisagno

ad Feritoris virentes ripas exercentur. Sed nulla lasciviendi aut procacius feminas appellandi libertas maior quam cum matronae phaselis litora pererrant et studio piscandi[246] in altum provehuntur. Tum enim eas stupri compellare, exprobrare[247] libidines, et obscenis percontationibus earum pudorem lacessere vel infimis[248] homunculis licet, sicut in ipsis vindemiis Neapoli vinarios baiulos in illustres etiam feminas illa tanta sed vectigali tamen empta licentia petulantius audere conspicimus.

80 ʹFeminae Genuenses, paucis ante annis, bombycinas albas togulas exsertis bracchiis induebant, quae non omnino[249] talares erant ita ut pulchellos pedes, pictas crepidulas, calceolos candenti ferro pernotatos ostenderent. Papillas et summa pectora, quod erat indecorum et ineptum, praealtis subuculis integebant. Baltheolis argenteae catenulae ternae nectebantur, e quibus haec omnia dependebant: crumina serica, gemini cum forficula caelatis manubriis cultelli, et nux myristica, argenteo reticulato globulo inclusa, qua nauseam sedarent.

81 ʹNunc vero hic amictus ut frugalis atque ridiculus pudori nobilioribus esse coepit, quae pallas villuta e purpura caudatas trahunt, nudatos sinus monilibus gemmatis exornant, et sumptuosiora rerum omnium ornamenta et unguentorum etiam delicias[250] ad insatiabilem luxuriem exquirunt. Facies earum ut plurimum a suavi quodam colore, nec eo quidem multum fucato, et a teneriore habitu periucundae. Nullis autem ingenium est absurdum: omnes dicacitate, facetiis, et salibus valent, et quamquam sermo e blaesula lingua corruptior ac ineptior effluere videatur, mollitudinem tamen quandam et venerem insuefactis auribus instillat omni exacta vel ad Etruscam normam elocutione[251] dulciorem.

River.[88] But there is no greater opportunity for lascivious behavior or for making impudent advances to women than when matrons in small boats cruise along the shores and sail into the open sea to catch fish. Then, even the lowest fellows can accuse them of fornication, reproach them for their lusts, and tempt their modesty with obscene proposals—just as in those grape harvests of Naples we see that the wine porters dare to behave in such rude ways, even toward illustrious women—and indeed by a license, so to speak, bought by their tax revenue.[89]

"A few years earlier, Genoese women used to put on little white 80 silken gowns from which their arms protruded. These were not quite ankle length, so that they exposed pretty little feet wearing small embroidered slippers, tooled by a hot iron. They covered their breasts and the tops of their chests with high undergarments, a thing both inelegant and boorish. Three little silver chains were attached to small girdles, from which all these things hung down: a silk purse; twin small knives with engraved handles along with scissors; and nutmeg, enclosed in a little silver mesh ball, to settle nausea.

"But nowadays this cheap and ridiculous manner of dress has 81 begun to be regarded by the more noble women as shameful. They trail long outdoor dresses trimmed in the back with purple velvet, adorn their bare breasts with jeweled necklaces, and with insatiable luxury seek out more sumptuous trappings of all kinds as well as special kinds of perfumes. Their faces are extremely attractive, mostly because of their smooth complexions which they do not cover with a great deal of makeup, and their youthful appearance. In none of these women, however, is the intellect undeveloped. All are skilled in sarcasm, clever banter, and witty remarks. Although their speech seems to flow forth impurely and awkwardly from lisping tongues, nonetheless it instills in ears that are accustomed to it a certain softness and charm, even when their whole manner of speaking is judged by the Tuscan standard.[90]

82   'Cum essem adolescens et propter consuetudinem studiorum
cum Ottobono Flisco, eodem longe nobilissimo atque optimo sacerdote, Genuam venissem, nympham vidi divino prope oris habitu puellam ex vetere Iustinianorum Graeca familia, quae multis
ante annis fato functa magnum apud Ligures desiderium et famam
immensae pulchritudinis reliquit. Aliquanto autem post duae, meo
iudicio, supra ceteras omnes excelluere: Theodora Spinula nupta
Sebastiano Saulio cui Bendinellus Cardinalis frater fuit et Pellota
Grimaldia Hieronymo Auriae collocata, quarum venustas et elegantia eo tempore singularis enituit, quo Iulianus Leonis Maximi
Pontificis frater, uxorem ex Allobrogibus Florentiam perducens, a
Genuensibus summo cum honore fuit exceptus.

83   'Verum cum Theodora multis puerperiis vividum formae decorem amiserit, et Pellotam immitia Fata rapuerint, nunc maxime ab
omnibus laudatur Catarineia Spinula, a festivis deliciis Meliboea
nuncupata,[252] quam multis expetendis corporis atque animi dotibus ante alias cohonestatam esse conspicimus. Est enim ei animus
excelsus liberalis nitidus pudicus venustate oris nulli secunda est,
cum facile prima exsistat in omni elegantia vel morum illustrium
vel Etruscorum carminum vel exquisitarum etiam munditiarum.[253]

84   'In Argentina Martini Centurionis, qui apud caesarem[254] legatum agit, manet adhuc formae dignitas erudita morum suavitate
sustentata.[255] In Saulia etiam domo, opibus splendore litteris atque
omni virtute ornatissima, duae sunt Tamesinae aetate florentes,
altera Lomellina altera Spinula, duobus fratribus nuptae, illa Nicolao summae fidei ac industriae mensario, haec vero ipsi Dominico
cum omnis elegantiae et optimarum litterarum tum maxime

"When I was a young man and had come to Genoa, following   82
the usual course of studies with Ottobuono Fieschi[91] (he being by
far the most noble and virtuous of priests), I saw a young woman
with a nearly divine countenance, a girl from the old Greek family
of the Giustiniani, who at her death left behind her among the
Ligurians a great longing and a reputation for immense beauty. A
little later, however, two women surpassed all others in my estimation: Teodora Spinola,[92] married to Sebastiano Sauli, whose
brother was the Cardinal Bendinello Sauli, and Pellota Grimaldi,[93]
given in marriage to Girolamo Doria.[94] Their beauty and elegance
shone forth uniquely at the time when Giuliano, the brother of
the great Pope Leo X, while taking his wife from France to Florence, was received with the highest honor by the Genoese.[95]

"But now that Teodora, through bearing many children, has   83
lost the lively charm of beauty, and the cruel Fates have snatched
away Pellota, Caterina Spinola,[96] called 'Meliboea' on account of
her playful charms, is the woman everyone praises the most. We
admire her as one who has been elevated above others by many
desirable endowments of both body and mind. For she has a lofty
mind; is honorable, refined, and modest; and is second to none in
beauty of countenance. She stands out easily as preeminent in every elegance, whether it is her illustrious character, her knowledge
of Tuscan poetry, or even her exquisite manners and taste.

"In Argentina,[97] the wife of Martino Centurione[98] (who is serv-   84
ing as a legate at the emperor's court), there remains as yet the
distinction of beauty, sustained by a well-instructed charm of
character. And in the family of the Sauli, adorned with wealth,
splendor, literary pursuits, and every virtue, there are the two
Tomasinas in the prime of life—one is Lomellini,[99] the other,
Spinola[100]—married to two Sauli brothers: the former to the
banker Nicolò,[101] a man of the greatest good faith and diligence;
the latter, to Domenico[102] himself, a man devoted to every elegance, to good letters, and particularly to the liberty of the state.

publicae libertatis studioso. Spinula, a puro quodam et aequabili corporis atque animi candore insignique pudicitia, marito ac omnibus est cara. Lomellina vero, totius oris et oculorum praeclara specie felicior,[256] ingenio adeo mobili et saepe etiam contumaci exsistit ut nihil eius gratia et familiaritate fragilius esse iudicetur.

85 'Perstrinxit etiam oculos cordaque perussit quibusdam insignibus viris inenarrabili mollium ocellorum fulgore Camogenia. Sed ea non est ex eo quem requirimus ordine nobilitatis. Lucretiam quoque Gentilem, quae suavitatem patrii moris Romanis salibus scitissime condivit, pervenusta lumina, roseae genae, nullis interlitae pigmentis, et sucus in toto nequaquam effluidus ac argenteo quodam nitore pernobilis eximie commendant.'[257]

86 Haec cum dixissem, 'Periucundum' DAVALUS inquit, 'tuum hoc, Iovi, de Venetis atque Liguribus iudicium fuit, ac eo etiam praeter exspectationem absolutius atque subtilius quoniam non modo feminarum sed virorum etiam ingenia et mores exquisitissime descripsisti ita ut iam aliquanto uberius de Florentinis dissertaturus esse videare, quando in earum civitate aliquot annos honestissima vitae condicione sis versatus.'

87 Ad id ego ⟨IOVIUS⟩ inquam, 'Ita est, Davale, nihil mihi notius ac exploratius Etruscis rebus ac moribus esse potest. Nam ab eo tempore quo Laurentius Medices[258] Iunior iuvenili intemperantia ab levi morbo sublatus est, et Iulius tum Cardinalis eo profectus ad cohonestandum funus regendae reipublicae gubernacula suscepit, modo hiemes, modo aestates, ut oportuit, Florentiae egimus usque ad eum annum quo ipse Hadriano mortuo pontificatum est adeptus. In eius adventu, ut diximus, respublica adeo benigne et

Spinola is dear to her husband and to all on account of a certain unsoiled and uniform purity of body and mind, and on account of her outstanding modesty. But Lomellini, who is the more blessed with extraordinary beauty in her face and eyes, shows herself to be so changeable in temperament, often even defiant, that nothing is judged to be more fleeting than her favor and friendship.

"Camogenia[103] too has dazzled the eyes and inflamed the hearts   85
of certain prominent men by the indescribable brightness of her gentle eyes. But she is not from that rank of nobility which we seek. Consider also Lucrezia Gentile[104] who with exceeding cleverness has seasoned with Roman humor the charm of her father's style. Also recommending her are very attractive eyes, cheeks rosy (and without applying any makeup), and in general a vitality that is by no means slipping away, and that is distinguished by a certain silvery sheen in her complexion."

Once I had said these things, D'AVALOS commented: "Giovio,   86
this evaluation of yours regarding the Venetians and Ligurians has been most pleasing, and it surpasses expectation all the more completely and precisely in that you've described the natural endowments and character not only of the women but also of the men in the most exquisite detail. You appear poised to speak about Florentine women somewhat more effusively, since you lived for several years in their city in a very elevated position."

To this I [GIOVIO] said: "That's right, d'Avalos. Nothing can be   87
better known and clearer to me than Tuscan matters and morals. After Lorenzo de' Medici the Younger[105] was carried off by a brief bout of illness that resulted from youthful intemperance,[106] and Giulio, then a cardinal, having gone there to pay respects to the deceased, took over the helm of state, we spent time in Florence — sometimes in winter, sometimes in summer, as required — up until that year when Adrian VI died and Giulio himself acquired the papacy.[107] On his coming to Florence, as I've said, the state was established with such goodwill and serious purpose that,

graviter constituta est ut propter eius viri aequitatem ac temperantiam, qui se minime liberos esse antea[259] putabant, libertatem ipsam recepisse faterentur, nos vero, qui in splendidiore eius tum
eramus comitatu, Romanarum[260] ambitionum obliviscaremur, laeto
et salubri[261] otio gauderemus amoenitateque et tranquillitate ornatissimae urbis magnopere teneremur. Itaque brevi in eorum amicitiam facile sum receptus qui vel insigni auctoritate, vel suavitate
ingenii, vel optimis studiis eruditisque artibus ceteris civibus prae-
cellebant,[262] per quos, et per ipsum praesertim Iulium ex officii
consuetudine, me in illustrium etiam feminarum familiaritatem ab
honesta quadam libertate periucundam[263] insinuavi.[264]

88 'In ea civitate mihi tum viri memorabiles esse videbantur provectae iam aetatis qui cum honores summos in republica gessissent
et obivissent[265] insignes legationes, essentque praediti usu rerum et
optimarum disciplinarum scientia, etiam senatoriae gravitati civilem et peramoenam comitatem addiderant. Ii fuere Franciscus
Aiacetus, Platonicae sectae philosophus, ut in academia tum
morte Marsilii Ficini[266] admodum deserta, singularis; Petrus item
Martellius, quo nemo erat vitae elegantia[267] et studiorum varietate
iucundior, cuius hodie filium Braccium cultu ubertateque ingenii
florentem[268] admiramur;[269] et Robertus Acciaiolus, qui Donati
patris vestigia secutus, Peripateticus esse malebat quam Platoni-
cus. Ioannes quoque Corsius, qui unum maxime Plutarchum ut
varium ac indefessum scriptorem admirabatur, cuius ipse aureolos
quosdam libellos Latinitate donavisset.[270]

89 'Ii apud Oricellarios fratres Ioannem et Pallantem, litteratos et
elegantes viros studiorumque similitudine ipsis coniunctissimos, in

thanks to his fairness and moderation, those who previously supposed that they were anything but free now declared that they'd received liberty itself. For our part, we who were then in his splendid retinue forgot Roman ambitions and took delight in pleasurable and restorative leisure, being held fast by the charm and peacefulness of that magnificent city. So in a short time I was easily received into the friendship of those who surpassed the other citizens either in the eminence of their authority, their charming dispositions, or their devotion to the humanities and learning. Through their agency and especially through that of Giulio himself, and by virtue of the everyday functions of my position, I insinuated myself into the friendship also of illustrious women, which was most pleasant because of the respectable freedom they enjoyed.

"Back then, in that city, there appeared to me to be remarkable 88
men, already advanced in age, who had held the highest honors in the republic and had gone on important embassies, and they were endowed with experience of affairs and knowledge of the finest branches of learning. Also they had added on to their senatorial dignity a civic[108] and very charming graciousness. These were Francesco Diacceto,[109] a philosopher of the Platonic school, a man unique in the academy once it had been abandoned by the death of Marsilio Ficino. Likewise, there was Pietro Martelli,[110] than whom nobody was more delightful either in elegance of life or in range of literary pursuits, whose son Braccio,[111] flourishing with refinement and an abundance of natural talent, we admire today. Also, there was Roberto Acciaiuoli[112] who, following in the footsteps of his father, Donato,[113] preferred to be a Peripatetic rather than a Platonist; and Giovanni Corsi,[114] who admired Plutarch above all others as a versatile and tireless writer. He himself translated into Latin certain of Plutarch's splendid little books.

"These men had been accustomed to meet in the extensive and 89
charming gardens at the home of the Rucellai brothers, Giovanni

423

latis et amoenis eorum hortis convenire erant soliti, ubi modo sub Ionica[271] porticu, modo sub platanis ad quorum umbram Oricellarius pater Latinos annales otiose conscripserat, inter ludicros sermones gravissimarum rerum colloquia serebamus. In eosdem etiam hortos saepe matronae insignes ventitabant; nam uxorem Pallas duxerat, in cuius nuptiis, praesidente Iulio Cardinale,[272] et choreae ductae et comoediae actitatae[273] fuerant, quas ipsi Oricellarii summa ingenii suavitate composuissent.

90 'Sed paucis annis tam liberalis et tam docta societas intermissa primo publicis quibusdam et privatis incommodis, et demum Aiaceti atque Martellii Ioannisque Oricellarii morte sublata est, ita ut iuventutem quae successit et nunc maxime floret, eam indolem sapientiae et moderationis[274] adhuc excepisse non liqueat, quamquam in aliquibus[275] optimarum litterarum flagrantiora studia videamus, et consilia plena vehementiae[276] quibus innixi per occasionem capti pontificis[277] negotium commutandae reipublicae susceperunt.[278] Quod facinus plerique nequaquam ingrati perfidique animi infamiam veriti, sibi[279] honestum et, pulsis Mediceis pueris,[280] tamquam recepta libertate gloriosum arbitrantur. Verum id factum postea plane probabimus nisi, ut complures male ominantur, haec inauspicata libertas, Mediceorum lenissimo dominatu multo acerbior atque funestior, pulcherrimae civitati diram vastitatem attulerit.

91 'Ceterum[281] cum hac etiam iuventute tamquam mihi magis aequali ac hilarioribus[282] voluptatum studiis accommodata, certis[283] temporibus periucunda erat consuetudo. Singulorum enim[284] humanitate aditus mihi facile patebat ad amicitiam cum iis

and Palla, learned and elegant men, to whom they were very close, owing to their common interests.[115] There, sometimes under the Ionic colonnade, sometimes under the plane trees in whose shade their father Bernardo had written Latin annals during his hours of leisure,[116] amid playful conversations we used to carry on discussions of the weightiest matters. Illustrious matrons too used to come regularly to these same gardens: for instance, Palla had taken a wife in whose wedding ceremony — Cardinal Giulio presiding — there had been dancing and the performance of comedies which the Rucellai themselves had composed with great charm and literary skill.

"But within a few years, this noble and learned association was 90 first suspended by certain public and private misfortunes, then ultimately was brought to an end by the deaths of Diacceto, Martelli, and Giovanni Rucellai.[117] It's not clear whether the young men who've succeeded them and now are flourishing have yet taken up in turn that inborn quality of wisdom and moderation. Still, in some of them we see a more ardent enthusiasm for the best literature and for debates full of intensity, in which they've taken up the business of transforming the state, driven by the opportunity afforded by the capture of the pope. Many of them, rather than fearing infamy for ingratitude and treachery, judge this criminal act honorable and glorious for themselves, on the grounds that liberty was recovered once the Medici nephews had been expelled. Doubtless afterward we shall come to approve that criminal act unless, as many people are maliciously predicting, this ill-omened liberty, more bitter and calamitous by far than the mild rule of the Medici, should visit dire destruction on a surpassingly beautiful city.

"However that may be, at certain times the company of those 91 youths was most delightful, as they were more my age and disposed to the lighter pursuits of pleasure. Indeed, thanks to the courtesy of individual men, the door stood open to me to enter

feminis ineundam, quae ipsos cognationis necessitudine contigissent, sic ut ad festos nocturnos ludos invitarer nuptiarumque convivia, et nonnumquam rusticaremur cum foris[285] ad iucundiorem liberioremque animi requiem insignes matronas a propinquis invitatas esse audiremus. Adolescente enim aestate et adulto demum autumno omnes familiae ditiores in amoenissimas possessiones effunduntur. Villas namque[286] habent Florentini non modo luculentis[287] aedificiis, verum etiam mirifica suavitate: sal[l]ientibus aquis, piscinis, topiariis, hortis lautoque apparatu maxime sumptuosas. Pecuniosi enim sunt, et publice magnifici, cum in re domestica continentiae et frugalitatis laudem quaerant.

92   'Sed id studium aedificandi vehementer etiam accendit peramoena[288] locorum facies, nam urbem longe omnium toto terrarum orbe pulcherrimam interfluente Arno in media nec multum ibi lata vallis planitie constitutam, hinc atque inde imminentes fructiferi colles circumdant e quibus nobili quodam[289] prospectu non modo incomparabilem urbis figuram contemplari, sed tecta ipsa singillatim agnoscere, ac enumerare facile queas. Arnus ipse, natura perspicuus, lascivis admodum meandris per immensam planitiem villis et oppidis frequentem, sic fertur ut nihil aspectu iucundius esse possit, quamquam rapidis ac maleficis undis cum plenis imbribus intumescit cum gemitu colonorum, et sata obruat et margines possessionum incitatus abripiat.

93   'Florentini uxores suas humaniter colunt et eas perblande semper appellant, tribuuntque non nihil earum[290] ingeniis et cupiditatibus, ut facilius in officio ac amore coniugali teneantur. Multis namque censoriis legibus, quo nihil muliebri animo gravius esse

426

into friendship with those women who were related to these men by connection of birth. Thus I was invited to festive parties at night and to wedding banquets, and on various occasions would spend time in the country when we heard that illustrious matrons from elsewhere had been invited by kinsmen for the purpose of more pleasing and unconstrained forms of relaxation. For from the beginning of summer on to the end of autumn, all the wealthier families flee to their supremely charming estates. The Florentines have lavish, marvelously attractive villas with beautiful buildings and gushing fountains, ponds, ornamental landscaping, gardens, and luxurious embellishments. They are rich and magnificent in public display, although in private matters they seek praise for self-control and frugality.

"But the exceedingly pleasing appearance of the landscape also 92 inflames the zeal for building; for that city, which is by far the most beautiful in the whole world, is built on a plain in the midst of a valley that is not very wide at that point. The Arno River flows through Florence, and fruit-bearing hills overlook the city, surrounding it on this side and that. From a certain majestic observation point in the hills one can see the incomparable layout of the city and easily distinguish and count the individual houses. The Arno itself, naturally clear, is carried along by frisky meanderings through an immense plain crowded with villas and towns in such a way that nothing can be more charming in appearance. But when it becomes swollen with plentiful rains, to the groans of farmers it swamps the crops with swift and harmful currents and, with its fast flow, both overwhelms and washes away the retaining walls of estates.

"The Florentines treat their wives with every kindness and al- 93 ways speak to them charmingly, and they thoroughly indulge their wives' talents and passions, so that they are more easily held true to their conjugal duty and love. Many stern laws, burdensome to women's natures, curtail their extravagance and luxury in

potest, in cultu superfluus earum luxus valde est castigatus, et viri dissimulanter aliqua sibi licere in amatoriis lusibus[291] arbitrantur. Quibus de causis, ad promerendos earum animos tuendumque pudorem, qui saepe una pecuniae egestate corrumpitur, commeatus omnes[292] domestici et fortunae familiares uxorum[293] fidei et diligentiae commendatae sunt atque concreditae. Quarum rerum disciplinam ab Aristotele ductam maxime salutarem experiuntur; nam sic se mulieres enixe et curiose exercent ut numquam in otio et mollissimis cogitationibus persistant, et viros facile[294] ab minutis impensis atque his familiaribus fastidiis liberent.[295]

94   ʽEae, in universum, si corporum figuram spectes, graciliore sunt habitu et propterea corpore admodum agili, ac ingenio maxime prompto, secus ac in Venetis accidere videmus. Ingeniorum autem amoenae quaedam[296] subtilitates cum[297] tersa facundia et peracutis sententiis eas commendant.[298] Porro civitatis mos est perantiquus delectari amictu nitido potius quam pretioso, nec eo quidem alicubi ad luxuriem conciso vel prodige nimium diffluenti. Pectora iugulo tenus linteis interulis opperiunt, aut pudoris causa aut dissimulata quadam arte gracilitatis integendae, nam si quae sunt sinu et papillis admodum venustae, nudata omnia studiose et alacriter ostendunt. Ipsae domi, in victu frugales et parcae bellariorum, et sermonum iucunditate cenas exornare solent, sunt et plurimum deditae religionibus. Quibus de rebus accidit ut ceteris Italiae feminis aliquanto castiores esse iudicentur utpote quas neque ullae cuppediae luxuriosius saginent, neque ulla inertia otia remolliant, neque ullae immoderatae custodiae ad perdendam pudicitiam invitent. Pudor enim in ipsis semper extremis discrimen adire

adornment, and men disguise their view that they have some degree of license in amatory dalliances. For these reasons, to win
over women's minds and to safeguard their chastity, which is often
ruined by a simple lack of money, all the shopping for the family
and the domestic finances have been entrusted to the good faith
and diligence of wives. They demonstrate that this responsibility,
drawn from Aristotle, is most salutary, for the women engage in it
so strenuously and so carefully that they have little time for leisure
and for more sensuous thoughts, and so without causing any difficulty they liberate men from dealing with small expenses and from
tiresome household chores.

"In general, if you consider the features of their bodies, they are 94
of rather slight build and therefore very agile. Their minds are
razor sharp, in a way different from what we see happening in
Venice. Florentine women are recommended by certain pleasant
refinements of their natural intelligence, along with polished eloquence and shrewd opinions. What's more, it is an ancient custom
of the city to take delight in clothing that's marked by elegance
rather than costliness: it's neither cut short to the point of inde-
cency at any spot, nor too prodigiously flowing. They cover their
breasts with linen undergarments that go up to the neck, either on
account of modesty or in order to hide their scrawniness by artifice and deception—for those who have the most attractive torsos
and breasts are quick and eager to put all that on display, laid bare.
At home, these same women, though frugal and sparing of sweets,
are in the habit of enhancing dinners with pleasant conversation,
and they are very much devoted to religious observances. Hence
they are judged to be a bit more chaste than the other women of
Italy, inasmuch as no delicacies fatten them too luxuriously, nor
does any idle leisure soften them, nor does any excessive supervision encourage them to squander their chastity. Modesty, as
a rule, is sorely tried by extremes: too-strict control arouses a

consuevit, quoniam et cura severior in femina libidinem accendat, et nimiam libertatem excitata lascivia subsequatur.

95   'Paucis ante annis, ut dixi, Florentiae plures erant cum formae tum generis ac ingenii dignitate conspicuae, quarum omnium laudes[299] in gratiam unius adamatae[300] Etrusco amoeniore quodam libello celebraram. Sed ex iis aliae perierunt; aliae vero senescentes, succedentibus novis nuptis ipsum summae pulchritudinis florem, vel invitae, reliquerunt. Nam et Cassandra Agenoria, elegantium matronarum decus, nuper interiit, et Ludovicam Tornabonam, qua nulla viduarum vel nuptarum doctior, facundior, aut morum suavitate condicior fuit, inexorabiles Parcae rapuerunt.[301] Et biennio ante, illa ipsa admirabilis Constantia Barda iniquitate Fati[302] in primo aetatis flore surrepta est, cuius immaturam mortem Etruscis octonariis elegis deflevit Aloisius Alamannus cum, ex contagione nefariae coniurationis qua Iulius Medices, ad pontificatum Fato reservatus, in templo trucidari debebat,[303] in Galliis exularet. Claricem quoque Magni Laurentii Medicis neptem quae Philippo Strozae Florentinae iuventutis principi litteris et libertate vitae[304] iucundissimo nupta est, ab irrequieta fecunditate[305] et gravi etiam morbo deformatam paene defecisse audimus, in qua et consilii magnitudo et ingenii eruditio morumque suavitas et illustris omnino pudicitia sic enitescunt ut eam facile tantis natalibus ortam appareat.

96   'Neria hodie Puccia, cui Laurentius Cardinalis est patruus, eximia facie et suavi colore et teretibus membris et crispo crine subrufulo, inter formosas et pudicas insignem locum promeretur. Ioannam etiam Tornabonam ⟨et⟩[306] modestus admodum vultus et nigri lucentesque oculi et incessus ad pudorem compositus maxime

woman's libido, but too much laxity leads to prurience and wantonness.

"A few years earlier, as I've said, more women in Florence ranked as outstanding in beauty, descent, and intellect. In order to win the favor of one beloved woman, I'd sung the praises of them all in a certain rather pleasant little book in Tuscan. But of those women, some have died; moreover, others, growing old, have left the flower of the highest beauty to the new brides succeeding them, albeit against their will. Even Cassandra Ginori,[118] the glory of elegant ladies, has recently died. The unyielding Fates have snatched away Ludovica Tornabuoni,[119] who surpassed all widows and wives in learning, eloquence, and a spicy charm of character. And two years earlier, that admirable woman Costanza de' Bardi[120] was stolen away by the injustice of Fate in the first flower of her youth. Luigi Alamanni lamented her premature death in *ottave rime* in Tuscan when he was in France as a result of his being tainted by the nefarious conspiracy in which Giulio de' Medici, reserved by Fate for the papacy, was supposed to have been slaughtered in a church.[121] And then there's Clarice,[122] the granddaughter of Lorenzo 'the Magnificent' de' Medici, who was married off to the surpassingly congenial Filippo Strozzi, foremost of Florentine youth in learning and in privilege. We hear that she's all but died, disfigured by constantly giving birth and also by a serious illness.[123] Greatness of counsel, erudition of wit, charm of character, and certainly illustrious modesty gleam in her with such brilliance that it's readily apparent she's descended from a great lineage.

"Today, Nera Pucci,[124] the niece of Cardinal Lorenzo Pucci, merits a distinguished place among the beautiful and chaste by her exceptional face, charming complexion, shapely limbs, and slightly reddish curly hair. Giovanna Tornabuoni[125] is greatly recommended by the purity of her countenance, her lively dark eyes, and her modest gait. Costanza Alberti,[126] who sometimes arranges

95

96

commendant.[307] Constantia Alberta, nonnumquam composito per admirabiles tricarum laqueos capillo, Faustinae Augustae effigiem, ut in antiquis nomismatis videmus, adeo eleganter expressit ut in Laurentii Iunioris nuptiis[308] Florentinorum omnium longe pulcherrima putaretur. Nunc honor omnis cum formae et ingenii tum castitatis atque natalium in una Catarina Medicea haud dubie refulget. Ea est Galeotto Medice genita, viro prudentia et civili virtute ornatissimo, sed nupta parum feliciter: nam vir eius Fabius Petrucius qui Senensium Rempublicam tenebat, amissis paternis[309] opibus, [dum][310] populari tumultu urbe exactus est et hostis liberae civitatis iudicatus.

97 'Sunt etiam honestae quaedam et nobiles matronae apud Senenses, quorum civitas inter beatissimas Italiae diceretur, si ad ubertatem agri ac urbis ipsius pulchritudinem animorum etiam consensus accederet: est enim misere divisa in factiones, cum genere multiplices tum maxime publicae libertati perniciosas quae, si propriis explicentur nominibus,[311] omnino ridiculae et ab insanis ingeniis ad perturbandam omnium quietem deductae videantur.

98 'Senenses puellae in universum, confessione totius Etruriae, Florentinas venustate oris antecellunt. E quibus Portiam, quae fuit Pandulfi Petrucii sapientissimi Senensium tiranni filia, peramoena quadam oris ac ingenii iucunditate praecellentem agnovimus. Sed una ab omnibus insigni cum laude celebratur, Honorata Tancredia, nobili[312] orta familia, quae meo iudicio super ceteras omnes singularem formam cunctarum prope virtutum et amoenitatum decore cumulavit. Est enim adeo communi omnium praeconio laudata ut, sicut divino oris habitu humanam speciem, ita etiam admirandis augustioris ingenii dotibus muliebrem captum

her hair in wonderful tangled coils, so elegantly imitated the appearance of Faustina Augusta (as we see on ancient coins) that at
the wedding ceremony of Lorenzo the Younger she was judged by
far the most beautiful of all the Florentines. At present every distinction of beauty, intellect, chastity, and origins doubtless shines
forth in one woman, Caterina de' Medici.[127] She was born to Galeotto de' Medici,[128] a man richly endowed with discretion and
civic virtue, but she married with too little luck: for her husband,
Fabio Petrucci, who used to be in charge of the Sienese Republic,
was driven out of the city by a popular rebellion once he'd exhausted his father's resources, and was declared an enemy of the
free state.[129]

"There are also certain respected and noble matrons among the   97
Sienese. Their community would be named among the most fortunate of Italy if a harmony of minds too were to be joined to the
fertility of the land and the beauty of the city itself, whereas in fact
it is wretchedly divided into factions that are both many in kind
and immensely ruinous to communal freedom. If only they might
be extricated from their respective factions, these would surely appear absurd things, traceable to insane minds aiming at disturbing
everyone's peace.

"Sienese girls in general, by the acknowledgment of all Tuscany,   98
surpass the Florentines in charm of countenance. Of these we
have declared Porzia,[130] the daughter of Pandolfo Petrucci, the
wise tyrant of Siena, to be exceptional for her delightful and pleasant countenance and disposition. But one woman is celebrated
with extraordinary praise: Onorata Tancredi,[131] born into a noble
family. In my view she, above all others, has gracefully brought to
perfection a matchless beauty comprising nearly all virtues and
charms. Indeed, she's been so lauded by universal report that,
since she transcends her human form physically by a divine quality
in her countenance and transcends in intellect the normal capacity of women, she should be proclaimed worthy of a more lofty

supergressa, praedicetur digna profecto celsiore fortuna mulier, ut tot opima gravissimarum virtutum semina velut latiore in campo ad multo copiosiorem stupendamque segetem et pullulare felicius et luxuriosius etiam florere videremus.'[313]

99   Haec cum absolvissem, DAVALUS ad Musetium conversus: 'Postquam,' inquit, 'Iovius non feminarum modo illustrium sed amoenissimarum etiam rerum et locorum facies Genuae atque Florentiae suaviter est persecutus, quo nam ore facundiore quam tuo et heroidum nostrarum laudes et haec ipsa tam felix ac amoena Parthenope poterit decantari? Nam sicut heroo et mollibus elegis haec littora peculiari amoenitate et Sirenum nobilitata monumentis amoresque tuos veteres aestuosos lepidissime celebrasti, ita tibi in hoc munere tam necessario quam pulchro, explicanda est alacrius perpetua vi[s][314] illa florentis et conditae mille leporibus eloquentiae, ut multo clariora haec et specie etiam augustiora, non breviter et in transcursu, sed diffuse ac ornatissime meritis praeconiis enarrentur.'

100   Tum vero ad id MUSETIUS: 'Recte,' inquit, 'Davale praecipis; sed utinam meae vires, quae nec tum cum illa iuvenis canerem ullo modo suffecerunt, ad communem voluptatem hodie maxime sufficiant. Longo enim intervallo et Venetas et Ligures et Etruscas feminae nostrates antecellunt, si nobilitatem amplis opibus et clariore vita sustentatam, vel mores illustri hominum consuetudine ad decus eximium conformatos, vel ingenia perennibus litterarum studiis altius provecta, aestimare velimus. Nullus enim apud eas principalis est luxus, nullus ad ornatum cultus paullo splendidior, nullae in iis vel splendoris vel munificentiae vel altioris consilii

status. Then we would see in a wider field, as it were, so many fertile seeds of the most majestic virtues both sprouting forth, producing a far more abundant and wondrous crop, and flourishing even more fruitfully and luxuriantly."

When I had finished summing up, D'AVALOS, having turned 99 toward Muscettola, said: "Now that Giovio has charmingly described the beauties not only of the illustrious women but also of the delightful customs and physical environments of Genoa and Florence, how could the praises both of our heroines and of this very city, the fortunate and pleasing Naples, be recited now by a mouth more eloquent than yours? After all, you've delightfully celebrated these shores in epic poetry and tender elegiac verses, ennobled by their special beauty and by the monuments of the Sirens, as well as your old summer loves. Just so, in this task as well, as necessary as it is beautiful, you must unleash the lasting power of your eloquence, flourishing and seasoned with a thousand charms as it is. In this way, Naples, more famous by far and also more majestic in appearance, may be described in no brief and cursory treatment, but fully and with the utmost elegance, with the public praises it merits."

Then MUSCETTOLA said in response, "D'Avalos, you advise us 100 well. But would that my force of words—which did not by any measure suffice when as a young man I used to extol those things —might today be utterly sufficient for our shared pleasure. For the women native to our own land surpass the Venetians, the Ligurians, and the Tuscans by a great distance if we take into account nobility that has been sustained by ample wealth and an illustrious life, or morals that have been trained to exceptional virtue by intimacy with illustrious persons, or natural intelligence that has been elevated by the constant study of literature. For among those women there stands out no princely luxury, no devotion to adornment that is even a little more splendid, no great acts either of brilliance or of generosity or of more elevated delibera-

virtutes enitescunt, quoniam certis civilis angustique animi legibus astrictae, neque exercere animos, neque humilia vel occupata ingenia sublevare, neque quicquam virile atque arduum meditari queant.

101 'Porro quae nam terrarum toto orbe ipsa Campania feracior amoenior salubrior poterit inveniri? Quaenam alia urbs, vel si illa ingens Antipodum fabulosa Temistitan ab Hispanis pro miraculo proferatur, vel opportunitate situs et maris, vel praeclara originis antiquitate, vel pulchritudine domorum, vel civium nobilitate, ipsi nostrae Neapoli poterit exaequari? Vincunt enim omnem humanae admirationis celebritatem haec amoena et beata Sirenum sedes, haec litora, lunatis sinibus, craterem hunc adeo laetum immensae fertilitatis a vasto mari complectentia, hicque ipse perpetuo vere florens Pausilipus, non minus iucundae Veneri quam opulenti[s] Baccho et Palladi dedicatus, urbs demum editis ornata speculis, et tot eximiis excelsa domibus, et ipse demum portus latis navalibus, mole magnifica, pharo insigni, trinisque arcibus munitissime circumsaeptus.

102 'Quid refero regios hortos ad Campanam arcem, omni voluptaria arte ac amoenitate constitutos, quos deliciis suis et genio dicavit Alfonsus Iunior? Ibi enim cultissimae aedes citriis circumvestitae nemoribus, opaci passim recessus salientibus lymphis, admirabilisque cenatio in ipsum depressa cavaedium, cum pavimentis signino et musivo opere vermiculatis,[315] quadrata item[316] saepta porticu, et nobili circa podium scamillorum[317] peristylio. Uberrimus fons e medio in porphyreticum erumpit labrum, et reiecta siphonculis aqua occultis excipitur canalibus. Et cum libet, rursus

tion. This is so because they are bound by inflexible, narrow-minded civil laws and are able neither to exercise their minds nor to elevate their natural abilities (which have been humbled or kept preoccupied) nor to contemplate anything manly and difficult.

"Furthermore, where in the entire world can you find a place   101
more fruitful, delightful, and salutary than Campania? Even if the Spaniards were to claim that that massive fabled Tenochtitlan on the other side of the world was a miracle, what other city could be put on the same level with this Naples of ours either in regard to its advantageous location on land and sea, its ancient and illustrious origins, its beautiful buildings, or its noble citizens? These things surpass every famous object of human wonder: this pleasant and blessed home of the Sirens, those shores that embrace the vast sea with their crescent-shaped bays, the volcano crater so rich and immensely fertile, and this Posillipo itself, perennially flourishing, dedicated no less to delightful Venus than to splendid Bacchus and Athena. Then there's the city itself, adorned with scenic vista points on its heights, and soaring aloft with so many excellent houses; and finally, there's the port, securely encircled, with wide docks, a magnificent pier, a prominent lighthouse, and three fortresses.

"What shall I say of the royal gardens in the Campanian cita-   102
del, appointed with every delightful artifice and amenity, which Alfonso II created for his pleasure and inspiration? There he had the most carefully tended dwelling wrapped round with citrus groves, shady recesses with gushing springs here and there, and a wonderful dining room sunk right into the inner courtyard, its floors inlaid in wave patterns of plaster and mosaic, and this enclosed in turn by a square portico with a noble peristyle around the base of the steps. A gushing fountain bursts forth from the center into a porphyry basin, and by means of small pipes the water is taken up by hidden conduits. Then, on command, it returns to surprise and drench the dinner guests when it is dis-

ad fallendos rigandosque convivas; subter sedilia intercluso et rursus laxato spiritu, pneumaticis machinationibus effunditur. Fenestrae ab ortu hippodromum despectant in quo generosi illi equi a decora iuventute ad decursiones et concursus exercebantur.

103   'Quid memorem Podii Regalis villam eiusdem Alfonsi opus, tanto sumptu amoenitati et voluptatibus indulgentis? Ibi saepta ferarum, ibi omnis generis aves liberis nutritae in campis, et ad regium aucupium reservatae, item piscinae saepto[318] marmore circumsaeptae nobilium piscium plenissimae, et aviaria intro picta reticulata, cantricium[319] volucrum multitudine referta.

104   'At quis modo regum beatiorem villam possidet? Ea enim est dignis condecorata picturis, quibus Hydruntini belli labores atque victoriae de Turcis immanibus partae ad veras hominum effigies referuntur. Quaterna ibi triclinia et bis totidem cubicula singulari symmetria ad omnes caeli conversa partes, praealta ac illustris porticus coniungit, quae marmoreis triginta columnis sustinetur. In proximo altera etiam porticus in sublime gradibus assurgit, quae iuncta est piscinis marmoreo podio et decenti columellarum corona conclusis, itemque lithostrotis[320] lavacris et balineis frigidariis, ad quae aditus est. Per occultos hortos perpetua illa citriorum viriditate florentes, ab hac celsa porticu cenantes maria despectant, et campos ad aucupia et venationes severa lege custoditos. Ibi circum mensas, tantum aquarum iucundo murmure variis occultatisque tubulis diducitur, et in omnes partes elaboratis aere siphonibus ad potum et voluptatem effunditur, ut discumbentes e marmoreis ingentibus carchesiis caelatisque labellis, natantes calices crystalinaque pocula et fulgentes pateras gestienti et madida manu corripiant.

charged by pneumatic machines with air stored up beneath the seats. From the east, windows overlook the hippodrome in which those well-bred horses used to be trained up by graceful young men for the purpose of military maneuvers and charges.

"What should I call to mind about that same Alfonso's villa of Poggio Reale, where no expense was spared for amenities and pleasures? In one place, we saw enclosures full of wild beasts; in another, birds of every kind, raised in the open fields and reserved for royal fowling; likewise, we saw pools, enclosed by marble walls, full of remarkable fish; and aviaries, painted on the inside and covered with nets, jam-packed with a multitude of songbirds. 103

"Well, then, what king possesses a more beautiful villa? It was decorated with worthy paintings, in which the labors connected with the War of Otranto and the victories over the savage Turks are narrated with true likenesses of the participants.[132] Nearby rises a lofty and splendid portico supported by thirty marble columns, which adjoins a set of four dining rooms and twice as many bedrooms, arranged with singular symmetry to face every part of the sky. Close by, another portico — this one joined with fishponds enclosed by a marble base and a handsome crown of small columns — rises upward by steps, providing access in like manner to tessellated baths and cold plunges. From this lofty portico the diners look down, through hidden gardens flourishing with the perpetual green of citrus trees, upon the sea and the fields reserved by severe laws for fowling and hunting. Around the tables in that room, an immense quantity of water is conveyed with a pleasant murmur by hidden pipes of various sizes and dispersed to all areas by siphons fashioned from bronze for drinking and pleasure, so that the diners, by dipping their eager hands into huge marble beakers and embossed bowls, may snatch up the floating goblets, crystal drinking glasses, and gleaming plates. 104

105 'Quid etiam illa suburbana plaga quae ad perforati Pausilipi cryptam perducit, vel piscationis opportunitate vel hilaritate prospectus, villarumque frequentia ac hortorum et xystorum amoenitate, iucundius esse potest?

106 'Verum ut ad ipsas feminarum laudes properemus, nonne haec quae in arce est, Ioanna Aragonia, Ascanio Columnae equitum magistro nupta, omnes omnium urbium quae numeratae[321] sunt aut a maioribus ingeniis enumerari possunt, admirabilium morum et inenarrabilis formae dignitate confessione omnium antecellit? Quam scilicet blanda Venus peperit mollissimeque lactavit, Iuno caelitum regina ad augustum habitum feliciter eduxit, studiose Pallas erudivit, Charites vero ipsae ad unum eam absolvendam feminam conspirantes, eius ori et moribus divina rerum omnium ornamenta contulerunt. Ea ut est Ferdinandi clarissimi regis ex filio neptis, et Castalliae nobilissimae ac pudicissimae feminae filia, et in huius demum Victoriae Columnae Ascanii coniugis sororis disciplinam traducta, tales docili illustrique animo mores hausit, ut eius pudicitia nihil limpidius, nihil ingenio cultius, nihil mente religiosius esse possit.'

107 Tum vero DAVALUS: 'Museti,' inquit, 'summa tantum atque communia summis digitis attingis, cum sermo penitus sit demittendus ad propiores dotes singillatim internasque virtutes quas tu in officio et cultu (ne dicam amoribus) provectarum matronarum vehementer occupatus, in his tenellis et regiis puellis agnoscere minime potuisti. Sunt enim corporis eius ac[322] animi infinitae quaedam amoenitates, quas et Iovius et ego longa et familiari consuetudine sic deprehendimus ut paene ambo in earum

"What can be more pleasant than that suburban stretch of land 105 leading to the tunnel piercing Posillipo,[133] either in its suitability for fishing or in the cheerfulness of view, in the abundance of villas and in the charm of gardens and open porticoes?

"But let's hasten back to the subject of praising women. Isn't 106 it the case that, by universal acknowledgment, this Giovanna d'Aragona[134] who is in the citadel, married to the cavalry captain Ascanio Colonna, surpasses in the distinction of her admirable character and indescribable beauty all the women of all the cities which we have considered or which can be counted up by greater minds than ours? She to whom alluring Venus surely gave birth and tender suck; whom Juno, the queen of the gods in heaven, felicitously raised to attain a majestic comportment; whom Athena devotedly educated—she it was whom the Graces themselves, acting in concert to put the finishing touches on her, granted every divine adornment of countenance and character. She is the granddaughter of the illustrious King Ferdinand through his son and is the daughter of Castellana, an exceedingly noble and chaste woman; and she has been given over to Vittoria Colonna, the sister of her husband Ascanio, for training. As a result, Giovanna, with her teachable and brilliant mind, has formed so fine a character that no one can be purer than she in chastity, no one more cultivated in intellect, no one more devout in contemplation."[135]

Then D'AVALOS, for his part, observed: "Muscettola, you 107 scarcely touch with the tips of your fingers upon the most superficial generalities, whereas the discussion needs to be brought down to the more particular endowments and to the internal virtues, one by one. Having been energetically occupied in the service and education of ladies advanced in years (to say nothing of your love affairs with them), you haven't at all been able to identify those qualities in these young and royal girls. Such girls have infinite charms of body and mind which both Giovio and I apprehended by long and friendly contact with them, so much so that we both nearly lost

admiratione perierimus. Nam id totum quod est eleganter ad citharam saltare, clavicimbala aenochorda⟨ta⟩ digitorum erudita gesticulatione pulsare, musicis accentibus ad librorum notas iucundam scite vocem applicare, decantare Etruscos rhythmos liberiore concentu et mollioribus numeris, et denique in ioco et convivio suavissime versari, et cuncta demum facetiis et salibus verecunda quadam hilaritate colludere, non insulse in cumulo totius venustatis computantur.'

108   Tum vero ego ⟨IOVIUS⟩ inquam: 'Davale, egregia haec sunt, et supra quam quisquam aestimare possit admiranda. Sed haec omnia profecto animos potius delectant quam inflamment vel sensus ipsos sedibus suis revellant. Oculi siquidem illi glauci ad augustiorem oris maiestatem potius quam ad lasciviarum illecebras accommodati, illa labella corallina, ille flavus capillus ad argenteum splendorem undulatus et ad ventilantem auram per eburnea colla niveosque umeros dispersus, illae exsultantes papillae, numquam ad oculorum satietatem satis ostentatae, illa regia proceritas, ille denique gestus ad gravitatem cum venustate compositus spectantes abripiunt, exanimant, et infixa memoriae perpetuo miseros torquent.

109   'Quid fecunditatem et natorum similitudinem, quid ingentes opes ad ornatum et exquisitissimum cultum commemoro? Quorum alterum est arridentis Fortunae alterum vero rarissimae felicitatis, quando propiora et magis peculiaria eius naturae bona sint numeranda. Id enim vere suum et proprium videtur, quod ea semper seipsa omnium pulcherrima pulchrior apparet, cum neglecta in brevicula chlamyde, nudis a cubito lacertis, soluto et incomposito

our hearts to them out of admiration. Consider what it is to dance elegantly to the lute; to play with skilled touch the keys of a metal-stringed clavicembalo;[136] to apply a pleasant voice expertly in correct rhythm to the notes in a songbook; to sing Tuscan rhymes to an improvised tune, and in more soothing meters; and finally, to take part in the sweetest way in jokes and conviviality, and in the end to make sport of everything in witticisms and wisecracks with a certain modest good humor. It is not foolish to include these things in the sum total of complete beauty."

Then I [GIOVIO] said: "D'Avalos, these are outstanding quali- 108 ties, and they must be admired more than anyone could reckon. But surely they all delight minds rather than inflaming them, let alone wrenching loose the very senses from their seats in the body. Giovanna d'Aragona's sparkling eyes serve to give majestic grandeur to her countenance rather than to entice wantonness. Those coral-red lips, that blond hair streaked with silvery splendor and blown over her ivory neck and snow-white shoulders by the breeze, those quivering breasts never displayed enough for the eyes' satiety, that regal tallness, and finally that bearing, combining beauty with authority: all these things seize hold of those who watch her, take their breath away and, once fixed in their memory, torture the wretches forever.

"Why enter d'Aragona's fertility into the record, and how closely 109 her children resemble her? And why mention the immense natural beauty that lends itself to adornment and the choicest refinement? The former of these comes from Fortune smiling upon her, but the latter is from the rarest good luck, inasmuch as the endowments of nature must be counted as nearer and more particular to her character. This indeed seems to be characteristic of her: that even though she is the most beautiful of all women, she appears still more beautiful every time one sees her; that even when she is ungroomed, in a very short cloak, with the skin bare from the elbows on down, and her hair loose and disheveled, those who get

capillo, sui videndi copiam arsuris et perituris facit, quando ea est inusitatae formae praerogativa, ut nullo fuco, nullis indumentis, nullis ad exactiorem comptum lenociniis indigeat.

110 'Sentit enim iniuriam importunae diligentiae natura sagax, nec eos[323] artus operiri artificio ullo patitur, quos ipsa liberaliter ad apertum decus absolverit, ita ut haec Aragonia opalo gemmae simillima videatur, quae in pretiosissima claritate semper fuit, quoniam in ea, et carbunculi micantior flamma et virentis smaragdi nitor ille translucidus, et amethistina purpura dilutior, incredibili quadam radiorum mixtura pelluceant, sicque eius confusi colores oculos delectent ut opalus[324] nihil operoso includente auro, nihil substrata bractea prorsus indigeat: nam exili tantum et simplici praecinctus funda longe pulcherrimus evadit quoniam, tum libere evibratus in omnes partes, varius et eximius ille fulgor eniteat.'

111 Tum vero MUSETIUS 'Praeclari,'[325] inquit, 'mihi fatiscenti in Aragonia celebranda adiutores exstitistis; nam certe tantarum eius virtutum reputatio meipsum obruerat, nisi quotam partem eius oneris benigne admodum subissetis. Sed quo ordine ceteras subiungam, postquam aequo prope certamine plures simul de claritate contendunt? Aliae enim amplissimis subnixae opibus, aliae exactiore forma conspicuae, aliae item fretae natalibus, aut maritorum honoribus provectae sese ceteris praestare arbitrantur. Vincet tamen omnem meum inevitabilis invidiae timorem unus pulcherrimarum respectus, eaque serie singulae citabuntur qua sensibus meis atque memoria fuerint collocatae, ita ut Nemesim pie atque sincere etiam contester, me nulla adductum gratia nulloque

the chance to see her even like this will burn and lose their hearts to her. Since she has the privilege of uncommon beauty she needs no makeup, no fancy clothes, and no sexy allurements to make her appear more *soignée*.

"Her perceptive temperament senses the detrimental effects of excessive attention to her appearance, and does not allow to be covered by any artifice those parts of the body which she herself has graciously brought to perfection in natural beauty. As a result, d'Aragona seems very much like the opal gem, always prized for its brightness, since there shine forth in her, with a certain incredible mixture of rays of light, a flame more glittering than a carbuncle, the translucent luster of a green emerald, and a violet paler than an amethyst's. Thus the opal's mingled colors delight the eyes in such a way that it doesn't in the least require an elaborately worked gold enclosure or gilding underneath; for surrounded only by a slight and simple setting, it proves to be the most beautiful by far because then its variegated and exceptional brightness is thrown off freely, shining out in all directions." 110

At this point MUSCETTOLA said, "You've been outstandingly helpful to me, tired as I am, in celebrating d'Aragona, for surely the reckoning of her great virtues would have overwhelmed me had you not been kind enough to take so much of the task upon yourselves. But in what order should I continue on with the other women, inasmuch as quite a lot of them are evenly matched in their rivalry for renown? Many believe themselves to excel the rest: some rely on their ample wealth; others are conspicuous for their carefully tended beauty; still others rely upon lineage or have been elevated on account of the honors of their husbands. Nonetheless, one consideration regarding the ranking of beauties will conquer all my fear of the inevitable odium: I will mention individual women by name in that sequence in which my senses and memory arrange them. Respectfully and sincerely, I call Nemesis[137] to 111

maligno impulsum iudicio, nemini proprium honoris locum esse praerepturum.

112 'Igitur quis huius Constantiae sororis tuae, Davale, et Alfonsi Picolominei Amalphii Reguli uxoris: decorem vel cogitatione perfecte concipere, vel exacte oculis contemplari, vel oratione aptissime poterit definire? Qui cum sit ab infinitis atque conspicuis elegantiarum omnium floribus exornatus et absolutus, eum tamen ingenitae candidiori animo virtutes eximiae, multo admirabiliorem efficiunt. Quas enim spirat veneres lata et serena fronte, nigris et micantibus oculis, roseis labellis, candidulis dentibus! Quas autem gestat cupidines lacteis cervicibus et palpitantibus papillis, verecundo incessu, sermone rariore blandulo, et tenerrimis[326] affectionum omnium illecebris! Quanta porro memoriae felicitas, quanta acuitas sublimioris ingenii, quantaque prudens simplicitas ac honestarum cogitationum delicata mollitudo![327] Nam solitam eam videmus et aliena carmina memoriter decantare, et sua scitissime lucubrata recitare, et nihil animo vel incautius vel simulatius agitare; et, quod usu in pulcherrimis et opulentissimis rarissimum semper fuit, affectiones omnes absque ulla superbia aut elatae vanitatis fastu rectissime moderari.

113 'Quae demum fecunditas! Qui liberi, sive pueros sive puellas malis! Qua illi specie, qua virtutis indole! Quae denique eius pietas et castimonia! Quis[328] amor, quae caritas erga coniugem Alfonsum etiam intemperanter alios amores meditantem, ut nulla iam credatur vel probatissima Vestalis Virgo ea religiosior et purior!

114 'Nec in latibulis remotioribus vel acerbiore custodia delituit, sed in luce hominum et in conspectu iuventutis et in civitate feminei pudoris maxime corruptrice versata est — atque ita versata ut, cum

witness that I shall not rip away the proper place of honor from anyone owing to favor or malice.

"So then, d'Avalos, let's consider this Costanza[138] who is both 112 your sister and the wife of Alfonso Piccolomini, ruler of Amalfi. Who could conceive her beauty fully in thought or survey it precisely with the eyes or define it suitably in speech? Although her beauty has been adorned and perfected by an infinite number of visible refinements, nonetheless her extraordinary virtues, innate to her pure soul, render it far more admirable. Indeed, what charms emanate from her wide and serene brow, her dark and twinkling eyes, rosy lips, and pretty white teeth! What longings she carries about in her milk-white neck and quivering breasts, her modest gait, her spare and pleasing speech, and the tender enticements of all her emotions! What a happy endowment of memory she possesses, what a keen and high-minded intellect, what judicious candor and feminine delicacy she shows in her noble mind! We see that she is accustomed both to repeat verbatim the poems of others and to recite her own compositions with consummate skill. She never acts unreflectively with too little caution or sincerity; and—a thing experience shows has always been rarest in wealthy and beautiful people—she controls her moods with the utmost propriety, without any pride, haughtiness, or vanity.

"Lastly, what fertility she enjoys! What children she has, 113 whether you prefer her sons or her daughters! How good looking and naturally virtuous they are! Finally, what piety and moral purity she has! What love and affection she shows to her husband Alfonso, despite his intemperate obsession with other love affairs. At present not even the most morally upright Vestal Virgin is believed more devout or pure than she.

"Nor has she hidden herself away in remote retreats or in a con- 114 finement that would be more cruel to us, but instead she has moved around in the sight of people, in the presence of youth, and in a community extremely corrosive of womanly modesty—and

447

eam multi illustres viri studiose coluerint, nonnulli etiam, ut credibile est, flagranti amore deperierint, et ad promerendam gratiam ingenia liberaliter exercuerint. Iaculationum equestrium comicorum et Lupercalium Ludorum spectacula ediderint, nullis umquam flecteretur obsequiis, et vera gloriosi sui nominis Constantiae laude frueretur. Quin etiam adeo benigne et temperate pervicax esse consuevit, non firmis modo gravitatis, sed humanitatis etiam vallata praesidiis ut sine ullo colentium ludibrio vel agrestiore contumelia tota ea parum pudicae cupiditatis obsequia repudiet ac eludat, adamanti nobilissimae gemmae persimilis cuius vis indomita nullis admotis ignibus concalescit.'

115   Tum ego ⟨IOVIUS⟩ inquam, 'Et quo spiritu dicendae laudis de Maria Aragonia uxore tua, Davale, te maxime praesente iudicium faciemus? In qua cum regii vultus alacritas et virginalis pudor, cum roseis malis tum nigris paetisque[329] oculis et serenae fronti summam afferant dignitatem; toto etiam vividi corporis habitu ad torquendos homines elegantia singularis exprimitur. Verum etsi illam pretiosae vestes, et gemmata monilia ad comptum e regiis opibus deprompta, semper exornarint, illo die tamen divina eius venustas enituit, cum in festa Lupercalium laetitia, in nympharum morem atque habitum compositam et cum virginibus suis ad citharam saltantem conspeximus. Super pallam illa crispo ex auro rigentem, tenue linteum aureis virgatum limbis induerat. Purpurea item brevior chlamys ad umerum aureo nodo revincta, et manicae a cubito ad omnem motum implente aura diffluentes, latusque ex auro balteus ab umero per medias papillas oblique reductus numeroso incessu vadentem honestabant. Flavos autem crines myrtea corona

has done so in such a way that, although many illustrious men have eagerly courted her, some, understandably, have even fallen hopelessly in passionate love with her, and have put their talents to use unstintingly for the purpose of earning her favor. They put on exhibitions of throwing, horsemanship, comedies and Lupercalian Games, but she was never won over by any acts of deference, and she delighted in the praise that truly lived up to her illustrious name, 'Constance.' Instead of giving in, she is customarily kind, temperate, and steadfast, surrounded as she is not only with the fortifications of seriousness but also with the garrison of gentleness, so that without in any way mocking or boorishly insulting those who court her, she rejects and parries all those solicitous but shameless attentions. She is like a hard, noble gemstone whose fierce strength glows without being lit by fire."

Then I [GIOVIO] added, "As far as praise is concerned, in what 115 spirit, d'Avalos, will we pass judgment concerning your wife, Maria d'Aragona,[139] especially with you present? In her the liveliness of regal countenance and virginal modesty contribute the greatest dignity both to her rosy cheeks and to her dark, playful eyes and serene brow. The entire demeanor and vitality of her body exudes a singular refinement suited to tormenting men. But even if costly clothes and jeweled necklaces from royal treasuries have always bedecked her, nonetheless her divine charm began to shine forth on the day when we saw her in the festive joy of the Lupercalia, done up into the manner and attire of the nymphs and, along with her maidservants, dancing to the lute. Over her mantle, stiff with crimped gold, she had wrapped a sheer linen cloth, accented by golden fringes. She wore a short purple cloak fastened at the shoulder with a golden knot, and its long sleeves, flowing away from the elbow, were puffed out by a breeze with her every movement; and a wide golden shoulder strap was drawn diagonally across her breasts. These adornments graced her as she moved with measured step. A crown of myrtle, attached by interlacings of

margaritarum nexibus obligata praecingebat ita ut peramoeno oris habitu[330] pulcherrima videretur. Sed tum etiam in se omnium ora atque animos maxime convertit, cum decoro cervicis ac umerorum gestu, et molli laterum flexu, et docto crurum alternantium tripudio, ad Maurisiacum[331] modulum choream variis gyris atque maeandris iucundissimam perduxisset.

116   'Quae omnia in occultis et puellaribus deliciis computantur; nam in publico ea est excelsa atque defixa gravitate, iisque moribus ad matronalem dignitatem conformatis ut, cum in oppidis Davalae familiae quae sunt ad oram Marrucinorum et Frentanorum ex imperio cuncta administraret, ii populi se non a sexdecim annorum puella sed a matrona usu rerum valde exercitata et prudenti moderate regi ac in pace contineri praedicarent.

117   'Sed ad quam vel summae virtutis frugem has duas minime perventuras arbitramur, cum domi tantum habeant exemplorum et illam praesertim quam imitentur ad effigiem priscae honestatis atque prudentiae Constantiam amitam, quae Federico Baucio Acerrano regulo coniuge orbata et, quod florentis aetatis auxit calamitatem, nulla prole suscepta, in admiratione hominum quondam fuit, propter divinae formae venustatem et studiorum optimorum, elegantiam singulari prudentiae laude cumulatam, adeo ut rex Ferdinandus glorioso cognomine Catholicus, cum eam Aenariae praefectura et Frentanorum principatus titulo donaret, omnino etiam vel nihil prohibente sexu, senatorio honore dignam dixerit, ut gravissimarum rerum consiliis interesset. Nec postea sapientissimi regis iudicium fefellit, cum in asperis pariter et secundis rebus, omne virilis administrationis decus, non modo implesse verum abunde superasse diceretur.[332] Quarum rerum dignitatem non

pearls, encircled her hair in such a way that she appeared utterly beautiful with her thoroughly pleasing countenance. But then, too, she drew everyone's faces and minds toward her especially when with graceful movement of the neck and shoulders, a gentle bending of the body, and an expert leaping from one leg to the other, she performed the dance with various circlings and meanderings, in harmony with the most pleasant Moorish music.

"All this is an assessment of her private, youthful pleasures, for in public she has a lofty and steadfast seriousness. Her mores have been fashioned so as to suit the dignity of a married woman, so that when in accordance with her family's authority she governed the towns belonging to the d'Avalos family on the shore of the Marrucinians and Frentanians,[140] those peoples claimed that they were being ruled in a moderate manner and kept together in peace, not by a girl of sixteen years, but by a matron exceedingly well practiced and experienced in the conduct of affairs. 116

"But we cannot conceive of these two women not attaining the fruits of the highest virtue, since they have such examples at home: especially their Aunt Costanza,[141] whom they ought to imitate as the portrait of pure honor and prudence. She was bereaved of her husband Federico del Balzo, the ruler of the Acerrians, and — what magnified the misfortune of her youth — she bore no children. Formerly people greatly admired her on account of her charming and divine beauty and her refinement in literary studies, perfected by a uniquely praiseworthy prudence. As a result, when King Ferdinand, endowed with the glorious epithet 'the Catholic,' made her the governor of Ischia and gave her the title of Duchess of Francavilla, he also declared her entirely worthy of senatorial honor — her sex in no way barred her from this — so that she might take part in deliberations of the weightiest matters. Nor thereafter did she fail to implement the judgment of that wisest of kings, both in violent circumstances and equally in favorable ones. She was said not just to have satisfied but to have surpassed abun- 117

eliso penitus vel[333] obscurato decore ita adhuc retinet ut quod prementibus annis vel evanidum vel offuscatum sit,[334] id totum egregie, perpetua vitae sanctimonia tueatur.'

118 'At huius,' inquit MUSETIUS, 'et superioris Aragoniae soror est Isabella Villamarini regiae classis praefecti filia, et subinde, rara utriusque felicitate, Ferdinando Sanseverino nupta principi Salernitano adolescenti procerum omnium longe nobilissimo atque pulcherrimo. Eius suavi ore nihil laetius, nihil oculorum iucunditate beatius, nihil ingenii eruditione ac ubertate florentius. Verum insigni forma et aetate praetenera maxime praecellentem praeclara studia musicae artis plurimum nobilitant, quibus ab ineunte aetate tanta sollertia se dedidit, ut non modo animum in otio honeste ad tuendum pudorem exerceret, sed in illis palam ad decus vitae principalis, cum opus foret, cum laude et multa coniugis delectatione versaretur.

119 'Nihil enim in nobili puella musicis exercitationibus aut salubrius aut iucundius esse potest. Illae enim, ut in segni otio saepe accidit, molliores cogitationes revellunt, ablegant taedia cuncta curasque mitigant, ac animum numerorum dulcedine delenitum ad moderationem, temperantiam, et lenitatem instituunt. Nec mirum est, cum ex numeris constare animos nostros, quibus adeo impense delectentur, Aristoteles tradiderit; Pythagorae secutus disciplinam, qui cuncta naturae corpora ex harmonica sympathia, aut aperte aut saltem surde sonantia, deprehensis occultis affectionibus existimavit. Et Plato ipse, ad superna divinaque[335] nequaquam

dantly every distinction of manly administration. She retains the dignity of her position with her beauty not in any way destroyed or degraded, so that she still preserves with distinction, thanks to her constant purity of life, all that which might either pass away or be obscured by the years weighing upon her."

"Well then, her companion and that of the elder d'Aragona," 118 MUSCETTOLA added, "is Isabella Villamarina,[142] the daughter of the admiral of the royal fleet;[143] she was promptly, with the uncommon happiness of both of them, married to the young Salernitan prince Ferdinando Sanseverino,[144] who is by far the most noble and handsome of his entire lineage. Nothing is more cheerful than her pleasing mouth, happier than the charm of her eyes, or more flourishing than the cultivation and abundance of her intellect. But most of all, the splendid studies of the art of music ennoble this woman, so outstanding for her beauty and in her exceptionally tender age. To these studies she has devoted herself from an early age with such great skill that not only has she disciplined her mind in leisure hours so as honorably to safeguard her modesty, but when it is needed for the adornment of a princely life, she has engaged in them in public, with acclaim and much to her husband's delight.[145]

"Nothing in a noble girl can be more wholesome and pleasing 119 than musical exercises. They drive out the pensive moods such as often occur in torpid leisure; they get rid of all objects of boredom and alleviate anxieties, and edify a mind calmed by the charm of rhythmic harmonies so as to attain moderation, temperance, and gentleness. Nor is this astonishing, since Aristotle [sic] taught that our minds are composed of numbers, by which they are so immoderately delighted.[146] In this he followed the teachings of Pythagoras, who regarded all natural bodies as resonating from harmonic sympathy either expressly or at least mutely once their hidden qualities had been discerned. And Plato himself, by no means blind to things celestial and divine (which had been divided

caligans, ex perfectissima numerorum proportione discissa, et ab
duobus paribus hemicyclis in absolutum orbem circumducta,
mundum universum a summo opifice fabrefactum esse perscripse-
rit. Propterea Athenienses hanc unam ex liberalibus disciplinis
maxime dignam ingenua muliere putaverunt adeo ut eius rudes
aut parum studiosas minime nobiles esse arbitrarentur. Quoniam
et in quiete suavis, et in negotio commoda, ac omni denique sexui
cunctaeque aetati aptissima atque honestissima videretur, vel una
praesertim ratione: quod conceptam animo iucunditatem mirifice
conservet, insidentem vero molestiam repente discutiat, et affectionibus demum cunctis absque ulla prorsus amaritie saluberrime simul ac iucundissime[336] medeatur.

120   'Porro et in ea laudem accumulant sermo urbanis plenus illecebris, mores naturali candore conspicui animusque totus ad pudorem ac[337] adamati coniugis obsequium conversus. Unde felicem
profecto eam prolem fore crediderim, quam summae virtutis et
pulchritudinis coniuges aliquando sustulerint.

121   'Summam inter has nostras aliquamdiu claritatem obtinuit Isabella Recasentia Raimundo Cardonio proregi nupta. Nam tum
haec Aragonia maior, quae ad ipsum proregem avunculum ventita-
bat, neque viro matura erat, neque illum nitentem sucum atque
illud absolutae formae decus induerat. Nec ipsa quoque Constantia Davala tanta sua venustate inenarrabiles[338] huius veneres tum
maxime florentes poterat obscurare. Factum est enim quod semper
rarissimum fuit felici conatu naturae blandientis ut haec inter se ad
torrendos iuvenes essent coniuncta: membrorum scilicet omnium
niveus candor, et argentei crines internitente quodam fulgore palli-
dioris auri, et oculi nigri fulgentes, radiosi paeta[339] mobilitate, ad

in two, according to the most perfect proportional relationship of numbers, and drawn around from two equal semicircles into a complete circle), wrote that the entire universe had been fashioned by the highest artisan.[147] Hence the Athenians supposed that out of the liberal disciplines, music alone was especially worthy of a freeborn woman — so much so that they supposed women who were unskilled or uninterested in it lacked nobility. This was so because it appeared to be both a pleasant activity in leisure and fitting in social situations, and finally very well suited and most honorable for each sex and for every age, and for one reason above all: namely, that it marvelously preserves intact a delight that has been conceived in the mind, while dispelling in an instant deep-seated vexation. Finally, it most healthfully and pleasantly heals all the moods without suffering.

"Furthermore, Isabella Villamarina wins praise for her speech 120 that is replete with sophisticated charms, her character that is distinguished by its natural sincerity, and her mind that is entirely directed toward modesty and toward obedience to her beloved husband. So I trust that the offspring that wives of the greatest virtue and beauty will someday rear will be truly blessed.

"Among these women of ours, Isabel de Requensens,[148] wife of 121 the viceroy Ramón de Cardona,[149] for some time maintained the highest fame. For at that time the elder d'Aragona (who used regularly to visit the viceroy, her maternal uncle) was neither ripe for marriage nor had she yet assumed the glowing vitality and the splendor of unqualified beauty belonging to a bride. Nor, likewise, had Costanza d'Avalos herself with her abundant beauty been able to eclipse the indescribable charms then very greatly flourishing. For it happened (a very rare occurrence) that, with the fortunate effort of obliging nature, the following features had been united in Isabel that might inflame the desires of young men: the snowy whiteness of all her limbs; silvery hair with a certain splendor of rather pale gold shining forth; and dark, gleaming eyes, radiant

Cypriae luminum effigiem fabrefacti, quae omnia adhuc integra manerent, si, secus quam ut nunc est atrata, et frontem et sinum nigris velis altius protecta, ad ornatum revocatis elegantiarum amoenitatibus, splendide amicta, prodiret in publicum.'

122   Tum ego ⟨IOVIUS⟩ 'Apage,' inquam 'Museti, ne putato eam in ulla vel aurea quam pulla in veste pulchriorem fore. Nigra enim candidas et aetate maxime provectas decent, meque imprimis ea vela obtenta mollibus oculis mirifice delectarunt adeo ut nihil iam pristini decoris in ea desiderem, postquam ingenium eius omni humanitate atque eruditione excultum esse longis sermonibus deprehendi. Tanta enim est eius excelsis moribus innata facilitas ut mihi prope ipsam mentis libertatem eripuerit, cum impetrante aegra matre cui ego propter assidebam[340] venas tangens ut mihi alienigenae morem gereret ad cytharam Ovidiana carmina de Didonis infaustis amoribus scitissime decantasset.'

123   ⟨Tum MUSETIUS inquit⟩,[341] 'Duae item sunt Neapoli nuptae e Gonzaga familia admodum illustres quas Iovius inter Mantuanas numerare debuisset: Dorothea atque Susanna, Federici Bozoli qui cum insigni laude Gallorum stipendia meret sorores, ambae pariter nobilissimis viris orbatae. Nam Susanna Petrum Cardonium, eundem pulcherrimum coniugem et ducem fortissimum, Mediolanensi bello, in ipsa prosperae pugnae victoria infeliciter amisit. Dorothea vero, Aquevivium regulum Betuntinum morbo nuper extinctum luget. In Susanna, quae est[342] aetate viridior ac[343] suco, et oculis et tota denique forma tenerior, splendoris elegantiae et liberalitatis studium viget. Dorothea autem quod[344] bona corpo-

with playful quickness, forged in the likeness of the eyes of Venus. All these things would still remain unimpaired, if, unlike the present moment, when she is dressed in black and her face and breast are covered by black veils, she were to take up again her delightful elegance and appear in public, splendidly attired."

Then I [GIOVIO] said, "Nonsense, Muscettola! Don't imagine   122 that she would be more beautiful in any other clothing, even were it made of gold, than in dark-colored attire. Black is becoming to fair-skinned women, and to those who are advanced in age. Especially those veils which have been stretched over her tender eyes have marvelously delighted me. I find lacking in her nothing of her earlier beauty, now that I have discovered through long conversations her natural gifts, polished with all humanity and learning. Her complaisance, native to a lofty character, is so great that she almost made me her vassal at a time when I was close by, keeping watch over her sick mother and taking her pulse. At her mother's request that she might oblige me, a foreigner, she'd most expertly sung to the lute the Ovidian verses about the ill-omened loves of Dido."[150]

Then MUSCETTOLA interjected: "Also in Naples there are two   123 outstandingly illustrious young wives from the Gonzaga family, whom Giovio ought to have listed among the Mantuans: Dorotea and Susanna, sisters of Federigo da Bozzolo, who serves the French with great distinction.[151] Both alike have been deprived of noble husbands: for Susanna, unhappily, lost don Pedro de Cardona,[152] a handsome spouse and a brave commander, in the moment of victory during a propitious battle of the Milanese war. Dorotea, on the other hand, mourns Acquaviva,[153] the marquis of Bitonto, who recently died from an illness. In Susanna, more youthful in age and vitality, more delicate in her eyes and in fact in her beauty as a whole, there flourishes enthusiasm for splendor, refinement, and liberality. Dorotea, however, because she foresaw that the goods of the body and of beauty in its prime would be

ris et florentis formae fluxa esse et caduca providebat, sic ingenium
subtile et peracutum litteris excoluit, sic mores qui matronale decus respicerent virtutibus iocis salibus exornavit ut ea plerisque
amabili ac erudita et florenti Catharina filia longe suavior esse videatur.'

124 'Haec inquam, Dorothea, vere deorum munus,[345] bonos poetas
humaniter colit, a quibus et ipsa iucundius observatur atque diligi-
tur. At qua gravitate animi coniugis obitum tulit ut cum tu, Iovi,
humanioris officii causa ad eam in pullatis stratis considentem, ut
aegram solareris, accessisses, et locos non vulgares ex philosophia
deprompsisses, sic eam siccatis plane lacrimis ratione firmatam
productis sermonibus invenisti ut cuncta remedia forti animo eam
antecepisse mirareris, plusque[346] tibi negotii mox fuerit in cohiben-
dis Matthei soceri lacrimis, cum ille et vir et longaevus et summus
professione philosophus, nulla adhuc crudo dolori paullo molliora
lenimenta reperisset. Quamobrem summum honorem huic feminae tribuendum puto, post unam Victoriam Columnam, quam
optimo iure semper excipio, propter admirabilem in ea praestantis-
simarum virtutum concursum, adeo ut eam omnino eripiendam e
turba mulierum, et in primos optimorum virorum ordines merito
deducendam esse iudicemus.'

125 Ad ea DAVALUS: 'Nudasti studia tua tandem,' inquit, 'Museti,
cum mulieres quas amantissime semper observaris, et imprimis
Dorotheam propter morum et studiorum similitudinem, merita
laude minime fraudasti adeo ut ipsa nostra Victoria, in hoc tuo
tam vehementi sermone, memoria prope exciderit! Sed habetote

transitory and fleeting, so developed her subtle and acute mind through literature, and so attuned her behavior to take account of the dignity proper to a married woman, with virtues, jests, and witticisms, that to many people she appears far more agreeable than her daughter Caterina,[154] who is amiable and learned and in her prime."

"This Dorotea, I say, is truly a gift of the gods. She graciously 124 promotes good poets, by whom she herself in turn is pleasantly courted and held dear. But she bore the death of her husband with such dignity that when you, Giovio, by reason of your compassion and sense of responsibility, had drawn near to comfort her in her grief as she was sitting on a couch of mourning, and you'd produced philosophical passages that were not commonplaces, you discovered that once her tears had dried and after extended conversation, she had been strengthened by rational reflection—so much so that you marveled that she had anticipated all your remedies in her courageous mind. And after that you had more difficulty restraining the tears of her father-in-law, Matteo,[155] both a venerable man and an eminent philosopher by profession, since as yet he'd found no remedies that even slightly soothed the rawness of his grief. For this reason, I think that the highest honor must be bestowed upon this woman—that is, leaving aside Vittoria Colonna, whom I always exclude with very good reason, on account of the wonderful combination in her of the most outstanding virtues. That is why in my judgment she must surely be picked out at once from the multitude of women and deservedly introduced into the foremost ranks of the best males."

In response D'AVALOS said, "At last, Muscettola: you've revealed 125 your loyalties, since you've not in the slightest cheated of deserved praise the women whom you've always most lovingly kept your eye on—and especially Dorotea, on account of the similarity in her character and studies to yours—but in so doing, in such forceful words, you've almost forgotten our very own Vittoria! You may be

pro constanti Iuliam Gonzagam quae Vespasiano Columnae nupta
est, puellam toto oris et corporis habitu prope divinam, harum
amitarum suarum famam ac nomen obscuraturam si in urbanam
lucem indulgentia coniugis proferatur. Nam simul ac Neapolitani
eam videbunt, morem certe Persarum imitabuntur qui, cum ori-
entem tantum solem suppliciter adorent, eum ad occiduas incli-
nantem partes et lucem ad Antipodas deferentem ita negligunt ut
nullo cultu et nullo vel exiguo honore dignum putent.

126   'Vidi enim eam nuper ad traiectum Minturnarum. Dii immortales, qui flos aetatis! Quae et quam iucunda proceritas! Qui totius
oris et cervicis candor! Quae laterum et lacertorum et membrorum
denique omnium venustas! Quae sermonis alacritas promptitudo
simplicitas! Ea neque habiliorem Dianam neque Venerem ipsam
formosiorem aut dulciorem esse putatote. Ingenio atque sermonibus severos capit, oculis undique spicula contorquet, motu corporis in omnes partes igniculos iacit, ac cum omnia apte atque decenter dicat et faciat, ante omnia tamen[347] longe elegantissime choreas
ducit, in quibus sive gravius ac numerosius incedendum sive lasci-
vius ac incitatius saltandum sit, cuncti chordarum moduli erudito
gestu in admirationem summae artis exprimuntur.'

127   Tum ego ⟨IOVIUS⟩ inquam, 'Davale, talem eam esse alias audi-
veram ut eam omnium si sucosior habitus accessisset, venustissi-
mam evasuram crederemus, ut referre solebat Pyrrhus eius frater,
eruditus imprimis et suavissimus iuvenis, quem benignitate pontificis cooptari in numerum cardinalium suis ac Federici patrui meritis audimus. Verum is, ut frater, de sororis laudibus aliquanto
parcius loquebatur ita ut haec omnia singillatim enumerando ut in

certain that Giulia Gonzaga,[156] who is Vespasiano Colonna's wife and a young girl nearly divine in the entire demeanor of her face and body, will eclipse the reputation and good name of those paternal aunts of hers, if her husband should indulge her by allowing her out in public. For as soon as they see her in Naples, they will surely imitate the custom of the Persians, who worship the sun as it's rising but ignore it as it inclines toward the western regions, carrying light to the antipodes, thinking it worthy of no reverence nor even the slightest honor.

"I saw her recently at the river crossing near Minturno. My 126 God, what blooming youth! How delightfully tall she is! How shining white are her face and neck! What beauty there is in her flanks and arms and indeed in all her limbs! What liveliness, promptness, and candor of speech! You cannot believe that Diana is more nimble, nor Venus herself more beautiful or charming. By her brilliance and her way of speaking, she takes stern men captive. She launches arrows everywhere with her eyes; she throws off sparks in all directions with the movement of her body. And although nothing she says and does lacks propriety and good taste, above all else she dances in what is by far the most elegant fashion. In these dances, whether one needs to promenade with deliberation and due measure or leap about playfully and swiftly, all modulations of the lute's strings are expressed with skilled movement in a marvel of high artistry."

Then I [GIOVIO] said: "D'Avalos, I had heard before that she's 127 the sort of woman who, if she weren't so thin, we'd trust to become an extremely beautiful woman, as Pirro, her brother, used to relate. We've heard that he, an exceptionally learned and very charming young man, is being elevated to the cardinalate by the kindness of the pope, owing to the youth's own merits and those of his uncle, Federico.[157] But as a brother, he used to be a bit too stingy in singing his sister's praises, with the result that by enumerating all these things singly he corroborates to us, his friends,

461

tenera aetate non maturuisse, sed certe propinqua esse summae dignitati, nobis familiaribus confirmaret.

128   'Duae etiam Sanseverinae sorores cum ab ipsa stirpe illustri tum ab excellenti etiam forma nobilitatem ferunt: Catarina Federico Caietano nupta et Maria, Henrici Ursini Nolani reguli uxor, cuius laudes adaugent mirifica studia Etruscarum litterarum et eximia benignitas hospitalis, quam regia liberalitate hac praesertim aestate in Neapolitanos cives exercuit, qui pestiferis Neapoli in populum omnem vulgatis morbis, sese Nolam periculi metu contulissent. Sunt et aliae duae Sanseverinae sorores: Aurelia, eximia facie et moribus luculentis, et Ariadna quae, marito extincto, multis lacessentibus procis, in tristi orbitate pertinacissime permansit.'

129   Tum vero sermonem abrumpens DAVALUS: 'Abstineto,' inquit, 'Museti, ab iis quae minime sunt dignae ut in angusta prima classe collocentur, et aequabilem institutae rationis tenorem observato. Nam si tuae libidini et tuis illis erga omnes formosas et eruditas flagrantibus studiis obsequamur, prius dies ipse deficiet quam tibi mulieres omnino deficiant quae merito cum honore numerandae et laudandae[348] videantur? Magna siquidem iniuria Venetis inferetur, Etruscisque item atque Liguribus apud quas multo plures formae gloria virtutibusque florere credendum est, quam[349] ipse Iovius anguste eas et lectissimas tantum recensendo longe parcissime laudarit? Consurgent et ante alias ipsae meae Insubres iusto contumeliae dolore compulsae, quarum ornatissimarum atque nobilium adeo magnus est numerus ut ea obrutus multitudine vix quattuor tantum et eas quidem mihi notissimas cum laude sim prosecutus.'

that at her tender age she hasn't ripened; but surely she approaches the highest rank of beauty.

"Also, two Sanseverino sisters display nobility both by their il- 128
lustrious lineage and by their outstanding beauty: Caterina,[158] the wife of Federico Caetani;[159] and Maria,[160] the wife of Enrico Orsini,[161] the ruler of Nola. Increasing the praises of Maria are her marvelous enthusiasm for Tuscan literature and her exceptional kindness as a host, which she exercised with regal liberality toward Neapolitan citizens, especially in that summer when the plague had spread among the entire populace of Naples, and out of fear of that danger people had betaken themselves to Nola. There are also two other Sanseverino sisters: Aurelia,[162] endowed with exceptional beauty and excellent character; and Andriana[163] who, after her husband died, although pressed by many suitors, has persisted tenaciously in sorrowful widowhood."

But then D'AVALOS, cutting the speech short, said: "Muscettola, 129
keep away from those women who aren't at all worthy to be placed in the narrow first class, and stick to the even tenor of our established procedure. For if we should gratify your fancy and these passionate enthusiasms of yours for all beautiful and learned women, daylight will run out on you before you run out of those who appear to deserve honor and praise. And thus a great injury will be caused to the Venetians and Tuscans and likewise to the Ligurians—among whom, it must be believed, there are many more beauties flourishing in fame and virtuous qualities than those whom Giovio himself praised sparingly while passing them in a cursory review, and even then only the most select of them. And these Insubrians of mine[164] are going to rise up in protest before other women, moved by justified pain at the affront. The number of surpassingly honorable and noble women among them is so great that, overwhelmed by that multitude, I've honored with praise scarcely four, and those indeed very well known to me."

130   'Ergo,' inquit MUSETIUS, ut ex rubore videbatur vehementer inflammatus, 'si cunctarum Italiae urbium haec nostra Neapolis formosarum et nobilissimarum mulierum feracior exsistit, neque numerum excedere neque virtutum pondera coaequare neque tantam fertilitatem in magnis excessibus conferre licebit? Quae malum enim ratio est eas silentio praeteriisse quae, si illustres ii dicionum tituli et decora illa vel magistratuum vel subiectorum oppidorum cognomina a principalibus feminis, quod dii avertant, una fortunae conversione detergeantur, profecto istae eae ut vultis secundae classis, et per se nobiles erunt et forma conspicuae et totis elegantis vitae moribus illustratae. Porro, si Iovio, quae sua est eximia pietas et officiosa memoria, aliquot non modo lurida macie carieque consumptas, sed morte ipsa penitus exstinctas licuit laudare, hoc, viri benignissimi, humanioribus studiis meis non dederitis, ut non modo vivas sed maxime etiam florentes quas colam et dignissimas putem, [non] nominem vel in transcursu et, ut pictores sine apparatu solent, solo saltem carbone absque ullis omnino coloribus depingam?'

131   Ad id ego ⟨IOVIUS⟩ inquam 'Progredere ut libet, Museti, et cunctis ut soles ambitiosius etiam fave, modo, ut recipis te facturum, pigmenta variis intrita conchis et scutellis et molliores penicilli ad opus faciundum minime deferantur. Quamquam illi tui peracuti carbones multum certe et scite quidem luminum contrahant, et contra, ut oportet, satis umbrarum explicent ut non magnopere colorum asciticias[350] amoenitates desiderent qui unam vim naturae diligentius expressam sine ullis lascivioribus velamentis admirantur.'

132   'Igitur,' inquit MUSETIUS, 'qua voce Lucretiae Scaleoniae venustatem[351] cum singulari proceritate[352] coniunctam laudaverim? Qua

"Well then," said MUSCETTOLA — and he looked flushed and 130
angry — "if, of all the cities in Italy, this Naples of ours is especially
fertile in producing the most beautiful and noble women, will it
not be permissible to extend their number or to do justice to the
weight of their virtues, or to discuss their great fertility in long
digressions? What the devil is the reason for passing over them in
silence? Even if, heaven forfend, one upheaval of fortune should
strip from princely women their illustrious titles to dominions and
their honors in magistracies or subject cities, surely these you
speak of — those of the second class, if you want to put it that
way — are noble on their own account, conspicuous in beauty, and
embellished with all the virtuous habits of an elegant life. Moreover, if Giovio, out of great loyalty and dutiful memory, has been
allowed to praise some women who not only have wasted away
with thinness and decay, but have actually died, wouldn't you,
most obliging of men, allow it to my even kindlier zeal to mention
by name in a cursory fashion those women who are not only living
but also flourishing brilliantly, whom I honor and think most worthy, or at least to portray them, as painters are accustomed to doing when without their kit, using only charcoal, without any
color?"

To this I [GIOVIO] said: "Go on as you please, Muscettola, and 131
even treat all of them, as you usually do, with lavish display — but
only provided that you agree that you won't bring in pigments
crushed from various shells in shallow bowls[165] and soft paint-
brushes to do the work — although these extremely fine charcoals
of yours may be capable of an assured and expert chiaroscuro, as is
fitting, so that those who admire the strength alone of nature, expressed quite accurately yet without any more sensual coverings,
do not much miss the borrowed charms of colors."

"Well, then," said MUSCETTOLA, "with what language ought I 132
to praise Lucrezia Scaglione's[166] beauty, conjoined with her remarkable height? With what eloquence ought I to extol the charms of

465

facundia pulcherrimi oris, radiantium luminum, exactissimi corporis, et iucundissimi animi veneres extulerim? Quae vel uno eo argumento tantae exsistunt ut iis facile capti irretitique iuvenes pro ea vel stolide mori non dubitent, ut modo vidimus in A. Sommeio insigni equitum praefecto, qui cum amore vecors, viro nuper orbatam et quartanae etiam morbo laborantem misere deperiret; neque illa alias aestuanti nisi pudicas aures praeberet, ita intemperanter eius corpori est insidiatus ut intempesta nocte e summo ipsius matronae tecto, a fune suspensus ad fenestram eius cubiculi se demitteret ut per eam sibi aditum ad eius lectum moliretur. Sed miser[353] dum alternis genibus, obseratas propellit fores, fallente vestigio, praeceps ab alto corruit ita ut eius foedus et miserabilis interitus, nobilem materiam Neapolitanis poetis attulerit.'

133   Tum vero ego ⟨IOVIUS⟩ inquam, 'Museti, promissis est standum, in quorum limine defuisse pudendum videtur. Pigmentis enim, et lascivo etiam penicillo (ne dicam carbonibus), non modo corporis ac animorum habitus, sed etiam amorum infelicium eventus properanti illa tua manu figurantur. Sed hoc lectissimae feminae prolixius detur, cuius humanitati non modo tu ipse, assiduus elegantiarum eius omnium contemplator, sed ego plane peregrinus repente obnoxius sim effectus, cum ex quartana decumbentem visitassem atque illa tum recentem ac acerbissimum Sommei casum, quo pudor ipsius ab omni calumnia praeclare esset redemptus moderatissimis sermonibus enarrasset.'

her exceedingly pretty face, shining eyes, perfect body, and most delightful disposition? This one example shows that these charms are so powerful that young men, readily captivated and ensnared by them, do not hesitate to die (and quite foolishly) for her, as we have seen just now in the case of A. di Somma,[167] the famous cavalry commander. Crazed with amorous desire, he was desperately dying of love for that woman, who was recently widowed and was also sick with quartan fever, but while he burned with lust for her, she offered nothing but chaste ears to him. So unrestrainedly was he lying in ambush for her body that, in the dead of night, hanging from a rope from that matron's lofty rooftop, he lowered himself to her bedroom window so that he might gain access to her bed. But while the unfortunate man was banging against the window shutters with one knee and then the other, he lost his foothold and fell headfirst to the ground from on high. His disgraceful and wretched death has provided great material for Neapolitan poets."

But then I [GIOVIO] interjected, "Muscettola, you must adhere   133
to what we have promised; right at the beginning you seem to have shamefully failed, for that agile hand of yours is fashioning with colors and also with a playful brush—and not with charcoals—not only conditions of body and states of mind, but also the results of unhappy loves. Still, we should allow a more expansive treatment to a surpassingly worthy woman, to whose kindness and nobility not only you yourself, assiduous as an observer of all elegances, but I, an obvious foreigner, was suddenly rendered vulnerable when I had visited her as she was lying ill with quartan fever. At that time she had related in detail, in very carefully controlled speech, the recent, bitter misfortune of di Somma, by which her very own modesty had been splendidly rescued from every calamity."

134 Tum vero ille ⟨MUSETIUS⟩ festinantius inquit, 'Iovi, ceteras percurram, nam si in Scaleonia longior fuisse sum visus, id accidit, quoniam te nihil de inusitato Sommei interitu audivisse arbitrabar.'

135 Hoc[354] loco subridens DAVALUS 'Sit hoc ut dicis,' inquit, 'in causa, Museti, modo tuum illud vetus studium ac obsequium ne dicamus amorem erga humanissimam mulierem infitiari minime videare.'

136 Tum vero MUSETIUS 'Parce' inquit, 'Davale, parce, cum meae tum Scaleoniae famae, ne honesta nomina temere iuvenilibus fabulis inferantur. Non enim edepol ad ipsum amorum meorum scopum his tuis iaculis rectissime colliniasti.[355] Ceterum ad alias obiter pergam.

137 'Est etiam egregiae formae et cordatae mansuetudinis decus in Aemylia Petro Antonio Caraffae, strenuo et iucundissimo nobilium alae signifero nupta. Portiam Blanciam magnopere cohonestant praeter ipsam suaviter et perite canendi iucunditatem capilli perlucentes, decentissimae[356] papillae, et in molliore tripudio motus laterum exquisitus. Fuit in fama et celebritate Violantilla Sangria cum nuberet, in qua est ocellorum nigrorum argutia singularis, multusque lepos et multa eruditio elegantiarum, quae ab Ariadna matre, virtute ornatissima, deduxit.

138 'In Isabella Gualandia, ille niveus color illeque mollior sucus, ab tanta fecunditate nequaquam decoxit, elucetque in ea minime fucata facie, caeruleorum oculorum obtutus, perblandae et castae benignitatis clarissimus testis.[357] Sed nec alteram siluerim Isabellam cognomento Bresenniam, quamquam ea, parentibus orta Hispanis et Hispano nupta, minime Neapolitana esse videatur. Est enim in ea tenera admodum puella, ipso Cupidine digna facies, munditiae praecellentes, tanta vero comitas cum singulari artis

But then MUSCETTOLA said rather hurriedly, "Giovio, let me   134
rush through the other women, for if I've seemed rather long-
winded in the matter of Scaglione, that happened because I was
thinking you'd heard nothing about di Somma's unusual demise."

At this point, D'AVALOS, smiling, said: "We accept what you   135
say in your own defense, Muscettola, provided you don't deny your
longstanding devotion and deference toward, not to say love for,
an exceedingly refined woman."

But then MUSCETTOLA said, "D'Avalos, spare both my reputa-   136
tion and Scaglione's, lest honorable names be recklessly injured by
youthful gossip. In fact you haven't aimed any too accurately at the
true target of my loves with these darts of yours, by God. Anyhow,
let me proceed to treat cursorily the other women.

"The adornment of outstanding beauty and prudent gentle-   137
ness is also found in Emilia,[168] the wife of Pietro Antonio Carafa,
the vigorous and highly congenial standard-bearer of the cavalry
squadron of the nobles. Combining to grant high honors to Porzia
Brancia,[169] aside from the true delights of her sweet and expert
singing, are her radiant hair, well-proportioned breasts, and the
exquisite movement of her body in the calmer dances. Violantilla
di Sangro[170] was famous and renowned when she was engaged to
be wed. She has a remarkable wit, the most charming dark little
eyes, and extensive training in refined manners, which she derived
from her mother Adriana,[171] an exceedingly virtuous woman.

"Isabella Gualandi's[172] great fertility hasn't at all diminished her   138
snowy complexion and gentle vitality; and from her face, which
has not been made up at all, there shines forth the gaze of her blue
eyes, a most illustrious witness to her charming and chaste benevolence. But I ought not to have kept silent about the other Isabella, whose last name is Brisegna,[173] even though she, born to
Spanish parents and married to a Spaniard, might seem not at all
to be Neapolitan. For in that tenderest of girls are a face worthy of
Cupid himself, surpassing elegance, and so much courtesy coupled

musicae peritia coniuncta, ut nihil eius ingenio ac forma suavius esse iudicemus.'

139   Tum vero ⟨IOVIUS⟩ inquam, 'Museti, postquam ad Hispanas usque descendis, scilicet voluptatis illecebris deductus, quonam in loco velut inter obscuras Cassandra Marchesia relinquetur, quam certe nonnullis iunioribus praetulerim?[358] Residet enim in oculis eius peramoenus quidam vigor, in eo etiam aetatis flexu, remanetque[359] candidior habitus. Verba eius autem Atticos[360] lepores redolent, et[361] mores expoliti libertatem ingenua matrona dignissimam, quibus rebus et fratris poetae Balthasaris et Actii Synceri nostri musas humaniter refovit, et ad praeclare canendum saepius excitavit.'

140   Tum vero DAVALUS: 'Satis superque et ambitiose quidem ab utroque vestrum Neapolitanarum gloriae video satisfactum; verum sol ad serum diei iam proclinatus te Iovi praesertim admonet, ut de Romanis aliqua augustae urbis amplitudine et maiestate digna proloquare, si ullae iam sunt incolumes, earum feminarum quae ante luctuosissimam cladem dignitate atque opibus et pulchritudine ac integra pudicitiae fama claruerunt.'

141   Ad id ego alte suspirans, 'Praestabo,' inquam, '"vel in gemitu," quod potero, ut vobis expetentibus mos geratur. Sed qua tranquillitate iucundioris animi, quave, ut operaepretium[362] foret, exsultantis ingenii alacritate, tot laudes totque decora Romanarum heroidum merito celebranda retulero, cum urbs ipsa ab augusta

with unusual expertise in the art of music that we believe that nothing is more delightful than her beauty and brilliance."

But then I [GIOVIO] said, "Muscettola, now that, evidently 139 drawn down by the enticements of pleasure, you're stooping all the way to Spanish women, in what place—perhaps even among women of no distinction?—will Cassandra Marchese[174] be left, whom certainly I would prefer to some younger women? For even in the stooped-over condition of old age, there is in her eyes a certain delightful vigor, and there persists a quite dazzling appearance. Moreover, her speech smacks of Greek oratorical charm, and her polished manners have the scent of that freedom most worthy of a freeborn matron. By these things, she has fostered anew in a generous way the poetic talents both of her brother, Baldassar,[175] and of our friend Sannazaro; and quite often she has stirred them to splendid compositions."

Next D'AVALOS said, "Doubtless enough attention and more, 140 even importunate attention, has been given to the glory of these Neapolitan women of yours, I see. But the sun, having now inclined toward a late hour of the day, admonishes you especially, Giovio, that you say some things about the Roman women who are worthy of the eminence and majesty of that venerable city— if there remain safe and sound any of those women who, before the most grievous of calamities, shone forth with dignity and wealth, as well as with beauty and an unblemished reputation for modesty."

At this, sighing deeply, I [GIOVIO] said: "I will answer, 'even in 141 a groan,' to the best of my ability so as to indulge your request. But how shall I be able to relate with a calm and pleasant attitude or a ready and dancing wit, enough to make the effort worthwhile, the many achievements and virtues of Roman heroines that deserve to be celebrated, at a time when that same city—by far the

semper dignitate longe omnium florentissima, atque illud paullo ante fortunatissimum sacrosancti imperii et Christianae religionis domicilium nefariae libidini cesserit atque inauditae crudelitati immanissimorum barbarorum? Qui inexplebili rabie supra omnem militiae morem vel humanitatis consuetudinem efferati, nullis corporibus, nullis fortunis, nullis denique deorum[363] immortalium delubris, vel mortuorum etiam sepulchris, pepercerunt, quin cuncta crudeli caede, immanibus suppliciis[364] et ruinis exsecrandis affligerent, et ad satietatem barbarae feritatis everterent.

142   'Verum in tanto luctu nos omnino consolari possunt illae ipsae, de quibus dicturi sumus, illustres feminae, quoniam aut absentes tot mala dirae calamitatis corporibus suis non senserint; aut, si quas inopinata clades in urbe deprehendit, illae aut egregiis praesidiis effusoque omni auro aut felici fuga[365] libertatem ac pudorem defenderint. Neque enim hoc loco dicendum est de iis quae, urbe capta, saevientibus undique barbaris, cum essent de una tantum castitate sollicitae ut ab imminentibus contumeliis corpora atque animos liberarent, quod certe Romanum fuit aut ab altis fenestris sese praecipites dederunt, aut propriis manibus ferro pudica pectora traiecerunt.'

143   Tum vero DAVALUS 'Vera,' inquit, 'narras, Iovi, nec te supra aequum tantae publicae iniuriae iustissimus dolor exagitat: nam innumerabilia — et ea quidem *Historiis* tuis dignissima — obstinatae ac inexpugnabilis pudicitiae exempla de Romanis mulieribus in exercitu recitantur, ita ut hanc nimis secundam fortunam plurimum detester quae, dum nostris intemperantius favet, eo immanium scelerum adegerit ut aliquando condignas nefariis[366] maleficiis poenas omnibus luendas credam.

most illustrious of all in its eternal and majestic dignity and the most fortunate dwelling place of sacrosanct authority and of the Christian religion — has yielded to the wicked caprice and unheard-of cruelty of the most monstrous barbarians? Savage with insatiable frenzy, beyond every norm of military conduct or custom of humanity, they spared no bodies, no fortunes, and indeed no churches — nor even the tombs of the dead — wreaking havoc everywhere with cruel slaughter, savage tortures, and the accursed destruction of buildings, sacking everything so as to sate their barbarous wildness.

"Yet even in the deepest mourning, these very illustrious women, 142 about whom we are going to speak, can greatly console us — either because, being absent, they did not experience in their bodies those many horrible misfortunes; or because, if unforeseen slaughter did overtake them, they preserved their freedom and chastity either by exceptionally strong garrisons and by giving up all their gold, or by a lucky escape. But we mustn't speak about those women who, once the city had been taken and the savage barbarians were everywhere, were so anxious about chastity alone that they delivered their bodies and minds from impending disgrace — assuredly a Roman characteristic — for either they threw themselves headfirst from high windows or with their own hands they thrust a sword through their pure chests."

Then D'AVALOS said: "What you say is true, Giovio, and the 143 grief from this great collective injury that so angers you is entirely justified and reasonable: for innumerable instances of resolute and impregnable chastity — things, indeed, worthy of your *Histories* — are told in the army about Roman women, so that I curse most that all too propitious fortune which, in favoring us to such an intemperate degree, drove us to such savage crimes. I do believe that at some time we shall have to suffer punishments — fully earned — in atonement for all our wicked offenses.

144 'Et certe, non putabam tanti esse Romae pudicitiam, quoniam ea tot antistitibus opulentis et tot ditibus inquilinis qui uxores non haberent et prodige lascivirent maxime prostrata diceretur. Memini enim cum Romae essem, et in Aurelianum[367] templum infinitae prope feminae religionis causa coivissent, earumque ora pervenusta pudicosque habitus admirarer, ab amicis qui me deducebant esse interrogatum an ex eo numero ulla prae aliis placeret; nam eam haud multo cum labore vel pretio in complexus meos esse perducturos. Neque id professis fides defuit, ita ut arbitrarer me brevi tempore haud inani coniectura si libidini paruissem, magnam illarum multitudinem esse corrupturum.'

145 Ad id ego ⟨iovius⟩ inquam: 'Davale, falleris et a lenonibus perpulchre[368] deciperis, si Romanas honestasque matronas fuisse existimas, quas illi ludibundis oculis lenones tuis[369] obtulerint. Neque enim palla obscurior, neque linteum a cervice per terga demissum, neque modestior incessus, neque oculi pudenter deiecti, Romanam efficiunt. Sunt enim ii toti habitus promiscue etiam inquilinis et scortis concessi, tametsi illud nuper Clemens lata lege prohibuerit. Eo siquidem cultu tamquam pudentiore[370] magnopere gaudent meretrices, quarum urbs tota plenissima semper fuit, quoniam ex[371] eo facilius atque lepidius advenarum crumenis insidiantur.

146 'Romanarum feminarum sunt tres classes, ut etiam totius populi quondam fuit. In prima collocantur heroides clarissimis ortae natalibus ac ipsis proceribus nuptae, quae sex domibus omnino concluduntur, Columnia scilicet Ursina Sabella Comite Caesarina Farnesia. In secunda autem sunt patriciae familiae, quae longo stemmate nobilissimas ab antiquis stirpibus origines ducunt.

"To be sure, I didn't suppose that the purity of Rome was 144
worth all that much, inasmuch as it was said to have been pro-
foundly debased by so many wealthy bishops and so many rich
visitors who didn't have wives and were leading extravagantly dissolute lives. I remember a time when I was at Rome, and a nearly
infinite number of women were flocking into the Aurelian church
for a religious service. As I was admiring their pretty faces and
chaste attire, the friends who were showing me around asked
whether, out of that number, one woman might particularly please
me, for without much effort or expense they could soon bring her
into my embraces. The people who made this claim were perfectly
credible, and it was not vain to suppose that if I gave in to lust, in
a short time I might have seduced a large number of them."

To this I [GIOVIO] said: "D'Avalos, you are mistaken, and the 145
pimps have splendidly deceived you, if you suppose that the
women they'd put before your frisky eyes were honorable Roman
matrons. For neither a dark mantle nor a linen cloth hanging
down from the neck behind nor a more decorous gait nor eyes
lowered modestly makes a woman Roman. All those styles of
dress have been conceded indiscriminately to noncitizen residents
as well as to whores, despite the fact that Clement VII recently
introduced a law prohibiting just that. The prostitutes, of whom
the entire city has always been chock full, are delighted to wear
this more modest style of dress, since using it they may ambush
the money purses of foreigners the more easily and charmingly.

"Of the Roman women, there are three classes, as formerly 146
there were in the entire population as well. In the first are placed
together the heroines born from very distinguished lineages and
those who married noble scions. These women are contained in
six houses in all: the Colonna, obviously, and the Orsini, Savelli,
Conti, Cesarini, and Farnese. Then, in the second class are patrician families, very noble because of their lengthy pedigree,
who trace their origins from an ancient lineage. Then come the

Reliquae porro sunt obscuriores vel insiticiae, quae nullam adhuc vetustatis vel opulentiae opinionem ceperunt.

147 'De primis cum claritate generis et magnitudine opum et praestantia animi ceteras antecedant, nefas esse puto de earum pudicitia disceptare, quando eam tantis virtutibus coniunctam esse minime dubitemus. At tertiam classem non modo ex faece illa Romuli pervetusta, sed Gothorum externarumque gentium colluvie, quae gentes evastatam totiens urbem incoluerint, constare putatote. Sanguis enim ille, variis affinitatibus permixtus, varios effinxit mores. Non linguarum siquidem unus et idem est sonus, non vestis, non convictus, non eadem pudicitiae cura, non idem prope deorum immortalium cultus, cum patriis addicti religionibus peculiares quosdam minores divos, ignotos aliis, venerentur. Habitant tamen in universum in propriis urbis regionibus, in quibus videmus xenodochia cum templis et gratuitas hospitales domos egregia et salutari pietate a peregrinis gentibus esse constitutas.

148 'Incolunt Hispani fere omnes Candidi Putei regionem; Galli et Germani ad Flor⟨a⟩e[372] Campum extenduntur; Illyricae gentes in Campo Martio coiverunt; Graeci Quirinalem tenent Collem; Langobardis, de nomine eorum cum platea sedes est ad curiam Caesaris; Iudei, a Capitolinis radicibus theatroque Marcelli ad Tullianum carcerem et ripam Tiberis, cuncta occuparant. In Transtiberina vero regione, Corsorum et Sardorum coloniam positam esse videmus. Britanni Pannonii Sarmatae certa quoque habent domicilia, sicut et Armenii ac Aethiopes, qui Vaticanas figlinas inhabitant. Sicut quemadmodum Romanus populus, magnis peregrinorum

remaining ones, who hitherto have garnered no reputation for antiquity or for opulence and are of humbler origin or of foreign blood.

"Women of the first two classes surpass the rest in renown of 147 family, greatness of wealth, and outstanding excellence of mind. I think it is forbidden to debate about their chastity, inasmuch as we shouldn't doubt at all that it has been conjoined to great virtues. But believe you me, the third class is composed not only of those ancient dregs of Romulus, but also of the foul sewage of Goths and of the foreign peoples which have taken up residence in the oft-devastated city. For that blood, indiscriminately mixed through a variety of marriage relations, has produced a variety of moral characters. Accordingly, the sound of their tongues is not one and the same, nor are their clothes, nor their way of life. Nor do they show the same degree of concern about chastity, and their worship of the gods is quite different because, enslaved to their ancestral religions, they venerate certain lesser deities unknown to others. Nonetheless, they live entirely in their own particular regions of the city, where we see that, with outstanding and salutary piety, foreigners have established inns for pilgrims along with churches and free accommodation for guests.

"Nearly all the Spaniards live in the region of the White Well.[176] 148 The French and Germans dwell in an area extending to the Campo de' Fiori. The Albanians have assembled in the Campo Marzio, and the Greeks hold the Quirinal Hill. For the Lombards, the base is along the street bearing their name, by Julius Caesar's senate house. The Jews have occupied the entire area from the bases of the Capitoline Hill and the Theater of Marcellus to the Tullian prison[177] and the bank of the Tiber. In Trastevere, moreover, we see that a colony of Corsicans and Sardinians has been established. The Britons, Hungarians, and Sarmatians also have certain haunts, just as also do the Armenians and Ethiopians who inhabit the Vatican pottery works. Just as the Roman people always flour-

ingeniis atque virtutibus, semper effloruit, ita cunctarum quoque nationum ac Italiae praesertim urbium eieticiae sordes excrementaque omnia Romam, tamquam in unam sentinam, confluxerint.

149 'Hinc est illa feminarum venalium impudica multitudo, quae occupatis et in caelibatu viventibus morigerari consuevit, dum saepe habitum probatissimarum atque nobilium mentiretur. Inter quas aliquamdiu principatum obtinuit Lucretia Claricia, in quota parte absolutae dignitatis stirpem Troiani sanguinis iactare solita. Quae, cum venustate oris et delicatis corporis lasciviis et ingenio Etrusce et Latine ad admirationem erudito, amplissimas opes esset consecuta, dum urbs caperetur, et ornatum omnem totamque illam lautissimam supellectilem quaestu corporis quaesitam puncto temporis amississet, vocem[373] cum pudica tum Romana dignam edidit: quod diceret nihil se tantarum rerum iactura commoveri, postquam incolumi pudore sese e[374] manibus praedantium eripuisset.

150 'In secunda vero classe, quae inter hanc plebeiam et illam longe clarissimam media consistit, haud dubie pudor habitat. Et modestia et integritas, et honestae artes et sana religio, et veteres denique illae Romanae virtutes enitescunt. Habentur eae domi admodum severe et frugaliter, nec studere deliciis et musicis artibus, nec mollioribus litteris operam dare permittuntur. Viri Romani etenim animo sunt erga feminas subagresti truculento suspicaci, ita ut in eas haud cunctanter animadvertant, si ulla vel obscura libidinis vestigia deprehenderint. Fit enim saepe ut non modo uxores ab iratis viris, sed matres ab impiis filiis, et sorores ab immanibus

ished by making use of the great talents and virtues of foreigners, so also the ones born defective, the dregs, and all the excrement of all nations and especially of the cities of Italy have drained into Rome as into a single hull, filled with bilgewater.

"Next, there is that shameless multitude of women for hire. 149 Although they've grown accustomed to gratifying men whose employment dictates that they not marry, these women often affect the demeanor of the most upright and noble. Among these, Lucrezia da Clarice[178] for some time secured pride of place. She was in the habit of boasting about the dignity that the substantial Trojan blood in her lineage had conferred upon her. She acquired immense wealth thanks to her beautiful face and the wanton lasciviousness of her body, and by a mind trained in Tuscan and Latin that elicited admiration.[179] Then Rome was sacked, and in an instant she had lost every adornment and all her sumptuous furniture acquired by the marketing of her flesh. Still, she uttered words worthy of a woman both chaste and Roman: she was not at all upset, she said, by the loss of her great possessions, since she had managed to escape from the hands of the brigands with her female honor intact.

"But in the second class—the mean which occupies the place 150 between the plebeian and the other, far more illustrious class —where doubtless female honor dwells, there shine forth modesty and integrity, both honorable arts and sober religious observance, and, finally, those ancient Roman virtues. With complete strictness and austerity these women are kept at home, and they are allowed neither to sink energy into pleasures and the musical arts nor to give attention to literature of a more amorous nature. The fact is that Roman men have such a crude, harsh, and mistrustful attitude toward women that they punish them without any hesitation if they have discovered any traces, however obscure, of lustfulness. For it's often the case that not only wives who have been caught in the act by angry husbands, but also mothers caught

fratribus deprehensae, quod veneno tollere minime sit gloriosum, crudelissime[375] iugulentur.

151 'Quibus de causis Romanae patriciae eas non habent Etruscarum aut Latinarum litterarum et exquisitorum morum amoenitates, quibus et circumpadanae nostrae et Neapolitanae vestrae delectantur. Probroque etiam ducunt olevisse unguenta indica, et manus vel aquilonaribus diebus protexisse illis pelliceis[376] velamentis quae singulos digitos exprimunt, ut promiscue apud alios, ipsae etiam ancillae, uti consueverunt. Ceterum eis summa est gratia, in seminudis papillis et decoris illis vultibus, ad amoeniorem veneris et verecundiae lineam directis, quos aqueo et subtiliore fuco sic expoliunt ut artem dissimulent, ⟨nec⟩ negligunt etiam capillum, quem, in spiras tricarum capiti convolutum, linteis integunt latioribus, quae etiam per tergum demissa ab extremis angulis velorum more succinguntur. Inter colores usurpavere violaceum et nigrum, tamquam honestiores, nulla collo monilia, nulla auribus, nulla cinctui, nulla denique digitis, praeter semuncialis anuli sigillum, ornamenta conspiciuntur.

152 'Verum in solemni caerimoniarum apparatu et sponsalibus epulis, adeo sumptuose instrui ac exornari mos est, ut nulla sit paullo nobilior quae non aureae pallae purpuream laciniam superinducat, e raso villutove Serico vel Damasceno, acanthi[377] et florum capreolis figurato; aut manicas a cubito, et fascias item ubera sustinentes, Phrygiis operibus pictas, margaritis undique fulgentibus, non ostentet. At oculis, quibus eximium nec simulatum quidem

by disloyal sons, and sisters by savage brothers, are most cruelly butchered, since to do them in by poison would not be at all glorious.

"For these reasons, Roman patrician women don't possess those 151 amenities of Tuscan and Latin literature and of refined manners by which both our women of the Po River valley and your Neapolitan women are amused. They regard it as disgraceful if they give off the scent of Indian ointments and if they protect their hands, even on days when the north wind blows, with those leather gloves that are tailored for each individual finger, the sort that elsewhere are worn indiscriminately, even by maidservants. But for these women, their greatest attraction lies in their half-naked breasts and those faces of theirs that they arrange to give a pleasant mien, neither lustful nor excessively modest but somewhere in between, and on which they daub moisturizer and more subtle colorings, while concealing their artifice. Nor do they neglect their hair either, which, wrapped into coiling tangles on their heads, they cover with broad linen bands. Hanging down across the back, these too are gathered up from the far corners like veils. Among the colors which they have usurped are violet and black, as if they were of higher social standing. No necklaces are visible, nor jewelry for the ears or the waistband or for the fingers, excepting a half-ounce signet ring.

"But when they dress up for important ceremonies and for wed- 152 ding banquets, the custom is to be expensively attired and adorned to such an extent that no woman of above average rank wears a golden cloak that lacks a purple fringe out of shorn or brushed silk or of damask, decorated with the shapes of flowers and of tendrils of acanthus. Long sleeves that flare out from the elbow, and likewise the broad ribbons supporting their breasts, are embroidered with Phrygian workmanship, pearls shining forth from every side. But, using their eyes to display a modesty that is indeed excellent and even unfeigned—an astounding thing—they entice the men

praeferunt pudorem, quod certe mirum videtur, ad cupidineos oc-
cultiores nutus inevitabili quadam illecebra contuentes alliciunt.

153   'Ex hoc ordine secundo, plures simul aequales inter se et formae
singularis et praeclarae nobilitatis dotes ferunt e quibus aetatis viriditate maxime florent: Hersilia Cafarella, Petro Mellino nobilissimo actorum Romani senatus scriptori et poetae longe tenerrimo
nupta; et Tarquinia Iacobatia, Dominici Cardinalis, qui in calamitate captae urbis interiit †lx† patruelis filia.[378] Item Antonina Vel-
leia, quam Aloisius Mattucius coniunx, dum Roma diriperetur,
navigio feliciter in Galliam asportavit; et Portia Bonaventura, Antonio[379] Pallucello in matrimonium collocata.

154   'Viget et in plerisque aliis matronale decus et pertinax etiam
pulchritudo, cum vetustissimi generis nobilitate copulata, ut in
Paulina Portia, M. Marcello Laenae nupta; et Ioanna Casalia, Iacobi Crescentii honestissimi equitis uxore; et Iacobella Mancina,
cui coniunx est Paulus Tophius, vir consularis; et Gloria Galla
Pauli Blondi quae Blondo historico prosocero gloriatur; et Iulia
Alberina, quae Curtio Fregepanio, arte musica et carminum studio
iuveni ornatissimo,[380] ex Divi Gregorii Romani Pontificis progenie,
nupsit.

155   'Habent et uxores pari nobilitate ac insigni oris venustate: Hieronymam Saxiam, Iordanes Serlupius; Cynthiam Cossariam, Ae-
milius Capisuccus; et Lauram Pallosiam, Hieronymus Benibenius;
et quae his est aetate tenerior, Aloisiam e Rusticorum genere per-
vetusto, Vincentius Mattheus; et Camillam Micinellam, Domini-
cus Cabellerius, quae est ex progenie cum puellarum tum marium
eadem numerosa atque pulcherrima.'

beholding them, irresistibly alluring as they are, into making covert nods of amorous assent.

"In this second rank several women of about the same age are 153 endowed with special beauty and outstanding nobility, thanks to which they flourish greatly in the greenness of their youth. Consider Ersilia Caffarelli,[180] wife of Pietro Mellini, the noble scribe of the proceedings of the Roman civic government[181] and by far the best of love poets; and Tarquinia Jacobacci,[182] daughter of a cousin of Cardinal Domenico Jacobacci, who perished in the calamity of the Sack of Rome.[183] Also, there is Antonina Velli,[184] whom her husband, Luigi Matuzzi,[185] fortunately carried off by ship to France while Rome was being sacked. And there's Porzia Bonaventura, given in marriage to Antonio Paluzzelli.[186]

"There also lives on in most of the others a matronly propriety 154 and enduring beauty conjoined with the nobility of a very ancient family, as we see in Paolina Porcari,[187] wife of Marco Marcello Leni;[188] and in Giovanna Casali,[189] wife of the very high-ranking knight Giacomo Crescenzi; and in Giacovella Mancini,[190] whose husband is Paolo di Toffia,[191] a man of consular rank; and in Paolo Biondo's wife, Gloria Gallo,[192] who takes pride in her husband's grandfather, the historian Flavio Biondo; and Giulia Alberini,[193] who married Curzio Frangipane,[194] a young man highly distinguished in the art of music and in the study of poetry, and descended from the family of St. Gregory, the Roman pontiff.[195]

"The following men, too, have wives of equal nobility and strik- 155 ingly beautiful faces: Giordano Serlupi has Giroloma de' Sassi;[196] Emilio Capizucchi has Cinzia Cossaria;[197] Girolamo Beneimbene has Laura Palosci;[198] Vincenzo Mattei[199] has Ludovica,[200] from the very ancient de' Rustici family, who is younger than these others; and Domenico de' Cavalieri[201] has Camilla Miccinelli,[202] who is from a lineage that abounds in women and men of exceptional beauty."

156   Tum vero MUSETIUS, 'Perstricte,' inquit, 'Iovi, et properanter eae tuae Romanae recitantur. Earum enim singillatim morum et lineamentorum omnium colores et articulos, te ut modo in aliis urbibus facere solebas, expressurum putabamus; sed te, ut arbitramur, earum amplior numerus omnino deterruit.'

157   Ad id ego ⟨IOVIUS⟩ inquam: 'Has iuvat in transcursu nominasse, ut non modo feminarum, verum et ipsarum quoque familiarum, quae claritudine et vetustate ceteras antecellant, nomina nosceretis. Neque oportuit tot et tantas minutias in iis describendis[381] morosius consectari, quoniam in illis vel morum vel[382] elegantiarum nulla prope varietas deprehendatur, utpote quae unam et aequabilem disciplinae rationem sequantur, nec aliquem praeter propinquos ad colloquium admittere soleant, et procul a viris domi inter nutrices et ancillas versentur, quibuscum saepissime etiam[383] cibum tumultuarie capiunt. Neque enim eas viri ab quadam subrustica et minus benigna consuetudine vel mensa vel cubili continue dignantur—quamquam hic magnus et frequens advenarum nobilium concursus, eorum dico qui fortunas suas et familias in communi omnium gentium patria collocarunt, illos mores per humaniora commercia magna ex parte molliverit.

158   'Sed nec propterea quod multas nominarim, duas omnino viduas silebimus, quae mihi paucis ante annis magnopere placuerunt: Hieronymam scilicet Bubalam, cuius oculis nihil blandius, nihil sucoso illo habitu tenerius atque candidius, nihil ipsis munditiis limpidius videtur; et Cassandram Bonaventuram Portiae sororem, quae delicati oris venustate cunctas aetate mea superavit.'

159   Haec cum dixissem, 'Vellem,' inquit DAVALUS, 'mi Iovi, ut harum omnium pudicitiae fama non a te, verum ab aliquo minus

But then MUSCETTOLA said, "Giovio, these Roman women of   156
yours are also being listed too tersely and hastily. For we were supposing that you would limn the qualities and particular features of
each individually, as you were just doing in the case of other cities,
but we think that the greater number of the Roman women has
utterly deterred you."

To this I [GIOVIO] said: "I like to mention them in passing, in   157
order that you might learn the names not only of the women but
also of their families, which surpass all the others in renown and
in their antiquity. Nor has it been necessary in describing them to
hunt out numerous minute details fastidiously, inasmuch as nearly
no differentiation either of morals or of refinement may be detected in them. This is as one might expect, since they follow one
and the same system of instruction, are not accustomed to engage
in conversation with anyone outside their kin, and are occupied at
home, far away from men, among wet nurses and maids, with
whom they also very often take their makeshift meals. Nor indeed
do the men, following a certain uncouth and less kindly custom,
consistently consider women worthy of either the dinner table or
the marriage bed. To be sure, that great and crowded concourse of
foreign nobles — I speak of those who have invested their fortunes
and their families in the common fatherland of all peoples — for
the most part have softened those customs through more civilized
social interactions.

"But although I have mentioned many women, I won't be en-   158
tirely silent about two widows whom I found greatly pleasing just
a few years ago: Giroloma del Bufalo,[203] who has the most charming eyes ever seen, the most tender and dazzling vitality in her
demeanor, and the most refined elegance of taste; and Cassandra
Bonaventura,[204] the sister[205] of Porzia who in the delicate beauty
of her face has surpassed all other women of my time."

After I'd said this, D'AVALOS remarked: "I wish, my dear Giovio,   159
that the reputation for chastity of all these women might be

pudenti et[384] Romanarum rerum peritissimo subtiliter excuteretur.
Nam mihi haudquaquam verisimile videtur,[385] eas in universum ut
modo visus es constanter affirmare, integra corporis atque animi
castimonia delectari, quoniam tantas, quas illis viri inferunt, contumelias tametsi palam penitus exsorbeant, concoquere tamen
exulcerato stomacho minime videantur. Et eae quidem matronae
spiritus prope illos veteris Romanae superbiae implacabilibus animis gerunt ita ut, cum viri passim et in oculis etiam scortentur, vix
eas credendum sit aequissime pati iura coniugalis tori violata, ac
dolorem atque iracundiam heroica virtute aliqua temperare; quin
talionis poena dissimulatas iniurias ex opportunitate vindicandas
arbitrentur, quando incluti opibus[386] decorique et longe liberalis-
simi corruptores numquam desint, qui usquequaque pudicas et
nobiles lacessant, ac vel acerbissime custoditas studiose[387] sollici-
tent.

160   'At fortasse illis in unam eam curam dies ac noctes excubantibus
aptissimae[388] mille modis occasiones non affulgent, cum illae ipsae
quae tam severa disciplina continentur, vetere illa et ad furta veneris maxime accommodata consuetudine omnes antiquae urbis regiones pro libidine religionis causa pererrent, in desertis et opacis
locis, diruta et obsita vepribus, sacella visitantes, vix comitantibus
singulis ancillis, quae amorum internuntiae et omnis pudoris ex-
pultrices allectae muneribus esse consueverint.'

161   Tum vero ego ⟨iovius⟩ inquam, 'Davale, non sum adeo ex-
pers ac imperitus urbanarum consuetudinum ut ullam omnino

486

scrutinized in minute detail not by you, but by someone less bashful yet highly expert in things Roman. To me, it seems quite unlikely that all these women take delight in purity of body and mind, as just now you seemed to be steadily affirming. Granted, the women swallow completely the many indignities which the men inflict upon them in public; yet they do not in the least appear to digest them, their stomachs being sore and upset, so to speak. In fact, these matrons stubbornly maintain the spirit of ancient Roman pride in their implacable hearts. So when men are consorting with prostitutes hither and yon, even in plain view, it is scarcely believable that the women endure with complete equanimity the violation of the rights of their marriage bed, and that they restrain both grief and anger by means of some heroic virtue. No, instead they reckon that the injuries that they have concealed must be avenged by punishment in kind when the opportunity presents itself, seeing that there is never a shortage of well-known seducers. Wealthy and handsome, this most 'gentlemanly' class of men assails chaste and noble women in every conceivable situation and eagerly solicits even women who are under the strictest guard.

"But perhaps thousands of highly suitable opportunities do not 160 dawn for these men who keep watch day and night with that one object because the very women who are held in strict confinement follow that old practice that is perfectly suited for illicit sex: under the pretext of religious observance, but actually out of lust, they wander about through all the districts of the old part of the city. In deserted and dark spots, they visit shrines that have been destroyed and overgrown by thorn bushes, with scarcely a single maidservant attending them. These maidservants, enticed by gifts, commonly become the lovers' go-betweens, banishing any sense of shame."

Then I [GIOVIO] countered, "D'Avalos, I'm not so green and 161 ignorant of city ways that I would say there exist no unchaste

impudicam inficier et omnes probatissimas esse contendam. Verum ea, quae de matronarum amoribus circumferuntur, potius ex levi et maligna hominum opinione famam ducunt, et ex unis aut alteris exemplis, quam quod ea flagitia usu a multis cognita compertaque sint. A iactabunda enim et petulanti iuventute optimis saepe mulieribus maculae quaedam consperguntur, quas brevi demum tempore detergi et deleri penitus videmus. Nam id omnino falsum et auditu etiam nefandum esse puto, quod plerique natura vel iniuria infensi mulieribus petulanter dicunt, et C. Catellia narrare solebat:

162   'Obstetrix erudita, et imprimis ab eo quaestu pernobilis et dives, et proinde amorum omnium tota urbe et secretarum conscia libidinum. Ea utpote quae in omni aetate fuisset impurissima, nullam prope paullo nobiliorem feminam pudicam esse testabatur; et certe occultas multarum flammas et stuprorum intercalationes, iras pretia abortivos[389] ac omnia denique singularum embolia noverat.

163   'Ea, cum familiares viros tamquam minus audaces serio et festive tamen increparet, quod non alacrius stupri feminas compellarent et cum iis manu iniecta liberius colluctari dubitarent, tres eius sexus aetates esse disserebat quas, si forte aliquae intacto ac illibato pudore percurrissent, vel saxeae vel mente commotae vel omnino animo divinae fuisse viderentur. Puellas, procaci quadam luxurie titillantes, fragili admodum earum pudore, donis atque blanditiis potius quam libidine capi, cum adhuc dulciora resolutae veneris

women, nor would I contend that they are all completely incorruptible. But those things which are spread around about the love affairs of matrons derive their notoriety from people's frivolous and spiteful opinions and from a few examples here and there, rather than because in practice those crimes have been discovered and verified by many witnesses. Certain aspersions are often spattered on the best women by boastful and impudent youth. Yet after a short time we see these stains entirely wiped away and effaced. Certainly I think it is altogether mistaken and even wicked to listen to what is said impudently by the many people who either because of their nature or on account of some injury are hostile to women. As a matter of fact, C. Catellia[206] used to tell this story:

"There was a skilled midwife, famous and rich beyond others of 162
that profession, and for that reason privy to all the love affairs and secret acts of lust in the entire city. Naturally, as one who had been utterly dissolute for her entire life, she used to claim that no woman was chaste who had even a drop of noble blood in her. And without any doubt, she knew the hidden passions of many a woman, the safest times of month to schedule illicit sex,[207] the quarrels, the money exchanged, the abortifacients, and, in short, all the escapades of every single woman.

"Moreover, when she was chiding male acquaintances (seriously, 163
but in a joking manner) for not being daring enough, in that they didn't more readily solicit women for illicit sex and, once having copped a pretty good feel,[208] were hesitating to tussle with them more wantonly, she was accustomed to say that there were three stages of female sexual development, and if perchance some women had passed through them with chastity intact and undiminished, they would appear to have been either made of stone, mentally deranged, or entirely divine. She said that girls whose chastity is quite fragile and who quiver at the thought of wanton licentiousness are won over by gifts and flattery rather than by lust, since up to that point they haven't yet sampled the sweeter

gaudia minime degustarint; adultas autem ac aetate integra florentes vera tentigine et iustis virorum desideriis inflammari, utpote
quibus natura ad progignendam subolem vehementiorem[390] appe-
titum et ad id requisitos acriores[391] stimulos indidisse videatur. In
ipso autem aetatis flexu et propinqua iam senectute, mulieres saeva
libidine sic accendi, quod florem aetatis ante neglexerint, ut stoli-
dae castitatis paenitentia adductae, oblatos demum[392] quosque ad
venerem corripere non dubitent, nec ab infinito pruritu exsatiari
queant.

164   'Quin etiam in castissimis[393] et diligentissime custoditis incerta
quaedam esse horarum ac temporum momenta quibus aestu quodam saevae libidinis incitentur adeo ut,[394] si ea colligere et loco
atque animo antecapere viris daretur, ii nullam omnino verecundius reluctantem essent inventuri; ut nuper, in nobili et alioqui
semper casta superioris Italiae matrona contigisse (inter molliora
fabularum colloquia referebat) quae, cum ante lucem in villam
profectura, extra gyneceum excitandis ad maturandum mulionibus
ceterisque ministris vagaretur, fortuito, inter scalarum angustias,
validi et vixdum pubescentis aurigae occursu, pressius attrectata et
protinus emollita, repentinam et numquam antea meditatam libidinem exsolvit—spectante forte ex occulto nobili vicino eius ama-
tore et fortunam suam pariter ac dominam diris persequente,
quando ipse frustra plures annos inanibus ingrati amoris obsequiis
impendisset.

165   'Quod factum impudicum et sordidum, non multo post, cum
ille subblandienti adhuc matronae et dulcioribus verbis ad proximas vindemias amoris fructum pollicenti tot simulatas illecebras
alienato iam pridem[395] virilique animo stomachatus obiectasset,

joys of unrestrained sensuality. But, she said, healthy and mature women in the prime of life are aroused by erections and by the legitimate desires of men, inasmuch as nature appears to have instilled by these means a fiercer appetite for bearing children and, toward that end, has implanted more ardent stimuli. During menopause, however, as old age is approaching, women are so inflamed by savage lust—something to which earlier, in the flower of youth, they'd been indifferent—that, induced by regret for their steadfast chastity, they don't hesitate to grab every man for sex who appears in their path, nor are they able to satiate the boundless itch of their desires.

"In fact, even in cases of the chastest and most carefully guarded 164 ones, there are certain unsafe times and hours when they are aroused by the heat of raging lust. So if men could analyze and anticipate these moments with respect to place and intent, they would surely find no woman too bashfully resisting. Thus it happened recently (this is one of her milder stories!) in the case of a noble matron of northern Italy who in other respects had always been chaste. Before daylight, when about to set out for a villa, she was wandering beyond the women's quarters, awakening the muleteers and other attendants and bidding them to make haste. As chance would have it, at that moment she came upon a very young but sturdy groom in a narrow stairway. She immediately softened in his strong grip and consummated an act of lust that had never before entered her head. As luck would have it, her suitor, a noble neighbor, was watching from a hiding place. He cursed his own bad luck and his lady alike, because he himself had devoted many years without success to vainly courting an ungrateful beloved.

"Not long after, when the matron was fawning over him and 165 with sweet words was promising the fruit of love at the next harvest, he brought up this shameful and sordid deed, having long since become indignant and alienated in his manly heart at so many feigned enticements. She replied with great wit and

491

illa constanter et facete admodum respondit: "An te propterea a me parum amari putas, atque etiam iniuria affici quod aurigam tibi praetulerim? Parata enim tum fueram tibi[396] morigerari si tu, semper infelix, in aurigae fortunati momentum incidisses." Quod acute et opportune dictum, cum vulgaretur, sic in proverbium cessit ut, cum amatoriarum rerum incursus in praecipiti quodam occasionis momento verti fateamur, propterea explorandum aurigae punctum cunctis amantibus esse praedicemus.'

166   Hoc[397] loco in cachinnum sese exsolvens DAVALUS 'Non agnosco' inquit 'quaecumque eius beati aurigae fortuna fuerit, haec tam propitia secundae Veneris momenta, si ea penitus e caelo astrorumque radiis deducantur. Neque enim ab occultiore vestra disciplina haec mihi umquam aucupanda putaverim, quando ea, ut usu praeclare compertum est, vehementi amantium studio, perennibus obsequiis, ac insigni maxime liberalitate facilius atque nobilius captentur. Quae omnia, etiam si desint, una loci commoditate parari felicissime videmus.'

167   Tum vero MUSETIUS 'Haec' inquit 'una loci commoditate cuncta caeli puncta rerumque omnium momenta concluduntur. Unde non insulsa ratione eos amantium beatiores esse constet, qui propinquorum ac affinium amore perusti, omnium horarum[398] consuetudine perfruuntur.'

168   Ad id ego ⟨IOVIUS⟩ 'Apagete,' inquam, 'hos amores omni prorsus vel ingenuo civilique homine indignos, et penitus exsecrandos; et revertamur ad tuendum feminarum decus, unde discessimus. Magna[399] profecto corruptela nequitiae hoc maxime tempore hominum animos invasit, ut unius aut alterius intemperantis feminae exemplo, totum earum genus impudicitiae flagitiis temeratum et

self-possession: 'Can it really be that you think yourself too little loved, even injured, because I preferred a muleteer to you? Well! At that time I was perfectly ready to gratify you, had you, hapless man, shown the impulsiveness of that lucky muleteer.' Once this story got around and was told in a sharp and suitable way, it became a proverb, so now when we acknowledge that the course of a love affair may be redirected by a certain head-over-heels impulse of the moment, we say that all lovers ought to give a try to the muleteer's 'quick pricking.'"[209]

At this point, D'AVALOS, laughing loudly, said: "Whatever the 166 luck of that fortunate coachman may have been, I don't see that these propitious moments of Venus' favor can be traced back entirely to heaven and to the effect of the stars. I wouldn't suppose that I'd ever have to lie in wait for these moments on the basis of this obscure science of yours since, as has been established very plainly in practice, these moments are obtained more easily and more nobly by lovers' intense zeal, persistent service, and especially by their remarkable generosity. We see that even if all that is missing, your goal may be successfully obtained by a well-chosen place alone."

Then MUSCETTOLA added, "All those 'pinpricks' of heaven and 167 the motions of all things are comprehended under the expression 'a well-chosen place alone.'[210] And so there is a sensible line of reasoning that the more blessed of lovers are those who, consumed by love of female kin and relations, enjoy their company at all hours."

To this I [GIOVIO] said: "Back off! That sort of love affair is 168 absolutely unworthy of any freeborn and civilized person, and must be utterly abhorred. Let's return to the topic we've left, our consideration of the beauty of women. Without question, great moral corruption and vice have invaded the minds of men especially in our time, so that thanks to the example of one or two licentious women, we might be willing to believe that their entire

corruptum esse credere velimus: quasi ea quae maledicentissime de earum intemperie memorantur, ut falsa magna ex parte aut certe minora vero saepissime non confutent atque redarguant et inspecta vita sincerius et probatissimi testes qui, ad tuendum pudicitiae decus cum opus est, prope divinitus offeruntur, et puris atque sanctissimis numquam desunt. Multa enim partim obtrectatione atque odio partim iactantia et levitate effundi necesse est, in coronis atque conviviis dissolutae maxim[a]e iuventutis quae, sicut in praesens[400] et notam inurere et bonam famam suggillare videntur, ita mox ut nullis veritatis subsidiis sustentata, quoniam mendacium celeriter evanescat, hominum silentio et conscientia facile diluantur.

169 'Magna hercle servando pudori praesidia legibus imposita, multa item claustra firmissimarum rerum adinventa et constituta esse videmus, ut ea non facile ab impudicis etiam animis eludi aut refringi posse sit putandum. Alias, propinquorum severitas et non dubiae mortis metus a flagitiis deterrent; aliae, religionibus tactae inferorum poenas exhorrescunt; aliae amittendi decoris periculo commoventur. Quo semel amisso, quae celsi sunt animi mulieres nihil reliquum se habere in hac vita vel honestum, vel carum, vel ulla mediocri laude dignum existimant,[401] nec iam, alacribus oculis, sceleris conscientia deiectae, caelestem hanc lucem contuentur.

170 'Ceterum ex ipsis procerum familiis, a Farnesia domo primus erit gradus ad summam praestantissimi ordinis claritatem. In qua est Laura, Iuliae Farnesiae feminarum omnium eius aetatis elegantissimae filia, Nicolao nupta Ruereo. Ea paucis ante annis, cum pulchritudine totius corporis tum maxime mollioribus argutiis oculorum, et infinitis amabilium morum illecebris omnes alias

sex has been defiled and corrupted by disgraceful actions—as if the things that are very scurrilously retold about the intemperance of women were not for the most part false or at least exaggerated, disproved and refuted by a careful inspection of their lives. Indeed, when it's necessary to protect the honor of a woman's chastity, completely trustworthy witnesses come forward almost as if by divine will, and these the holiest and purest of women never lack. Yes, inevitably, in the entourages and dinner parties of the most dissolute youths many things are said, in part out of disparagement and hatred and in part out of boasting and frivolity. At the present time, they appear to stigmatize and give a black eye to a good reputation; but since a lie that is not bolstered by the support of truth quickly disappears, they are soon easily washed away just as quickly by men's silence and remorse.

"By God, we see that many protections for preserving modesty 169 are imposed by law, and likewise many cloisters of the strongest materials are devised and set up, so that we mustn't think they can be escaped from or broken into easily, even by those of unchaste minds. The strictness of kinsmen and fear of certain death deter some women from misdeeds. Others, moved by religious scruples, tremble at the punishment of hell. Still others are disturbed by the risk of losing their honor: for once it's lost, women who are of a lofty mind reckon that no possession remains to them in this life that is either honorable or valuable or worthy of even modest praise, and so, downcast by the consciousness of their crime, they no longer look upon the light of heaven with eager eyes.[211]

"Of the families of the high nobility itself, that of the Farnese 170 holds the first rank for its high fame and excellence. It includes Laura—the daughter of Giulia Farnese, the most elegant of all women of her time—who is married to Nicola della Rovere.[212] Just a few years ago, no doubt, she surpassed all other women in the beauty of her entire body and especially by the soft expressivity of her eyes and the countless allurements of her charming charac-

haud dubie superavit; et manet adhuc integra effigies incomparabilis venustatis, quamquam assiduis pituitae stillicidiis contracta macies, illum vividiorem habitus florem abstulerit.[402]

171   'Collocavit nuper geminas filias Io. Georgius Caesarinus Romanorum splendidissimus: alteram, cui nomen est Iuliae Tibaldio Simoni, fortissimo equitum praefecto;[403] alteram, nomine Semideam, in Bubala familia.[404] Quarum ea est dignitas, ut cum singulari forma, mores nitidi et perspicua castitas facile contendant. At Comitum domus, sicut orbata est viris, ita duabus maxime viduis matronis floret. Altera est Hieronyma, cuius aspectu proceritate modestia et sermone nihil venustius; altera Iulia est, quae Anthimo Sabello nupta erat: eadem formosa strenua fecunda, ex eadem quoque gente Hieronymo Pepulo nupsit, cuius stata forma pudicorum morum ornamentis honestatur.[405]

172   'E Sabella autem domo nobiles pleraeque matronae profluxerunt. Sex ante alias ab Romana virtute lectissima videtur: Portia, huius Virginii Ursini mater; verum si corporis decus et florem aetatis et, iunctam cum eo, praeclaram pudicitiam sequamur, Tarquinia, Carolo Polio nuper orbata, ceteras omnes antecedet. Admirati etiam saepe sumus subtile et temperatum ingenium et pulchritudinem non ad lascivias sed ad fecunditatem opportunam in Paula, quae Troili Sabelli uxor fuit. Porro ex Ursina gente in honore sunt praecipuo Maria, magni Virginii ex Iordane filio neptis, quae cum Antonio Cardonio, Padulio duci fortissimo, antea nupsisset, cum Rentio Anguillario Cerite secundas nuptias fecit. Ea est casta, fecunda, mitis, modesta, fortis, aequissimo namque animo. Cum in arcem, urbe capta, confugisset, et viri calamitatem et patriae

ter. She still remains the complete exemplar of incomparable beauty, although (it is said) an emaciation caused by a chronic rheum has stolen away the vigor and youthfulness of her physical constitution.

"Recently, Giovanni Giorgio Cesarini,[213] the most illustrious of Romans, married off his twin daughters. One, named Giulia,[214] wed Simone Tebaldi,[215] the very brave cavalry commander; the other, named Semidea,[216] married into the del Bufalo family. Such is their distinction that their shining character and evident chastity easily rival their exceptional beauty. But the house of the Conti, while orphaned of its male members, flourishes exceedingly thanks to two matronly widows. One is Girolama,[217] whose facial countenance, height, modesty, and speech are of matchless beauty. The other, Giulia,[218] who had been married to Antimo Savelli,[219] is likewise beautiful, vigorous, and fertile. She has married Girolamo de' Pepoli[220] from that same clan. Her beauty, though average, is graced with the adornment of chaste character. 171

"Numerous noble matrons have sprung forth from the Savelli family. Six are seen to surpass the rest in the choicest Roman virtue. There is Porzia,[221] the mother of Virginio Orsini. But if we should use as our guide physical beauty and youth conjoined with outstanding modesty, then Tarquinia,[222] recently widowed by the death of Carlo de' Conti di Poli, will outstrip the others. In Paola,[223] who was the wife of Troilo Savelli, we have often admired a fine and temperate nature, and a beauty suitable for fecundity rather than acts of lust. Next from the Orsini clan in exceptional honor comes Maria,[224] granddaughter of Virginio the Great by way of his son Giangiordano. Although previously she'd been married to Antonio de Cardona, the powerful marquis of Padula, she married a second time, to Renzo Orsini da Ceri of Anguillara. She is chaste, fecund, mild, proper, strong, and certainly endowed with great patience and resignation. When, after Rome had been taken, she fled into the papal fortress, she endured both the misfortune 172

interitum, et quae imminebant atrocia pericula et foedae conclu-
sionis incommoda toleravit.

173 'Huius noverca est Felix Iulio Pontifice genita cuius pulchritudinem in hac aetate evanidam plerique etiam admirantur. Ceterum
eius mulieris eximia est probitas,[406] incredibilis vigilantia, ac industria singularis; regendae familiae et gubernandis oppidis accommodata, ingenium autem ab optimis litteris haud absurdum, mores
vero festa iucunditate cultissimi. Huius privigna est Carlotta, Tamisio Pico[407] Mirandulae nupta, facie et moribus peramabilis; de
qua plura diceremus, si ingenium a paternis oppidis quae sunt ad
Sabatinum Lacum, in urbanam lucem protulisset.'

174 Hoc[408] loco DAVALUS 'Quid est hoc,' inquit, 'ingenium in urbanam lucem minime protulisse? An non satis illustres fuere Sabi-
nae, quae quondam in subagresti vita summam pudicitiae laudem
meruerunt?'

175 Tum ego ⟨IOVIUS⟩ 'Sint,' inquam, 'ut libet, vel nobilissimae et
castimonia vel antiquis Sabinis exaequentur. Nequaquam enim
hac tempestate hoc solum consectamur pudicitiae nomen, sed
amoenitates etiam eruditas, quas non ab ancillis rusticanisque ministris, sed ab illustri virorum insignium ac matronarum consuetudine generosae puellae facile suscipiant. An tibi fortasse stultus
ineptusque videbitur in *Phaedro* Platonis Socrates cum, in eo extra
urbem herbido et molli umbrosoque secessu, ingenue fateretur
se numquam antea praeterfluentem illam aquolam vidisse, cuius
perenni irrigatione illa diffusa et pluribus[409] sermonibus potius
quam ramis insignis platanus excrevisset, utpote qui, intra

of her husband and the ruin of her country as well as the dreadful dangers that threatened us and the hardships of being shut in the castle.

"Her stepmother is Felice della Rovere,[225] the daughter of Pope Julius II, whose beauty, reduced though it is at her time of life, most men still admire. Besides the extraordinary uprightness of this woman, she is incredibly vigilant and exceptionally diligent, and is suited to running the family and to governing towns. She has an intelligence in tune with great literature, and her highly refined manners are joined to a happy vivacity. Felice's stepdaughter is Carlotta,[226] the wife of Tamisio Pico della Mirandola,[227] a woman whose appearance and character are easy to love. We might say many more things about her, had her brilliance been brought forth from her father's towns on the Sabatine Lake[228] into the light of the city."

At this point, D'AVALOS said: "What do you mean by a brilliance that has not been brought forth into the light of the city? Were not the Sabine women illustrious enough when once upon a time they merited the highest praise of chastity despite their somewhat rustic life?"[229]

Then I [GIOVIO] said: "As you wish; let these too be either ranked as the noblest in purity or regarded as equal to the ancient Sabines. In our times we by no means strive only for a reputation for chastity, but also for attractions which require a good upbringing. Well-bred girls easily pick these up, not from servant girls and peasant attendants, but from distinguished company, by association with eminent men and women. Or perhaps Socrates in Plato's *Phaedrus* seems to you stupid and foolish when in that grassy, soft and shady retreat outside the city he admitted ingenuously that never before had he seen that tiny stream flowing by. Irrigated by its waters that plane tree grew up, more famous for the many conversations that took place there than for its spreading boughs.[230] Socrates' admission was that of a man accustomed to staying

173

174

175

Athenarum moenia se continere esset solitus, ut in frequenti hominum commercio ea facile disceret quae ex ipsa sapientiae ratione ad excolendos mores maxime conducerent, quando per opacas silvas et florentia rura otiose et solitarie secedendo, nihil quod ad optimum vitae genus pertineret ab arboribus umquam et liquidis fontibus doceretur.

176 'Habet domi Franciottus Ursinus Cardinalis[410] Caeciliam, filiam lenis limpidi castique ingenii feminam, quam Alberto Pio Carpensi regulo summae auctoritatis philosopho[411] Leonis liberalitate collocavit.[412]

177 'Ad has ipsae Columniae succedunt. Hortensia, M. Antonii clarissimi ducis filia, quae Hieronymo[413] Pallavicino Insubri regulo nupsit, haec proceritate insigni et[414] candore corporis, flavoque item capillo et[415] altitudine animi,[416] patris specimen referre videtur. Pulchritudine[417] vero, quae in ea est admodum liberalis, a Lucretia matre venustissima deducit. Haec[418] Iulium Pontificem avunculum et Galeotum Cardinalem fratrem sanguine respicit, quorum alterum prolatis Sacri Imperii finibus, et reipublicae fortiter atque feliciter gestae inexstinguibilis gloria caelo consecravit; alterum tamquam humani generis delicias aetate forma gratia fortunisque florentem, properantes[419] Parcae, lugente Romano Populo, rapuerunt. Ceterum in Hortensia, cum praeclarae disciplinae multae virtutes emineant, ante omnia musicis studiis adeo subtiliter se extulit ut Romanam Sirenem quod paternum in galea et scuto pro insigni Columniae familiae gestamen fuit, dulcedine vocum effingere dicatur.

178 'Magnam quoque tum exactae formae tum absolutae virtutis indolem praebet Victoria nubilis puella, quam Petrus Franciscus Columna, honestus et eruditus[420] eques, ex Laura Sommeia

within the town walls of Athens, so that by frequent interaction with men he might easily learn from wise reasoning things which were especially conducive to cultivating character. For nothing which pertains to the best kind of life is ever learned from trees and flowing springs, that is, by withdrawing through dark woods and flowering fields, in idleness and in solitude.[231]

"Cardinal Franciotto Orsini[232] has in his family his daughter   176
Cecilia,[233] a woman of singular modesty and noteworthy honor, of a gentle, pure, and chaste disposition, whom he gave in marriage, through the liberality of Leo X, to Alberto Pio, prince of Carpi, a philosopher of the highest reputation.[234]

"Next come the Colonna women. Ortensia,[235] daughter of the   177
very illustrious commander Marcantonio Colonna — she who married Girolamo Pallavicini, the ruler of Insubria — appears to recall the model of her father in the distinctive height and whiteness of her body and in her blond hair and loftiness of mind. But she derives her beauty, which is especially ladylike, from her very attractive mother, Lucrezia.[236] In blood ties, she looks back to her maternal uncle, Pope Julius II, and her brother, Cardinal Galeotto.[237] The inextinguishable glory of a state bravely and successfully governed and an ecclesiastical empire expanded consecrated the former of these to Heaven; the latter was the darling of humankind, flourishing in youth, beauty, gracefulness, and social prestige, but the Fates were in a hurry to snatch him away, to the grief of the Roman people. But while many virtues of outstanding education stand out in Ortensia, she has chiefly exalted herself with her exacting musical studies, so that in sweetness of voice she is said to imitate a Roman Siren — an image that has been a lineal ornament of the Colonna family, used as an insignia on helmet and shield.

"Also, Vittoria,[238] a young girl of marriageable age, displays great   178
innate qualities both of exquisite beauty and absolute virtue. Pierfrancesco Colonna, an honorable and learned knight, took over guardianship of her from Laura di Somma,[239] a most

muliere lectissima suscepit. Est et mite ingenium et suavissima forma Laviniae Mutii filiae, quae Ioanni Bentivolio nupsit. Clarescit et virilis animi virtus ad compensandam oris venustatem in Beatrice, quam Fabritius ex paelice sustulit. Eam, ut est Rodulfo Camertis reguli filio nupta, dum ille novercae et Camertibus[421] bellum molitur, arma impigre tractare, auxilia cogere, et strenue divisis cum viro muneribus bellum gerere audimus. Sed ante omnes, in Iulia Prosperi Columnae Rubrobarbi uxore animus immensus, vehemens industria, pudor incorruptus magnopere splendescunt, cum ipsa paucis ante annis etiam matronali venustate fuerit insignis.[422]

179 ‘Sed quibus tamquam summae artis sculptoriae praestantibus instrumentis huius Victoriae Columnae veram effigiem habitum figuram, quibus aptis atque delectis facundiae coloribus animi similitudinem ad peculiares virtutum omnium, tamquam naturalium naevorum, notas referre poterimus, cum in ea cuncti artus a natura definite perfecti ad singularem respondeant decorem, et excelsi animi clarissimae dotes, inenarrabili quodam concentu, in se ipsas ad absolvendam verae virtutis speciem concurrere videantur? Vincit enim haec una mulier ceteras omnes, sicut Roma ipsa, quae talem ad gloriam tulit, singulas terrarum orbis civitates augusta claritudine superavit, si in unam cuncta naturae atque fortunae munera, tum ab illa, tum ab hac largissimis manibus congesta computemus. Quod certe non ad adulationem compositum sed aequabili feminarum omnium ac hominum consensu, verissimum esse deprehenditur.

180 ‘Hanc enim unam illae Heroides humanis et divinis donis superbae, quae merito pares ferre nequeunt, ita sibi ac omnibus

excellent woman. Also, both a gentle temperament and delightful beauty belong to Muzio's[240] daughter Lavinia,[241] who married Giovanni Bentivoglio. In Beatrice[242] too, Fabrizio's daughter by a mistress, there begins to shine forth a manly virtue of mind, balancing out a beautiful countenance. She has married Rodolfo,[243] son of the ruler of Camerino, and we hear that while he is stirring up a war against his stepmother and the Camerinians, Beatrice, having divided the labors with her husband, is tirelessly wielding weapons, mustering troops, and waging war with great vigor. But before all other women, Giulia,[244] wife of Prospero 'Redbeard' Colonna, is beginning to manifest on a large scale immense courage, energetic diligence, and uncorrupted chastity, whereas a few years earlier this very woman had also been well known for matronly beauty.

"But what fine tools, like those of the highest kind of sculpture, will allow us to render the true likeness, image, and character of our Vittoria Colonna?[245] What apt, what choice colors of eloquence will enable us to relate the likeness of her mind to the special qualities of all her virtues, which belong to her like natural birthmarks? How, indeed, when all her limbs, precisely perfected by nature, match her singular grace, and it appears that in her the very qualities of a most illustrious mind are assembled together with a certain indescribable harmony to complete the appearance of true virtue? For this one woman prevails over all the others — just as Rome herself, which advanced to such great glory, surpassed in august renown all the individual states of the world — if we should add up all the gifts that nature and fortune have conferred with their bountiful hands upon this one woman. And this description is certainly not composed to flatter her, but will be recognized as absolutely true by the universal consensus of all women and men. 179

"Those heroines of old,[246] glorying in their gifts human and divine, who rightly cannot abide equals, admit to themselves and 180

superiorem esse confitentur, ut non modo eam fatali Victoriae nomine, quod tamquam bene auspicatum ab ipso lustrico die susceptum fuit, verum et "unicae optimae[423] maximae"[424] cognomento
dignissimam praedicent. Est enim ea mulier ingenio, forma et totis
denique virtutibus praealtorum instar montium, qui cum procul
spectantibus haud multum ingentes appareant, appropinquantibus
demum et paullatim ad radices succedentibus, excelsiores, et a
sublimiore cacumine insuperabiles iudicantur.

181   'Id quoque, quod[425] rarum est, ei divinitus inditum esse videtur,
ut numquam longa eius praesentia amicis et familiaribus vel tae-
dium pariat vel contemptum, verum admirationem quandam incredibilem assiduaque reputatione maxime diuturnam. Tantum
vero abest ut absentia ullam inducat oblivionem, ut desiderium
tantarum eius amoenitatum flagrantissima atque infinita cupiditate proferatur.

182   'Et hercle, id dictu perfacetum et re ipsa verissimum esse liquidissime constat, quod Gibertus noster de Victoria collata ceteris
mulieribus dicere solebat, cum eam propterea sanctissime coleret
magnopereque suspiceret: omnibus scilicet feminis praeterquam
uni huic, accidere ut musivi et tessellati operis picturis similes essent, cuius artificii figurae humanaeque facies procul spectantibus
admirabiles atque pulcherrimae videntur; quod[426] si propius succe-
das et collatis oculis id opus subtiliter contempleris, laxiores com-
missurae protinus apparent, et calculorum ruditer insertorum hiatus enormes et frequentes tumultuariae prope artis inconcinnitates,
quae cuncta manifeste oculis deprehensa, totam operis existimationem convellunt.

183   'Sic enim accidit cum feminas familiarius intuemur, nam in
summa saepe generis claritate, fastus vehementer eminet, qui dignitatem spectantibus gravem atque ridiculam reddit. At corporis

to all that she is so superior that, they say, she is most worthy not only of the fateful name 'Vittoria'—her well-omened baptismal name—but also of the epithet 'the unique, best, and greatest.' For in brilliance, beauty, and virtues this woman is comparable to the highest mountains: although to those gazing from afar they do not appear very large, to those who approach them, arriving little by little at their bases, they are judged to be loftier; and from their highest peak, they are judged to be unsurpassed.

"There also seems to have been bestowed upon her by divine 181 agency this characteristic, which is rare: never does she cause either boredom or contempt to arise in friends and acquaintances, even after long exposure to her, but instead she arouses an incredible and enduring admiration that stands up to uninterrupted consideration. Her absence in no way leads to her being forgotten; rather, the longing for her great charms is prolonged by an ardent and boundless desire.

"And by God, it's indisputably agreed that what our friend Gi- 182 berti used to say about Vittoria is not only clever but absolutely true. Since he honors her most reverently and esteems her greatly, he would say this about her in comparison to other women: that it was the lot of all besides her alone to be like the images of a mosaic composed of small pieces of stone. To those looking from a distance, the figures and human faces of this work of art seem admirable and beautiful; but if you approach the work more closely and examine it more minutely and with focused attention, immediately seams appear to view, and both the enormous gaps and the crowded awkwardness, the almost haphazard workmanship, of the crudely inserted pebbles—all discerned clearly by the eyes—shatter one's entire opinion of the work.

"So it happens when we observe women more closely. For often 183 in the high splendor of a lineage there is a strong trait of haughtiness which conveys to observers an obnoxious and ridiculous self-esteem. But sometimes a foolish or unsound moral character

pulchritudinem inepti vel improbi mores nonnumquam deturpant, ingenia vero praeclara splendorem illum egregiae laudis facile deperdunt, aut propter gloriolam vanitate animi conceptam, aut propter insuperabiles libidines quae illa[427] saepissime comitantur. Castimoniam porro ipsam aliquando inusitata morum durities deformat, et religiosior ad fastidium severae vitae consuetudo minus illustrem efficit et penitus contemnendam.

184   'Igitur haec ipsa Victoria neque elata generis claritate contumescit, neque in ea corporis decus animi viciis obumbratur, neque acutissimi atque anhelantis ingenii ferventiores motus pudicitiae qui⟨c⟩quam[428] officiunt, neque puram castamque mentem ab ipso decenti civilis et iucundae vitae proposito detorquent. Namque haec quattuor simul virtutes sic in unum coeunt ad eam exacte perficiendam, ut illa totidem naturae generantis elementa, quae tametsi ab diversis potestatibus omnino sint contraria, egregie tamen ad numeros caelestis rationis inter se colligantur.

185   'Sed de claritudine, ingenio et pudore, quae manifestis morum ac operum monumentis et constantissima hominum fama continentur, postea dicemus, quando nunc ipsius pulchritudo sit enarranda, ut qui illam ab aliarum virtutum praeconio vel absentes et incogniti venerari solent, etiam ab insigni forma, quae animum per oculos capit, ab hac perstricta descriptione plenius admirentur. Nam cum in ea sit totius corporis perquam apta habilisque figura—nec paullo obesior ad quadratum habitum, nec ad exilitatem gracilis staturae procerior—etiam singuli artus aequabili per totum eximia specie ad singularem mensuram egregie correspondent.

disfigures physical beauty, while distinguished natural endowments easily lose that splendor of outstanding praise either because of the petty glory to which vanity of mind gives rise or because of the insurmountable desires which so often accompany those things. In turn, an unusual austerity of morals sometimes disfigures chastity itself; and the practice of an austere life that is too scrupulous with respect to fastidiousness makes chastity less illustrious and even quite despicable.

"Well, this Vittoria doesn't puff herself up because of the high distinction of her lineage, nor is the beauty of her body overshadowed by vices of the mind. None of the more torrid passions of an exceedingly keen and breathless temperament impede her modesty, nor do they divert a pure and chaste mind from the very proper aim of a pleasing life of service to her city. Certainly these four virtues[247] together join into one to bring her exactly to perfection—just as the four elements produced by nature,[248] even if they are entirely opposed to one another on account of their disparate capacities, are nonetheless bound together among themselves admirably well in accordance with the mathematical structure of divine reason. 184

"But let us speak later on about her renown, brilliance, and modesty, which are safeguarded by conspicuous reminders of her morals and achievement and by unwavering public opinion. Right now we need to describe her beauty. In this way those who are absent or don't know her, but customarily revere her from reports of her other virtues, may more fully admire her beauty—which captivates the mind via the eyes—from our brief description. For as her body as a whole is extremely well proportioned and shapely—neither too plump for a thickset physique, nor too tall for someone of lean and slender build—so too her individual limbs are beautifully well proportioned throughout and conform to the measure appropriate for each. 185

186 'Sed tria sunt in ea muliere, quae natura, cum gravitate lasciviens, ad admirationem effinxisse videtur, et eae quidem, mirificum rarumque in aliis visu, pulcherrimarum rerum concentum efficiunt: oculi scilicet, manus, papillae. Quibus maxime in locis, ut
poetae ferunt, protervi cupidines, dum miseris mortalibus insidiantur, habitare atque inde tela et faces emittere consueverunt.

187 'Sunt oculi etenim colore nigri ac ambiente velut nitido ebore
convestiti, quales ipsius Veneris fuerunt; nec tamen ludibundi,
sed grata micantium luminum iucunditate pervenusti. Pinnatae et
comantes palpebrae eos et molliter custodiunt et decenter exornant. Supercilia vero disiuncta inter se, quod ingenuae frontis est
signum, vix arcuata et sensim desinentia, sic honestant ut eleganter etiam coronent.

188 'Circa hos alludunt capilli ad hebenum auro interlitum nigrican-
tes, ut in Laeda fuisse poetae ferunt: a vertice tenui discrimine per
tempora diffusi et molliter nitente ac leni glutino castigati, sic ut
nihil importune obrepant et latam ob idque liberalem et serenam
frontem condecorent. Quos etiam genae sustineant, pudico rubore
et lactea suavitate refulgentes, laeto admodum earum ductu rece-
dente ad aures, et eas quidem adeo absolutas et breves, ad exacti
iudicii similitudinem exprimendam, ut cum ex infima auricula
mirabiles saepe gemmae unionesque penderent, ab iis statim
ornamentis, ad earum tantum contemplationem, spectantium oculi
verterentur.

189 'At quae non inest venustas naso ipsius a fronte, delicata linea
sensim directo? Qui ad probitatem et regiam dignitatem sic est
productus, quemadmodum in Persarum Arsacidis gentilicium fuit,

"But in this woman there are three things which nature, playful   186
amid its serious business, appears to have fashioned for the purpose of admiration.[249] And indeed these things, marvelous and
unusual to see in others, bring about a harmony of exceedingly
beautiful elements: namely, her eyes, hands, and breasts. In those
sites most of all, as the poets relate, shameless desires have become
accustomed to dwell while they lie in ambush for unfortunate
mortals, and from there they let loose the arrows and flames of
love.

"Take her eyes, dark in color and, as it were, completely sur-   187
rounded by shining ivory, like those of Venus herself. Yet they are
not playful, but extraordinarily attractive, with the agreeable charm
of glittering lights. Thick, feathery eyelashes both tenderly guard
and gracefully embellish them. Moreover, her eyebrows, separated
one from the other (a thing which betokens a noble countenance),
are slightly arched and gradually taper off, adorning her eyes in
such a way that they also tastefully crown them.

"Nearby frolics her hair, verging on black ebony daubed with   188
gold, as the poets relate was the case for Leda. Lightly parted, it
flows from the top of her head down across her temples, and is
held in place by a tenderly shining and smooth gel in such a way
that it covers nothing inappropriately and adorns her forehead,
which is wide, and on that account noble and serene. Also supporting her tresses are her cheeks, gleaming with a modest blush
and milky-white sweetness, happily sweeping back toward ears
that are small and just perfect—expressing a likeness to her precise judgment—so that when marvelous gems and pearls hang
from her earlobes, as they often do, the eyes of observers are immediately diverted from those ornaments toward the contemplation of her ears alone.

"But what beauty is not present in this same woman's nose, ex-   189
tending delicately in a straight line from her forehead? It has been
lengthened (as was the case in the Arsacid dynasty in Parthia) to

ut natura illum ad decus prominulum collem a medio sustulerit, quem tamen potius exprimat quam ostentet, atque ea quidem sollertia aptaque temperie ut nihil ab ea parte quae virilem speciem praeferret femineae venustatis austeritate inducta demeretur.

190   'Porro quem decorem quamve symmetriam et ad lacertos et ad totum denique habitum in ipsis manibus esse conspicimus, si eas detractis forte velamentis nudatas ostendat! Marmora namque candore quodam eximio, expolita vero ebora nitido levore, et zebellinarum denique tergora mollitudine superarent. Explicantur oblongi digiti nullis exstantibus nodis sic ut anuli cedente suco libenter exsiliant, circum iuncturas eminent foruli, fossulae recedunt perlucentque nitidae et rubentes unguiculae, cum tota manus resupinata protenditur.

191   'At illa orbiculata ubera ipso nitenti argento candidiora, quam molliter, quam decenter ad anhelitus modulos e castigantibus severe fasciolis resultant et cubantium palumbularum instar suavibus intervallis contumescunt! Quae pectori, tam lato ab umeris quam ad ilia reducto, natura sic infixit ut inclusa, non appensa esse, interiecto illo mollissimo sinu videantur. Ergo non mirum erit si et illas partes absolute formosas esse dixerimus quas pudor occultavit, nec ullus omnino mortalium praeter virum, eo praestanti naturae dono dignissimum, aut pressit[429] aut inspexit. Postquam et ipsi oculi aliena lumina evibratis late radiis perstringunt, et attrectatae vel conspectae manus cunctos medullitus inflammant, et mamillae turgescentes non iam lacte sed caelesti quodam nectare corda remolliunt.

192   'Quae vero labiis atque ori probe complanatis, quae sucosiori mento, et in toto cervicum gestu gravitas sine severitate, hilaritas sine levitate, iucunditas sine proterva mollitie conspicitur. Is vero

show probity and regal dignity; in its middle, for the sake of adornment, nature has raised a very slight bridge, though without drawing too much attention to it.²⁵⁰ And in fact it does so with such subtle skill and modesty that that feature, which could convey a manly aspect, does not deprive her of any of her feminine beauty, even though it gives her a stern look.

"Moreover, what beauty and what symmetry we observe in her 190 hands in relationship to her upper arms and her whole posture when she chances to take off her gloves and show them naked! They surpass marble in their extraordinary whiteness; in their sleek smoothness, they outstrip ivories; in softness, they surpass ermine. Her fingers are so slender and regular in shape that she can slip off her rings whenever she wants to.

"But those orblike breasts, whiter than shining silver itself, 191 spring back softly and becomingly from their sternly chastising little bindings in time with the musical beat of her breathing and, like little turtledoves sleeping, they swell at sweet intervals. Nature has firmly affixed her breasts to her chest, broad at her shoulders and narrowing to her waist, in such a way that they seem to be framed within it, not made to droop down, and the most delicate cleavage is visible between them. So it will be no wonder if we have depicted as perfectly formed those parts of the body which modesty has hidden; nor has any mortal man ever viewed or caressed them other than her husband, a man extremely deserving of such an extraordinary gift of nature. After her eyes with their widely vibrating rays touch lightly on everyone else's, then her hands, whether touched or seen, arouse all men to their marrow, and her breasts, swelling now not with milk but with a certain heavenly nectar, soften their hearts.

"What is more, in her lips and a mouth smoothed out in ac- 192 cordance with good manners, in a rather fleshy chin, and in the entire movement of her neck there is dignity without severity, cheerfulness without frivolity, and pleasantness without wanton

est neque obstipi neque tener⟨i⟩[430] nimis flexuosi corporis motus, ut saepe inter illustres matronas humano velut ancillari incessu vadentes, augustiorem speciem temperatis passibus praeferret. Et quo non virili ausu, dum cum viro venaretur, incitatis in fugam cervis Hibericos equos agitavit? Quas nemorum asperitates coniugis innixa vestigiis pulcherrimo succinctu minime superavit?

193 'Cui nam vel eruditissimae feminae in ducendis choreis palmam non praeripuit, ac tum maxime cum Bona Sfortia, Sigismundo Sarmatarum Regi desponsata, legatis Neapoli traderetur? Hungaram enim choream quae est solitarii tripudii genus ad peregrinum sonum ceteris feminis ad id rudibus atque stupentibus voluit aemulari, idque tanta cum venere et dignitate doctius explicavit ut cum sola a nullo deducta iuvene saltaret in amplissimo conclavi et frequenti, totius populi corona etiam ipsa una prae admiratione spectaretur. Nihil enim iucundissimis illis motibus quando omnia revocabat ad numeros venustius fuit, vel cum plumeum flabellum ad ciendas auras dissimulanter agitaret, vel manicas colligeret diffluentes, vel ipsa latiore veste descriptis mollissimis orbibus pavimenta converreret; et ad tibicinis modulos modo gradatim ad harmonicam requiem suspensa, modo subsultim circumacta in obliquos meatus, modo convolutim curvatis spatiis incitata, velut labentibus in lubrico vestigiis deferretur.

194 'At qua in veste haec tanta ac erudita studia propalavit, ut summae et exquisitae arti par honos haberetur! Ea erat aurea ad

licentiousness. Moreover, the movement of her extremely flexible body can neither be crowded nor contained, so that often, when she is among illustrious matrons who are stepping along with an obliging gait, like that of servant girls, she displays a more majestic appearance with her measured steps. And what about the time when she went hunting with her husband, and the deer had been driven to flight—with what masculine daring did she not manage the Iberian horses? What hardships of the woods did she not overcome, very beautifully girded for action, following in the traces of her husband?

"From what woman, even the most skilled, did she not snatch 193 away first prize in performing the dance, especially at that very moment when Bona Sforza,[251] promised in marriage to King Sigismund I of Poland, was being handed over to his ambassadors at Naples? She wanted to perform a Hungarian dance, which is a type of solo ritual dance accompanied by foreign-style music; the other women, being untrained in it, were dumbstruck at her performance. She carried it out knowledgeably, and with such charm and dignity, that when she performed it alone with no young man accompanying her in the spacious yet crowded room, everyone formed a circle around her and gazed with admiration. Nothing was more attractive than when, with the most pleasing gestures, she matched all her movements to the rhythms of the dance, whether she was pretending to wave her feathery fan to stir the air or was gathering up her long, flowing sleeves, or when she swept the floor with her wide skirts tracing delicate circles. And step by step, in tune with the rhythms of the flute player, sometimes raised on tiptoe for a harmonic rest, at other times following a circular path by taking little sideways leaps, and at still other times with whirling motions in curving paths, she was borne along perilously with gliding steps.

"But in what wonderful attire did she display these great and 194 skillful exertions, so that equal honor was given to that most

effigiem crispantis et leviter commoti maris, revolutis colorum luminibus undulata a cinctu ad imam fimbriam, purpureis distincta
limbis, quos praetexta emblemata caelato pictoque auro fabrefacta,
paribus intervallis exornabant. In iis expressa erat in frutice balsa-
mus cum hac inscriptione, "HUIC ANIMUS SIMILIS," ad argumentum incorruptae vitae, quoniam nullo tempore balsami lacrima
corrumpatur. Quae palla, in eam tantum festam diem ostentata,
multis[431] milibus aureis stetit, ita ut aliquanto tamen pluris aesti-
maretur in erudito sumptu iucundae eius inventionis alacritas. Sed
quas ipsa in toto femineo cultu rerum omnium amoenitates non
induxit, cum incredibili quodam artificio laetioris ingenii elegantiarum omnium esset novatrix, et nemo ea vel totius amictus ornamenta subtilius reperiret, vel crinem concinnaret habilius aut
aptius, vel splendidius margaritas et gemmas suis in sedibus collocaret!'

195   Tum vero ego ⟨IOVIUS⟩ inquam: 'Davale, rarissimae[432] haec quidem sunt dotes nobilioris puellae, quae iuvenes potius quam senes
alliciant. Sed multo in ea praestantiores et speciosiores exsistunt,
quae viri aetate[433] provecti ac eius maxime familiares admirantur, e
quibus neque ego neque ipse Musetius in postremis sumus; quamquam tu ea omnia plenissime noveris, cum ab incunabulis prope
ipsis cum ea sis educatus. Nam ubi primum Victoria ex materno
utero lucem aspexit, fatali quadam sorte et Piscario tuo patruelli
desponsata est et in Davalam domum traducta, laetis ad tot ingentes victorias auguriis, quae postea familiam vestram longe clarissimam fecere.

196   'Nos itaque iis admodum neglectis, utpote quibus illa et ceteris etiam humanae vitae voluptatibus omnino renuntiarit,

elevated and refined art! Her gown was gilded in the likeness of a rippling and lightly agitated sea, billowing with rays of colors rolled back from the waistband to the bottommost fringe, decorated with purple borders and fringed edges, embroidered with chased and painted gold, adorned at regular intervals. On these was depicted a balsam tree with this inscription on its trunk, 'THE SOUL IS LIKE UNTO THIS,' a symbolic representation of an uncorrupted life, the explanation being that the gum of the balsam tree never decays.[252] This mantle, which went on display only on that feast day, cost many thousands of gold ducats, but the liveliness of its pleasing originality was valued still more for the good taste of the expenditure. But what charming feminine fashions has this woman introduced! With incredible skill and fertile imagination she has been an innovator with respect to every elegance, and there is no one who discovers all these adornments of attire more finely, or fixes her hair more handily and aptly, or positions pearls and gems in their places more strikingly!"

Then I [GIOVIO] said: "D'Avalos, these are indeed the exceed-   195 ingly rare endowments of a noble girl, and they entice young men rather than old ones. But there exist in her far more outstanding and more splendid attributes which men advanced in age and her closest friends admire — groups that include, not least, both Muscettola and myself. But you know all these things perfectly well, since you were raised with her almost from the cradle. For as soon as Vittoria came out of her mother's womb and saw the light of day, she was promised by a kind of preordained fate to your paternal uncle, Pescara, and transferred into the d'Avalos household amid abundant auguries of the numerous great victories which afterward have made yours by far the most illustrious of families.

"Let us therefore honor these admirable virtues of hers, even   196 though they have been rather disregarded [at the moment] as things she has completely renounced, along with the other

admirabiliores virtutes veneramur: scilicet animi magnitudinem
splendorem prudentiam castimoniam pietatem, quibus aditus in
caelum munitur, et gloria indelebilis certissima cum laude comparatur ad quam boni omnes et praeclara ingenia sine dissimulatione
semper anhelarunt. Iis enim ipsa Victoria non modo supra muliebrem captum sese mirabiliter extulit, sed cum probatissimis ac sapientissimis viris exaequavit. Quae partim avo materno, Federico
Feltrio sapiente ac invicto imperatore, partim a Fabritio patre An-
nesinaque matre ducta, partim a Piscario coniuge imbibita fuisse,
credi par est, quamquam inepte paene dicamus haec eximia dona
in eam ab altis stirpibus omnino profluxisse: cum illam omnes
omnium virtutes studiose collegisse et cuncta item vicia repudiasse
prorsus appareat adeo ut nulli mortali feminae vel Natura benignius, vel Fortuna propensius, vel ipsae denique stellae felicius ar-
riserint.

197 'Quae pulcherrima deorum munera non illi quidem ut saepe fit
invidiam conflavisse, verum apud omnes matronas incomparabilem gratiam atque observantiam peperisse videntur. Quod mirum
certe est atque difficile, cum ab ipsa natura feminae in aliena per-
sona omnem exsuperantiam virtutis oderint, et nimium excedentis
formae decus aegris et malignis oculis semper aspexerint. Illud
imprimis avitum est: adversus omnes cupiditates omnesque fortunae iniurias invictum animum praetulisse, cum in tantis opibus, in
tanta vitae libertate in tantaque saeculi et corruptorum morum licentia, aliquanto maius fuerit non peccare quam omnino illustrem
clarioribus virtutibus evasisse.

198 'At quam excelsa et summo digna philosopho gravitate, incredibilem amisso viro dolorem temperavit atque lenivit ut, cum

pleasures of human life,[253] to wit, magnanimity, personal distinction, prudence, chastity, and piety. By these virtues one gains access into heaven, and by them imperishable glory is united with the most certain praise, toward which all good people and brilliant minds have always striven breathlessly and undisguisedly. By these qualities not only has Vittoria raised herself marvelously beyond womanly capacity, but she has equaled the most widely esteemed and wisest men. It is reasonable to believe that she has derived them partly from her maternal grandfather Federico da Montefeltro, a wise and invincible commander, and partly from her father Fabrizio and her mother Agnese, and that she has imbibed them as well from her husband Pescara. Yet is would be foolish to say that these extraordinary gifts have all come to her from her high ancestry, for it is absolutely clear that she has herself been zealous to acquire every single virtue and likewise has repudiated every vice — so much so that upon no mortal woman has Nature smiled more kindly, or Fortune more favorably, or the stars themselves more felicitously.

"These most beautiful gifts of the gods seem not to have 197 aroused envy, as indeed often happens, but even among the matrons, every one of them, they seem to have produced incomparable goodwill and deferential regard. This is surely astonishing and difficult to believe, since by their very nature women have hated every superiority of virtue in another person, and they have always regarded an excessive endowment of surpassing beauty with wounded and spiteful eyes. This quality, especially, is an ancestral one: her display of unyielding resistance to all cupidity and to all injuries of fortune. To someone enjoying such wealth and freedom, and in a licentious age marked by corrupt morals, it would have been a great accomplishment to refrain from sin, let alone to win renown for the finest virtues.

"Then, after her husband died, she has tempered and assuaged 198 her incredible anguish with sublime seriousness worthy of the

acerbissimi luctus causa eius animo insideat sempiterna, ea tamen velut[434] siccatis lacrimis moderatione finita videatur. Porro ille qui in eius domo latissime refulget aequabilis et perpetuus vitae splendor a matre deductus est. Ea enim, ut clarissimi ac splendidissimi viri filiam decebat, Columniam domum invectis peristromatum et aulaeorum ornamentis[435] lectorum[436] mensarumque munditiis illustravit, cum antea in universum Romani proceres politioris lautitiae rudes essent et militari quadam illuvie subagrestes.

199 'Patet enim domus hospitibus non modo bonis et studiosis, quod peculiare eius benignitatis semper fuit, verum etiam ignotis et advenis quos variae necessitudines obtulerint; eos adeo laute ac hilariter excipere consuevit, ut ii demum insatiabili cum laude admirationeque discedant. Disciplina etenim familiae adeo honeste ac liberaliter instituta est ut nihil ad apparatum opulentius, vel ad obsequium paratius, vel ad iucundam celeritatem expeditius possit inveniri. Namque eruditus et cum ratione largus dispensator, et acutus ac diligens architriclinus, per industrium et vigilantem obsonatorem, ac expertum ac nitidum coquum, celeres et Pythagoricos pueros, rem esculentam distinctis muneribus administra[n]t. Moderati vero abaci praefectus nitido potius quam capaci et[437] vario et multae artis argento, beneolentibus mappis et candidis mantelibus, mensas instruit; cuncta floribus aut virentibus foliis eleganter exornat.

200 'Ipsa etiam, quamquam est abstemia, deligendis vinis studium adhibet, ne quid a convivis omnino desideretur. Totam vero convictus voluptatem desiderio potius quam satietate metitur,

greatest philosopher. As a result, although the abiding reason for her bitter lamentation lies heavy on her mind, it seems to have been limited and brought under control, as if her tears had been dried. Moreover, that steady and constant splendor of life which shines forth so extensively in her home has been derived from her mother: indeed, as was fitting for the daughter of so distinguished and illustrious a man, she added luster to the House of Colonna thanks to the adornments she introduced: bed coverings and tapestries and elegant tables and couches—whereas previously, Roman nobles were entirely ignorant of the more refined forms of luxury and were more boorish with their filthy military ways.

"Her house lies open not only to good and learned men—that 199 has always been a distinguishing feature of her liberality—but also to unknown people and immigrants whom various difficulties have brought to her. She has been accustomed to receive these people so lavishly and cheerfully that in the end they depart with unwearying praise and admiration. And indeed, the orderly operation of the household has been set up so creditably and unstintingly that it would be impossible to find a house more richly supplied, better served or so pleasantly quick in its operations. There's an administrator who is both well trained and munificent (within reason), and an astute and assiduous butler who manages the foodstuffs through the agency of a diligent and watchful provisioner, a cook both skilled and elegant, and servants who are quick to action and Pythagorean.[254] Moreover, the chief server in charge of the carefully regulated sideboard tends efficiently to the scented napkins and bright white tablecloths, and sets the tables with silver that is shining rather than capacious and is variegated and of fine workmanship. He decorates all things tastefully with flowers or verdant leaves.

"Vittoria herself, too, though abstemious, brings enthusiasm to 200 choosing the wines, lest the guests find anything lacking. Moreover, she measures the delight of the feast in accordance with

splendoremque ipsum non in epulis nimia cura atque luxuria conquisitis, sed in salubribus et teneris obsoniis et in structoris elegantia perpetuisque munditiis reponit.

201 'Feminae ancillantes tum maxime conticescunt. Nullae domesticae sollicitudines familiam excruciant, nullae eam occultae agitant simultates, nullae verborum altercationes concordiam dissolvunt, quando haec omnia liberalibus et severis excubantis dominae legibus gubernentur, quoniam omnis vel servilis obsequii vel officii veteris ac benevolentiae remuneratrix ab ineunte aetate semper fuit, ac indefessa etiam adiutrix egenorum bonorumque omnium, quibus largissima et paene prodiga manu semper subvenit, cum ex adverso impudentiae sceleris ignaviae, simulationis, supra quam dici possit, inimica semper exstiterit.

202 'Sed quid proferre opus est e domestica disciplina consilium eius, prudentiam, rationem, quae multo clarioribus exemplis enituerint[438] cum[439] Samnites Picentinos Aquinates Arpinatesque regeret, et quae in Latio sunt paterna oppida, in pace ac officio temperata legum aequitate contineret, talisque esset ad quietem atque opulentiam iis populis parandam ut, cum saepius clementia et lenitate esset dulcis, aliquando ad exactam iustitiam virili severitate asperior ab inquietis atque maleficis sentiretur. In ea enim vis illa divinaque virtus cernitur ut ea, quae agenda sunt mature deliberet, perite concludat et celeriter administret. Propterea non modo Columnii proceres in suscipiendis gravissimarum rerum negotiis eam consiliorum omnium participem esse voluerunt.

desire rather than satiety, and she gauges its splendor, not in terms of recherché, elaborate, and extravagant dishes, but in healthful and delicate provisions as well as elegant and consistently immaculate service.

"The serving women keep particularly silent during feasts. No domestic worries torment the household, no hidden quarrels trouble it, and no verbal altercations destroy the harmony, seeing that all these things are governed by the rules — at once liberal and stern — of the mistress keeping watch over the house. From the earliest age she has always been someone who rewards all deference of servants or old obligations and goodwill, and is also a tireless helper of the deserving poor; to them, she has always provided support with a hand that is so very generous as almost to be prodigal — although by the same token she has always been, more than can be expressed, a conspicuous enemy of impudence, criminality, faintheartedness, and pretense. 201

"But what need is there to produce instances of her wise counsel, practical understanding, and good judgment from her household management, when she has provided much more illustrious examples of these qualities when governing the Samnites, Picentines, Aquinates, and Arpinates as well as her father's towns in Latium — all places she kept tranquil and loyal by enforcing the law with restraint and impartiality. And in providing peace and wealth to those peoples she acted in such a way that, although she was more often indulgent and showed clemency and mildness, sometimes she was perceived by the restless and criminal as too harsh, having exacted justice with manlike severity. You can see this strength and divine virtue in her: she decides in good time what needs to be done, quickly attends to it, and expertly concludes it. That is why the leaders of the Colonna family, and others too, have wanted her participation in all their deliberations when undertaking the most serious matters. 202

203 'Verum et ipse Piscarius, absens, tantae prudentiae dux et tantae felicitatis, cum inusitatis artibus res bellicas vehementius agitaret, consulendam saepe uxorem ac in omni actione magnifaciendas eius sententias arbitraretur. Quis enim ea vel certius de occultis principum voluntatibus, vel de castrensi disciplina salubrius, vel de nummariis et frumentariis difficultatibus explicatius, vel denique de toto bellorum eventu divinius umquam iudicavit? Neque haec velut delecta ex libris, quos fere omnes memoriter tenet,[440] sumpsisse putatote, cum haec tanta maximorum et clarissimorum ducum filia, neptis, uxor, cognata ac in domo armorum tropheorumque plenissima viriliter educata didicerit.

204 'At quanta animi aequitate et quanta sine fremitu patientia viri Piscarii absentis famosos amores atque lascivias tulit, cum se ab eo supra omnes vere amari ac observari intellegeret! Dicebat enim aequum esse, ut Mars bellicosus ludibundae Veneris amore teneretur, quoniam natura eosdem corporis ac animi virtutibus magnos et libidinosos pariter effinxisset; unde natam esse Martis ac Veneris fabulam apud poetas, humanarum affectionum causas figuratis rerum involucris abscondentes, quam Aristoteles naturae interpres sollertissimus aperuit.

205 'Quanta vero animi firmitate atque alacritate pudicitiam, qua nihil in muliere formosius esse potest, viro superstite custodivit! Et nunc, eo orbata, quantis religionis et diligentiae praesidiis consaepsit. Institutis enim castissimis et ingenuis artibus erudita, non conscientiae modo et veritati sed famae etiam flagrantissime serviendum arbitratur. Nam cum pudicitia ipsis penitus medullis sit

"But even a wise and successful commander like Pescara, when 203 absent in order to prosecute a war more energetically and with innovative stratagems, often felt the need to consult his wife and gave great weight to her views in every one of his actions. For who ever exercised judgment more reliably than she about the secret objectives of princes, or more profitably about military discipline, or more clearly about the difficulties of provisioning troops with money and food, or with more foresight concerning the overall outcome of wars? And don't imagine that she just picked this knowledge up from books—though she has a tenacious memory for nearly all her reading. In fact, as the daughter, granddaughter, wife, and cousin of the greatest and most illustrious commanders, she learned it all from her manly upbringing in a household filled with arms and trophies.

"Yet she endured with great equanimity of mind and patience, 204 and without grumbling, the well-known love affairs and dalliances of her absent husband Pescara, because she understood that he truly loved and respected her above all other women. She used to say that it was fair enough for warlike Mars to be held fast by love for frisky Venus, inasmuch as nature had fashioned the two of them to be great and lusty, with excellences of body and mind in equal measure. She used to say that this was what gave rise to the fable about Mars and Venus in the poets, who hid the motives of human affections in figurative wrappings—a fable that Aristotle, the most skilled interpreter of nature, explicated.

"But while her husband was alive, she safeguarded her chas- 205 tity—than which nothing in a woman can be more becoming— with great strength and keenness of mind. Even now, though bereft of him, she has fenced it in with garrisons of religious observances and watchfulness. Indeed, having been brought up in the chastest habits and in the arts worthy of gentlefolk, she is of the opinion that one must ardently subordinate one's actions, not only to conscience and truth, but also to reputation. Since her purity

inclusa, omnes animi corporisque delicias non occultavit ut iis in abdito frueretur, sed omnino resecavit.

206 'Duae ante omnia vetulae, ab tristi virginitate non minus superbae quam feroces cottidiana assiduitate, ei stationem habent, tamquam duo feri ac ingentes molossi ad fimbriam excubantes; qua re, adversus improvisae libidinis repentinos impetus atque obviorum vel familiarium fortuitam ac insanam temeritatem, neque cautius neque salubrius quicquam poterit inveniri. Ceterum, quae summa eius est et incredibilis pietas, florem aetatis ieiunio subigit; non linteo sed laneo subuculae thorace latera illa mollia circumdat; in diuturnis supplicationibus ante statuas divorum genua atterit vertebrasque debilitat; et quod [in]indignum est, etiam pudicas corporis partes aculeatis flagris flagellat.

207 'Sed quid [non] possent sacra perpetua continuatis prope horis audita? Quid divinae Instrumenti Veteris ac Novi lectiones, quid cogitationes sanctissimae, quamquam ipsa excelso proloquio fateatur castimoniam non esse positam in multo difficilique labore, sed in quadam constanti et firma inductione animi, et bona ac studiosa voluntate?

208 'Quam cunctae mulieres continuo essent habiturae, si, ut Milesius Thales dicere erat solitus, deos omnia cernere et cuncta vel abstrusiora etiam loca diis plena esse existimarent, et ipsas enixe colerent virtutes quae pudoris fidelissimae tutrices esse consuevissent! Propterea et tum cum in summo luxu viveret et humanis deliciis in praeclara luce frueretur, et nunc cum orbata coniunge, reiectis omnibus vitae blandimentis, vix unis tantum tenuioribus alimentis vitam sustentet, nihil superstitiose, nihil simulanter, nihil

and virtue truly belong to her inmost nature, she has not suppressed all delights of mind and body in order to indulge them in secret, but instead she has curtailed them entirely.

"First of all, two elderly women, fierce, proud, and unremitting 206 thanks to their own stern virginity, maintain a guard over her like two huge and wild mastiffs keeping watch at her feet. No more cautious or secure step could have been taken to thwart sudden, unforeseen urges of lust as well as chance, insane acts of rashness on the part of members of her household or other persons encountered. Still, such is her lofty and incredible piety that she subdues the flower of her youth by fasting; she covers her delicate flanks not with a silken but rather a woolen vest as her tunic; she wears out her back and knees with daily supplications before statues of the saints; and she even lashes private parts of her body with the stinging blows of a whip, a punishment undeserved.

"But why may[255] perpetual divine services be heard at almost 207 every hour? Why are there holy readings from the Old and the New Testament, why the pious meditations, when even she herself would acknowledge in a lofty preamble that chastity does not reside in great and difficult labor, but in a certain steadfast and firm application of the mind and in a good and zealous will?

"Just think how all women would come immediately to be re- 208 garded if, as Thales of Miletus was accustomed to say, they should reckon that the gods see all things and that all places, even the more remote ones, are replete with the gods, and if they should assiduously cultivate those very virtues that have customarily been the most faithful guardians of chastity. For this reason, both at that time when she was living in the greatest luxury and enjoying the delights of human life in the bright light of day, and also now when, deprived of her husband, with all the charms of life cast off, and scarcely sustaining life with a single scant meal a day, she still commits no superstitious, feigned, or foolish action, and she is

inepte facit, ut castitatis decus sollicite tueri videatur, quando alias nullum in suspiciosa et facile maledica civitate locum sermoni obtrectatorum omnino reliquerit.

209 'Familiariter enim et iucunde et cum dignitate semper salutantes excipere consuevit, et de amatoriis affectionibus, de totoque genere humanarum voluptatum, si adsint viri elegantes et praesertim litteris exornati, luculentissime fabulatur; et cum neque tristes neque severas habeat aures, suoque sale et alienis facetiis delectetur; nullum tamen verbum exit ex ore eius nisi pudicum iucundum honorificum. Nam si quando aculeata scommata, quod est urbanioris ingenii, contorquet, nullam amaritiem quae altius descendat in perstrictorum animis relinquit, ita ut nihil ingenio eius apertius sit atque candidius. Irridet enim eas quae, ut castimoniam simulent, religiosa quadam rusticitate ad teneriores facetias frontem et supercilia velut stomachantes contrahunt, quando difficilis admodum sit virtutis simulatio diuturna.

210 'Quid enim modo magis ineptum magisque ridiculum fuit Ioannae Castriotae iudicio? Quae cum esset admodum formosa inter Isabellae Reginae virgines, proptereaque et saepe quidem sine rivali seipsam flagranter adamaret omnesque mortales virginali ipsius flore putaret indignos, eo superstitiosae vanitatis ac insaniae animum provexit, ut ioco compellari vel digito attingi vel avidis oculis spectari piaculum duceret: adeo ut cum lavaretur, ancillae oculos vittis obligaret, numquam nisi exstincto lumine nudaretur, naturae gratias ageret quod pulices caecos effinxisset, et cum maxima animi sollicitudine theologos percontaretur an mortui cum omnes resurgent ante tribunal Dei, ex vitae moribus de toto

seen to safeguard carefully the honor of chastity, seeing that, besides, she has given no occasion at all for disparaging gossip in a suspicious city that turns so easily to slander.

"In fact, she always has been accustomed to receive those calling 209 upon her in a friendly, pleasant and dignified fashion; and if elegant men are present, and especially those renowned in literature, she converses beautifully about matters of the heart and about the entire range of cultivated pleasures. And since she has ears that are neither gloomy nor severe, she takes pleasure in her own wit and in the jokes of others. Nonetheless no word leaves her mouth that is not modest, pleasant, and honorable. If ever she lets fly sarcastic barbs — a thing characteristic of the more sophisticated wits — she leaves behind no bitterness that might penetrate deeper into the minds of the wounded, so that nothing can be more open hearted and more candid than her temperament. Indeed, she laughs at those who, in order to counterfeit chastity, frown ill temperedly and furrow their brows at slightly salacious jokes with a kind of religious boorishness; her view is that it's difficult to keep up a pretense of virtue on a daily basis.

"What judgment recently has been more foolish and ridiculous 210 than that of Giovanna Castriota?[256] Among the young girls in Queen Isabella's retinue, she was especially beautiful, and on that account she often used to admire herself a great deal as if she had no rival and supposed that no mortal was worthy of the flower of her virginity. Thus she took superstitious and unsound vanity to such a level that she thought it a sin if she were spoken to flirtatiously, or someone laid a finger on her, or even if she were looked at by hungry eyes. So obsessed was she that when she was being bathed, she would bind the eyes of the maidservant with linen bands. Never would she be stripped nude unless the lights were put out. She even used to thank nature for having made the fleas blind! And with extreme anxiety, she used to ask theologians whether, when all the dead rise again before the tribunal of God,

hominum genere iudicantis, nudi penitus sine tunicis essent consti-
turi, et an ipsa ex merito observatae virginitatis saltem linteolum,
quo pudenda velarentur, ab Deipara Virgine esset impetratura.'

211   Ad ea cum ego risum sustulissem, DAVALUS 'Ne putato,' inquit,
'Iovi, mulierem ullam Castriota pudoris fastu vaniorem umquam
exstitisse. Obiter,[441] etiam a Pyrrho Epirotarum et Antigono[442]
Macedoniae regibus originem se ducere haud dubie praedicabat.
Et profecto tibi stomachum movissent tot in hac pudoris cura[443]
fastidiosae religiones ad ostentandam virginitatem, cum tu affectionem omnem cum gestus tum[444] verborum libero animo nequaquam feras, et cum puellis nostris Gallica familiaritate libenter io-
ceris.

212   'Sed tum maxime prae nimio risu praecordia dirupisses si tibi
eius sollemne convivium spectare contigisset: nam cum id celebra-
retur[445] in triclinio regalibus aulaeis exornato in quibus nobili Bel-
gica texturae arte iudicium Paridis erat depictum, ipsa egregie
pudica, ne convivarum oculi argumento minus verecundo offende-
rentur, trium dearum femora et clunes supra consutis totidem
candidis mantelibus praetexit, admirante id primo et mox ridente
convivio, cum sciscitanti Penelope Caraciola, muliere curiosa et
erudita, quonam casu tam insigne aulaeum fuisset erosum aut
vitiatum, illa respondisset id quidem esse incolume, verum se dearum partes, quas poetarum more pictor lascivus sub tenuissimo et
transmittenti velo naturaliter expresserat, honestius convelare voluisse.[446]

and He passes judgment on all humans on the basis of how they've lived, they will stand entirely naked—and whether she herself, as a deserved reward for her well-guarded virginity, might be able to obtain by request from the Virgin Mother of God at least a strip of linen to cover her genitals."

When I had let out a laugh at this, D'AVALOS said: "You can't imagine, Giovio, that there has ever existed a woman who was more vain and arrogant about her chastity than Castriota. (Incidentally, she also used to say that without doubt she was descended from King Pyrrhus of Epirus and King Antigonus of Macedonia.) And undoubtedly the many religious scruples she invoked out of concern for her modesty and to make a show of her virginity would have vexed you, seeing how, when with Gallic familiarity you joke as you please with our maidens, you don't allow *them* to express their feelings freely by word or gesture.[257]

"But if you had happened to witness a certain solemn feast, you would have burst your guts laughing on the spot. Since the feast was being celebrated in a dining room adorned with regal tapestries on which the judgment of Paris had been depicted by the noble Flemish art of weaving, to prevent her guests' eyes from being offended by this less-than-modest subject, our ever-so-chaste woman herself cloaked over the thighs and bottoms of the three goddesses with three white tablecloths that had been sewn together. The guests' surprise soon turned to laughter when Penelope Caracciolo,[258] a woman curious and learned, inquired how it had happened that so notable a tapestry had become worn or damaged. The Castriota woman responded that it was in fact intact, but that she had wished to cover more decorously the parts of the goddesses' bodies which the lascivious artist, in the manner of the poets, had portrayed in their natural state under a very thin and translucent veil.

211

212

213   'Verum[447] Piscarius tantam eius pudicitiae ostentationem salsis-
simo scommate aliquando ita perstrixit, ut a tota Neapoli Castriotae castimonia, proverbii loco habita, rideretur. Nam cum ab
eo, salibus colludente, liberius esset interrogata an ulla[448] umquam
nubendi libido quae acrius stimularit pudicum eius animum laces-
sisset, argute illa (ut ipsi videbatur) "semel in omni vita tantum"
respondit, et eo quidem tempore quo legiones Helvetiae Gallos
(quibus propter Aragoniam factionem erat infensa), totis Italiae
finibus pepulissent. Incomparabili enim se tum amore Helvetiorum fuisse captam, ac illi tam forti populo virtutis causa nubere
cupivisse. Ad quod repente Piscarius: "Non aliter," inquit, "tam
diuturnis desideriis, mi domina, peregregie consuluisses, nisi validus et numerosus quidem populus ad luculentas nuptias, pro uno
tantum homunculo ut nos sumus, fuisset expetitus."'

214   Quod festive et praepilate[449] dictum cum nobis placuisset et
propterea rideremus, MUSETIUS: 'Luciae' inquit 'Caeselliae haec
nostra Castriota similis videtur quae, cum esset vidua et valde
formosa et cum multo luxu multisque deliciis vitam traduceret, et
a pluribus procis ad eius nuptias ambientibus sollicitius amaretur,
"Quid mihi" inquit "tam assidue et petulanter molesti estis, quando
ego nubere nolim nisi in ipsa *Politia* Platonis, in qua bonae mulieres sine ulla mollioris vitae infamia, plenissima veneris voluptate
poterant satiari?"'[450]

215   Tum vero ego ⟨IOVIUS⟩ inquam: 'Haec tua Caesellia, Museti,
in rabida[451] tentigine castissima fuisse videtur, sed facessant ab iis
verecundis sermonibus eae feminae quae in praecipiti etiam aetate
furiosa libidine peruruntur, et ad Victoriae laudes in transcursu
saltem absolvendas aliquando redeamus. In qua adeo illustres atque elegantes litterae ad admirationem hominum refulgent ut

"But then Pescara criticized her ostentatious chastity in a sur-   213
passingly witty gibe, with the result that the purity of the Castriota family was made proverbial and was laughed at throughout
Naples. For when he asked her jestingly whether her modest soul
had ever been assailed by a compelling desire for marriage, she replied cleverly (or so she thought), 'only once in my entire life'; and
indeed, 'it was at the time when the Swiss armies had driven the
French beyond the boundaries of Italy.'[259] (Being of the Aragonese
faction, she was bitterly hostile toward the French.) She said that
back then, indeed, she had been captivated by an incomparable
love of the Swiss and, moved by their virtue, had desired to be
married to so brave a nation. To this Pescara instantly replied, 'My
ladyship, to service in distinguished fashion such a long-standing
desire you could not have done otherwise than to seek a brilliant
marriage with a strong and populous nation, rather than one little
man like me.'"

When we had enjoyed the story and laughed at Pescara's blunt-   214
tipped witticism, MUSCETTOLA said: "This Castriota of ours
seems similar to Lucia Caselli,[260] an exceedingly beautiful widow
leading a life of great luxury and enjoyment. When she was being
courted too attentively by numerous nobles with a view to marriage, she asked: 'Why are you bothering me with such aggressive
persistence? I don't want to be married unless I can do so in Plato's
Republic, where good women could satisfy themselves with the full-
est sensual pleasure without incurring infamy for living too voluptuous a life.'"[261]

Then I [GIOVIO] added: "This Caselli of yours, Muscettola,   215
seems to have been perfectly chaste while in a state of rabid lust,
but let those women who are consumed with wild sexual desire,
even in their declining years, be gone from these respectable conversations of ours; and let us finally return, at least briefly, to
complete the praises of Vittoria. Distinguished and elegant scholarship shines forth in her to the admiration of men—so much so

praeclarae illae praestantissimorum morum dotes vix in parte summae[452] laudis et gloriae censeantur, quoniam ea sese a teneris annis tanta discendi cupiditate omnium prope disciplinarum studiis imbuerit, ut disceptantem et scribentem philosophi laudibus extollant; theologi prope rigentes auscultent; humaniorum vero studiorum cultores et poetae penitus admirentur, quoniam tot et tanta non perpetuis hausta lectionibus sed divinis potius afflatibus concepta fuisse credantur.

216   'Eius enim Etrusca carmina quae verecundo ipsius[453] animo renitente ac penitus invito, circumferuntur, quibus nam tenerioris eloquentiae floribus depicta? Quibus interlita celsioris ingenii luminibus? Quibusque numerorum artificiis exornata esse conspicimus? Quam porro gravitatem, quod virile decus, quem denique leporem ferunt innumerabiles eius epistolae de gravissimis ac honestissimis rebus ad summos et doctissimos viros et maximos reges conscriptae? Non fugacem enim haec et cito perituram, sed omnino sempiternam laudem promerentur. Litterae profecto in hac una divina muliere tot et tantis virtutibus impositae sic elucent ut sint illis ingentibus ignibus omnino persimiles qui in cacumine pyramidum in magnis victoriis et publica laetitia ab Aegyptiis regibus excitantur. Ii enim, per se magni, quanto sublimius ab excelso illarum fastigio sese attollunt, tanto eos latius homines ab remotis Africae regionibus ipsisque Nili ostiis et maritimis cursibus contuentur.'

217   Haec cum dicerem, a pueris nobis est renuntiatum portarum custodes aegerrime fer⟨r⟩e quod tam diu ipsorum officia moraremur. Iam enim corniculata luna et stellae ipsae, sole penitus

that her famous gifts of exceptional character are reckoned as only a part of her high glory and praise. This is the case because from a tender age she imbued herself with an enormous desire for learning in nearly all fields, so that philosophers praise her argumentation and writing; theologians are thrilled[262] as they listen to her; and poets and the devotees of humanistic studies admire her without reservation, since they believe that she has not imbibed her many great thoughts from assiduous reading, but rather from divine inspiration.

"Consider her Tuscan poems, which are in circulation despite   216
her bashful resistance and absolute unwillingness that this should be so. How beautifully have they been painted with flowers of tender eloquence! What sparkling gems of lofty intellect have been interlarded among them! We may note too the metrical skill that adorns them. Then there are her almost innumerable letters: what authority, what manly decorum, and what charm these display, written as they are to the loftiest and most learned men and to the greatest kings, and concerning the most weighty and honorable matters? These accomplishments merit praise that is neither fleeting nor perishable, but absolutely immortal. The scholarship that so many and such great virtues have unquestionably placed in the control of this one divine woman shines forth in such a way that it is certainly very like those massive fires which are stirred up by Egyptian kings at the summit of pyramids after great victories and during periods of public rejoicing. For the higher that those fires, already great in themselves, fly up from their lofty summit, the more widely are they visible to mankind, as far away as remote regions of Africa, and the mouth of the Nile Delta, and ships plying the waters of the sea."

While I was making these remarks, the servant boys reported   217
to us that the gatekeepers were greatly vexed that we had so long delayed them in the discharge of their duties. For already, the sun had hidden his head, and the little crescent moon and the stars

occultato, aliam lucem invexerant, ita interrupto potius quam confecto sermone, ex amoenissimo reginae scopulo ad naviculas descendimus et in arcem rediimus.

FINIS

had sailed in, bearing a different kind of light. So, our conversation interrupted rather completed, we descended from the delightful Queen's Rock into the small boats and went back into the citadel.

THE END

APPENDIX

1 Cum in ipso incredibili et longe luctuosissimo totius paene religionis et Romanae civitatis interitu gravis pestilentia super tot accu-
   mulatas clades Hadriani molem invasisset, in qua Clemens iam
   deditus et senatus barbarorum custodia servabantur, totque circum me iactis fulminibus totam veteris atque perpetui officii mei
   cum pontifice consuetudinem abrupisset, arce eiectus in Aenariam
   veni ad Victoriam Columnam, feminam cum forma et pudicitia
   illustrem tum omni virili laude longe dignissimam, *quam tu quoque,*
   sicut in amore tardus et gravis, ita demum stabilito iudicio et pertinax et
   vehemens super omnes coluisse videris, cuius amoris tui nunc maxime
   fructum sentis et eius mirificam voluntatem in hac privata tua calamitate
   feliciter experiris. Sciebam enim illam tanta esse animi magnitudine
   atque virtute ut nihil *antiquius atque* praestantius duceret quam
   naufragio et saevis adversae tempestatis eiectos fluctibus excipere,
   nec eos ulla fortunae iniuria mergi pati, ac demum conservatos

APPENDIX

Since the opening of Dialogue One was heavily revised, a reconstruction of the first draft version is provided here, along with an English translation. Italics in the text indicate elements subsequently deleted or replaced. The notes indicate how the altered passages ultimately read. While Giovio left undeleted the line in the title dedicating the dialogue to Giberti, the revised version is reoriented in ways that deemphasize Giberti's captivity, an event long past by the time of the later revisions.

In the very midst of the incredible and most lamentable destruction of practically the whole of religion and of the city of Rome, on top of so many accumulated disasters, a severe pestilence attacked Castel Sant' Angelo, where Clement, who had already surrendered, and the cardinals were being held in custody by the barbarians. Amid so many thunderbolts that had fallen round about me, the pestilence broke off my entire association with the pope — a longstanding and uninterrupted attendance. Cast out of the citadel, I came to Ischia — and to Vittoria Colonna. She is a woman both outstanding in beauty and purity and worthiest by far of the kind of praise normally reserved for men. *You, also, Giberti, appear beyond all others to have cultivated her friendship. Just as you are deliberate and dignified in your affections, so in the end you are both steadfast and strong once your judgment is established. And now, especially, in this personal calamity of yours, you feel the benefit of her affection toward you and are finding out her marvelous generosity.* For I was aware that she is endowed with such magnanimity and virtue that she considers nothing finer *and more important* than to rescue those cast out by shipwreck and by the savage waves of a hostile storm and not to allow them to be drowned by any wrong of fortune and,

benigne et liberaliter recreare, et eos quidem ante alios qui aliquam ab optimis litterarum studiis commendationem ac laudem meruissent. Neque vero id sum veritus quominus ab ea insignis humanitas cum summa liberalitate foret exspectanda, ut offenso animo acerbissimarum cladium memoriam retineret, quarum magnitudine Columnius ager Latino bello a nostris exercitibus atrociter fuerit evastatus; hunc enim domestici doloris sensum virtutis amor penitus *absterserit*,[1] ad eam unam siquidem inflammata plenis passibus fertur, eximiaque pietate reiectis humanae vitae illecebris viam sibi ad gloriam in caelum munire contendit.

2   Itaque ea caritate eoque liberali animo sum receptus ut me non amicum modo vel necessarium clientem, sed exoptatum aliquem propinquum advenisse ceteri familiares existimarent. Certatum enim est exquisita atque perpetua benignitate cum ab ipso Alfonso Davalo duce *fortissimo*,[2] tum etiam ab huius amita Constantia Davala, cuius ingenio nihil nobilius *nihil mitius* aut sanctius reperitur. *Quibus de rebus fiebat ut, qui fortunas ipsas et spes prope omnes amiseram, amicorumque praecipuos aut inusitatis miseriarum iactatos fluctibus aut publica clade exstinctos videbam, postquam tantis essem ereptus periculis, perbeatum me ac fortunatum esse putarem, nisi apud vos[3] obligatum constanti fide religioneque animum omnino reliquissem. Quis enim tam alieni ferreique animi, tam inhumanae impiaeque mentis fuerit, qui vel in tutissimo portu ac iucundissimo heroum ac Musarum domicilio laetari, aut laxare animum vel maerore vacuus et molestissimis curis liberatus esse possit, cum sacrosanctum pontificem et senatum fere omnem captum teneri, te vero immanioribus barbaris ad nefariam crudelitatem deditum esse conspiciat?*

once they have been saved, kindly and generously to restore them to health, especially those who have derived some commendation and praise from the excellent study of literature. Nor in fact did I entertain any fears that her outstanding kindness combined with exceeding generosity might not await me or that she would rancorously harbor the memory of the terrible, large-scale disasters by which, during the war in Latium, the Colonna estate was shockingly devastated by our armies. Her love of virtue thoroughly cleansed her sense of domestic grievance, since to virtue alone she is carried with passion and at full stride. With her extraordinary piety she has cast aside the allurements of human life and hastens to pave for herself a path to heavenly glory.

And so I was welcomed with such love and generosity that the   2 others in the household supposed that I had arrived, not just as a friend or an invaluable dependent, but as some longed-for close relation. Indeed the *exceedingly brave* commander Alfonso d'Avalos and his aunt Costanza d'Avalos contended with each other in their exquisite and continual kindness toward me. He himself is highly distinguished in statesmanship and martial prowess, and she has the noblest, gentlest, holiest character that one could possibly find. *I had just lost my own fortune and practically all my hopes, and was seeing my closest friends either tossed about by unusual waves of misery or killed in the general slaughter. After I had been rescued from great danger, I should have thought myself very blessed and fortunate, had I not left behind with you a heart altogether obligated by steadfast loyalty and by religious obligation. For who could have been so unsympathetic and hard-hearted, so inhuman and impious, that he could either rejoice in the safest port and the most delightful dwelling of the heroes and the Muses or could relax his mind, even though himself liberated from the most distressing concerns, when he observed that the Holy Father and nearly the entire Curia were being held captive—and what is more, that you, Giberti, have been given over to the unspeakable cruelty of savage barbarians?*

2a   *Verum duo mihi maxime conceptum maerorem levant perturbatumque animum mirifice consolantur: illa tua invicti animi divina fortitudo cum his tum aliis saepe spectata periculis, qua te admodum patienter contumelias cruciatus catenas et denique vel taeterrimae mortis genus laturum scio, cum iam pridem puram castamque mentem, corporis dolore contempto et despecta omni casuum atque fortunae acerbitate, ad verae virtutis ac religionis contemplationem revocaris; alterum est spes ipsa, quam nemo umquam vita purus atque integer in Dei Optimi Maximi ope atque auxiliis frustra collocavit. Neque enim existimandum est Deum et divos omnes, qui humanarum rerum curam gerunt et ad poenam et praemium ex merito mortalium bona pariter ac mala rectissime dispensant, tam aversos a salute vestra fore ut ad satietatem sceleratissimorum hominum et religionem et virtutem omnem excisam velint. Ceterum quales exitus haec dira tempora conturbatis ac afflictis rebus dederint, tales certe ad exsecrabilem impiorum memoriam et ad gloriam proborum sempiternam litterarum monumentis demandantur. In hoc enim praepingui castissimoque otio librum huius anni rerum admodum insignem Historiis adieci nostris, quas deorum beneficio e tanta clade ereptas, ne iterum pereant, publicare constitui.*

2b   *Sed ubi allatum est te pro obside traditum et catenis vinctum perpetuis Cimbrorum excubiis in carcere custodiri, cohortante Victoria, dialogum conscripsi* De viris et feminis aetate nostra florentibus, *ut animum tuum inusitatis angoribus et corporis incommodis fatigatum honestissima peramoenae commentationis voluptate delinirem, si (quod vix crediderim) fortasse mens ipsa, assiduis sacrarum litterarum lectionibus recreata atque evecta altius haec humaniora vitae oblectamenta, certis nonnumquam intervallis admiserit.*[4] *Porro dialogum conscripsi ea fide et sermonis libertate qua*

But two things above all lighten my solemn mourning and marvelously 2a
console my troubled mind. First, there is that divine fortitude of your un-
conquered spirit, often seen in these and other perils, by which I know that
you will endure with the utmost patience the insults, tortures, chains and,
ultimately, even the foulest form of death. For having disregarded physical
pain and despised all the hardships of circumstances and fortune, you have
directed your mind, pure and pious for so long, back to the contemplation of
true virtue and true religion. My second consolation is hope itself, for no
one of a pure and innocent life has ever based his hope in vain on the help
and assistance of God Most High. God and all the saints manage the care
of human affairs, and they dispense both the good and the bad with the
utmost justice, so as to reward and punish mortals in accordance with their
deserts. Surely we should not suppose that they would be so unfavorably
disposed toward your well-being that they would wish both all religion and
all virtue destroyed just to satisfy the appetites of the most criminal of men!
And yet, whatever outcomes these dire times should give to our unsettled
and ruined circumstances, surely those outcomes are entrusted to the monu-
ments of literature to curse the memory of the impious and glorify the righ-
teous everlastingly. And so, in this most opulent and unspoiled retreat, I
have added a suitably noteworthy book, dealing with the events of this year,
to my Histories. *Since the latter work was snatched from the midst of*
great ruin by the good offices of the gods, I have decided to publish it lest it
be lost a second time.

But when it was reported that you had been handed over as a hostage, 2b
bound with chains, and were being kept in prison under the constant watch
of German guards, I then, at Vittoria's urging, composed a dialogue, Notable Men and Women of Our Time, *so as to sooth your soul, ex-*
hausted from unaccustomed vexations and bodily discomforts, with the
perfectly honorable pleasure that comes from a delightful account. —Assum-
ing, that is (as I can scarcely believe), that your mind, refreshed and carried
aloft as it is by continual readings of sacred literature, might from time to
time permit itself more human amusements such as these.[1] *At the same*
time, I have composed the dialogue with that honesty and candor of speech

inter nos ego et Davalus atque Musetius sumus collocuti, cum in amoenis-
simo recessu apud lacum inter myrtos familiariter atque otiose sederemus.[5]

3   Venerat tum forte ex Umbris ab exercitu Davalus, ut has illustres feminas sanguine atque amore sibi coniunctissimas inviseret;
nam cum, oppressa caesaris classe et Genua subinde capta, Andreas Auria Gallicae praefectus classis a Thyrreno mari et Venetae
triremes a Siculo freto Campaniae oram maxime terruissent, plerique cariores res suas in hanc munitissimam arcem perbeatae insulae conferre coeperant. Ipsique ante alios Ascanius Columna et
Alfonsus Amalfius Regulus Ioannam Aragoniam et Constantiam
Davalam uxores suas, quibus pulchriores sol non videt, cum infantibus liberis ad Victoriam sororem et Constantiam Davalam Seniorem amitam deduxerant. Itemque Davalus etiam ex ora Picentinorum Mariam uxorem acciverat, quae sicut Aragoniae soror est,
ita eius formam atque elegantiam statim aequatura videtur, cum
adamati coniugis emollita atque excitata blanditiis puellarem verecundiam exuerit.

4   Has omnes Davalus incredibili studio ita colebat ut nullam
omnino praetermitteret occasionem *ludorum omnis generis et piscatio-*
nis et aucupii et venationis, qua muliebris animus iucundissima voluptate
oblectari ⟨e⟩ff⟨u⟩nderetur. Saepe enim spectantibus feminis sese hasta gla-
dio, iaculis ingentique folle cum robustissimis centurionibus exercuerat cepe-
ratque aliquot ingentes cervos in proximis montibus, cum totus venationis
apparatus, ferarum fugae variusque canum ac hominum discursus, e sum-
mae arcis fenestris spectarentur. Sed cum ad exercitum esset rediturus, tria

with which d'Avalos and Muscettola and I talked among ourselves when
we were seated in a familiar and leisurely fashion among the myrtles in a
delightful secluded spot alongside the lake.

At that time, as it happened, d'Avalos had come from the army 3
in Umbria to visit these illustrious women, bound to him by ties
of blood and by affection. Recently, after the emperor's fleet had
been defeated and Genoa thereupon captured, Andrea Doria, the
admiral of the French fleet, had terrorized the coast of Campania
from the Tyrrhenian Sea, and Venetian ships had done so from
the Straits of Messina. And so, many people had begun to convey
their treasures into the exceedingly well-fortified citadel on the
blessed isle of Ischia. Above all others, Ascanio Colonna and Alfonso Piccolomini, the duke of Amalfi, had brought to this place
their respective wives, Giovanna d'Aragona and Costanza d'Avalos
the Younger. No one under the sun is more beautiful than they.
Along with their infant children, these women came to stay with
Ascanio's sister Vittoria and his wife's aunt, Costanza d'Avalos the
Elder. In like manner, Alfonso d'Avalos too had sent for his wife,
Maria, from the coast of the Picentians. The sister of Giovanna
d'Aragona, she appears poised to equal her beauty and elegance as
soon as, softened and stimulated by the blandishments of her
dearly loved husband, she will have cast off girlish bashfulness.

D'Avalos was looking after all these women with such extraor- 4
dinary zeal that he let slip no opportunity *for games of every sort,*
fishing and fowling and hunting, in order that their womanly minds could
be delighted by the most agreeable amusements. Indeed, while the women
watched, he often (along with his most robust officers) had busied himself
with spear, sword, javelins, and a huge sack, and in the nearby hills had
caught several large deer. Meanwhile, all the hunting equipment, the wild
beasts in flight, and the dogs and men running to and fro, were observed
from the highest windows in the fortress. But when at last he was on the

demum continuato triduo varii generis spectacula edidit in gratiam femina-
rum.

4a   *Primo die supra eam orae plagam quam castra Romana incolae appel-*
lant, perdices rubripedes nobilissimo aucupii genere consectatus est. Inde
enim se insula ab oriente in meridiem recurvat praealtis aspera cotibus sed
iis summo in vertice peramoeno nemore virentibus dumetisque passim ac
filicetis ad alendas atque occultandas huiusce generis aves a natura constitu-
tis. Perdices itaque multo venantium canum hominumque strepitu et cla-
more, suis exturbatae sedibus ad subiectum mare pellebantur. Provolantes
ac trepidas improvisi hierofalcones sinuoso per aera praecipitique volatu ac
aduncis unguibus invadebant. Spectabatur e subiecto mari iucunda atque
admirabilis pugna, cumbarum classis huc atque illuc adigebatur, ut propior
voluptas et tenendae spes praedae gestientes dominas impulissent, eae cum
alternis puellarum choris erudito et blandiore concentu venantibus applau-
debant. Perdices captae honoris causa mulieribus dono dabantur, cunctaque
litora et concavae rupes astrepente terra marique iuvenum ac puellarum
multitudine laetitiam atque victoriam resonabant. Opima paucis horis
perdicum praeda facta est, nec ullis omnino desideratis hierofalconibus qui
vel infida libertatis libidine vel petulanti alacrioreque volatu ad ipsas usque
nubes effugissent.

5   *Secunda* dies,[6] cunctis diis atque deabus maris ad exoptatam
tranquillitatem mire faventibus, celeberrima piscatione fuit insignis. *Exquisitis enim artibus summoque*[7] apparatu ad piscosissimam
stationem, quae ambustis adiacet petris, omni prope piscium generi feliciter insidiati sumus. Horrida est supra litus et confragosa
loci facies antiquis Aenariae incendiis deformata; *mille*[8] enim ante
annis[9] quam Vesevus arserit, Aenariam summo cacumine evomuisse flammas atque hunc tractum percoctis *et*[10] eliquatis cotibus

point of returning to the army, for each of three days in succession d'Avalos
staged a performance for the women's delectation.

    On the first day, on the stretch of the shoreline which the inhabitants call   4a
"The Roman camp,"[2] he hunted red-footed partridges using the finest form
of fowling. From that point, rising from the east into the south, the harsh
island curves up to lofty cliffs. But in a delightful verdant grove on the high-
est peak, in thickets and ferns here and there, birds of every kind were
hidden by nature and nourished. Thus the partridges, flushed from their
homes by the noise of the hunters and the baying of the dogs, were driven
toward the sea below. The falcons, appearing without warning with a div-
ing and spiraling flight through the air, attacked the frightened partridges
with curved talons as they were flying away. This pleasing and admirable
battle was visible from the sea below. A fleet of ships was being assembled
here and there now that the imminent pleasure and the hope of possessing
the spoils had driven forward the delighted ladies, and, in accomplished and
charming unison with alternating choirs of girls, they applauded the hunt-
ers. With due respect for honor, the captured partridges were presented to
the women as gifts and, as the multitude of young men and girls on both
land and sea cheered, all the shores and the hollow cliffs echoed the joy of
victory. Within a few hours, a splendid booty of partridges was taken. Not
a falcon had fallen in battle. On account either of a treacherous lust for
liberty or a brash eagerness for flight, they had escaped all the way to the
clouds.

    The second day was extraordinary for its successful fishing, since   5
all the gods and goddesses were wonderfully propitious in providing the calm sea we'd hoped for. *With meticulous technique and the*
finest gear, we successfully lay in ambush for nearly every kind of
fish at the anchorage near the scorched rocks, which absolutely
teems with them. Above the shore, the appearance of the place is
rough and rugged, disfigured by the ancient fires of Ischia. Indeed,
it is known that *a thousand years[3]* before Vesuvius erupted, Ischia
spewed forth flames from the highest peak and totally devastated
this region with the molten lava it poured out. From this was born

penitus evastasse constat, natamque exinde fabulam poetarum carminibus de Typhoei gigantis supplicio quem, superbe caelitibus
bellum minantem ac saevos ore et naribus spirantem ignes, tota
simul insula, supino reluctantique imposita, Iuppiter iratus et ultor
oppresserit. Sed quantum atrae et squallidae sterilitatis ea incendia
proximis insulae partibus intulerunt, tantum natura, humanis usibus semper benigna, apud subiectum litus certa *semper*[11] ac fertili
piscatione compensavit.

5a   *Igitur cum ab ea mole qua oppidum Iscla, cum summa arce praeciso*
undique scopulo impositum insulae, velut oblongo ponte committitur, fre-
quenti comitatu soluissemus, ingens atque praescriptus maris tractus, pis-
cantium naviculis est occupatus. Videres alios in alto expandere atque colli-
gere minora retia, alios a litore ingentes plagas lunatis cornibus magno
conatu, sed multo maxima exspectatione pertrahere; porro alia in parte
antelocatis nassis, melanuros et picturatos salpas educi, nonnullos praetenta
arundine defixos considere in scopulis, alios hamata plurifariam linea resi-
lientibus argenteis bellonis verrere maria. Peritos vero aliquos nobiliore arte,
errantes sargos et lupos intenta fuscina consectari, alibi pueros insuefactos e
scopulis maculosas murenas sibilis ad escam evocare atque comprehendere,
alios quoque mirabili patientia urinantes profundo mergi, echinos et odora-
tas spondilorum conchas, quas recens rubrica pertinxit, evellere atque of-
ferre, toto vagari vado, lascivire in delphinorum morem, et modo huc,
modo illuc, ad conspectum dominarum reflantia capita exserere atque iti-
dem occultare.

5b   *Nox ipsa demum tantae voluptati finem imposuit, cum in incredibili*
copia et varietate piscium vel satiari animus vel oculi tam longo spectaculo
expleri nequivissent. Nihil etiam eo reditu festivius et alacrius fuit, nam in

the tale in the verses of poets concerning the punishment of the giant Typhoeus: when he arrogantly threatened the gods with war and breathed out savage fires from his mouth and nostrils, angry and avenging Jupiter crushed him, covering him with the whole island as he lay on his back struggling. But to the extent that those fires scorched the nearby regions of the island and made them sterile, nature, always obliging to human needs, has compensated for the damage with *consistently* reliable and abundant fishing near the shore below.

And so, when we had cast off with a full crew from the jetty by which 5a *the town of Ischia is joined as though by a long bridge to its high citadel, placed on a cliff cut off from the island on all sides,*[4] *a huge and delimited portion of the sea was occupied by the boats of fishermen. You might have seen some men spreading out and gathering up smaller nets on the open sea; others, with great effort but still greater anticipation, trawling huge tracts of the sea with seine nets. In another area, you would have seen men dragging wicker traps that had been set out beforehand, drawing up black-tailed fish and variegated saupes; others, with fishing rods outstretched, were settled on the cliffs; others were sweeping the seas using lines with multiple hooks as the silver needlefish leaped backward. What is more, you might have seen certain men, expert in a finer art, chasing after wandering sars and pikes, aiming tridents at them. Elsewhere, you would have seen boys trained to lure spotted morays away from the cliffs toward the bait and to capture them; and you would have seen others diving and staying under-water with marvelous endurance. These men would pluck out and then display sea urchins and fragrant mussels which the recent run-off of clay had tinted red. They wandered through the shallows, frolicking like dol-phins, and now here, now there, in the sight of the ladies, lifted their heads from the sea to breathe and then disappeared again.*

At last night itself put an end to these great pleasures, although neither 5b *could the heart be sated nor the eyes sufficiently filled with the sight of the incredible abundance and variety of fish. Nothing, certainly, was more*

triumphi morem, dum arcem subiremus, capaces cistae accumulatis intro
piscibus, infixorumque iuncis mulorum et pagrorum coronae pulcherrimae
praeferebantur, nec deerant qui inditia virtutis et navatae feliciter operae
vinctos nobiliores sinoduntas et contumaces polypos, praetentis dextris os-
tentarent.[12]

6   Ultima *vero*[13] dies iucunditate novitateque spectaculi haud dubie superiores antecessit; cum fulicis enim incredibili cum voluptate uberrimoque victoriae proventu pugnavimus. Lacus est paullo
supra ambustas petras in circuitu decem fere stadiorum naturali et
pulcherrimo inclusus amphitheatro quod undique frondosi colles,
velut circino in orbem circumducti, ad singularem spectantium
voluptatem repraesentant;[14] a septentrionibus effracti *colles*[15] ad
exitum aquarum depressas fauces praebent, atque inde, velut ab
ingenti porta, late maria prospectantur, *hinc atque inde duo promon-*
toria in speculas editiores clementer assurgunt vestita perennibus arbustis.
In dextro insigne templum conspicitur,[16] ad levam virentia succedunt
prata, quae ab amoenis lacus ripis ad ipsos molliter assurgentes
colles, curvatis spatiis extenduntur. Totae margines partim iuncis
et lentisco, partim frequentibus myrtetis, *consaeptae exornataeque*[17]
sunt. Ab austro incipiunt altissimi et in summo culmine exesi
montes, in quorum radicibus[18] salubri scaturigine calidae manant
aquae,[19] ibique terna sunt balinea, paribus divisa labris atque siphunculis egregioque opere concamerata. In medio autem lacu insula est manu facta, superiacta[s] moles congestis cespitibus, et
protracto in linguae similitudinem lapideo ad continentem isthmo,
ut per viam silice constratam Neptuni templum, quod in ea perantiquum est, vel pedibus adiretur. Infinitam fulicarum multitudinem lacus alit ab immo herbidus, et ob id ad pinguem ac nobilem

*festive and cheerful than that return, for we came back to the fortress as in
a triumphal procession, holding before us beautiful crowns of mullets and
crabs. Some even put on display the evidence of their excellence, industry,
and success by holding out before them in nets the finer specimens of sea
bream and defiant octopi.*

But the final day in its turn surely surpassed the earlier ones in   6
pleasantness and novelty of spectacle, for we fought with waterfowl both with immense pleasure and with an abundant yield of
victory. A little above the scorched rocks is a lake, enclosed within
a circumference of almost ten stadia by a very beautiful natural
amphitheater which the leafy hills on all sides, as if drawn in a
circle by a compass, display to the singular delight of observers.
Broken open in the north, the hills provide deep channels for
the outflow of waters, and from there, as if from a mighty gate,
one can gaze out far and wide upon the seas *from this point and
that. Two promontories dressed in evergreens rise up gradually toward the
higher lookouts. On the right, one catches sight of a famous church.* On
the left are verdant meadows, which, with their curved, open
spaces, spread out from the pleasant shores of the lake to the
gently rising hills themselves. All the edges have been *adorned and
marked off either with hedges* consisting of reeds and mastic trees, or
with crowded myrtle groves. In the south begin the tallest mountains, hollowed out at their peak. At their base, next to the lake, a
salubrious spring pours forth hot waters that are healing to human
ailments. Here one finds three baths, separated by basins and siphons, and vaulted by a splendid structure. In midlake, moreover,
is an artificial island. A mound of earth was piled over with grassy
turf, and a stone isthmus like a tongue was extended to the mainland, so that the temple of Neptune, which is the most ancient
thing on the island, can be approached on foot via a road paved
with lava stone. The lake bed is quite grassy, feeding an infinite
multitude of waterfowl and enticing them to fine, rich pasturage,

pastionem aves alliciens, *sicut et in eo sapidissimi pisces a perpetua vivae et salubris aquae scaturigine maxime nutriuntur.*

7   *Davalus qui id genus aucupii saepe antea subitario tantum apparatu praetentarat, imperatis operis lacus fauces laxari iubet, perfecta fossa et per eam ad sescunciam lacu derivato*, plures cumbae *a* mari in lacum *subiectis* scutulis *hominumque*[20] umeris impelluntur. Armata perticis *atque arcibus*[21] iuventus, et canes palustribus assueti venantionibus, ripas corona obsident. Nos cum feminis cumbas conscendimus,[22] instructi arcubus, quibus argillaceae pilae ad certos ictus excutiuntur. Excitatae fulicae huc et illuc provolant. Ab omni parte infestos hostes inveniunt, undique cum plausu et mutua gratulatione dissipantur et creberrimis pilis *configuntur*.[23] Eo modo natando et revolando fessae, debilitatae ictibus varioque periculo terrefactae, ad densissimos iuncos totis ripis se recipiunt.[24] Ibi *novum atrox*[25] varium et maxime cruentum instauratur proelium. Canes enim trepidis et sese occultantibus allatrare insultare capere mordicus; ipsi venatores *discalciati*[26] eas latebris extrudere, saxis fustibusque necare, manu comprehendere, aut in adversas cumbas unde pilarum procella continenter effundebatur pavidas compellere; ita cum aliquamdiu pugnassemus, tanta earum strages est edita ut interfectis[27] amplius trecentis dominarum cumbae complerentur.

just as the tastiest fish are nourished in it by the perennially bubbling spring of fresh and healthful water.

D'Avalos, who often before had done that kind of fowling with only 7
improvised equipment, commanded that the outlets of the lake be opened up using forced labor. After the channel was finished, an eighth of the lake was drawn off through it. Once the narrows had been opened and deepened, a number of boats were conveyed on skids and men's backs from the adjacent sea into the lake. Young men armed with poles, and dogs trained in swamp hunting, formed a blockade along the shores. We, along with the womenfolk, boarded the boats as did many men equipped with bows with which they shoot clay missiles with precision. The startled waterfowl flew out this way and that, encountering the enemy in every direction. They were scattered and *attacked* on every side by a constant rain of missiles accompanied by applause and mutual congratulations. Thus exhausted by swimming and flying round and round, disabled by blows, and terrified by the ever-changing danger, they retreated from the entire shoreline into the dense reeds. Nor did they dare to fly out either into the hills or out to the adjacent sea since they were too fat, sluggish, and timid to make the extraordinary effort required. There a *new, fierce* battle was begun in a different and exceedingly gory form. Even as the frightened birds were seeking cover, the dogs were barking, leaping upon them, and catching them in their teeth. The *barefooted* hunters themselves flushed them out from their coverts, killing them with stones and clubs or catching them by hand, or driving them, terrified, toward the boats opposite, from which an unremitting shower of missiles was pouring. When we had fought this battle for some time, such a huge aviary massacre was entailed that the ladies' boats were filled with more than three hundred birds dead or captured.

Note on the Text and Translation

꽃ᯬ꽃

THE MANUSCRIPTS

The *Dialogus de viris et feminis aetate nostra florentibus* as it has come down to us is unfinished and in many places quite rough. Only one manuscript of each of the three books, or dialogues, is known to have survived. In the eighteenth century all three were in the possession of the author's heir, Giovan Battista Giovio, and today they are preserved in two locations in Como: the Società Storica Comense owns the manuscripts of Dialogues One and Two, which are in Fondo Aliati, cassetta 28, in the Centro Studi "Nicolò Rusca," housed in the Seminario Vescovile di Como; the manuscript of Dialogue Three is held in the Biblioteca Civica di Como, Fondo Giovio, segnatura 1.6.16. Each of the three manuscripts poses distinct challenges to the editor.

That of Dialogue One is by far the most intractable. Those wishing a thorough and erudite analysis of its peculiarities can now find one in the new critical edition of the text by Dr. Franco Minonzio, described below. Here, a brief description may indicate the particular challenges of its editor's task. The manuscript of Dialogue One comprises forty-eight folio pages in the midst of which three smaller, folded sheets of differing sizes have been inserted but are not attached. Whereas the folios are numbered in arabic in the upper right-hand corner of the recto side, these unattached pages bear the lower-case letters "a," "b," and "c," respectively. Combining as they do new text with variant drafts of material elsewhere in the manuscript, they are not easy to integrate. Determining what to do with these inserted pages, however, is the least of the editor's problems. The manuscript is in three hands, including Giovio's own, and many pages include both his autograph and

a scribal hand. On occasion, a page marked with Giovio's auto-graph changes has been recopied onto another folio in a scribal hand. Conversely, some of the pages that are entirely in Giovio's own hand rewrite passages that survive in scribal drafts, often in more complete and polished form, elsewhere in the manuscript. The current ordering of pages is owed to Giovan Battista Giovio, who writes at the end of the manuscript (fol. 48v) of the immense effort he put into assembling it.[1] That effort is abundantly evident; its success, markedly less so. In short, Dialogue One has remained until recently a very rough draft (or drafts), incompletely and problematically organized.

The manuscript of Dialogue Two poses different problems. It lacks both its opening and its conclusion.[2] There is no indication of the frame, and the surviving manuscript both begins and ends in midsentence. It comprises nineteen folio pages. The body of the text is written in a single elegant hand by one of the two scribes used for Dialogue One. Most but not all of the marginal addenda and corrigenda are in Giovio's hand.

The body of the text of Dialogue Three, written in the same scribal hand as Dialogue Two, includes far more addenda and delenda in Giovio's hand. It concludes neatly with a closing frame that ends with the word "Finis," but it is not so complete as that might suggest. Some transitions are jarring, and the precise place in the text where marginal additions are to be inserted is not al-ways indicated. For reasons that are unclear, part way down on fol. 13v (numbered in arabic as 26) several blank line spaces separate the discussion of Bolognese (and, in passing, Modenese) women from the section on Genoese women. Was something intended to be added there, or does the gap result from the section on Genoa having been rewritten first, with surplus space having been left for the later insertion of the revised text on Bologna and Modena? Like the other two parts of the dialogue, Dialogue Three remained an unfinished draft.

EARLIER PUBLISHED EDITIONS

Until 2011, Giovio's *Dialogus* had appeared only in Latin. In the eighteenth century Giovan Battista Giovio lent the second part to Girolamo Tiraboschi, who published it in 1781 as an appendix to his *Storia della letteratura italiana*.[3] Tiraboschi's edition had the virtue of widely disseminating this previously inaccessible work, and indeed Jacob Burckhardt drew upon it in his *The Civilization of the Renaissance in Italy* (1860). But Tiraboschi provides only a basic transcription with a minimal apparatus that essentially consists of glossing some of the names of humanists in the text. The transcription itself is riddled with typographical errors.

The first complete edition of the *Dialogus* was that of Ernesto Travi and Mariagrazia Penco, printed in the Italian national edition of Giovio's works in 1984.[4] Given the massive effort involved in editing the manuscript, one must lament that the published product is so deeply flawed. Errors in transcription abound, often over a dozen per page. On occasion the editors have omitted words and even phrases. Frequently they do not signal where they have incorporated material from marginal addenda, and they often do not indicate the pages of the draft where ultimately deleted words and passages appeared. Most seriously, they provided their own idiosyncratic arabic numeration of the pages without ever explaining adequately how those numbers correspond to the numbers actually on the manuscript or where the material is drawn from the loose leaves (a, b, or c). The introduction to the edition, by Ernesto Travi, remains important and merits consultation. But the edition itself should be consulted only with extreme caution. Happily, it has now been entirely superseded by a new, far superior edition.

The recent edition and Italian translation of the *Dialogus* by Dr. Franco Minonzio is a major contribution to Giovio scholarship.[5] Its two volumes comprise, in addition to the text and translation themselves, a 170-page introduction, a 31-page "note" on the text, a

48-page critical apparatus, and an entire second volume of explanatory notes. The editor not only lists marginalia but indicates where on the page they occur and often seeks to establish in what year they were added. This new edition will be essential for anyone doing advanced work on this text, or indeed on any aspect of Giovio's life and work. Moreover, its well-indexed notes provide copious bibliography on the hundreds of contemporaries that Giovio mentions in the work. It is an encyclopedic contribution that will be of enduring significance.

That very encyclopedism, however, perforce renders the edition less approachable for nonspecialists. Minonzio has sought to reproduce faithfully the orthography, and often even the capitalization and punctuation as they appear in the manuscripts. But that spelling and capitalization are far from consistent, and the punctuation bears little resemblance to today's standards. The text is not broken into paragraphs, and the translation often goes dozens of pages without a break. This approach reduces editorial intrusion into the work's structure, but at significant cost to ease of reading. The priorities of the present edition, as will be seen, are quite different.

PROTOCOLS FOLLOWED IN THE PRESENT EDITION

In keeping with the norm of ITRL series books, this edition strives not only for precision and consistency but for concision and accessibility. The text as printed presents in principle only the final redaction of the manuscript. Rather than trying to identify the different stages of revision — a task nearly as conjectural as it is cumbersome — the present edition distinguishes the final redaction only from the earliest version, insofar as that can be established. (This earliest draft is indicated in the notes with the siglum *d*.) On occasion, substantial marginal addenda were subsequently deleted. Since those passages represent intermediate redactions,

parts neither of the initial draft nor of the last redaction, they are here omitted. Scholars interested in further details regarding the evolution of the text may consult the Minonzio edition, where such issues are discussed *in extenso*.

In keeping with the protocols of this I Tatti series, spelling, capitalization, and punctuation have been modernized. The present edition adopts the preferred spellings of the *Oxford Latin Dictionary* (excepting only that "u" and "v" are here distinguished), supplemented where necessary, for postclassical vocabulary, from Lewis and Short's *Latin Dictionary*. Occasionally, words or idiosyncratic usages not found in either of those dictionaries appear in René Hoven's *Lexique de la Prose Latine de la Renaissance*, 2nd edition (Leiden: Brill, 2006), whose spelling is followed in these cases. All these changes, as well as the standardization of Latinized forms of names, have been made silently.

This orthographical standardization comes at some cost: the reader loses the flavor and on occasion the precision of Giovio's use of archaisms. But it must be emphasized that Giovio and his scribes were by no means consistent, even within the single books of this work, in their orthographical choices. Usually, for example, Giovio uses the spelling "cum" only for the preposition, otherwise preferring "quum"; but that preference is not consistent, while one of the scribal hands uses "cum" consistently throughout for both the preposition and the relative adverb. Giovio also likes to use the variant "uti" for "ut." In this edition the word "uti" is only used as the infinitive of "utor." Other orthographical standardizations here include changing "queis" to "quibus," and "tralatio" to "translatio." This privileging of classical over postclassical spelling is no doubt anachronistic to a degree, but the result, it is hoped, is a far more accessible text. Fortunately, readers interested in following the evolution of and variations in Giovio's orthographical preferences can find an ample treatment of these issues in Minonzio's edition.

In the Latin text of the present edition, editorial insertions and conjectures are enclosed in angled brackets, ⟨ ⟩; deletions, in square brackets, [ ]. Illegible words in the manuscripts are generally noted and, where possible, conjecturally restored. Daggers (††) enclose words and phrases that hitherto have defied interpretation. Redundancies that have been corrected within the manuscript have been silently omitted. The ultimate redactions of the three manuscripts of the *Dialogus* (each comprising one dialogue, or book, as described above) are indicated, respectively, with the sigla C_1, C_2, and C_3.

The Minonzio edition was not available to the present editor until this volume was in its final stages of preparation. Although this has meant extensive duplication of labor, particularly in the identification of some of the more obscure individuals mentioned in the text, it has the silver lining that the present edition is in no way parasitical upon its predecessor. Happily, the two agree closely in their reconstruction of the labyrinthine text of Dialogue One. The one major difference in interpretation comes in its opening frame: the present edition understands as deleted from the final version a long passage that Minonzio includes. That passage, on fols. 1v–2r (= §2) of the manuscript, appears here, both in Latin and in translation, in the Appendix.

The Appendix reconstructs insofar as possible the original draft of the opening frame of Dialogue One. All the text that was subsequently deleted appears in italics both in the Latin and in the English translation; the subsequent revisions are recorded in the endnotes. Thus the reader can see clearly the extent of Giovio's efforts to revise the text so as to reduce the role of its original dedicatee, Gian Matteo Giberti.

The two principal ways in which the present edition engages with that of Minonzio are in the Latin text and in biographical details in the notes. Differences in transcription that affect mean-

ing are detailed in the apparatus, Minonzio's readings being indicated with the siglum *m*; banal printing errors are passed over in silence. In the notes to the English translation, those details drawn from Minonzio's notes are clearly identified as such, with page and note references provided for the reader's convenience. It is the firm belief of the present editor that these two editions are complementary, each contributing in its own way to rendering this important text at last both accessible and usable.

THE TRANSLATION

To make the translation readable in twenty-first-century English, the editor has often reduced pleonasm of adjectives, changed passive constructions to active ones, eliminated inflationary uses of the comparative and superlative degrees, converted participial phrases to adjectives, regularized rhetorical schemes such as hendiadys, and so forth. It is hoped that the reader will appreciate the smoother text that results from such interventions, which seek to move the text fully into English rather than leaving the translation suspended, uncomfortably, in limbo between the two languages.

NOTES

1. Dialogus Primus, fol. 48v: "Incredibilis prope labor in hisce digerendis Pauli Iovii Ep⟨iscop⟩i Nucerini Dialogis suoque loco exesis dispersisque chartis collocandis insumptus est a Comite Ioanne Baptista Iovio anno 1775. Mense Septembri."

2. For analysis of hypotheses regarding how much of the opening and closing of Dialogue Two are missing, see Minonzio, 1:CLXXXIII–CLXXXV.

3. In the first edition (1781) it appeared as an appendix to vol. 9. I have consulted the text in a later edition: Girolamo Tiraboschi, *Storia della letteratura italiana*, vol. 7, pt. 2 (Milan: Società Tipografica de' Classici Italiani, 1824), 2444–99.

4. *IO* 9:147–321.

5. Paolo Giovio, *Dialogo sugli uomini e le donne illustri del nostro tempo*, ed. and trans. Franco Minonzio, 2 vols. (Turin: Nino Aragno Editore, 2011).

Notes to the Text

꽃숲꽃

SIGLA

C₁   final version of the text of Dialogue One
C₂   final version of the text of Dialogue Two
C₃   final version of the text of Dialogue Three
d   earliest draft
m   Minonzio edition
t   Travi edition

DIALOGUE ONE

1. *For the original version of §§1–7, see Appendix*

2. *after* certa, *d writes* semper

3. cura *m*

4. connestitae *m*

5. fascis *m*

6. nec *d*

7. Romae *added in* C₁

8. Philibertus *added in* C₁

9. *after* Belga, *d writes* nullorum stipendiorum adulescens ceterum numquam

10. ceterum primorum stipendiorum adulescens *added in* C₁

11. atque *d*

12. *after* deprecantes, *d writes* e quarum conspectu divelli non poterat

13. *after* ut, *d writes* et

14. *after* proximis, *d writes* concitato et nonnumquam contento passu et sublata etiam voce

15. *after* evocarunt, *d writes* Iam plane fatigatum et

16. e tanta] publica e *d*

17. magna *d*

18. salvas et *added in* C₁

19. *after* pretio, *d writes* et demum Vespasiani Columnae fidei commendatas

20. tot *omitted in m*

21. scyphis et tot pateris meis erudita arte fabrefactis] poculis et pateris meis *d*

22. meam pariter] eas *d*

23. aliquantoque *d*

24. perpetuis bellis ac odiorum inveteratae libidini effuse] odiis inveterataeque libidini *d*

25. cunctos fere] Franciscum Regem Summumque Pontificem et Ludovicum Pannonium et ipsum nunc quoque caesarem *d*

26. exitus *m*

27. *after* Et, *d writes* me

28. atque *d*

29. provinciis] (*lac.*) omnibus *d*

30. cuius est primus Christiani hominis respectus] adversus deos penitus *d*

31. insanientibus *d*

32. *after* capta, *d writes* ac incensa

33. contentus scilicet . . . sunt collocatae *added in* C₁

34. deos *d*

35. Nec adhuc] Et negant propterea *d*

36. profitentur *added in* C₁

37. saepe *m*

38. *after* animi, *d writes* tui

39. et *added in* C₁

40. ut credi par est vere pio et Christiano ac] et pio et *d*

41. quinque *d*

42. ac *d m*

43. Laetabar equidem . . . minaretur. Et] Sed *d*

44. et *d*

45. cum *m*

46. incorruptoque] et incorrupto *d*

47. et sapientiae *added in* C₁

48. Ex *d*

49. *after* illuvie, *d writes* tantum

50. tantum *added in* C₁

51. Lydiis Cariis] Lyciis *d*

52. qui modo Pannonicum . . . evertit *added in* C₁

53. Sapheram *m, perhaps correctly*

54. Sapherum classis praefectum alioqui virum fortissimum] Sapheram classis praefectam aliqui viram fortissimam *d*

55. avarius ac acerbius se gesisse] et iniquus et venalis et rapax *d*

56. gesserunt *d*

57. sic *d*

58. animalia *m*

59. ⟨perf⟩ectione] ⟨mundi ra⟩tione *m*

60. mundum *m*

61. *omitted in m*

62. Sunt enim qui haec ipsa mortalia . . . tandem in seipsa pl⟨. . .⟩ *added in* C₁ *(partly illegible owing to damaged paper)*

63. inusitati *d*

64. abdita *d*

65. *after* Museti, *d writes* et

66. et *omitted in m, perhaps correctly*

67. Ad id DAVALUS "Uter" inquit "incipiat non refert . . . de facilitate et comitate sim concessurus *added in* C_1

68. ac animorum] enim *d*

69. asseveranter retulisse] ser⟨. . .⟩usius referre *d*

70. ab *d m*

71. nequeunt *m*

72. Quamquam ea quae tam anxie . . . philosophus esse voluerit *added in* C_1

73. Ita *d*

74. veniam ut pio homini] igitur veniam ut Christiano et *d*: veniam ut pio homini et *m*

75. *after* coluerim, *d writes* tum Graecis tum Arabibus

76. igitur *added in* C_1

77. hominis] imprimis humanam *d*

78. et ceterorum animantium genera, uno perfectionis perpetuo tenore propagata cum humana specie conferantur *added in* C_1

79. effinxerit *d*

80. successivus C_1

81. ut in se ipsa perfecta] et integra *d*

82. a summa naturali potestate deduci] remitti *d*

83. et *m*

84. Sed *d*

85. *after* gratissimo, *d writes* oculis

86. oculis nostris offeratur] esse videatur *d*

87. in rotatione retardari vel incitari] retardari omnino *d*

88. esse *added in* C_1

89. docileque] docile flexibileque *d*

90. *after* tum, *d writes* et

91. mortalium animos] animos mortalium *d*

92. *after* parent, *d writes* sic ut operosos pontes tamquam iuga et servitutis impositae monumenta defugere, superba libidine videantur

93. Quin et alia] Alia etiam *d*

94. *after* exarescere, *d writes* fiunt

95. siccarique] siccari quoque *d*

96. scaturriunt *d*

97. non alia ratione quam cum *added in* C₁

98. atque *d*

99. decorem *d*

100. decorentur] atque frequentia celebrentur *d*

101. frequentiae *added in* C₁

102. *after* depravato, *d writes* iam

103. in corpus sensusque suos] corporis sensuumque suorum *d*

104. *after* enim, *d writes* omnium

105. a diversa ingeniorum potestate, ac immoderatis morum excessibus, constantes aut imbecilli, feroces aut mansueti, turbidi aut lenes et dociles reddantur] acuti segnes infirmi constantes mansueti leves turbidi dociles feri pertinaces et immoderatis excessibus subiecti atque obnoxii penitus efficiantur *d*

106. in universum *added in* C₁

107. rigida *d*

108. *after* nos, *d writes* omnes

109. *after* transpadanos, *d writes* et

110. intenti *added in* C₁

111. vivos coepissent ac subinde] honore omni *d*

112. *after* metu, *d writes* atque iniuria

113. vel *added in* C₁

114. *after* gentibus, *d writes* et

115. aliquanto *d*

116. *after* superbiores, *d writes* et acerbiores

117. *after* Hispanis, *d writes* ac saeviores

118. inferendae vastitatis] crudelitatis *d*

119. pariter ac] et *d*

120. atque *d*

121. *after* sublatisque, *d writes* magna ex parte

122. sceleratissimorum *d*

123. *after* per, *d writes* omnia

124. Probitate *d*

125. aequitate *added in* C₁

126. certissime] haud dubie *d*

127. *after* improbe, *d writes* et perverse

128. in tantis malis *added in* C₁

129. hominum primordiaque *added in* C₁

130. ac *d*

131. *after* urbium, *d writes* hominumque et rerum omnium

132. aut vano] vanoque *d*

133. intimis] ipsis *d*

134. est enim ut] enim est *d*

135. reperitur *d*

136. contrariis *m*

137. *after* Quis, *d writes* enim

138. ipse *added in* C₁

139. cum firmissima valetudine . . . favebatur *added in* C₁: fruebatur *m*, *perhaps correctly*

140. ipso conciderent] eo corruerunt *d*

141. melior et sapientior] maior *d*

142. vel *added in* C₁

143. Turcarum] sub Turcico *d*

144. explodendos] coarguendos explodendosque *d*

145. tam anxia] et tanta *d*

146. de astris] Museti *d*

147. certius *d*

148. *after* Iovi, *d writes* ea

149. ab adulescentia *added in* C₁

150. *after* commotus, *d writes* ea

151. Verum *d*

152. et foedo] foedoque *d*

153. *after* eae, *d writes* profecto

154. vos *d*

155. quas ab usu rerum . . . disciplina deducuntur] quae ex usu rerum et veterum auctorum lectione deduximus *d*

156. pravitate et transalpinarum gentium iniuria] consuetudine barbarorumque iniuria opulentiae et *d*

157. *after* artes, *d writes* fora et

158. iniurii *m*

159. Radagasius et Totila immanitate ruinis et cladibus exsultarent] Totila immanitate saevitia ruinis et cladibus exsultaret *d*

160. nisi mercennarius *added in* C₁

161. et *omitted in* m

162. admirationem *m*

163. gloriosissimo *d*

164. Tum Musetius quamquam inquit] Sane Musetius inquit quamquam *d*

165. ut poetae dicunt *added in* C₁

166. cum *m*

167. magnetis usus et *added in* C₁

168. posterorum *m, perhaps correctly*

169. cum] utpote qui *d*

170. ipso *d*

171. aliunde *t m*

172. vestrorum *t m, perhaps correctly*

173. *after* existimationi, *d writes* et

174. peregregiae *m, perhaps correctly*

175. ad summam cum potentiae tum laudis opinionem *added in* C₁

176. pariter *added in* C₁

177. notam *d*

178. carnifices *d*

179. vitam *m*

180. et *d*

181. prontibus *m, perhaps correctly*

182. *after* quam, *d writes* sero: *m treats* sero *as undeleted*

183. crimina *added in* C₁

184. pertimeat C₁] pertineat *corrected by m*

185. cum *d*

186. *after* flumen, *d writes* in agro Laudensi

187. dimittuntur *m, perhaps correctly*

188. conferantur *d*

189. Bracciani Sfortiadae Picinnini et Coleones] Carmagnolae Picinnini Coleones Sfortiadae *d*

190. atque *d*

191. et *d*

192. equitatu *d*: equitato C₁

193. coniuncti cum Germanis *added in* C₁

194. lacrimabili *d*

195. pertinere *d*

196. modo *d*

197. paene *added in* C₁

198. nobis *added in* C₁

199. erat *d*

200. bene *added in* C₁

201. *after* ut, *d writes* mihi

202. dubitem] sit dubitandum *d*

203. praeclara *d*

204. indoles *d*

205. siquaturos *d*

206. destrinxit *is my conjecture:* distrinxit C₁ *m*

207. summae] vel summae vel mediocri *d*

208. *After* adulescens, *d writes* maioribus postea

209. postea maioribus *added in* C₁

210. et Roma capienda *added in* C₁

211. *after* pontificis, *d writes* vel Gallorum

212. alio *d*

213. pariter *added in* C₁

214. umquam ipse] ipse umquam *d*

215. experiti *m*

216. seniorum *m*

217. *after* construendis, *d writes* acutior

218. *after* picturae, *t and m both add* de

219. libidine *m*

220. quandocumque *m*

221. semiviva *m*

222. pro solacio *added in* C₁

223. visurum *added in* C₁

224. coniunctorum *m*

225. et dissidentium regum animos . . . extremo quodam voto] esse conspecturum *d*

226. Christianique imperii ac Italiae *added in* C₁

227. *after* equitatum, *d writes* et

228. virtutes *m*

229. gradum *d*

230. viridaeque *m*

231. de *added in* C₁

232. summorum *added in* C₁

233. cum omnibus Italis tum] suis *d*

234. reliquamus *m*

235. sicut audimus *added in* C₁

236. virtutum *d*

237. vir *added in* C₁

238. princeps *added in* C₁

239. scriptorumque memoria *added in* C₁

240. eripit venenum] linguam eripit *d*

241. etiam *d*

242. *after* Pontifex, *d writes* alacri passu

243. Sed certe Clementi . . . fuerit decoquendum *added in* C₁

244. vetere *d*

245. numina *added in* C₁

246. nostra *added in* C₁

247. diminuta C₁

248. divertisti C₁

249. videmus *d*

250. ulturus avum . . . interfectum *added in* C₁

251. in rusticano] ignobili et in *d*

252. insignia] stipendia *d*

253. *after* Neapolio, *d writes* cognomento

254. Abbas *added in* C₁

255. In *d*

256. nihil dicam qui . . . pro] qui cum *d*

257. Ursinae familiae viris hostibus *added in* C₁

258. *after* militasset, *d writes* vis ingenii nobilis vis ardens cum singulari militaris iudicii constantia. Ita ut nisi a familiae rationibus defecisset, aliquanto tam clarior esset atque probatior

259. conspicitur *added in* C₁

260. clarissimi *d*

261. Anthonius *m*

262. *after* modo, *d writes* ab

263. nequaquam exaequantur sed nec his etiam] iam plane degenerant sed ab his *d*

264. imperio] reges regno *d*

265. *after* Itali, *d writes* nostri

266. impensae C₁: impensa *m*

267. quum *m*

268. alam *d*

269. scilicet *added in* C₁

270. *after* praefectus, *d writes* cuius filium Franciscum Borellium ab eximia prudentia et locum in secretiore senatu et censurae officium in recognosendis equitum turmis promeruisse conspicitis

271. aliquamdiu *added in* C₁

272. valent *d*

273. ex *added in* C₁

274. unus admodum conspicuus fuisset] praeesset *d*

275. Carolo *added in* C₁

276. contra caesaris voluntatem *added in* C₁

277. perfidiose nobiscum de pace legatos mittentem] omnibus perfidiae cruor apertum sceleribus *d*

278. limite *m*

279. in illa *added in* C₁

280. eum] laborantem *d*

281. arce educere *added in* C₁

282. Nagereus omnium in exercitu consiliorum] ipse Nagereus exercitus *d*

283. prorex ipse *added in* C₁

284. Romam venisset] Roma esset *d*

285. ulla pietatis vel humanitatis ratione induci potuit ut *added in* C₁

286. inediae *added in* C₁

287. et pestibus] pestis ac mediae *d*

288. cibariorum *added in* C₁

289. recrearet] recreare voluit *d*

290. *after* minime, *d writes* sua

291. videntur *m*

292. ut ipsi ditarentur *added in* C₁

293. caesar indigeat] indiget caesar *d*

294. Venetos *m*

295. ut gloriosum et longe iustissimum bellum contra vero⟨s⟩ hostes geratur *added in* C₁

296. item *d*

297. nobis *added in* C₁

298. proclamantibus *m*

299. horibus *d*

300. vester *d*

301. vivum *added in* C$_1$

302. quisque *m*

303. *or possibly* tantam

304. exaequantur C$_1$ (*a before* e *appears to be expunctuated*): exaequantur *m, perhaps correctly*

305. geram *added in* C$_1$

306. *perhaps* cum

307. milite *added in* C$_1$

308. ad exemplum in] gratia in rege et *d*

309. paganorum *d*

310. Persinus *m, perhaps correctly*

311. ad Seminariam *added in* C$_1$

312. *after* alternis, *d writes* saepe

313. inutile *m*

314. Petraeam *m*

315. aliquanto *d*

316. potuerit *m*

317. equestres *d*

318. ab his] a Gallis *d*

319. manifestum *d*

320. in temone *added in* C$_1$

321. auctoritati *m*

322. prope Mediolanum *added in* C$_1$

323. ac *d*

324. ingenio *added in* C

325. simus *m*

326. putatur *m*

327. *after* circumvertere, *d writes* edoctos

328. perite tum] tum perite *d*

329. parca quidem] perarguta *d*

330. Regium et Mutinam *added in* C₁

331. *after* feliciter, *d writes* appli *(sic)*

332. putem *added in* C₁

333. cum *m*

334. aliquando *m*

335. disciplina *added in* C₁

336. universa *m*

337. praeclara *m*

338. denique *m*

339. Sed nec Franciscus . . . umquam disceptavit *added in* C₁

340. via *m*

341. *after* laudis, *d writes* vel infamiae

342. apud Bononiam *added in* C₁

343. strunui C₁, *corrected to* strenui *in m*

344. recedunt *m, perhaps correctly (a hole in the paper occurs between* d *and* n*)*

345. ⟨Marmir⟩olum *added in* C₁

346. mitis *d*

347. etiam *d*

348. gentibus *added in* C₁

349. semper *added in* C₁

350. *after* bellici, *d writes* decoris

351. *after* denique, *d writes* religionis diligentiarum et

352. equites *added in* C₁

353. Ghingatam *d*

354. Porro *added in* C₁

355. *after* Vitellium, *d writes* quoque

356. ne *added in* C₁

357. *after* vigilantia, *d writes* et fide

358. Feltrii *m, perhaps correctly*

359. §§144–47 *exist in an intermediate draft found on inserted leaf (a), recto-verso, as described in the Note on the Text and Translation*

360. *after* MUSETIUS, *d writes* inde

361. *after* Mediolano, *d writes* peperistis

362. *after* adversus, *d writes* et

363. *after* nam, *d writes* in eo

364. crimen] armorum *m*

365. aut caesar ipse . . . malignitas obtuderit *added in* C₁

366. Nam certe gravissimas causas . . . et est ingenio] Est enim ingenio *d*

367. difficultate] asperitate *d*

368. *after* constantem, *d writes* perpessa

369. septem menses *added in* C₁

370. penitus *added in* C₁

371. multitudinis] amicorum *d*

372. dedita *added in* C₁

373. et summo salutis *added in* C₁

374. *after* metu, *d writes* mortis

375. et tacite minabundus . . . occasionem opperiretur] eam patrandi sceleris occasionem *d*

376. *after* milites, *d writes* eius capiti

377. gravibus *d*

378. tum *m*

379. *after* haereret, *d writes* illi etiam nudatis capitibus tamquam incolumi principatus fortuna, haud malignis vultibus assurger

380. *after* transiremus, *d writes* illi

381. propter singularem . . . meam fidem *added in* C₁: *not considered part of final draft in* m

382. salutis *d*

383. propositis *added in* C₁

384. semper *m*

385. et *m*

386. male auspicata] inauspicata *d*

387. communem *added in* C₁

388. militat castris] castris militat *d*

389. enim *d*

390. *after* robusta, *d writes* vis

391. in dicendis sententiis nihil umquam] numquam *d*

392. de libertate et fuga cogitantem *added in* C₁

393. *after* exciperet, *d writes* educeret

394. patrando *added in* C₁

395. super *d*

396. Pauli filius *added in* C₁

397. cohortes *added in* C₁

398. *after* imbutas, *d writes* cohortes

399. *after* fortitudo, *d writes* conspicitur

400. *after* conspiciuntur, *d writes* florent

401. For §§154–55, *the version of the text in the bound manuscript is superseded by inserted leaf (b) recto (see Note on the Text and Translation). Inserted leaf (b) recto is therefore treated here as part of* C₁, *the final draft*

402. excelsa *added in* C₁

403. in proeliis *added in* C₁

404. quod in milite rarissimum est *added in* C₁

405. *after* amoenissimarum, *d writes* etiam

406. et studio carminum *added in* C₁

407. quoque bello] multis bellis *d*

408. erudito] et maxime *d*

409. a Borbonio] totius *d*

410. nuper *added in* C₁

411. Elucet enim in eo liberalitas . . . in miseros afflictosque] Est enim in hoc urbis excidio admodum pius et in miseros et ad afflictos *d*

412. In ingenio item . . . dignitatis efflorescit *added in* C₁

413. et *d*

414. Simon *m*

415. *after* animos, *d writes* naturam

416. ac *added in* C₁

417. ipsisque etiam hastarum motibus *added in* C₁

418. artibus *m*

419. tuerique] ac tueri *d*

420. et denique ad imperatoris nomen et laudem feliciter aspirant *added in* C₁

421. Proelia namque multos] Namque multos proelia *d*

422. pericula deterruere] deterruere pericula *d*

423. minime decorum] indecorum *d*

424. contra *added in* C₁

425. militares ac] atque *d*

426. et luculenter . . . maledixerit *added in* C₁

427. qui *m*

428. *after* ab, *d writes* ipsis

429. *after* stipendiis, *m writes* quia omnes, *as it seems*

430. centuriis *d*

431. alas demum et *added in* C₁

432. atque *d*

433. *after* consequamur, *d writes* Huius itaque classis cum Ugonem Pepulum et Ioannem Saxatellum et Ianum Fregosium Ligurem ut strenuos praestandaeque operae avidos probem. Etiam vel a multis stipendiis vel ab omni nobilitate testatisque operibus laudandos puto Hannibalem Bentivolium Bernabovem Vicecomitem Paulum Camillum Trivultium Ludovicum Balbianum Philippum Torniellum Luduvicum Pallavicinum (*compare §163, below*)

434. Haec *added in* C₁

435. tum *m*

436. *after* constitutis, *d writes* Italiae

437. sedata *d*

438. cum *m, perhaps correctly*

439. et *d*

440. *after* ut, *d writes* sperem

441. confusis *d*

442. ac *m*

443. *after* Trivultium, *d writes* et Bernabovem Vicecomitem et Nicolaum Vitellium ut

444. laudandum *is my correction (see n. 433 above)*: laudandos C₁

445. qui a Gallis ad nos transivit *added in* C₁

446. qui *d*

447. qui *d*

448. ab inclutus] gloriosis et a *d*

449. convictissimus *m, perhaps correctly*

450. *after* Vigent, *d writes* et

451. diligenti *d*

452. duces *d*

453. Mamfronios *corrected in m*: Mamfronos *d*: Manfronos C₁

454. *after* cupide, *d writes* et intemperanter

455. tantisper *d*

456. qui vel semel serio tubarum cantum audierint *added in* C₁: audierim *m*

457. matricula *d*

458. traduxisse *added in* C₁

459. ac *d m*

460. quoniam] et certe *d*

461. atque *d*

462. cedere *d*

463. proprio iudicio *added in* C₁

464. fama vel indole vel rebus gestis probatiores] probatiores fama aut indole aut rebus gestis *d*

465. enim *added in* C₁

466. oreque terribili *added in* C₁

467. etiam *added in* C₁

468. atque *d*

469. ipse *added in* C₁

470. atque *d*

471. Sed quaecumque . . . amisisse praedicarint *added in* C₁

472. eos *added in* C₁

473. enim *d*

474. possunt *d*

475. iam *d*

476. iam *added in* C₁

477. *Perhaps* Alantur *should be read in d and* C₁

478. enim *added in* C₁

479. *after* crudelitati, *d writes* enim

480. latrociniis *d*

481. nilque *d*

482. parant *m*

483. cum *m, perhaps correctly*

484. ita ut caesari . . . compresso gemitu feramus *added in* C₁

485. omnino *added in* C₁

486. ac *m*

487. infamiae *m*

488. *after* libidinem, *d writes* comprimere

489. velareque *added in* C₁

490. Messanae *added in* C₁

491. efflavit *m*

492. efferateque *m*

493. et suas *added in* C₁

494. Ab illa siquidem] Ut non mult⟨um⟩ *d*

495. *after* barbaricas, *d writes* importat

496. *after* persequantur, *d writes* Itaque

497. aequo *d*

498. laborem *added in* C₁

499. *after* aestu, *d writes* laborem

500. *after* nidificant, *d writes* iactatam

501. ut sperandum est . . . clementia singulari *added in* C₁

502. Davale *added in* C₁

503. explicare non graveris] impartire rogamus *d*

504. igitur *added in* C₁

505. quo] quod ipsi *d*

506. *after* studium, *d writes* et singularem diligentiam

507. Genuenses] Celtiberi Ligures *d*

508. cum misera essent] impensae magnitudine deterriti aut misera *d*

509. sint soli hodie] soli sint *d*

510. *after* onerariae, *d writes* et eae naves

511. utuntur *d*

512. remigio insignibus] quae remigio utuntur *d*

513. quando iis imperent navarchi] cum his imperent tetrarchi *d*

514. serviant *d*

515. cadant *d*: concedant *m*

516. multa *d*

517. sub pontifice dudum merebat. Is *added in* C₁

518. noxiis *added in* C₁

519. *after* patria, *d writes* Pentagonium

520. e *m*

521. qui nostri operis sunt duces *added in* C₁

522. quos *d*

523. numeravimus *d*

524. illos hercle *added in* C₁

525. *after* meliores, *d writes* ac omnino superiores

526. *after* et, *d writes* peramplum atque

527. cum largissimis mensis *added in* C₁

528. egregium ducem] ducem egregium *d*

529. *after* atrocius, *d writes* nihil periculosius

530. animo *d*

531. ut rudiore saeculo erat solitum *added in* C₁

532. tremat *d*

533. crepitet *d*

534. et caecis *added in* C₁

535. integras cohortes et turmas crudeli morte prosternunt] horribiles morientium strages repraesentant *d*

536. tum *m*

537. mente *d*

538. enim *d*

539. et liberis] liberisque *d*

540. ut pote quae] quae acres et *d*

541. *after* cunctatione, *d writes* excipi et

542. praeprospere *m*

543. Quam infelix . . . discrimen adduxit *added in* C,

544. propterea tamen *added in* C,

545. ipsae *added in* C,

546. denique *added in* C,

547. scilicet *added in* C,

548. definitum] atque perpetuum *d*

549. varie *d*

550. repentinus *m, perhaps correctly*

551. et cuncta] atque omnia *d*

552. quattuor rebus maxime] tum severitate commixta comitati et una plerumque felicitate eventuum *d*

553. constantissime *d*

554. pulcherrimae ac] praeclarae atque *d*

555. *after* certe, *d writes* multo

556. imperatores ac milites *added in* C,

557. suis *d*

558. ac existimationem *added in* C,

559. etiam *added in* C,

560. *after* furiosae, *d writes* etiam

561. optimo cuique requisitas *added in* C,

562. vitiorum] ac extremis *d*

563. sic *d*

564. *after* ut, *d writes* etiam

565. atque *d*

566. atque *d*

567. subinde *added in* C₁

568. hominem *added in* C₁

569. Zeusis C₁

570. ut Helenam] Helenam ut *d*

571. nitidis *d*

572. paene *m*

573. gestus *d*

574. virtute *d*

575. *after* is, *d writes* a

576. alio *added in* C₁

577. Navarrum arbi⟨tror⟩ *(partly illegible) added in* C₁

578. inquam *added in* C₁

579. ut de eo suprema censura finiatur *added in* C₁

580. eum *added in* C₁

581. illud *added in* C₁

582. servum *d*

583. *after* quo, *d writes* virtus

584. *after* et, *d writes* simplicium

585. Didacum *d*

586. *after* altissimo, C₁ *adds* Albanus Princeps *in margin, without an insertion mark*

587. etenim] et enim C₁

588. eius et *added in* C₁

589. militum *added in* C₁

590. quisque *m*

591. excelsum *d*

592. Guillermus *added in* C₁

593. seniorem *d*

594. Odectus F⟨usii⟩ cognomento *added in* C₁

595. exitiorum *d*

596. vehementer *m*

597. scimus *d*

598. omnium *d*

599. et penitus] ac *d*

600. vel *d*

601. saepius *d*

602. Admirante *added in* C₁

603. Boninetto *m*

604. *after* properavit, *d writes* ut brevi Gastonis Fusii patruelis qui ad Ravennam victor interiit

605. felicius ut *added in* C₁

606. *after* ipsa, *d writes* demum

607. uno *added in* C₁

608. rerum *d*

609. tum *m*

610. enim in eo animi robur cum summa perseverantia] in Obegnino qui Eberardum patruum moribus bellicis refert *d*

611. *after* cupidissime, *d writes* legum

612. *sc.* Franciscus (*see Notes to the Translation, Dialogue One, n. 322*)

613. *after* ardentissimi, *d writes* liberalis gloriae flagrantissimi

614. *after* tenuit, *d writes* Ceterum ut ad intermissum sermonem aliquando redeamus necesse est

615. ut ad intermissum sermonem aliquando redeamus *added in* C₁

616. usus fueris] sis usus *d*

617. ipsius et aliorum] aliorum et ipsius *d*

618. exsistimatote *d*

619. *after* vobis, *d writes* omnino

620. et *d*

621. et *d*

622. quod *d*

623. exploratamque] ad exploratam *d*

624. re *d*

625. certam parari] parari certam *d*

626. fortia et aspera] praeclara *d*

627. ex adverso *added in* C_1

628. quisque *m*

629. tam *d*

630. mortisque] et mortis *d*

631. *after* dicere, *d writes* enim

632. *The text here from §206 to §211 incorporates material from insert (c) and omits material from the bound manuscript, the latter considered as belonging to an intermediate draft*

633. tantum C_1: tam *insert (c)*

634. equuleo *d*

635. eam *added in* C_1

636. *after* numquam, *d writes* enim

637. diceret *added in* C_1

638. quae dicta laudavimus] extemplo respondimus *d*

639. etiam *added in* C_1

640. vel . . . vel] aut . . . aut *d*

641. veris de hoc homine] vero *d*

642. primas cohortes educentem *added in* C_1

643. effluido] e fluido *m*

644. iudicaret *d*

645. restrinxit *m*

646. *after* maxime, *d writes* et

647. Laudi Pompeiae (Pompeia *m*) *added in* C_1

648. excitaverit *m*

649. *after* fortitudine, *d writes* atque industria

650. summae *added in* C₁

651. dolorem *d*

DIALOGUE TWO

1. *The manuscript of Dialogue Two (= C₂) appears to lack its opening pages.*

2. maxima *d*

3. experimur *added in* C₂

4. magno *d*

5. cura *m*

6. et *omitted in m*

7. e *omitted in m*

8. sui *added in* C₂

9. cecinisset] *(illeg.)* proluo luculentissimis quos modo in philosophiae edidit libellis *d*

10. Horum sicut] sicuri *m*

11. *after* Actio, *d writes* nostro

12. tum *m*

13. Spero tamen eum . . . ad imitandum admirentur *added in* C₂

14. aliquando *m*

15. aliquando *m*

16. dura *m*

17. quisque *m*

18. *after* Cosentinus, *d writes* valde pacatus et diligens grammaticus (valde *remains undeleted, evidently by mistake*)

19. et Noctu volantem cicindelam *added in* C₂

20. ingenium *m, perhaps correctly*

21. Ludit enim saepe . . . fortunatus et sapiens *added in* C₂

22. Martialis *m*

23. nec valde ineptum . . . app⟨ellabat⟩ *added in* C₂

24. et *d*

25. desecare *m*

26. *after* qui, *d writes an illegible word beginning with* V

27. Hic ego: Benigne . . . ad Martialem redeamus *added in* C₂

28. cum *m*

29. et *added in* C₂

30. *d writes* innumerabiles *after* alii

31. et ante alios *added in* C₂

32. ut illo maxime . . . in Capitolio posuisset *added in* C₂

33. nec plane quidem . . . lacrimis *added in* C₂

34. quod *is my correction:* qui C₂ *m*

35. post *added in* C₂: *m reads* primum

36. ceteris *m*

37. *d writes* Alfonsusque Genarius poetarum ditissimus *after* clarus

38. *d writes* et *after* hominum

39. ut hic ipse Pomponius . . . pro lacrimis risum extorsit *added in* C₂

40. penitus *m*

41. Verum iis omnino . . . haurire praecipiunt *added in* C₂; *m reads* proripiunt

42. varia *added in* C₂

43. *d writes* erudita *after* ingenii

44. pernobilis] et fortuna pariter nobilis *d*

45. *m adds* omnino *after* crediderim

46. Cinna *m*

47. *after* decantare, *d writes* ut modo Romae vidimus in Dominico Venerio legato Veneto qui tametsi personam longe gravissimam sustinebat

dum tamen cum eruditis viris animum laxaret cum lepore et sale versibus ludebat

48. flebat *m*

49. *m adds* omnes *after* ante

50. fortasse *added in* C₂

51. *m adds* me *after* saeculo

52. perque *m*

53. propriores *m*

54. et suaves *omitted in m*

55. *A change of speaker is my conjecture; not indicated in* C₂

56. lenissimus *m*

57. sum *m*

58. etiam alii] alii etiam *m*

59. Nullus enim ex hac poetarum . . . proceri videantur *added in* C₂

60. *d writes* Nicolaus *after* alacer

61. *after* salsus, *d writes* et Beccatianus quamquam Latino melior in multo et praepingui suco ut libet aculeatus et lenis

62. viri nobiles *added in* C₂

63. Georgius *added in* C₂

64. Alexander *added in* C₂

65. Hyphigeniam *is added in right margin, without clear insertion mark;* Medeam *is ambiguously deleted in d, with underline instead of strikethrough*

66. inventore tamen Trisino *added in* C₂

67. Sed Trisinus etiam reconditas artes . . . fortasse displicuit *added in* C₂

68. *d and m add* personatos *after* lepidissime

69. *after* transmutatur, *d writes* Sua est et insignis gloria in his amatoriis lusibus Bandellio cucullato, quamquam licentius quam par sit sacrato viro acutissimi ingenii facibus, ut videatur, duobus

70. *d writes* et Alexandro item Arelogio *after* insignis

71. Romae cognitum] cognitum Romae *m*

72. *after* Pansa, *d writes* ipseque Auria Henricus, qui nobile scortum multo cum lepore ab incunabulis, eruditis sed inverecundis excultum lasciviis, publicavit

73. Sed hic velut ab ioco . . . felicius se exercet, ingenium traduxit *added in* C$_2$

74. excolere] *an illegible word ending in* -ssere *d*

75. locutionis *d*

76. *after* exsultat, *d writes* Berna vero noster qui Etruscis salibus iucundissimum adversus malos poetas opus publicavit tantam in scribendo scitae urbanitatis elegantiam consequitur ut poetarum omnium cum eruditione facetissimus habeatur

77. qua *m*

78. illo *omitted in m*

79. *Perhaps* Niliacam *should be read; see Notes to the Translation, Dialogue Two, n. 125*

80. ex his qui in parando stilo non ignobiliter desudant *added in* C$_2$

81. *d writes* et acer dialecticus et subtilis astronomus *after* libet

82. tu *omitted in m*

83. *Perhaps* Niliaca (*see n. 79 above*)

84. memoria *m*

85. *m adds* omnino *after* genus

86. reparatae *m*

87. *after* perscribit, *d writes* Floret adhuc Lucae religiosissimus senex Nicolaus Tegrimius qui Castrucii Lucensium tiranni disciplinaeque bellicae in Italia reparatoris vitam Latinarum litterarum memoriae commendavit

88. I. *is my correction (see Notes to the Translation):* T. C$_2$

89. Rosanensem *m*

90. orationibus *m*

91. humanis *d*

92. perfalse *m*

93. *m reads* videtur, *perhaps correctly*

94. externi *m*

95. *m reads* Samnionum, *perhaps correctly*

96. iis *d*

97. aetatis *m*

98. tum *is my correction:* cum C₂

99. Aesopos et C₂] et Aesopos *m (see his explanatory note)*

100. *d writes a word, perhaps* non, *after* nobilissimis

101. opinato *d*

102. quae *d*

103. colluvionem *d*

104. interruptis ieiunisque] interruptisque *m*

105. Suscipiunt *m*

106. Suspiciunt etiam viri doctissimi . . . exilii fortunam exaequantur *added in* C₂

107. Chaldaicisque *added in* C₂

108. excussam C₂

109. *after* legimus, *d writes* et Hieronymus Balbus Gurcensis qui cum sit in omni doctrinae varietate vehementer exercitatus etiam suaviores Musas in exacta aetate solicitat

110. est *m*

111. subtiliori *m*

112. festorum *m*

113. Bono⟨m⟩o] Bononio C₂

114. et hilaris *added in* C₂

115. stile *m*

116. *after* ordinis, *d writes* Petrum quoque Philippum Pandulphinum Florentiae nobilem ardenti ille ingenio non modo Aelianum quem Latinum facit verum et graviora feliciter ausurum esse putamus

117. usitata semper et admodum superbe] usitata tam superbe *d*

118. unctionibus *m*

119. arbitramur *d*

120. sine compendio *added in* C₂

121. topiariis *m*

122. ceterarum *m*

123. impeditura *m*

124. discendo atque docendo senex factus *added in* C₂

125. et Franciscus Conternius et Hieronymus Fondulius et Petrus Crassus *added in* C₂

126. hos *m*

127. excidisset *m*

128. Tum vero inquam recte sentis . . . melius eo scripsisse iudicetur. Sed *added in* C₂

129. nobiliore *d*

130. *d writes* ii *after* modo

131. observare *m*

132. Ceterum postea cottidianus . . . admirabilisve proveniet *added in* C₂

133. ac item] et *d*

134. artificium *m*

135. diducere *m*

136. Magis enim est ingenuum . . . emptosque cremare cogeretur. Sed unum *added in* C₂

137. et *added in* C₂

138. unicus *d*

139. tam *added in* C$_2$

140. solent *m*

141. *m conjecturally adds* non *after* quaeque

142. *m reads* facundos, *perhaps correctly*

143. varietateque] et varietate *d*

DIALOGUE THREE

1. *after* animi, *d writes* et exercendi corporis

2. angulae *d*

3. arcuatae *d*

4. et hiasminarum C$_3$: hiasminarum etiam *d*

5. et *added in* C$_3$

6. clarorum *m*

7. *after* decerpi, *d writes* omnino

8. pontibus] binis trabibus *d*

9. insulas *added in* C$_3$

10. *after* sicut, *d writes* illa

11. et *d*

12. infantia *m*

13. topiarii operis] topiarum *d*

14. his quos videtis] proximis *d*

15. ac *added in* C$_3$

16. ⟨non⟩ videre] videre ⟨non⟩ *m*

17. audivimus *m*

18. pulcherrimarum *m*

19. acutorumque *d m, perhaps correctly*

20. *after* perspicue, *d writes* nihil distincte

21. fuisse *added in* C$_3$

22. hoc *d*

23. scilicet *added in* C₃

24. et religione] pudicius aut denique gravitate religione pietate constantius aut *d*

25. prope] sordidae atque *d*

26. deleverit *d*

27. et *d*

28. prosperisque Lotrechii successibus] atque victoriis *d*

29. pro iure imperii *added in* C₃

30. et *d*

31. Sed profecto *added in* C₃

32. ipse *added in* C₃

33. qui *d*

34. urbana iucunditate] et (?) civili perurbanaque virtute vestra *d*

35. tum commoda tum] et commoda et *d*

36. nihil *m*

37. *after* omnium, *d writes* memorabilium

38. novit *d*

39. habebantur *d*

40. cum . . . civitatis] vel quietem constitutae civitatis vel seniorum consilia *d*

41. Tantum *m*

42. viderentur *d*

43. muliebribus] et mulieribus *d*

44. et patriae *added in* C₃

45. conserentur *m*

46. optimae *added in* C₃

47. sed *d*: vero *m*

48. ut Graecorum . . . adducendas *added in* C₃

49. diffisus esset] diffidisset C_3

50. *after* Athenae, *d writes* ipsae

51. *after* universas, *d writes* terrarum

52. cum aequalium tum] et aequalium et *d*

53. barbaras gentes etiam hodie] Persas tamen *d*

54. ut *d*

55. mollitiam *corrected:* molliciem C_3

56. numerentur *corrected:* enumerentur C_3

57. praeclare *m*

58. quae *corrected:* qui C_3

59. et laudem *added in* C_3

60. interdictis nobilioribus officiis *added in* C_3

61. inferuntur *m*

62. magnitudinem *d*

63. vitae fructum] fructum vitae *m*

64. certe *d*

65. officiisque . . . denique] ossibus ac *d*

66. *after* infusae, *d writes* et

67. et in iis . . . vigere *added in* C_3

68. *Here follows a long addendum, in a different hand, with corrigenda in Giovio's hand; it was, however, entirely deleted and therefore is omitted from the present edition as representing an intermediate redaction*

69. siquidem *added in* C_3

70. vel . . . vel] aut . . . aut *d*

71. *after* quae, *d writes* maxima atque

72. vexillum de manu . . . euntibus] signum et vexillum contra euntibus Hispanis *d*

73. Sugambris *corrected:* Sicambris C_3

74. atque *d*

75. felicius *d*

76. renovandi belli *added in* C₃

77. industria *possibly deleted*

78. Quae nam huius . . . abruperint *added in* C₃

79. metu *added in* C₃

80. sic *d*

81. *after* exsequeretur, *d writes* segnes castigaret, inflammaret dubios, et semel erectos ad spem libertatis vehementius incitaret, adeo ut

82. iniquo *d*

83. difficillime *m*

84. *after* summum, *d writes* et incomparabile

85. illos *added in* C₃

86. indomiti *added in* C₃

87. *after* animi, *d writes* auctoritate abstinentia

88. *after* moderatione, *d writes* et ubi expediret cum severitate, tum lenitate

89. cum . . . tum] et . . . et *d*

90. ac *d*

91. Apage *d*

92. vero *m*

93. *after* ea, *d writes* et

94. contumeliosissima *d*

95. *after* Sed, *d writes* ea

96. neque *d*

97. nequeant] no⟨n⟩ possint *d*

98. concisura *corrected:* concasura C₃

99. satis honestum] honestissimum *d*

100. et nequaquam obscure nobilitant *added in* C₃

101. quidem *corrected:* quidam C₃

102. quidem voto facilius imaginato concipi] desiderari atque animo concipi facilius *d*

103. in ipso rerum usu omnino *added in* C₃

104. illam *added in* C₃

105. *after* mulierem, *d writes* illam

106. et morum ac *added in* C₃

107. ab institutione . . . nutriciis et] praestantius *d*

108. maxime *added in* C₃

109. splendidissimi *d*

110. quae non minus a caelo quam a parentibus ducitur *added in* C₃

111. animos *added in* C₃

112. autem *added in* C₃

113. feminas *added in* C₃

114. ac *d*

115. ipsius integri] integerrimi *d*

116. famosissimae *d*

117. et religiose] ac religiosissime *d*

118. item *added in* C₃

119. mirabiliter *added in* C₃

120. pollucens *m*

121. omnium *d*

122. quin . . . reputetur *added in* C₃

123. ex *added in* C₃

124. consideratius *added in* C₃

125. non multum] minime *d*

126. at (et?) *d*

127. praeclaraque] praeclara *m*

128. et maxime luxuriosa] atque luxuriosissima *d*

129. inferti *m*

130. cuncta pretiosa] ea *d*

131. Quin et *added in* C₃

132. lasciviora in multam noctem] in multam noctem lasciviora *d*

133. coepere *added in* C₃

134. tam *d*

135. *after* venerem, *d writes* quam Valentinorum equitum crebrae illae salutationes, quae molli tantum capitis nutu a mulieribus in fenestris excipiuntur dum illi phaleratis mulis per Urbem vecti et saepius eadem revecti incurvata cervice ad conspectum despectantis dominae capita denudant

136. vero *d*

137. siccioribus *d*

138. Ita ut in Politicis . . . fas esset *added in* C₃

139. veteratores *added in* C₃

140. probrosis *m*

141. etiam hodie *added in* C₃

142. et pretexto concisoque] stragula coccinea aut praetexte *d*

143. *after* expresserint, *d writes* Propterea aliae spadices albipedes aliae gilvos nigra fasciola clunes et media terga distinguente pecuniis aut adulteriis parant. Unam ex iis ego novi quae candidos pares guttatos difficillima conquisitione in aemulationem alterius ab amatoribus impetravit.

144. martolarum *m, perhaps correctly*

145. Scythicae mittunt sylvae pretiosis] Scythicus mittit oceanus pretiosissimis *d*

146. femoralia furtorum veneris] subligacula femorum furtorum *d*

147. unguentis *d*

148. indica unguenta in suffitus adolentur] moscus ambra zebettum myrrha in suffitus adolentur et cubicula ac triclinia puris odoribus replentur *d*

149. floribus odoratis quod ex ipsa domestica hortorum fecunditate facile paratur ad delicias pertinet] suavissimis floribus ad delicias narium pertinet, vel e iasminis citrinis nardinisque oleis *d*

150. ut ab incognito . . . quidem maxime (maxime *possibly deleted, as in m*)] tantum et *d*

151. maximis *d*

152. evastatam esse opulentam] convulsam esse opulentissimam eam *d*

153. acerbissime *d*

154. inquam Desine nos Davale] Desine inquam Davale nos ipsos *d*

155. et *d*

156. *after* Comum, *m adds* ⟨abhinc⟩

157. primo contra fidem publicam *added in* C₃

158. demum penitus *added in* C₃

159. *after* ut, *d writes* et

160. amoenissimi *d*

161. obsecro *perhaps deleted*

162. *after* credebatur, *d writes* et (*m reads as undeleted*)

163. credebatur publico sed iniquo quidem iudicio in quaestione *added in* C₃

164. in exercitu legatus *added in* C₃

165. Petrus *added in* C₃

166. fateamur *m, perhaps correctly*

167. Castellioniam Hieronymi iurisconsulti eloquentissimi nurum familia nobili et pervetusta] Castelliam familia non aeque nobili sed vetustissima *d*

168. *An additional paragraph appears approximately at this point in d, replaced in the final draft by* §§50–52: Secundum locum obtinet Matalena Sanseverina Ferrerio quaestori pecuniosissimo atque nobili quondam nupta. In ea ut in summis educata delitiis quae in liberiore vidua excogitari munditiae, ac ornamenta deferri possunt ad principalis luxus effigiem spectantur. Ita ut forma corporis per se excellens non a gemmis et purpura quas

orbatae non admittunt commendationem accipiat sed a multis liberalis ingenii argutiis atque leporibus. Rabinia etiam Beatrix in qua una pulchritudo ante alia venit maxime laudanda tantam et tam grata venustate modestiam vultu incessu atque oculis praesefert ut ab ea nativae propioresque lasciviae artificio quodam recondi et publice dissimulari videantur.

169. propriores *m*

170. audiant *m*

171. quodam *m*

172. munus *m*

173. quicumque *m*

174. nequaquam huius ordinis . . . multis de causis] tenuioris ordinis atque fortunae *d*

175. *after* opportuna, *d writes* civitate; *m reads* civitate *as undeleted*

176. paene *added in* C₃

177. Et hercle . . . secessu sentiuntur. Nam senatus] Cuncta enim ibi rerum omnium copia et varietate laetissima cuncta pacata atque tranquilla summa bonis omnibus ac modestis perducendae hilarius vitae iucundissima libertas commoditas item incredibilis et voluptas navigandi nulli umquam tumultus nulli bellorum strepitus nullae publicae nulla privatae iniuriae sentiuntur. Senatus *d*

178. incredibili *added in* C₃

179. honestum *d*

180. et circumpadanis *added in* C₃

181. ineptae C₃, *m*

182. crassiculis *d*

183. oblectare *corrected:* oblectari C₃ *m*

184. *after* comptui, *d writes* et

185. atque item] et *d*

186. a ceteris *added in* C₃

187. facile *d*

188. earum *added in* C₃

189. *after* ut, *d writes* et

190. *after* munificis, *d writes* et cupidis

191. *after* desint, *d writes* Ad tuendam patriciarum pudorem secretiores quaedam libidinum officinae in angiportibus sunt institutae quae diligenti vetularum laenarum ministerio continentur ad quas ultro eunt impudicae mulieres. Quae pretii spe vel explendae veneris cupiditate ab ignotis hominibus comprimuntur. Vidimus nos Eugeniani summae claritatis laenam per cellas puellarum manus in certos formae ac aetatis et morum ordines digessisse ita ut profiteretur se cunctis vel salacissimorum hominum cupiditatibus egregie responsuram.

192. vestales *d*

193. Proinde *d*

194. praetextuque] et praetextu *d*

195. cum eam *added in* C₃

196. *after* ulcisci, *d writes* properare

197. properabant *added in* C₃

198. vasa argentea] argentea vasa *d*

199. itemque *added in* C₃

200. etiam *added in* C₃

201. parabantur *added in* C₃

202. erant *added in* C₃

203. Ceterum *added in* C₃

204. *after* Matronae, *d writes* autem

205. Isabella *added in* C₃

206. incitetur *d*

207. nivea *added in* C₃

208. etiam *added in* C₃

209. Venetiis reperitur, Aryadnam *added in* C₃

210. a vobis *added in* C₃

211. non minus copia et specie quam fama nobilissimos *added in* C₃

212. parum pudicas] impudicas *d*

213. scilicet *added in* C₃

214. acuti *d*

215. praeclara *added in* C₃

216. secundae *m*

217. quietissimae *d*

218. equitum magistrum] magistrum equitum *d*

219. quae tua est etiam erga hostes singularis humanitas *added in* C₃

220. Sunt et in eo Padi tractu . . . merito numeretur *added in* C₃

221. Mantuae Isabella Boscheta Calvisiani *deleted in* C₃, *probably in error; the words are reinserted here to preserve the sense of passage*

222. et *m*

223. in tota vitae cursu . . . aspirante. Haec singillatim] totius vitae aequabilem disciplinam quae omnia *d*

224. castissimoque] et castissimo *d*

225. Chioppa *m*

226. heroicarum elegantiarum *added in* C₃

227. suavi quadam *added in* C₃

228. etiam nunc vigere] sublevari *d*

229. sunt admodum suculentae ab nitida] bene pastae suculentae ab obesa *d*

230. cervices arvinosae pleniores et] turgidae cervices arvinosa pectora *d*

231. apta *d*

232. quam liberrimae iucunditati *added in* C₃

233. ipsi contra longe pulcherrima marium iuventute decorentur] Iuventus ipsa non aeque pulchra vel habili oris et corporis figura decoretur. Propterea apud Bononienses frequens est proverbium illud, leves et pulposos clunes, et mollia femora ob deformem et minus elegantem vultum sapientibus nequaquam esse refutanda. Ex iis tamen est cum forma, tum

ingenio et moribus haud iniucunda, natalibus amplis et praeclara castitate *is added in d; after* decorentur *the page is blank for several lines before resuming with* §75

234. *after* indecorum, *d writes* est

235. comparatus sorte quadam] comparatis et sortitis *d*

236. exercebantur *d*

237. Per *added in* C₃

238. *after* quam, *d writes* cuiquam

239. *after* Aestate, *d writes* autem

240. citriisque] et citriis *d*

241. tanta est] est tanta *m*

242. frequentia *d*

243. manibus *m*

244. operosae] operosissimae ipsius *d*

245. vel elati portus vel exculti] situs ac elati *d*

246. *after* piscanti, *d writes* cum retibus

247. *corrected in m:* exprobare C₃

248. humilibus *d*

249. non omnino *added in* C₃

250. ornamenta et unguentorum etiam delicias] et unguentorum ornamenta *d*

251. *after* elocutione, *d writes* composita

252. a festivis deliciis Meliboea nuncupata *added in* C₃

253. *after* munditiarum, *d writes* Emersit etiam nuper in urbanam lucem
M(*illeg.*) Gentilis in qua stupens iuventus admiratur absolutae formae ac
eximiae proceritatis decus et nigrorum luminum fulgorem roseasque ge-
nas et labra ipsa nullis interlita pigmentis. Verum illi insunt ut semper in
astricta et minus liberali educatione accidit mores subrustici et paullo
rudiores qui tamen facile molliri polirique poterunt si Pasqual⟨i⟩ coniunx

more urbano eam ceteris matronis et iuventuti excolendam erudiendamque permiserit.

254. caesaris *m*

255. *after* sustentata, *d writes* neque ⟨civilibus praes⟩ulae spectatissimae virtutis matronae quicquam vere de pristina dignitate excurrentes anni detraxerunt

256. feliciorum *m, perhaps correctly*

257. Perstrinxit etiam oculos . . . eximie commendant *added in* C$_3$

258. Medices *added in* C$_3$

259. ante *m*

260. urbanarum *d*

261. laeto et salubri] salubri et laeto *d*

262. vel optimis studiis eruditisque artibus ceteris civibus praecellebant] cum optimis studiis tum eruditis artibus valebant *d*

263. suavissimam *d*

264. *after* insinuavi, *d writes* Quamobrem quicquid tota urbe aut iucundum visu aut dignum cognitione fuerat id diligentium meum et curiositatem nequaquam effugerit.

265. obivissent *added in* C$_3$

266. Ficini *added in* C$_3$

267. alacritate *d*

268. florentiae *m, perhaps correctly*

269. cuius hodie filium Braccium cultu ubertateque ingenii Florentem admiramur *added in* C$_3$

270. *after* donavisset, *d writes* Quintus accedebat Franciscus Victorius cuius grave iudicium stabilesque sententias aliquanto pluris quam litteras faciebant.

271. Dorica *d*

272. praesidente Iulio Cardinale *added in* C$_3$

273. recitate *d*

274. humanitatis *d*

275. quibusdam *d*

276. *after* vehementiae, *d writes* et virilis omnino rationis

277. per occasionem capti pontificis *added in* C₃

278. susceperint *d*

279. nequaquam ingrati . . . veriti, sibi] si non plane fidele, sibi tamen valde *d*

280. pueris *added in* C₃

281. Verum id factum . . . attulerit. Ceterum] Ex iis fuere Laurentius Bartolinus Baucius Cavalcantes Petrusphilippus Pandulphinus et is qui in commotae reipublicae tumultu octovir factus est Ioannes Neretius *d*

282. ac hilarioribus] et alacrioribus cum litterarum tum *d*

283. *after* certis, *d writes* et exquisitis

284. Singulorum enim] Quorum singulari *d*

285. cum foris] in proximis et luculentissimis villis cum in illas *d*

286. enim *d*

287. insanis *d*

288. peramoena] praeclara et amoena *d*

289. nobili quodam] incredibili *d*

290. carum *m*

291. lasciviis *d*

292. omnes *omitted in m*

293. commeatus omnes domestici et fortunae familiares uxorum] fortunae omnes familiares et domestici commeatus *d*

294. facile *added in* C₃

295. liberent *added in* C₃

296. quaedam *added in* C₃

297. et *d*

298. eas commendant] exprimuntur *d*

299. *after* laudes, *d writes* erant eae triginta quinque

300. adamatae *added in* C₃

301. *after* rapuerunt, *d writes* Et Constantia pariter Acelina, venustate mollibusque deliciis insignis, fato concessit

302. iniquitate Fati *added in* C₃

303. qua Iulius Medices ad pontificatum Fato reservatus in templo trucidari debebat *added in* C₃

304. litteris et libertate vitae *added in* C₃

305. *From* §95 et gravi etiam morbo, *to* §98 quae meo iudicio super ceteras, *the text in the ms. has been canceled* (= *f*. 17v). *Although the passage appears to belong to a redaction intermediate between d and* C₃, *it is necessary to the coherence of the narrative and therefore has been included here.*

306. et (?) *d*

307. *after* commendant, *d writes* In Constantia vero Pandulphina Zenobio Bartolino nupta viro luculento haec eminent et laudem ferunt. Virilis adunco naso facies tornata habilisque statura liberalis atque alacer animus cum muliebri venustate mollitudineque coniuncta Contessiae Castellanae grata proceritas obtutus admodum blandus et candor eximius multos perussit.

308. in Laurentii Iunioris nuptiis *added in* C₃

309. amplissimis *d*

310. *after* dum, *d writes* pontifici studeret

311. *after* nominibus, *d writes* et externis

312. Portiam quae fuit Pandulfi Petrucii sapientissimi Senensium tiranni filia, peramoena quadam oris ac ingenii iucunditate praecellentem agnovimus. Sed una ab omnibus insigni, cum laude celebratur Honorata Tancredia nobili] unam sat erit insigni cum laude celebrasse: ea est Hon⟨inusi⟩ a Picolominea pontificia *d*

313. Est enim adeo . . . etiam florere videremus *added in* C$_3$

314. via *m*

315. cum pavimentis signino et musino opere vermiculatis *added in* C$_3$

316. item *added in* C$_3$

317. scamillorum *added in* C$_3$

318. secto *m*

319. canorum *d*

320. lithostratis *m*

321. numerata *m*

322. et *m*

323. eas *m*

324. opalus *corrected:* opali *d:* opalis C$_3$

325. Praeclare *m, perhaps correctly*

326. tenerissimis *m*

327. multitudo *m*

328. Qui *d*

329. laetisque *m*

330. habitu *added in* C$_3$

331. *sc.* maurusiacum

332. prudentiae laude . . . superasse diceretur *added in* C$_3$

333. ac *d*

334. *after* sit, *d writes* affectum

335. divinaque] ac divina *d*

336. saluberrime simul ac iucundissime] medellae tam gratae salubriter omnino *d*

337. et *d*

338. inenarrabiles *corrected:* innerrabiles C$_3$

339. picta *m*

340. assidebant *m*

341. *The third-person reference to Iovius in the following line suggests that Musetius begins speaking here.*

342. *after* est, *d writes* et

343. et *d*

344. quam *m*

345. inquam Dorothea vere Deorum munus *added in* C₃

346. plusquam *m*

347. tamen *omitted in m*

348. *after* laudandae, *d writes* omnino

349. quum *m*

350. asciticias *corrected (see Hoven s.v.):* adscititias C₃

351. venustatem] incomparabilem speciem *d*

352. humanitate *d*

353. miser *added in* C₃

354. *d gives a different version of the passage from §135 to §137* alae signifero nupta *continuing Musetius' speech*: Tantum vero abest ut eius singularis feminae laudes absolvisse confitear ut multo satius putem omnino de ea siluisse quam tam pauca et ceteris etiam mulieribus fere communia protulisse. Altera est Lucretia Caraffae Bellingerii filia in qua peramabilem et oris et totius corporis venustatem itemque mores ad promerendam gratiam idoneos non iuventus modo sed aemulae etiam mulieres saepissime laudarunt. Est etiam egregiae formae dignitas Victoriae Herbeiae quae nuper nobili et strenuo iuvene marito Hieronymo Columnae orbata est placet et candidus suci plenus et alacer habitus Iuliae Crisoniae viris elegantibus.

355. colliniasti *corrected:* collimasti C₃ *m*

356. praeter ipsam suaviter et perite canendi iucunditatem capilli perlucentes, decentissimae] capilli perlucentes, flavi, turgidulae leves *d*

357. elucetque . . . clarissimus testis *added in* C₃

358. nonnullis iunioribus praetulerim] paene istis omnibus praetulerim si aliqua mihi Neapoli ad animi laxamentum et totius vitae iucunditatem foret excolenda *d*

359. in eo etiam aetatis flexu remanetque] in integra ac viridi aetate (*illeg.*) *d*

360. *after* Atticos, *d writes* et eruditissimos

361. et *added in* C₃

362. operaepretium *corrected in* m: operepretium C₃

363. deorum] tectis deorumque *d*

364. *after* suppliciis, *d writes* nefariisque rapinis

365. aut felici fuga *added in* C₃

366. exsecrandis *d*

367. Aurelianum *added in* C₃

368. etiam *d*

369. lenones *added in* C₃: *m inserts* lenones *after* tuis, *perhaps correctly*

370. *after* pudentiore, *d writes* amictu

371. ex *added in* C₃

372. Florae *m*

373. *after* vocem, *d writes* quod

374. e *added in* C₃

375. pugionibus *d*

376. pelli *d*

377. acanthi *corrected:* achanti C₃: vitium *d*

378. *after* filia, *d writes* et Faustina Cincia Christophori Stati uxor

379. Antonio] C. *d*

380. arte musica et carminum studio iuveni ornatissimo *added in* C₃

381. *after* describendis, *d writes* scrupulosius et

382. vel morum vel] aut morum aut *d*

383. etiam *added in* C₃

384. et *added in* C₃

385. videatur *m*

386. opibus *added in* C₃

387. ac vel acerbissime custoditas studiose] et acerbissime custoditas omnino *d*

388. aptissime *m, perhaps correctly*

389. abortivos *added in* C₃

390. ap⟨p⟩aratiorem *d*

391. vehementiores *d*

392. demum *added in* C₃

393. pudicissimis *d*

394. quibus aestu quodam saevae libidinis incitentur adeo ut] ad exprimendam impetrandamque venerem maxime opportuna quae sicut nulla arte nullaque observatione provideri possunt ita *d*

395. iam pridem *added in* C₃

396. *after* tibi, *d writes* corpore atque animo

397. *§166 through §168* unde discessimus *omitted in d*

398. horum *m*

399. Magna] Sed magno *d*

400. in praesens *corrected:* impresens C₃

401. putant *d*

402. *after* abstulerit, *d writes* Sunt etiam viduae sorores duae, Beatrix et Contarena Farnesiae, ingenua quadam animi liberalis alacritate et morum et eloquentiae urbanique leporis elegantia, nullis secundae.

403. Tibaldio Simoni, fortissimo equitum praefecto] in Tibaldio (*sic*) familia *d*

404. familia *added in* C₃

405. *an intermediate draft, deleted in* C₃, *writes* altera Iulia est . . . honestatur; *the passage is included here for the sake of coherence*

406. constantia *d*

407. Pico *added in* C*₃*

408. §§174–175 *added in* C*₃*

409. illa diffusa et pluribus] usu distribu⟨ta⟩ plurium *m, perhaps correctly*

410. *after* Cardinalis, *d writes* Portiam Octavi filii uxorem quae Petiliani neptis fuit praeclara fecunditate singulari modestia insignique pudore et: *m reads* singulari modestia insignique pudore *as part of* C*₃, perhaps correctly*

411. Caeciliam filiam . . . summae auctoritatis philosopho] et Caeciliam quoque filiam Alberto Pio *d*

412. *after* collocavit, *d writes* Fuit etiam spectatae pulchritudinis Ursina duobus Columnis Stephano atque Alexandro praenestinis regulis mater, in qua nunc et effigiem pristini decoris et singularem prudentiam et raram gravitatem suspicimus.

413. Hieronymo *added in* C*₃, omitted in m*

414. et *added in* C*₃*

415. item capillo et] capillo *d*

416. *after* animi, *d writes* ac habitu denique toto

417. Pulchritudinem *m*

418. haec] Ea *d*

419. properantes] properatae *m*: inexorabiles *d*

420. honestus et eruditus] honestissimus et eruditissimus *d*

421. et Camertibus] Camertib⟨us⟩que *d*

422. *after* insignis, *d writes* Huic fratres sunt duo prenestini, quos modo memoravi, sed nequaquam eadem matre progeniti

423. *after* optimae, *m adds* ac

424. optimae maximae] et maximae ac optimae *d*

425. quod *added in* C*₃*

426. quibus *m*

427. ea *d*

428. qui⟨c⟩quam *corrected:* quiquam C₃

429. sensit *d*

430. tenere C₃

431. tribus *d*

432. rarissime *m*

433. acuti *m*

434. velut *added in* C₃

435. *after* ornamentis, *m adds* et

436. lectorum *added in* C₃

437. quam capaci et] et capaci quam *d*

438. enituerit *m*

439. cum *added in* C₃

440. tenent *m*

441. Obiter] Ab iis *m*

442. a Pyrrho Epirotarum et Antigono] ⟨ab⟩ Alexandro Magno et ceteris *d*

443. tot in hac pudoris cura] fabulosi stemmatis ineptiae Graecienses et *d*

444. affectionem omnem cum gestus tum] portenta *d*

445. celebraret *m*

446. Sed tum maxime . . . convelare voluisse *added in* C₃

447. Sed *d*

448. nulla *m*

449. propilate *m*

450. sociari *m*

451. rabiosa *d*

452. summae *omitted in m*

453. eius *d*

APPENDIX

1. abstersit C_1

2. fortissimo *d*: duce ⟨civili⟩ et bellica virtute ⟨clariss⟩imo C_1 *(restorations from t)*

3. *in an intermediate draft,* vos *was replaced with* pontificem

4. *After* admiserit, *an intermediate draft (subsequently deleted) adds:* Neque hoc scribendi genus aut ieiunum aut parum illustre videri debet quando in eo duos Graecorum et Latinorum eosdem philosophos graves et historiarum scriptores longe praestantissimos Xenophontem et T. Livium divina sua ingenia exercuisse constat. Neque materia etiam erit ignobilis. Nam in primo libro Davalus cum aliud agere videatur plenissime docet quibus maxime virtutibus fiat illustris et valde conspicuus imperator. In secundo autem de toto litterario munere ad parandam laudem variis sententiis cum hilari ingeniorum censura disp⟨utatur⟩. Postremo honestissimus ad admirationem nobilis matronae habitus cum insignium feminarum la⟨udibus⟩ quadam orationis amoenitate describitur.

5. Quibus de rebus . . . otiose sederemus *added in d*

6. ludorum omnis . . . nubes effugissent. Secunda *d*] exercitationum varii generis ac ludorum qua muliebris animus iucundissima voluptate posset oblectari. Namque aliquot ingentes cervos sic agitavit et cepit in proximis montibus ut totus venationis apparatus, ferarum fuga et varius canum et iuvenum discursus e summae arcis fenestris spectarentur. Ab ea quoque parte qua insula praealtis aspera cotibus sed his summo in vertice peramoeno nemore virentibus ab oriente in meridiem recurvatur perdices nobilissimo aucupii genere consectatus est cum mansuefacti hierofalcones per aera sinuoso praecipitique volatu exturbatas sedibus ac in mare provolantes invaderent. Altera C_1

7. Exquisitis enim artibus summoque *d*: Exquisito enim C_1

8. multis C_1

9. saeculis C_1

10. ac C_1

11. semper *added in* d

12. Igitur cum ab ea mole qua oppidum Iscla cum summa arce praeciso undique scopulo praetentis dextris ostentarent *added in* d

13. porro C_1

14. *after* repraesentant, C_1 *adds* verum

15. colles *added in* d

16. hinc atque inde duo promontoria in speculas editiores clementer assurgunt vestita perennibus arbustis. In dextro insigne templum conspicitur *added in* d

17. consaeptae exornataeque d: convestitae consaeptaeque C_1

18. *after* radicibus, C_1 *adds* iuxta lacum

19. *after* aquae, C_1 *adds* mortalium morbis salubres

20. Sicut et in eo sapidissimi . . . lacum subiectis scutulis hominumque d] Itaque laxatis et depressis angustiis plures cumbae ab attiguo mari in lacum scutulis atque hominum C_1

21. atque arcibus *added in* d

22. *after* conscendimus, C_1 *adds* atque item complures

23. impetuntur C_1

24. *after* recipiunt, C_1 *adds* Neque enim ut nimium obesae inertes et timidae egregio conatu vel in montes vel in mare proximum evolare audent

25. novum atrox d: ergo C_1

26. discalciati *added in* d

27. *after* interfectis, C_1 *adds* aut captis

Notes to the Translation

꽃꿍꽃

ABBREVIATIONS

Ady
Julia Mary Cartwright Ady, *Baldassare Castigione, The Perfect Courtier; His Life and Letters 1478–1529*, 2 vols. (New York: E. P. Dutton, 1908).

Altamura
Antonio Altamura, *L'Umanesimo nel mezzogiorno d'Italia: Storia, bibliografie e testi inediti* (Florence: Bibliopolis, 1941).

Altieri
Li Nuptiali di Marco Antonio Altieri pubblicati da Enrico Narducci, introd. Massimo Miglio, with documentation and name index by Anna Modigliani (Rome: Roma nel Rinascimento, 1995).

Amayden
Teodoro Amayden, *La storia delle famiglie romane*, ed. Carlo Augusto Bertini (Rome: Collegio Araldico, 1910–14; repr. Bologna: Forni, 1967).

Ammirato
Scipione Ammirato, *Delle famiglie nobili napoletane*, 2 vols. Part One (Florence: Giorgio Marescotti, 1580); Part Two (Florence: Amadore Massi da Furlì, 1651).

Arfaioli
Maurizio Arfaioli, *The Black Bands of Giovanni: Infantry and Diplomacy during the Italian Wars (1526–1528)* (Pisa: Edizioni Plus, Pisa University Press, 2005).

Argegni
Condottieri, capitani, e tribuni, fino al Cinquecento, ed. Corrado Argegni, 3 vols. (Milan: Tosi, 1936–37).

Balsamo
Jean Balsamo, with Franco Tomasi, *Poètes italiens de la Renaissance dans la bibliothèque de la Fondation Barbier-Mueller: de Dante à Chiabrera: catalogue*, 2 vols. (Geneva: Droz, 2007).

615

Becker   Michael Becker, *Genealogien zur Papstgeschichte*, rev. Christoph Weber, 6 vols. (Stuttgart: Anton Hiersemann, 1999–2002).

Bembo   Pietro Bembo, *History of Venice*, ed. and trans. Robert W. Ulery, Jr., vols. 1–3 (The I Tatti Renaissance Library, 28, 32, and 37) (Cambridge, MA: Harvard University Press, 2007–9).

Benedetti   Alessandro Benedetti, *Diaria de bello carolino (Diary of the Caroline War)*, ed. and trans. Dorothy M. Schullian (New York: Ungar, 1967).

Berni   Anne Reynolds, *Renaissance Humanism at the Court of Clement VII: Francesco Berni's Dialogue Against Poets in Context. Studies, with an edition and translation* (New York: Garland, 1997).

Biblioteca modenese   Girolamo Tiraboschi, *Biblioteca modenese*, 6 vols. (Modena: Società tip., 1781–86).

Cath Ency   *Catholic Encyclopedia* (New York: Robert Appleton Company, 1913), available online at www.newadvent.org/cathen

CathEn   Charles George Herbermann et al., *The Catholic Encyclopedia: An International Work of Reference on the Constitution, Doctrine, Discipline, and History of the Catholic Church*, 19 vols. (New York: Appleton, 1907–12).

CE   *Contemporaries of Erasmus: A Biographical Register of the Renaissance and Reformation*, ed. Peter. G. Bietenholz and Thomas B. Deutscher, 3 vols. (Toronto: University of Toronto Press, 1985–87).

Colapietra   Raffaelle Colapietra, *I Sanseverino di Salerno: Mito e realtà del barone ribelle* (Salerno: Pietro Laveglia, 1985).

Commynes — Philippe de Commynes, *The Memoirs of Philippe de Commynes*, ed. Samuel Kinser and trans. Isabelle Cazeaux, 2 vols. (Columbia, SC: University of South Carolina Press, 1969–73).

CompNLS — Jozef Ijsewijn, *Companion to Neo-Latin Studies*, vol. 1, 2nd ed. (Louvain: Louvain University Press, 1990).

Conte — Emanuele Conte, *I maestri della Sapienza di Roma dal 1514 al 1787: I rotuli e altre fonti* (Fonti per la storia d'Italia 116; Studi e fonti per la storia dell'Università di Roma, n.s., 1) (Rome, 1991).

Coryciana — *Coryciana*, ed. Jozef Ijsewijn (Rome: Herder, 1997).

Cosenza — M. E. Cosenza, *Biographical and Bibliographical Dictionary of the Italian Humanists and of the World of Classical Scholarship in Italy, 1300–1800*, 6 vols. (Boston: G. K. Hall, 1962–67).

Cox — Virginia Cox, *Women's Writing in Italy, 1400–1600* (Baltimore: Johns Hopkins University Press, 2008).

Croce (1894) — *Versi spagnuoli in lode di Lucrezia Borgia duchessa di Ferrara e delle sue damigelle*, ed. Benedetto Croce (Naples, 1894).

CTC — *Catalogus Translationum et Commentariorum: Mediaeval and Renaissance Latin Translations and Commentaries; Annotated Lists and Guides*, ed. Paul Oskar Kristeller, F. Edward Cranz, Virginia Brown, et al., 9 vols. to date (Washington, D.C.: Catholic University of America Press, 1960–).

Cuestión — *Cuestión de Amor (Valence: Diego de Gumiel, 1513)*, ed. Françoise Vigier (Paris: Publications de la Sorbonne: Presses Sorbonne nouvelle, 2006).

CV — *Condottieri di ventura*, maintained by dott. Roberto Damiani, www.condottieridiventura.it

D'Amico   John F. D'Amico, *Renaissance Humanism in Papal Rome: Humanists and Churchmen on the Eve of the Reformation* (Baltimore: Johns Hopkins University Press, 1983).

DBI   *Dizionario biografico degli italiani* (Rome: Istituto della Enciclopedia Italiana, 1960–).

DELI   *Dizionario enciclopedico della letteratura italiana*, 6 vols. (Rome: Laterza, 1967–70).

DLI   Julia Haig Gaisser, *Pierio Valeriano on the Ill Fortune of Learned Men: A Renaissance Humanist and His World* (Ann Arbor: University of Michigan Press, 1999).

DPR   *Donne di potere nel Rinascimento*, ed. Letizia Arcangeli and Susanna Peyronel (Rome: Viella, 2008).

Ellinger   G. Ellinger, *Geschichte der neulateinischen Literatur Deutschlands im sechzehnten Jahrhundert*, 3 vols. (Berlin: de Gruyter, 1929–33).

Elogi   Paolo Giovio, *Elogi degli uomini illustri*, ed. Franco Minonzio (Turin: Einaudi, 2006).

ER   *Encyclopedia of the Renaissance*, ed. Paul F. Grendler, 6 vols. (New York: Scribner's, 1999).

Eubel   Konrad Eubel, *Hierarchia catholica medii aevi, sive Summorum pontificum, S. R. E. cardinalium, ecclesiarum antistitum series*, 3 vols. (Regensburg: Monasterium, 1913–23).

EWR   *Encyclopedia of Women in the Renaissance: Italy, France, and England*, ed. Diana Robin, Anne R. Larsen, and Carole Levin (Santa Barbara, CA: ABC-CLIO, 2007).

Frede   Carlo De Frede, *I lettori di umanità nello studio di Napoli durante il Rinascimento* (Naples: L'arte tipografica, 1960).

Geanakoplos

Deno John Geanakoplos, *Greek Scholars in Venice* (Cambridge, MA: Harvard University Press, 1962).

Genmarenostrum

(Società Genealogica Italiana) *Enciclopedia genealogica del Mediterraneo* (www.genmarenostrum .com).

Giraldi

Lilio Gregorio Giraldi, *Modern Poets* (*De poetis nostrorum temporum*), ed. and trans. John N. Grant (The I Tatti Renaissance Library, 48) (Cambridge, MA: Harvard University Press, 2011).

Gnoli

Domenico Gnoli, *La Roma di Leon X* (Milan: Ulrico Hoepli, 1938).

Gouwens

Kenneth Gouwens, *Remembering the Renaissance: Humanist Narratives of the Sack of Rome* (Leiden: Brill, 1998).

Gragg

Paolo Giovio: An Italian Portrait Gallery, ed. and trans. Florence Alden Gragg (Boston: Chapman and Grimes, 1935).

GSLI

Giornale storico della letteratura italiana (1883–)

Guicciardini

Francesco Guicciardini, *Storia d'Italia*, ed. Silvana Seidel Menchi, 3 vols. (Turin: Einaudi, 1971).

Hallam

Henry Hallam, *Introduction to the Literature of Europe in the Fifteenth, Sixteenth, and Seventeenth centuries* (New York: F. Ungar Publishing, 1970 [reprint of 1873 edition]).

Hallman

Barbara McClung Hallman, *Italian Cardinals, Reform, and the Church as Property* (Berkeley: University of California Press, 1985).

Hook

Judith Hook, *The Sack of Rome, 1527* (London: Macmillan, 1972).

Hoven

René Hoven, *Lexique de la Prose Latine de la Renaissance*, 2nd ed. (Leiden: Brill, 2006).

Hyde   Helen Hyde, *Cardinal Bendinello Sauli and Church
                    Patronage in Sixteenth-Century Italy* (Wood-
                    bridge, Suffolk: Boydell and Brewer, 2009).

Imber   Colin Imber, *The Ottoman Empire, 1300–1650: The
                    Structure of Power* (New York: Palgrave Mac-
                    millan, 2002).

Imhoff   Jacob Wilhelm Imhoff, *Genealogiae viginti illustrium
                    in Italia familiarum* (Amsterdam: ex officina
                    Fratrum Chatelain, 1710; repr. Sala Bolognese:
                    Forni, 1973).

IO   *Pauli Iovii opera*, 10 vols. to date (Rome: Istituto
                    Poligrafico dello Stato, 1957–).

Iter   Paul Oskar Kristeller, *Iter Italicum: A Finding List
                    of Uncatalogued or Incompletely Catalogued Hu-
                    manistic Manuscripts of the Renaissance in Italian
                    and Other Libraries*, 7 vols. (Leiden: Brill,
                    1963–97).

Kidwell   Carol Kidwell, *Sannazaro and Arcadia* (London:
                    Duckworth, 1993).

Knecht   R. J. Knecht, *Renaissance Warrior and Patron: The
                    Reign of Francis I* (Cambridge: Cambridge Uni-
                    versity Press, 1994).

Litta   Pompeo Litta, *Famiglie celebri di Italia*, 10 vols. plus
                    2 supplements (Milan: P. E. Giusti, 1819–83).
                    (Numeration follows that in pencil in a copy
                    in the Vatican Library, shelf mark Italia.Folio.3
                    [1–12]. Cons.)

Lodi   *Lodi di dame napoletane del secolo decimosesto dall'
                    'Amor prigioniero' di Mario di Leo*, ed. G. Ceci
                    and B. Croce (Naples: [V. Vecchi] 1894).

Mallett (1973)   Michael Mallett, "Venice and Its Condottieri,
                    1404–1454," in *Renaissance Venice*, ed. J. R.
                    Hale (London: Faber and Faber, 1973).

Mallett (1974)   Michael Mallett, *Mercenaries and their Masters: Warfare in Renaissance Italy* (Totowa, NJ: Rowman and Littlefield, 1974).

McIver   Katherine A. McIver, *Women, Art, and Architecture in Northern Italy, 1520–1580* (Aldershot: Ashgate, 2006).

Minonzio   Paolo Giovio, *Dialogo sugli uomini e le donne illustri del nostro tempo*, 2 vols., ed. and trans. Franco Minonzio (Turin: Nino Aragno, 2011).

Muratori   *Rerum italicarum scriptores: raccolta degli storici italiani del cinquecento al millecinquecento*, original edition by L. A. Muratori; new edition, revised, enlarged, and corrected, ed. Giosuè Carducci (Città di Castello: S. Lapi, 1900–).

MusRed   *Musae Reduces*, ed. P. Laurens and C. Balavoine, 2 vols. (Leiden: Brill, 1975).

Negri   Giulio Negri, *Istoria degli scrittori fiorentini* (Ferrara: Bernardino Pomatelli, 1722).

Oman (1902–30)   Charles Oman, *A History of the Peninsular War*, 7 vols. (Oxford: Clarendon Press, 1902–30).

Oman (1979)   Charles Oman, *A History of the Art of War in the Sixteenth Century* (New York: AMS Press, 1979).

Pastor   Ludwig von Pastor, *The History of the Popes from the Close of the Middle Ages*, 3rd ed., tran. F. I. Antrobus et al., 40 vols. (London: Kegan Paul, 1901–33).

Pecchiai   Pio Pecchiai, *Roma nel Cinquecento* (Bologna: Cappelli, 1948).

Pitts   Vincent J. Pitts, *The Man Who Sacked Rome: Charles de Bourbon, Constable of France (1490–1527)* (New York: Peter Lang, 1993).

Poesia umanistica latina   *Poesia umanistica latina in distica elegiaci. Atti del convegno internazionale Assisi, 15–17 maggio 1998*, ed. Giuseppe Catanzaro e Francesco Santucci (Assisi: Accademia Properziana del Subasio, 1999).

Poeti estensi   *Poeti estensi del rinascimento*, ed. Silvio Pasquazi (Florence: F. Le Monnier, 1966).

Pontificate of Clement   *The Pontificate of Clement VII: History, Politics, Culture*, ed. Kenneth Gouwens and Sheryl E. Reiss (Aldershot: Ashgate, 2005).

Rendina   Claudio Rendina, *I capitani di ventura: Storia e segreti* (Rome: Newton Compton, 1985).

Repertorium   *Repertorium Pomponianum* (www.repertorium pomponianum.it)

RLV   *Renaissance Latin Verse: An Anthology*, ed. Alessandro Perosa and John Sparrow (London: Duckworth, 1979).

Robin   Diana Robin, *Publishing Women: Salons, the Presses, and the Counter-Reformation in Sixteenth-Century Italy* (Chicago: University of Chicago Press, 2007).

Sannazaro   Jacopo Sannazaro, *Latin Poetry*, ed. and trans. Michael C. J. Putnam (I Tatti Renaissance Library, 38) (Cambridge, MA: Harvard University Press, 2009).

Sanuto   Marino Sanuto, *I diarii di Marino Sanuto*, 58 vols. (Venice: Visentini, 1879–1902).

Serio   Alessandro Serio, *Una gloriosa sconfitta: I Colonna tra papato e impero nella prima età moderna* (Rome: Viella, 2008).

Setton   Kenneth M. Setton, *The Papacy and the Levant (1204–1571)*, 4 vols. (Philadelphia: The American Philosophical Society, 1984).

Shaw (2006)   *Italy and the European Powers: The Impact of War,*
                  1500–1530, ed. Christine Shaw (Leiden: Brill,
                  2006).
Shaw (2007)   Christine Shaw, *The Political Role of the Orsini Fam-*
                  ily from Sixtus IV to Clement VII: Barons and
                  Factions in the Papal States (Rome: Istituto
                  Storico Italiano per il Medio Evo, 2007).
Smith   William Smith, ed., *Dictionary of Greek and Roman*
                  Biography and Mythology, 3 vols. (London: Tay-
                  lor and Walton, 1844).
Spreti   Vittorio Spreti, *Enciclopedia storico-nobiliare italiana,*
                  8 vols. (Bologna: Forni, 1981)
Stevenson   Jane Stevenson, *Women Latin Poets: Language, Gen-*
                  der, and Authority, from Antiquity to the Eighteenth
                  Century (New York: Oxford University Press,
                  2005).
Thérault   Suzanne Thérault, *Un cénacle humaniste de la Re-*
                  naissance autour de Vittoria Colonna, châtelaine
                  d'Ischia (Florence: Sansoni, 1968).
Tiraboschi   Girolamo Tiraboschi, *Storia della letteratura ital-*
                  iana, 9 vols. (Rome: L. P. Salvioni, 1782–85).
Toscano   Tobia R. Toscano, *Letterati corti accademie. La let-*
                  teratura a Napoli nella prima metà del Cinquecento
                  (Naples: Loffredo, 2000).
Treccani   www.treccani.it, website of the Istituto
                  dell'Enciclopedia Italiana
Ubaldini   Federico Ubaldini, *Vita di Monsignor Angelo Co-*
                  locci, ed. Vittorio Fanelli (Vatican City: Biblio-
                  teca Apostolica Vaticana, 1969).
Varchi   Benedetto Varchi, *Storia florentina,* ed. Gaetano
                  Milanesi, 3 vols. (Florence: Successori Le
                  Monnier, 1888).
Varillas   Antoine Varillas, *Histoire de Charles VIII* (Paris:
                  Claude Barbin, 1691).

Vecce (1990a) Carlo Vecce, "La Gualanda," *Achademia Leonardi Vinci: Journal of Leonardo studies and bibliography of Vinciana* 3 (1990): 51–72.

Vecce (1990b) Carlo Vecce, "Paolo Giovio e Vittoria Colonna," *Periodico della Società Storica Comense* 54 (1990): 65–93.

Vida Marco Girolamo Vida, *Christiad*, ed. and trans. James Gardner (The I Tatti Renaissance Library, 39) (Cambridge, MA: Harvard University Press, 2009).

Volpati (1934) Carlo Volpati, "Paolo Giovio e Venezia," *Archivio veneto* 15 (1934): 132–56.

Volpati (1936) Carlo Volpati, "Paolo Giovio e Napoli," *Nuova rivista storica* 20 (1936): 347–62.

Zimmermann T. C. Price Zimmermann, *Paolo Giovio: The Historian and the Crisis of Sixteenth-Century Italy* (Princeton: Princeton University Press, 1995).

DIALOGUE ONE

1. Gian Matteo Giberti (1495–1543), who served as Pope Clement VII's datary, was among the hostages handed over to the imperial troops to ensure that the pope would meet his obligations. On Giberti, see the Introduction.

2. Vittoria Colonna (1492–1547), a daughter of Fabrizio I Colonna and Agnese da Montefeltro of Urbino, was Giovio's host on Ischia in 1527–28. See *EWR*, 88–91; *DBI* 27:448–57.

3. On September 20, 1526, members of the Colonna family, including Vittoria's cousin, Pompeo, led a military assault on the Vatican. In retaliation, that November and December Clement dispatched an army under the command of Vitello Vitelli to devastate and conquer Colonna-controlled lands in Latium. See Pastor, 9:341 and n. 1. Giovio described the campaign in his *Life* of Pompeo Colonna: *IO* 6:173.

4. Alfonso d'Avalos, marchese del Vasto (1502–46). The son of Iñigo (II), marchese del Vasto, and Laura Sanseverino, he was orphaned young

and raised by his aunt Costanza, the duchess of Francavilla. He served in the military under his cousin Ferdinando Francesco d'Avalos, marchese di Pescara, Vittoria Colonna's late husband. See *DBI* 4:612–16; Arfaioli, 125; Argegni, 1:230–31; and Giovio's eulogium of him in *IO* 8:462–63; *Elogi*, 910–12.

5. Costanza d'Avalos the Elder (ca. 1460–1541). See *DBI* 4:621–22.

6. This is Charles V (1500–1558), who became king of Spain (as Carlos I) in 1516 and then was elected Holy Roman Emperor as Charles V in 1519. Technically, he was emperor-designate until his coronation in Bologna in 1530.

7. Andrea Doria (1466–1560), a Genoese admiral, had worked primarily for France since 1513. In the summer of 1528, believing that he had been insufficiently remunerated by Francis I, he would go over to the service of Emperor Charles V. See *DBI* 41:264–74; Argegni, 1:307–310; and Giovio's eulogium of him in *IO* 8:485; *Elogi*, 962–63.

8. Ascanio Colonna (1500–1557), a brother of Vittoria, was married to Giovanna d'Aragona. See *DBI* 27:271–75; Argegni, 1:181–82.

9. Alfonso Piccolomini, duke of Amalfi, husband of Costanza d'Avalos the Younger. See Argegni, 2:424.

10. Giovanna d'Aragona (1502–75), born to Ferdinando d'Aragona, duke of Montalto (an illegitimate son of Ferrante I d'Aragona by his mistress, Diana Guardato), and Castellana de Cardona (daughter of Ramón de Cardona). She married Ascanio Colonna in 1521. See *DBI* 3:694–96.

11. Costanza d'Avalos the Younger (ca. early 16th cent.–1575), duchess of Amalfi. She was the daughter of Iñigo (II), marquis del Vasto, and Laura Sanseverino. She and Alfonso Piccolomini had two children, Iñigo and Vittoria. See *DBI* 4:622–23.

12. Maria d'Aragona (1503–68), marchioness del Vasto. Like her sister Giovanna (see n. 10 above), she was born in the castle on Ischia. In 1523 she married Alfonso d'Avalos, marquis del Vasto (the namesake of Giovio's interlocutor here). *DBI* 3:701–2.

13. An early version of this story appears in Hesiod, *Theogony* 820–70.

14. I.e., Giovanni Antonio Muscettola. See Introduction, p. xiv.

15. Hugo de Moncada (1476–1528), a Spanish captain, would die in the Battle of Capo d'Orso against Filippino Doria. See Argegni, 2:279–80.

16. Charles de Lannoy (ca. 1487–1527), imperial viceroy of Naples. On his actions as viceroy, see especially Hook, *ad indicem*, and Pastor, 9: *ad indicem*.

17. In a letter of October 1, 1527, Sigismondo Fancino, then in Rome, wrote to Venice that Moncada had sent for both d'Avalos and Urbina, with the intention of getting them to accept the emperor's decision to elevate Orange as lieutenant-general of the imperial forces in Italy (under Alfonso I d'Este, the duke of Ferrara, who was then the captain-general). See Sanuto, 46: col. 220.

18. Lannoy had arrived in Rome on May 28, 1527, but was utterly ineffective in getting control over the troops. By June 8, following a Spanish mutiny, he had been driven from the city. See Hook, 209; Sanuto, 45: cols. 316, 324; on d'Avalos' role, see ibid., cols. 312–14, 324.

19. Philibert de Châlon (1502–30), Prince of Orange.

20. In July of 1527, Orange, rather than d'Avalos, was appointed to serve as lieutenant-general of the imperial forces in Italy. See Sanuto, 45: cols. 588, 591; and n. 17 above.

21. Charles de Bourbon (1490–1527), Constable of France, rebelled against King Francis I in 1523. Subsequently in the service of Charles V, he led the army that sacked Rome on May 6, 1527, himself being killed in the initial assault. See Pitts.

22. The bishopric of Nocera, available because of the death of Cardinal Jacobacci, was conferred upon Giovio on July 6, 1527. See Zimmermann, 86 and 315 n. 3.

23. On the loss and recovery of the *Histories*, see Zimmermann, 67–68.

24. Captain Hernando Alonzo de Herrera of Córdoba.

25. Captain Antonio Gamboa of Navarre.

26. A learned joke: the Latin text alludes to *postliminium*, the legal process by which a Roman soldier captured by the enemy could recover his rights as a citizen once he returned to Roman territory.

27. Selim I (the Grim; 1470–1520), Turkish sultan. See Giovio's eulogium of him in *IO* 8:403–4; *Elogi*, 774–76.

28. Süleyman I (the Magnificent; 1494–1566), Turkish sultan (1520–66). See *ER* 6:100–101; and Giovio's eulogium of him in *IO* 8:484–85; *Elogi*, 960–61.

29. In January 1517, a merchant named Christen Kauffman wrote a report to Pope Leo X in which he stated that Selim I visited the Church of the Holy Sepulcher in Jerusalem, asked to attend a service, and distributed 20,000 akches to the Franciscan monks. See Feridun M. Emecen, *Yavuz Sultan Selim* (Istanbul: Yitik Hazine Yayinlari, 2010), 248.

30. In his *Commentary on Turkish Affairs*, Giovio mentions a victory of Selim near this shrine, which was approximately five miles from Cairo (identified at times in sixteenth-century writings with Memphis). According to the Coptic tradition, on the flight into Egypt the Holy Family stopped at that place, and the infant Christ performed a miracle causing balsam trees to spring forth. See respectively Giovio, *Commmentarii delle cose de Turchi* (Venice: In casa de' figliuoli: di Aldo, 1541), 22–23, and Otto F. A. Meinardus, *Two Thousand Years of Coptic Christianity* (Cairo: The American University in Cairo Press, 1999), 21.

31. In his *Life* of Pope Adrian VI, Giovio praises Süleyman for having forbidden that Rhodes be sacked. See Zimmermann, 52. According to dispatches from Venetians in Crete, however, the sultan initially did intend to raid the church's treasury. The Grand Master prevailed upon him not to do so, and ultimately Süleyman took only an Annunciation scene depicted in gold that had belonged to the Grand Master himself. Pasha Ahmed wanted the relic of the arm of St. John the Baptist, whom he claimed as an ancestor, but in the end the Grand Master was allowed to keep it. See Sanuto, 34: cols. 11, 13.

32. Süleyman entered Buda in September 1526. Shortly before, he had routed the Hungarian army in the Battle of Mohács (August 29, 1526).

According to one contemporary, Kemalpashazade, the sultan's men in Buda did in fact despoil the king's palace and the armory. Rather than being distributed among the victors, the goods were inventoried and sent to Belgrade. Three (not two) statues that had been taken were put on display atop stone columns in the Hippodrome in Istanbul. See Kemalpashazade, *Histoire de la Campagne de Mohacz*, ed. Abel Pavet de Courteille (Paris: Imprimerie Impériale, 1859), 116. On the despoiling of the palace see also Sanuto, 43: col. 113.

33. I.e., "old" St. Peter's Basilica.

34. The "official guarantee" Muscettola mentions is the truce made by the imperial viceroy of Naples, Lannoy, with Clement VII. The armistice was settled on March 15, 1527 and ratified on March 29. See Hook, 131–41.

35. At least by his own account, Alfonso d'Avalos had absented himself from the imperial army before it sacked Rome. See Zimmermann, 315 n. 14.

36. The exact nature of this injury at Milan is unclear. It may have been d'Avalos' loss of some troops to the command of the prince of Orange upon the latter's arrival in Milan with the landsknechts in December of 1526, upon which Bourbon elevated Orange from being commander of the light cavalry to leading the vanguard. D'Avalos remained co-commander (with Antonio de Leyva) of the infantry. In any case, d'Avalos was in fact subject to "grave danger" while in Milan. Already in April and June of 1526, before Bourbon's arrival, there had been rioting, and d'Avalos and de Leyva nearly lost control of the city. That autumn, d'Avalos was among the officers who gave money out of pocket to help keep the soldiers (whom Bourbon then had no resources to pay) from following through on their threats of mutiny. See Pitts, 438, 445.

37. Ferdinando Francesco d'Avalos (1489–1525), marquis of Pescara, had married Vittoria Colonna in 1509. His fame as a military commander becomes the focus of discussion late in the first "day" of this dialogue. See *DBI* 4:623–27; Argegni, 1:232; *IO* 8:412–13; *Elogi*, 795–96; and Giovio's *Life* of Pescara (cited in n. 104 below).

38. Despite the absence of a subject noun, the implicit subject of the verbs *suscepit* and *moliretur* must be Clement VII. See the following note.

39. From context, the pronoun *eum* is here taken to refer to Pope Clement. The Latin passage rendered in this and the preceding sentence is entirely in scribal hand, but its grammatical awkwardness and ambiguities suggest that it is an incomplete reworking of the original text. An intermediate draft (not extant) might have revealed where Giovio had been making changes so as to cast Charles V in a more favorable light, without however offending the pope—a move Giovio clearly made in autograph revisions elsewhere in the manuscript.

40. Giovio's "Bostanges" is Dukaginzade Ahmed Pasha, who was married to Selim's daughter Fatma Sultan. From the prominent Dukagjin clan of Albania, he evidently served at one point in the Corps of Gardeners in the sultan's palace (hence Bostanges, from the Turkish *Bostanji*, = gardener). In early 1515, shortly after his appointment as grand vizier, he was executed in Amasya because Selim suspected him of involvement in a janissary rebellion in that city. In his *Histories*, Giovio writes that Bostanges had earlier formed a secret agreement with Selim: he was promised the hand of Selim's daughter in exchange for betraying Bayezid II, which he did in 1512. In the *Histories* Giovio adds the detail that when Bostanges' corpse was put on display, the head had been severed from the body, and observes that this made a show both of the condemned's wretchedness and of the sultan's cruelty. See *IO* 3:284, 440–41. The execution is mentioned in a dispatch in Sanuto, 20: col. 49.

41. Louis II Jagiello, king of Hungary 1516–26, died while fleeing from the battle of Mohács (August 29, 1526), in which the Turks soundly defeated his troops. See Setton, 3:249.

42. Ja'fer Bey, a *kapudan* (admiral), was executed in 1520, the first year of Süleyman's reign. The event is noted in passing in a dispatch from the Venetian *bailo* in Constantinople, dated October 15, 1520. See Sanuto, 29: col. 392.

43. "Others" renders ⟨ali⟩i as a supplement to the lacuna. The previous sentence is perhaps also lacunose; one expects "the astrologers" (*astrologi*) or the like as its subject.

44. Literally, "those things," here taken to refer (despite its being in the neuter) to the "celestial motives" (*caelestes causas*) mentioned in the preceding §.

45. This account of earlier standards of warfare is highly idealized and inaccurate. For correctives, see William J. Caferro, *Mercenary Companies and the Decline of Siena* (Baltimore: The Johns Hopkins University Press, 1998); Mallett (1973); and Mallett (1974).

46. Marcantonio I Colonna (1478–1522), *signore* of Paliano, of the Genazzano branch of the family. He died in the French siege of Milan. See *DBI* 27:365–68; *CV* # 0487; Argegni, 1:186; and Giovio's eulogium of him in *IO* 8:404–5; *Elogi*, 777–79.

47. Suspected of having helped to lead a conspiracy to poison Pope Leo X in 1517, Cardinal Petrucci was deprived of his ecclesiastical dignities, imprisoned in the Castel Sant' Angelo, and executed there. See Giovio's account of Petrucci's demise in the *Life* of Leo X, *IO* 4:85–86. For a balanced recent reconstruction of the conspiracy, see Hyde, 131–72.

48. I.e., in the conspiracy of 1517.

49. In astrology, the Alchocoden is an individual's "vital planet," related to the calculation of one's expected lifespan.

50. This was Bartolomeo da Petroio, called "Brandano" (ca. 1488–1554). On Holy Thursday 1527, while Clement was blessing the crowd in St. Peter's, Brandano denounced the pope as a "sodomite bastard" whose sins would bring about Rome's destruction if he did not repent. See *DBI* 6:752–55.

51. Notable among these was the astrologer Luca Gaurico. See Paola Zambelli, "Fine del mondo o inizio della propaganda? Astrologia, filosofia della storia e propaganda politico-religiosa nel dibattito sulla congiunzione del 1524," in *Scienze, credenze occulte, livelli di cultura: Convegno internazionale di studi, Firenze, 26–30 giugno 1980* (Florence: Olschki, 1982), 291–368.

52. Deucalion is said to have been a king in Thessaly who survived the flood.

53. The particular reference is to the Aristotelian philosopher Agostino Nifo (ca. 1470–1538), who published a tract critical of these predictions of a flood, *De falsa diluvii prognosticatione: quae ex conventu omnium planetarum qui in piscibus continget anno 1524 divulgata est* (1520), which he dedicated to Emperor Charles V. See the entry on Nifo in *ER* 4:320–21.

54. Petrarch's poem "Italia mia" had similarly described the foreign military presence on the peninsula with an image of flooding: "O diluvio raccolto / di che deserti strani / per inondar i nostri dolci campi!" (*Rime sparse* 128, lines 28–30). Compare the metaphor of Fortune as a river in Machiavelli's *The Prince*, chap. 25. Zimmermann, 318 n. 36, observes that "[i]t is easy to suppose that by 1527 Giovio could have seen one of the MSS of *The Prince* in Florence."

55. Giovanni Gioviano Pontano (1426–1503) was the leading humanist in late fifteenth-century Naples. The circle of literati that clustered around him there was known from 1471 as the "Accademia pontaniana." See *ER* 5:118–20.

56. This refers to Constantine's moving the administrative center of the Roman Empire from Rome to the city of Byzantium, which he renamed "Constantinople."

57. "Trualongi" is an error. Perhaps Giovio intended the Thuringi (Toringi) or the Thervingi (Tervingi, Teruingi).

58. I.e., the northern coast of modern France.

59. Odoacer (or, "Odovacar") (ca. 435–93) was chieftain of the Heruli, Sciri, and Rugii (all Germanic peoples). After he had served Rome as a mercenary, in 476 his troops revolted and proclaimed him their king. He went on to depose Romulus Augustulus, the last of the Roman emperors in the west until the coronation of Charlemagne in 800.

60. Alaric I (ca. 370–410), the Visigothic king who sacked Rome in 410.

61. Radagasius, probably an Ostrogothic chief, invaded Rhaeta soon after he evidently formed an alliance with Alaric (400). His forces were defeated by Stilicho in 405/6 and he was beheaded.

62. Totila (or "Baduila"), d. 552, was the last king of the Ostrogoths (541–52).

63. Giangaleazzo Visconti (1351–1402), whose family had long controlled Milan, became its sole ruler in 1385, and in 1395 he received imperial investiture as its duke. See ER 6:276–77; Argegni, 3:369–70. He was originally called the "Count of Virtues" because he had obtained the county of Vertus in Champagne as a dowry from his first wife, Isabelle de Valois.

64. On Giangaleazzo's military innovations and especially his tying of mercenaries to the state by means of land grants, see Mallett (1974), 50–54; and William Caferro, *John Hawkwood: An English Mercenary in Fourteenth-Century Italy* (Baltimore: Johns Hopkins University Press, 2006), 255–56.

65. On Nicholas V (pope, 1447–55) see ER 4:316–17.

66. Alberico da Barbiano, "The Great" (ca. 1348–1409), was captain of the Company of St. George, a mercenary army said to have been composed entirely of Italians (unlike that of John Hawkwood, in which Alberico had previously served). See Caferro, *Hawkwood*, 228 and passim; *DBI* 1:639–41; *CV* # 0150; and Argegni, 1:67.

67. Francesco I Sforza (1401–66), a mercenary captain, became duke of Milan in 1450. See ER 4:139–40; Argegni, 3:237–38; and especially Giovio's eulogium of him in IO 8:334–35; *Elogi*, 626–28.

68. Braccio Fortebracci da Montone (1368–1424). See Argegni, 1:403–4.

69. Bartolus de Saxoferrato (1313–57).

70. Baldus de Ubaldis (1327–1400).

71. This is presumably the jurist Raphael Comensis, who died in 1427.

72. Raffaele Fulgosio of Piacenza (1367–1427) taught at Padua, 1407–27. See Luigi Mensi, *Dizionario biografico piacentino* (Piacenza, 1899; repr. Sala Bolognese: Forni, 1978).

73. On Biagio Pelacani, called "Biagio da Parma," d. 1416, see Cosenza.

74. Torrigiano de' Torrigiani (d. ca. 1350) was renowned as a commentator on Galen's *Ars medica*. See William F. Edwards, "Niccolò Leoniceno and the Origins of Humanist Discussion of Method," in *Philosophy and*

Humanism: Renaissance Essays in Honor of Paul Oskar Kristeller, ed. Edward P. Mahoney (Leiden: Brill, 1976), 283–305, at 286–87.

75. On Gentile da Foligno (1230?–ca. 1310), see *DBI* 53:162–67.

76. Giotto di Bondone (1267/75–1337).

77. Cimabue (Bencivieni di Pepo), ca. 1240–ca. 1302.

78. Filippo Brunelleschi (1377–1446).

79. Andrea Pisano (ca. 1295–1348/49?). See *ER* 5:38–40.

80. Presumably a reference to the bronze-door reliefs (1330–36) of the Florentine baptistery. Andrea Pisano's baptistery panels actually depict scenes from the life of John the Baptist and images of the cardinal and theological virtues.

81. Donatello (ca. 1386/87–1466).

82. Ludovico II Sforza, "Il Moro" (1452–1508). See *DBI* 66; Argegni, 3:244–46; and Giovio's eulogium of him in *IO* 8:373–76; *Elogi*, 706–12.

83. Alfonso II d'Aragona, king of Naples, 1494–95.

84. Alexander VI (pope, 1492–1503).

85. In fact, the use of guns in Italy is documented as early as 1326. See Alan Williams, *The Knight and the Blast Furnace: A History of the Metallurgy of Armour in the Middle Ages & the Early Modern Period* (Leiden: Brill, 2003), 850. Humanist historians, however, following the account of Flavio Biondo in his *Roma triumphans* (1455–63), routinely "attributed its invention to a mid-fourteenth-century German, and its first use to the Venetians in their war of Chioggia (1378–81) against the Genoese." J. R. Hale, "Gunpowder and the Renaissance: An Essay in the History of Ideas," in idem, *Renaissance War Studies* (London: The Hambledon Press, 1983), 389–420, at 391.

86. Williams, 866–70, details the use of handguns in early sixteenth-century Italy and Europe, giving particular attention to the battles of Ravenna, Novara, Marignano, Bicocca, and especially Pavia, all of which are discussed below in the present dialogue. The impact of gunpowder on warfare was critical in the case of cannons used in sieges.

87. See *Sil.* 8.654.

88. See n. 85 above on the misattribution of the invention of firearms to a fourteenth-century German.

89. Christopher Columbus (1451–1506) was from the Republic of Genoa.

90. See Cicero, *On Duties* 1.81.

91. Cyrus the Great (d. 529 BCE), king of Persia and founder of the Persian Empire.

92. Alexander the Great (Alexander III, king of Macedon), 356–323 BCE.

93. Philip II (382–336 BCE), king of Macedon, was Alexander the Great's father.

94. Allegations that mercenaries were low-class and wicked were commonplace at least from the fourteenth century onward, but in general these charges were untrue. Caferro, *Siena*, 5–7, notes the difficulty of distinguishing between the "knight" and the "mercenary" in the fourteenth century. Mallett (1974), 221–27, observes that *condottieri* usually were not social upstarts but were well educated and often collected books. Many were also patrons of religious institutions. Their armies included a significant number of local men, including conscripts as well as professionals.

95. Maximilian I (1459–1519), Holy Roman Emperor (r. 1493–1519).

96. The references are specifically to the *condottieri* Braccio da Montone (1368–1424), Francesco I Sforza (1401–66), Niccolò Piccinino (1386–1444), and Bartolomeo Colleoni (ca.1395/1400–1475).

97. In his eulogium accompanying a portrait of the Vitelli brothers, Giovio asserts that Paolo Vitelli, thinking it unworthy that common foot soldiers could kill their social betters with such weapons, ordered that captured arquebusiers be punished by having their eyes put out and their hands cut off. See Giovio, *IO* 8:365; *Elogi*, 686.

98. The Battle of Caravaggio on September 14, 1448, was critical to Milanese autonomy. See the analysis in Mallett (1974), 178–80.

99. Gentile da Leonessa (1408–53) would be freed that October. In April of 1451, he would be elevated as governor-general of the Venetian forces. See CV # 0873; Argegni, 1:439.

100. Francesco Sforza fought for the short-lived Ambrosian Republic, but in 1450 he took Milan for himself. See CV # 1836 on Sforza's role at Caravaggio.

101. Directly conflicting with Giovio's account, Andrea Navagero, who was Venice's official historian following Marcantonio Sabellico's death, described the mortality at the Battle of Caravaggio as high. See Navagero, *Historia veneta ab origine urbis usque ad annum 1498*, in Muratori, 23 (1733), cols. 919–1218, at 1112c. On Navagero's poetry see below, Dialogue Two, §§37, 38.

102. This is the Battle of Riccardina (or, Molinella) in 1467, in which Federico da Montefeltro led Florence and Milan in defeating the troops of Venice and Ferrara, who were led by Colleoni. CV # 1159, on Federico da Montefeltro, estimates that six hundred men died. Machiavelli, by contrast, claimed that "no one was killed; only some horses were wounded and a few prisoners taken on each side." See Niccolò Machiavelli, *Florentine Histories*, trans. Laura F. Banfield and Harvey C. Mansfield, Jr. (Princeton: Princeton University Press, 1988), 299 (Bk. 7, §20).

103. Federico da Montefeltro (1422–82), duke of Urbino. See ER 4:174–76; DBI 45:722–43; Argegni, 2:302.

104. Gonzalo Fernández de Córdoba (1453–1515), duke of Terranova and Santangelo, known as "El Gran Capitán." A critical edition of Giovio's *Vita* of Gonzalo ("Gonsalvo"), edited by M. Cataudella, is forthcoming in volume seven of IO. For a modern edition of a sixteenth-century translation of that text into Italian, see Giovio, *Le vite del Gran Capitano e del Marchese di Pescara*, trans. Lodovico Domenichi, ed. Costantino Panigada (Bari: Laterza, 1931).

105. Granada fell to Ferdinand of Aragon and Isabella of Castile in January of 1492.

106. Hernán Cortés (1485–1547), best known for conquering the Aztec Empire in Mexico (1519–21).

107. In ancient ethnography, notably in Arrian's *Anabasis of Alexander*, Dionysus (Bacchus) and Heracles (Hercules) were credited with having conquered and brought civilization to India. See Grant Parker, *The Making of Roman India* (Cambridge: Cambridge University Press, 2008), 83–84.

108. The *condottiere* Fabrizio Maramaldo (1494–1552) subsequently became infamous for his murder of Francesco Ferrucci after the latter had surrendered in the Battle of Gavinana (August 3, 1530). See *DBI* 69:398–401; Arfaioli, 164; *CV* # 1000; Argegni, 1:198.

109. The "dearth of commanders" is a theme that recurs at §167 and §187; it is an ancient topos; see Cicero, *In Verrem* 2.5.2 and 25; *Pro Fonteio* 42–43.

110. Fabrizio I Colonna (ca. 1450/60–1520) was married to Agnese, the daughter of Federico da Montefeltro, duke of Urbino. He had six children: Ascanio, Federico (d. at age 19 serving Maximilian), Camillo, Sciarra (illegitimate), Vittoria (who married Pescara), and Beatrice (who married Rodolfo Varano). See *DBI* 27:407–12; Argegni, 1:182–83.

111. Prospero Colonna (1460?–1523). See *DBI* 27:418–26; Argegni, 1:189–90.

112. On Marcantonio I Colonna, see above, n. 46.

113. Muzio Colonna (ca. 1480–1516) was the illegitimate son of Lorenzo Oddone Colonna (d. 1484), an apostolic protonotary. See *DBI* 27:389–90; Serio, 107 and Table 4; *CV* # 0490; and Argegni, 1:187–88.

114. Vespasiano Colonna (b. between 1480 and 1490; d. 1528), son of Prospero, married Giulia Gonzaga in 1526. On Vespasiano see *DBI* 27:447–48; Argegni, 1:191.

115. On Ascanio Colonna, see n. 8 above.

116. On the Battle of Frosinone, see Setton, 3:258–59; Hook, 120–21. On Lannoy's truce with Clement VII (March 15, 1527) and its immediate aftermath, see Hook, chap. 9 ("Lannoy's Truce"; 131–46).

117. Although the Latin is ambiguous, Giovio here evidently writes of Lannoy rather than Ascanio Colonna. Stricken with the plague while in occupied Rome, Lannoy died at Naples on September 23, 1527.

118. Giulio Colonna (d. 1530 or later) fought on the imperial side in the Sack of Rome and against Lautrec the following year. See *DBI* 27:347–48.

119. Marcello Colonna (d. 1528) fought on the imperial side in 1527. See *CV* # 0488; Argegni, 1:187.

120. Pompeo Colonna (1479–1532), created cardinal in 1517, was a staunch ally of Emperor Charles V and a frequent antagonist of Pope Clement VII. Pompeo dedicated to his cousin, Vittoria Colonna, a work in praise of women. See *DBI* 27:407–12.

121. Shaw (2007), Table Colonna III, notes a Giangirolamo (fl. 1521) who was Marcello's son. This is probably the Girolamo Colonna (d. ca. 1525) listed in *CV* # 0483 who took part in the Battle of Bicocca (April 1522).

122. This is Prospero (di Cave) Colonna (d. September 1528), son of Giordano, and cousin of Ascanio, Vittoria, and Sciarra. See Serio, Table 4; Argegni, 1:189, s.n. Prosperetto.

123. Sciarra Colonna (d. ca. 1545) was the illegitimate son of Fabrizio I, and so a half-brother of Vittoria and Ascanio. See *DBI* 27:432–33; *CV* # 0497; Argegni, 1:191.

124. Venetian and papal troops had laid siege to Cremona in August and September of 1526. See Hook, 89–91.

125. *Sic.* Seemingly an error, given that four deceased Colonna men (Fabrizio, Prospero, Marcantonio, and Muzio) are identified above in §81.

126. Stefano Colonna (d. 1548), of the Palestrina branch of the family, was the son of Francesco Colonna (d. before 1512) and Orsina Orsini. See *DBI* 27:443–45; Serio, Table 2; *CV* # 0499; Arfaioli, 176.

127. Virginio Orsini (ca. 1445–97), the son of Napoleone Orsini (d. 1480), was duke of Bracciano. See Shaw (2007); *CV* # 1343; Argegni, 2:359.

128. This is Niccolò II Orsini (1442–1510), sixth count of Pitigliano. See Treccani; Argegni, 2:367–68.

129. Bartolomeo d'Alviano (1455–1515) was married to Bartolomea Orsini, who may have been Virginio's sister (but see *DBI*, which identifies her as Virginio's cousin). He had served under Virginio's father, Napo-

leone. Shaw writes that he "was practically adopted into the Orsini family" and became its "virtual head," even though he was not Orsini by birth. See Shaw (2007), 85; *DBI* 2:587–91; Argegni, 1:38–39; Arfaioli, 23; and Giovio's eulogium of him in *IO* 8:388–89; *Elogi*, 741–44.

130. Renzo da Ceri (Renzo degli Anguillara da Ceri), 1475–1536, was in charge of the defense of Rome when the imperialists attacked it on May 6, 1527. See *DBI* 3:309–12; Arfaioli, 155, 157, 173.

131. Clement VII's father was Giuliano de' Medici, murdered in the Pazzi Conspiracy in 1478.

132. A close paraphrase of Horace, *Carmina* 1.1.36: "sublimi feriam sidera vertice."

133. Andrea Gritti (1455–1538) was doge of Venice, 1523–38. On his life and career, see DBI 59:726–34. Robert Finlay, *Politics in Renaissance Venice* (New Brunswick, NJ: Rutgers University Press, 1980), 155–56, briefly describes Gritti's imprisonment by the Turks and his capture by the French. See also Giovio's eulogium of Gritti in *IO* 8:456–57; *Elogi*, 726–34.

134. The Battle of Novara, June 6, 1513. For a brief account of Gritti's escape, see Robert Finlay, "Fabius Maximus in Venice: Doge Andrea Gritti, the War of Cambrai, and the Rise of Habsburg Hegemony, 1509–1530," *Renaissance Quarterly* 53 (2000): 988–1031, at 1001–2.

135. On Gritti's flight from this battle, which took place at La Motta on October 7, 1513, see Finlay, "Fabius Maximus," 1002–3.

136. Giovio adapts Cicero's self-description as a "toga-clad leader and commander" (*Catilinarians* 2.28 and 3.23).

137. The virtue here left unnamed may well be that of liberality. On Giovio's comparison of Clement's parsimony to the liberality of his cousin, Leo X (Giovanni de' Medici; pope, 1513–1521), see T. C. Price Zimmermann, "Guicciardini, Giovio, and the Character of Clement VII," in *Pontificate of Clement*, 19–27, at 20.

138. See the famous comparison of Leo and Clement in Guicciardini, 3:1666–69 (bk. 16, chap. 12).

139. See Cicero, *Fam.* 3.19: "Sine eum errare et putare me virum bonum esse nec solere duo parietes de eadem fidelia dealbare"; Erasmus, *Adages*

1.7.3. Here, this may also allude to Clement's *impresa*, CANDOR IL-LAESVS.

140. An allusion to Tacitus, *Germania* 33.2: "with the fates of the empire closing in" (*urgentibus imperii fatis*).

141. Gianantonio Orsini (d. 1562), of the Gravina branch of the family, was active in the defense of Rome during the Sack. He was the son of Francesco Orsini and Maria Todeschini Piccolomini. See *CV* # 1297; Shaw (2007), Table Orsini VIa; Argegni, 2:362.

142. Camillo Orsini (1492–1559), marquis of Atripalda and Monte-fredane, prince of Amatrice and lord of Mentana. The son of Paolo Orsini (d. 1503) in the Lamentana branch of the family, Camillo was active in the defense of Rome during the Sack. See *CV* # 1284; Argegni, 2:356–57.

143. I.e., Ludovico Orsini, seventh count of Pitigliano (d. 1534), who succeeded his father, Niccolò II, in that position. See Argegni, 2:364–65.

144. Aldobrandino Orsini (d. 1472), fifth count of Pitigliano. See *CV* # 1281; Argegni, 2:354.

145. Valerio Orsini (1504–50), duke of Ascoli, took part in the defense of Rome during the Sack. He was the son of Giulio Orsini (d. by 1514) of the Monterotondo branch. See *CV* # 1341; Argegni, 2:375; see Shaw (2007), Table Orsini VII, which errs in dating his death to 1580.

146. (Gentile) Virginio Orsini, of the Anguillara branch, was the son of Carlo Orsini and Porzia Savelli (Carlo was the son of Virginio the Great). See Shaw (2007), Table Orsini V; Argegni, 2:359–60.

147. Napoleone Orsini (1501–33), abbot of Farfa, was the son of Gian-giordano Orsini (d. 1517; son of Virginio the Great) by his first wife, Maria Cecilia d'Aragona. Napoleone was imprisoned in early 1527 for conspiring with Ascanio Colonna against the pope, and then was re-leased after the conquest of Rome. See *CV* # 1316; Shaw (2007), Orsini Table V.

148. Mario (or, Marzio) Orsini was the son of Giulio Orsini of the Monterotondo branch. In early 1527 he served with imperial forces (his brother Valerio and most of the family fought on the other side). After

the Sack of Rome, Mario went over to fight for France against Charles V's troops in Italy. He died December 16, 1529, in the defense of Florence against an imperial army. See *CV* # 1314; Cecil Roth, *The Last Florentine Republic* (New York: Russell and Russell, 1968), 225–26; Shaw (2007), 88; Argegni, 2:365.

149. Giampaolo degli Anguillara da Ceri (Giovanni Paolo Orsini) (d. ca. 1560), son of the more famous Renzo, took part in the defense of Rome against Bourbon's troops. See *CV* # 0448.

150. Luca di Pandolfo Savelli (d. ca. 1515), of the Rignano branch of the family, fought for Milan against France in the Battle of Novara (1515). See Shaw (2007), Table Savelli I; *CV* # 1732; Argegni, 3:143.

151. Silvio Savelli (d. 1515) was son of Piergiovanni (fl. 1473), in the Aricia branch of the family. Silvio also fought for Milan. See Shaw (2007), Table Savelli II; *CV* # 1738; Argegni, 3:146.

152. Troilo Savelli (1465–1517) was son of Mariano, of the Palombara branch of the family. See *CV* # 1740; Rendina, 469–70; Shaw (2007), Table Savelli I; Argegni, 3:146–47.

153. Probably Antimo di Cristoforo Savelli, who took part in the baronial revolt against Pope Julius II that Pompeo Colonna led in 1511. See Serio, 63; Shaw (2007), Table Savelli II; Argegni, 3:138.

154. Giacomo (or, Jacopo) Savelli (d. ca. 1525), of the Palombara line, was Troilo's brother. See *CV* # 1730; Shaw (2007), Table Savelli I; Argegni, 3:141.

155. Gianbattista (Giovanni Battista) Savelli (1505–51), son of Giacomo Savelli and Camilla Farnese, took part in the defense of Rome against Bourbon's troops in the Sack. See *CV* # 1727; Shaw (2007), Table Savelli II; Rendina, 470–72; Argegni, 3:142–43.

156. The Latin phrase "Grappellia . . . comitum familia" would appear to mean the "Grappelli family of counts," as here translated. A passage in the *Histories* regarding distinguished Roman families, praising the "Ursinis vero Comites cognomento Grapellii," could be taken to indicate that they are not counts but instead a branch within the distinguished Conti

family. In Domenichi's Italian translation the phrase is rendered "i Conti per sopranome Grapelli." *IO* 3:12; Giovio, *Delle istorie del suo tempo. . . ,* trans. Lodovico Domenichi (Venice: Francesco Rocca, 1565), 8.

157. This Ranuccio Farnese (1509–28) was the son of Alessandro Farnese, the future Pope Paul III, by Silvia Ruffini. Ranuccio distinguished himself in the unsuccessful defense of Rome against Bourbon's troops, making stands at the Porta Settimiana and at the Ponte Sisto, both on the route the troops took into the main part of the city. See *DBI* 45:147–48; *CV* # 0657.

158. This Ranuccio Farnese (d. 1495) was *signore* of Gradoli and of Canino. See *DBI* 45:144–47; *CV* # 0656; Argegni, 1:371–72.

159. Pier Luigi Farnese (1503–47) was a son of Alessandro (the future Paul III). On his military career, see Rendina, 376–80; Argegni, 1:367–68.

160. Ferrante (or, Ferdinando) Sanseverino (1507–68), prince of Salerno. In 1516 Ferrante married Isabella Villamarina. See Colapietra; Argegni, 3:122.

161. Pietrantonio (Pietro Antonio) Sanseverino (1508–59), fourth prince of Bisignano, first married Giulia Orsini, the daughter of Giangiordano Orsini and Felice della Rovere (Julius II's daughter). Upon learning of Giulia's infidelity, Sanseverino would have her strangled (1537). In 1538 he would remarry, to Irena Castriota Skanderbeg. See Colapietra; *Lodi*, 34.

162. Alfonso Piccolomini, duke of Amalfi. See n. 9 above.

163. Alfonso Piccolomini did go on to Siena, from which he was ousted in November 1530.

164. Giovanni (or, "Sergianni") Caracciolo (1487–1550), prince of Melfi, was usually in the service of France. He fought at the Battle of Ravenna (1512). In November 1529, Charles V would strip him of the principate of Melfi and confer it upon Andrea Doria. In 1530 Caracciolo would fight in the unsuccessful defense of Florence against imperial troops. See *DBI* 19:380–84; *CV* # 0377; Arfaioli, 107, 146, 195–97; Argegni, 1:140–41.

165. Ettore Pignatelli (d. 1536), duke of Monteleone, was viceroy and captain of Sicily. See Argegni, 2:433.

166. Troilo Pignatelli (d. 1537), the duke of Nocera. See *CV* # 1472.

167. Giulio Cesare da Capua (Giulio Cesare d'Altavilla), d. ca. 1535, was prince of Capua. He was active in the imperial defense of Naples against Lautrec in April 1528. See *CV* # 0370.

168. Perhaps the "Franciscum Capuanum, astuto ingenio iuvenem" whom Giovio mentions in narrating events of the year 1495 in his *Histories, IO* 3:129. A "Francesco da Capua conte di Altavilla" receives passing mention in *Monumenti storici pubblicati dalla R. deputazione veneta di storia patria*, ser. 1: "Documenti" 10 (1901): 204.

169. Guidone Fieramosca of Capua (1479–1531), count of Mignano, spent much of his career in the service of Emperor Charles V. See *DBI* 47:421–23; *CV* # 0671; Argegni, 1:383.

170. Cesare Fieramosca (ca. 1480–1528) was Guidone's brother. He would die fighting on the imperial side in the Battle of Capo d'Orso. See *DBI* 47:416–18; *CV* # 0669; Argegni, 1:381; Arfaioli, 176.

171. On Rinaldo Fieramosca (d. 1496), see *CV* # 0672; Argegni, 1:383–84.

172. Rossetto (Rosso) Fieramosca (1420–85) had fought in the Battle of Caravaggio (1448). Later he served as captain for Alfonso, duke of Calabria. See *CV* # 0373; Argegni, 1:384.

173. Ettore Fieramosca (ca. 1475–1515), brother of Guidone and Cesare. See *DBI* 47:418–21; Rendina, 257–62; *CV* # 0670; Argegni, 1:381–83; Arfaioli, 176.

174. The Challenge of Barletta, a chivalric tournament held outside the walls of the besieged city, took place in 1503. See Renato Russo, *La disfida di Barletta: L'epoca e i suoi protagonisti* (Barletta [Bari]: Rotas, 1999); and Giuliano Procacci, *La disfida di Barletta: tra storia e romanzo* (Milan: Mondadori, 2001).

175. Cesare Fieramosca, as a representative of the imperial viceroy Lannoy (and therefore of the emperor), brokered the armistice with Clement

VII in mid-March 1527. On March 29, Lannoy, by then in Rome, ratified the treaty with the pope. This is the treaty that Bourbon either would not or could not honor. See Hook, 132–34.

176. I.e., Cesare Fieramosca's (although grammatically, the pronoun could refer instead to Emperor Charles V).

177. Dispatched by Lannoy to Bourbon's camp with news of the truce, Cesare Fieramosca was ill received — in fact, according to one account, the troops tried twice to kill him. See Hook, 138, 140–41; Sanuto, 44: col. 353.

178. This is Fernando Marín, the abbot of Nájera and imperial commissioner-general, who would die in mid-July 1527. See Setton, 3:276 n. 25.

179. Lannoy died on September 23, 1527.

180. Giovio refers to Sallust, *Catiline* 58.2, part of a speech attributed to Lucius Sergius Catilina, the conspirator famously denounced by Cicero, before the battle of Pistoria (January 62 BCE).

181. Gaspare Sanseverino carried the banner of Francesco Maria della Rovere, duke of Urbino, in Leo X's *possesso* (April 11, 1513). Sanseverino died in Rome on June 3, 1519, in desperate poverty. See Ady, 1:350, 357 and 2:34; Argegni, 3:123.

182. Teodoro (or, Girolamo Teodoro) Trivulzio (1454–1532). See CV # 2034; Argegni, 3:332.

183. Pescara's infantry captured Teodoro Trivulzio in November of 1521.

184. See Giovio's account of the battle at Seminara (June 28, 1495) in his *Histories*, bk. 3, in *IO* 3:96–99.

185. I.e., Ferdinand II ("Ferrante II," "Ferrandino"), king of Naples (1469–96; ruled 1495–96).

186. This is Bernard Stewart (Bérault Stuart) (ca. 1452–1508), lord of Aubigny, a Scot who was in the service of the French king. See the index to Giovio's *Histories*, *IO* 5:304, s.n. Obegninus aut Obigninus Eberardus.

187. Charles VIII of France (king, 1483–98).

188. On the Battle of Fornovo (or, "Taro"), which took place on July 6, 1495, see Giovio, *Histories*, bk. 2, in *IO* 3:82–84; Benedetti, 89–115 (bk. 1, §§37–63); Commynes, 2:523–36; Antonio Santosuosso, "Anatomy of Defeat in Renaissance Italy: The Battle of Fornovo in 1495," *International History Review* 16 (1994): 221–50; Mallett (1974), 241–48.

189. François de Toursel, sieur de Précy, receives detailed treatment in Giovio's *Histories*. See the index in *IO* 5:307, s.n. Persivus.

190. This battle is also described in Guicciardini, 1:209–10 (bk. 2, chap. 10); and Varillas, 455–58. Passero gives its date as September 24, 1495 (cited in Guicciardini, 1:209 n. 39).

191. This is Giovanni Tommaso Carafa, count of Maddaloni (pre-1450–1520/21). See *DBI* 19:570–71; Giovio, *Histories*, in *IO* 3:126–28; Guicciardini, 1:209 n. 38.

192. This battle took place in April of 1503 between the town of Gioia Tauro and the Petrace River, in the province of Reggio Calabria. See Giovio's *Histories*, *IO* 3:176; Guicciardini, 1:531–32 (bk. 5, chap. 15); and Francesco Campennì, "La terra murata: i secoli XVI–XVIII," in *Gioia Tauro: Storia, cultura, economia*, ed. Fulvio Mazza (Soveria Mannelli: Rubbettino, 2004), 66. On Hugo de Cardona, see Giovio's *Histories*, *IO* 3:97, 105, 176; Guicciardini, 1:472 and n., 505, 519, 545. On d'Aubigny see n. 186 above.

193. Giovio's description of the French horsemen as "victorious" is problematic here. The passage in the manuscript is in Giovio's own hand, and so the words *victori* and *victor* cannot be attributed to scribal error (e.g., for *victo* and *victus*, respectively). See Guicciardini, 1:531–32, where the defeat of d'Aubigny's advance force is described.

194. The battle at Cerignola took place on April 28, 1503. See Guicciardini, 1:533–35 (bk. 5, chap. 15). For a brief account of the battle's significance, see Mallett (1974), 250–51.

195. Louis d'Armagnac (1472–1503), count of Guise and duke of Nemours.

196. This is the Battle of Garigliano of December 27–29, 1503, in which imperial forces under Gonsalvo the Great (see n. 104 above) and Bartolomeo d'Alviano soundly defeated a substantially larger French army under the command of Ludovico II del Vasto, marquis of Saluzzo. See Guicciardini, 1:580–86.

197. The real-life Alfonso d'Avalos did himself have difficulty getting along with those with whom he shared commands. See *DBI* 4:612–16.

198. This is the Battle of Agnadello (May 14, 1509). See the analysis in Mallett (1974), 252–54. Giovio witnessed the battle while he was a student at Pavia. See Zimmermann, 11.

199. In using the epithet "Cunctator," or "Delayer," for Niccolò II Orsini of Pitigliano, Giovio here explicitly invokes the ancient Roman general Quintus Fabius Maximus "Cunctator," whose strategy of delay assisted in the defeat of Carthage in the Second Punic War.

200. On Bartolomeo d'Alviano, see n. 129 above.

201. On Gritti, see above, §§92, 93 and nn. 133–35. Gritti was one of the two Venetian *provveditori generali* who had been dispatched to the army that was under the joint command of d'Alviano and Orsini. See Setton, 3:57, 59.

202. See Mallett (1974), 252–54.

203. On the Battle of Ravenna (April 11, 1512), see especially Guicciardini, 2:1030–41 (bk. 10, chap. 13); F. L. Taylor, *The Art of War in Italy, 1494–1529* (Cambridge: Cambridge University Press, 1921), 180–204 (= appendix A); and Thomas Arnold, *The Renaissance at War* (London: Cassell, 2001), 147–50.

204. Pedro Navarro (ca. 1460–1528), a Spanish captain, was taken prisoner later on in the battle. On his career see *CV* # 1239; Argegni, 1:324, s.n. "Pietro Navarra"; Arfaioli, 106–7, 132; and especially Giovio's eulogium of him, *IO* 8:436–38; *Elogi*, 844–48.

205. I.e., Fabrizio Colonna.

206. Gaston de Foix (1489–1512), duke of Nemours (1507–12). See Giovio's eulogium of him in *IO* 8:384–85; *Elogi*, 723–24.

207. See Giovio, *Histories*, IO 3:176.

208. On the Swiss victory over the French in the Battle of Novara (June 6, 1513), see Setton, 3:148–49.

209. Gian Giacomo Trivulzio (1441–1518), called "The Great." See Argegni, 3:330–31.

210. Louis de la Trémoille (1460–1525), viscount of Thouars and prince of Talmont, fought for the French in major battles including Fornovo (1495), Agnadello (1509), Marignano (1515), and Pavia, in the last of which he died. His name appears frequently in the early books of Giovio's *Histories*: see IO 5: *ad indicem*. For Giovio's eulogium of him, see IO 8:392–94; *Elogi*, 751–54.

211. The Battle of La Motta (October 7, 1513). See also n. 135 above.

212. Giovio's elliptical account here leaves out details necessary to understanding the maneuver. As de Cardona (the Spanish viceroy in Naples) was leading his legions in retreat, d'Alviano pursued them impetuously. But then Pescara, who was bringing up the rear with his Spanish infantry, turned them around to form a new battle line which then proceeded to defeat d'Alviano's forces. For a brief account of the battle, see Oman (1979), 57.

213. The Battle of Marignano (September 13–14, 1515), which took place several miles south of Milan.

214. The Battle of Bicocca (April 27, 1522).

215. Odet de Foix (1483/84–1528), viscount of Lautrec and (from 1511) marshal of France. For his important role in Italy in the 1520s, see Zimmermann, 38, 102, 104, 275, 322 n. 92; Setton, vol. 3 (*ad indicem* in vol. 4); Hook, 197, 226–31, 233–34, 236–37, 243, 249; Pastor, 9: *ad indicem*; and Giovio's eulogium of him, IO 8:432–33; *Elogi*, 835–38.

216. Jacques (II) de Chabannes (1470–1525), seigneur de la Palice, succeeded Gaston de Foix as French commander in Italy (1512) and in 1515 became grand marshal of France. He died in the Battle of Pavia. See Setton, 3:68–69, 118, 129–30, 224. He is mentioned in Giovio's *Histories*: see IO 3:22, 180, 183, 200, 218, 337, 345, 382; 4:7.

217. The Battle of Pavia (February 24, 1525).

218. On Vitellozzo Vitelli (ca. 1458–1502), see *CV* # 2188; Argegni, 3:385–86; and especially the portrayal of him in Giovio's eulogium of the Vitelli brothers, *IO* 8:364–66; *Elogi*, 685–89.

219. Mallett dates the Battle of Soriano to January 24, 1497. See Michael Mallett, *The Borgias: The Rise and Fall of the Most Infamous Family in History* (Chicago: Academy Chicago Publishers, 1987), 158.

220. Guidobaldo da Montefeltro (1472–1508) had become duke of Urbino following the death of his father, Federico, in 1482. See Argegni, 2:303–4; *ER* 4:176.

221. A reference to the tactics of the German landsknecht companies, trained pikemen who were noted for their mobility.

222. See the similar observation in Giovio, *Histories*, *IO* 3:169.

223. This battle took place in 1508 near Pieve di Cadore. See Mallett (1974), 251–52.

224. Alfonso I d'Este (1476–1534), duke of Ferrara, Modena, and Reggio. Giovio's *Life* of Alfonso is forthcoming in *IO* 7. See also *DBI* 2:332–37; Argegni, 1:331–32.

225. This encounter, sometimes called the Battle of La Polesella, took place just before dawn on December 22, 1509. Giovio's account errs on several points. Whether or not Alfonso d'Este directed strategy, it was Ippolito d'Este who commanded the Ferrarese forces and who had cannons spaced out along the Po during the night of the 21st–22nd. The flagship of Angelo Trevisan, the captain-general of the Venetian fleet, was sunk (he himself was injured but managed to escape). The two galleys that did reach safety were led not by Trevisan but by Girolamo Contarini. See Robert Finlay, "Venice, the Po Expedition, and the End of the League of Cambrai, 1509–1510," *Studies in Modern European History and Culture* 2 (1976): 37–72, at 54–55.

226. *IO* 5:280, s.v. "Fossa Giliola," identifies it as the Scolo Franiolo, a canal that issues from the Po River near Argenta (a town midway between Ferrara and Ravenna). Guicciardini describes the encounter using slightly different terminology, referring to "la bastia del fossato di Genivolo." See Guicciardini, 2:999–1000 (bk. 10, chap. 9).

227. Taylor, *Art of War in Italy*, 209–10, works out the probable route by which Alfonso so efficiently moved the heavy guns to the Spanish right. See also Arnold, *Renaissance at War*, 147–50, with an annotated map (148–49) detailing the course of the battle.

228. Francesco Maria della Rovere (1490–1538), dispossessed of the duchy of Urbino by Leo X, has often been blamed for his tendency to delay taking action and especially for his failure to lead his troops to Rome to attempt to free the pope after the city was taken. See *DBI* 50:47–55; Argegni, 1:262–63. For a careful revisionist account more sympathetic to della Rovere while not entirely absolving him of responsibility, see Cecil H. Clough, "Clement VII and Francesco Maria della Rovere, duke of Urbino," in *Pontificate of Clement*, 75–108. See also Giovio's eulogium of him in *IO* 8:454–56; *Elogi*, 891–95.

229. In 1511 della Rovere had stabbed to death Cardinal Francesco Alidosi (b. 1455), who was suspected of traitorous contact with the French. On the murder and Julius II's absolution of della Rovere for it, see Clough, "Clement VII and Francesco Maria della Rovere," 79 n. 15.

230. Federico da Montefeltro (1422–82), duke of Urbino (see n. 103 above). Federico's daughter Giovanna, who married Giovanni della Rovere, was Francesco Maria's mother.

231. Cremona capitulated on September 25, 1526.

232. On the military career of Federico II Gonzaga, duke of Mantua (1500–40), see *CV* # 0789; *DBI* 45:710–22; Argegni, 2:19–20.

233. Hook, 90, offers a less sympathetic assessment of Federico's avoidance of military activity.

234. In 1492–96, Francesco II Gonzaga (1466–1519) created a *barco* (hunting reserve) on the family property at Marmirolo. The *villa suburbana* (or, *palazo novo*), designed in part by Giulio Romano, was built in 1523–25 and became Federico II's favorite residence. The gardens and waterworks there were renowned in the 1520s and 1530s. When Charles V visited on March 27, 1530, "hidden water jets were turned on to drench the surprised and amused monarch." See Molly Bourne, *Francesco II Gonzaga:*

The Soldier-Prince as Patron (Rome: Bulzoni, 2008), 109–36 (quotation at 135 n. 135); Amedeo Belluzzi, "The Palace at Marmirolo," in *Giulio Romano*, ed. Manfredo Tafuri, trans. Fabio Barry (Cambridge: Cambridge University Press, 1998), 243–46. On Francesco II himself, see Giovio's eulogium in *IO* 8:399–400; *Elogi*, 763–66.

235. Michele Antonio del Vasto (1495–1528) became marquis of Saluzzo upon the death of his father, Ludovico II, in 1504. On his military career see Argegni, 3:102–3.

236. See Petrarch, *Rerum familiarium libri* 22.14, which also faults Italian soldiery for gambling.

237. See Cicero, *Verrines* 2.5.35, describing his policy as quaestor in Sicily.

238. This is the Battle of the Spurs (August 16, 1513). See C. S. L. Davies, "Tournai and the English Crown, 1513–1519)," *The Historical Journal* 41 (1998): 1–26.

239. The military career of Vitello Vitelli (1480–1528) is detailed in *CV* # 2187; Argegni, 3:385. See especially Giovio's eulogium of the Vitelli brothers in *IO* 8:364–66; *Elogi*, 685–89.

240. This passage refers to events that took place in March 1517 during the War of Urbino.

241. These events took place in February–March 1527.

242. I.e., Francesco II Maria Sforza (1495–1535), duke of Milan, son of Ludovico "il Moro." See Argegni, 3:241–42; and especially Giovio's eulogium of him in *IO* 8:448–49; *Elogi*, 874–78.

243. I.e., Francesco I Sforza (1401–66), duke of Milan. See above, n. 67.

244. Francesco II Sforza surrendered the citadel of Milan on July 22, 1526, and left it under imperial escort two days later. See Pitts, 437.

245. On Guido Rangoni (1485–1539), see *CV* # 1578; Arfaioli, 161.

246. On Federico Gonzaga da Bozzolo (1480–1527), see *DBI* 57:726–29; *CV* # 0788; Argegni, 2:19; and Arfaioli, 40, 53.

247. This injury is described in the account of Federico's career in *CV* # 0788, which dates it to May of 1527.

248. Malatesta Baglioni (1491–1531), son of Giovan (Gian) Paolo Baglioni (1471–1520). On the Baglioni dynasty's tumultuous rule in Perugia, see William Heywood, *A History of Perugia*, ed. R. Langton Douglas (London: Methuen, [1910]), 305–23. On Malatesta Baglioni in particular, see *DBI* 5:230–33; Argegni, 1:61–63.

249. I.e., syphilis, which ravaged the armies in the Italian Wars that began in 1494.

250. On Mercurio Bua (1478–1542), see *DBI* 14:747–48; and especially *CV* # 0304.

251. I.e., he had been a mercenary leader of "stradiots," light cavalry from Albania, which Venice introduced into Italian use in the 1460s and 1470s. Riding unarmored horses, they were usually equipped with light lances and javelins, and the only armor they wore was a breastplate and a shield. The stradiots tended to lack discipline, as was abundantly evident at the Battle of Fornovo. Generally, however, the light cavalry were important because highly maneuverable, and they played an increasing role in the decades that followed. See Mallett (1974), 119, 152–53.

252. Roberto Ambrogio Sanseverino (d. 1532), third count of Caiazzo. In 1519 he married Ippolita Cibo, sister of Cardinal Innocenzo Cibo. See Imhoff, 282; Sanuto, 28: col. 42.

253. I.e., Roberto Sanseverino d'Aragona (1418–87), who was count of Caiazzo as well as of Colorno. See Colapietra, 28, 31, 35, 56, 58, 78, 172; Argegni, 3:125–26.

254. On Cesare Fregoso (ca. 1502–41), see *DBI* 50:392–94; Argegni, 1:414.

255. Pietro Maria (Piermaria) de' Rossi (1502–47) would leave papal service for that of the emperor in June 1528. See *CV* # 1658; Argegni, 3:58–59.

256. Alessandro di Paolo Vitelli (1500–1554) would take part in the imperial siege of Florence (1529–30). See *CV* # 2173; Argegni, 3:380–81.

257. This is the Luigi Gonzaga called "Rodomonte" (1500–1532), who was the nephew of Federico Gonzaga, prince of Bozzolo. See *DBI* 57:817–24; Arfaioli, 178; Argegni, 2:32–33.

258. This is Luigi Alessandro Gonzaga (1494–1548/49), son of Rodolfo. See *DBI* 57:814–17; *CV* # 0799; Argegni, 2:33.

259. Rodolfo Gonzaga (1452–95). See *DBI* 57:838–39; *CV* # 0802; Argegni, 2:34–35.

260. Ferrante Gonzaga (1507–57), brother of Federico II Gonzaga, duke of Mantua (see above, §§140–41). On Ferrante see *DBI* 57:734–44; Argegni, 2:21–22.

261. Alessandro Gonzaga (d. 1532), count of Novellara; see *CV* # 0779; Argegni, 2:15.

262. The military career of Gianfrancesco "Cagnino" Gonzaga (d. 1539), brother of Luigi "Rodomonte" and nephew of Federico di Bozzolo, is detailed in *CV* # 0782; Argegni, 2:28; and Adele Bellù, "Figure femminili nei Gonzaga del ramo di Sabbioneta e Bozzolo: Antonia del Balzo e la sua famiglia," in *Vespasiano Gonzaga e il ducato di Sabbioneta: Atti del Convegno Sabbioneta-Mantova 12–13 ottobre 1991*, ed. Ugo Bazzotti, Daniela Ferrari, and Cesare Mozzarelli (Mantua: Accademia Nazionale Virgiliana di Scienze Lettere ed Arti, 1993), 356–73, at 365.

263. I.e., of Luigi "Rodomonte" Gonzaga; see above, n. 257.

264. The brothers Braccio and Sforza Baglioni would both die in 1532. See Heywood, *History of Perugia*, 304.

265. On Orazio Baglioni (1493–1528), see *DBI* 5:234–37; *CV* # 0131; Rendina, 329–30; Argegni, 1:63; Arfaioli, 16, 37, 46, 95.

266. Gentile Baglioni (ca. 1466–1527), son of Guido (1425–1500). See *DBI* 5:215–17. Among the other victims was Galeotto Baglioni, the brother of Braccio and Sforza. See Heywood, *History of Perugia*, 314.

267. Girolamo Mattei (d. ca. 1530), a cavalry captain in Clement VII's guard, took part in the defense of Rome during the Sack. See *CV* # 1055; and Giovio's description of him in his *Dialogo dell'imprese militari e amorose*, *IO* 9:400.

268. Simone Tebaldi (d. 1529) was distinguished in his defense of Rome during the Sack. See CV # 1920.

269. The career of Guido Vaina (d. 1544), which included service as a cavalry commander under Francesco Maria della Rovere, is detailed in CV # 2072; Argegni, 3:342–43.

270. Cesare Filettino served the Colonna family as an infantry commander against papal forces in 1526. See Guicciardini, 3:1786, 1808. Perhaps a relative of Marcantonio Filitino (d. 1514), a Roman, on whom see CV # 0679.

271. Giambattista Castaldo (1493–1563), described in CV # 0407 as possibly from Nocera, served as a captain under Pescara and subsequently under del Vasto. He was a longtime friend of Giovio, who dedicated his Life of Pescara to Castaldo. See Volpati (1936), 359–60; Zimmermann, 76, 217, 225, 238, 251–52; Argegni, 1:155–56.

272. Paolo Luzzasco (d. ca. 1555) had taken part in the Battle of Pavia. See CV # 0901; Argegni, 2:112; Arfaioli, 58, 139.

273. Taylor, Art of War in Italy, 70–76, details the precedence Italians came to give to light-armed horse over heavy cavalry starting in the mid-1490s.

274. This club is the Turkish bozdogan (iron mace).

275. Giovio may be referring here to armor made by the Austrian manufacturer Konrad Seusenhofer, employed by Emperor Maximilian I, who reduced its weight "by utilizing fluted plates, the glancing property and strength of which were increased by an ingenious corrugating of the sheet metal." This type of armor is known today as "Maximilian." See Henrietta Larson, "The Armor Business in the Middle Ages," Bulletin of the Business Historical Society 14:4 (1940): 49–64, quotation at 54. Another possibility is that the armor here described was personalized to accommodate the distance between joints in particular men's arms and legs.

276. Sinibaldo Fieschi (or, "Flisco") (ca. 1485–1531/32), a prominent Genoese patrician, whose son Gianluigi would later lead an unsuccessful conspiracy against the Doria. See DBI 47:518–21; and Argegni, 1:391–92.

277. On Ugo de' Pepoli (1484–1528), see Arfaioli, 16, 133–34, 137, 164; *CV* # 1419; Argegni, 2:414.

278. On Giovanni da Sassatello (d. 1530), called "Il Cagnaccio," see *CV* # 1714; Argegni, 3:137. His son Francesco fell at Vicenza in the Battle of La Motta.

279. I.e., the Battle of La Motta, described above, §125.

280. On Paolo Camillo Trivulzio (d. 1528), see *CV* # 2031.

281. Ludovico da Barbiano di Belgioioso (1488–1530) had long fought on behalf of France, doing so with distinction at the Battle of Pavia in 1525. In August of the following year, after a falling out with Federico Gonzaga da Bozzolo, he went over to the imperial side. See *DBI* 6:206–11; *CV* # 0177; Argegni, 1:69; and Guicciardini, 3:1781 and n. 10.

282. On Alberico da Barbiano, see above, n. 66.

283. On Filippo Tornielli (d. ca. 1556), see *CV* # 1993. In 1527–28 he was fighting in the imperial army, in Piedmont and Lombardy.

284. This is Giovanni Matteo Beccaria (d. ca. 1535) of Pavia. See *CV* # 0173.

285. Giampaolo Manfron (1442–1527/28 or later). According to *CV* # 0993, he was killed by an arquebus shot in October 1527. But see Giovio, who mentions him (s.n. Paulus Manfronus) in the *Histories*: *IO* 3:123, 135, 221, 228, 375, 376; and in *IO* 4:90, where Manfron is described (in Book 26, concerning the year 1528) as still fighting vigorously as an octogenarian. See also Argegni, 2:195.

286. Ambrogio da Landriano (d. ca. 1530). See *CV* # 0859; Argegni, 2:86–87. Giovio includes Landriano in the *Histories* (see *IO* 3:167–68).

287. Pietro Zanchi di Longhena (1474–1533). See *CV* # 0885; Giovio's *Histories* (*IO* 3:14, 257, 334; 4:29, 90).

288. Giovanni de' Medici (1498–1526), the famous mercenary leader, died in the fighting at Governolo. See Giovio's eulogium of him in *IO* 8:427–28; *Elogi*, 823–26. See also Hook, 107–8; Argegni, 1:239–41; and especially Arfaioli, xiii–xvii, 1–23. At xiii–xv, Arfaioli emphasizes that while this

Giovanni de' Medici is known to history as "Giovanni of the Black Bands," he was not called that within his lifetime, and indeed his mercenary troops were not even known as the *bande nere* until after his death.

289. The following passage through §172 surveys, not without schadenfreude in the manner of Lactantius' *On the Deaths of the Persecutors*, the deaths of the "four chief instigators" (§172) of the loss of Italian liberty.

290. Alfonso II d'Aragona (king, 1494–95) was succeeded by his son, Ferrante II (king, 1495–96).

291. On Paolo Giustinian and Alban d'Armer, see Giovio, *Histories*, in IO 5: *ad indicem*. On Giustinian (with first name given as "Polo"), see also Argegni, 2:11.

292. I.e., commanders of land troops.

293. Probably Niccolò II, count of Pitigliano. See above, n. 128.

294. Probably Gian Giacomo Trivulzio. See above, n. 209.

295. Prospero Colonna (d. 1523); see above, n. 111.

296. On Francesco II Gonzaga (1466–1519), see n. 234 above.

297. The anecdote comes from Cicero, *On Invention* 2.1–3.

298. Hernando de Alarcón (1500–1540), historically significant above all for his navigation along the western coast of Mexico.

299. On Alarcón taking custody of the pope, see Sanuto, 45: col. 134 (from a copy of an undated letter from Castel Sant' Angelo by Francesco Pesaro, archbishop of Zara). On the letter, see Setton, 3:270–71 n. 4.

300. On Juan de Urbina (d. 1529), who participated in the Sack of Rome and subsequently became Alfonso del Vasto's camp master, see Arfaioli, 129, 161; and Zimmermann, 304 n. 60, with added bibliography.

301. Originally from Basque Navarre, which Ferdinand of Aragon had conquered, Navarro fought with distinction under Gonsalvo. Following Navarro's capture in the Battle of Ravenna (1512), King Ferdinand refused to ransom him, and so after languishing in a French prison for two years, Navarro entered the service of Francis I. By calling him "Navarrogallus" (here rendered "Gallo-Navarran"), Muscettola draws a playful

parallel between the political division of Navarre into Spanish and French territories and Navarro's move from Spanish to French service.

302. The dangers of "long peace" (*longa pax*) were a topic of ancient historiography: Tacitus, *Agricola* 11.4; *Histories* 2.17.1.

303. Fernão Pires de Andrade is best known for his role in negotiating trade between Portugal and China in Canton in 1517. See K. G. Jayne, *Vasco da Gama and his Successors, 1460 to 1580* (New York: Barnes and Noble, 1970), 227–29. See also Guicciardini, 1:530, 531 n. 15.

304. I.e., in the Battle of Seminara in 1503. On his victory over d'Aubigny, see above, n. 186.

305. Diego Hurtado de Mendoza (1468–1536) fought in major battles including Ravenna (1512) and Pavia (1525).

306. Don Iñigo de Velasco helped to put down the *Comuneros* revolt in Spain, in which Juan Padilla was executed. On Padilla see Dialogue Three below.

307. Juan de Manriquez, marqués de Aguilar.

308. This is the French campaign into Castile in 1521 under André de Foix, de l'Esparre. Having just taken Pamplona in Navarre, l'Esparre proceeded to besiege the town of Logrogno (Logroño), on the Ebro River in Castile, but the Spaniards resisted and defeated the French. See William Robertson, *History of the Reign of Charles the Fifth, with an Account of the Emperor's Life after his Abdication by William H. Prescott* (London: Routledge, n.d.), 151.

309. Antonio de Leyva (1480–1536), a Spanish captain, had assumed Pescara's command following the latter's death (December 2–3, 1525). In 1527 he was one of Charles V's representatives in the Italian campaign, active primarily in Lombardy. See Setton, 3:261, 283n, 285–86; Zimmermann, 77, 110, 128, 244, 264; and Giovio's eulogium of de Leyva, *IO* 8:451–52; *Elogi*, 883–86.

310. Georg von Frundsberg (1473–1528) was commander of the German landsknechts who joined forces with Bourbon in his march on Rome. In mid-March 1527, shortly after confronting his mutinous troops, Frunds-

berg suffered a stroke that prevented his continuing with the army. See Setton, 3:256, 259, 261–62; Hook, *ad indicem*; and Giovio's eulogium of him, *IO* 8:431–32; *Elogi*, 833–34.

311. This is Marc Sittich von Hohenems. See *IO* 3:379, 384, 385, 445.

312. Giovio wrote extensively in the *Histories* about von Rogendorf. See *IO* 5: *ad indicem*.

313. On Lautrec see n. 215 above.

314. Such street fighters ("urban gladiators") are discussed at length in Dialogue Two, §84.

315. On Louis de la Trémoille (1460–1525), see n. 210 above.

316. On de la Palice, see n. 216 above.

317. This is Guillaume Gouffier, seigneur de Bonnivet (ca. 1488–1525), who had been made admiral of France in 1517. He died in the Battle of Pavia. See Setton, 3:217 n. 66, 312; Knecht, 43 and passim.

318. Thomas de Foix, seigneur de Lescun (d. 1525). See Setton, 3:166, 173, 196n, 224.

319. John Stuart, duke of Albany, was brother-in-law of the deceased Lorenzo de' Medici (duke of Urbino). See Pastor, 9:275–76.

320. Claude de Lorraine (1496–1550), the son of René II, duke of Lorraine, became count (1506–1528) and then duke of Guise (1528–50). See Giovio's *Histories*, *ad indicem*.

321. Giovio has "Ioannes" (Jean), a clear mistake for François de Bourbon-Vendôme (1491–1545), count of St. Pol, of whom Giovio had written in his *Histories* (*ad indicem*, *IO* 5:263). See also Knecht, *ad indicem*.

322. Antoine de Lorraine (1489–1544) became its duke in 1508.

323. Jean de Guise (1498–1550), cardinal of Lorraine. See Knecht, *ad indicem*; Giovio, *Histories*, *ad indicem*.

324. This Charles de Bourbon (1489–1537) became duke of Vendôme in 1515. See Knecht, *ad indicem*.

325. Louis II de Bourbon de Vendôme (1493–1557), created cardinal in 1517.

326. On this incident see Pitts, 390.

327. Louis de Lorraine (1500–28) became count of Vaudémont in 1522. A veteran of the Battle of Pavia, he died of plague while fighting under Lautrec in the siege of Naples.

328. On Anne de Montmorency (1493–1567), who would be made constable of France in 1538, see Knecht, *ad indicem*; Setton, 4: *ad indicem*; and ER 4:182–83.

329. Philippe de Chabot, seigneur de Brion (1480–1543), defended Marseille against Bourbon in 1524. Following the Battle of Pavia, in which he was captured, Chabot became Admiral of France (1525). See Knecht, especially 224, 226, 252–53.

330. C_1 has *regibus* (hence "members of the royal family"); he has in mind, above all, Francis I.

331. This maneuver by Pescara at the Battle of La Motta is discussed above in §125.

332. On "filling the minds of all with admiration and terror" (*omnium animos admiratione terroreque complevit*), see Machiavelli, *Il Principe*, bk. 7, regarding the murder of Ramiro de Lorqua, which his master, Cesare Borgia, had ordered: "La ferocità del quale spettaculo fece quelli populi in uno tempo rimanere satisfatti e stupidi."

333. This is Prospero Colonna (d. 1523). See above, n. 111.

334. Pierre du Terrail Le Vieux (1473–1524), seigneur de Bayard, whom Francis I made a knight of the order of St. Michel. On the story of King Francis I having himself knighted on the battlefield by Bayard, see the sources cited in Knecht, 77 n. 28.

335. A reference to Giovio's work on his *Life* of Pescara.

336. From Cicero, *On the Laws* 3.18.

337. Ippolito Quinzio, here described as governor of the island, would serve as secretary to del Vasto when the latter governed Milan. See Abd-el-Kader Salza, *Luca Contile: Uomo di lettere e di negozi del secolo XVI* (Florence: G. Carnesecchi e figli, 1903), 12, 28, and 215. The interlocutors discuss Quinzio's poetry below in Dialogue Two, §61.

DIALOGUE TWO

1. The present edition follows scholarly consensus (e.g., Travi, Zimmermann; see Minonzio, who dissents) that the beginning of the manuscript of Dialogue Two is lost (see the description of the manuscripts in this volume). Here, Giovio writes of Cardinal Pompeo Colonna. Initially Giulio de' Medici's rival for the papacy, when Colonna's own elevation appeared impossible, he provided support essential to Giulio's election. But in late 1526, after Pope Clement joined in the League of Cognac against Charles V, the staunchly pro-imperial Colonna led a military attack on the Vatican. The cardinal did not support the pope again until after the meeting here described, on June 1, 1527.

2. Francesco Armellini (1470–1528; created cardinal, 1517). As *camerlengo* (chamberlain) of the Holy Roman Church — effectively, the pope's chief financial officer — he was widely hated for perceived avarice. In a consistory meeting at which Armellini suggested imposing new taxes, Pompeo Colonna is said to have quipped that "the most useful, honest, and expeditious course of all" for gaining the needed revenue "would be to have Cardinal Armellini flayed, to send his pelt through the states of the church, and to make anyone wishing to look at it pay a *quattrino*." Hallman, 22–24.

3. Giovanni Battista Valentini (ca. 1450–1515), called "il Cantalicio" after his home town, Cantalice, in Latium. After teaching in cities including Urbino and Siena, he was called to Rome by Alexander VI to tutor Pier Luigi Borgia, whom the humanist then followed to Naples. His compositions include many epigrams, a lengthy poem on the war between the Aragonese and Charles VIII, and another dedicated to Gonsalvo "the Great," which Giovio may here have in mind: *De bis recepta Parthenope. Gonsalvia* (Naples: Mair, 1506). See Luigi Allevi, "Umanisti camerinesi, il Cantalicio e la corte del Varano," *Atti e memorie della Deputazione di storia patria per le Marche* 2:2 (1925): 169–95; Frede, 25, 45, 118; *DELI* 1:556–57.

4. Widely lambasted as a poetaster, Girolamo Casio de' Medici (1464–1533), from the Bolognese Apennines, had grown rich as a merchant of

luxury goods, including precious stones. Giuliano de' Medici, duke of Nemours, conferred upon him the Medici coat of arms and surname, Leo X named him a knight (*cavaliere*), and Clement VII made him a poet laureate (*laurea*). His chief work is *La Clementina* (Bologna?: Faelli?, 1528?), a collection of lyric poems composed mostly around the time of Clement's elevation to the papacy (1523). "Bejeweled" (*Gemmatus*) probably refers to the large agate intaglio that Casio wore on his courtier's hat as his personal device (an *impresa* that Giovio, in his *Dialogo dell'Imprese* [1551], would call "ridiculous"). Berni, 5–13 and passim. For Giovio's account of Pope Clement laughing at Casio's description of his *impresa*, see *IO* 9:378. The identification of *Cassius Gemmatus* with Casio de' Medici is established by Minonzio, 2:530–31.

5. Niccolò Leonico Tomeo (1456–1531) taught Aristotle to great acclaim at the University of Padua and translated the *Parva naturalia* and *De partibus animalium*. Giovio commemorated him with a eulogium (XCI), praising his brilliance, learning, and character. See *CE* 2:323–24; *IO* 8:114–15; Gragg, 129–30; *Elogi*, 268–70.

6. Pietro Bembo (1470–1547), a Venetian patrician, excelled in writing both Latin and the Tuscan vernacular. In a letter to Gianfrancesco Pico (1513), he defended the imitation of Cicero as a stylistic ideal. Himself an outstanding Ciceronian stylist, Bembo served as domestic secretary to Leo X (pope, 1513–21). In 1530 the Venetian Republic would make him its librarian and official historian, in which capacity he was to continue the history of the city that Marcantonio Sabellico had begun. In 1539 Pope Paul III would create him cardinal. See *ER* 1:201–2; *CE* 1:120–23; *DBI* 8:133–51. His Latin verse, along with his dialogue *Aetna*, was published in this I Tatti Library (2005, vol. 18, corrected edition 2012), trans. Mary P. Chatfield and Betty Radice.

7. The pastoral poet Jacopo Sannazaro (1458–1530) led the Neapolitan academy starting in 1504 (Pontano had died the previous year). Among his most famous works are the *Arcadia* (authorized ed. 1504) and *De partu Virginis* (1526). See *ER* 5:394–96. His Latin poetry has been published in this I Tatti Library (2009, vol. 38), with a translation and notes by Michael C. J. Putnam.

8. The work referred to is Bembo's *Prose della volgar lingua* (Venice: Tacuino, 1525).

9. The dialogue to which Giovio refers is Bembo's *De Guido Ubaldo Feretrio deque Elisabetha Gonzaga Urbini ducibus* (Venice: Sabbio, 1530). Guidobaldo da Montefeltro (1472–1508), duke of Urbino, was the husband of Elisabetta Gonzaga (1476?–1526), whom Castiglione made the host of the conversations in his *Il libro del cortegiano*.

10. Angelo Poliziano (1454–94), an exceptional philologist and noted poet, spent most of his career in Florence, where he enjoyed the patronage of Lorenzo "il Magnifico" de' Medici. See *ER* 5:114–16; *CE* 3:106–8.

11. The work referred to is Poliziano's unfinished poem, *Stanze cominciate per la giostra del magnifico Giuliano di Piero de Medici* (1475/78, first published 1494).

12. Included in Poliziano's *Sylvae*. The work has been published in this I Tatti Library (2004, vol. 14), trans. Charles Fantazzi.

13. Baldassare Castiglione (1478–1529) had begun writing *Il libro del cortegiano* in 1513–14 and completed it by 1524. Although it was first published only in 1528, Vittoria Colonna had a manuscript copy in her possession well before Giovio's arrival on Ischia in 1527.

14. Against Minerva's will: *invita Minerva*, a proverbial phrase found in Cicero's *De officiis* 1.31.10 and Horace's *Ars poetica* 385, was used to describe uninspired work; see Erasmus' *Adagia* 1.1.42.

15. Marco Girolamo Vida (ca. 1485–1566), from Cremona, went to Rome in 1510. There he enjoyed the patronage of Gian Matteo Giberti, Leo X, and Clement VII. On the strength of his epic poem on the life of Christ, the *Christiados libri sex* (Cremona: Ludovico Britannico, 1535), Vida came to be called "the Christian Vergil." See *CE* 3:391–92; and James Gardner's introduction to his edition and translation of Vida, *Christiad*, published in this I Tatti Library (2009, vol. 39).

16. Vida, *De arte poetica lib. III. Eiusdem De bombyce lib. II. Eiusdem De ludo scacchorum lib. I. Eiusdem Hymni. Eiusdem Bucolica* ([Rome: Ludovico Vicentino, 1527]).

17. Vida presented the *Christiad* to Clement VII in 1532. It was printed three years later. See n. 15 above.

18. Marcantonio Flaminio (1498–1550), from the Veneto, studied in Rome, Naples (where he met and befriended Sannazaro), Bologna, and Padua. He first published poetry in 1515. In 1524 he met Gian Matteo Giberti, who would be his patron in Rome and, from 1528 on, in Verona. See Carol Maddison, *Marcantonio Flaminio: Poet, Humanist and Reformer* (Chapel Hill: University of North Carolina Press, 1965); *DBI* 48:282–88; Balsamo, 1:346–48.

19. *Sic.* Actually, he was born in Serravalle (now part of Vittorio Veneto).

20. The best brief account of the life of Pierio Valeriano (1477–1558) is that of Julia Haig Gaisser in the introduction to her edition of Valeriano's *De litteratorum infelicitate*: *DLI*, 2–23.

21. The work that Giovio here describes is Valeriano's *Hieroglyphica* (Basel: Palma Ising, 1556), a 58-book compendium which took several decades to complete.

22. Count Nicolò d'Arco (1492/93–1546), of the province of Trent, is best known for his collection of Latin poems, *Numerorum Libri IV* (Verona: Typis Marci Moroni, 1762).

23. On Arco and Giovio, see Zimmermann, 9–10, 128. No copy of the *Anterotica* is known to exist.

24. Francesco Maria Molza (1489–1544), from an old noble family in Modena, studied in Bologna before going to Rome, initially at the court of Julius II. In his eulogium of Molza (no. CIV, in *IO* 8:125; *Elogi*, 304–6), Giovio faulted him for his extravagance and especially his constant involvement in love affairs, which led to his contracting a venereal disease that ultimately proved fatal. Molza spent three decades in Rome supported by a variety of patrons, and in the late 1530s he and Giovio both took part in the Accademia della Virtù that Claudio Tolomei established there. See *Elogi*, 305–6; Balsamo, 1:503–5.

25. This account of Andrea Marone (1475–1528) complements Valeriano's description of Marone's gift for extemporaneous versification, in

DLI, 184–87 (= bk. 2, §25). On Marone's career and the loss of most of his works in the Sack of Rome, see Gaisser's account in *DLI*, 305, with further bibliography. For the art of performing extemporaneous Latin verse, see F. Alberto Gallo, *Music in the Castle: Troubadours, Books and Orators in Italian Courts of the Thirteenth, Fourteenth and Fifteenth Centuries* (Chicago: University of Chicago Press, 1995), chap. 3.

26. Quintianus Stoa (Giovanni Francesco Conti, 1484–1557) took his Latin name from his hometown, Quinzano d'Oglio, near Brescia. In 1509 King Louis XII of France crowned him poet laureate in Milan. He published extensively on language, e.g., *De syllabarum quantitate* (Paris: Johannes Parvus, 1500?), on religious topics, e.g., *Christiani opera* (Paris: Petit, 1514), and a tragedy on the life of Christ, the *Theoandrathanatos* (Lyon: Hylaire, 1515). See Tiraboschi 7, 3:364–70; Cosenza, 4:2982–84; *DBI* 28:429–31.

27. Elephantis was an ancient author (probably female) of erotica. According to Suetonius in his *Lives of the Twelve Caesars*, the Emperor Tiberius furnished some of the rooms in his retreat on Capri with the books of Elephantis as an inspiration toward the indulgence of lust. Suetonius, *Tiberius*, 43; see also Martial, bk. 12, epigram 43.

28. Giovanni Maria Cattaneo (after 1480–1529/30) of Novara studied under Merula (Giorgio Merlani; see n. 83 below) and Demetrius Chalcondyles in Milan. His publications include an edition of the letters of Pliny (Milan, 1506); *Genua*, a lengthy poem in praise of Genoa (Rome, 1514); and an unpublished epic on the First Crusade. Cattaneo served as secretary to Cardinal Bendinello Sauli, in whose household in Rome he and Giovio became well acquainted. Both humanists appear in Sebastiano del Piombo's painting of *Cardinal Bendinello Sauli and Three Companions* (1516). See Hyde, 92–94; *CE* 1:286–87; *DBI* 22:468–71; *DLI*, 52.

29. Cattaneo's commentary on Pliny the Younger's *Epistulae* was published in Milan in 1506 and a second edition in the same city in 1518. See Lucia A. Ciapponi, "Plinius Caecilius Secundus," in *CTC* 9:111–121.

30. The reference is to Godfrey of Bouillon's conquest of Jerusalem (1099) in the First Crusade. His opponents there were the Fatimids.

31. Benedetto Lampridio (1478–1540) of Cremona was a member of Paolo Cortesi's household in Rome. Following Leo X's death in 1521, he went to Padua, where he enjoyed the patronage of Pietro Bembo. Lampridio rendered Pindaric odes into Latin and wrote letters in hexameter and epigrams. See *RLV*, 429–32; *DELI* 3:322; *DBI* 63:266–69; Balsamo, 1:431–32.

32. Fabio Vigili (ca. 1480?–1553) of Spoleto became secretary to Cardinal Raffaele Riario in 1511. In Rome, Vigili became active in Goritz's sodality, and several of his poems appear in the *Coryciana*. In the 1530s he would become domestic secretary to Pope Paul III, and in 1540 would be made bishop of Spoleto. See Saul Levin and T. C. P. Zimmermann, "Fabilo Vigile's *Poem of the Pheasant*," in *Rome in the Renaissance: The City and the Myth*, ed. Paul A. Ramsey (Binghamton: Center for Medieval and Early Renaissance Studies, 1982), 265–78, with further bibliography.

33. Carlo Cappello (1492–1546), a Venetian patrician and distinguished diplomat, had studied under Marco Musurus. His compositions include *De observanda et, secundum Deum, colenda divina ecclesiastica maiestate ex sanctorum apostolorum constitutionibus et decretis* (Venice: s.n., 1544). See *DBI* 18:767–72.

34. This is probably Bernardino Martirano of Cosenza (ca. 1490–ca. 1548), a student of Aulo Giano Parrasio, who edited his teacher's commentary on Horace's *Ars poetica* (Naples: Sulzbach, 1531); he became secretary of the Regno di Napoli. He was not, however, a cleric (Minonzio suggests that on this point Giovio confused Bernardino with his younger brother, Coriolano). Minonzio, 2:553–54; Toscano, 265–98; *DBI* 71:336–41.

35. Antonio Telesio (1482–1534) of Cosenza taught eloquence in Milan and Rome. He was a protégé of Gian Matteo Giberti and also associated with Pompeo Colonna. Skilled in a variety of poetic genres, he is best known for his tragedy, *Imber aureus* (Venice: Bernardino Vitale, 1529), reprinted in 1530, 1545, and 1566. Three of his poems appear in the *Coryciana* (nos. 333–35). See *DELI* 5:253; Altamura, 183–85; *RLV*, 224–26; *Coryciana*, 224–25.

36. Telesio, *De coronis libellus* (Rome: Calvo, 1525). Giovio encouraged Telesio to publish this work. See Zimmermann, 310 n. 27.

37. For the *Lucerna* and *Reticulum*, see Telesio, *Poemata* (Rome: Calvo, 1524).

38. Telesio's *Cicindela* is printed in with an edition of his *Libellus de coloribus* (Paris: Wechel, 1529).

39. Publio Francesco Modesti (1471–1557) of Rimini. His *Venetias* (Venice: Bernardus dei Vitali, 1521) concerns Venice's war against Maximilian, 1505–8. That edition includes as well his *Sylvarum liber unus*.

40. Girolamo Fracastoro (ca. 1478–1553) of Verona studied astronomy, philosophy, medicine, and anatomy at the University of Padua, the last subject under Marcantonio della Torre, with whom Giovio also studied. In 1505 he joined the college of physicians in Verona. The *Syphilis sive morbus gallicus* (Verona: [S. dei Nicolini da Sabbio and Brothers], 1530) is his most famous work. See *DBI* 49:543–48; *CE* 2:49; Balsamo, 1:353–55. An edition of his complete Latin poetry is in press with the I Tatti Renaissance Library, translated by James Gardner.

41. Giovanni Aurelio Augurelli (ca. 1456–1524) of Treviso studied in Venice and Padua. Pietro Bembo's father, Bernardo, introduced Augurelli to Poliziano and Ficino in Florence. Starting in 1485, he taught in Treviso, next in Venice, and then ended his career in Treviso. He dedicated the *Chrysopoeia*, a didactic poem on alchemy, to Leo X. Other works include Petrarchan verse in the vernacular and a hexameter poem on Giuliano de' Medici's joust in 1475 (the subject also of Poliziano's *Stanze*; see above, n. 11). See *DBI* 4:578–81; *DELI* 1:208; and Zweder von Martels, "Augurello's 'Chrysopoeia' (1515) — a turning point in the literary tradition of alchemical texts," *Early Science and Medicine* 5 (2000): 178–95.

42. Marco Antonio Casanova (ca. 1477–1528) of Rome was famed for his Latin epigrams. Few of his poems appeared within his lifetime (see, however, nos. 10, 11, 107–110, 112–15, 142, and 162 in the *Coryciana*). Casanova enjoyed Leo X's patronage, but fared less well under Clement VII, perhaps because of the poet's adherence to Pompeo Colonna. Following his capture and torture during the Sack of Rome, he found refuge briefly in Colonna's household but was expelled from it and subsequently died on

the streets. Giovio commemorated him in Eulogium no. LXXVI. See especially Gaisser's account in *DLI*, 276–77; *DBI* 21:171–74; *IO* 8:100–101; *Elogi*, 221–23; Gragg, 110–11.

43. Casanova himself wrote about the episode in an elegy, *Ad divum Pompeium*, which survives in manuscript in the Vatican Library, MS. Vat. lat. 5227, vol. 1, fol. 11ᵛ. See *DBI* 21:171–74.

44. Blosio Palladio (d. 1550) of Sabina, near Rome, was a *scriptor* in the papal court who became a private secretary to Clement VII and Paul III. Involved in the salon of the courtesan Imperia and active in the academies of Colocci and Goritz, he edited two major collections of poetry: the *Suburbanum Augustini Chisi* (Rome: Mazzocchi, 1512), celebrating the Sienese banker Agostino Chigi's villa on the outskirts of Rome (now the Villa Farnesina); and the *Coryciana* (Rome: L. de Henricis and L. Perusinus, 1524; ed. Jozef IJsewijn, Rome: Herder, 1997). The latter comprised poems that members of Goritz's sodality had written annually, for over a decade, in celebration of the feast of St. Ann (July 26). See *CE* 3:46–47; D'Amico, 59.

45. Palladio's oration in Leo's honor was written ca. 1518, but Leo died before the dedication ceremonies for the statue could take place. By June of 1521 the statue, by Domenico Amio of Bologna, was finished and placed in the Palazzo dei Conservatori on the Capitoline hill. For a summary and analysis of the oration, see D'Amico, 134–37. The episode is analyzed in Hans Henrik Brummer and Tore Jansen, "Art, Literature, and Politics: An Episode in the Roman Renaissance," *Konsthistorisk Tidskrift* 45 (1976): 79–93.

46. Angelo Colocci (1474–1549), from the town of Jesi, became a member of Pontano's academy in Naples in 1490. Eight years later he moved to Rome and began accumulating ecclesiastical offices. By the early 1500s he was living in what had been Pomponio Leto's house on the Quirinal and had become the leader of an academy that lasted for several decades. Giovio knew Colocci in Rome and praised him highly in passing in his eulogium of Elisio Calenzio (*IO* 8:75; *Elogi*, 135). See *DLI*, 53–57; *DBI* 27:105–11; *CE* 1: 330–31; and above, Introduction, n. 18.

47. Pietro Corsi (d. before December 1548), from Carpineto Romano, was in Rome at least by 1509. A participant in the sodalities of Colocci and Goritz, Corsi was frequently criticized for the rusticity of his Latin. His compositions include a poem on the Sack of Rome, *Romae urbis excidium* (see n. 48 below); and the *Defensio pro Italia ad Erasmum Roterodamum* (Rome: Antonio Blado, 1535), in which he defended Italian military prowess against a passing criticism Erasmus made in his *Adagia*. Valeriano made him an interlocutor in his *De litteratorum infelicitate*. See *DLI*, 59–61; Gouwens, 73–102; *DBI* 29: 579–81; *CE* 1: 344.

48. Pietro Corsi, *Ad humanis generis servatorem in urbis Romae excidio Petri Cursii civis Romani deploratio* (Paris: Estienne, 1528). In the poem's dedicatory letter to Louise of Savoy, Corsi implores her to exhort her son, King Francis I, to send a French army to rescue the Romans.

49. Tommaso Pighinuzzi (d. before 1548), called "Pietrasanta" after his native city. Valeriano made him an interlocutor of his *De litteratorum infelicitate*. Pighinuzzi appears to have been a patron of Marco Antonio Casanova, and also to have been one of the chief supporters of Celso Mellini's attack on Christophe de Longueil (see n. 192 below). *DLI*, 65–67.

50. Pietro Mellini (b. after 1491; d. after 1548?), from a distinguished and wealthy aristocratic Roman family, was not only a poet but a patron of other humanists. Valeriano made him an interlocutor in the *De litteratorum infelicitate*, a dialogue set in 1529 in Mellini's palazzo near Piazza Navona. During the Sack of Rome, Mellini, like Giovio and the pope, had found refuge in the papal fortress. See *DLI*, 62–65 and passim.

51. Giano Vitale, *De monstro nato* (Rome: [s.n.], 1512). See the discussion in Ottavia Niccoli, *Prophecy and People in Renaissance Italy* (Princeton: Princeton University Press, 1990), 48–50; and Niccoli, "High and Low Prophetic Culture in Rome at the Beginning of the Sixteenth Century," in *Prophetic Rome in the High Renaissance Period*, ed. Marjorie Reeves (Oxford: Clarendon Press, 1992), 203–22, at 218–19. From a noble family in Palermo, Vitale (1485–1559) moved in 1510 to Rome, where he gained the patronage of Leo X and was active in the academies. His *Imperiae panaegyricus* ([Rome: Beplin, ca. 1512]) celebrated the courtesan Imperia. A

number of his poems appear in the *Coryciana*. He also wrote a lament on the death of Vittoria Colonna's husband, the marquis of Pescara (d. 1525): *Lachrymae . . . in obitum Francisci Ferdinandi Davali Aquinatis, Magni Pischariae marchionis* (undated). See *DELI* 5:476; *Coryciana*.

52. Marcello Palonio, *Clades ravennas* (Rome: Mazzocchi, 1513). In a lateral gloss, this poem also describes a monster: see Niccoli, *Prophecy*, 41, 45–46, 49–50. One of Palonio's poems appears in the *Coryciana* (no. 219), and he is mentioned by Arsilli in the *De poetis urbanis* (published as an appendix to the *Coryciana*), which was dedicated to Giovio.

53. Menicocius remains to be identified.

54. Perugino had in fact died in 1523.

55. Perugino's paintings on the walls of the Sistine Chapel include the famous fresco *Christ Handing the Keys to St. Peter* (1481–82).

56. Originally from Palermo, Pietro Gravina (1452/53–1528) was active in the Aragonese court in Naples and in Pontano's academy. In Rome he participated in Paolo Cortesi's academy in the 1490s, and he delivered a sermon before Alexander VI in 1493. Sannazaro admired his epigrams. Gravina wrote a poem in heroic verse in honor of Gonsalvo the Great, parts of which have survived and are published in Gravina's *Poematum libri ad illustrem Ioannem Franciscum de Capua Palensium Comitem, Epigrammatum liber. Sylvarum et elegiarum liber. Carmen Epicum*, ed. Scipione Capece (Naples: Sulzbach, 1532), fols. 59r–70r. Giovio's Eulogium LXXIV is on Gravina. See *DBI* 58:770–72; *DLI*, 296; Altamura, 114–16; Gragg, 108–9; *IO* 8:98–99; *Elogi*, 215–17.

57. Girolamo Carbone (later 15th cent.–1528) of Naples, who served the Aragonese on diplomatic missions, became a student and friend of Pontano, and he led the academy after his mentor's death (1503). Carbone died from the plague in Naples during Lautrec's invasion. See *DLI*, 275; Altamura, 122–24; *DBI* 19:695–98.

58. Girolamo Angeriano (1470–1535) was active in Pontano's academy in Naples and was a friend of Sannazaro. His *Erotopaegnion* (Florence, 1512) includes 178 of his epigrams. He also wrote a poem in two books entitled

De principum miseria opusculum (Florence: Giunti, 1522). See *DELI* 1:134; Altamura, 142–43; Balsamo, 1:55–56.

59. Ancient Lucania lay to the south of Naples.

60. Giano (Giovanni Francesco) Anisio (ca. 1465/75–post-1540) was in Pontano's academy. A skilled imitator of Pontano's Latin verse style, Anisio wrote a pastoral lament following his teacher's death. His publications include *Varia poemata et satyrae* (Naples: Sulzbach, 1531), which he dedicated to Cardinal Pompeo Colonna; and a sacred tragedy entitled *Protogonos* (Naples: Sulzbach, 1536). See *Coryciana*, poems 119, 143; *DBI* 3:332–33; *DELI* 1:143; Altamura, 116–20.

61. Antonio Sebastiani (ca. 1500–1574), called "Il Minturno" after Minturnae, the ancient Roman town on the site of his birthplace, Traetto. He studied with the philosopher Agostino Nifo in Naples, and then followed Nifo to posts in Rome and Pisa. He tutored the children of Ettore Pignatelli, who served as viceroy of Sicily from 1517 until his death, in 1534. Minturno accompanied the Pignatelli children to Ischia. See Zimmermann, 316 n. 18; Thérault, 290–95, 473; Balsamo, 1:498–500.

62. The latter of these is the *Poemata ad Illustrissimum Principem Marcum Antonium Columnam* (Venice: Valuassor, 1564).

63. Pomponio Gaurico (1481/82–1528/30?). From the province of Salerno, Gaurico spent time in the Aragonese court of Naples until around 1500. After stints in Padua and Rome, he returned to Naples where he held the chair in Greek and Latin from 1512 to 1519. There, he wrote a book of Latin elegies (Naples, 1523). In Eulogium LXXV, Giovio says that Gaurico "would have been remarkable for the vigorous productivity of his ardent genius in various branches, if he had not been led astray by his volatile temperament and, in his feverish haste and pursuit of novelty, failed to attain the dignity of sound knowledge in any subject through his lack of accuracy and industry in all." Gragg, 109–110. See also *IO* 8:99–100; *Elogi*, 218–220; *DBI* 52:705–7; *DELI* 3:48–49.

64. This is Antonio Matteazzi (d. 1523), called "Marostica" from the town near Vicenza where he was born. A friend of Trissino, Lascaris, and Valeriano, he served as secretary to Cardinal Francesco Pisani. See *DLI*, 308.

65. Giorgio Anselmi (before 1459–1528) of Parma was a friend of Francesco Carpesani (see n. 67 below). His most notable publication is *Epigrammaton libri septem: Sosthryides. Peplum Palladis. Aeglogae quattuor* (Venice: Pasini, 1528). See *DBI* 3:378–79.

66. Bernardino Dardano (1472–1535) of Parma was in Rome by 1524. The *Coryciana* includes several of his poems (nos. 171–86; also, he is described in no. 400, Francesco Arsilli's *De poetis urbanis*, lines 313–26). Dardano's poem commemorating Giason del Maino appears in Giovio's *Elogia*, no. LXVI (*IO* 8:92; *Elogi*, 194). See also Jean Michael Massing, *Erasmian Wit and Proverbial Wisdom: An Illustrated Moral Compendium for François I* (London: The Warburg Institute, University of London, 1995), 19–21, 81–84.

67. Francesco Carpesani (1451–1528) of Parma, where he became a canon of the cathedral. His writings include *Commentaria suorum temporum* (*1476–1527*), ed. Giacomo Zarotti (Parma: Deputazione di Storia Patria per le Province Parmensi, 1975), with a detailed introduction.

68. Bartolomeo Crotti (or, "Croto") (d. 1541) from Reggio Emilia. A longtime adherent of the Farnese family, he would eventually be appointed master of the Papal Chapel (1535–1540) by Pope Paul III. His writings include *Epigrammatum elegiarumque libellus* (Reggio Emilia: Ruggeri, 1500). Giovio's *Elogia* includes a poem Crotti wrote in memory of Berardino Rota (Rutilius): Eulogium XCVI (*IO* 8:119; *Elogi*, 282). See *Biblioteca modenese*, 2:197–202; Ubaldini, 115; José María Llorens Cisteró, "Los maestros de la Capilla Apostólica hasta el pontificado de Sixto V (1585–1590)," *Anuario musical* 43 (1988): 35–65, at 6–11.

69. Riccardo Bartolini (ca. 1475–ca. 1529), from Perugia, who served as a chaplain to Cardinal Matthäus Lang for five years (1514–19) and then held the chair in rhetoric at the University of Perugia (1520–26). His twelve-book epic, *Ad divum Maximilianum . . . de bello Norico Austriados* (1516) celebrates Maximilian's role in the Bavarian Succession War (1504–5). See *CE* 1:97–98; *DBI* 6:625–27.

70. Mariangelo Accursio (ca. 1489–1546), from Aquila, was a philologist, epigrapher, and antiquarian. At least by late 1513 he was in Rome. Amid a decade in the service of princes of the Hohenzollern family, he spent

four years in the court of Charles V in Spain (1525–29). See CE 1:4–5; *DBI* 1:126–32; *Coryciana*.

71. Accursio, *Diatribae in Ausonium Solinum et Ovidium* (Rome: Silber, 1524).

72. Accursio, *Osci et volsci dialogus ludis Romanis actus* ([Rome: Beplin, 1515?]), which he dedicated to the humanist Tommaso Pighinuzzi (Pietrasanta). Composed soon after the accession of Leo X to the papacy in 1513, its targets are Giambattista Pio and his followers. See CE 1:4.

73. Andrea Navagero (1483–1529), a Venetian patrician, studied initially under Marcantonio Sabellico. In 1508 he joined the retinue of the Venetian general Bartolomeo d'Alviano, whose defeat at Agnadello he witnessed. Navagero succeeded Sabellico as Venice's official historian and as librarian of the Marciana. Although he published little, he took part in editing the Aldine Lucretius, Ovid, and Vergil. From 1523 to 1529, he served Venice as an ambassador to Spain and then to France. See CE 1:8–9 (which errs in dating his death to 1527).

74. The poet L. Arruntius Stella, known for the love elegies he wrote for his future wife Violentilla. His friend Statius dedicated Book 1 of the *Silvae* to him, and its second poem (1.2) is an epithalamium for the nuptials of Stella and Violentilla. Martial also mentions Stella (6.21). See Statius, *Silvae*, ed. and trans. D. R. Shackleton Bailey (Cambridge, MA: Harvard University Press, 2003), 24.

75. The poet C. Licinius Calvus, a close friend of Catullus. See Erich S. Gruen, "Cicero and Licinius Calvus," *Harvard Studies in Classical Philology* 71 (1967): 215–33, with further bibliography.

76. C. Pedo Albinovanus, a contemporary and friend of Ovid, wrote both epic verse and epigrams. See Smith, 1:90.

77. Domitius Marsus was a Roman poet of the Augustan age whom Martial admired for the licentiousness and satirical edge of his epigrams. Smith, 2:962.

78. On "Goritz's statues" and poetry contests, see Julia Haig Gaisser, "The Rise and Fall of Goritz's Feasts," *Renaissance Quarterly* 48 (1995): 41–57, with further bibliography.

79. Francesco Arsilli of Senigallia (ca. 1472–soon after 1540) knew Giovio in the Rome of Leo X. His *De poetis urbanis libellus*, dedicated to Giovio, appeared in print in 1524 as an appendix to the *Coryciana* (see above, n. 52). See *Coryciana*, 344–64; *DBI* 4:342–43.

80. Bembo's *Prose della volgar lingua* (see n. 8 above) was a major intervention in the so-called *Questione della lingua*.

81. The thought appears to be incomplete.

82. Ermolao Barbaro (1454–93) of Venice studied as a youth under Pomponio Leto and Theodorus Gaza in Rome. Among his best-known works is the *Castigationes plinianae* (1492/93). See *DLI*, 265–66; *CE* 1:91–92.

83. "Merula" is Giorgio Merlani (1430/31–1494) of Alessandria. A student of Francesco Filelfo in the early 1440s, he went on to play an active role in philological debates of the later fifteenth century. See Giovio's eulogium of him in *IO* 8:68–69; *Elogi*, 113–14.

84. On Poliziano, see n. 10 above.

85. Girolamo Aleandro (1480–1542) of Motta (near Treviso) is best known as a papal nuncio who was a staunch opponent of Luther. Over the decades Aleandro had a fraught and at times vitriolic relationship with Erasmus. He had left Rome in March of 1527, initially for Brindisi. See *CE* 1:28–32.

86. Bernardo Accolti (1458–1535) of Arezzo was known for his quick wit and verse improvisations. Active in the courts of Naples, Rome, and Mantua, he is most identified with Urbino thanks to Castiglione, who gave his name to an interlocutor in *Il libro del Cortegiano*. He wrote extensive lyric poetry and also a comedy, *Virginia* (1494). See *DBI* 1:103–4.

87. Ludovico Ariosto (1474–1533) of Ferrara. When it first appeared in print in 1516, the *Orlando Furioso* was forty cantos long. So, too, was the second, revised edition of 1521. Giovio evidently alludes to work on what would be the third and definitive edition, comprising forty-six cantos, which appeared only in 1532. See *ER* 1:97–103.

88. Girolamo Benivieni (1453–1542) of Florence was learned in Greek, Hebrew, and Latin, and in the Tuscan writings of Dante and Petrarch. He became a close friend of Giovanni Pico della Mirandola, whose interest in Platonism he shared. Like Pico, Benivieni became a devoted follower of Girolamo Savonarola. His *Opere* (Florence: Giunti, 1519) includes both early love poetry and later religious works, including *laudi*, ten *stanze in passione Domini*, and vernacular translations of Psalms 65, 73, and 94. See *DBI* 8:550–55; Balsamo, 1:118–21.

89. Pico wrote the *Commento* on Benivieni's *Canzone d'amore celeste e divino*, which was a synopsis in verse of Marsilio Ficino's commentary on Plato's *Symposium*. Many years later, when preparing materials for a new edition of his complete works, Benivieni decided to reproduce the original poem, now juxtaposed with a rewritten, thoroughly Christian version of it, so as to enable the reader "to distinguish the gold of Christian love / from the alchemy of Platonic love." See the introduction to Giovanni Pico della Mirandola, *Commentary on a Canzone of Benivieni*, trans. Sears Jayne (New York: Peter Lang, 1984), especially 15–20 (quotation at 16). See also Balsamo, 1:118–21; Donald Weinstein, *Savonarola and Florence: Prophecy and Patriotism in the Renaissance* (Princeton: Princeton University Press, 1970), 205–8, 216–20.

90. Niccolò Amanio (1468/69–ca. 1528) of Crema became a citizen of Cremona in 1520 and served as *podestà* of Milan in 1524. His poems were widely anthologized. See *DBI* 2:632–33.

91. Amanio's distinguished target, here unnamed, was most likely Clement VII. See Minonzio, 2:591–92.

92. Girolamo Verità (ca. 1465–1552) of Verona was a pupil of Guarino Guarini. His friends included Lodovico Ariosto, Pietro Aretino, Gian Giorgio Trissino, and Mario Equicola. See Lamberto Carlini, ed., *Girolamo Verità, filosofo e poeta veronese del secolo XVI* (Verona: Franchini, 1905), which details Verità's political service to Verona and edits ninety-six of his poems.

93. Girolamo Cittadini, who wrote vernacular poetry, was in contact with the court of the Gonzaga in Mantua at least by 1514. From 1524 to

1527, he was in Venice, representing Gonzaga interests there. See Massimo Danzi, "Girolamo Cittadini poeta milanese di primo Cinquecento," in *Veronica Gambara e la poesia del suo tempo nell'Italia settentrionale: atti del convegno (Brescia–Correggio, 17–19 ottobre 1985)*, ed. Cesare Bozzetti et al. (Florence: Olschki, 1989), 293–322, with an appendix (316–22) editing nine of Cittadini's poems.

94. Niccolò Tiepolo (d. 1551), a Venetian patrician, was a friend of Vincenzo Querini, Gasparo Contarini, and Giambattista Cipelli (called "Egnazio"). Along with Contarini, Tiepolo was for a while a follower of the ascetic religious reformer Tommaso Giustiniani. He served with distinction as Venice's ambassador, including an extended stay at the imperial court starting at least by the time of Charles V's coronation in Bologna (1530). See Setton, 3:338n, 347, 358, 360n; Elisabeth G. Gleason, *Gasparo Contarini: Venice, Rome, and Reform* (Berkeley: University of California Press, 1993), 9, 20–21, 27.

95. Niccolò Delfino (late fifteenth century–1528), or Dolfin, was a friend of Bembo and of Trifone Gabriele. See Minonzio, 2:593–94. Some of his poems appear in *Rime del Brocardo et d'altri authori*, ed. Francesco Amadi (Venice: n.p., 1538).

96. Giovanni Francesco Valerio, the illegitimate son of a Venetian nobleman, was a friend of Isabella d'Este, Bembo, Ariosto, and of Castiglione, who originally used his name for an interlocutor in Book 2 of *Il cortegiano*. See Ady, 1:272, 354; 2:369.

97. Gian Giorgio Trissino (1478–1550) of Vicenza studied Greek in Milan (ca. 1507–8) under Demetrius Chalcondyles. After spending time in Venice and Florence, in 1514 he moved to Rome, where he served as a diplomat for Popes Leo X, Clement VII, and Paul III. Trissino is noted for his efforts to reform the vernacular by blending Italian dialects into a shared "courtly" language, and especially for his proposal that letters from the Greek alphabet be introduced into Italian. The *Sofonisba*, written in 1514–15, was published in 1524. See ER 6:171–72: DELI 5:335–37.

98. Alessandro de' Pazzi of Florence translated *Iphigenia* from Greek into Latin and into Tuscan verse. His Latin rendition of Aristotle's *Poetics*,

completed in 1524, was dedicated in 1527 to Niccolò Leonico Tomeo and published posthumously (1536). He also wrote tragedies and poetry of his own. In his eulogium of Alessandro's brother, Cosimo de' Pazzi (no. CXLVI), Giovio acknowledges the quality of Alessandro's translation of the *Poetics* but writes harshly of his dramatic compositions: ". . . the Tuscan actors, who thought that at all costs they must avoid the hisses of the populace as a deadly peril, would have none of his poems, because they were written in imitation of the Greeks in verse a foot longer than that to which they were accustomed, a form novel and strange to our ears and pleasing to no one except the Grecophiles, because it was considered abnormal and awkward in measure and rhythm" (Gragg, 164). See *IO* 8:142; *Elogi*, 378–79; Negri, 22–23; and *Le tragedie metriche di Alessandro Pazzi de' Medici*, ed. Angelo Solerti (Bologna: Commissione per i Testi di Lingua, 1969).

99. According to Beatrice Corrigan, Trissino's *Sofonisba* "is considered the first regular tragedy observing classical rules written in the vernacular in Europe, and its extensive use of blank verse, an innovation followed by Rucellai, established that meter as the accepted form for Italian tragedy." See *Two Renaissance Plays. Ariosto, Il Negromante. Trissino, Sofonisba*, ed. Beatrice Corrigan (Manchester: Manchester University Press, 1975), 10.

100. Palamedes, a mythological Greek hero of the Trojan War, was credited with having invented the alphabet.

101. In his *Epistola de le lettere nuovamente aggiunte ne la lingua italiana* (Letter Concerning the New Letters Added to the Italian language; 1524), which he addressed to Pope Clement VII, Trissino proposed expanding the Italian alphabet to include Greek letters, various consonants and vowels, for sounds unaccounted for in the Roman alphabet. See *ER* 6:171–72.

102. Evidently Giovio was unaware that Machiavelli had already died (June 21, 1527).

103. Giovio refers to it as the *Nicia*. Whereas Machiavelli modeled several plays on writings of Plautus and Terence, the *Mandragola* evidently draws upon Livy and Boccaccio (especially *Decameron* 2.9 and 7.7). See *ER* 4:9.

104. Giangiacomo (Giovanni Giacomo) Calandra of Mantua (1488–1543) spent his career in the Gonzaga court. He wrote in the vernacular a now-lost work entitled *Aura*. Another lost work, composed between 1507 and 1511, lauded Isabella d'Este. Calandra succeeded his father, Silvestro, as castellan for the Gonzaga. He also served as a secretary to the marquis Francesco II Gonzaga (d. 1519), his wife Isabella d'Este, and their son Federico II (d. 1540). A friend of Mario Equicola and of Nicolò d'Arco, he helped manage the Mantuan court's dealings with literati and with artists including Titian. See *DBI* 16:427–31; Ady, 2:21, 144, 148; Zimmermann, III, 128.

105. Bonaventura Pistofilo (d. 1535) of Ferrara served as Alfonso I d'Este's secretary for twenty-five years. His biography of Duke Alfonso was published only in the nineteenth century. See *CE* 3:95.

106. Pietro Barignano (late fifteenth century–1540/50) may have been from Pesaro rather than Brescia. In the early Cinquecento he was active in the courts of Pesaro and of Urbino, where he participated in debates on the *questione della lingua*. Some of his poems are included along with those of Veronica Gambara in *Rime di diversi eccellenti autori bresciani*, ed. Girolamo Ruscelli (Venice: Plinio Pietrasanta, 1554). See *DBI* 6:365–67.

107. Sasso de' Sassi of Modena, called "Pamphilus" (ca. 1455–1527). A friend of Giovanni Aurelio Augurelli (see above, n. 41), he published a collection, *Opera del preclarissimo poeta miser Panfilo Sasso modenese. Sonetti CCCCVII. Capituli XXXVIII. Egloge V* (Venice: de' Viani, 1511). See *Biblioteca modenese*, 5:22–34.

108. Marco Antonio de' Marsi, called the "Neapolitan Epicurus" (1472–1555). From Abruzzi, Marsi was active in Pontano's academy. Mentioned in Giovio's correspondence, he was known for his Latin and vernacular poetry and for his skill at devising *imprese*. His *Cecaria* (or *Dialogo delli tre ciechi*; ca. 1525) and *Mirtia* (or *Trebatia*; ca. 1535–40) are important in the history of pastoral drama. See Altamura, 180–83; *DBI* 43:19–22 (s.n. Epicuro, Marcantonio); Antonio Marsi, *I drammi pastorali di Antonio Marsi detto l'Epicuro napolitano*, ed. Italo Palmarini, 2 vols. (Bologna: Romagnoli–dall'Acqua, 1887–88).

109. Giovio mentions Baldassar Marchese in a letter of 1534–35 to the Neapolitan humanist Girolamo Scannapeco (*IO* 1:177–78): "Mi ricordo, in Ischia, che leggendo Sua Signoria [Muscettola] il Dialogo nostro, nel quale introduco esso proprio, che parla del Sanazzaro [*sic*], e parendogli che io mi fussi con giocondissime tirate assai diffuso in lodarlo, disse la signora Marchese di Pescara: — Non dite, signor Musetola, ch'el sia lodato assai, perché dice Baldassar Marchese ch'el non si contenterebbe di sì poco, quando vedrà tutto il Dialogo." See also Balsamo, 1:333–34.

110. The Cistercian monk Severo Varini (d. 1549), from Piacenza, was active in Goritz's academy in Rome. A language tutor of Cardinal Alfonso Petrucci, he managed to escape Rome in 1517 when the cardinal and others were arrested for suspected complicity in a conspiracy to assassinate Leo X. See *DLI*, 97 n. 19. For the identification of Varini with the "Severinus Antonius" of this dialogue, see Minonzio, 2:604.

111. Lucas Gavius has not been identified definitively. See Minonzio, 2:604–5.

112. Paolo Pansa served as secretary to the Ligurian patrician Sinibaldo Fieschi (d. 1532) and tutor to Fieschi's son Gianluigi, who would conspire unsuccessfully against the Doria family in 1547. Pansa wrote lives of the two popes who came from the Fieschi family (Innocent IV and Adrian V), as well as Latin and Italian verse that Ariosto praised. Giovio in his *Dialogo dell'imprese* describes Pansa as "dottissimo." See Emanuele Celesia, *The Conspiracy of Gianluigi Fieschi: or, Genoa in the Sixteenth Century*, trans. David H. Wheeler (London: Sampson Low, Son and Marston, 1866), 81–82; *IO* 9:399. Minonzio, 2:605, incorrectly identifies Pansa's employer as Ottobuono Fieschi.

113. On Ippolito Quinzio see Dialogue One, n. 337 above.

114. Claudio Tolomei (ca. 1492–ca. 1556) of Siena studied law in Bologna and then taught it in Siena (1516–18). In 1526, as a partisan of the Medici, he was exiled from Siena. Subsequently, he became a secretary to Cardinal Ippolito de' Medici and then entered the service of Pier Luigi Farnese. His writings include lyric poetry, two dialogues concerning orthographic reform of the vernacular (*Il Polito*, 1525; *Il Cesano*, 1555), and a tract on

how to imitate ancient meters in Italian verse, *Versi et regole de la nuova poesia toscana* (1539). In 1529, he delivered an oration urging Clement VII to establish peace between France and Spain. See *DELI* 5:288; Treccani; Tiraboschi 7,3:189–94.

115. Giulio Camillo (or, "Camillo Delminio") (ca. 1480–1544), from Friuli, studied at Venice and Padua. He wrote tracts on literary imitation but is best known for planning to construct a large theater of memory which would enable an orator to have mastery over all knowledge. Camillo's works, including *L'idea del teatro* and tracts on literary imitation, appeared only posthumously. See *CE* 1:248–50; *DBI* 17:218–30.

116. Leandro Signorelli da Perugia (1490–1530) won distinction both as a poet and as a military commander. He gained the favor of Leo X and of Adrian VI. See Giovanni Battista Vermiglioli, *Biografia degli scrittori perugini e notizie delle opere loro*, 2 vols. (Perugia: Vincenzo Bertelli and Giovanni Costantini, 1829), vol. 2, pt. 1: 290–92; Varchi, 2:149 (s.n. Leonardo Signorelli).

117. Sempronio Amaranti (d. 1539) of Spoleto became a doctor to Pope Clement VII. On May 20, 1528, by a *motu proprio* the pope made him chancellor and fiscal procurator of Spoleto. See Gaetano Marini, *Degli Archiatri pontifici*, suppl. and ed. Mandosio (Rome: Pagliarini, 1784), 1:344–46.

118. Gabriele Maria Cesano of Pisa (ca. 1490–1568) was an interlocutor in learned debates about the *questione della lingua*, and as such he is portrayed in Claudio Tolomei's *Il Cesano: De la lingua toscana* (1525; pub. 1555). After serving Clement VII on diplomatic missions, by 1529 he became attached to Ippolito de' Medici (who was elevated to the cardinalate that year; d. 1535), and by 1540 he had entered the service of Cardinal Ippolito d'Este. See *DBI* 24:129–32.

119. Trifone Gabriele (1470–1549), known to contemporaries as "The Venetian Socrates." He did not publish but significantly influenced other literati and theorists including Bembo, for whom he read drafts of works including the *Asolani* and the first two books of the *Prose della volgar lingua*. Independently wealthy, he had no need to be a secretary or to court

potential patrons. See Lino Pertile, "Trifone Gabriele's commentary on Dante and Bembo's *Prose della volgar lingua*," *Italian Studies* 40 (1985): 17–30, at 18–20; *DELI* 3:2; *DBI* 51:44–47 (s.n. Gabriel).

120. Girolamo Britonio (ca. 1491–1549), from Sicignano degli Alburni, near Salerno. Renowned as a musician and poet, he was active in the reformed academy in Naples following Pontano's death and spent time on Ischia in the service of Costanza d'Avalos the Elder and Vittoria Colonna. At some point during Leo X's pontificate he went to Rome where, as a participant in Colocci's sodality, he was ridiculed for his ineptitude at improvising. In the Battle of Pavia in 1525 he served under Pescara, the subject of the vernacular poem that Giovio here calls the *Davaliad*: i.e., the *Trionfo de lo Britonio nel quale Parthenope Sirena narra e canta gli gloriosi gesti del Gran Marchese di Pescara* (Naples: Evangelista di Presenzani, 1525). His final composition, *I canti e i Ragionamenti* (Venice, 1550), was dedicated to Costanza d'Avalos the Younger. See *DBI* 14:347–49; *DELI* 1:480; *Elogi*, 912 n.4; Balsamo, 1:162–63; and especially Gianni Ballistreri, "Due umanisti della Roma cocciana: il Britonio e il Borgia," in *Atti del Convegno di studi su Angelo Colocci, Jesi, 13–14 settembre 1969* (Jesi: Amministrazione Comunale di Jesi, 1972), 169–76.

121. Berardino Rota (1508–1575), a Neapolitan nobleman, was well known for his love sonnets. Recent collections of his poems include *Egloghe pescatorie*, ed. Stefano Bianchi (Rome: Carocci, 2005) and *Rime*, ed. Luca Milite (Parma: Guanda, 2000). See also Hallam, 2:88–89; and especially Toscano, 299–325.

122. "Epicuro" here is Marco Antonio de' Marsi (the "Neapolitan Epicurus"; see above, n. 108).

123. Dragonetto Bonifacio (ca. 1500–ca. 1526). See his *Rime*, ed. Raffaele Girardi (Fasano: Schena, 1996); and Erasmo Pèrcopo, "Dragonetto Bonifacio, marchese d'Oria, rimatore napolitano del sec. XVI," *GSLI* 10 (1887): 197–233; *DBI* 12:193–94.

124. Ludovico Martelli of Florence (b. 1500) did not, in fact, die before the dialogue's fictive date but instead probably in 1528. His *Risposta alla epistola del Trissino* (1524) defends the Florentine vernacular against the

orthographic and linguistic reforms proposed by Trissino. Martelli also wrote a *Trionfo della Pace*, addressed to Clement VII, and a verse account of the Battle of Capo d'Orso in 1528, *Stanze sopra la rotta marittima che ebbono gli Spagnuoli*. See Balsamo, 1:474–75; Negri, 363–64; and especially Minonzio, 2:610–12, 725–47.

125. Unidentified, but possibly the portico in the Piazzetta del Nilo where Pontano met with the members of his academy; see Notes to the Text, Dialogue Two, n. 79.

126. I.e., the contemplative and active lives; Giovio as a philosopher and doctor lives both kinds of life.

127. Jacopo Sadoleto (1477–1547) studied under Niccolò Leoniceno in Ferrara before going to Rome ca. 1499. He served as domestic secretary to Leo X and to Clement VII. In mid-April 1527, just weeks before the Sack of Rome, he left the city for his diocese in France, not returning to Rome until 1536. See CE 3:183–87; and Richard M. Douglas, *Jacopo Sadoleto, 1477–1547: Humanist and Reformer* (Cambridge, MA: Harvard University Press, 1959).

128. In August of 1524, Clement VII issued a bull that reined in the usurious practices of the Jewish moneylenders in Provence, but in 1525 a delegation to Rome obtained a reinstatement of their practices in exchange for their paying a new tax. See Douglas, *Jacopo Sadoleto*, 49. On Armellini's reputation for avarice, see n. 2 above.

129. On Navagero, see n. 73 above.

130. On Bartolomeo d'Alviano, see Dialogue One above. Leonardo Loredan (1436–1521) was doge of Venice, 1501–21. The two orations were printed in *Andreae Naugerii patricii Veneti Orationes duae, carminaque nonnulla* ([Venice]: Tacuino, 1530).

131. Marcantonio Coccio (ca. 1436–1506) studied in Rome under Pomponio Leto, in whose academy he took the name "Sabellicus." After teaching in Udine for a decade, in 1484 he went to Venice. In 1485 he obtained the post of second lecturer at the Scuola di San Marco, and he went on to be Venice's official historian. See DLI, 281–82; CE 3:181–82; DBI 26:510–13.

132. According to Martin Lowry, Navagero became Venice's official historian in 1516 (rather than immediately upon Sabellico's death in 1506, as some have supposed). See CE 1:8–9. He died without completing the history. In 1530, Pietro Bembo was named to succeed Navagero as historian of the Venetian Republic. See CE 1:121.

133. Paolo Emili (d. 1529) of Verona studied theology in Paris and by 1489 had become the official historian of the monarchy of France. Contemporaries called him the "French Livy." His ten-book magnum opus is the *De rebus gestis Francorum* (Paris: Vascosan, 1539). Daniele Zavarizzi of Verona finished the last of its books. See CE 1:429.

134. Polydore Vergil (ca. 1470–1555) of Urbino studied in Padua and then held church offices in England until 1553. His most famous work is *On discovery* (*De inventoribus rerum*, 1499); published in this I Tatti Library (2002, vol. 6), ed. and trans. Brian P. Copenhaver.

135. Polydore Vergil, *Anglicae historiae libri vigintiseptem* (Basel: Thomas Guarinus, 1570).

136. Giovanni Battista Sanga (1496–1532) served as secretary to Cardinal Bibbiena (Bernardo Dovizi; d. 1521) before becoming principal secretary to Gian Matteo Giberti. Active in Goritz's sodality, he contributed poems to the *Coryciana*. Francesco Berni made him an interlocutor in his *Dialogo contra i poeti* (1526), and he is discussed in Giraldi, 96–97. Later he would serve Pope Clement as an apostolic protonotary (1528–31). See Berni, 87–102; *DELI* 5:37.

137. Lorenzo Grana (ca. 1494–1539) of Rome was a canon of the Church of S. Giovanni in Laterano and became bishop of Segni in January of 1528. A participant in Goritz's academy, he appears as an interlocutor in Valeriano's *De litteratorum infelicitate*. See *DLI*, 61–62.

138. Copies survive of Grana's funeral orations for the prominent Roman humanist Celso Mellini (1519), Cardinal Egidio da Viterbo (1532), and Pope Clement VII (1534). See *DLI*, 61 n. 221.

139. Vicenzo Pimpinella (d. 1534) lectured on rhetoric at La Sapienza. He was elevated as archbishop of Rossano in July of 1525. See Eubel, 3:286; *DLI*, 235 n. 147.

140. Gian Maria del Monte (b. 1487), the future Pope Julius III (1550–55), was elevated as bishop of Siponto (Manfredonia) in March of 1513 and would be promoted to the cardinalate in December of 1536. Under Clement VII, del Monte twice served as governor of Rome. See J. N. D. Kelly, *The Oxford Dictionary of the Popes* (Oxford: Oxford University Press, 1986), 262–64.

141. Del Monte was among the ten hostages given over to the imperialists by an agreement of June 5, 1527, to serve as surety for Clement VII's adherence to the terms of that agreement (Gian Matteo Giberti, the initial dedicatee of the present dialogue, was another). See Pastor, 9:421–22.

142. Tommaso "Fedra" Inghirami (1470–1516) of Volterra, renowned for his oratorical skill, studied under Pomponio Leto in Rome. He gained his nickname from his success in the title role of Seneca's *Phaedra*, produced by Pomponio and members of his academy in 1486, and subsequently he was active in Goritz's sodality. In 1514 he succeeded Pomponio as professor of rhetoric at the University of Rome. See *DLI*, 297–98; CE 2:223–25.

143. Camillo Porcari (d. by November 1521) taught at La Sapienza under Julius II and Leo X. A skilled orator, he collaborated with his mentor and friend Inghirami in producing the festivities for the bestowal of Roman citizenship upon Giuliano de' Medici in 1513. In 1519 he delivered the funeral oration for Lorenzo de' Medici, duke of Urbino. A member of Goritz's sodality, he contributed poems to the *Coryciana*. See *DLI*, 319–20; *Coryciana*.

144. Gottifredi remains obscure. References to him in Gnoli and in Ubaldini (42 n. 50) are drawn from the present passage. *Iter* notes a Giovanni Battista Gottifredi and a Giuseppe Gottifredi. Amayden, 1:428–30, offers a disordered genealogy of the Gottifredi family that his editor, Bertini, clarifies at 429 n. 2. Giovio's "Gottifredus" may be the Giacomo Gottifredi who was a *cameriere segreto* of Leo X.

145. Giulio Pomponio Leto (1428–98) is one of the most influential figures in the intellectual culture of Renaissance Rome. Soon after he began teaching at the University of Rome (ca. 1465), he founded the Roman

academy, an informal gathering of scholars interested in antiquities, the classics, and more generally the revival of ancient Roman culture. In 1468 he and others in his academy were imprisoned by Pope Paul II on charges of conspiracy, paganism, and sexual immorality. He returned to teaching in 1570, and in 1578, under Sixtus IV (pope, 1471–84), revived the academy, now as a religious sodality. See *DLI*, 318–19; *Repertorium*; *ER* 3:415–16.

146. Quintus Roscius Gallus (d. 62 BCE).

147. Ermolao Barbaro (1454–93). See n. 82 above.

148. Themistius, *Paraphrasis in Aristotelem*, trans. Ermolao Barbaro (Treviso: Bartolomeo della Fonte and Morellus Gerardinus, 1481).

149. I.e., Blosio Palladio (see n. 44 above).

150. On these festivities see Anthony M. Cummings, *The Politicized Muse: Music for Medici Festivals, 1512–1537* (Princeton: Princeton University Press, 1992), 53–66 (chap. 4: "Giuliano de' Medici's Capitoline Investiture").

151. The word *cynocephalus* (referring to the Egyptian baboon) invokes current debates over imitation, in which slavish (and often incompetent) imitators of ancient models were derided as mere "apes." On "apish" imitation in the Renaissance, see Kenneth Gouwens, "Erasmus, 'Apes of Cicero,' and Conceptual Blending," *The Journal of the History of Ideas* 71 (2010): 523–45.

152. Nikolaus von Schönberg became archbishop of Capua in 1520 and was created cardinal in 1535. He was one of Clement VII's chief advisors and, in contrast to Giberti, he favored the papacy's allying with Emperor Charles V. See Eubel, 3:23, 151. Hook, s.n. Schomberg; Pastor, 9: passim.

153. Federigo Fregoso (ca. 1480–1541) of Genoa. Upon the death of his father, Agostino, in 1487, he moved to the court of his maternal grandfather, Duke Federico da Montefeltro, in Urbino, where he became acquainted with Bembo and Castiglione. While in religious orders (he became archbishop of Salerno in 1507 and a cardinal in 1539), he was active in politics. Exiled from Genoa in 1510, he returned in 1513 when his brother Ottaviano became doge and appointed him commander of the army, but was forced out again when Charles V's troops took the city in

1522. Federigo appears as an interlocutor in Bembo's *Prose della volgar lingua*. See *DBI* 50:396–99.

154. Agostino Giustiniani (ca. 1470–1536), a Dominican from Genoa, became bishop of Nebbio (on Corsica) in 1514 thanks to the support of his kinsman Cardinal Bendinello Sauli. His *Psalterium octuplex* (1516) presented the Psalms in parallel in the Hebrew, Septuagint, Aramaic Targum, and Arabic, along with Latin translations of the first three. His subsequent publications included editions of Hebrew grammars and a translation into Latin of Maimonides' *Guide of the Perplexed* (1520). See *CE* 2:102–3; *DBI* 57:301–6; Hyde, 95–99. For Giovio's brief eulogium (no. CXXX) of Giustiniani, see Gragg, 156–57; *IO* 8:136; *Elogi*, 355–56.

155. Paul of Middelburg (1446–1534) became physician to Francesco Maria della Rovere, duke of Urbino, upon whose advice Pope Alexander VI made Paul bishop of Fossombrone in 1494. A student of astronomy, he advocated reform of the calendar. See Eubel, 2:156, 3:198 and n.; *Cath Ency.*

156. Pietro Bonomo (1458–1546) became bishop of Trieste in 1502. From 1496 to 1500 he had served as Emperor Maximilian's emissary at the court of Ludovico Sforza. He served as chancellor of Austria, 1521–23. See *CE* 1:169–70; *DBI* 12:341–46.

157. Gian Pietro Carafa (1476–1559) would be elevated to the cardinalate (1536) and then become Pope Paul IV in 1555. He was made bishop of Chieti (1505) and Brindisi (1518), but resigned both offices in 1524 and became a Theatine. See Eubel, 3:141–42, 311; *CE* 3:56–57 (s.n. Paul IV).

158. Filippo Sauli (ca. 1492–1528), created bishop of Brugnato (in Liguria) in 1512, developed a reputation for high moral character and for his efforts at reform of the Church. He translated from Greek into Latin some writings on the Psalms by the early twelfth-century Byzantine theologian Euthymius Zigabenus: *Euthymii monachi Zigaboni commentationes in omnes psalmos* (Verona: Nicolini, 1530). Sauli's library included over three hundred Greek manuscripts. See Hyde, 59–67.

159. Giambattista Cipelli, called "Egnazio." Born in Crema, he is said to have become a cleric in his adolescence, but despite repeated assertions that he would join the monastic order of Camaldoli, he never did so, in-

stead remaining a teacher in Venice. In 1520 the Venetian government appointed him to a public lectureship in Latin. See *CE* 1:424–25; *DBI* 25:698–702.

160. See Hoven, s.v. *coronis*.

161. Egnazio (i.e., Cipelli) published this work on the emperors in 1516. See, e.g., the edition in the Library of Congress, *Caesarum vitae post Suetonium Tranquillum conscriptae* (Lyons: Gryphius, 1551).

162. His *Racemationes* was published in 1502.

163. Gregorio Cortese (ca. 1480/83–1548), of Modena, studied at Padua and Bologna. After 1500, he became a secretary to Cardinal Giovanni de' Medici (the future Leo X) but left that post to enter the Benedictine monastery of Polirone near Mantua. In 1515 he was appointed prior of the island monastery of Lerins. In 1526 he became an abbot, and in 1542 would be raised to the cardinalate by Paul III. A copy of his Latin translation of Gregory of Nazianzus' *Oratio de pauperibus diligendis* survives in the Biblioteca Nazionale di Firenze, Carte Rinuccini, filza 8. See *DBI* 29:733–40.

164. The reference is to Lilio Gregorio Giraldi. Originally from Ferrara, he taught in Modena before going to Rome around 1514. The work is his *Libellus quomodo quis ingrati nomen et crimen effugere possit* (Florence: Lorenzo Torrentino, 1547) and/or the *Liber adversus ingratos in quo multiplices ingrati criminis radices convellentur, variisque tum historiis tum naturae exemplis ingrati refelluntur* (Florence: Lorenzo Torrentino, 1548), both written around 1521. See *DBI* 56:452–55; and especially the introduction to Giraldi, *Modern Poets*, ed. and trans. John N. Grant, for this I Tatti Library (2011, vol. 48).

165. Girolamo Negri of Venice (d. 1557) studied in Padua and held a benefice there. He went to Rome during the pontificate of Julius II. From 1529 to 1533 he served as secretary to Cardinal Francesco Cornaro of Venice, and from 1538 to 1541 he was Cardinal Gasparo Contarini's vicar in the diocese of Belluno. A number of his letters from Rome to his friend Marcantonio Michiel in Venice are preserved in *Lettere di Principi*, 3 vols. (Venice: Ziletti, 1581). See Douglas, *Jacopo Sadoleto*, 250 n. 4, with further bibliography.

166. Achille Bocchi (1488–1562) of Bologna studied with Giambattista Pio and went on to teach at the University of Bologna. On commission from the Bolognese senate, he wrote the city's history to the year 1263. See *DBI* 11:67–70; *CE* 1:157–58.

167. Domenico Nani Mirabelli, *Polyanthea* . . . (Venice: [P. Liechtenstein], 1507); Albrecht von Eyb, *Margarita poetarum* ([Venice: Vercelli, 1493]); and Pietro Martire Vermigli, *De rebus oceanicis et novo orbe, decades tres* (Basel: Joannes Bebelius, 1533), of which several decades had been published by the time at which the present dialogue is set.

168. M. Petreius Cassiatus remains to be identified. See the suggestions in Minonzio, 2:630–31.

169. I.e., choler.

170. *Phaedrus* 275a–b.

171. Benedetto Giovio (1471–1545), elder brother of Paolo, practiced law in Como. Learned in Greek and Latin, he wrote a history of Como to 1532 as well as poetry and antiquarian studies. See Zimmermann, passim, with further bibliography at 291 n. 7.

172. In 1515 Leo X praised Book 8 of the manuscript of the *Histories* (these comprise Books 13–14 of the ultimate version of the text). Zimmermann, 15, 300 n. 34.

173. Giulio de' Medici (1478–1534), created cardinal in 1513 and elevated as Pope Clement VII in 1523. Giovio gained his patronage in 1517.

174. *Sic.*

175. Luis Fernández de Córdoba, duke of Sessa. On this invitation see Zimmermann, 65.

176. *De piscibus* (1524).

177. Felice Trofino (d. 1527) became archbishop of Chieti in August of 1524, following Carafa's resignation. See Eubel, 3:311; Zimmermann, 17, 65, 222.

178. Francesco Chieregati (1479–1539) of Vicenza became bishop of Teramo in September of 1522 and served Adrian VI as papal nuncio to the Diet of Nuremberg. He saw to it that Calvo published Giovio's *Libel-*

lus de legatione Basilii magni principis Moschoviae (Rome, 1525), based upon
Giovio's conversations with Dimitri Gerasimov, the grand duke of Mos-
cow's ambassador to Rome during that Jubilee year. See CE 1:301; Eubel,
3:112; Zimmermann, 65–66. Giovanni Ruffo de Theodoli (d. 1527), mentioned here, had become archbishop of Cosenza in 1511. See Eubel, 3:183.

179. Girolamo Massaini (ca. 1460–after September 8, 1528) from Poppi,
was educated in the Florentine Studio. In 1505 Julius II appointed him an
apostolic notary in the Curia, and by 1512 he was a protonotary. While in
Rome he took part in Goritz's sodality. Captured in the Sack of Rome,
Massaini eventually escaped to Venice but died soon thereafter. Evidently
his only original publication is the dedicatory letter, addressed to Roberto Pucci, for an edition of Leon Battista Alberti's writings, *Opera*
([Florence: Bartolomeo de' Libri, 1499]). See Nelson H. Minnich, "Girolamo Massaino: Another Conciliarist at the Papal Court, Julius II to
Adrian VI," in *Studies in Catholic History in Honor of John Tracy Ellis*, ed.
Minnich et al. (Wilmington, DE: Glazier, 1985), 520–65; Luca D'Ascia
and Stefano Simoncini, "Momo a Roma: Girolamo Massaini fra l'Alberti
ed Erasmo," *Albertiana* 3 (2000): 83–103; DLI, 194–96, 308.

180. The unpublished work to which Giovio here refers is Massaini's
De conciliis. Written in 1512 at the request of Cardinal Niccolò Fieschi,
the tract's harsh criticism of theologians and churchmen and of the
papacy's claims to *imperium* so offended Fieschi that Massaini believed
himself in mortal danger. Although he thought it prudent not to publish
the *De conciliis*, he continued to revise and expand it, all the while hiding
his reformist convictions under a mask of dissimulation. In 1523 Massaini
presented it to Adrian VI who, however, died later that year, and the
work was never published. See D'Ascia and Simoncini, "Momo a Roma,"
88–94; Minnich, "Girolamo Massaino." On the state of the manuscripts,
see ibid., 521–23, n. 2.

181. Lattanzio Tolomei (1487–1543) of Siena was, at least by the late
1530s, a friend and correspondent of Gasparo Contarini. Francisco de
Holanda made him an interlocutor, along with Vittoria Colonna, Mi-
chelangelo, and Holanda himself, in his *Quatro diálogos da pintura antigua*
(Oporto: Joaquim de Vasconcellos, 1896), set in Rome in 1538/39. See
Gleason, 261–62.

182. Romolo Quirino Amaseo (1489–1552), from Udine, moved in 1509 to Bologna, where his friends included Achille Bocchi and Giambattista Pio. He spent most of his career at the University of Bologna, where he lectured in Latin and Greek (1513–20 and 1524–44). He published translations of Xenophon's *Anabasis* (Bologna: Jo. Baptista Phaellus, 1533) and Pausanias' *Graeciae descriptio* (Florence: Lorenzo Torrentino, 1551). His son Pompilio edited his orations for publication: *Orationum volumen* (Bologna: Joannes Rubreus, 1564). See *CE* 1:39; *DBI* 2:660–66.

183. Benedetto Tagliacarne (1480–1536) was born at Sarzana, near La Spezia. He became tutor to Francis I's sons in 1524, went to Spain with them when they became hostages in 1526, and remained there until their release in 1530. See *CE* 3:305–6. In February 1535, in a letter to Rodolfo Pio da Carpi, Giovio would make reference to his praise of Tagliacarne in the *Dialogus*: "Al dotto Teocreno [i.e., Tagliacarne] raccomandate il nome mio, com'io ho raccomandato il suo alli immortali discorsi delle Muse nel mio Dialogo." *IO* 1:143.

184. Lazzaro Bonamico of Bassano, in Friuli (1477/78–1532). By 1499 Bonamico was attending the University of Padua, where he studied Latin, Greek, and philosophy under Giovanni Calfurnio, Marcus Musurus, and Pietro Pomponazzi, respectively. From 1510 to 1527 he taught privately in Mantua, Bologna, Genoa, and then Rome, where he cultivated friendships with Angelo Colocci and Jacopo Sadoleto. He left Rome shortly before the city was sacked, and from at least 1530 until his death he taught at the University of Padua. His few publications, comprising poems, letters, and a tract in Italian on the Latin language, appeared in print only posthumously. *CE* 1:166; *DBI* 11:533–40.

185. Girolamo Borgia (1475–ca. 1550), from Lucania, participated in the Neapolitan academy of Pontano, whose close friend he became. Upon Pontano's death in 1503, he became attached to the *condottiere* Bartolomeo d'Alviano, whom he followed to Venice in 1507. After d'Alviano died in the siege of Brescia (1515), Borgia went to Rome, where he enjoyed Farnese patronage. His as yet unpublished *Historiae de bellis Italicis ab anno 1494 ad 1541* is one of the sources that Francesco Guicciardini consulted for his *Storia d'Italia*. A manuscript copy survives in the Biblioteca Marciana in Venice, Marc. Lat. X 98 (formerly XXII 162 [coll.

3506])). Ultimately Borgia returned to Naples, where he was in the service of the imperial viceroy don Pedro da Toledo. He wrote lyric and heroic verse that was published within his lifetime. See Ballistreri, "Due umanisti," 173–76; *DELI* 1:442; *DBI* 12:721–24.

186. The father is Lorenzo Campeggio (1474–1539), created cardinal in 1517, who had been bishop of Bologna 1523–25. Alessandro Campeggio became bishop of Bologna in March of 1526. See Eubel.

187. Ranuccio Farnese (1509–29), the son of Cardinal Alessandro Farnese (the future Paul III) and Silvia Ruffini.

188. Celio Calcagnini (1479–1541) of Ferrara taught Greek and Latin at the university there. His published compositions include dialogues, poems, and numerous letters. See *CE* 1:242–43; *RLV*, 203–6; *DBI* 16:492–98.

189. Francesco Conterni of Verona was a teacher of Francesco III Gonzaga. *Iter* lists letters he wrote to Paolo Manuzio, Benedettus Rhambertus, and evidently to Barth. Paiellus. A collection of his poems, with a preface to Cardinal Niccolò Ridolfi, is preserved in the Biblioteca Marciana of Venice, MS Marc. Lat. XII 113 (coll. 4444).

190. This is probably Girolamo Fondulo, or Fundulus, of Cremona, documented 1518–40. Fundulus studied Greek under Marcus Musurus. By 1520 he was in Paris as a client of Louise of Savoy, subsequently becoming a royal secretary for Francis I. See *CE* 2:42.

191. Gian Pietro Grassi (d. 1538) of Bologna, a familiar of Cardinal Niccolò Ridolfi, would become bishop of Viterbo in 1533. He was noted for his learning in the classics and in mathematics. Perhaps because of the latter skill, Pinzi suggests, "Clemente VII lo volle presente quando il celebre Vindmostadio nel 1533 venne in Roma a spiegargli il sistema di Copernico." C. Pinzi, "Il castello e la villa di Bagnaia, già signoria dei vescovi viterbesi," *Bollettino storico-archeologico viterbese* 1 (1908): 89–112, at 98 n. 21.

192. Christophe de Longueil (1488–1522), known as Longolius, from Mechelen, had by 1516 settled in Rome, where he gained a reputation as a leading advocate of a strict Ciceronianism. Two other outstanding Ciceronian stylists — the papal secretaries Pietro Bembo and Jacopo Sado-

leto—championed Longueil, who rose rapidly in the clerical bureaucracy and participated in Goritz's academy. His enemies in Rome, including Angelo Colocci, Lorenzo Grana, and Tommaso Pighinuzzi, made known that years earlier Longueil had delivered an oration (pub. 1512) celebrating the Franks as the true heirs of classical Roman culture. In 1519, after Longueil had been approved for the honor of Roman citizenship, Celso Mellini pressed a charge of treason against him, but after Longueil submitted (*in absentia*) orations in his defense, the city council found in his favor. That same year Longueil moved to Reginald Pole's household in Padua, where he died three years later. His publications included letters, orations, and an attack on the followers of Luther (1520). Erasmus lamented that the Ciceronianism of the last of these hampered its effectiveness in defending the faith. Giovio would commemorate Longueil in Eulogium no. LXVII. See Gragg, 100–101; *IO* 8:92–93; *Elogi*, 195–97; *DLI*, 302–3; *CE* 2:342–44.

193. Rudolf Agricola (1444–85), born near Groningen, studied at Erfurt, Cologne, and Louvain. He spent 1468–79 living in Italy (Pavia and Ferrara). His chief work is the *Dialectica: seu de inventione dialectica libri tres* (Louvain: Martinus, 1515). In his eulogium of Agricola (no. XXXII), Giovio expressed wonder at the rapidity with which Agricola mastered Hebrew, Greek, and Latin, and he mourned his having died young. See *IO* 8:64–65; *Elogi*, 98–99; Gragg, 62–63; *ER* 1:17–20; *CE* 1:15–16.

194. For this view of eclectic imitation, see Poliziano's letter to Paolo Cortesi, in *Ciceronian Controversies*, ed. JoAnn DellaNeva and trans. Brian Duvick, in this I Tatti Library (2007, vol. 26), 2–5, and Gianfrancesco Pico's letters to Pietro Bembo in ibid., 16–43 and 91–125.

195. An allusion to the *lupa* that suckled Romulus and Remus.

196. The artists Dosso Dossi (ca. 1490–1542) and Battista Dossi (ca. 1490–1548).

197. Pietro Alcionio (1490s?–1528) studied Greek in Venice under Marcus Musurus, then taught in Florence before going on to limited success in Rome. Giovio's Eulogium no. CXXIII ridicules Alcionio's breeding, manners, and academic dishonesty. With reference to his *Medices legatus: de exsilio* (Venice: Aldus and Andrea Asulanus, 1522), Giovio wrote that

"in a brilliant work on *Enduring the Misfortune of Exile* he so vindicated his reputation for learning and eloquence that many supposed he had concocted it from Cicero's treatise on *Glory*, which he had then impiously and spitefully destroyed. For they observed that in it, as in a varied patchwork, were interwoven brilliant threads of rich purple, while all the other colors were dim." Gragg, 152–53; *IO* 8:133; *Elogi* 340–43. See also *DLI*, 262–63; Kenneth Gouwens and Christopher S. Celenza, "Humanist Culture and Its Malcontents: Alcionio and Sepúlveda on the Consequences of Translating Aristotle," in Celenza and Gouwens, eds., *Humanism and Creativity in the Italian Renaissance: Essays in Honor of Ronald G. Witt* (Leiden: Brill, 2006), 347–80, at 347–51.

198. Juan Ginés de Sepúlveda (ca. 1490–1573), from humble origins in a town near Córdoba, studied at the University of Alcalá (1510–13) and at Bologna (1515–23), where he worked with Pietro Pomponazzi. In the 1520s his patrons included Alberto Pio, prince of Carpi, and Giulio de' Medici (both as a cardinal and then as Pope Clement VII). In 1536 he became official chronicler and chaplain to Emperor Charles V. He is best known today neither for his histories nor for his extensive translations of Aristotle into Latin, but instead for his defense of the Spaniards' enslavement of the Indians of the New World, a position he justified on Aristotelian grounds in his *Democrates alter seu de justis belli causis.* See *CE* 3:240–42; Gouwens and Celenza, "Humanist Culture and Its Malcontents."

199. Alcionio's translations of Aristotle into Latin, including *De generatione et interitu* and ten books on animals (Venice: B. dei Vitali, 1521), were soon attacked in print by Sepúlveda (*Errata Petri Alcyonii in interpretatione Aristotelis* [Bologna: s.n., 1522]). On the conflict between Alcionio and Giovio, see Gouwens, 42–44. On the feud between Alcionio and Sepúlveda and the rumors of the former burning copies of the latter's *Errata,* see Gouwens and Celenza, "Humanist Culture and Its Malcontents."

200. Giovan Battista (or, Giambattista) Pio (1460–ca. 1540) of Bologna studied under Filippo Beroaldo and taught in several cities before Paul III appointed him to the University of Rome in 1534. The description here anticipates Giovio's eulogium (no. CII) of Pio (s.n. Baptista Pius) as priding himself on his obscure diction: "He misguidedly sought out

musty and obsolete old words to the admiration of the ignorant mob of his pupils but the open derision of men with any taste. Indeed the strangeness of his speech and writing recalled in its crudity and harshness the dialects of Oscans and Aborigines, which some might desire to learn for sport if they were not afraid of catching the infection. . . ." Gragg, 140–41, at 140; IO 8:123–24; Elogi, 297–300.

201. Catullus 66.39: "Invita, o regina, tuo de vertice cessi." See also Vergil, Aeneid 6.460.

202. Guillaume Budé (ca. 1467–1540) of Paris studied law and in 1497 became secretary to King Louis XII, a position he held until the king's death in 1515. Budé applied humanist philological methods to his study of Justinian's Digest, and in so doing contributed to the development of textual criticism. He corresponded frequently with Thomas More and with Erasmus. CE 1:212–17; ER 1:313–14.

203. Budé's De asse (1515; second ed., 1516) detailed the systems of coinage in antiquity and sought to establish the values of ancient currency. The treatise also included moral reflections on contemporary attitudes toward wealth, including on the part of the Church. See John M. Headley, "The Problem of Counsel Revisited Once More: Budé's De asse (1515) and Utopia I (1516) in Defining a Political Moment," in Humanism and Creativity, ed. Celenza and Gouwens, 141–68.

204. Jean Ruel (1474–1537) served as a physician of Francis I, to whom he dedicated his botanical manual De natura stirpium (Paris: Colinaeus, 1536). He is the subject of Giovio's Eulogium no. XCIII. See IO 8:116; Elogi 275–76; Gragg, 131–32; CE 1:415 (s.n. Du Ruel).

205. Guillaume Cop (d. 1532) studied in his native Basel before going to Paris, where he continued university studies and became a medical doctor (1496). At least by 1523 he had become one of Francis I's royal physicians. Having studied Greek with Lascaris and Aleandro, he went on to publish translations of medical writings by Paul of Aegina (1511), Hippocrates (1511–12), and Galen (1513, 1528). See CE 1:336–37.

206. Jacques Lefèvre d'Étaples (ca. 1455–1536), born in Picardy, studied and then taught at the Collège du Cardinal Lemoine in Paris. He published extensive paraphrases, commentaries, translations, and new

editions of writings of Aristotle, including of the *Nicomachean Ethics* (Paris: Joannes Higman and Wolfgangus Hopyl, 1497) and the *Metaphysics* (Paris: Henri I Estienne, 1515). He also wrote extensively on Scripture, including commentaries on the Pauline Epistles and his *Quincuplex Psalterium* (Paris: Henri I Estienne, 1509). In 1521 he helped his patron, Briçonnet, to reform the diocese of Meaux. By 1525 his questioning of the spiritual authority of the priesthood, and of the efficacy of the sacraments when faith was lacking, led to suspicions of heterodoxy, but he was well protected by patrons including Francis I and Marguerite de Navarre. See *ER* 3:396–97; *CE* 2:315–18.

207. Lazare de Baïf (ca. 1496–1547) went to Rome around 1516 with Christophe de Longueil but returned to France by 1521, entering the service of Cardinal Jean de Lorraine in 1525. The *De re vestiaria* (Basel: Johann Bebel, 1526) was his first work. In 1529 Francis I would appoint him ambassador to Venice. See *CE* 1:87–88.

208. Pierre Brisson, a professor of arts and medicine at the University of Paris, renowned as a philosopher and mathematician. See Marshall Clagett, *Archimedes in the Middle Ages* (Philadelphia: The American Philosophical Society, 1988), 3:74; Balsamo, 1:113.

209. Louis II de Bourbon de Vendôme (1493–1557), created cardinal in 1517.

210. Jean de Lorraine (1498–1550) was created cardinal in 1518. On his career see *CE* 2:350.

211. This stone is mentioned in Moritz Anton Cappeller, *Prodromus crystallographiae* (Lucerne: H. R. Wyssing, 1723), 31: "Arenae aureae quadrulae in Hamochryso Lapide."

212. François de Ponchier (d. 1532) was created bishop of Paris in 1519. Among works dedicated to him are Girolamo Aleandro's edition of Sallust (1511) and Nicolas Bérault's edition of Appian (1521). See Eubel, 3:270; *CE* 3:112; Cosenza 5:1460–61.

213. Guillaume Briçonnet (ca. 1472–1534), a church reformer and diplomat, was created bishop of Meaux in 1516. See *CE* 1:198–99.

214. Jean du Bellay (1498–1560), made bishop of Bayonne in 1524 and created cardinal in 1535, frequently served Francis I on diplomatic missions. A book of his Latin poems was published with Jean Salmon's *Odarum libri tres* (Paris: Robert Estienne, 1546). See CE 1:407.

215. Upon Francis I's taking the throne in 1515, he appointed Antoine du Prat (1463–1535) as chancellor of France. (In 1507, at the behest of Louise of Savoy, du Prat had become Francis' tutor.) Made bishop of Sens in 1525, he was created cardinal in the consistory of November 21, 1527. See CE 1:412–13.

216. Jean Grolier (1479–1565) of Lyon served as treasurer of Milan when it was under French occupation (1510–12, 1515–21), then as treasurer of the French army, and would ultimately become treasurer-general of France in 1547. A patron of scholars including the Alsatian humanist Beatus Rhenanus, he was renowned for his collecting of books. See CE 2:136–37.

217. A reference to Francis I's capture in the Battle of Pavia and his subsequent imprisonment.

218. Thomas Linacre (ca. 1460–1524) spent the years 1487–99 in Italy, studying Greek and Latin in Florence under Demetrius Chalcondyles and Angelo Poliziano and medicine at the University of Padua. In 1509 he became physician to Henry VIII, and in 1514 to Henry's sister Mary Tudor upon her marriage to King Louis XII of France. In 1518 Linacre founded the College of Physicians (later, Royal College of Physicians), over which he presided until his death. In 1523 he was appointed tutor to the future Queen Mary I of England. See CE 2:331–32.

219. For an edition of Linacre's translation, see *Procli De sphaera liber . . .*, ed. Marcus Hopper (Basel: [Heinrich Petri], 1547).

220. At the time of the setting of the *Dialogus*, Thomas More (1477/78–1535) was chancellor of the duchy of Lancaster. In October 1529 he would leave that position to serve as Henry VIII's lord chancellor, the post that he would resign in 1532. See CE 2:456–59.

221. Richard Pace (ca. 1483–1536) studied in Padua, Bologna, and Ferrara, where he worked under Niccolò Leoniceno. From 1509 to 1514 Pace

was in Rome in the service of Cardinal Christopher Bainbridge. He entered Wolsey's service in 1515, and for the following decade was involved in diplomatic missions around Europe. In 1525, while in Venice, he became seriously ill. He returned to England and convalesced for the remainder of his life. Pace's most important work is his *De fructu qui ex doctrina percipitur* (Basel: Froben, 1517). His translations of Lucian and Plutarch into Latin, some of which appeared in print as early as 1514 or 1515, were collected in one volume, *Plutarchi Cheronaei Opuscula: de garulitate; de avaritia; quomodo poterit quis ab inimicis aliquid commodi reportare; eiusdem, de modo audiendi; ex Luciano, Demonactis philosophi vita. Omnia per eximium R. Paceum Angliae oratorem elegantissime vera* (Venice: B. Vitali, 1522).

222. Reginald Pole (1500–1558), of the Plantagenet line, was a cousin of King Henry VIII of England. He studied at Oxford under Thomas Linacre and William Latimer. From 1521 to 1526/27, with King Henry's financial support, Pole attended the University of Padua, where he studied under Niccolò Leonico Tomeo and befriended Christophe de Longueil and Pietro Bembo. He would again live in Padua (1532–36), by which time his advocacy of Church unity set him against Henry VIII. See *CE* 3:103–5; *ER* 5:105–7; and especially Thomas F. Mayer, *Reginald Pole: Prince & Prophet* (Cambridge: Cambridge University Press, 2000).

DIALOGUE THREE

1. Giovanna IV d'Aragona of Naples (1478/79–1518) was queen consort to Ferrante II (= Ferdinand II) of Naples (1469–96; ruled, 1495–96), who was also her nephew. After his death she did not remarry. She was the daughter of Ferrante I (= Ferdinand I) of Naples and Giovanna III d'Aragona of Naples (Juana of Aragon; 1454–1517), who was also an *infanta* of Aragon.

2. Alfonso II of Naples (r. 1494–95) abdicated in favor of his son, Ferrante II.

3. Sancia d'Aragona (Sancha of Aragon; 1478–1506) became princess of Squillace in 1494 when she married Gioffre (or, Jofrè) Borgia, a son of Pope Alexander VI. See *DBI* 3:704.

4. Costanza d'Avalos "the Elder" (ca. 1460–1541), duchess of Francavilla, the *chatêlaine* on Ischia. The daughter of Iñigo (I) d'Avalos and Antonella d'Aquino, she married Federico del Balzo (d. 1483). In 1501 she followed her brother Iñigo (II) to the safety of Ischia. When he died in 1503, she personally directed the island's defense through four months of siege by a French fleet. See *DBI* 4:621–22.

5. Camilla di Sangro is identified by Vigier as a daughter of Carlo di Sangro, prince of San Severo, a Neapolitan baron of the Angevin faction. See *Cuestión*, 352 n. 844. On the di Sangro family, see Spreti, 6:88–90.

6. Sista has not been identified.

7. Perhaps the Angela Castriota (d. 1518) from the Scanderbeg lineage (the family had emigrated from the Balkans) who married Ferdinando Orsini (d. 1549), fifth duke of Gravina. Her well-known tomb is in Gravina, in the church of S. Sofia. See Maltagenealogy.com.

8. Violantilla Grappini married Ferrante Diaz Carlone, of the counts of Alife, the feudal seat in Caserta, in the region of Campania. See Minonzio, 2:663 n. 20.

9. Isabella del Balzo (1465–1533), daughter of Pirro del Balzo, prince of Altamura, and Maria Donata Orsini, became the second wife of Federico IV (also known as Federico I) of Naples (r. 1496–1501). Her brother, Federigo del Balzo (d. 1483) had been married to Costanza d'Avalos the Elder. See *DBI* 62:623–25.

10. Beatrice d'Aragona of Naples (1457–1508), daughter of Ferdinand I of Naples and Isabella of Taranto. In 1476 she married Matthias Corvinus (d. 1490), thus becoming queen of Hungary. Following Corvinus' death, she married his successor, Ladislaus Jagiellon (d. 1516).

11. Isabella d'Aragona (1470–1524), daughter of Alfonso II of Naples, had married Gian Galeazzo Sforza, duke of Milan, in 1488. Their daughter Bona Sforza, born in the year of Gian Galeazzo's death (1494), went on to become queen of Poland in 1518. On Isabella see *DBI* 62:609–15; and especially Giovio's eulogium of her (the only one of a woman) in *IO* 8:421–22; *Elogi*, 812–15.

12. A reference to the first two "days" of the dialogue.

13. The thought appears to be incomplete.

14. In Latin, this can also mean "the emperor's Fortune," i.e., that Charles V has Lady Fortune on his side.

15. I.e., so far removed from Lycurgus' stern decrees regarding education.

16. Aristotle, *Politics* 2.1269b.

17. A reference to Plato's statement that children should be of unknown paternity and held thus in common, being considered the offspring of all members of the guardian class; see *Republic* 5, passim. Giovio's criticism extends that of Aristotle in *Politics* 2.1261b and following.

18. I.e., ethics. Like Aristotle, Giovio does not distinguish strongly between the teachings of Plato and those of Socrates, the chief interlocutor of the *Republic*.

19. Cicero, *De fato* 5.10, says that when the physiognomist Zopyrus characterized Socrates as *mulierosus*, Alcibiades let out a loud guffaw. The point of the anecdote, however, is that Socrates admits he is naturally lustful but has controlled this disposition to vice by reason.

20. This refers to the Battle of Chaldiran, in Azerbaijan, in August of 1514, in which Selim I won a resounding victory over Shah Ismail I. See Imber, 45.

21. This recalls Cato the Elder's statement, made in opposition to repealing one of those sumptuary laws, that "the instant women become your equals, they will be your superiors."

22. This is Isabella of Castile, spouse of Ferdinand of Aragon, whose daughter Joanna "the Mad" was the mother of Emperor Charles V.

23. Margaret of Austria (1480–1530) became regent of the Netherlands in 1506 on behalf of her fraternal nephew, Charles (the future Emperor Charles V).

24. Louise of Savoy (1476–1531), the mother of Francis I and Marguerite de Navarre (d'Angoulême).

25. The Battle of Pavia (February 24, 1525), in which forces of Emperor Charles V decisively defeated French troops and took Francis I prisoner.

26. Louise served as regent in Francis' stead from the time of his capture in the Battle of Pavia (February 24, 1525) until his return from captivity in Spain (March 17, 1526).

27. Marguerite de Navarre (or, "d'Angoulême"), 1492–1549, is best known as author of the *Heptameron*, as a patron of the arts and of literature, and for her sympathy for advocates of religious reform including Briçonnet, with whom she corresponded regularly in the years 1521–24. Her *Miroir de l'âme pecheresse* (Alençon: S. Du Bois, 1531) elicited attacks from the Paris theologians that prompted Francis I himself in 1533 to intervene to protect her. See *CE* 2:386–88; *ER* 4:37–38.

28. Marguerite traveled to Madrid in September of 1525 to try to negotiate King Francis' release from captivity. On November 27, when the terms of ransom that the French proposed were rejected, she left Madrid for France. Francis' release was secured under the Treaty of Madrid (January 14, 1526), and he returned to France on March 17, 1526. See Knecht, 245–48.

29. María Pacheco y Mendoza was from a noble family of Toledo. Her father, Iñigo Lope de Mendoza, second count of Tendilla, took part in the reconquest of Granada and thereafter was made its captain-general, and so Maria was raised there. Her brother was the famous humanist Diego Hurtado de Mendoza. In 1510 she married Juan de Padilla. See Stefania Pastore, "La rivoluzione di Doña María Pacheco a Toledo: Riflessi letterari e costruzione storica," in *Donne tra saperi e poteri nella storia delle religioni*, ed. Sofia Boesch Gajano and Enzo Pace (Brescia: Morcelliana, 2007), 265–80.

30. When leading the *Comuneros* revolt, Juan de Padilla was captured in the Battle of Villalar (April 23, 1521) and executed.

31. From May 1521 to February 1522, she led the final, unsuccessful resistance of Toledo against royal forces. She fled to Portugal, where John III refused to accede to Charles V's requests that she be extradited. In 1531 she died in Porto, in extreme poverty. Giovio's praise of María Pacheco's political and military role runs counter to the Habsburg-dominated historiography, in which she was portrayed as the antitype of feminine excellence—the ruinous, treacherous "political" woman. Thus, in the domi-

nant narrative, she served as a counterexample to the celebrated Isabella of Castile. See Pastore, "La rivoluzione"; *DPR*, 442.

32. This is the first appearance in Dialogue Three of its most celebrated subject, Vittoria Colonna (1490/92–1547), marchioness of Pescara, lyric poet, and patron of arts and letters, who was Giovio's host on Ischia in 1527–28. For a brief biographical sketch see *EWR*, 87–91; and especially *DBI* 27:448–57. She is mentioned above at the outset of Dialogue One.

33. This is the *sacro catino* ("holy basin") of Genoa, long supposed to be an emerald. Housed today in the Museo del Tesoro di San Lorenzo, it is now known to be made of glass.

34. See *Republic* 5.468b–c.

35. The phrase "obtrectatione alienae gratiae" may echo Livy 2.40.11, "sine obtrectatione gloriae alienae."

36. On sable furs as aphrodisiacs for women, see Girolamo Cardano, *De subtilitate*, bk. 10.

37. On de Leyva's reputation and his harsh treatment of the Milanese citizenry, see Giovio's eulogium of him: *IO* 8:451–52; *Elogi*, 883–86.

38. In late 1521, after the French army occupying Como surrendered to Pescara, the latter's troops proceeded to sack the city. Giovio's brother Benedetto was among those tortured. Contrary to what the interlocutor *Iovius* asserts, the subsequent imperial occupation, if at times onerous, did not cause continuous destruction. See Zimmermann, 39–40; Minonzio, 2:673 n. 79.

39. Larius is the geographical region that includes Como.

40. Chalcondyles (or, Chalkondylas) was a prominent teacher of Greek. See above, Dialogue Two, nn. 28, 97, and 218.

41. The rhetorician Giano Parrasio of Cosenza. Giovio had heard both him and Chalcondyles teach in Milan at some point in the years 1501–6. See above, Dialogue Two, n. 34; and Zimmermann, 6.

42. Damigella Trivulzio (1483–1527), countess of Montechiarugolo, was married to Francesco Torelli. See *DPR*, 604 and n.; Maria Olivieri, *Damigella Trivulzio Torelli, Contessa di Montechiarugolo (1483–1527)* (Parma: A.

Zerbini, 1909); A. Ronchini, "Damigella Trivulzio Torelli, Contessa di Montechiarugolo," *Atti e memorie delle R. Deputazioni di Storia Patria per le provincie dell'Emilia*, n.s. 7:2 (1882): 229–57.

43. Agostino Trivulzio (1485–1548), created cardinal in 1517, was taken hostage in the Sack of Rome. See *DLI*, 157 n. 67.

44. For contemporaries' praises of Damigella's learning and character, see Olivieri, *Damigella Trivulzio Torelli*, 6–11.

45. Ippolita Sforza (1481–ca. 1520), who married Alessandro Bentivoglio of Bologna, was a patron of the writer of *novelle*, Matteo Bandello. See Cox, 41, 284 n. 67.

46. Bergonzio (Bregonzio, Bregoncio) Botta of Tortona (ca. 1454–1504), a favorite of Ludovico "Il Moro" Sforza, had been a functionary in Ludovico's court. Daria Pusterla (see below) was his second wife. See *DBI* 13:362–64; Monica Pedralli, *Novo, grande, coverto e ferrato: gli inventari di biblioteca e la cultura a Milano nel Quattrocento* (Milan: Vita e pensiero, 2002), 615–16, especially n. 656; Stefano Meschini, *Luigi XII duca di Milano: gli uomini e le istituzioni del primo dominio Francese, 1499–1512* (Milan: FrancoAngeli, 2004), 133; and n. 48 below.

47. This Chiara, who married Pietro Pusterla, was the daughter of Galeazzo di Guido Visconti by his second wife, "Catterina Masi francese." See Becker, 4:967. See also Marie Alphonse René Maulde-La-Clavière, *The Women of the Renaissance: A Study of Feminism*, trans. George Herbert Ely (London: Swan Sonnenschein and Company, 1901), 223, who (calling her "Clara") describes her dazzling appearance at a "celebrated ball given by the court of France in 1518": "devoted to white," she "made a brilliant figure with her silver embroideries and ropes of pearls. . . ." According to Guicciardini, 3:1529, she was famous both for her physical beauty and for Prospero Colonna's love for her.

48. Although Giovio terms Daria the *amita*, or "paternal aunt" of Chiara, this may refer to Daria Pusterla, whose husband Bergonzio Botta had died in 1504. In 1515, she hosted King Louis XII of France in her home in Milan. In 1516, she along with a number of other Milanese nobles was taken to France as a hostage. See the entry on "Botta, Bergonzio," in *DBI* 13:362–64.

49. This may be (1) Ippolita Castiglioni (b. 1488), the daughter of Gian-francesco and Rosanna di Lancellotto di Majno: this Ippolita married Giangaleazzo Trotti; or (2) Ippolita Castiglioni, daughter of Guarnerio Castiglioni (brother to the first Ippolita) and Anna di Luigi Gallerati (who married in 1496): this Ippolita married Gerolamo Dugnani. See Litta, 2:107 (Famiglia Castiglioni di Milano; Table Two). See also Minonzio, 2:675 n. 94, who identifies her as the wife of Tito Girolamo Sempronio Castiglioni.

50. Literally, "snoring exceptionally into each ear of the two," a play on the adage "Utramvis dormire aurem" ("To sleep sound on either ear"), meaning to rest easy, free from care. Erasmus glosses it in *Adagia* 1.8.19.

51. *peramabilis* is attested in Petrarch; see Hoven, 256.

52. Isabella was the daughter of Galeazzo Sforza, who ruled Pesaro until 1512 (he was the last of the Sforza line to govern the city).

53. The following paragraph from the earliest redaction (*d*) was suppressed here: "In order to preserve the decencies certain bawdy houses were set up in the alleyways which were managed carefully by aged procuresses, and to these shameless women voluntarily came. There, in hope of gain or to slake their lust, they would couple with unknown men. We ourselves saw a famous procuress distributing into individual chambers whole squads of girls, arranging them in order by beauty, age and moral habits. She claimed she was responding outstandingly to all the desires of men, no matter how lascivious."

54. Literally, "Salian." The Salii, a group of priests in classical Rome, were known for their sumptuous banquets.

55. Girolamo Adorno was from a Genoese family opposed to the Fregosi, who were then ruling Genoa. See Zimmermann, 44.

56. Isabella Giustinian was the daughter of Girolamo Giustinian (d. 1532) and Agnese Badoer. She had married Vittore Grimani in 1521. See Volpati (1934), 144.

57. Vittore, a grandson of Antonio Grimani (doge of Venice, 1521–23), was a Venetian senator noted for his skill in oratory.

58. This is Lucrezia Zorzi (d. 1531), wife of Marcantonio Venier. For the identification, see Minonzio, 2:676 n. 104.

59. Lucia was probably the daughter of either Francesco Barbarigo or the doge Agostino Barbarigo. See Volpati (1934), 146–47.

60. On Benedetta, daughter of Doge Andrea Gritti of Venice, see Becker, 2:775 (Table Pisani 1 [Venezia]).

61. This is Cardinal Francesco Pisani's brother, Giovanni Pisani, who married Benedetta Gritti in 1528. See Becker, 2:775 (Table Pisani 1 [Venezia]).

62. Francesco Pisani, created cardinal in 1517 (d. 1570). Becker, 2:775 (Table Pisani 1 [Venezia]); Hallman, 70.

63. Elisabetta Diedo is listed among the Venetian gentlewomen that Paolo Barbo celebrated in verse. See Emmanuele Antonio Cicogna, *Delle iscrizioni veneziane*, vol. 6, pt. 1 (Sala Bolognese: Forni, 1969), 100. On the Diedo family, see Spreti, 8:21–22.

64. Giovanni Cornaro (or Corner) (1488–1551) was the nephew of Caterina Cornaro (1454–1510), who was queen of Cyprus from 1474 to 1489. His siblings included two cardinals: Marco (created cardinal 1500; d. 1524) and Francesco (created cardinal 1527; d. 1543). See Becker, 1:268; Hallman, 6–7.

65. This "Ariadne" is Andriana (or Adriana) Pisani, daughter of the Venetian procurator Alvise (or Luigi) Pisani (1467–1528), who married Giovanni Cornaro in 1516. See Becker, 2:775.

66. Girolamo Adorno was in Venice in December 1522 on a mission from Charles V. See Zimmermann, 48–49, 51.

67. This is Leonardo Loredan, doge of Venice, 1501–21. The law here referenced is dated August 9, 1514. See Volpati (1934), 137 n. 1.

68. Ippolita Fioramonte (d. ca. 1555), the daughter of Ettore Fioramonte (a general and favorite of Ludovico "il Moro" Sforza), was the wife of Ludovico Malaspina, marquis of Scaldasole. Active in literary sodalities, she was also famed for taking part in defending the walls of Pavia when it was besieged by the French starting in November 1524. See *Dizionario*

biografico delle donne lombarde 568–1968, ed. Rachele Farina (Milan: Baldini and Gastoldi, 1995), 457–58; Ady, *ad indicem*. Giovio also lauds her exceptional beauty in his dialogue on *imprese* (devices); see *IO* 9:376–77.

69. Thomas de Foix, lord of Lescun (d. 1525), was the brother of the famous military leader Odet de Foix, viscount of Lautrec. See above, Dialogue One, §200 and n. 319.

70. Veronica Gambara (1485–1550) of Brescia, a celebrated poet and generous patron of literati and artists, married Giberto X, lord of Correggio, in 1509. From his death in 1518 until her own, she ruled Correggio, and already in 1520 she changed its allegiance from Francis I to Charles V. Her major achievements as patron and poet largely postdate the Ischian Dialogue. See *DBI* 52:68–71; *EWR*, 160–62.

71. Isotta Gambara may have been named for her great-aunt, the humanist Isotta Nogarola.

72. In his *Epistola in lode delle donne* (ca. 1525), Agnolo Firenzuola praised Isotta Gambara for her letters written in Ciceronian style. See Cox, 51–52, 284 n. 68.

73. On Uberto Gambara, see *DBI* 52:63–68.

74. Angela de' Rossi (1505–73) married the condottiere Vitello Vitelli in August of 1522. She was the daughter of Troilo de' Rossi and Bianca Riario. She later remarried, to Alessandro Vitelli. See Becker, 6:820.

75. Virginia Pallavicini-Gambara (ca. 1511/14–ca. 1559), daughter of Gianludovico II Pallavicini, marquis of Cortemaggiore (d. 1527), married Ranuccio Farnese (1509–August 1528) less than two years before his death. In late 1529 she remarried, to Bruno Gambara (d. 1570s), the brother of Veronica Gambara (1485–1550) of Correggio. See McIver, 26, 45, 54, 56; *DPR*, 603, 605n.

76. This marriage postdates the setting of the dialogue. See n. 75 above.

77. This is Ludovica, daughter of Pallavicino Pallavicini (1426–84/86), marquis of Busseto, and Caterina Fieschi. See McIver, tables.

78. This is Margherita Pio (d. after 1524), daughter of Marco II Pio of Carpi (d. 1493). Around 1495 she married Antonio Maria Sanseverino

(1454–1509), following whose death she entered a convent in Carpi. See Kleio.org online; Becker, 4:781.

79. Isabella Boschetti (1500–?), whose first marriage was to Franceso Cauzzi Gonzaga, count of Calvisano. See Minonzio, 2:680 n. 135.

80. I.e., Federico II Gonzaga (1500–1540), whom Charles V elevated in 1530 to be duke of Mantua. Minonzio, ibid., identifies Isabella Boschetti as Federico's mistress.

81. Isabella d'Este (1474–1539), marchioness of Mantua, was the daughter of Ercole I d'Este, duke of Ferrara. In 1490 she married Francesco II Gonzaga (1466–1519), marquis of Mantua. Best known for her patronage and collecting of art, Isabella played a major role in Mantuan government following her husband's death, upon which their son, Federico II Gonzaga (1500–1540), inherited the marquisate. See *EWR*, 130–33; *ER* 2:295–97.

82. Her mother was Eleonora d'Aragona.

83. Eleonora Gonzaga (1493–1550) was the firstborn child of Francesco II Gonzaga and Isabella d'Este. She married Francesco Maria della Rovere, duke of Urbino, in 1509, and bore their son, Guidobaldo (1514–74). See DBI 42:422–25; Cecil H. Clough, "Clement VII and Francesco Maria della Rovere, Duke of Urbino," in *Pontificate of Clement*, 75–108.

84. This is Laura Brenzona Schioppi of Verona (ca. 1470–1532), to whom humanists addressed much poetry. In her youth she wrote a 966-verse Vergilian epic about the deeds of the *condottiere* Roberto Sanseverino d'Aragona (1418–87) in the War of Ferrara (1482–84). See Cox, 2, 12–13, 267 n. 69 and passim.

85. The daughter of Sigismondo d'Este, Diana was married to Uguccione dei Contrari. She is celebrated in Ariosto's *Orlando Furioso*, 42.90: "Non guardar (dice il marmo scritto) ch'ella / Sia altiera in vista, chè nel core umana / Non sarà però men ch'in viso bella."

86. The negator is not in the manuscript.

87. On this fountain, see Girolamo Bertolotto, *La fontana dell'Amore e gli umanisti genovesi. Conferenza tenuta alla società di letture e conversazioni scien-*

tifiche di Genova la sera del 25 giugno 1894 (Genoa: Tipografia di Angelo Ciminago, 1894). Citation drawn from Minonzio, 2:682 n. 152.

88. Pliny had identified a river running between Genoa and Bisagno as the "Feritor."

89. This refers to a custom that was part of the summer-long festival, the "Spassi di Posillipo," during which the well-to-do of Naples, including all the nobility, frolicked in small boats along the coast from Mergellina to Posillipo. A Frenchman who visited Naples in 1632 described how, during the celebration of their harvest, the grape pickers were allowed to hurl whatever insults they liked at people of any station. See Jean-Jacques Bouchard, *Voyage dans le royaume de Naples*, in idem, *Journal*, ed. Emanuele Kanceff, 2 vols. (Turin: G. Giappichelli, 1976), 2:437; John A. Marino, *Becoming Neapolitan: Citizen Culture in Baroque Naples* (Baltimore: The Johns Hopkins University Press, 2011), 65–66. An earlier account appears in Pierre de Brantôme, *Recueil des dames, poésies et tombeaux* (Paris: Gallimard, 1991), 659–60.

90. See the discussion of Genoese enunciation above in Dialogue Two, §41.

91. Ottobuono Fieschi was a brother of Sinibaldo Fieschi (see Dialogue One above, §161 and n. 276). On his friendship with Giovio see Zimmermann, 6, 47.

92. Teodora was the daughter of Cristoforo Spinola (of the Spinola di S. Luca branch of the family). In 1502 she had married Sebastiano Sauli (d. 1536). They had seven sons and one daughter. Hyde, [xiv], Fig. 2; Natale Battilana, *Genealogie delle famiglie nobili di Genova* (Sala Bolognese: Forni, 1971), "Spinola di S. Luca," Table 8.

93. Volpati (1938), 184, mentions Pellota Grimaldi's marriage to a "Gerolamo" Doria but provides no further details.

94. Evidently not the Girolamo Doria who was created cardinal in 1529: he had been married to Luigia Spinola (d. 1528). See Becker, 1:373.

95. Giuliano di Lorenzo de' Medici's wedding to Filiberta of Savoy took place in France in February 1515.

96. On Caterina Spinola, see Ernesto Travi, *Lingua e vita tra '400 e '500* (Milan: Vita e Pensiero, 1990), 148, where she is called the "stella dell'ambiente genovese quando Giuliano de' Medici, fratello di Leone X, vi fece sosta mentre accompagnava la sposa novella dalla Francia a Firenze."

97. Argentina Pinelli, a daughter of the Genoese merchant Benedetto Pinelli, married Centurione in 1505. See Luisa d'Arienzo, "Francesco Pinelli banchiere del papa, collettore e nunzio apostolico in Spagna all'epoca di Cristoforo Colombo," in *Cultura e società nell'Italia medievale: Studi per Paolo Brezzi*, 2 vols. (Rome: Istituto Palazzo Borromini, 1988), 1:247; and Alberto Boscolo, "Il genovese Francesco Pinelli amico a Siviglia di Cristoforo Colombo," in *Presencia italiana en Andalucía, siglos XIV–XVII: actas del I coloquio Hispano-Italiano*, ed. Bibiano Torres Ramírez and José Jesús Hernández Palomo (Seville: Escuela de estudios hispano-americanos, 1985), 249–65, at 256; Boscolo article reprinted in *Nuova rivista storica* 68 (1984): 355–66.

98. Martino Centurione (fl. 1469; d. 1534) was the business partner of Argentina's father, Benedetto. He spent much of his career in Spain. See *DBI* 23:629–31.

99. This is Tomasina Lomellini, daughter of Nicolò Lomellini (d. 1505) and Bianca Centurione Becchignone. She married Nicolò Sauli in 1525; they had four children. See Hyde, [xv], Fig. 3; Battilana, *Genealogie*, "Lomellini," Table 27.

100. Tomasina Spinola (d. 1541), the daughter of Giorgio Spinola (of the Spinola di Luccoli branch) and Maria di Antonio Spinola. She was famed for her beauty. See Hyde, [xv], Fig. 3; Battilana, *Genealogie*, "Spinola," Table 84.

101. Nicolò di Antonio Sauli, a brother of Filippo Sauli, the bishop of Brugnano (see Dialogue Two above). Hyde, [xv], Fig. 3.

102. Domenico di Antonio Sauli (1490–1570), a brother of Filippo and Nicolò. See Hyde, [xv], Fig. 3. From 1507 to 1515 he served as depositor general to the papacy. Hyde, 7.

103. "Camogenia" has not been identified.

104. Lucrezia Gentile remains to be identified. Perhaps she is a member of the Gentile Pignolo family of Genoa (see Becker, 4:581–92, but Becker does not appear to mention a Lucrezia in the appropriate generation).

105. I.e., Lorenzo de' Medici, duke of Urbino (d. 1519).

106. Giovio here reflects the consensus of the time that Lorenzo de' Medici, duke of Urbino, died from syphilis. Recent scholars, while concurring that Lorenzo had syphilis, attribute his death instead to tuberculosis. See Ann Carmichael, "The Health Status of Florentines in the Fifteenth Century," in *Life and Death in Fifteenth-Century Florence*, ed. Marcel Tetel et al. (Durham: Duke University Press, 1989), 29–31.

107. I.e., 1523.

108. I.e., appropriate for an average citizen, along the lines of the image that Lorenzo "Il Magnifico" de' Medici cultivated.

109. Francesco Cattani da Diacceto (1466–1522). See *DBI* 22:507–9.

110. Pietro Martelli (d. 1523), who studied under Diacceto, was active in the gatherings of Florentine intellectuals in the Rucellai Gardens. He was learned in Greek, Latin, Hebrew, and mathematics. See *DLI*, 306.

111. Braccio Martelli (1501–61), Pietro's son, served Clement VII as a diplomat. According to Pierio Valeriano, he was among those who found refuge in Castel Sant' Angelo during the Sack of Rome. He became bishop of Fiesole in 1530, and would go on to participate in the Council of Trent. See *DLI*, 203.

112. Roberto Acciaiuoli (1467–1539) was a Florentine philosopher and a politician of the Medici faction.

113. Donato Acciaiuoli wrote commentaries on Aristotle's *Nicomachean Ethics* and *Politics* and also translated Plutarch's *Vita* of Demetrius into Latin. See Arthur Field, *The Origins of the Platonic Academy of Florence* (Princeton: Princeton University Press, 1988), especially chap. 8.

114. On Giovanni Corsi, who wrote a biography of Marsilio Ficino, see *DBI* 29:567–70.

115. On the importance of these discussions, see Felix Gilbert, "Bernardo Rucellai and the Orti Oricellari: A Study on the Origin of Modern Po-

litical Thought," *Journal of the Warburg and Courtauld Institutes* 12 (1949): 101–31.

116. Bernardo Rucellai, *De bello italico commentarius*, ed. John Brindley (London: William Bowyer, 1724).

117. Giovanni Rucellai died in 1525.

118. This is Cassandra Bartolini Salimbeni (d. 1527), who in 1500 married Carlo Ginori (1473–1527). Both died of the plague: he at the end of September and she a few days later. See the entry on Carlo Ginori in *DBI* 55:31–32.

119. This Ludovica Tornabuoni remains to be identified. Since Giovio here situates her death two years after that of Costanza de' Bardi (see following note), and so probably in 1527, she cannot be the Ludovica di Giovanni Tornabuoni portrayed in a fresco by Ghirlandaio ca. 1485–90, since that Ludovica, who married in 1489, died in childbirth at age 15.

120. Costanza di Agnolo de' Bardi had married Girolamo Guicciardini (1497–1556), brother of Francesco and Luigi, in 1524. She was the sister of Camilla de' Bardi, whom Jacopo Guicciardini (also a brother of Girolamo) had married in 1504. Costanza died within a few days of giving birth to a son, Agnolo, on December 27, 1525. See Randolph Starn, "Francesco Guicciardini and his Brothers," in *Renaissance: Studies in Honor of Hans Baron*, ed. Anthony Molho and John A. Tedeschi (Dekalb, IL: Northern Illinois University Press, 1971), 409–44, at 416–17; entry on Agnolo Guicciardini in *DBI* 61:84–88.

121. Luigi Alamanni (1495–1556) was one of the conspirators against Cardinal Giulio de' Medici in 1522. He fled initially to Venice, and then to France. He returned to Florence in May of 1527, shortly after the expulsion of the Medici, and went on diplomatic missions on behalf of its new government. On Alamanni's role in the conspiracy, see Patricia J. Osmond, "The Conspiracy of 1522 against Cardinal Giulio de' Medici: Machiavelli and *'gli esempli delli antiqui,'*" in *Pontificate of Clement*, 55–72, at 56, 57, 59, 64, and 65; and *DBI* 1:568–71.

122. Clarice de' Medici (1493–1528) was daughter of Piero de' Medici and his wife, Alfonsina. She married Filippo Strozzi in 1508. See Natalie

R. Tomas, *The Medici Women: Gender and Power in Renaissance Florence* (Aldershot: Ashgate, 2003), *ad incidem*.

123. Clarice died May 3, 1528, but was already seriously ill the previous fall. See Melissa Meriam Bullard, *Filippo Strozzi and the Medici: Favor and Finance in Sixteenth-Century Florence and Rome* (Cambridge: Cambridge University Press, 1980), 172 n. 84.

124. Nera Pucci (d. 1547) married Alessandro di Gherardo Corsini in 1516. She was the daughter of Alessandro di Antonio Pucci (1454–1525) and Sibilla di Francesco Sassetti, who married in 1483. Cardinal Lorenzo Pucci (1458–1531; created cardinal, 1513) was her paternal uncle. See Becker, 4:797–98 (Tables Pucci 1–2 [Firenze]).

125. This Giovanna Tornabuoni is probably the daughter of Lorenzo Tornabuoni and Giovanna di Tommaso degli Albizzi. She married Alessandro Antinori in 1513. See Litta, 8:136; and Minonzio, 2:691 n. 205, with archival sources.

126. Costanza Alberti has not been identified.

127. This Caterina is not to be confused with the more famous Caterina (Catherine) de' Medici, who was the daughter of Lorenzo, the duke of Urbino. This Caterina was the daughter of Galeotto de' Medici and Maddalena di Francesco Girolami (see the following note). Clement VII arranged for Caterina's marriage to Fabio di Pandolfo Petrucci (d. 1529), which took place in 1525. Subsequently she married Pietro Baglioni Colonna di Castel di Piero. See J. N. Stephens, *The Fall of the Florentine Republic 1512–1530* (Oxford: Clarendon Press, 1983), 169; and Litta, 4:353.

128. Evidently not a close relative of the line of Lorenzo "il Magnifico" de' Medici. A "Galeottus de Medicis" (married to "Magdalena" Girolami, 1503), son of Averardus (*gonfaloniere* in 1485 and 1513), appears in Imhoff, 119 (Table Medici 9). No daughters, however, are shown there.

129. On Fabio Petrucci's political fortunes, see Litta, 4:353.

130. Porzia Petrucci was one of Benvenuto Cellini's most important patrons. He describes meeting her in the villa outside Rome that the Sienese banker Agostino Chigi had built (subsequently called the Villa Farnesina). Her sister, Sulpicia Petrucci, was married to Sigismondo

Chigi, Agostino's brother. Cellini mistakenly identifies Porzia as Sigismondo's wife. In 1525 she did marry, but to Boncompagno Agazzari of Siena. See Benvenuto Cellini, *La vita di Benvenuto Cellini scritta da lui medesimo*, ed. Gaetano Guasti (Florence: Barbèra, 1890), xxvi, 45–46; Becker, 4:749.

131. Perhaps the Onorata Tancredi to whom Lattanzio Benucci dedicated his unpublished *Dialogo della lontananza* (1563), cited by Cox, 96.

132. In 1480–81 the fortress of Otranto in southern Italy was captured by the Turks, who were ultimately driven out by forces under the command of the future Alfonso II, son of Ferrante I, king of Naples.

133. Here the focus shifts abruptly from Poggio Reale, outside the eastern gate of Naples, to Posillipo, a peninsula separating Pozzuoli from the Bay of Naples, on the west side. The tunnel to which Giovio refers is the *crypta neapolitana*, which connects Piedigrotta and Mergellina. It dates to the first century BCE. In April of 1528, the prince of Orange, fearing that French troops would use the *crypta* as a route of attack, destroyed Sannazaro's villa in Mergellina (near where the tunnel debouched) to prevent it from serving the French as a secure base within the city. See Kidwell, 168.

134. Giovanna d'Aragona (1502–75), duchess of Tagliacozzo, was born and raised on Ischia. The daughter of Castellana de Cardona and Ferdinando d'Aragona, duke of Montalto (an illegitimate son of King Ferrante I of Naples), she was renowned for her beauty. Raphael was commissioned by Cardinal Bibbiena to paint her portrait in 1518. Her marriage to Ascanio Colonna (June 5, 1521) was unhappy. In 1535, following the birth of their son Marcantonio, she would leave Ascanio and go to live in the castello on Ischia. See *DBI* 3:694–96; *EWR*, 22–24; and above, Dialogue One, §3, which places her on Ischia at the time of the dialogue.

135. By the late 1530s Giovanna d'Aragona, like Vittoria Colonna, would become a follower of the religious reformer Juan de Valdés.

136. The meaning of the combination *clavicimbala aenochorda* is obscure. A clavicembalo, like the harpsichord, was a keyed instrument with strings sounded by plectra. *Aenochorda(ta)* is here taken as "metal-stringed"; but

aenochorda may instead be a variant of *enneachordum*, an ancient nine-stringed instrument whose invention the fifteenth-century musicologist Florentius attributed to Prophrastus of Pieria. See Florentius de Faxoli, *Book on Music*, published in this I Tatti Library (2010, vol. 43), ed. and trans. Bonnie J. Blackburn and Leofranc Holford-Strevens, at 34–35.

137. I.e., the Goddess of Justice.

138. This is Costanza d'Avalos the Younger (ca. early 16th cent.–1575), duchess of Amalfi. She was the daughter of Iñigo (II), marquis del Vasto, and Laura Sanseverino. She and Alfonso Piccolomini had two children, Iñigo and Vittoria. See *DBI* 4:622–23. In Dialogue One, §3, Giovio places her on Ischia at the time of the dialogue.

139. Maria d'Aragona (1503–68), marchioness del Vasto, was the daughter of Ferdinando d'Aragona, duke of Montalto (son of Ferrante I of Naples by his mistress, Diana Guardato) and his second wife, Castellana de Cardona (daughter of Ramón de Cardona). Like her sister Giovanna, she was born in the castello on Ischia. In 1523 she married Alfonso d'Avalos, marquis del Vasto (the namesake of Giovio's interlocutor here). *EWR*, 24–26; and Dialogue One above.

140. I.e., on the southeastern Adriatic coast of Italy.

141. I.e., Costanza d'Avalos the Elder (ca. 1460–1541). See n. 4 above.

142. Isabella Villamarina de Cardona (1503–59). See Colapietra, passim; *DPR*, 564; Thérault, 340–41; Laura Cosentini, *Una dama napoletana del XVI secolo: Isabella Villamarina, principessa di Salerno* (Trani: V. Vecchi, 1896).

143. This is the admiral Bernardo de Villamarín, conte di Capuccio (d. 1516). Isabella was his second child.

144. The wedding between Isabella Villamarina and Ferdinando ("Ferrante") Sanseverino took place in 1516 (he was not yet ten years old). See Colapietra, 124.

145. Isabella Villamarina also governed Salerno, with the assistance of Agostino Nifo, while her husband was away for three months in early 1527. See Colapietra, 145.

146. Giovio errs in attributing this teaching to Aristotle; it would be more accurately attributed to Plato in the *Timaeus*.

147. A garbled account of Plato's discussion of the creation of the soul in *Timaeus* 36c.

148. On Isabel de Requesens (Isabella de Requensens), 1500–1577, who married Ramón de Cardona in 1509, see *DPR*, 670 n. 3; Thérault, 212, 337–38; Croce (1894), 55–56. Her portrait (previously believed to be of Giovanna d'Aragona), painted by Giulio Romano and Raphael in 1518, hangs in the Louvre.

149. Ramón de Cardona was viceroy of Naples from 1509 until his death in 1522.

150. Presumably a musical setting of Ovid, *Heroides* 7.

151. On Federigo da Bozzolo, see Cecil Roth, *The Last Florentine Republic* (New York: Russell and Russell, 1968), 29–31, 186, 341–42. He, Dorotea (d. 1550), and Susanna were children of Gianfrancesco Gonzaga of Sabbioneta and Anna (or, Antonia) del Balzo (d. 1530). See Becker, 5:436.

152. On don Pedro de Cardona of Sicily (d. 1522), see Giovio's *Histories* (*IO* 4:51); Becker, 5:215. Susanna Gonzaga was his second wife.

153. This is Gianfrancesco (Giovanni Francesco) Acquaviva, marquis of Bitonto. The eldest son of Andrea Matteo Acquaviva (1458–1529), he died in October of 1527. See Becker, 3:10.

154. Caterina Acquaviva, married to Enrico Pandone, was the daughter of Dorotea Gonzaga and Gianfrancesco Acquaviva, marquis of Bitonto. See Antonio Colombo, "Il palazzo dei principi di Conca alla strada di S. Maria di Costantinopoli," in *Napoli nobilissima: Rivista di topografia ed arte napoletana* 7–9 (1898–1900), 129–32, at 131; Ammirato, 2:66–67. See Becker, 3:11, who lists Gianfrancesco and Dorotea's daughter Isabella Acquaviva as having been married first to Enrico Pandone. Becker does not list a "Caterina."

155. I.e., Andrea Matteo Acquaviva.

156. Giulia Gonzaga (1513–66), duchess of Fondi, was the daughter of Lodovico Gonzaga, duke of Sabbioneta, and Francesca Fieschi of Genoa.

In 1526 she married Vespasiano Colonna. Upon his death in 1528, she inherited his titles and property on the condition that she not remarry. Subsequently she sponsored literary gatherings at Fondi. There, too, she was courted by Cardinal Ippolito de' Medici, to whom she was betrothed just weeks before his death in August 1535. In 1536 she moved to Naples, where she spent her remaining three decades in a convent. See *EWR*, 166–70; Robin, *ad indicem*.

157. Pirro Gonzaga (d. 1529) was created cardinal in 1527.

158. Caterina Sanseverino (d. 1539) was one of six children of Bernardino Sanseverino, prince of Bisignano, and Dianora Piccolomini, who was the daughter of Antonio I Piccolomini, duke of Amalfi. See Ammirato, 1:31; Becker, 6:862.

159. Federico Caetani d'Aragona (d. 1528) was count of Morcone. His father was Onorato Caetani, duke of Traetto and prince of Altamura. See Becker, 6:862.

160. Maria Sanseverino was daughter of Bernardino Sanseverino, prince of Bisignano, and was the sister of Caterina. Maria's marriage to Enrico Orsini took place in June 1513. See Becker, 6:862.

161. Enrico Orsini, count of Nola, count of Tricarico, and prince of Bisignano, was of the Pitigliano branch of the Orsini family. He was the son of Gentile Orsini and Caterina d'Aragona. See Ammirato, 1:31; Becker, 6:862.

162. Aurelia Sanseverino (d. 1562), daughter of Tommaso Sanseverino. She married Giovanni di Giovanni Antonio Sanseverino di Luca in 1512. Giovanni Sanseverino was the brother of Alfonso, duke of Somma, and of Cardinal Antonio Sanseverino (d. 1543; created cardinal in 1527). See Croce (1894), 61; Becker, 6:863–64 (Tables Sanseverino 10–11); Imhoff, 295, 297.

163. Andriana Sanseverino, Aurelia's sister, was widowed by Federico Grisone. The instrument for the return of her dowry to her natal family reads as follows: "1523, 3 luglio, XI Napoli — Istr. per not. Gregorio Russo di Napoli — Quietanza della dote di Andriana Sanseverino, vedova di Federico Grisone, rilasciata a Giovanni Sanseverino, cognato di Andri-

ana, da Camilla Tomacelli, madre di Federico e balia e tutrice dei figli di lui." See Archivio di Stato di Napoli, *Archivi privati; inventario sommario*, 2 vols. (Rome, 1953–54), 20.

164. "Giovio is the Insubrian, not d'Avalos, but C₃ clearly reads "meae."

165. Vitruvius thus described the extraction of a choice purple dye: "When these [sea] mollusks are gathered, they are cut all round with iron blades, and from these wounds a purple ooze, flowing out like tears, is shaken into mortars and prepared by grinding. Because it is extracted from the shells of marine mollusks, it is called oyster-purple, and because it is so salty it quickly becomes desiccated unless it has honey poured over it." Vitruvius, *Ten Books on Architecture*, trans. Ingrid D. Rowland (New York: Cambridge University Press, 1999), bk. 7, chap. 13. A proximate source, which Giovio praised in Dialogue Two, is Sannazaro's *Piscatorial Eclogues*. In the second eclogue, *Galatea* (lines 36–41), Lycon promises Galatea purple shellfish as a source of Tyrian dye to color soft wool. See Jacopo Sannazaro, *Latin Poetry*, in this I Tatti Library (2009, vol. 38), with a translation and notes by Michael C. J. Putnam, pp. 114–15.

166. Lucrezia Scaglione di Aversa, daughter of Giovan Luigi Scaglione and Maria d'Alagno, had married the Neapolitan patrician Paolo Carafa, of the Stadera line of the family, who died in 1522. She was present on Ischia in 1528. See Genmarenostrum; Thérault, 334–37, 486 n. 129; and especially Kidwell, 111–29, with nn. on 229–34.

167. A. di Somma is possibly to be identified with Alfonso Sanseverino, duke of Somma, listed by Becker (6:863) with the dates "1506/29."

168. This is Emilia Carafa, the second wife of Pietro Antonio Carafa, count of Palicastro (the first was Laura di Biondo Tolomei of Siena). She was the daughter of Antonio di Fabrizio Carafa (1471–1525) of the Stadera branch of the family, and Crisostoma d'Aquino, of the Grottaminarda branch. See Litta, under "D'Aquino di Capua," Table 21; Becker, 1:186, 297; 3:193.

169. Porzia Brancia, daughter of Bernardino Brancia and Eleonora del Tufo, was married to Giovan Carlo Brancaccio (d. 1548). See Croce (1894), 60; Becker, 3:112.

170. This is Violante di Sangro, daughter of Giovanni di Sangro (Alfonso II's majordomo) and Adriana Dentice. She married Paolo di Sangro, marquis of Torremaggiore (d. 1528). See Croce (1894), 61.

171. This is Adriana Dentice, wife of Giovanni di Sangro, majordomo of Alfonso II. See Croce (1894), 61.

172. Isabella Gualandi (b. ca. 1491) was the daughter of Ranieri Gualandi (d. 1492) and Bianca Gallerani. Carlo Vecce, a prominent scholar of Leonardo da Vinci, argues that she was the model for the *Mona Lisa*. See Vecce (1990a).

173. Isabella Brisegna (or, Briseña) (1510–67), from a noble Spanish family, was educated in Naples. She was married to the Spanish captain don Garcia Manrique, who is mentioned in Giovio's *Histories* (IO 3:240–41; 4:44, 57). See *EWR*, 60; *DPR*, 722 and n., 729, 733; Croce (1894), 51.

174. Cassandra Marchese had married early, unhappily, to Alfonso Castriota. Leo X issued an annulment of their marriage in 1518. She and the poet Sannazaro were close friends. At the time of the Ischian dialogue's setting, she would have been around forty-eight years old. See Kidwell, chap. 7 ("Naples and Cassandra Marchese"), 111–29.

175. On Baldassar Marchese, see above, Dialogue Two, §60 and n. 109.

176. This area was so notorious for prostitution that at least by the early sixteenth century the expression "una puttana di pozzo bianco" ("a whore of the White Well") had become proverbial.

177. The prison in which, according to tradition, Sts. Peter and Paul were imprisoned.

178. This Lucrezia was nicknamed "Matrema non vole" ("my mother doesn't want [me to]") because her mother Clarice—a prostitute—did not want her to follow her example. By the 1520s Lucrezia was one of the foremost courtesans in Rome. See Georgina Masson, *Courtesans of the Italian Renaissance* (New York: St. Martin's Press, 1976), 70–79.

179. Aretino, in his *Ragionamenti*, ridiculed Lucrezia da Clarice for her affectation of being an expert on correct Italian style and usage. See Masson, *Courtesans*, 78–79.

180. Ersilia di Antonio Caffarelli married Pietro di Mario Mellini in February of 1521. See Gasparo Alveri, *Roma in ogni stato*, 2 vols. (Rome: V. Mascardi, 1664), 2:52; Stella P. Revard, "Lampridio and the Poetic Sodalities in Rome in the 1510s and 1520s," in *Acta Conventus Neo-Latini Bariensis: Proceedings of the Ninth International Congress of Neo-Latin Studies, Bari, 29 August to 3 September 1994*, ed. Rhoda Schnur et al. (Tempe: Medieval and Renaissance Texts and Studies, 1998), 499–507, at 503 and n.; see Becker, 3:158, who identifies the year of marriage as either 1521 or 1525.

181. I.e., he was the *scribasenatus*, the official who recorded the resolutions of the Capitoline (or civic) councils. On Mellini, see above, Dialogue Two, §27 and n. 50.

182. Probably Tarquinia Jacobacci, the daughter of the apostolic abbreviator Nicola Jacobacci *de Faceschis* and Antonia de Mezzabufalis, whom he married in 1493. This Tarquinia married Gaspare de Amadeis in 1519. See Becker, 4:616 (Table Giacobazzi/Jacovazzi 5 [altra linea]); Altieri, 106*.

183. Domenico Jacobacci (d. 1528) was created cardinal in 1517. Becker, 4:612 (Table Giocobazzi/Jacovazzi 1 [Roma]); Hallman, 6; Eubel, 3:16. Amayden, 1:458, errs in dating his death to July 2, 1527. On the Jacobacci family see Altieri, 15; Pecchiai, 21–22, 364, 399.

184. Antonina Velli was the sister of Marcello, Adriano, and Berardo Velli. See Becker, 2:613.

185. Luigi Matuzzi (Mattuzzi) was the son of Giorgio Matuzzi (d. 1490) and Anastasia del Cavaliere. See Becker, 2:613.

186. On Porzia Bonaventura and her husband, see Becker, 3:71; Amayden, 1:160.

187. This may be Paolina di Cencio Porcari. See Anna Modigliani, *I Porcari: storie di una famiglia romana tra Medioevo e Rinascimento* (Rome: Roma nel Rinascimento, 1994), *ad indicem*.

188. Evidently the Marco Marcello Leni who was the son of Vincenzo Leni. On December 17, 1501, Marco and five other "Roman gentlemen" were part of an entourage escorting Lucrezia Borgia to Ferrara. See Ivana Ait and Manuel Vaquero Piñeiro, *Dai Casali alla fabbrica di San Pietro,*

I Leni: Uomini d'affari del Rinascimento (Rome: Ministero per i beni e le attività culturali, 2000), 41. However, on February 6, 1500, this Marco Marcello Leni married Lucia, daughter of Antonio Angelo *Palutii de Albertonibus*. See Ait and Vaquero Piñeiro, 45 n. 198.

189. This is Giovanna Casali di Bologna, whose marriage to "Jacomo" di Virgilio Crescenzi is attested in Becker, 1:283.

190. Giacovella Mancini is the daughter of Alessandro di Giuliano Mancini and Ambrosina Fabi. See Becker, 4:664 (Table Mancini 2).

191. This is Giovanni Paolo Orsini di Toffia. See Becker, 4:664 (Table Mancini 2).

192. On the Gallo family, see Spreti 3:334–35. There are two *nipoti* of Flavio Biondo named Paolo: one, the son of Gaspare Biondo and Lucrezia Margani; the other, the son of Francesco. Information provided by Dr. Paola Farenga.

193. Giulia Alberini (d. 1551), daughter of Giovanni Battista Alberini. She married Frangipane in 1530. See Marcello Alberini, *Il Sacco di Roma: L'edizione Orano de I ricordi di Marcello Alberini*, introd. Paola Farenga (Rome: Roma nel Rinascimento, 1997), 495 (Appendix IV B, Table 2); Becker, 3:550).

194. Curzio Frangipane (d. 1554, at age 55) is the son of Antonino Frangipane (d. 1545) and Antonina di Stefano del Bufalo. A banker, Curzio would later become a steward to Cardinal Alessandro Farnese. See Becker, 3:550; Zimmermann, 202.

195. Gregory I "the Great" (pope, 590–604). (This cannot be Gregory VII, since he was not canonized until the later sixteenth century.)

196. On Giordano Serlupi (d. 1528) and Girolama Sassi degli Amateschi, see Minonzio, 2:711 nn. 320–21.

197. Although Giovio wrote "Cossaria" (perhaps for the Italian "Cosciari") as her surname, he most probably intended Cintia (di) Beccaluva, wife of Emilio Capizucchi, the son of Piero Ludovico Capizucchi and Lucia Cesarini (sister of Cardinal Giuliano Cesarini). Their noted son, Cencio, was born on January 25, 1525. See Becker, 1:182–83; *DBI* 18:566–68, s.n. Cencio (Innocenzo) Capizucchi.

198. Laura Palosci is attested for providing a dowry for her daughters, Cecilia and Marzia Beneimbeni, to the Monastero di San Sisto all'Appia on January 17, 1544. Both daughters went on to become prioresses. Raimondo M. Spiazzi, *Cronache e fioretti del Monastero di San Sisto all'Appia* (Bologna: PDUL Edizioni Studio Domenicano, 1993), 386.

199. Vincenzo Mattei (d. before 1548) was the son of Pietro Antonio di Lodovico Mattei and Antonia Capodiferro. See Becker, 2:607; Altieri, vii.

200. Ludovica de' Rustici is attested as Vincenzo Mattei's wife in Becker, 2:607.

201. Perhaps the Domenico de' Cavalieri who helped post bail for Cardinal Raffaele Riario when the latter had been implicated in the conspiracy against Leo X in 1517. See Warren Kirkendale, *Emilio de' Cavalieri "gentiluomo romano": His Life and Letters, His Role as Superintendent of All the Arts at the Medici Court, and His Musical Compositions* (Florence: Olschki, 2001), 15. On Domenico, the son of Giorgio de' Cavalieri and Ambrogina di Tommaso di Lorenzo Rusticelli, see Becker, 3:332–33 (De' Cavalieri 1–2 [Roma]; the name of that Domenico's wife is not, however, listed by Becker).

202. On the Miccinelli family of Rome and Viterbo, see Spreti, 4:581–82. Camilla has not been identified.

203. Giroloma del Bufalo was a daughter of Cristofero del Bufalo (d. 1499) and Francesca Orsini (d. 1524). In her mother's testament (December 31, 1524) she is called the widow of Gregorio de Erulis. Information provided by Professor Patricia Waddy. Becker, 3:351–52, lists Cristofaro [*sic*] di Agnolo del Bufalo, cancelliere perpetuo del Popolo Romano, whose first wife was Francesca Orsini. Becker does not however include a "Girolama" among their issue.

204. Probably Cassandra di Mario Bonaventura, who married Mario Orsini di Mugnano (adopted, de' Cavalieri) in 1509. See Becker, 3:71, 6:735.

205. *Sic.* While Becker, 3:71, lists no sister of this Cassandra Bonaventura, Porzia (who is mentioned above at n. 186) was her niece.

206. C. Catellia has not been identified.

207. Giovio evidently plays on adjustments to the calendar by the insertion of days (*intercalationes*) and the scheduling of trysts. Minonzio, 2:712 n. 334, proposes that this has to do with determining where in the lunar calendar (and so, the menstrual cycle) to schedule sexual intercourse with the least risk of conception.

208. The Latin also carries the legal sense of having "laid claim to them."

209. Giovio puns on *punctum*, which can mean either a moment of time (here, the groom's having seized the "moment") or a pinprick. See Montaigne, *The Complete Essays . . .*, trans. Donald M. Frame (Stanford: Stanford University Press, 1965), 241: "As the story says: Handsome and gentlemanly as you may be, when you have had no luck, do not promptly conclude that your mistress in inviolably chaste; for all you know, the mule driver may get his will with her" ("Of the Inconsistency of Our Actions"). A variant of this story, with a very different tone and moral, appears in Marguerite de Navarre's *Heptameron*, story 20.

210. Here, *cuncta caeli puncta* is a double entendre, with the fitting arrangement of all points in the universe, mapped out geometrically, corresponding to the ideal circumstances of sexual conquest. See the astrological discussion in Dialogue One.

211. I.e., they commit suicide.

212. Officially Laura Orsini (b. 1492) was the daughter of Orsino Orsini and Giulia Farnese (a sister of Alessandro, the future Pope Paul III), who had married in 1489. Many, however, supposed that her biological father was Rodrigo Borgia (Alexander VI, pope, 1492–1503). Laura married Nicola Franciotti della Rovere in 1504. See Becker, 3:76; Mandell Creighton, *A History of the Papacy during the Period of the Reformation* (London: Longmans, Green, 1882–94), 4:71, notes that the wedding took place in the Vatican, and that her "parentage was generally attributed to Alexander VI."

213. Giovanni Giorgio Cesarini (d. 1532), the son of Gabriele Cesarini and Giulina Colonna, whose marriage to Marzia Sforza in 1504 provided the occasion for Marco Antonio Altieri's composition of *Li Nuptiali*. He

was made Gonfaloniere of the Roman People by Pope Alexander VI in 1499. See Gaetano Moroni, *Dizionario di erudizione storico-ecclesiastica da S. Pietro sino ai nostri giorni.* . . (Venice: Tipografia Emiliana, 1840–61), 31:277. In 1513 he carried the banner of Rome in Leo X's *possesso*, "armed from head to foot and wearing a red silk mantle": see Ferdinand Gregorovius, *History of the City of Rome in the Middle Ages*, trans. Annie Hamilton (London: Bell, 1902), vol. 8, pt. 1:182. See also Becker, 3:250–51.

214. Giulia Cesarini was daughter of Giovanni Giorgio Cesarini and Marzia Sforza. See Becker, 3:251.

215. Simone Tebaldi (d. 1529) was the son of Marco Tebaldi and grandson of the Simone Tebaldi who had served as a doctor to Pope Calixtus II. He died while fighting under Lautrec at the siege of Brindisi. On his military career, see *CV* #1920. On his marriage to Giulia Cesarini, see Becker, 3:251. He is mentioned above in Dialogue One, §156. Compare Minonzio, 2:713 n. 341, who cites Alfonso Ceccarelli da Bevagna, *Istoria di Casa Cesarina*, as indicating to the contrary that in fact Giulia Cesarini married Bandino Bandini of Castel della Pieve, and after being widowed remarried to Filippo de' Pepoli.

216. Semidea Cesarini, daughter of Giovanni Giorgio Cesarini and sister of Giulia, married Cristofero di Angelo del Bufalo, a nephew of the Girolama del Bufalo glossed in n. 203 above. Information provided by Professor Patricia Waddy. Semidea does not appear in the genealogical chart in Becker, 3:251, which shows Giulia Cesarini.

217. Girolama Conti remains to be identified.

218. This is Giulia de' Conti di Poli, the daughter of Giovanni di Bruno Conti. See Becker, 1:265 (Table Conti 5).

219. The marriage is attested in Becker, 1:265. On Antimo Savelli, see above, Dialogue One, n. 153. In a document from 1523, she is described as Savelli's widow: see Umberto Gnoli, *Topografia e toponomastica di Roma medioevale e moderna* (Rome: Edizioni dell'arquata, 1984), 155n.

220. Becker, 2:741–42 lists "Maria Giulia di Giovanni Conti da Roma" as wife of Girolamo de' Pepoli (d. 1551). But in Becker, 1:265, a Julia di Ioannes di Bruno Conti is identified as wife first of "Antimus Sabellus" and then of "Io. Franc. de Marerijs"; no mention is made there of Pepoli.

221. Porzia Savelli di Ariccia was the wife of Carlo Orsini, of the Anguillara branch of the family. Their children were (Gentile) Virginio and Brigida. See Shaw (2007), 102, who discusses the intertwining of the two families: "All four branches of the Savelli were related to the Orsini by marriage by the 1530s."

222. Tarquinia Savelli was the daughter of Antimo Savelli and Giulia de' Conti di Poli. See Shaw (2007), Table Savelli II.

223. Paola was the daughter of Giulio Orsini di Monterotondo (d. 1513). Troilo Savelli was the son of Mariano and nephew of Cardinal Gianbattista. See Becker, 6:742; Shaw (2007), 103.

224. "Maria" is an error for Francesca, the daughter of Giangiordano Orsini (son of Virginio the Great), probably by his first wife, Maria Cecilia d'Aragona (illegitimate daughter of King Ferrante d'Aragona). Francesca married twice: first, to Giovanni, marquis of Padula (evidently Giovio's "Antonio [sic] de Cardona, the very powerful marquis of Padula"), and then to Lorenzo Anguillara (= Renzo da Ceri) (she was his second wife). Felice della Rovere, Giangiordano Orsini's second wife, was Francesca's stepmother. See Shaw (2007), 85, 192; Becker 6:704.

225. On Felice della Rovere (ca. 1483–1536), illegitimate daughter of Pope Julius II, see the popular biography by Caroline P. Murphy, *The Pope's Daughter: The Extraordinary Life of Felice della Rovere* (New York: Oxford University Press, 2005). Felice married Giangiordano Orsini in May of 1506.

226. Carlotta Orsini was Giangiordano's daughter by his first wife, Maria Cecilia d'Aragona (d. 1504). See Becker, 6:704.

227. Carlotta married Giantommaso della Mirandola in 1523. See Becker 6:778; Shaw (2007), Table Orsini V.

228. I.e., Lago di Bracciano, adjoining which the Orsini family held property.

229. Ancient Sabina and sixteenth-century Sabatina are geographically distinct from each other. Perhaps *d'Avalos* puns on the similarity of the names.

230. Plato, *Phaedrus* 229a–230e; see Cicero, *De oratore* 1.28–29; Pliny, *Nat. Hist.* 12.4–5.

231. Plato, *Phaedrus* 230d; see *Crito* 52b, 53a.

232. Franciotto Orsini (1473–1534) was the son of Orso (Organtino) Orsini (d. 1495), of the Monterotondo branch of the family, and Costanza di Giacomo Savelli, *signore* of Ariccia. Following the death of his wife, Violante di Pierfrancesco Orsini (of the Mugnano branch of the family), Franciotto was created cardinal (1517) by Pope Leo X, his first cousin and friend since childhood. See Becker 6:733, 745.

233. On Cecilia Orsini (1493–1575), see Becker 4:778. Alessandro Luzio, "Isabella d'Este e il Sacco di Roma," *Archivio storico lombardo*, ser. 4, 35 (1908): 15, 365.

234. Cecilia married Alberto Pio in February of 1518. She was his second wife. See Becker 4:779; CE 3:86–88, at 87.

235. Ortensia Colonna, daughter of Marcantonio Colonna (d. 1522). Serio shows her as having married Paolo Pallavicini (not Girolamo) in 1524. See Serio, 110, 114–15, and Table 3. Compare Becker, 5:249, who shows her as having married Bartolomeo Martinengo, count of Villachiara.

236. This is Lucrezia della Rovere, daughter of Luchina della Rovere (a sister of Pope Julius II) and her second husband, Gabriele Garra of Savona. Julius adopted Luchina's children (including Lucrezia), giving them the della Rovere surname. See George L. Williams, *Papal Genealogy: The Families and Descendants of the Popes* (Jefferson, NC: McFarland and Company, 2004), 54–55.

237. This is Galeotto della Rovere, Lucrezia's half brother, the son of Luchina della Rovere and Gianfrancesco Franciotti. Julius' favorite nephew, he was created cardinal of S. Pietro in Vincoli in 1503. He died in September of 1508. See Christine Shaw, *Julius II: The Warrior Pope* (Oxford: Blackwell, 1993), 228; Williams, *Papal Genealogy*, 54.

238. This younger Vittoria Colonna, the daughter of Pierfrancesco Colonna and Laura di Somma, married Camillo Colonna. See Becker, 5:258 (Colonna di Palestrina, Table 1); Litta, 2:194 (Famiglia Colonna di Roma, Table 5).

239. Laura di Somma was the daughter of Fabrizio di Somma, baron of Miranda, and Paola Colonna, the daughter of Antonio Colonna, prince of Salerno. Laura married Pierfrancesco Colonna, of the Palestrina line. See Shaw (2007), Table Colonna I; Becker, 5:258; Litta, 2:194 (Famiglia Colonna di Roma, Table 5). On Fabrizio di Somma, see Serio, 40, 110.

240. This is Muzio Colonna, illegitimate son of the apostolic protonotary Lorenzo (Oddone) Colonna (d. 1484). Muzio married twice: to Laura di Girolamo Frangipane, and to Ginevra Varano, daughter of Rodolfo Varano and Camilla d'Este. See Serio, Table 4; Shaw (2007), Table Colonna II; Becker, 5:248 (Table Colonna di Paliano 9).

241. Lavinia Colonna, illegitimate daughter of Muzio (d. 1516), married Giovanni Bentivoglio in April 1524. See Serio, 276, 292 n. 104.

242. Beatrice Colonna, illegitimate daughter of Fabrizio. She married twice: to Rodolfo Varano, and then to Francesco Valignani. See G. B. Belluzzi, *Diario autobiografico (1535–1541)*, ed. Pietro Egidi (Naples: Riccardo Ricciardi, 1907), 168; see also Serio, 213 n. 25, and Shaw (2007), Table Colonna II, who follows Litta (rather than Egidi) in calling Valignani "Ferdinando."

243. Rodolfo Varano (d. November 1527) was an illegitimate son of Giovanni Maria Varano, duke of Camerino, who had died on August 10, 1527. In his will Giovanni Maria had appointed his wife, Caterina Cibo, as governor of the duchy, and specified their sole child, Giulia (then four years old) as his heir, initially under Caterina's guardianship. Assisted by Sciarra Colonna, Rodolfo made war on Camerino, took the city, and imprisoned Caterina, but in October papal forces laid siege to Camerino, and Rodolfo had to flee. He himself was imprisoned, and then executed, the following month. See John Law, "The Ending of the Duchy of Camerino," in Shaw (2006), 77–90, at 81–83; CV # 2099.

244. Giulia Colonna (d. 1571), daughter of Pietro Colonna of the Palestrina line, married Pietro Margani (1485–1516), a Colonna ally who had been imprisoned by the French along with Prospero Colonna (d. 1523; of the Genazzano branch of the family) in 1515. Following Margani's death, she remarried to Prospero "di Cave" Colonna (d. 1528) of the Paliano line.

See Serio, 352, Table 4; Shaw (2007), 114, 117, 190, and Table Colonna I; Becker, 5:259; and CV # 1016 (on Margani's military career).

245. I.e., Vittoria Colonna, widow of the marquis of Pescara.

246. The Latin is *heroides*, which recalls the title of Ovid's noted collection of metrical epistles from famous mythological females to their absent lovers.

247. The "four virtues" are those highlighted in the previous sentence, i.e., nobility of birth, physical beauty, chastity, and civic responsibility.

248. I.e., earth, water, air, and fire.

249. On the topos of nature's serious play, see Paula Findlen, "Jokes of Nature and Jokes of Knowledge: The Playfulness of Scientific Discourse in Early Modern Europe," *Renaissance Quarterly* 43 (1990): 292–331.

250. I.e., nature has given her a Roman or aquiline nose.

251. Bona Sforza (1494–1557; queen of Poland, 1518–56) was the daughter of Gian Galeazzo Sforza, duke of Milan, and Isabella d'Aragona, the daughter of King Alfonso II of Naples. In 1517 the Polish ambassadors arrived in Naples, where the pact (i.e., the *capitoli*) for her marriage to King Sigismund I of Poland was finalized on December 6. She was crowned queen in Kraków the following April. See Giovanna Motta, "Bona Sforza, una regina del Rinascimento," in *Regine e Sovrane: Il potere, la politica, la vita privata*, ed. eadem (Milan: FrancoAngeli, 2002), 11–25.

252. Presumably a reference to opobalsamum, or the Balm of Gilead; see Genesis 37:25 and Jeremiah 8:22 and 46:11. The resin was used for medicinal purposes and as part of the embalming process in ancient Egypt.

253. I.e., on account of her being in mourning over the death of her husband.

254. Very possibly referring to Pythagoras, the wine steward of Nero, known for mixing lavish cups of wine; see Martial 11.6.10. He is probably the same Pythagoras mentioned in Tacitus, *Annals* 15.37, where the historian describes with disgust Nero's same-sex marriage to the man, with Nero playing the female part.

255. The manuscript includes a negator, so technically this ought to read "shouldn't." Omitting the negator is an editorial conjecture.

256. This is Giovanna Castriota Skanderbeg, the daughter of don Ferrante Castriota, marquis of Civita Sant' Angelo and count of Spoltone, who died in the Battle of Pavia. Her mother, Maria Zandari, had been wet nurse to Giovanna IV d'Aragona. See Minonzio, 2:19–20 n. 389, with extensive further bibliography. Giovanna III d'Aragona, in her testament made in 1502, bestowed titles upon Giovanna Castriota in thanks for "l'osequj et grata servitù, per molto tempo, et anni, et sua gioventù dispersi nel nostro beneplacito, et volere, non curandosi di toglier marito, nè d'haver figliuoli, ma tutto ha abbandonato per nostro amore, si anco per l'altre sue virtudi quali conoscimo molto singolari in essa per le quali saria degna de maggiore remunerazione. . . ." In 1513 this Giovanna Castriota founded in Naples a church called "dell'Ospedaletto," to which was attached a hospital for the care of indigents of high birth. See Carlo Padiglione, *Di Giorgio Castriota Scanderbech e de' suoi discendenti* (Naples: Francesco Giannini, 1879), 4–5 (quotation at 5).

257. The last phrase, as written, is surely ironic.

258. Penelope Caracciolo remains to be identified.

259. *Semel in vita*: alluding probably to the famous remark of Lucilius that Crassus had only once laughed in his entire life; see Cicero, *De finibus* 5.30.92 and *Tusculanae Disputationes* 3.15.31.

260. Giovio writes "Caesellia." She remains to be further identified.

261. Referring to the famous passages in Book 6 where Plato, through the mouth of Socrates, calls for common possession of women for sexual purposes. See the discussion of this subject in §21 above.

262. Literally, "become rigid" (rigentes); a sexual double entendre is possibly intended here.

APPENDIX

1. *Here, an intermediate draft (subsequently deleted) adds:* Nor should this genre of writing seem either dry or undistinguished, since we know it was used by two important philosophers, Xenophon and Livy, who were by far the best historians writing in Greek and Latin, respectively. Nor, besides, will the subject matter lack distinction. For in the first book, al-

though he might appear to do otherwise, d'Avalos shows in abundant detail the virtues by which a captain is made famous and illustrious. Then, in the second book, with a lighthearted appraisal of talents, we debate about the task of writing as a whole, so as to set out what deserves praise in a variety of views. In the last book, the most wondrously honorable comportment of a noble matron and the praises of outstanding women are described and a certain charm of speech.

2. Today known as the Carta Romana.

3. a thousand years *d*] many centuries C_1

4. The Castello Aragonese, built in 1441 by Alfonso V of Aragon, who constructed the stone bridge connecting it with the town.

Bibliography

EDITIONS

Travi, Ernesto, and Mariagrazia Penco, eds. *Paulus Iovius: Dialogus de viris et foeminis aetate nostra florentibus*. In *Pauli Iovii opera*, 10 vols. to date. Rome: Istituto Poligrafico dello Stato, 1957–. Text in vol. 9, pp. 147–321.

Minonzio, Franco, ed. and trans. *Paolo Giovio: Dialogo sugli uomini e le donne illustri del nostro tempo*. 2 vols. Turin: Nino Aragno Editore, 2011. Latin critical edition with Italian translation and extensive commentary.

RELATED WORKS

Bembo, Pietro. *History of Venice*. Edited and translated by Robert W. Ulery, Jr. 3 vols. The I Tatti Renaissance Library, 28, 32, and 37. Cambridge, MA: Harvard University Press, 2007–9.

Berni, Francesco. *Dialogue Against Poets*. In Anne Reynolds, *Renaissance Humanism at the Court of Clement VII: Francesco Berni's Dialogue Against Poets in Context. Studies, with an edition and translation*. New York: Garland, 1997.

Boccaccio, Giovanni. *Famous Women*. Edited and translated by Virginia Brown. The I Tatti Renaissance Library, 1. Cambridge, MA: Harvard University Press, 2001.

Ciceronian Controversies. Edited by JoAnn DellaNeva. Translated by Brian Duvick. I Tatti Renaissance Library, 26. Cambridge, MA: Harvard University Press, 2007. Texts by Angelo Poliziano, Paolo Cortesi, Gianfrancesco Pico, Pietro Bembo, Giambattista Giraldi Cinzio, Celio Calcagnini, and Antonio Possevino.

Coryciana. Edited by Blosio Palladio. Rome, 1524. Modern edition by Jozef Ijsewijn. Rome: Herder, 1997. The latter includes Francesco Arsilli's *De poetis urbanis* on 344–64.

Giovio, Paolo. *Elogi degli uomini illustri*. Edited and translated by Franco Minonzio. Turin: Einaudi, 2006.

———. *Elogia virorum illustrium*. Edited by Renzo Meregazzi. In *Pauli Iovii opera*, 10 vols. to date. Rome: Istituto Poligrafico dello Stato, 1957–, vol. 8.

Giraldi, Lilio Gregorio. *Modern Poets*. Edited and translated by John N. Grant. The I Tatti Renaissance Library, 48. Cambridge, MA: Harvard University Press, 2011.

Guicciardini, Francesco. *The History of Italy*. Edited and translated by Sidney Alexander. Princeton: Princeton University Press, 1969. (Abridged edition.)

———. *Storia d'Italia*. Edited by Silvana Seidel Menchi. 3 vols. Turin: Einaudi, 1971.

Sanuto, Marino. *I diarii di Marino Sanuto*. 58 vols. Venice: Visentini, 1879–1902.

Valeriano, Pierio. *Pierio Valeriano on the Ill Fortune of Learned Men: A Renaissance Humanist and His World*. Edited by Julia Haig Gaisser. Ann Arbor: University of Michigan Press, 1999. Contains a critical edition and English translation of Valeriano's *De litteratorum infelicitate*.

MODERN LITERATURE

Arfaioli, Maurizio. *The Black Bands of Giovanni: Infantry and Diplomacy during the Italian Wars (1526–1528)*. Pisa: Edizioni Plus, Pisa University Press, 2005.

Cox, Virginia. *Women's Writing in Italy, 1400–1600*. Baltimore: Johns Hopkins University Press, 2008.

D'Amico, John F. *Renaissance Humanism in Papal Rome: Humanists and Churchmen on the Eve of the Reformation*. Baltimore: Johns Hopkins University Press, 1983.

Gouwens, Kenneth. *Remembering the Renaissance: Humanist Narratives of the Sack of Rome*. Leiden: Brill, 1998.

Hook, Judith. *The Sack of Rome, 1527*. London: Macmillan, 1972.

Kidwell, Carol. *Sannazaro and Arcadia*. London: Duckworth, 1993.

Mallett, Michael. *Mercenaries and their Masters: Warfare in Renaissance Italy*. Totowa, NJ: Rowman and Littlefield, 1974.

Pastor, Ludwig von. *The History of the Popes from the Close of the Middle Ages*. 3rd ed. Edited and translated by F. I. Antrobus et al. 40 vols. London: Kegan Paul, 1901–33.

The Pontificate of Clement VII: History, Politics, Culture. Edited by Kenneth Gouwens and Sheryl E. Reiss. Aldershot: Ashgate, 2005.

Robin, Diana. *Publishing Women: Salons, the Presses, and the Counter-Reformation in Sixteenth-Century Italy*. Chicago: University of Chicago Press, 2007.

Setton, Kenneth M. *The Papacy and the Levant (1204–1571)*. 4 vols. Philadelphia: The American Philosophical Society, 1984.

Thérault, Suzanne. *Un cénacle humaniste de la Renaissance autour de Vittoria Colonna, châtelaine d'Ischia*. Florence: Sansoni, 1968.

Zimmermann, T. C. Price. *Paolo Giovio: The Historian and the Crisis of Sixteenth-Century Italy*. Princeton: Princeton University Press, 1995.

Index

Publication of this volume has been made possible by

The Myron and Sheila Gilmore Publication Fund at I Tatti
The Robert Lehman Endowment Fund
The Jean-François Malle Scholarly Programs and Publications Fund
The Andrew W. Mellon Scholarly Publications Fund
The Craig and Barbara Smyth Fund
for Scholarly Programs and Publications
The Lila Wallace–Reader's Digest Endowment Fund
The Malcolm Wiener Fund for Scholarly Programs and Publications